JOSEPH HAYDN'S
KEYBOARD MUSIC

Joseph Haydn at the keyboard. Engraving by Neidl after a
painting by Zitterer (1795?). The music on the keyboard is
Symphony No. 94 in G major, Andante (the "Surprise" movement). (Author's collection)

JOSEPH HAYDN'S
Keyboard Music
SOURCES AND STYLE

A. Peter Brown

INDIANA
UNIVERSITY
PRESS

Bloomington

This book is published with the assistance of
a grant from the John Simon Guggenheim
Memorial Foundation.

Manufactured in the United States of America

Library of Congress Cataloging-in-Publication Data

Brown, A. Peter.
  Joseph Haydn's keyboard music.

  Bibliography: p.
  Includes index.
    1. Haydn, Joseph, 1732–1809. Keyboard music.   2. Haydn, Joseph, 1732–1809.
Chamber music.   3. Keyboard music—18th century—History and criticism.   4. Cham-
ber music—18th century—History and criticism.   I. Title.
ML410.H4B86   1986   786'.092'4   85-45029
ISBN 0-253-33182-X

I   2   3   4   5   90   89   88   87   86

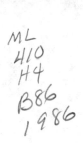

For
C.V.B. *and* H.E.V.B.

Through his keyboard pieces [Haydn] has at last become the favorite of all connoisseurs. Not only are they substantial and suited to the instrument, but distinguished above all by the unusual beauty of their melodies.

Christian Friedrich Daniel Schubart,
Ideen zu einer Ästhetik der Tonkunst
[1784].

CONTENTS

PART TWO: *Style*

PLATES

TABLES

PREFACE

Keyboard music and keyboard instruments were of primary concern to Haydn throughout his life. He was an effective performer who used keyboard instruments for personal, social, commercial, professional, and compositional pursuits. Indeed, during the 1760s Haydn almost single-handedly changed the Viennese keyboard sonata from a work of little consequence to one that forms a core of the keyboard repertoire. His decisive contributions to the history of the symphony and the string quartet have long been acknowledged; it is fitting that we recognize his pre-eminence in cyclic works and individual pieces for keyboard instruments.

The present study is organized topically rather than chronologically and is divided into two parts: sources and style. The word "sources" is used in its most expansive sense, including philological and bibliographic matters, the documentary/historical background, and Haydn's stylistic heritage. Although each essay was envisioned as a discrete entity, the unifying thesis that underlies the entire volume is Haydn's consuming interest in keyboard music. All the extant documents concerning this repertoire are presented in Essay II—sketches and drafts, revisions, anecdotes, correspondence, contracts, dedications, announcements, and reviews. This essay buttresses the revisionist view of the opening chapter and provides the necessary documentation upon which much of the remainder of the book rests.

Questions of authenticity and chronology for Haydn's keyboard works are far from settled. A comparison of any two editions and/or musicological studies will immediately reveal that even the best informed and most astute editors and commentators cannot agree on even a canon of works, much less their chronological order. In part this situation is due to the nature of the evidence: for the early works the lack of reliable data forces one to base conclusions on internal clues rather than on hard evidence. In Essays III and IV my goal is to give a sense of the directions that current Haydn research is taking in order to bring these problems under better control, as well as to offer my own conclusions as far as the present state of knowledge permits.

Essay V is devoted to the central issue for eighteenth-century keyboard music—which instrument is most appropriate for a given work. Since Haydn is known to have played the organ, clavichord, harpsichord, and *fortepiano*, all of which were at his disposal throughout most of his creative life, it is my view that he did not always compose exclusively for any one instrument. Thus, rather than trying to view the change from the harpsichord to *fortepiano* as a Rubicon crossing, I see it as a more fluid and gradual metamorphosis from a style for touch-insensitive instruments to a style for touch-sensitive ones. This chapter concludes with specific recommendations as to which instruments are best suited to the realization of each keyboard work. The care with which Haydn wrote for the various idioms further attests to the central place of keyboard music within his *oeuvre*.

The musical environment for Haydn's keyboard music is the concern of the next pair of studies. Essay VI pursues Viennese repertoire and style during the mid-eighteenth century in the realms of solo, accompanied, and concerted keyboard music; while Essay VII looks at Haydn's most frequently mentioned stylistic model, C. P. E. Bach. In all instances Haydn maintained his individuality. As a young composer, even in some of his smallest and technically easiest works, Haydn made a decisive break with the tradition of Wagenseil and his circle. Haydn did not necessarily take as his model the sonatas of C. P. E. Bach but the principles of the *Versuch*, which he adapted to his own inclinations. From an early date Haydn absorbed and transformed everything to which he was exposed.

The second part of this volume consists of three essays on the development of Haydn's musical language. Essay VIII seeks to show the interrelationships among the various genres and settings, while Essays IX and X discuss structure and style in each category. The final two chapters have a chronological presentation, although the various units of the ritornello structure are stressed in the essay on the concertos, and the development of the sonata, variation, and part forms is pursued in the final essay on the solo and accompanied works. My intent is both to elucidate some of the individual characteristics of the keyboard works and to examine them within the context of Haydn's own developing style.

Space constraints do not permit a side-by-side presentation of all documents in their original language and in English; although most of the documents are therefore given only in translation, the original keyboard terminology is retained. I use the italicized term *fortepiano* to refer to the instrument of Haydn's time but not for dynamics or for today's product. For quotations from the Haydn correspondence, Dénes Bartha's transcriptions were translated. Most of the other English translations are based on the original documents, with those from the German by Paul Borg, from the French and Italian by Austin B. Caswell.

The abbreviations for the bibliographic references are based on the system used by W. S. Newman in his *History of the Sonata Idea*. The bibliography lists only the works cited in the text. For a comprehensive bibliography of literature, the reader should consult Brown and Berkenstock, *Joseph Haydn in Literature: A Bibliography* for entries through 1972, and Horst Walter's supplement in *Haydn-Studien* (III/3–4, V/4).

One cannot prepare a work of this nature without the assistance of a number of people and institutions. For financial aid I am first of all indebted to my wife, as it would have been impossible to pursue my research program of the last decade without her sustaining full-time employment; second, to the John Simon Guggenheim Memorial Foundation for a fellowship during 1978–79 that allowed me to devote a full academic year to research and writing; and third, to the Office of Research and Graduate Development at Indiana University for grants-in-aid and two summer fellowships. For the loan, use, and/or duplication of materials in their collections, I thank the following persons and institutions: Otto Biba (Gesellschaft der Musikfreunde, Vienna), Rudolf Elvers (Staatsbibliothek, Preussischer Kulturbesitz, Berlin), Ernst Hilmar (Stadtbibliothek, Vienna), István Kecskeméti (National Széchényi Library, Budapest), Karl Heinz Köhler (Deutsche Staatsbibliothek, Berlin), Ortrun Landmann (Sächsische Landesbibliothek, Dresden), the late Christa Landon (Vienna), H. C. Robbins Landon (Vienna), François Lesure (Bibliothèque Nationale, Paris), the late Albert Vander Linden (Conservatoire Royal de Musique, Brussels), Salvatore Pintacuda (Instituto Musicale, Genova), Peter Riethus (Gesellschaft der Musikfreunde, Vienna), Mlada Rutova (Národní Múzeum, Prague), and Jiří Sehnal (Moravské Múzeum, Brno).

For answering inquiries and providing information, I am indebted to Georg Feder, Michele Fillion, Karl Heinz Füssl, A. Hyatt King, H. C. Robbins Landon, Jan LaRue, Peter Lindenbaum, Sheila Lindenbaum, Nicholas McGegan, Darina Múdra, William S. Newman, Carla Pollack, Robert Schwarz, László Somfai, Alan Tyson, and Rachel Wade.

For research assistance including cataloguing, typing, constructing scores and tables, and other numerous services I am indebted to my past and present research assistants at the Indiana University School of Music: Peter Alexander, Richard Griscom, Beverly Heinlein, Suzanne LaPlante, Therese Lutz, Adrienne Meconi, Mary Sue Morrow, René Ramos, and Julie Schnepel. Among these a special acknowledgment is due Mr. Alexander, who accompanied me during the autumn of 1978 to Vienna, Brno, and Kroměříž and rechecked some Haydn sources in Berlin; and Ms. Morrow, who checked and rechecked the entire manuscript. I especially thank Constance Cook Glen, Mara Parker, and Julie Schnepel, who prepared the indexes. My wife, Carol, skillfully gave the book its most critical reading.

Many of the ideas and hypotheses stated herein find their origin in the work of other scholars, who are acknowledged in the footnotes. In particular, the work of Karl Päsler, Hermann Abert, H. C. Robbins Landon, László Somfai, William S. Newman, Christa Landon, and Georg Feder has proved to be the most stimulating. That issue is taken with some of their conclusions and doubts are expressed concerning others, should not be misconstrued. Most importantly, the influence of Jan LaRue, who during the last fifteen years has shared with me his bibliographic expertise and analytical acumen for eighteenth-century music, should be self-evident.

IDENTIFICATION OF
HAYDN'S WORKS

I have tried to identify Haydn's works in the manner in which they are best known. Symphonies are identified according to the old Mandyczewski numbers, string quartets according to the standard *opera*. All other instrumental works are designated according to their numbers in Hoboken/WERKVERZEICHNIS. Vocal works are referred to by their title and/or Hoboken number.

The keyboard works dealt with here belong to the following six groups established by Hoboken:

Hob. XIV	accompanied divertimentos and concertinos
Hob. XV	keyboard trios
Hob. XVI	solo sonatas
Hob. XVII	*Klavierstücke* (keyboard pieces)
Hob. XVIIa	keyboard music for four hands
Hob. XVIII	keyboard concertos

Within these groups Hoboken has identified each work by an arabic number following the roman numeral (Hob. XVI:2) or by a letter indicating key in combination with an arabic numeral (Hob. XVI:C2).

Movements within cyclic compositions are indicated for all the instrumental works by the last number following a slash; e.g., Hob. XVI:1/1 is the first movement of Hob. XVI:1, but String Quartet Op. 20/3/4 is the fourth movement of the third quartet of Op. 20.

For ease of reference, collations of various edition numberings for the solo sonatas and the keyboard trios follow.

Collation of Numberings of Haydn's Keyboard Trios

Key	Hoboken Catalogue	Doblinger (H.C.R. Landon)	Haydn Werke (Stockmeier and Becker-Glauch)	Peters (Hermann)	Breitkopf & Härtel (David)
G	XIV:6, XVI:6	3			
C	XIV:C1	16			
g	XV:1	5	I/9	19	16
F	XV:2, XIV:2	17	I/11	26	25
G	XV:5	18	II/1	28	28
F	XV:6	19	II/2	25	23
D	XV:7	20	II/3	10	21
B♭	XV:8	21	II/4	24	22
A	XV:9	22	II/5	15	9
E♭	XV:10	23	II/6	20	17
E♭	XV:11	24	II/7	16	11
e	XV:12	25	II/8	7	10
C	XV:13	26	II/9	14	8
A♭	XV:14	27	II/10	11	24
G	XV:15	29	II/12	31	31
D	XV:16	28	II/11	30	30
F	XV:17	30	II/13	29	29
A	XV:18	32		13	7
g	XV:19	33		17	14
B♭	XV:20	34		9	13
C	XV:21	35		21	18
E♭	XV:22	36		23	20
d	XV:23	37		22	19
D	XV:24	38		6	6
G	XV:25	39		1	1
f♯	XV:26	40		2	2
C	XV:27	43		3	3
E	XV:28	44		4	4
E♭	XV:29	45		5	5
E♭	XV:30	42		8	12
e♭	XV:31	41		18	15
G	XV:32	31			
D	XV:33	8 (lost)	I/App.		
E	XV:34	11			
A	XV:35	10	I/10		
E♭	XV:36	12	I/1		
F	XV:37	1	I/3		
B♭	XV:38	13	I/4		
F	XV:39	4			
F	XV:40	6	I/8		
G	XV:41	7	I/7		
C	XV:C1	2	I/2		
D	XV:D1	9 (lost)	I/App.		
f	XV:f1	14	I/6		
D		15			

Collation of Numberings of Haydn's Solo Sonatas

Hoboken Catalogue	Universal (C. Landon)	Henle Urtext (Feder)	Haydn Werke (Feder)	Breitkopf & Härtel (Päsler)	Schirmer (Klee and Lebert) and Presser	Peters (Martienson)	Breitkopf & Härtel (Zilcher)	Universal (Rauch)	Associated (Raymar)	Augener (Pauer)	Key
XIV:5 (recte XVI:5a)											D
XVI:1	10		I	1		D.1					C
XVI:2	11		I	2		22	40				Bb
XVI:2a	21		I/App.							lost	d
XVI:2b	22		I/App.							lost	A
XVI:2c	23		I/App.							lost	B
XVI:2d	24		I/App.							lost	Bb
XVI:2e	25		I/App.							lost	e
XVI:2g	26		I/App.							lost	C
XVI:2h	27		I/App.							lost	A
XVI:3	14		I	3		D.2	41				C
XVI:4	9		I	4		D.3					D
XVI:5	8		I	5		23					A
XVI:6	13		I	6		37	36	22		15	G
XVI:7	2		I	7		D.5					C
XVI:8	1		I	8		D.4					G
XVI:9	3		I	9		D.6	42				F
XVI:10	6			10		43					C
XVI:11	5		I/App. mvts. 2 & 3	11		11	31				G
XVI:12	12		I	12		29	28	5		11	A
XVI:13	15		I	13	17	18	18	4		7	E
XVI:14	16		I	14	14	15	15	3	2	4	D
XVI:15				15							C
XVI:16			I	16							Eb
XVI:17				17							Bb
XVI:18	20		I	18	18	19	30	28		8	Bb
XVI:19	30	I/3	I	29	9	9	19	16		20	D
XVI:20	33	I/5	II	20		25	24	26		27	c
XVI:21	36		II	21	15	16	16	23		5	C

Key	Hob.										
E	XVI:22	37		II	22		40	39	19	8	26
F	XVI:23	38	I/7	II	23	20	21	21	10	6	10
D	XVI:24	39		II	24		31	32			
E♭	XVI:25	40		II	25		32				
A	XVI:26	41	I/8	II	26	11	33	12	1		1
G	XVI:27	42		II	27	12	12	13	9		2
E♭	XVI:28	43		II	28	13	13	14	21		3
F	XVI:29	44		II	29		14	35	6		14
A	XVI:30	45		II	30		36	29	15	7	25
E	XVI:31	46	I/9	II	31	19	30	38	18	5	13
b	XVI:32	47	II/13	III	32		39	20	11		9
D	XVI:33	34	I/10	III	33		20	2	14		33
e	XVI:34	53	I/11	II	34	2	2	5	2		22
C	XVI:35	48	I/12	II	35	5	5	6	20		31
c♯	XVI:36	49		II	36	6	6	7	17		30
D	XVI:37	50		II	37	7	7	34	32		29
E♭	XVI:38	51		II	38		35	17	24		6
G	XVI:39	52		II	39	16	17	10	8		19
G	XVI:40	54	II/14	III	40	10	10	26	13	4	18
B♭	XVI:41	55	II/15	III	41		27	27	27		17
D	XVI:42	56	II/16	III	42		28	11			
A♭	XVI:43	35		III	43		41	4	33		23
g	XVI:44	32	I/6	I	44	4	4	25	30		21
E♭	XVI:45	29		I	45		26	8	31		28
A♭	XVI:46	31	I/4		46	8	8	33	7		16
F	XVI:47	57		I	47		34				
e	XVI:47/2	17	I/1								
E	XVI:47/3	18	I/2								
E	XVI:47/4	19									
C	XVI:48	58	II/17	III	48	3	24	23	29		24
E♭	XVI:49	59	II/18	III	49		3	3	25		32
C	XVI:50	60	II/21	III	50		42	22			
D	XVI:51	61	II/20	III	51		38	37	12		12
E♭	XVI:52	62	II/19	III	52	1	1	1	34		34
G	XVI:G1	4	I								
D	XVII:D1	7	I								

LIBRARY SIGLA

A—Österreich

A-Eh	Eisenstadt, Haydn-Museum
A-Gk	Graz, Akademie für Musik und Darstellende Kunst und Landesmusik-schule (ehem. Steiermärkisches Landeskonservatorium)
A-Gl	Graz, Steiermärkische Landesbibliothek (am Joanneum)
A-GÖ	Göttweig, Benediktinerstift Göttweig, Musikarchiv
A-HE	Heiligenkreuz, Zisterzienserstift
A-L	Lilienfeld, Zisterzienser-Stift, Musikarchiv und Bibliothek
A-Lambrecht	Lambrecht, Benediktiner-Stift, Musikarchiv
A-M	Melk an der Donau, Benediktiner-Stift Melk
A-Ssp	Salzburg, St. Peter (Erzstift oder Benediktiner-Erzabtei), Musikarchiv
A-SCH	Schlägl, Prämonstratenser-Stift Schlägl
A-SEI	Seitenstetten, Stift
A-SF	St. Florian, Augustiner-Chorherrenstift
A-ST	Stams, Zisterzienserstift
A-Wgm	Wien, Gesellschaft der Musikfreunde in Wien
A-Wlandon	Wien, Privatbibliothek H. C. R. Landon
A-Wn	Wien, Österreichische Nationalbibliothek (ehem. k. k. Hofbibliothek), Musiksammlung

B—Belgique/Belgie

B-Bc	Bruxelles (Brussels), Conservatoire Royal de Musique, Bibliothèque

CH—Schweiz (Confédération Helvétique/Suisse)

CH-E	Einsiedeln, Kloster Einsiedeln, Musikbibliothek

CS—ČSSR (Czechoslovakia)

CS-Bm	Brno, Moravské múzeum-hud. hist. odděleni
CS-BRnm	Bratislava, Slovenské národné múzeum, hudobné odděleníe (mit den Beständen aus Kežmarok und Svedlár)
CS-KRm	Kroměříž, Umělecko-historické múzeum
CS-Pnm	Praha, Národní múzeum-hud. oddělení

D-brd—Bundesrepublik Deutschland

D-brd-B	Berlin, Staatsbibliothek (Stiftung Preußischer Kulturbesitz)
D-brd-DO	Donaueschingen, Fürstlich Fürstenbergische Hofbibliothek
D-brd-F	Frankfurt/Main, Stadt- und Universitätsbibliothek, Musik- und Theater-abteilung Manskopfisches Museum
D-brd-HR	Harburg über Donauwörth, Fürstlich Öttingen-Wallerstein'sche Bibliothek, Schloß Harburg
D-brd-Mbs	München, Bayerische Staatsbibliothek (ehemals Königliche Hof- und Staatsbibliothek), Musiksammlung
D-brd-MGmi	Marburg/Lahn, Musikwissenschaftliches Institut der Philipps-Universität, Abteilung Hessisches Musikarchiv
D-brd-NEhz	Neuenstein, Kreis Öhringen (Württemberg), Hohenlohe-Zentralarchiv
D-brd-SI	Sigmaringen, Fürstlich Hohenzollernsche Hofbibliothek
D-brd-ZL	Zeil (Bayern), Fürstlich Waldburg-Zeil'sches Archiv

D-ddr—Deutsche Demokratische Republik

D-ddr-A	Altjessnitz, Schlossbibliothek
D-ddr-Bds	Berlin, Deutsche Staatsbibliothek (ehem. Kgl. Bibliothek; Preußische Staatsbibliothek; Öffentliche Wissenschaftliche Bibliothek), Musikabteilung
D-ddr-Dlb	Dresden (Sachsen), Sächsische Landesbibliothek, Musikabteilung (ehem. Kgl. Öffentliche Bibliothek)
D-ddr-GOl	Gotha (Thüringen), Landesbibliothek (ehem. Herzogliche Bibliothek)
D-ddr-LEb	Leipzig (Sachsen), Bach-Archiv
D-ddr-LEm	Leipzig (Sachsen), Musikbibliothek der Stadt Leipzig (Musikbibliothek Peters und verschiedene Sammlungen in der Leipziger Stadtbibliothek)
D-ddr-SWl	Schwerin (Mecklenburg), Mecklenburgische Landesbibliothek (ehem. Mecklenburgische Regierungsbibliothek), Musikabteilung
D-ddr-WRtl	Weimar (Thüringen), Thüringische Landesbibliothek (ehem. Grossherzogliche Bibliothek), Musiksammlung

F—France

F-Pc	Paris, Bibliothèque du Conservatoire national de musique (in F-Pn)
F-Pn	Paris, Bibliothèque nationale
F-Sim	Strasbourg, Institut de musicologie de l'Université

GB—Great Britain

GB-Lbm	London, British Museum (British Library)
GB-Lcm	London, Royal College of Music
GB-Ltyson	London, Privatbibliothek Alan Tyson

H—Magyarország

H-Bn	Budapest, Országos Széchényi Könyvtár (Nationalbibliothek Széchényi)
H-KE	Keszthely, Országos Széchényi Könyvtár, "Helikon"-Könyvtára

I—Italia

I-Bc	Bologna, Civico Museo Bibliografico-Musicale (ehem. Liceo Musicale "G. B. Martini")
I-Gi(l)	Genova, Istituto musicale (Biblioteca del Liceo Musicale "Paganini")
I-Mc	Milano, Biblioteca del Conservatorio "Giuseppe Verdi"
I-MOe	Modena, Biblioteca Estense

US—United States of America

US-BLl	Bloomington, Indiana University, Lilly Library
US-NYp	New York, New York Public Library at Lincoln Center
US-NYpm	New York, Pierpont Morgan Library
US-Wc	Washington, Library of Congress, Music Division

ABBREVIATIONS

auto.	autograph
deest	not present
E.	additions to Köchel Fux Catalogue (see Federhofer/Riedel/FUX)
*EK**	*Entwurf-Katalog*
frag.	fragment
*HBV**	*Haydn Bibliothek Verzeichnis*
*HNV**	*Haydn Nachlass Verzeichnis*
Hob.*	Hoboken Haydn Catalogue
*HV**	*Haydn Verzeichnis*
*JHW-HI**	*Joseph Haydn Werke*
K	Closing material
K.*	Köchel Mozart or Fux Catalogues
LV	London Catalogue
m. (mm.)	measure(s)
mvt.	movement
N	New material
P	Primary material in the tonic key
S	Secondary material presented initially in a related key or the solo in a concerto
T	Transition material, usually of a modulatory character
*WWV**	*Wagenseil Werkverzeichnis*
*Wq.**	*Wotquenne C. P. E. Bach Catalogue*

*See Bibliography

The analytical symbols K, N, P, R, S, and T used for movements in sonata form derive from the system developed in LaRue/GUIDELINES. Letters preceded by Arabic numerals define constituent parts of a function (e.g., 1P, 2P). Lower-case letters a, b, c, d, etc., following the upper-case letters indicate phrases or smaller-dimension portions of a function; while x, y, z following a, b, c, d, etc., identify a still smaller component. Thus, the initial motive of the beginning of a Primary section of an exposition would be Pax; the second idea of the second phrase of the second motive of the Secondary area would be 2Sby. Parentheses are for derivations: S(P) means that the Secondary area derives from the Primary material. Superscript numerals signal a variant: e.g., Pa^1 indicates a variant of Pa. A superscript k (e.g., P^k) means that a closing function is present at the end of the main function.

For forms other than sonata form, the standard upper- and lower-case letters are used (e.g., Rondo: ABACA).

When necessary, the dimensions (i.e., number of measures) of each part, section, etc., are given in Arabic numerals directly below the analytical symbols.

In the schematic examples, the morphological structure of a phrase, statement, section, etc., is indicated as follows:

2 + 2	Balanced classical phrase remaining within a tonal orbit
4 × 2	Sequence of four repetitions of a two-measure unit in which the materials change pitch level with each reiteration

The strength and nature of a cadence may be indicated as:

AIS   Authentic Imperfect Strong
APS   Authentic Perfect Strong
HC   Half Cadence

Finally, tonal changes are pointed out by the usual Roman numerals; a jagged line (⟿) signals tonal instability, while a horizontal arrow (→) identifies an area of stability. An arrow pointing downward (↓) indicates a structural downbeat.

PART ONE
Sources

Essay I

INTRODUCTION:
HAYDN AND THE KEYBOARD,
A REVISIONIST VIEW

There has been a tale in the air that Haydn did not have much sympathy for key-board instruments and that his works are not well suited to them.[1] This belief can be attributed to a convergence of social practice, aesthetic taste, and a remark that stems directly from the composer himself. During the eighteenth century, key-board music was not on the elevated plane of the string quartet, a genre then re-served for men.[2] Rather, it was more diversionary and required less of the per-former, both technically and spiritually; the vast number of facile keyboard sonatas and pieces offered by publishers for performance by the lady of the house attests to this characterization.

Our view of Haydn as a keyboard composer has also been determined to a great extent by the legendary reputation of his erstwhile student Beethoven; the Beethovenian concept of instrumental style, particularly in keyboard music, has been the most significant generator of musical taste throughout the nineteenth and twentieth centuries. Consequently, the keyboard works of Haydn have been largely absent from the repertoire, while those of Beethoven form the core of one program after another. Those works that do make an occasional appearance—the Sonatas Hob. XVI:20, 49, 50, 52, and the Variations XVII:6—are the precursors of the aesthetic that Beethoven, his contemporaries, and successors so thoroughly developed.

Finally, there is Haydn's own statement, "I was not a wizard on any instrument . . . ; I was not a poor *Klavier* player,"[3] which has made a negative impression on subsequent generations. After all, both Mozart and Beethoven were keyboard vir-tuosos and composers; certainly, one would think, their works were more idiomatic for the instrument. Yet the evidence does not support this view, as the following historical survey reveals.

As early as his fifth or sixth year, while living with a relative at Hainburg, the young Haydn probably began to play a keyboard instrument. Later, at the choir school in Vienna (1740–1749), he studied the clavichord, harpsichord, and organ with very fine masters. Beginning in the early 1750s, Haydn taught both clavichord and harpsichord, composing sonatas and trios for his students. During this same decade he was organist at the hospital of the Barmherzigen Brüder in Leopoldstadt and for the chapel of Count Harrach in Vienna; in these posts he must have been required to improvise, and he certainly composed several organ concertos for his own use. Also during this decade, he apparently mastered the art of accompaniment, under the supervision of Nicola Porpora. While serving in both Vienna and Bohemia as Kapellmeister to Count Morzin (*ca.* 1758–1760), Haydn gave the Countess keyboard lessons.[4]

By the 1750s the keyboard had become more than a professional vehicle for Haydn; playing it apparently provided him with solace. As an old man he remembered his life in less-than-desirable quarters in an attic on the Michaelerplatz, and, according to Dies,

> The severe loneliness of the place, the lack of anything to divert an idle spirit, and his quite needy situation led him to contemplations which were often so grave that he found it necessary to take refuge at his worm-eaten *Klavier* . . . to play away his melancholy."[5]

With his formal appointment in 1761 as Vice-Kapellmeister to the Esterházy court, which continued to be his full-time employer for nearly thirty years, Haydn's responsibilities at the various residences of the Hungarian magnate can be more fully documented. Two of the provisions of his contract of 1 May 1761 were that he should be prepared to provide music in both the mornings and the afternoons and to play all the instruments familiar to him.[6] Traditionally it has been assumed that works with the baryton or for full orchestra were performed; it is rarely mentioned that string quartets, trios, and, of course, keyboard music could well have satisfied these provisions. Since the Vice-Kapellmeister was a keyboardist as well as a violinist, violist, and baryton player, it seems likely that Haydn himself may have performed keyboard concertos, divertimentos, concertinos, sonatas, and possibly trios.

Haydn was certainly the keyboard player for the 1764 performances of his brilliant soprano aria from "Qual dubbio omai" (Hob. XXIVa:4) with orchestra and keyboard obbligato and in the chorus from "Al tuo arrivo felice" (Hob. XXIVa:3), both celebratory cantatas for Prince Esterházy. Indeed, Haydn may also have intended to perform the obbligato in the "Applausus" cantata, written for the occasion of the fiftieth year of the ordination of the abbot at Stift Zwettl, but found that impossible; hence, the famous letter of 1768 with instruction for its performance.[7] It has recently been documented that a keyboardist performed during the visit of Maria Theresa to Esterháza castle in 1773;[8] this performer must again have been Haydn himself.

After his promotion to full Kapellmeister following the death of Gregor Werner in March 1766, Haydn returned to playing and composing for the organ; his duties as chamber musician were now augmented by his assumption of the responsibility for the music in the Prince's chapel. With the death of the Eisenstadt castle organist Franz Novotny in the summer of 1773, Haydn also took up the task of playing the organ while the musical entourage spent the winter in Eisenstadt; the tenor and castle schoolmaster, Joseph Dietzl, occupied this position while Haydn was absent in the non-winter months.[9] During this post-Werner period, Haydn produced three liturgical works in which the organ takes on a soloistic function: the Great Organ Mass, written at the end of the 1760s; the Salve Regina, composed in 1771; and the Little Organ Mass, traditionally dated during the mid-1770s.

In a report from J. A. P. Schulz from *ca.* 1770 we have the first document concerning Haydn's compositional routine:

> I get up early, and as soon as I have dressed, I kneel down and pray to God and the Holy Virgin that things may go well today. After some breakfast, I sit at the *Klavier* and begin to improvise. If I hit upon something soon, then things go further without much effort. But if nothing comes to me, then I see that I have through some lapse lost grace; and I pray again for mercy until I feel that I am forgiven.[10]

Later reports from the early 1800s given by Haydn's biographers Dies and Griesinger, his amanuensis Johann Elssler, and his longtime friend the Abbé Maximilian Stadler also emphasize Haydn's use of the keyboard for composing works of all genres.[11]

By 1776 the musical interests at the Esterházy court had changed radically from church and chamber music to the theater. Thus, Haydn's activities as a keyboardist in solo and ensemble capacities were superseded by that of operatic conductor at the harpsichord *continuo*.[12] Perhaps at this time Haydn decided to broaden his study of *continuo* realization; he owned not only the famous treatises by Mattheson and Emanuel Bach but also other books devoted to the realization of the *continuo* line by Carissimi, Daube, Gugl, Heinichen, Kellner, Marpurg, and Münster.[13]

During these years as full Kapellmeister Haydn produced many important compositions for the clavichord, harpsichord, and *fortepiano*. Between the mid-1760s (after the composition of the Capriccio Hob. XVII:1 and the Variations Hob. XVII:2) and 1784, he wrote some thirty solo sonatas—including a series of impressive single sonatas extending to *ca.* 1771 (Hob. XVI:18, 45, 19, 46, 44, 20); the Esterházy Sonatas of 1774 (Hob. XVI:21–26); the "sonatas of the year 1776" (Hob. XVI:27–32); the Auenbrugger Sonatas (Hob. XVI:35–39 [20]), published in 1780; and those for Marie Esterházy (Hob. XVI:40–42), published in 1784—as well as three harpsichord concertos (Hob. XVIII:3, 4, 11). After 1784 the number of solo works decreases appreciably to five sonatas and two important *Klavierstücke*; under pressure from English and Continental publishers, Haydn turned to the composition of keyboard trios.

In the winter months, when operatic performances at Esterháza ceased, Haydn went to Vienna with his Prince, took up residence at the Esterházy *Palais* on Wallnerstrasse, and allowed himself to enjoy the social and musical amenities offered in the houses of the dilettantes. Haydn's keyboard trios and solo sonatas were performed in the home of Marianna von Genzinger in the Schottenhof.[14] His lieder with keyboard accompaniments also received an audience; as he was to do later in England, Haydn would perform at the clavichord or *fortepiano* and sing his newest songs, an act he considered his "prerogative."[15]

Accounts of these contacts with both connoisseurs and dilettantes during the 1780s broaden our knowledge of Haydn's keyboard interests. His concern with the amateur extended beyond the composition of keyboard music to its actual presentation, for he complained to his publisher Artaria in 1784 of the "terrible engraving" and "many aggravating mistakes"; the sections that were "unreadable, wrong, or badly arranged and laid out"; and caustically concluded "anyone who buys them will curse the engraver."[16] His works also began to appear in arrangements and transcriptions for keyboard. Here, Haydn's main concern was with their suitability for the instrument; an entire movement or several variations might be deleted. Concerning an arrangement of Symphony No. 69, "The Laudon," Haydn told Artaria: "The last or 4th movement is not practicable on the *Clavier*, and I don't think it necessary to print it."[17] At this time, Haydn also began to express an interest in the special attributes of various instruments, complaining that Herr Walter's were expensive and too inconsistent in quality and recommending those of Herr Schanz to Frau von Genzinger.

With the death of Prince Nikolaus in September 1790, Haydn's operatic and other musical duties came to an abrupt halt; by the end of the month the entire musical establishment was dissolved, and the former Esterházy Kapellmeister moved to Vienna. On the eighth of December, Johann Peter Salomon struck a deal with Haydn for concerts in London, and on the first of January 1791 the two set foot on English soil. This first venture outside the environs of Vienna had a profound effect on Haydn's activities as a composer: his high production of first-rate keyboard works ceased as Haydn concentrated on new symphonies and the opera *L'anima del filosofo*.

However, during his first English visit the keyboard was at the center of Haydn's public appearances at the Salomon orchestral concerts in the Hanover Square rooms; as the newspaper notices stated—and Charles Burney confirmed—Haydn "presided at the pianoforte." Subsequent historical commentary has been reluctant to take this statement at face value, explaining that it merely meant that the composer conducted from the keyboard, that the keyboard *continuo* was an unnecessary part of the texture in his late symphonies, and that, in any case, the keyboard could not be heard. On the other hand, it is difficult to believe that in fact Haydn did not play a *continuo* part and that in this capacity he did not provide rhythmic and harmonic support to the ensemble, as he had done in the theater at Esterháza for some fourteen years. In 1792 Haydn even incorporated a solo into the finale of Symphony No. 98. As Samuel Wesley recalled:

> His performance on the piano-forte, although not as such to stamp him a first rate artist upon that instrument, was indisputably neat and distinct. In the finale of one of his Symphonies is a passage of attractive brilliancy, which he has given to the

piano-forte, and which the writer of this Memoir remembers him to have executed with utmost accuracy and precision.[18]

Haydn also performed a number of times as an accompanist; his appearances are documented in one of several performances of "Arianna a Naxos" in February 1791 and in a "difficult English Aria by Purcell" ("From rosy bower") for the benefit concert of Madame Mara in June 1792.[19]

In 1793, during the respite in Vienna between the two London journeys, Haydn composed the F-minor Variations (Hob. XVII:6), which presents a microcosmic but complete view of his late keyboard style. Armed with the power of this work, Haydn undertook the second London journey and apparently entered another phase of intensive compositional activity in 1794–1795. During this period he probably produced three solo sonatas (Hob. XVI:50–52), fourteen or fifteen keyboard trios (Hob. XV:32, 18–29, 31), and vocal works with obbligato keyboard parts: fourteen songs with English texts, two duets with Italian texts, and the occasional piece "Dr. Harrington's Compliment."

Even though Haydn complained to Frau von Genzinger of his overwhelming social schedule at the beginning of his first London journey,[20] this new repertoire must have increased his appeal to the English capital's society: his singing and playing of the newly composed Canzonettas among royalty, nobility, and gentry seem to have been a highlight of British party life that could only be matched by owning the printed copy of the first set autographed by the composer.[21]

> After his introduction [to George III], Haydn, by desire of the queen, sat down to the pianoforte, and surrounded by Her Majesty and her royal and accomplished daughters, sang and accompanied himself admirably in several of his *canzonets*.[22]

While in London Haydn took an active interest in English developments and experiments in keyboard construction. In *The Morning Herald* of 27 April 1792 he addressed a letter to Mr. Clagget, the proprietor of a musical museum:

> I called at your house, during your absence, and examined your improvements on the Pianoforte, and Harpsichords, and I found you had made them perfect instruments. I therefore, in justice to your invention, cannot forbear giving you my full approbation, as by this means you have rendered one of the finest instruments ever invented, perfect, and therefore the fittest to conduct any musical performance, and to accompany the human voice.[23]

Another report tells us that Haydn went to Stodart's place of business on Lad Lane to see his *fortepiano* of grand dimensions in the form of a bookcase. He supposedly expressed delight not only with its "new possibilities" for case-making but also with the quality of its sound.[24]

During his time in London Haydn must also have had the opportunity to become familiar with many more virtuoso keyboardists than he had encountered previously. Although in Vienna there were Mozart and Beethoven, London—with its active public concert life and its attraction of immigrant musicians from revolution-

ary Paris—was populated by both amateur and professional players of unusual skill
in remarkable numbers. In his London Notebook from 1791–1792, Haydn provides us with what may be the best list of pianists active in the British capital during the 1790s: Muzio Clementi (1752–1832), Johann Ladislaus Dussek (1760–
1812), Adalbert Gyrowetz (1763–1830), Joseph Diettenhofer (*ca.* 1743–1797?),
Charles Burney (1726–1814), Miss Esther Burney (1749–1832), Nicolas-
Joseph Hüllmandel (1751–1823), Johann G. Graff, Miss Cecilia Barthelemon,
Johann B. Cramer (1771–1858), Johann Nepomuk Hummel (1778–1837),
Therese Jansen [Bartolozzi] (*ca.* 1770–1843), and Heinrich Gerhard von Lenz
(1764?–1839).[25]

From Haydn's final return to Vienna in 1795 until his death in 1809, his in-
volvement with keyboard performance and composition seems to have been minimal; only a single accompanied sonata (Hob. XV:30) was completed, although he
repeatedly expressed an intent to compose more. His vocal quartets and trios contain obligatory *fortepiano* parts, as do the numerous arrangements of Scottish and
other national songs produced by Haydn for Thomson and Napier. Solo passages
for the organ are present in the "Nelson" and "Creation" masses—two of six composed for the Princess Esterházy's name day between 1796 and 1802. The single
documented performance for this final period was a semi-public one at an entertainment given by the Princess Esterházy for the Archduchess Pawlowna on
31 October 1800.[26]

During his final years, when he was no longer able to compose, the old man
derived a great deal of comfort from hearing the *fortepiano*, although at times he
was hypersensitive to its sound, as his Swedish student Paul Struck reports in December 1804:

> Recently I had to play something for him. To begin with, he sat next to the *Forte-
> piano*, but he immediately carried the chair to the [other] end of the room because
> the *Fortepiano* was far too loud for him. There, however, he sat for a long time and
> said that he enjoyed listening.[27]

This condition probably caused Haydn to sell his *fortepiano*, an event ruefully recorded in his "Krakauer Schreibkalender" (see Plate 1). Thus, in his last years he
probably used the clavichord exclusively. Even in his final months he played "Gott
erhalte Franz den Kaiser" at this quiet instrument with regularity until five days
before his death: "I have often found support and consolation from it on restless
days—I can't do otherwise; I must play it once a day. I feel quite contented whenever I play it and for a little while after, too."[28]

The picture that emerges is not the traditional one of a composer disinterested in
the keyboard and his own keyboard music, but rather one in which the instrument
and its music had a compelling place in his life. Haydn not only performed on the
instrument with precision and an uncommon expression but also used it as a means
for developing ideas that later emerged as full-fledged compositions. In addition,
the keyboard was for him something more personal: it provided psychological com-

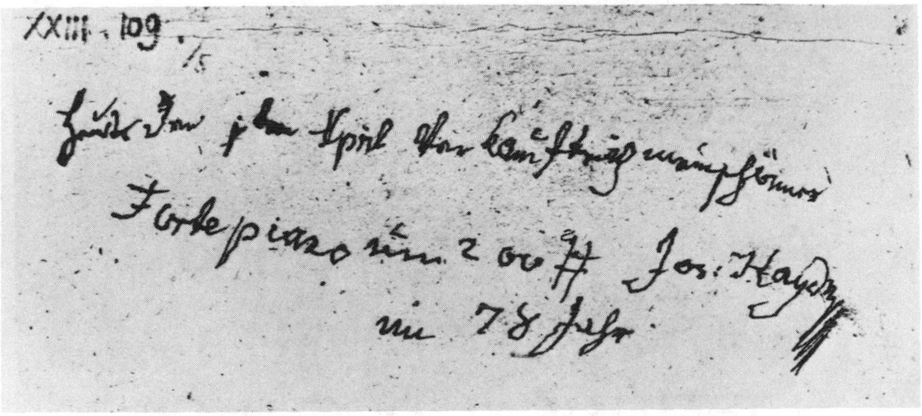

PLATE 1. Haydn's last entry in a "Krakauer" *Schreibkalender*. (A-Wn) "Heute den 1ten April verkaufte ich mein schönes Fortepiano um 200 Dukaten Jos: Haydn mp im 78 Jahr." (Today, the 1st of April I sold my beautiful *Fortepiano* for 200 ducats Joseph Haydn mp in my 78th year.) (A-Wn)

fort, and served as a social lubricator for his presence in the Viennese and London salons. Haydn also kept himself abreast of the newest developments in the design of these instruments, the special characteristics of the products of individual makers, and the current crop of *virtuosi* in both Vienna and London. Finally, Haydn was always concerned with the presentation of his keyboard works and the suitability of arrangements and transcriptions to the instrument's idiom. Indeed, no other instrument seems to have consistently occupied him so completely.

Thus, it is time to revise our view of Haydn and the keyboard. The overwhelming evidence is that the keyboard was at the very center of Haydn's musical life and interests from a tender age until mere days before his death at the age of seventy-seven.

Essay II

THE KEYBOARD WORKS IN BIOGRAPHICAL, CRITICAL, AND MUSICAL DOCUMENTS

Viennese and Esterházy Works to 1791

While it may be assumed that keyboard sonatas, solo pieces, trios, ensemble divertimentos, and concertos were among the earliest mediums in which Haydn composed, there exists little documentary evidence to dispute or to support such a claim. The only direct biographical reference to works including the keyboard from the early years comes more than half a century after the fact, from Georg August Griesinger's conversations with the aging composer:

> Many of his easy *Klavier* sonatas, trios, and the like fall into this period, and in them he mostly took into account the need and capability of his students. Only a few originals have remained with him; he gave them away and considered it an honor if people took them. He did not realize that music dealers did a good business with them, and he used to enjoy stopping in front of the shops where one or another of his works was displayed in print.[1]

Since this paragraph seemingly refers to circumstances in the 1750s, it must be viewed with some reservation: we know of no publication of Haydn's keyboard music—or in fact of any of his works—from this time.[2] The account is therefore more credible if "copies" is substituted for "print," as there is evidence that during the 1750s Haydn's works were being distributed without authorization by professional Viennese copyists. It may be that observing others profiteering from his works stimulated the young composer to work directly with the professional scribes, even though his correspondence suggests he never trusted them.[3]

Only three early keyboard works, Hob. XVI:6, Hob. XIV:11, and Hob. XVIII:1, survive in autographs, and only the Concertino (Hob. XIV:11) carries a contemporary date of 1760;[4] other early works survive only in copies. However, it is generally assumed that before his employment with the Esterházy family began in May 1761, Haydn had composed about sixteen solo keyboard sonatas, nearly all of the early keyboard trios and ensemble divertimentos, and most of the concertos. Some of these works may have been composed for Haydn himself, but the larger number, as Griesinger states, were probably for his students. Although most of Haydn's pupils are known to us only through these sonatas, two keyboard players of fine repute were students of the young Haydn during these years: Marianna Martines (1744–1812) and a Countess Thun.[5]

Haydn's association with Fräulein Martines, the daughter of the papal ambassador, began with his engagement as her teacher of singing and keyboard in 1751.[6] She was being tutored by the court poet, Metastasio, who lived in the Michaelerhaus at the same time as Haydn. She became well known as a keyboardist, singer, and composer and was honored by election to the Philharmonic Academy of Bologna.[7] Burney saw her with Metastasio on several occasions in 1772 and noted: "Her performance indeed surpassed all that I had been made to expect. . . . She displayed a very difficult lesson, of her own composition, on the harpsichord, with great rapidity and precision."[8] According to the Irish tenor Michael Kelly, "Mozart was an almost constant attendant at her parties, and I have heard him play duets on the piano-forte with her, of his own composition. She was a great favourite of his."[9] During the 1790s she hosted one of the leading Viennese musical salons on Sunday evenings.[10]

Our knowledge of the other early Haydn student, the Countess Thun, comes from a romanticized biographical pamphlet written by Nicolas Étienne Framery—based on information from Haydn's student Ignaz Pleyel—and published in Paris shortly after Haydn's death:

A woman of quality does not renounce a project which is firmly lodged in her head: the Countess was only searching for the composer of her sonata; she wished to be certain of his talents rather than his morals: thus she persists in her quest, and finally discovered the very modest retreat in which our young composer was hidden. A valet arrived there on her behalf: is forced to climb to the attic, where poor Joseph, ashamed of the miserable surroundings in which he is surprised, passes himself off as his own servant. "You will announce to your master," says the messenger, "that Mme. the Countess Thun wishes to see him, and that he should not fail to present himself at her home tomorrow morning." Joseph promises. But how can he keep his word? In his tatters of clothing, his shreds of shoes; will he dare appear in such condition before a lady of such rank? Spangler, his landlord, almost as poor as he, can't make him the smallest loan; nor can he because of the great difference in their height even lend him the bare necessities from his own wardrobe: nonetheless the command is precise; his fortune could depend upon this visit; he decides; he will go. The next morning he arranges what he can reassemble of his clothing as well as possible so as to cover his near nakedness to some extent, arms himself with courage, and arrives at the house of the countess; he is received by the same valet who had seen him before, and who examining him from head to foot, is astonished to find him so ill-dressed, even for the servant of a musician, and concludes by asking if his master will soon arrive. "I have no master," says the young man: "I am Haydn: please announce me." The valet is not sure that he can believe this; but his mistress wishes it: Joseph is introduced. Mme. de Thun is no less surprised to see a man of this profession in such a condition; she thinks she has been fooled. "Are you Mr. Haydn," says she, "whom I have sent for?" "I am he, Madame."—"But I wish to see the composer of this sonata" (it was on the music rack of her harpsichord).—"I am he, Madame."—"How old are you then?" "Madame, I am sixteen years old." She then examines more carefully this pitiful pale figure proclaiming his misery, and perhaps worse. "There must be a reason," she thought to herself: no doubt debauchery has reduced him to this condition. "Have you composed," she adds, "any other sonatas of this type?" "Yes, Madame, I have composed a number of them for some music lovers who have had the goodness to seek them: this is the latest." "And haven't these pieces earned you enough to allow you to dress decently?" "When I wrote the first ones, Madame, I was a choir boy at St. Stephen's, where I was completely provided for: the gifts that I received there were only for spending money; this one I composed since I was dismissed." "You were discharged."—"Yes, Madame, at seven o'clock in the evening in the Autumn." "As a bad student, because of misconduct?" "It is true, Madame, that I was treated that way, but it isn't so that I deserved it." "Anyway, this piece you have no doubt written it for someone who did not get it free?" "No, Madame, it earned me some florins which I gave to a benefactor who took me in my distress, and who shared his table to feed me: since I never go out, I have no need of clothes: but I need to show my appreciation to my friend: I cannot keep anything for myself since it ought to be his."

In spite of suspicions, the Countess appeared touched by these sentiments: she wished to know how and why he was expelled from the cathedral. With all the decency possible Joseph delivered an account of his disgrace, naively, as he was beginning to understand it. The injustice and cruelty Reitter [Reutter] had used in his case had reached a scarcely believable extent: even Mme. Thun thought the account exaggerated; but since it seemed plausible, she wanted to at least suspend her judgment. "Here is 25 ducats," she said to him; "use it to clothe yourself in a more presentable manner; to find a modest but comfortable lodging; and to settle your accounts with your friend. If everything you have told me is true, and if you always behave yourself, I will from now on be your protectress; every day you will give me lessons on the *clavecin* and in voice, and I will not allow you to lack anything; but if I learn that you turn to debauchery, I will shut my door to you and take back my benefits." [11]

The identity of this Countess Thun has been debated. Several Countesses Thun were active in Vienna at this time, but only Wilhelmine née Uhlfeld gained a reputation as an accomplished keyboardist and is a possibility in terms of age. If one dismisses some of the embroideries of a good story and rearranges some of the sequences of events so that this incident could be placed not in the late 1740s or early 1750s, but closer to Haydn's Morzin appointment (1758–1760), she seems the most reasonable possibility. [12]

During the 1760s Haydn's keyboard works were distributed outside of the Viennese environs: in Leipzig J. G. I. Breitkopf brought out several works, and in Amsterdam J. J. Hummel printed a set of six keyboard trios. Breitkopf offered his first sonata attributed to Haydn in his 1763 thematic catalogue (Hob. XVI:5) [13] and in subsequent years listed copies of accompanied keyboard divertimentos, trios, solo pieces, concertos, and additional solo sonatas. [14] More than thirty years later, in December 1799, Griesinger, as Breitkopf's emissary, questioned Haydn about the authenticity of some of these works; in light of our knowledge today, the old man's responses were not particularly reliable.[15] Hummel's print of keyboard trios (Op. 4) issued in 1767 consisted of four authentic works (Hob. XV:1, 37, C1, and XIV:1 [with two horns]), "grab bags" of solo sonata movements with added accompaniments (Hob. XIV:6 and XV:39), and one completely spurious movement (Hob. XV:39/2).[16] While Hummel's print is neither authentic nor of textual value, it did serve as the basis for other publications sold by Chevardière in Paris (*ca.* 1770) and Bremner in London (1772). Indeed, it may also have been the text of the Hummel edition that Leopold Mozart was familiar with when in August 1771 he requested the music for a Haydn Keyboard Trio in F major, probably Hob. XV:37.[17]

This wide distribution of his earliest works during the 1760s and early 1770s successfully established Haydn as a keyboard composer, but it also provoked the North German critics, and Haydn felt their wrath for some time to come. The first known denunciation appeared in Hiller's *Wöchentliche Nachrichten* in 1768: "Herr *Haydn*, a famous and estimable composer in other genres, has also written various things for the *Clavier*. It seems, however, that this instrument is not as congenial to him as other instruments which he puts to use in the most fiery and gallant symphonies. . . ."[18]

A year after Hiller's statement, a scathing review appeared in Hamburg, denouncing all Haydn's instrumental works save for the symphonies: "Only in his symphonies is he to be endured because of certain excellent ideas, not, however, due to taste or profundity. *Clavier* works or even trios and quartets by him are truly bad music."[19]

These criticisms were apparently more prevalent than the few surviving examples might seem to indicate. Charles Burney remarked about them in his article on Haydn in *The General History of Music*;[20] and in his autobiographical sketch from 1776 Haydn himself mentions such critics.[21]

However, by the time these notices appeared, Haydn had already changed his keyboard style. There is no apparent explanation for this metamorphosis.[22] It seems to have begun sometime around the year 1765 and is signaled by the composition of the Capriccio Hob. XVII:1 and the Variations Hob. XVII:2. The one-movement Capriccio is based on an Austrian folk melody, whose title, "Acht Sauschneider müssen seyn," is notated on the autograph with the date 1765. The song, in an Austrian dialect, begins:

Acht Sauschneider müassn sein,	Eight good men, it takes no more,
müassn sein,	takes no more,
wenns an Saubärn wulln schneidn.	Then you can castrate a boar.
Zwoa vorn und zwoa hintn,	Two in front, two behind,
zwoa holtn, uana bintn	Two to hold, one to bind,
und uana schneidt drein, schneidt drein,	Also, one to do the chore, do the chore.
iahna achti müassn sein.	Eight good men, it takes no more.
Siebn Sauschneider müassn sein,	Seven good men, it takes no more,
müassn sein,	takes no more,

wenns an Saubärn wulln schneidn.	Then you can castrate a boar.
Zwoa vorn und zwoa hintn,	Two in front, two behind,
uana holtn, uana bintn	One to hold, one to bind,
und uana schneidt drein, schneidt drein,	Also, one to do the chore, do the chore.
iahna siebni müassn sein.	Seven good men, it takes no more.
Sechs Sauschneider müassn sein,	Six good men, it takes no more,
müassn sein. . . .	takes no more. . . .

Since a musical version close to the Capriccio has not been found, it is impossible to determine whether Haydn quoted the tune directly or modified it to fit his own needs.[23] The Capriccio is one of the watersheds in the history of keyboard music, not only for its forward-looking harmonic language but also for its effective use of sonorities.[24] And while harmonic adventure is not a characteristic of the Variations Hob. XVII:2, the work represents a virtual compendium of variation technique.

After 1765, Haydn composed a series of sonatas that, together with the works of his Viennese contemporary Joseph Anton Steffan, broke radically from the cyclic works by Georg Christoph Wagenseil, Leopold Hofmann, and the earlier compositions by Steffan himself. Hob. XIV:5 (*recte* XVI:5a), XVI:47 in the E-minor/E-major version, 45, 19, 46, 18, 44, and 20 are larger in dimension and deeper in expression than the compositions previously associated with the genre. In addition, Haydn composed seven sonatas that are known to us only by their incipits in the *Entwurf-Katalog* (*EK*) (see Plate 2).[25] All fifteen sonatas from this period are remarkable for their emphasis on the minor as the principal mode of the cycle: we know of only the F-minor and G-minor Keyboard Trios (Hob. XV:f1 and 1) from the 1750s and early 1760s, but from the mid-1760s to the early 1770s Sonatas in E minor/major (Hob. XVI:47), C minor (Hob. XVI:20), and G minor (Hob. XVI:44), as well as two lost works in E and D minor (see Plate 2), are known.

The seven "lost" sonatas might provide more clues to the evolution of this new style, which is hinted at in Hob. XIV:5 (*recte* XVI:5a), but there seems to be little hope for their recovery. One of them, in the unusual key of B major, figures in a curious story:

> Around the year 1770, Haydn was afflicted with a high fever, and the doctor had strictly forbidden him to busy himself with music during the course of his gradual recovery. Soon thereafter, Haydn's wife went to church, sternly admonishing the maid beforehand to keep an eye on her master so that he would not go to the *Klavier*. In his bed, Haydn acted as if he had heard nothing of the order, and no sooner had his wife left, but he sent the maid out of the house on an errand. Hurriedly, he leaped to his *Klavier*; at the first touch, the idea for a whole sonata came to him and the first part was finished while his wife was at church. When he heard her returning, he quickly threw himself into bed, and there, composed the rest of the sonata, which he could not identify to me more precisely than that it had five sharps.[26]

Except for this anecdote, nothing is known of the origin of any of the sonatas from the 1760s and early 1770s. Those that survive in autograph are, save for

EK 19

PLATE 2. The pages of keyboard entries in the *Entwurf-Katalog*. (D-ddr-Bds)

EK 20
PLATE 2 (*continued*)

EK 21
PLATE 2 (*continued*)

EK 22
PLATE 2 (*continued*)

EK 23
PLATE 2 (*continued*)

TABLE II-1

Alternate Versions and Settings of Keyboard Works from the 1760s and Early 1770s

Non-keyboard version	Date	Keyboard version	Remarks
Baryton Trio XI:37/1	end 1766–Sept. 1767	XVI:3/1	1st movement transcription
Baryton Trio XI:38/1	end 1766–Sept. 1767	XVIIa:1/1, "Il maestro e lo scolare"	Melodic similarities of theme
String Quartet Op. 9/2/2	*ca.* 1769–1770	XVII:3	Theme used for variations
Baryton Trio XI:103/1,2 ⎫ Baryton Duo XII:13 (lost) ⎭	Jan.–Mar. 1772	XV:2/1,3 XIV:2/1,3	Transcription and recomposition
Baryton Trio XI:110/1,2	April 1772	XIV:8/1,2	Transcription and recomposition

Hob. XVI:20, in fair copies and thus tell us little about their genesis. However, we do have alternate versions and settings of movements from other chamber works, as listed in Table II-1. With the exception of the variations on the theme from the String Quartet Op. 9/2, one cannot be certain which version came first. For example, if we accept Feder's theory on the notation of appoggiaturas,[27] the Sonata Hob. XVI:3 preceded the baryton version. On the other hand, Haydn habitually increased the speed of his tempo markings in revisions and subsequent versions. Using the latter criterion, all the settings with baryton would precede the keyboard versions.[28]

Of the works listed in Table II-1, only Hob. XVIIa:1, "Il maestro e lo scolare," achieved popularity. Here, each phrase is played first by the master and then echoed by the student in a tiresome, pedagogical routine. Two early reviews present differing reactions, which are still voiced today:

> Since among the fashionable pieces of today are those for two people at one *Clavier*, which are composed by many more or less well-known and celebrated composers and are sought by friends of music, this work will also be welcome; since it is pleasant and entertaining for two friends to play together at one instrument. This sonata contains an Andante with eight variations which in turn keeps both players adequately occupied. At the end is a Tempo di Menuetto.[29]

> A melodic chain of the most select passages is supposed to be heard, of which each member is incessantly stated twice, once in the bass and once in the treble. This must necessarily arouse as much disgust as a collection of the best, the wittiest remarks, if they were to be spoken first by a master in a bass voice and then by a pupil in a high one.[30]

In 1773 Haydn was working on a set of six sonatas (Hob. XVI:21–26), which were to be the first works printed under his own supervision. They were announced in the *Wienerisches Diarium* on 26 February 1774 and were dedicated to

Prince Nikolaus Esterházy, Haydn's patron since 1762.[31] *EK* lists them as "6 gedruckte Sonaten von 774."

Prince Nikolaus Esterházy (1714–1790) was one of many connoisseurs of music among the Imperial nobility. He played the baryton[32] and had a passionate interest in it from around 1765 to the early 1770s, but by the time his new castle, Esterháza, was built at Fertöd in the Hungarian marshlands, his interest had changed to the theater and opera. Haydn provided incidental music for the former as well as overall direction and some new works for the latter. It was not so much his interests that distinguished the Prince from other aristocrats, but the wealth with which he was able to support these diversions on a grand scale.

Nothing is known directly of the Prince's musical taste of this time except from the repertoire used in the chamber, theater, and church at the Esterházy court. From Haydn's numerous works including the baryton, it can be surmised that the Prince's tastes tended toward the so-called *galant* style, which features sonata-form movements in a moderate tempo with a basic subdivision of the eighth note, variation movements as well as rudimentary contrapuntal movements of the Fuxian type, slow movements employing a cantilena style, and aristocratic minuets. The movements are often organized into a standard Viennese trio sonata cycle of the time: Slow–Fast–Minuet.

The degree to which Haydn continued to follow the preferences displayed in the baryton works is somewhat lessened in these six keyboard Sonatas Hob. XVI:21–26. However, one can point to a number of parallels: five of the first movements are in a moderate tempo, two of the finales are minuets, and one of the slow movements is a siciliana. In addition, the "al rovescio" minuet, which is transcribed from that of Symphony No. 47, recalls the artifices of the contrapuntal movements. In general, the sonatas are larger in dimension and of greater sophistication than the baryton works. Perhaps Haydn's awareness of this difference underlies the obsequiousness of the dedication:

> Most Serene Highness! Among the unique attributes, and much noted qualities, which adorn Your Most Serene Highness, is also found the complete command of all music, not only of the violin, and of the baryton, which you play exquisitely and equal to any expert teacher. This knowledge and the goodness with which Your Most Serene Highness has never hesitated to look upon my faithful service, as well as to bestow upon my compositions, makes me eager to dedicate to the superabundance of your merit this small portion of my talent. May Your Most Serene Highness deign to receive with your customary Magnanimity, as always encouraging and honoring with your high patronage he who humbly commends himself with the same offering [and] who bows in deepest respect,
>   of Your Most Serene Highness
>   the most humble, devoted, respectful
>   servant
>   Joseph Haydn.[33]

This first authentic Haydn print, published by Joseph Kurzböck, was set in type rather than engraved on plates, resulting in a text of less than first-rate clarity (see Plate 3). Nevertheless, the sonatas received wide distribution. In the same year

PLATE 3. The title page to the Kurzböck print of Hob. XVI:
21–26, the first authentic print of works by Haydn. (A-Wn)

Hummel of Amsterdam engraved them as Op. 13. These plates were taken over by
Longman & Broderip in 1781 and reissued in 1784 with an optional violin accompaniment by none other than Charles Burney. Other early printings were subsequently offered by firms in Vienna, London, and Paris.[34]

The following review appeared in 1778 in Germany:

> We can recommend the above-mentioned sonatas to friends of the *Klavier* as very
> agreeable and entertaining pieces. The strong and original humor that prevails in
> this composer's new quartets and quintets is not to be found here; rather [one finds]
> a very pleasant humor and an amusing wit.[35]

Six years later a review of debatable substance was published in England:

> From the engraving of these Sonatas, we imagine they were either printed in
> Germany or in Holland, and that the publishers have prefixed English titles to them.
> We do not hint this to lead the public to suppose they are incorrectly given: on the
> contrary, the note is a very good one, and there are very few faults to be met in the
> whole work.
>
> Although these Sonatas abound with great variety of thoughts, and a vast fund
> of invention, yet they are not so free and so generously open as most of this happy
> composer's works are generally found to be: some of them are confined, and others
> pedantick; but then it should be known they were intended to burlesque the man-
> ners of some German musicians, who, either from envy or ignorance, had entered
> into combinations against our author, and criticized his works with great severity in
> periodical pamphlets. Instead of answering them, however, in their own way, he

composed and printed three or four sets of Sonatas, in which, without announcing it to the public, he took them all off in so artful a manner, that each one beheld his own stile held forth in a ridiculous light, and yet none of them could claim one bar of the music!—It would be endless to particularize every passage throughout this work; but we cannot pass over the minuet to the fifth sonata, in which Haydn had Bach of Hamburg in his eye, whose compositions now and then are somewhat in the old stile, often consisting of *imitations* and *fugues*. This minuet that we are now pointing out being a regular canon, the answer of which is in the *unison*; in the first part the treble takes the lead, in the second part the bass begins, and the treble follows. This minuet is not a very pleasant one, because it is bound down by the rigid fetters that must encircle that species of music called a canon; so that what we lose of the pleasantry of the air, ample amends is made by the contrivance and ingenuity of the art.

Another curiosity (perhaps more so than the above) is the minuet to the sixth Sonata, which, when you have played the first part through, instead of repeating it, you begin with the last note of that part, and perform all the bars backwards; and the same is observed in the second part of the minuet, the whole of which is so contrived as to make good harmony, and is as agreeable to the ear backwards as forwards. This, by the bye, is a school trick; and examples of this kind are to be found in some of the works of our old English masters, such as Bird [*sic*] and Morley.[36]

Haydn's "second opus" of sonatas, Hob. XVI: 27–32, was composed *ca.* 1774–1776 or, perhaps in the case of the first sonata, as much as ten years earlier, even though the set is listed in *EK* as "6 Sonaten von Anno 776."[37] They bear no dedication and were originally distributed not in authentic prints but in copies—some of them dated—from a professional Viennese shop.[38] Like the 1774 set, they were also engraved by Hummel in Berlin and afterwards in England and at other points on the Continent.[39] Once again the Longman & Broderip edition with an added violin part was taken directly from the Hummel print Op. 14. Sentiments similar to those expressed about the 1774 sonata set appeared in a second English review from the same journal:

> These sonatas, like the former set [Hob. XVI: 21–26], are in many places intended to imitate the whimsical stiles of certain masters: and they are very well executed, for they abound with odd flights, strange passages, and eccentrick harmonies. The most natural and simple of them all is the first; after which he shews you with how much ease and address he can adopt the stiles of other authors, and blend their absurdities with his own good sense and pleasant melody.[40]

Haydn's third set of sonatas, Hob. XVI: 35–39 and 20, marks an important turning point in the distribution of his keyboard works, the beginning of his association with the publisher Artaria, a relationship that continued until the end of the composer's creative life (see Plate 4). In the numerous letters between Haydn and this Viennese house we see not so much the "Papa Haydn" but the shrewd businessman, who pitted Artaria against other firms desirous of his latest compositions. Unfortunately, the correspondence is one-sided; only the letters from Haydn were preserved in Artaria's once-rich archive.

The first letter, dated 31 January 1780, informs us that Haydn was sending the

PLATE 4. The title page of the Artaria edition of Hob. XVI:
35–39, 20. (Author's collection)

sixth sonata (C-minor Sonata Hob. XVI:20), which he had begun as early as
1771,[41] "because it is the longest and most difficult," and promised the fifth one,
probably the G-major Sonata Hob. XVI:39.[42] (On 8 February 1780 he sent the
G-major Sonata to be engraved.) The letter also reveals Haydn's continued concern, first expressed in the biographical sketch of 1776, with the reception of his
work: "I hope to gain a little recognition with these works, at least with the dis-
cerning public. Criticism of them will be made only by those who envy me (of
whom there are many)."[43] Within three weeks Haydn was returning the proofs and
again expressing concern with the reception of this "Opus 30":

> In addition, in order to anticipate the criticism of some half-wits, I find it necessary
> to add the following on the back side of the title page, underlined:
>   NOTICE
> In these six sonatas there are two single movements in which several measures show
> the same idea. The composer has done this intentionally to demonstrate different
> methods of treatment. For naturally, I could have selected a hundred other ideas for
> this one, but in this way no fault can be found with the whole opus on account of one
> intentional detail (which the critics and especially my enemies could interpret in the
> wrong way). So, I believe this advertisement, or something similar, must be added,
> since it could otherwise be detrimental to sales. I defer in this matter to the judicious
> opinion of the two Misses v. Auenbrugger, to whom I send my respectful attentions
> [*Hankuss* (sic)].[44]

The "Avvertissement," which Artaria did print, suggests that the C-minor Sonata was not the only work that originated some time before publication.

In a letter of 20 March Haydn expressed his satisfaction with the edition, but wished that the dedication to the "Misses von Auenbrugger" could have been his.[45] This letter reveals a common practice in music publishing: the dedication often came from the publisher rather than the composer. However, in this instance Haydn seemed more than pleased. And well he should be, for Katharina and Marianna—daughters of the famous physician from Graz, Leopold von Auenbrugger (1722–1809)—were highly accomplished keyboardists, and their home was a center of musical activity.[46]

Concerning Katharina (1755 or 1756–1825) and Marianna (1759–1782), Leopold Mozart remarked: "Both of them, and in particular the elder, play extraordinarily well and are thoroughly musical."[47] About 1781 Artaria published a keyboard sonata by Marianna together with an ode by Salieri, with whom she studied counterpoint. She died, possibly of consumption, on 25 August 1782.[48] At the age of ten or eleven, Katharina was mentioned in the 1766 listing of Viennese musicians in Hiller's *Nachrichten*.[49] She has been described as a "fiery beauty,"[50] and in 1796 she was still considered "one of the foremost artists on the *Fortepiano*, which she played not only with accomplishment but also with taste."[51]

Artaria's print was announced in the *Wiener-Zeitung* on 12 April 1780, by which time the sonatas had already reached Hummel in Berlin (according to Haydn's letter of 29 March, requesting author's copies of the sonatas from Artaria[52]). Hummel's edition appeared in September of the same year; editions by Longman & Broderip as well as by other English and French houses followed.[53] In a review of Artaria's edition, the *Almanach Musical* commented: "These sonatas present novel characteristics, some full of daring. It is to be hoped that this opus will cause the works which don't match the fame of this composer and which have errors and harshness of style to disappear."[54]

During the early 1780s the London music publisher Beardmore & Birchall issued an unauthorized print of three sonatas: Hob. XVI:33, 34, and 43. They are also known from Viennese copies, one of which, Hob. XVI:33, carries the date 17 January 1778.[55] To view these works as one opus is incorrect even though they all seem to come from the 1770s and/or early 1780s. Two of them, Hob. XVI:43 and 34, and Hob. XVI:15—that ever-present inauthentic arrangement of the Divertimento Hob. II:11—were republished together in 1785 by Le Duc in Paris. This French print was reviewed in Cramer's *Magazin der Musik* (1787).

> Although these sonatas are written in a very good style, they have a certain character which remains constant throughout each piece; and although they belong in every respect among the best sonatas for the Flügel or the *Fortepiano*, this reviewer would admit his doubts that they really come from Haydn's pen and are not merely appearing under his name—if only there were not in them so many ideas and turns of phrase that seem to betray a composer who could only be Haydn. Haydn would then have given his admirers three excellent sonatas in this collection, whose only fault is that they call to mind even more excellent products of his genius, which in contrast can be quickly recalled. The sonatas are easier than their predecessors, and

thereby, since the composer has perhaps taken special care to make them easy, the flight of his inspiration has naturally been somewhat curbed. We like the first one in A flat [Hob. XVI:43] the best. The initial Moderato is a fine web of the moderate feelings of youthful joy in which each thread adds to the beauty. From the second in D major [Hob. XVI:33], the Adagio in D minor is a lovely song and demands an especially warm heart in performance. The last one in C major [Hob. XVI:15] is quite short and has at its end a small Aria with five easy variations, of which the first four vary the upper part and the fifth the bass part.[56]

As early as the summer of 1782, Artaria had begun to request of Haydn some keyboard and violin works (probably trios); around 24 or 25 August Haydn wrote, "Concerning the *Clavier* sonatas with violin, you will have to remain patient for a long time, since I am now composing a completely new Italian opera [*Orlando Paladino*]. . . ."[57] The absence of new keyboard trios by Haydn since the mid-1760s also resulted in a letter from Königsberg published in Cramer's *Magazin* (April 1783):

> Herr Joseph Haydn, . . . who gave so many *Clavier* players an *Antispasmatica* against sadness and misfortune in his splendid sonatas; could he misconstrue it if such a considerable number of longing violinists beg of him here in the most friendly and respectful manner to remember them and to treat them again soon with an opus of violin sonatas? . . . As far as concerns the effort of a great man, is it not already payment when every violinist offers his unaffected thanks to the fine man? . . . Should this paper come to his attention, may he fulfill the wishes of the German violinists who honor him.[58]

The editor of this music journal of wide readership, C. F. Cramer, was one of the North German enthusiasts of Haydn's works. He possibly sent an advance copy to Artaria or to Haydn himself, as he was to do with his own lengthy review of an aria from *La Fedeltà Premiata* in early 1784.[59] Despite these urgings, in June 1783 Haydn was still overly occupied with his duties as *Opernkapellmeister*: "concerning those *Clavier* sonatas with violin and bass, you must still have patience since I am now writing a new *opera seria* [*Armida*]."[60]

The previous three authentic sets adhered to the eighteenth-century norm of six works of three movements each; that convention was now abandoned for a set of three solo Sonatas Hob. XVI:40–42, each in two movements. Perhaps this total of six miniature movements was partially a result of Haydn's preoccupation with his duties as an opera conductor and composer. Nevertheless, they are among Haydn's most beautiful creations in a lighter style. They were dedicated to Princess Marie Hermenegild Esterházy, née Liechtenstein, who had married the future Prince Nikolaus Esterházy II on 15 September 1783. The sonatas may have been a wedding present for the woman who was to gain the distinction of having more works by Haydn inscribed to her than to any other person.[61] The Preston edition of the Keyboard Trios Hob. XV:21–23 carries her name in dedication, and the six late masses (Hob. XXII:9–14) were commissioned for the celebration of her name day. In retrospect that is not surprising, for the Princess apparently had a special regard for Haydn. She visited him frequently during his last years; and, as he told Dies, "every visit is a new proof of her charity."[62]

That the sonata set Hob. XVI:40–42 was not published by Artaria is indicative of Haydn's growing contacts beyond the rather provincial Imperial capital.[63] Although the engraving of the text is not totally satisfactory, the first edition published as Op. 34 by Bossler in Speyer, advertised in the *Frankfurter Staatsristretto* on 31 August 1784, seems to have been the authorized one. Haydn himself performed from the Bossler print: this statement is written in Pater Rettensteiner's copy of the print located at Stift Michaelbeuren in Bavaria: "The following 3 sonatas were given to honor us by Herr Joseph Haydn at Esterháza on the 3rd of June 1785 during an entertaining hour-long visit when he played them."[64] A review of the Bossler edition in Cramer's *Magazin* uncannily communicates their spirit and style:

> These sonatas are written according to a different taste from previous ones by this famous master, though they are not any less valuable. The first in G major is actually only a short, very melodic movement in which each part has 8 measures. Then follows the *minore* in G. Both are then varied in an excellent manner. The final Presto in G major is put together in the same way. The finest taste prevails in the variations. The 2nd sonata in B-flat major is a masterpiece of its kind, just like its final Allegro molto. The 3rd in D major also has a *minore* and is almost more exquisitely varied than the first. In these variations, which are so well suited to the instrument, the composer proves to be like a skillful, tasteful singer when she repeats her aria. Moreover, the sonatas are more difficult to perform than one initially believes. They demand the utmost precision and much delicacy in performance.[65]

Haydn finally composed one new keyboard trio (Hob. XV:5). He sold it to the English publisher William Forster in 1784 along with two other trios, Hob. XV:3 and 4, which were actually written by Ignaz Pleyel. Through the detective work of Alan Tyson,[66] this strange tale can be thoroughly documented. It is first known from an anecdote apparently originating from Pleyel himself:

> Wishing to profit by the excellent lessons he [Pleyel] had received, he set himself assiduously to the composition of some sonatas for *clavecin*, whose quality is well known. After having been gone for some time, the pupil sent to the teacher as indications of his talent, two of these sonatas, composed at Strasbourg, where he then lived, and where he was having great success. This gift, which was only the homage of recognition, had an effect which may have confused these two men each so little inclined to esteem and love himself. Some time after, Haydn, having met with a music publisher from London, whose name, I think, is Forster, he [Forster] wrote and asked for three new sonatas of his, and that he fix a price for them, and that he send them as soon as possible: the master, then occupied with a large work, didn't wish to interrupt it for this trifle; but not wishing either to turn down the favorable price which had been offered him, he sent the publisher, along with one sonata he had just composed, the two with which his student had honored him, having no scruple to pass them off as his own, convinced that Mr. Pleyel would have no other use for them.

At almost the same time one of the associates of the house of Longmann & Broderip, another London music publisher, staying in Strasbourg, heard a number of
compositions by Mr. Pleyel, whose reputation was beginning to spread, specifically
the two sonatas which he had written for Haydn; seemed charmed by them, bought
some of his works, and also asked if he might have these two sonatas. "No," said the
composer, "I composed these for my teacher, and the thanks he sent me is the only
price I want for them." "At least allow me," said Longmann, "to publish them under
your name for the sake of your reputation." He insisted so strongly, that Mr. Pleyel
consented, not imagining that Haydn had already used them on his own account.

Haydn's pieces and those of Pleyel were published in London at almost the same
time; but the first purchaser, Forster, astonished that the house of Longmann had
dared to publish under the name of Pleyel two sonatas by Haydn himself, and which,
in his opinion, could only be by him, took his case to his lawyers, who in turn were
no less surprised that he had published under the name of Haydn two sonatas by
Mr. Pleyel of Strasbourg, as known by the entire city: they responded to the suit by
a long similar suit. It is known how severely the English execute the laws on copy-
right, plagiarism, and other excesses which music and book publishers occasionally
permit themselves: all of which attracted the interest of London music lovers, unable
to decide what judgment to give.

While this was going on, and while the trial was educating everyone, our Kapellmeister, having received a vacation from his Prince, came to London, where the
pleas of these same music lovers had long since attracted him; upon his arrival he
was informed of this suit of which he was the object, and, recalling that naturally the
two sonatas in question were those of his student, he could be nothing but embar-
rassed. Shortly thereafter, by an equally unique accident, Mr. Pleyel became interested in seeing London, without knowing that his old teacher was also there; when
he found out he was all the more eager to make the trip. The affair was brought to
their attention; but, neither wishing to trouble the other, they were both at a loss as
to how they should respond to the judges before whom the litigants, making use of
[the composers'] reunion in the city, had had them called: they could find nothing
better to recount than the simple truth, which in effect, in almost all occasions,
serves better than the most adroit invention. The judges and the publishers themselves acknowledged the good faith of the two composers: instead of a judgment,
which would have been ruinous, they made an accommodation: Haydn was released
of court costs, which in truth are enormous in London, and he gave three new sonatas of his own to each of the two publishers.[67]

Thus, by mid-1784 Haydn was finding himself unable to fulfill all the demands
resulting from his growing reputation. In this case, Haydn responded by pirating
the trios of another composer. In a broader context, this incident affects the entire
question of establishing the canon of Haydn's works: here authentic documents assert his authorship for two patently spurious trios.

On 25 October 1784 Haydn wrote to the Parisian music publisher Nadermann
that he would "take great pains to send you at the first opportunity the *Clavier*
piece you asked for. . . ."[68] Since Nadermann never published a *Klavierstück* of
Haydn's from this period, it can only be assumed that either the piece was never
delivered or Nadermann failed to print the work Haydn sent him.[69]

Finally, on 26 November 1785, comes the first mention of the Keyboard Trios

Hob. XV:6–8, Haydn's first set of wholly original and modern works for this setting:

> I beg that you let me know by the Monday Prince's Hussars if my sonatas have already been engraved and when you will send them to the Countess Witzey. The reason I would like to know is that before our departure, which will take place in no more than two weeks, I would like to pay a visit to the Countess on her estate. I waited, nevertheless, for the first copy of the sonatas so that I could correct them because there is a mistake which must be rectified. Therefore, please write me again next Monday. . . .[70]

This set of trios as published by Artaria (see Plate 5) was dedicated to Marianne the Countess Witzey (Viczay)—née Countess Grassalkovics, a niece of Prince Nikolaus Esterházy—who lived on her husband's estate, Gross-Losing (Nagylozs), near Esterháza. (After the death of Prince Nikolaus in 1790, the family of the Countess (the Grassalkovics) tried to persuade Haydn to become their Kapellmeister in Pressburg.[71]) Haydn was not able to make the presentation in mid-December, for it is learned from the letter of 10 December to Artaria that there were more problems with the trios than the one mistake Haydn wished to correct.

> The day before yesterday, I received the *Clavier* sonatas with greatest astonishment on account of the terrible engraving and so many aggravating mistakes which are

PLATE 5. The title page of the Artaria edition of Hob. XV: 6–8. (Author's collection)

found in all the parts, especially the *Clavier* part. I was at first so furious that I
wanted to send you your money back and immediately send the score of the sonatas
to Herr Hummel in Berlin because, owing to the places that are here and there unreadable, wrong, or badly arranged and laid out, my reputation will gain little and
you will get little benefit from them. Anyone who buys them will curse the engraver
when he reads through them and will stop playing.[72]

The letter then details all the problems in the text of these trios. As a result, their
plates were apparently completely redone or carefully corrected in Mainz, for on
3 January 1786 the famous publisher Bernhard Schott wrote to one Kanon
Batton: "Artaria asked me to repair the spoiled *Klaviertrios* for the Countess
Witzey. So, I will engrave them promptly."[73] Published as Artaria's Op. 40, these
trios were therefore not announced in the *Wiener-Zeitung* until 26 April 1786. The
dedication to the Countess Witzey was still indicated as the publisher's rather than
the composer's even though Haydn himself probably intended it.

     The rondo-finale of Hob. XV:7 is one of the few keyboard works by Haydn for
which a sketch exists. In this instance, what is available should be characterized as
a *Melodieskizze* and *Particellskizze*.[74] The sketch (Example II-1)[75] contains the
opening theme of the rondo in its final form; the harmony and bass line at the beginning reflect the complete sonority. The next fragment begins at bar 63, skip-
ping forty-seven measures of the final product. At this stage Haydn had already
decided not only that the B section was to be a *Minore* based on the material of A,
but that the entire movement was to be essentially monothematic. Hence he proceeded to the next compositional problem: the retransition, which ultimately leads
to the restatement of the primary material in the key of B minor, approached from
its major mode through the tonic of the chord of E flat, respelled enharmonically as
D sharp. Thus, the sketch concerns itself with the working-out of the main idea
and the most complex harmonic gesture of the movement.

     In 1786 Haydn signed a contract with William Forster of London that included
a number of keyboard works: Opus 40 (Hob. XV:3–5) and 42 (Hob. XV:9, 2,
10). It begins: "I acknowledge to have received of Mister William Forster, mer-
chant and music publisher, living in the Strand at London, the sum of seventy
pounds Sterling for the Symphonies, Sonatas, and other pieces of music composed
by me, as enumerated below."[76] This document is extraordinary in two respects: it
was made after the publication of some and delivery of all the works listed therein,
and in it Haydn continued the masquerade concerning the two Pleyel trios in Hob.
XV:3–5. It thus suggests that Forster was attempting to reaffirm his rights to the
works and Haydn's authorship of them.

     As it turns out, on 28 January 1786 Bossler announced *his* publication of the
Haydn/Pleyel trios in the *Frankfurter Staatsristretto*. It is assumed that Haydn had
also sold the trios to Bossler; the title page suggests authenticity, as it reportedly
contains "a very true silhouette" of Haydn (see Plate 6).[77] But Hob. XV:3–5 was
not the only questionable action in the contract with Forster: included in a second
set of trios, which Forster advertised in the *Morning Herald* on 4 February 1786,
was Hob. XV:2, an antiquated work from the late 1760s or early 1770s. This

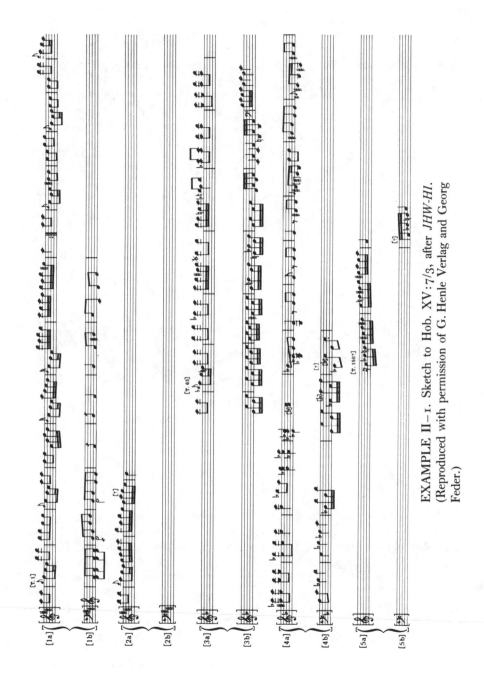

EXAMPLE II–1. Sketch to Hob. XV:7/3, after *JHW-HI*.
(Reproduced with permission of G. Henle Verlag and Georg
Feder.)

PLATE 6. The title page of Bossler's edition of Hob. XV:
3–5. The silhouette is believed to be an authentic one.
(A-Wlandon)

set—the other trios were Hob. XV:9 and 10—was also published by Hummel and
reviewed in Cramer's *Magazin der Musik*:

> Among the many excellent compositions by this great man for the *Flügel* and
> other instruments, these three sonatas claim one of the foremost places. The initial
> Adagio from the first one in A major has an inexpressible charm and makes a very
> pleasing contrast with the following Vivace. In the Allegro of the second one in F
> major, the contraction of the phrase in the sixth measure surprises the listener, per-
> haps too unexpectedly for many people. The theme of the final Adagio, with four
> variations, is made very original by the expansion of the phrase in the seventh mea-
> sure. However, the most beautiful sonata among these beauties is still the third one
> in E-flat major, in which Haydn's genius soars to its greatest heights. It is also
> harder to play than the previous ones. If the horde of composers, who write for
> *Clavier* accompanied by a violin or some other instrument *ad libitum*, would hear
> these sonatas executed well, should they not, at least some of them, take it to heart
> and be ashamed of their hybrid works?—But of course, if one eschews work or can-
> not work, what is then to be expected![78]

In the mid-1780s three of Haydn's keyboard concertos (Hob. XVIII:3, 4, and
11) began to appear in printed editions, although all of them were probably com-

posed earlier than their publication dates suggest; in February 1780, a Fräulein von Hartenstein probably performed one of these works at a private concert in Vienna.[79] Hob. XVIII:3 had the least activity: it was printed only in an unauthorized edition as Haydn's "Troisieme Concerto" (the first two being XVIII:11 and 4) by Le Duc in 1787.[80] The appearance of the work itself in the Breitkopf catalogue in 1771 and its listing in the main columns of *EK* corroborate its much earlier date of composition.

Hob. XVIII:4 appears in the margins of *EK*—justifying a date of composition later than that of XVIII:3—and among others in two early copies at Kroměříž;[81] it was printed in apparently unauthorized editions by Boyer and later by Schmitt, Bland, and Hummel. The concerto was performed in Paris in April 1784 by the blind Viennese keyboard virtuoso, pedagogue, and composer Maria Theresia Paradies (1759–1784) and was given notice in the *Journal de Paris* at the end of April 1784: "Mlle. Paradis exécutera un nouvelle concerto de clavecin de M. Haydn." This notice was repeated on the title page of Boyer's edition, where it is indicated that this G-major Concerto was indeed the one she performed. It seems unlikely that Haydn gave her this work, possibly composed ten years earlier, for her musical tour of Central Europe, France, Belgium, and England beginning in 1783, since she performed it only this one time.[82]

The D-major Concerto Hob. XVIII:11, excepting perhaps the Trumpet Concerto of 1796, is Haydn's most popular work of the genre. Among its earlier prints were those by Artaria, Boyer, and Le Menu (summer 1784); Longman & Broderip (early fall); and Schott (December). It is also known—among many others—from a Viennese copy located at Kroměříž in the hand of Radnitzky, a scribe at times associated with Haydn.[83] It gains some of its appeal from the finale, a "Rondo all'Ungarese," which might be among Haydn's earliest and most successful applications of an eastern European folk style.[84] A reviewer, however, found more to admire in the first movement:

> The first movement of this Concerto breathes the true and genuine spirit of its author; it is neat, sprightly, and beautiful; and although it is not very difficult, if played with spirit and vivacity, will set a performer off to very great advantage.
>
> The second and the last movements are by no means equal to the first in point of merit and yet they bear indelible marks of Haydn's pen.[85]

Both Hob. XVIII:4 and 11 were reviewed in Cramer's *Magazin* (1785) from the print by J. Schmitt of Amsterdam:

> These days one has become a little distrustful that everything appearing under Haydn's name is really by him. In these 2 concertos a few traces of Haydn shine through: however, whether they are entirely by him we will not venture to claim. Nonetheless, we do not intend to say that these concertos are therefore bad; they are very well written, appear to be entirely new and only seem to have been composed for particular amateurs.[86]

Finally, Hob. XVIII:11 is also seemingly referred to in Haydn's letter to the London publisher William Forster on 8 April 1787:

After a long silence, I must finally inquire about your health, and at the same time
report that the following new works are available from me: 6 magnificent symphonies, a big *Clavier* concerto, 3 small *Clavier* divertimentos for a beginner with
violin[s?] and bass, and one sonata for *Clavier* alone.[87]

This author's hypothesis is that the divertimentos were Hob. XIV: 7–9[88] and that
the keyboard sonata was either Hob. XVI: 33, 34, or 43. If so, it is no wonder that
Forster seems not to have accepted: he had already been swindled by Haydn, and
the concerto and all three sonatas had previously reached print in London.[89]

The latter years of the 1780s are remarkable for the number of keyboard works
Haydn composed as well as for the tangled and overlapping negotiations for their
sale. It must have been this period that Haydn had in mind when he complained in
his old age that he used to be capable of working on several projects at once.[90] The
keyboard works produced include seven trios (Hob. XV: 9–16), two to eight solo
sonatas (Hob. XVI: 48, 49, and possible lost works), the C-major Capriccio
(Hob. XVII: 4), and the little C-major Variations (Hob. XVII: 5). Publishers to be
wrangled with included John Bland from London, Sieber in Paris, Breitkopf in
Leipzig, and, of course, Artaria in Vienna. It should be noted that during this time
Haydn was also composing symphonies, quartets, and works in other genres, while
fulfilling his duties as musical director of the Esterházy opera.

The relevant keyboard documents for this period begin with a letter to Artaria
dated 10 August 1788:

Since I am now in a situation where I need some money, I am offering to write for
you by the end of December either 3 new quartets or 3 new *Clavier* sonatas with
violin and violoncello accompaniment.[91]

Artaria must have answered immediately with a request for keyboard trios, which
were to become Hob. XV: 11–13, for on 17 August Haydn wrote: "My industry
with the 3 *Clavier* sonatas with violin and violoncello accompaniment which you
requested will be the guarantee of my keeping your friendship for the future."[92]
Some two months later (26 October 1788) Haydn requested another advance from
Artaria:

In order to compose your 3 *Clavier* sonatas well, I was compelled to buy a new *Fortepiano*. Now, since you must have long been aware that from time to time even the
learned are short of money, which is the case with me now, I must entreat you, Sir, to
pay 31 gold ducats to Herr Wenzl Schanz, the organ and instrument maker, who
lives on the Leimgruben at the "Blauen Schiff," No.22. I will repay these 31#
[ducats] with thanks by the end of January next year 1789.[93]

Three weeks later (16 November 1788) Haydn told Artaria that "one and one half
[of the sonatas] are already finished."[94] However, in a letter dated 8 March 1789,
Haydn was still promising "the third sonata in a week."[95]

In a letter now lost, Artaria apparently requested that Haydn rewrite the first
movement of the third sonata, Hob. XV: 13. On 29 March the trios were
completed:

I am sending the 3rd sonata which, according to your taste, I have newly rewritten with variations. . . . During a humorous hour, I composed an entirely new Capriccio for *fortepiano*, which most certainly will be well received by connoisseurs and others alike on account of its good taste, singularity, and exceptional construction. It is only a single movement, somewhat long, but not at all too hard; as you always get precedence in acquiring my works, I offer it to you for 24 ducats. The price is somewhat high, but I assure you that it will be profitable.[96]

The "new Capriccio" does not refer to the 1765 work in G major (Hob. XVII:1) but a new one in C major, which Artaria did publish with the title "Fantasia" (Hob. XVII:4). This work is an almost programmatic piece based on the melody and the narrative of "Dö Bäuren håt d'Kåtz valor'n":

Dö Bäuren håt d'Kåtz valor'n,	The farmer's wife cannot find the cat
Woaß nit, wo's is,	She knows not where it is.
Geht ums Haus um ad um:	Running about the house she screams:
Muitzarl, wo bist?	Mutzerl where are you?
's Muitzarl is g'fånga worn,	The cat has been captured,
Sitzt en Arrest,	It sits in prison,
D'Bäuren håts Geldl nit,	The farmer's wife does not have the money
Daß sös auslest.	to redeem it.
Da Baua, dear is zorni worn,	The farmer loses his temper,
Schreit en Haus um ad um:	He screams in the house:
Bäuren, dö Kåtz muaß hear,	Woman, bring back the cat,
Bring di sünst um.	Otherwise I will kill you.
Baua, sei oanmål stat,	Man, be quiet,
D'Kåtz is en Haus;	The cat is in the house.
Sitzt a da Kåma drauβt,	It sits in the room over there,
Und fångt a Maus.[97]	and is catching a mouse.

The contract was settled by 6 April, when Haydn wrote to Artaria:[98]

I am sending the two signed, secured receipts you asked for, together with the Capriccio, which I assure you, no other soul will receive from my hands. I am sorry that, owing to the work I put in on it, I cannot lower this price of 24# [ducats] by one kreuzer. I only ask that the sonatas [trios] as well as the Capriccio be cleanly and readably engraved.[99]

According to Haydn's letter of 5 July, the trios (Hob. XV:11–13) were available; they had been announced in the *Wiener-Zeitung* on 1 July. For some reason, however, the Fantasia (Hob. XVII:4) was not advertised until 5 September.

For the 3 sonatas [trios] and the Fantasia you sent recently, my most obliging thanks. I only regret that here and there a few errors have crept in which can no longer be corrected, because they are already distributed and offered for sale. It is always painful for me that not a single work issued from you has been free of mistakes.[100]

The trios Hob. XV: 11–13 received glowing reviews in the *Musikalische Real-zeitung* and the *Allgemeine deutsche Bibliothek*:

> The original style of this composer, his beautiful modulations, and his wealth of ideas are already too well known for us to find it necessary to say anything further to recommend the announced composition. Neither the main part nor the accompany-ing parts are so encumbered with difficulties that the sonatas demand especially skilled players. The violin part exceeds c''' only once in the Andante of the last (or second) sonata, and even this spot, which might seem difficult to an inexperienced player, lies well under the hand.[101]

> For a long time we have received no sonatas which could challenge the superi-ority of these three. As a whole, they are most favorably distinguished by the well-known originality of their composer. The writing is outstanding and mostly in a serious manner. Herr Haydn has shown, especially in the C-major middle movement found on p.26, how attractive an ordinary tune can become through masterly han-dling. These sonatas do require a not unskilled player, mostly because of the fre-quent excursions into distant keys—which often require many accidentals, even double ones—rather than actual difficult passages needing highly accomplished per-formers. Even if someone were not able immediately to sight-read them without trouble, their efforts would be richly rewarded. For when played cleanly in all parts and with the proper expression, they yield the greatest enjoyment that this kind of music can provide.[102]

In the meantime, Haydn apparently agreed to compose a set of six sonatas for Breitkopf. In February 1789 the following notice appeared from the Leipzig firm:

> From the publishing house of the Breitkopf bookshop in Leipzig six *Clavier* sonatas by the beloved Capellmeister *Joseph Haydn* will appear in print this summer. In order to facilitate purchase by amateurs, subscriptions for 1 Rhinethaler, 12 Groschen will be accepted through August of this year, and the delivery of the copies will be announced in the newspapers in due time.[103]

The interest in subscribing to this set was apparently not sufficient to make the publication a worthy risk, since the sonatas never appeared.

Yet again, on 8 March 1789, Haydn dispatched a message to Johann Traeg, Breitkopf's Viennese agent, not about the projected six sonatas but about a single work in C major, Hob. XVI:48. Breitkopf had apparently written to Haydn or carried out negotiations through Traeg, who was to act as a middleman for the Leipzig publisher until that role was partly taken over by Georg August Grie-singer after the turn of the century. Haydn wrote "that the new *Clavier* sonata that Herr Breitkopf requested will be finished by next week."[104] The C-major Sonata for Breitkopf was actually not ready until 5 April 1789: "I am sending the new *Clavier* sonata through Herr Traeg in the full hope that it will meet with the world's approval. . . . I only ask a clean engraving and to be allowed to receive a couple of copies."[105] E. L. Gerber reviewed the work in the 1812 edition of his *Lexikon der Tonkünstler*:

In this sonata you will find everything Eman. Bach produced in his heyday—great-
ness, nobility, novelty and surprise in melody, harmony, and modulation—not only
in [an] incomparably high degree, but also bound up with charm, grace, and a certain cheerful mood which is characteristic only of Haydn. Generally, if it should
matter to discover the style of a composer to which Haydn comes nearest, then this
could be no other than Phil. Em. Bach's style.[106]

On 5 April 1789 Haydn also wrote to the Paris music publisher Jean Georges
Sieber:

I am very surprised that I still have received no communication from you, since (as
Herr Tost wrote me some time ago) you are supposed to have bought 4 symphonies
and 6 *Clavier* sonatas for one hundred Louis d'or. . . . Herr Tost has no claim at all
on the 6 *Clavier* sonatas. Thus, he has deceived you and you can pursue your rights
in the matter in Vienna.[107]

The sonatas mentioned in the letter are difficult to identify, since by this date all of
them—beginning with the 1774 Esterházy set—had already been published in the
major European centers. To which sonatas was Haydn referring? One possibility is
the six works intended for Breitkopf. Perhaps the scenario occurred in this manner:
Haydn secured the services of Johann Tost, a violinist with associations to the Esterházy court,[108] to deliver the works personally to Sieber for the pre-established
price; in order to assure Sieber of the exclusivity of the sonatas being offered, Tost
took autographs for which Haydn failed to make copies, and the sonatas were
somehow lost. Sieber did claim, however, on the title pages of the editions for Hob.
XV: 11–13 and 24–26 "sur l'original de l'auteur," but these trios could not have
been the ones referred to in this particular letter. If indeed Haydn was attempting
to sell Hob. XV: 11–13 or some other already printed works as a part of the pack-
age, he certainly indicted himself again. The latter possibility is supported by his
somewhat matter-of-fact reaction to the theft.

As the above suggests, Haydn's nearly exclusive relationship with Artaria
ended during the late 1780s. The authority of some of the Artaria prints from this
time, especially those of Hob. XVI: 17–19, 44–46; XVII: 1, 2, 3; and XVIIa: 1,
could be questioned merely because of the lack of existing correspondence. However, Haydn resided in Vienna during some of this time and could very well have
dealt with Artaria in person. Neither can the status of these prints be definitely
established from their texts, as the correspondence includes Haydn's complaints to
Artaria that he was not receiving proofs for some publications, and therefore even
works published with his authorization were appearing with errors. Perhaps the
strongest argument is that many of the prints are of works that originated twenty
or more years earlier.

The most peculiar aspect of Artaria's publication from the late 1780s is that five
prints (Artaria/Botstiber Nos. 33–37 [i.e., Hob. XVI: 17–19, 44–46, XVII: 3,
2, and XVIIa: 1]), were either announced or advertised in Frankfurt not Vienna.[109]
None of them should be considered authorized; Hob. XVI: 17 has even been
proven to be a sonata by Schwanberg (Schwanenberg[er]). Furthermore, the print

of Hob. XVII: 1 omits two measures (175 and 183) from the central modulatory episode found in the autograph, an alteration whose authenticity cannot be completely ruled out.[110] Also, Artaria/Botstiber no. 38 (Hob. XVI:47) contains a very odd first movement.[111]

Finally, when Hob. XVI:49 appeared under Artaria's aegis in August 1791, Haydn believed that it had been stolen and feared reprisals from the patron who commissioned it. So while Haydn's correspondence with the Viennese house demonstrates that he was financially squeezing his publisher, Artaria probably could have had any of Haydn's works, although not always for the earliest edition or the lowest price.[112]

In November 1789 Haydn was visited by John Bland, a London music dealer with whom he would do business until Bland's publishing activities ceased around 1792–1793.[113] When Bland left Haydn, he took with him or had sent to him three accompanied keyboard sonatas (Hob. XV: 15–17), the cantata "Arianna a Naxos," and a series of string quartets—among them the "Razor." In a recently recovered letter of 12 April 1790, Haydn wrote that he was enclosing the first (Hob. XV: 16) and would deliver the second sonata (Hob. XV: 15) within a week and the third sonata (Hob. XV: 17) as soon as possible.[114] When Bland began to publish the trios in 1790, they carried the following note:

> This & the Two following Trios were wrote [sic] at the particular request of the Publisher when he was with Mr. Haydn in Novr. last, at which time he settled Connection with him, Mess.ʳˢ Hoffmeister, Kozeluch, Mozart, Vanhall &c. &c. whose Works will come out in this manner with all possible expedition; they are absolute property and Enter'd as such; J. Bland thinks this sufficient notice to other Publishers not to pirate the same.[115]

Despite this notice, these trios, with the flute as an option for the violin, were also available in Artaria prints, announced in the *Wiener-Zeitung* on 20 October 1790 and 22 November 1792.[116] To Artaria, however, Haydn had applied some "hard sales" tactics in early 1790:

> This is to advise you that I received a letter this very day from M. Bland in London, in which he begs me for *Clavier* sonatas with violin and violoncello accompaniment. However, I am giving you precedence in this case, and also am informing you that the first sonata is ready now, the 2nd in two weeks, and the 3rd by the end of Carnival and each is to be had for the usual 10 ducats. Be so good as to let me have your decision by tomorrow morning.[117]

For Hob. XV: 17/1 two groups of sketches exist of thirteen and nine measures respectively (Example II-2)[118] for what was to become mm. 40–45. In both sketches Haydn prunes his material so that the entire development section seems to evolve from a large homogeneous section in the first sketch to a multi-faceted one divided into two large parts (mm. 33–53 and 54–62), within which are a series of subsections including mm. 40–45. The result is not only greater variety but a remarkable control of rhythm and harmony.

Sketch

EXAMPLE II–2. Sketch and compositional stages of Hob. XV:17/1, after Feder/SKIZZEN. (Reproduced with the permission of Sieghard Brandenburg and Georg Feder.)

First Draft

EXAMPLE II−2 (*continued*)

Second Draft

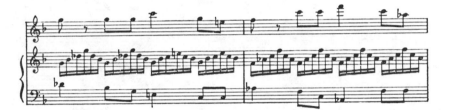

EXAMPLE II–2 (*continued*)

Final Version

EXAMPLE II–2 (*continued*)

E. L. Gerber took notice of Hob. XV:15 and 16 in his *Neues Lexikon der Tonkünstler*. Once again we find a reviewer skeptical of their paternity.

> Wit, caprice, modulation, etc. make Haydn's genius unmistakable in this opus. Nevertheless, specific peculiarities distinguish it from his other *Klavier* trios. The flute is obbligato and probably because of this is placed above the *Klavier* part, at least in this Hummel print. At the same time a certain something prevails in the development of the figures which gives the whole a kind of harshness otherwise uncharacteristic of Haydn. It is precisely because of this that these sonatas, which seem so easy at first glance, nonetheless, present more difficulties in performance than are usually found in Haydn's *Klavier* works of this period. At first this aroused the suspicion that this opus might be by Michael Haydn, many of whose works, it is asserted, are supposed to have come into Joseph's *oeuvre*.[119]

It was for one of Haydn's closest friends and admirers, Maria Anna von Genzinger (1750–1793), the wife of Prince Esterházy's physician Dr. Peter von Genzinger, that the E-flat major Sonata Hob. XVI:49 was conceived.[120] The von Genzinger family resided in the so-called Schotten-Hof, where their house was a veritable center of music making; Haydn, Mozart, Dittersdorf, and Albrechtsberger were frequent and welcome guests. Maria Anna's musical education was good enough for her to participate fully in the musical activities of such distinguished company. She was a fine performer and could skillfully transcribe symphony movements for the keyboard.

The warm relationship between Frau von Genzinger and Haydn began with a letter written by the *gnädige Frau* in June 1789. According to one Johann Schönauer, "Haydn appears to have bestowed not merely artistic attentions on this woman, but also more delicate feelings."[121] The E-flat major Sonata Hob. XVI:49 is first discussed in their correspondence of 6 June 1790:

> BETWEEN US! Your Grace should know that our Mademoiselle Nanette has commissioned me to compose a new *Clavier* sonata for you, which may be given out to no one else. I consider myself fortunate to have received such an order. Your Grace will receive this sonata in two weeks at most. The above-named Mademoiselle [Nanette] promised me some payment for it. But Your Grace can easily understand that I will always refuse any; for me the greatest reward will constantly be to hear that I have received some approval.[122]

The Mademoiselle Nanette was Fräulein Jelerschick, housekeeper for Prince Esterházy, who later was to marry the shady Johann Tost.

Although from the letter of 20 June 1790 one can surmise that Haydn had sent Frau von Genzinger one of the accompanied sonatas written for Bland, perhaps Hob. XV:17, Haydn also reveals some particulars about the composition of "her" sonata:

> This sonata is in E-flat, entirely new and forever meant for only Your Grace. It is curious that the last movement of this sonata contains the very Minuet and Trio that Your Grace asked from me in your last letter. This sonata was intended for Your

Grace already a year ago; only the Adagio, which I highly recommend to Your Grace, has been finished quite recently. There is much in it that I will point out to Your Grace when there is an opportunity. It is somewhat difficult, but full of feeling. What a shame that Your Grace does not have a *Fortepiano* by Schanz, as Your Grace would be able to get so many effects from it.

N.B.: The Mademoiselle Nanette must not know that this sonata was already half finished, because otherwise, she might get different ideas which would be damaging to me; I must be very careful not to lose her good will. Meanwhile, I count myself happy that I can, at least, be a tool of her enjoyment, especially since the offering is meant for you, my dearest Frau v. Genzinger. Oh, I would wish that I could play through this sonata a couple of times; how gladly would I again be contented to remain for awhile in my solitude.[123]

The autograph of this work, entitled "Sonata per il Forte-piano Composta—da me giuseppe Haydn mp 1 Juny 790," seems to confirm the above narrative: in the first gathering of the manuscript leaves 3—4 and 9—10 have been altered, presumably resulting from revisions to the Adagio, which begins with side 10. Apparently Haydn recopied the last part of the Adagio and the earlier composed finale (beginning of side 16), while retaining most of the first movement as copied out previously. Then the two gatherings were brought together, as shown in Diagram 1.

Its history continues with letters from 27 June, 4 July, and 11 July 1790:

27 June 1790
Your Grace will, without doubt, have received the new *Clavier* sonata; if not, perhaps you will get it with my letter. Three days ago I had to play the sonata for Mademoiselle Nanette in the presence of My Prince. At first I doubted whether I would get any applause because of the difficulty; but then, I was convinced of the opposite, since I received from [her?] own hand a gold tobacco box as a gift. Now I only wish that Your Grace might be satisfied with it, so that I can earn greater recognition from my benefactor. For just this reason, I ask Your Grace to let her know, if not personally at least through your husband, that I have been too delighted to conceal her generosity, the more so because I am convinced that Your Grace shares all the kindnesses shown to me. What a pity that Your Grace does not own a *Fortepiano* by Schanz since everything is expressed better on it. I think that Your Grace

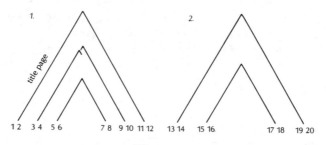

Diagram 1.

should give your still good *Flügel* to the Fräulein Peperl and buy a new *Fortepiano* for yourself. Your beautiful hands and the disciplined technique in them deserve this and still more. I know that I should have written this sonata for your type of *Clavier*, but it just was not possible, because I am not at all used to it any more.[124]

In the letter of 4 July, Haydn is even more insistent about a new instrument: "It is most necessary for Your Grace to have a good *Fortepiano*, and my sonatas gain so much by it."[125] One week later Frau von Genzinger wrote to Haydn:

I like the sonata very much: only one thing I might wish that I could have altered (if such does not detract from the beauty of the piece), namely this: the 2nd part of the Adagio where the hands cross; since I am not used to this, it is quite difficult for me, so please let me know how this might be changed.[126]

It is not known whether Haydn responded to her request. However, someone considered the sonata quite publishable. Haydn learned in London that Artaria had printed it. On 2 March 1792 he wrote to Frau von Genzinger:

I was very shocked when I had to read the unpleasant news about the sonata. By God! I would rather have lost 25 ducats than to hear about this robbery; and no one else but my own copyist could have done it. But, I hope to God to make up for this loss, again through the offices of Madame Tost. For, I do not want to be reproached by her. Your Grace must, therefore, be indulgent towards me until the end of July when I myself will have the pleasure to give you the sonata.[127]

It has been conjectured that the replacement was the Trio Hob. XV:32, which itself was published in London.

Nevertheless, Hob. XVI:49 was reviewed with great approbation:

As long as Haydn continues to work with the fiery imagination and the original genius that is the rule in his compositions to date, the public will continue to receive each product of his muse with acclaim. And there is no doubt that this single sonata will share a like fortune since it has been written in his well-known style. The Adagio cantabile is a model of a beautiful song.[128]

Knowing that Haydn was preparing to leave for London, on 22 November 1790 Artaria exacted a promise from him to complete and deliver the *Liebhaber* Variations Hob. XVII:5: "I the undersigned promise and pledge myself to hand over the 6 new variations for *Fortepiano* to H[err] Artaria in one week."[129] With Hob. XVII:5 Haydn concluded his output before the London experience and the final chapter in the composition of pieces for less-accomplished keyboardists. Six years later a paragraph in Schönfeld's *Jahrbuch* for 1796 revealed that few of the *Kenner* in Vienna were aware of the type of keyboard compositions Haydn wrote during his London years: "His *Klavier* pieces are mostly pleasant, simple, and easy to play and for this very reason, so much more usable, since today's composers mostly go in for obstacles and demand from students a power that is often difficult for the master."[130]

Works Written in and for London, 1791–1795

During his stay in London, Haydn kept a series of four notebooks in which he recorded virtually everything that interested him. In the fourth one, now lost, Haydn inscribed a catalogue of works written in and for London. Fortunately, it was copied by both Dies and Griesinger and incorporated into their biographies, but not without some inconsistencies.

As can be seen in Table II-2, there are two important discrepancies between Haydn's two early biographers: Dies credits Haydn with three sonatas for "Miss Janson," whereas Griesinger allows only two; and at the very end of Dies's list there are an additional three sonatas for Broderip. With regard to the "Janson" Sonatas, Griesinger seems more plausible; Hob. XVI:51 is totally different in style from Hob. XVI:50 and 52. The three sonatas for "Miss Janson" in Dies are probably the Trios Hob. XV:27–29, and the three additional sonatas for Broderip refer to the three works for Rebecca Schröter. By collocating both lists, it is possible to gain a more plausible interpretation of Haydn's original.[131]

Thus, during his first London journey, Haydn seems not to have produced any keyboard works except possibly Hob. XV:32, which was published in London by both Preston (1794) and Bland (1794);[132] instead, he depended on existing pieces such as the Fantasia Hob. XVII:4 and the keyboard Trio Hob. XV:14, both of which he reported receiving by mail from Maria Anna Genzinger on 2 February 1792.[133] However, if he intended to publish these works in London, he was apparently not yet aware that the Fantasia had been issued by Artaria's London agent, Longman & Broderip, in 1789.[134]

Haydn did use the A-flat major Trio Hob. XV:14 for the Hanover-Square concert in Salomon's series on 20 April 1792;[135] the keyboard part was played by the thirteen-year-old Master Johann Nepomuk Hummel, who later became Haydn's assistant when the Esterházy *Kapelle* was revitalized. The occasion was also the first known performance of a Haydn trio at a public concert, which brought forth its publication by Longman & Broderip in September 1792: "A favorite Sonata for the Piano Forte or Harpsichord with Accompaniments for a Violin and Violoncello as performed by Master Hummell at Mr. Salomon's Concert [Hanover Square composed by Dr. Haydn] Op. 68."[136]

Although it appeared in Haydn's London catalogue, the Variations in F minor Hob. XVII:6, a work that some consider his finest solo keyboard composition, was actually composed after his return to Vienna in 1793. According to an authentic copy signed by Haydn, these variations were composed for one of Vienna's finest performers, Barbara (Babette) von Ployer, a student of Mozart, who had established herself as a highly respected keyboardist. It was for her that Mozart composed the concertos K. 449 and 453, and they performed together the Sonata for Two Keyboards K. 448 (375a).[137] Both Mozart and Haydn had written compositions in her *Stammbuch*: the *Trauermarsch* K. 453a and the "Oxford" Canon with the first commandment text, which was signed by Haydn with the inscription "from your worshipper and admirer."[138] Unfortunately, no contemporary description of her playing comes down to us except for the usual terse statement found in

TABLE II-2

Haydn's London Keyboard Works
(in the order found in Griesinger/NOTIZEN)

Hoboken number	Griesinger	Dedications	Dies
Hob. XV:18–20	Drey Sonaten für Broderip	Princess née Hohenfeldt Esterházy	3 Sonates for Broderip
Hob. XV:21–23	Drey Sonaten für Preston	Princess Marie Esterházy	3 Sonates for Preston
Hob. XVI:50, 52 and/or Hob. XV:27–29	Zwey Sonaten für Miss Janson	XVI:52—Magdalene von Kurzböck/ Therese Janson Bartolozzi	3 Sonates for Ms. Janson
Hob. XVII:6	Eine Sonate in F minor	Ployer/von Braun	1 Sonata in F minore
Hob. XV:32	Eine in g		1 Sonate in g
Hob. XV:31/2	Der Traum	Therese Janson and violin-playing friend	The Dream
Hob. XV:24–26		Rebecca Schröter	3 Sonates for Broderip

Zinzendorf's diary for 23 March 1784: "then to a concert at the agent [Gottfried Ignaz] Ployer's where I heard his daughter [*sic*] play the *clavecin* marvelously."[139] After 1793 we know nothing further of Fräulein Ployer except that she married a Herr von Buganovitz and died in Hungary some time before *ca.* 1820.[140]

According to the autograph and an authentic copy, Haydn seemingly could not decide whether to compose an independent set of variations or a cyclic composition. The title page of the autograph states "Sonata," implying that perhaps Haydn intended to compose a cycle commencing with a set of variations using two themes contrasted by mode (e.g., Hob. XVI:40 and 48). Later he changed his mind, for on the authentic copy dedicated to Fräulein Ployer the title reads "Un piccolo Divertimento." Whether to make it a single- or multi-movement work seems to have been decided by the time the variations themselves were completed, for Haydn inscribed "Laus Deo" at their conclusion.

The layout of the two themes, each with two variations, seems not to have been altered; it was their conclusion that caused some difficulty. Haydn's first decision seems to have been to end the set in the major mode after the second variation, with five additional measures in major expanding upon the beginning of the second strain of the final variation (Example II-3). Since "Laus Deo" is lacking at the end of these five measures, this conclusion was apparently not satisfactory. Haydn then composed a lengthy coda, which was to be prefaced by a partial recapitulation of the initial theme without repetitions. The second strain of this theme is interrupted after only ten measures by the coda, reinforcing the effect of structural disruption. The coda itself has one substantial change: the nine bars originally composed (beginning in m. 180, see Example II-4) are removed and replaced by fourteen measures, which are notable for their heightened rhythmic activity.

The structure of the autograph confirms this interpretation: the original version without the coda was written on a single bi-folio, while the coda seems to have been inscribed on an additional half sheet, as shown in Diagram 2. Unfortunately, the autograph has been cut and bound so that this scheme cannot be verified.

EXAMPLE II-3. Hob. XVII:6, the original ending without the coda, to be inserted after m. 145(?).

EXAMPLE II−4. Hob. XVII:6, the measures deleted by
Haydn from the coda replaced by mm. 180−93.

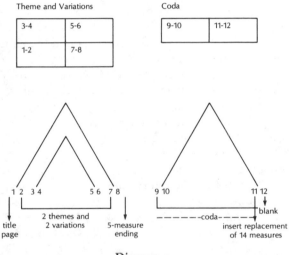

Diagram 2.

While Haydn was in England, another authentic copy of Hob. XVII:6 was
prepared by Elssler for an unknown Mrs. Montlieu: a "Sonate in F minor for the
pfte" consisting of eleven oblong folio pages signed and corrected by Haydn.[141] As
the variations are also listed as a "Sonate in f minor" in Haydn's catalogue of London works, one is led to wonder whether Haydn later used this work for the first
movement of a sonata. It seems more likely, however, that the title page of the
Elssler copy was simply taken from the autograph, which may have remained in
Haydn's possession at least until after his final return to Vienna in 1795.[142]

The variations were finally published in January 1799 by Artaria as Op. 83,
with a dedication to another pianist of fame: the Baroness Josephine von Braun,

wife of Peter Freiherr von Braun, the director of the court theaters in Vienna.[143] It was to her that Beethoven was to dedicate his *opere* 14 and 17. The print was reviewed in the *Allgemeine Musikalische Zeitung* in May 1799:

> A melancholy Andante in F minor, varied as only a master can do, so that it almost sounds like a free fantasy. The first section is already not easy; so, it can be imagined that its further elaborations will have their difficulties—now and then, especially with regard to the indications for new ideas of sound, more than even better players will accomplish at first. None the less, another worthy contribution![144]

Beginning with the second London visit, one can document Haydn's association with Therese Jansen Bartolozzi. Haydn wrote as many, if not more, keyboard works for her than for his beloved Princess Marie Esterházy. Certainly Hob. XVI:50 and 52, XV:27–29, the "Dream Sonata" (Hob. XV:31/2); possibly Hob. XV:32; and—according to tradition—XVI:51 were written for Therese Jansen, one of the finest pianists of her day. Bertini named her, along with Cramer and Field, as Clementi's three most outstanding pupils. Clementi himself dedicated his Piano Trios Op. 33 to her, as did Dussek his *opere* 13 and 43. Haydn witnessed her marriage in May 1795 to Gaetano Bartolozzi, son of the famous engraver; the composer's signature is found in the St. James parish register.[145]

Therese Jansen (*ca.* 1770–1843), was the daughter of M. Jansen, "the first dancing master of his age in Germany." After coming to England with her parents, she and her brother Louis, who was also a Clementi pupil, began teaching keyboard and—in Louis's case—dancing. They were tremendously successful, earning more than two thousand pounds per year and counting among their students members of the highest families. Therese's marriage to Bartolozzi produced one daughter, the famous dancer Madame Vestris.[146] The "Capital" female performer described in an essay entitled "Desultory Remarks on the Study and Practice of Music Addressed to a Young Lady while under the Tuition of an Eminent Master Written in the Years 1790–1 and 2" may possibly be Therese Jansen. She is not mentioned by name, but the essay contains allusions to Louis Jansen.

> It is a matter much deserving the attention of a lady, how she is to present and deport herself while at the Piano-Forte. I have repeatedly noticed some Capital Performers, who, while they highly gratified the Ear, have very much offended the Eye, by a most ungraceful, not to say distorted Position of their Body, and a disgustingly awkward motion with their arms and hands. I know one lady, whose demeanor, in general, is admired, but who places her Chair at a distance from the Instrument, like a Rustic seated at the table of his Lord with a plate half a yard from him; whence the Body, in either case, is bent forward, and the Arms are on the full stretch to reach their object. This Lady's manner of applying her Fingers to the Keys, is also unpleasing, and rather ludicrous, for, in their whole length, they drop perpendicular on the Instrument with a laxity and tremulation of every joint, as if they had been wetted and she was shaking them dry. It is, I allow, easier far to point out Defects than to give Instruction in the case before us. Defects are obvious and strike instantaneously; but to acquire a graceful deportment and a proper display of the Hands

and Arms while at the Desk, must depend greatly on making these a constant object of regard—and though "herein the Patient must minister to herself," yet can the skillful and accomplished [Louis] J[anse]-n assist you with some prescriptions that will prove efficacious.[147]

The only authentic Haydn anecdote concerning Therese Jansen involves Hob. XV:31: its second movement was originally a single-movement sonata (the "Dream Sonata"). A first movement was added some time before Haydn left England.[148] The tale of the second movement as a violin sonata, as related by Dies, explains the bizarre violin part shown in Example II-5.

In London he [Haydn] was closely acquainted with a German music lover who had achieved a skill on the violin that bordered on virtuosity, but had the nasty habit of always going sharp on the uppermost notes, next to the bridge. Haydn resolved to see if it were not possible to cure the dilettante of his habit and instill in him a feel for solid playing.

The dilettante often visited a Miss J[ansen] who played the pianoforte with great accomplishment while he usually accompanied. Quite in secret Haydn wrote a sonata for pianoforte with the accompaniment of a violin, entitled "Jacob's Dream" and had it sent by trusted hands to Miss J[ansen], sealed up and anonymous. She did not put off trying what appeared to be an easy sonata in the company of the

EXAMPLE II–5. Hob. XV:31/2, "Dream Sonata." Violin part portraying Jacob's Ladder, mm. 22–55, 89–95.

PLATE 7. The title page of Hob. XVI:50 in an English edition signed by Therese Bartolozzi. (Author's collection)

dilettante. What Haydn foresaw, indeed, happened. The dilettante got stuck on the high notes with which the passages were filled. And as soon as Miss J[ansen] realized the situation, that the unknown composer had intended to depict the heavenly ladder that Jacob saw in his dream, and then noticed that the dilettante climbed up and down on this ladder, now clumsily, uncertain, stumbling, now staggering or jumping—well, it all seemed so funny to her that she could not hide her laughter, while the dilettante insulted the unknown composer and impudently maintained that he did not know how to write for the violin.

Only after five or six months was it discovered that the sonata had Haydn for its composer, who then received a gift from Miss J[ansen] for it.[149]

In addition, Hob. XVI: 50 and 52 were without question written expressly for Therese Jansen; she apparently possessed their autographs and proceeded to publish them *ca.* 1800. In the case of XVI: 50, she signed the title page of the print (Plate 7), and the autograph of XVI: 52 states that it was expressly for her.

When Haydn published Hob. XVI: 52 with Artaria in 1798, a new dedication appeared on the title page—to Magdalene von Kurzböck (Plate 8). Reichardt tells us that she "was introduced to me as the greatest lady pianist of the local musical world."[150] Another description affirms how appropriate the dedication of this powerful work was to her style of playing in that she could effectively reproduce a fully orchestrated work at the *fortepiano*.[151] The appearance of this "Grand Sonata" was greeted by a review that indicates the complementarity of work and player:

> Grand Sonata, rich and difficult also, both in the content and in its manner. It is true that the reviewer must copy this exclamation from others for the hundredth time: Haydn is inexhaustible and never gets old. Again, what a personal gait here! No self parody. Whoever can completely master this extremely fine sonata (actually written for the connoisseur)—his earlier ones can hardly compare with respect to difficulty—and can execute it precisely without missing the least thing, he can let it be said that he plays. It speaks well for the lady named on the title page that the honorable Haydn, who most likely has no inclination nor time to give empty compliments, had dedicated such a sonata especially to her.[152]

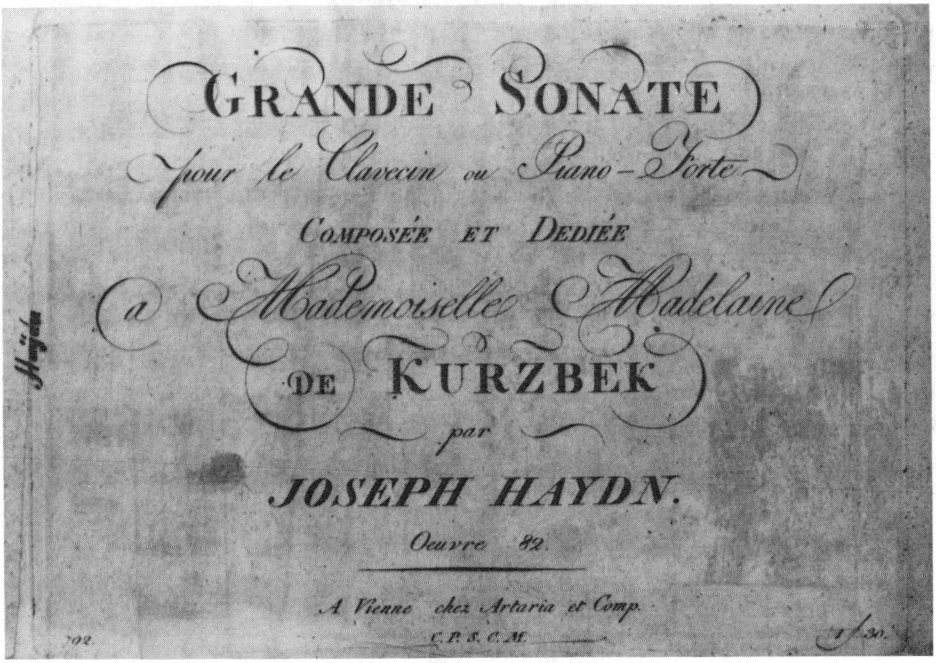
GRANDE SONATE
pour le Clavecin ou Piano-Forte
COMPOSÉE ET DEDIÉE
a Mademoiselle Madelaine
DE KURZBEK
par
JOSEPH HAYDN.
Oeuvre 82.
A Vienne chez Artaria et Comp.
C.P.S.C.M.

PLATE 8. The title page of the Artaria edition of Hob. XVI: 52. (US-BLl)

The set of keyboard trios written for Mrs. Bartolozzi (Hob. XV:27–29) is in the same big and daring style of the two solo sonatas, with striking key relationships among the movements, as the English theorist Kollman noted in 1799:

> In regard to [the relation between different movements], I must mention four cases of abrupt changes of the key from one movement to another, which are found in Haydn's *Sonatas* Op. 75. The first is in Sonata 1, where the first movement is in C Major, and the second in A Major. This change is allowable, according to the rules of abrupt modulation by omission, . . . for C is the key, and the triad of A the leading chord to a related key; but A is retained, and made a substituted key. The second case is the same Sonata, where the second movement ends in A Major, and the third one begins in C Major, which, as it is too great a skip in harmony, ought not be imitated by young composers. The third and fourth case is in Sonata III, where the first movement is in E-flat Major, the second in B (or C-flat) Major, and the third in E-flat Major again. Both these changes of the key are very good, according to the rules mentioned just now.

Kollman also remarks that these trios as well as Hob. XV:11–13 "are set with very interesting Accompaniments, contain the finest Solo passages, and deserve to be studied."[153]

Among the women to whom Haydn dedicated keyboard works, Rebecca Schröter was perhaps the closest to him. She was the widow of Johann Samuel Schröter, Johann Christian Bach's successor in 1782 as "Master of the Queen's Music."[154] A love affair between Mrs. Schröter and Haydn during his London visits is documented by their correspondence from the first London residence, which Haydn copied into the second London Notebook (1791–1792). The dedication of the Piano Trios Hob XV:24–26 as published by Longman & Broderip in 1795 and her signature on a Haydn contract from August 1796[155] indicate that the affair continued through the second London stay, even though there is no record of correspondence, probably because of the proximity of their living quarters. According to Dies, Haydn stated that "although she was already sixty years old, she was still a lovely, charming woman whom I might easily have married if I had been single then."[156]

Rebecca Schröter's trios contain some of Haydn's most remarkable and popular musical creations: the Finale of the second trio, in G major—the Rondo "in the Gypsies' stile" (all' Ongarese); and the entire third trio, in F-sharp minor. There has been some question as to which was the original version of this music: the trio setting, or the one used for the slow movement of Symphony No. 102, which is in F major. Although Landon claims that the symphony setting takes precedence,[157] the corrections in the viola, cello, and bass lines of the symphony autograph suggest that Haydn was working from a version in F-sharp major, i.e., Haydn used the trio as a *Particellskizze* for the orchestral version[158] and mistakenly placed sharps before C in the viola and F in the cello and bass parts.

The D-major Sonata Hob. XVI:51, which was not entered in the London catalogue, was written for a lady in England,[159] traditionally Therese Jansen Bartolozzi, but Rebecca Schröter seems in many respects a more likely candidate: its style is quite different from the other two Bartolozzi solo sonatas discussed above. The following letter in English from Haydn to John Parke from 22 October 1794 could refer to this work or possibly to the F-minor Variations: "I am much obliged to you for the two so charming Prints, I tack [sic] me the liberty to send for the Mistris [Maria Hester] Park a little Sonat [sic], and to come to Her next Friday or Saturday between 1 and 2 o'clock." [160] When Hob. XVI: 51 was finally published by Breitkopf & Härtel around 1805, it received the following notice in the *Allgemeine Musikalische Zeitung*:

> This sonata is appearing really for the first time before the public; it is, however, probably from a very early period of this master and perhaps was written as an occasional piece for someone who was still not too experienced as a *Klavier* player yet wanted to play something by Haydn. It consists only of two movements: a simple, singable Andante, like many in Haydn's early *Klavier* pieces, and a Finale which is set forth [either] by the beautiful blossoms of genial humor, and thus of profound art, as they have unfolded richly and abundantly in the best recent pieces of this kind, or by smaller buds, though unmistakable even to only partially practiced eyes. If then, the little piece is to be recommended mainly to less experienced players, it still has something attractive for more serious friends of art. [161]

Last Years in Vienna, 1796–1803

In contrast to the flurry of keyboard music that was produced during Haydn's second visit to London, the completion of only one new keyboard trio (Hob. XV: 30) can be documented after his return to the Imperial capital. With the exception of the string quartet, Haydn devoted himself almost entirely to vocal music until he ceased composing in 1803. Although, as the following documents show, Haydn had every intent to compose additional keyboard sonatas, keyboard music occupied him only as social and business activities demanded.

Trio Hob. XV: 30 is mentioned for the first time on 16 April 1796 in a letter to the publisher Christoph Gottlob Breitkopf. [162] Nearly eight months passed (9 November) before the trio was sent to Leipzig in the care of Haydn's student Joseph Weigl, who was entrusted with both the music and some money Haydn owed Breitkopf. [163] The print was reviewed in Breitkopf's own house publication, the *Allgemeine Musikalische Zeitung*, in the longest and most technical review to appear during Haydn's lifetime, from which come the following excerpts:

> The present sonata has been engraved for the first time from an autograph sent to the publisher by Haydn. His imagination is unmistakable in it. The character of the first Allegro moderato in E-flat major is generally gentle, rising now and then to moderately fiery. In all the three movements which constitute this sonata, well-selected modulations, transitions, and figures reveal the master's hand. . . . When the Andante con moto, the character of which stands between gentle and cheerful, is played immediately after the Allegro without a noticeable pause, then the key of C major in which it is written, makes an agreeable contrast with the previous key of E-flat major.

The preparatory transition between the Andante and the final Presto is surprisingly beautiful. In this Presto one notices Haydn's well-known learned style in which he presents the theme now with counterpoint placed over the subject (*dans le Contrepoint au dessus du Sujet*), now in inversion (*all' roverscio*), now with variations. Also, he often places it in different keys. . . .

Haydn possesses the skill to give such artificial devices a pleasing façade, though many might unjustly consider them empty schoolish devices. In this connection merely consider the whole fabric in its relationship to the episodes, and you will be satisfied with it.

From this and the above it is evident that this sonata is a substantial work, above all for cultivated musicians and amateurs. What might be the main difficulty in it for many are the chromatic passages and the diversions into the most distant keys—even those needing double flats—, the ligatures which are often stumbled over, and the passages mentioned earlier. . . .[164]

With Hob. XV:30 Haydn closed his activities as a composer of keyboard music. However, he seems to have intended to create more works for the instrument, as we have his contract of August 1796 with the English publisher Frederick Augustus Hyde for two keyboard *opere*:

Three Sonatas for the Piano Forte with an accompaniment for a Violin and Violoncello £75
Three Sonatas for the Piano Forte without accompaniment . . . . 60 [165]

A sketch in D major (Example II-6)[166] suggests, and the following letter to the Esterházy valet, Kürchner, on 1 June 1798 seems to corroborate such an intent: "For this favor, I will call on your dear daughter upon my arrival in Eisenstadt with a new *Clavier* sonata."[167] Yet by 12 June 1799 Haydn had not yet fulfilled any of his keyboard obligations under the 1796 contract, according to Griesinger's letter to Breitkopf & Härtel:

His publisher in England is a Mr. Bay [*recte* Banger or Hyde], a rather unimportant man as Haydn calls him, but who is associated with Clementi and Broderip. His agreement was set up for 5 years, of which 3 have already elapsed. . . . Because of an overload of projects, however, he has sent only a few quartets to England in these three years, and those quite recently. Though Bay is pressing especially for *Clavier* sonatas, he has as yet not been able to fulfill his wishes.[168]

As late as 1 July 1800 Haydn was still promising a keyboard sonata, this time to G. C. Härtel: "but just now I regret that I am in no position to serve you with another new *Clavier* sonata. As soon as *The Seasons* are finished, you shall be the first to be provided a *Clavier* sonata. . . ."[169] Five years after signing the English contract, Haydn had yet to complete his obligations, as he wrote to Hyde and Clementi on 28 April 1801: "I thank you for the 100 guineas you sent me. But, I also hope that I will receive the rest of the money as soon as possible, for which, however, I will endeavor to provide you with three good *Clavier* sonatas by the end of the summer."[170]

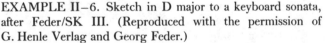

EXAMPLE II–6. Sketch in D major to a keyboard sonata, after Feder/SK III. (Reproduced with the permission of G. Henle Verlag and Georg Feder.)

In addition to his work on *The Seasons* and other compositions, at the end of the 1790s Haydn was, to a limited degree, supervising the publication of his *Oeuvres Complettes* by Breitkopf & Härtel, which was announced in 1799:

Complete Edition of J. Haydn's Works

We trust that we will fulfill the wish of every lover of excellent, and especially of Haydn's, music when we announce a complete, elegant and extremely inexpensive edition of the collected works of this great man—first of all, his *Klavier* compositions—to be done in our publishing house with the consent and authority of the composer himself. The often deceived public need not fear that something will appear in the edition that Haydn himself does not recognize as his own.

Our edition of Mozart's works is well known;—with Haydn's we will retain the same lay-out, the same print, the same elegance and accuracy, the same decorations and the same price—a volume of 25 to 30 sheets of paper at 1 Laubthaler or 1 thaler, 12 groschen, Saxon—in advance, and the fifth copy free, for which price the volumes will be delivered enclosed in tasteful covers. After the subscription period has run out, a volume will cost 3 thalers.— The first volume is already being printed and will appear this very summer. This will be followed within the year by at least four, and if the public wishes, even more volumes. The list of subscribers will be added to one of the following volumes. For the purpose of subscribing, please go to the nearest book and music dealers.

Furthermore, we hope that our edition of Haydn's works will not be confused with another one announced recently by a Herr Lehmann in Leipzig.

Leipzig, May 1793
BREITKOPF & HÄRTEL[171]

The edition was prefaced by the following remarks, presumably from Haydn:

Preface to the Oeuvres Complettes
Vienna, the 20th December 1799

The desire of many music lovers to own a complete edition of my *Klavier* works I recognize with delight as a flattering witness to their success. And I will be happy to ensure that nothing is included in this collection which has until this time wrongly carried my name or which, as an early work, does not deserve to be preserved here.

If my increasing age and my occupations permit, I will gladly fulfill the wish of the publisher to increase the desirability of this collection with a few new works.

JOSEPH HAYDN

Oeuvre Complettes began to appear, not as early as hoped, but in early 1800 with a volume of keyboard sonatas. It was not completed until December 1806.

In July 1803, Hob. XV:31, which was finished in London, became the subject of a dispute between Haydn and the Viennese music dealer Traeg. As reported by Griesinger:

After some time, Traeg asked for it back [the autograph to *L'isola disabitata*, which Haydn had borrowed] or else compensation of 12 ducats. Haydn, furious over this demand, had Traeg come to him and in the presence of others, gave him as rough a dressing down as possible. However, in order to avoid all problems, he finally gave up the sonata in question [Hob. XV:31], which he had composed in London.[172]

Traeg published this English sonata, which contained the "Dream" movement, later in the year, for it was announced in the *Wiener-Zeitung* on 27 August 1803. The dedication, like that of the Viennese edition of Hob. XVI:52, was to Fräulein von Kurzböck.

Sometime in the late fall of 1803, Prince Esterházy asked Haydn to write a sonata for Madame Moreau, the "beautiful and talented Creole wife of General Jean Victor Moreau."[173] Since Haydn was no longer able to compose, he presented her with Hob. XV:31 as a violin sonata merely by deleting the cello part; because of this omission, the work was incorrectly referred to in the Nadermann edition (*ca.* 1820) as the "Dernière Sonate." The dedicatory letter, dated 1 November 1803, is couched in ambiguity, as Haydn had not composed anything new for the keyboard in seven years:

Prince Esterházy did me the honour of informing me that you wish to have a Sonata of my composition. Nothing more than the great desire to please you would be necessary to compel me to begin this work; my age and my sicknesses have prevented me from accomplishing anything during the past two years, and I fear that you may not perceive this fact: but indulgence was always the handmaiden of charm and talent, and I am sure that I may count on yours. My doctors lead me to hope for a mitigation of my ills; and I wish for nothing more, *Madame*, than to repair the weakness of my work—by doing you homage in a new composition. I hope that it will be worthy of you and *M. le général* Moreau; I tremble that he might judge me sternly, and that he only remember that it was Timotheus alone who had the privilege of singing for Alexander.[174]

In 1803 Haydn also tried to authenticate some of his juvenilia from the files of Breitkopf & Härtel and to sell the publisher various works, including the early organ concerto (Hob. XVIII: 1).[175]

Essay III

AUTHENTICITY

The problem of authenticity remains at the forefront of late eighteenth-century musical scholarship, presenting bibliographical puzzles related to attribution, setting, cycle, and text. In part the situation can be ascribed to the flourishing musical life: publishers in London, Leipzig, Paris, and later Vienna could barely keep pace with the demand for new works from the most famous composers. In this environment of heated competition, the label on the product was at times a false one; that is, a more famous name was substituted for one of relative obscurity in order to promote sales. Thus, a large number of the works circulated under the name of Joseph Haydn did not flow from his pen.·

Carelessness in the storage and distribution of music, as well as problems of orthography and legibility, also resulted in false attributions. As it was the practice in many shops to have music copied without the scribe's knowing the identity of the composer, when the supervisor placed the cover with the composer's name around the completed copy, the possibilities of misattribution were very real; in many cases, but apparently not often enough, the situation was avoided by inscribing the incipit on the cover. Then, too, the covers themselves became worn, torn, or lost; such a circumstance may have resulted in a new cover by a Regens Chori, archivist, or librarian, who might inscribe the composer's name based on memory or assumption. Today, therefore, one must be suspicious of any attribution in a later hand or found on covers not contemporaneous with the contents. Another difficulty is that of deciphering the script itself; irregular practices of spelling and the progressive mutations that might occur in a series of secondary copies could cause a name like Lang, for example, to become Bach.[1]

In many instances authorship cannot be firmly established from either available external (i.e., derived from copies and prints themselves) or internal (i.e., style analysis) evidence. At other times the external evidence provides adequate data to support a tentative conclusion, but stylistic observations do not support it. Therefore, some works cannot be declared either spurious or unquestionably authentic, but they can be placed on a continuum of probability, using the categories authentic, probably authentic, plausible, doubtful, and spurious.[2] While this labeling may be viewed as "avoiding the question," it is certainly to be preferred in instances where the evidence is not decisive.

Although our methods of style analysis have become more sophisticated, the first line of attack must still be reserved for external data.[3] For Haydn in general and the keyboard works in particular, a relatively large body of authentic information (i.e., emanating from the composer) of varying reliability is available for determining authenticity: autographs, catalogues, correspondence including contracts, and early copies and prints. Since the autographs that survive for the keyboard works are relatively few in number and provide almost foolproof evidence, one can turn first to the five catalogues kept by Haydn, authorized by Haydn, or created at the time of his death: the *Entwurf-Katalog* (*EK*), the *London Verzeichnis* (*LV*), the *Haydn Verzeichnis* (*HV*), the *Haydn Bibliothek Verzeichnis* (*HBV*), and the *Haydn Nachlass Verzeichnis* (*HNV*).

The earliest of these, the *Entwurf-Katalog* (*EK*),[4] was apparently begun by Haydn sometime during the mid-1760s. It has been hypothesized that the origin of *EK* relates to a letter of complaint written in 1765 to Prince Nikolaus Esterházy by the old, apparently cantankerous, and ill Esterházy Kapellmeister Gregor Joseph Werner concerning the state of musical affairs under Haydn's direction.[5] In a letter, the Prince ordered Haydn to compose with greater diligence and to send to the Prince the first copy of all his new compositions.[6] The entries in *EK* are fairly complete through the 1770s, but after that date Haydn apparently felt it less important to keep a current record of his compositions. Although some of the listings were inscribed by Haydn's copyists Joseph Elssler, Sr., and Johann Schellinger, all those for keyboard works are in Haydn's hand and (with one exception) occupy pages 19–23 (see Plate 2). The keyboard listing commences with the concertos and continues with works mainly for solo keyboard, interspersed with a few accompanied divertimentos. It has been accepted that a considerable number of keyboard works written by Haydn before the mid-1770s were never entered in *EK*: entire groups of compositions (i.e., the early keyboard trios and concertinos), a few of which survive in copies of possibly authentic status, are not represented by a single incipit, possibly because the works themselves were no longer in Haydn's possession.[7]

The catalogue of works composed by Haydn in and for London (*LV*) was part of the fourth London Notebook, which is no longer extant. Its contents are known only from its publication in the three authentic biographies by Dies, Griesinger, and Carpani.[8] Unfortunately, their texts are not identical: Dies lists only short titles and the persons for whom the works were written; Griesinger includes full titles and the number of sheets for the autographs of each composition; and Carpani's list seems to be derived from Dies's. Despite some confusing entries, the significance of this catalogue is second only to *EK*.

The *Haydn Verzeichnis* (*HV*),[9] written by Haydn's amanuensis, Johann Elssler, dates from 1805, a time when the composer occupied himself with the organization of his musical legacy. The importance of *HV* has diminished, as it has recently been proven to include two works by Johann Vanhal and six by Romanus Hofstetter, and since Jens Peter Larsen's work in the late 1930s is recognized as being derived from *EK*, the available volumes of the *Oeuvres complettes* issued by Breitkopf & Härtel, and Pleyel's edition of the string quartets. The importance of *EK* and Breitkopf's *Oeuvres complettes* in compiling *HV* is immediately apparent in the keyboard listings: in *EK* are found later notations referring to Breitkopf & Härtel's volumes, and the order of the themes in *HV* corresponds to the contents of *EK* and the *Oeuvres complettes*.

The motivation for the compilation of the *Haydn Bibliothek Verzeichnis (HBV)*,[10] also in the hand of Johann Elssler, may have been the same as for *HV*: to bring in order the *musicalia* owned by Haydn. In addition to the composer's own compositions, whether in autographs, copies, or prints, it contains musical and theoretical works by Haydn's contemporaries. It is somewhat puzzling that some of the authentic keyboard works listed in this inventory are not entered in *HV*. Thus, *HV*, in contrast to *HBV*, did not even include all the works present in Haydn's own house. Compiled by the Viennese Schatzmeister and publisher, Ignaz Sauer, the *Haydn Nachlass Verzeichnis (HNV)*[11] of 1809—that is, the public record of Haydn's possessions at the time of his death—closely approximates *HBV*.

Although they do not come directly from Haydn, the catalogues of the Viennese collector and musicologist Aloys Fuchs (1799–1853) and the Leipzig music dealer Breitkopf are also of some importance. The Breitkopf catalogue,[12] which was issued in six parts (1762–1765) and sixteen supplements (1766–1787), is of great value for the period before 1774 in that it provides the only known dated early citation for some of Haydn's keyboard works. The two general catalogues by Aloys Fuchs, from 1839 and 1840,[13] are significant only insofar as they corroborate attributions; in cases where a work is not listed in Breitkopf the incipits from Fuchs are possibly based on early sources of Viennese provenance no longer extant.

Of particular importance in verifying the keyboard music is Haydn's correspondence with publishers both domestic and foreign: Artaria and Traeg in Vienna, Hummel in Berlin, Breitkopf & Härtel in Leipzig, Sieber in Paris, and John Bland and William Forster in London.[14] Unfortunately, Haydn's extant correspondence begins only in the 1780s. These letters, combined with the *Stichvorlage*—that is, the copy from which a plate is engraved—provide not only confirmation of authorship but also information concerning chronology and text criticism. Related to this body of correspondence is that between Georg August Griesinger and Breitkopf & Härtel; Griesinger persuaded Haydn to pass judgment on compositions attributed to him from the Breitkopf collection. Although Griesinger's material was destroyed during the Second World War, notes and extracts made by C. F. Pohl and Carl Maria Brand have preserved its core.[15]

Some prints must be regarded as authentic because of other documents. For example, although the Bossler edition of the Sonatas Hob. XVI:40–42 has all sorts of textual problems, it is inscribed on a copy of the print itself that Haydn performed from this edition in 1785; therefore, one presumes it authentic.[16] However, without corroborating evidence, prints whose title pages indicate that they were engraved from Haydn's autograph must to some degree be questioned.

In terms of textual importance, manuscript copies seem to be more valuable than prints. Despite his reservations about the professional Viennese scribes,

Haydn relied heavily on them and their Esterházy counterparts even during the years when his works were being engraved. Copies by such scribes as Viennese Nos. 2 and 3 and the so-called Fürnberg copyists are seemingly so directly connected with Haydn [17] that music produced by them has nearly as strong a claim to authenticity as those by Esterházy scribes. Even after the printing of his first set of solo sonatas (Hob. XVI: 21–26, dedicated to Prince Nikolaus), Haydn apparently chose to distribute his next set (Hob. XVI: 27–32) through a professional Viennese copy shop.

Works that are not a part of the above documents must be scrutinized for the reliability of the archive, collection, or publisher from which they are known. Lacking a decisive stylistic profile, many of the early works must be so judged. Among the most important and largest of the currently extant archives for Haydn's early keyboard music is the archbishop's music collection at Kroměříž, in Moravia. For the most part the copies are in the hands of professional scribes from Vienna, a few of which are by the so-called Fürnberg group. Unfortunately, one of the collection's peculiarities is the duplication of works, indicating either that at some point the archive was consolidated with others or that the collection itself lacked organization during the eighteenth century. [18]

Despite all the available evidence, complete agreement as to Haydn's keyboard output is still to be achieved: one need only compare the various modern editions by C. Landon, H. C. R. Landon, Georg Feder, and Karl Päsler and read the subsequent revisions by their editors. [19] Based on a re-examination of the evidence, herewith is one additional attempt at a definitive list.

In the following discussion the strength of the authenticity of the keyboard works attributed to Haydn will be explored. Each genre will be considered separately, as will arrangements and any remaining questions of setting. While one cannot present all the details of the evidence within the text for every piece, tables summarizing the available data are provided at the end of each section; these together with the documents of the previous essay supply all the essential external information regarding each work. For works not included in volume one of Hoboken's catalogue or lacking incipits, complete incipits are given here. In Table III-8, at the end of this essay, the authenticity of each work is assessed as to the strength of the evidence—both external and internal—on a continuum from authentic to spurious.

Solo Sonatas

Of the more than eighty solo keyboard sonatas attributed to Haydn in contemporary sources, only twelve survive in autographs: Hob. XVI: 6, 18, 19, 20, 21, 22, 23, 26, 29, 45, 49, and 52. The appearance of the autograph fragment of Hob. XIV: 5 (*recte* Hob. XVI: 5a) indicates that this work too is for solo keyboard. Besides the series of "lost" sonatas, only four solo keyboard sonatas that do not survive in autograph are entered with their incipits in *EK*: Hob. XVI: 3, 4, 14, and 46. In this same inventory are two inscriptions without incipits: "6 gedruckte Sonaten

EXAMPLE III–1. "Göttweig" Sonatas.

v. 774" and "6 Sonaten von Anno 776." These works can be identified as those dedicated to Nikolaus Esterházy and printed by Kurzböck (Hob. XVI:21–26) and those distributed by professional Viennese copyists (Haschke?) in 1776 (Hob. XVI:27–32).[20] In addition to those not surviving in autograph, or without an inscription in *EK*, another dozen are found in *HV*: Hob. XVI:34, 35, 36, 37, 38 39, 40, 41, 42, 44, 47, and 48. As expected, all these works are published in Breitkopf's *Oeuvres complettes*; many are also referred to in Haydn's correspondence. Finally, *LV* lists "3 Sonatas for Miss Janson," which could refer to either the

EXAMPLE III–2. "Frankfurt" Sonatas.

EXAMPLE III–2 (*continued*)

three solo sonatas Hob. XVI:50–52 or the three trios dedicated to her (Hob. XV:27–29).[21] Regardless, the slow movement of Hob. XVI:50 and all of XVI:51 and 52 are also published in *Oeuvres complettes*.

The remaining solo sonatas do not survive with any authentic documentation. Hob. XVI:5 and 7–13 first appear in the Breitkopf catalogues; Hob. XVI:1, 2, 15, 16, 17, 33, 43, C1, D1, Es1, G1, B1, XVII:D1, and XIV:C1 exist under Haydn's name only through copies.[22] Twelve sonatas not originally in Hoboken should also be mentioned: three at Göttweig (Example III-1) published in an edition by Ernst Fritz Schmid in 1937 and later shown by him to be by Franz Anton Hofmeister;[23] six sonatas at the Landesbibliothek in Frankfurt (Example III-2);[24] a sonata (XVI:C2) from Genoa (Example III-3); and two sonatas discovered by Georg Feder in the collection from the Benedictine Monastery at Rajhrad (now in the Moravské Múzeum in Brno), which he dubbed Es2 and Es3 (Examples III-4 and 5), a continuation of Hoboken's numbering.[25]

Four sonatas for keyboard four hands are also attributed to Haydn: Hob. XVIIa:1, 2, C1, and F1, the last being listed in Hoboken's supplement (Example III-6). Hob. XVIIa:1 appears in both *EK* and *HV* as well as in numerous other

EXAMPLE III−3. Hob. XVI:C2.

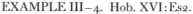

EXAMPLE III−4. Hob. XVI:Es2.

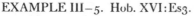

EXAMPLE III−5. Hob. XVI:Es3.

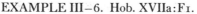

EXAMPLE III−6. Hob. XVIIa:F1.

catalogues, copies, and prints. The three remaining works have, in general, weak traditions.

A number of these sonatas lacking verification in authentic sources can be dismissed immediately. Hob. XVI:C1 is known only from a single copy in the Österreichische Nationalbibliothek, entitled "Sonata per cembalo Del Sigre Giuseppe Häydn" with "Spect: ad me J. H." in the lower right-hand corner (Example III-7). It is one of several spurious works with the provocative "shown to me, J. H." on the copy, which does not stand for Joseph Haydn but for Joseph Georg Haroldt (1720–1772), who was Claviermeister and Regens Chori at St. Ulrich's in Vienna. The copy is therefore an early one and shows the demand for Haydn's keyboard music before 1772. Considering the unreliability of Haroldt, the cyclic make-up, and the unskilled syntax, it is hard to accept this work as authentic or as a divertimento/sonata in any sense, unless it represents one of Haydn's very earliest efforts. The single-movement sonata Hob. XVI:C2 is known only from a copy of Italian provenance. Neither the source nor the style supports Haydn as a possible author. Hob. XVI:D1 also survives in a single copy, this time at the Bibliothèque Nationale in Paris (Conservatory Collection). The work, "La conquista d'Occzakau . . . 1788," belongs to the popular genre of the military or battle sonata, in this case portraying the victory of the Russians over the Turks, with descriptive indications for the sections. Since this genre is unknown in Haydn and the composer's name was added at a later date, it must be summarily rejected. It may well

EXAMPLE III–7. Hob. XVI:C1.

EXAMPLE III–8. Hob. XVI:Es1.

EXAMPLE III–9. Hob. XVI:B1.

be a creation of Ferdinand Kauer (1751–1831).[26] Hob. XVI:Es1, a transcription
by Pietro Polzelli, is a one-movement work, known from Haydn's estate (*HNV*
516), with a Vivace assai coda (Example III-8). Originally it was a trio from the
pasticcio *Circe* performed at Esterháza in 1789. Another copy from Donaueschingen reveals that Es1 was also circulated as a battle sonata with commentary in
the music. It has no authentic basis as a keyboard work. Hob. XVI:B1, also known
from a single copy at the Österreichische Nationalbibliothek, by the same scribe as
Hob. XVI:C1, is highly doubtful on the basis of style. The sonata consists of two
fast movements, a cyclic structure not duplicated by Haydn in any other multi-
movement instrumental work (Example III-9). In addition, the cadence formulas
used to close sections speak against Haydn's authorship. The so-called Frankfurt
Sonatas, with a watermark from the Wolfegg paper mill in Württemburg (1740–
1785), are six works "par Mr. Hayde" from the Nachlass of the Domkapellmeister
Keller, now at the Landesbibliothek in Frankfurt.[27] The bibliographic situation—
non-Austrian paper and scribe—as well as the overall style indicate that the probable composer is a North German.

Of the remaining sonatas, a large number were acknowledged by Haydn in
1803, when he was questioned by Griesinger.[28] However, his memory was not very
reliable: in one case, Hob. XVI:13, Haydn confirmed and then denied his authorship, while in another he accepted a sonata, Hob. XVI:17, which has been shown
to be by the Braunschweig Kapellmeister Johann Schwanenberger (Schwanenberg[er]s) (1740–1804).[29] Indeed, some of these early works, e.g., the first movements of Hob. XVI:12 and 5, have been doubted for reasons of style—the former
on grounds of the large-dimension structure (it lacks the customary double bars
with repeats) and the generally disjointed presentation of the material, the latter on
its use of *Fortspinnung*. Hob. XVI:12 has to some extent been rehabilitated because of its similarity to an early aria that Haydn may have composed.[30] It is most
disturbing that many of these copies seem to emanate from Breitkopf in Leipzig,
and few are to be found in collections closer to Vienna.[31] However, this generally
weak source situation is at times compensated for by the quality of the music itself.

Among the early works not known to Breitkopf, Hob. XVI:15 is an inauthentic arrangement of movements from the popular divertimento "Der Geburtstag"
(Hob. II:11). Hob. XVI:16[32] survives only in a single copy of Viennese origin in a
Bavarian collection not known for Haydn's early keyboard music; its style is possible only as a very early work. Hob. XVII:D1 survives in a single Viennese manu-

script but is, in contrast to the incipit given by Hoboken, in three movements and therefore a sonata rather than a *Klavierstück*. Hob. XVI: 33 and especially 43 are surprisingly weak bibliographically, considering their later date of origin, but their style is not to be doubted.[33] Finally, Hob. XVI: G1 is a more plausible Haydn creation than Hob. XVI: 11 from both the cyclic layout and the distribution of the sources. The Andante from Hob. XVI: 11, although musically attractive, has no claim to Haydn's authorship except in copies that perhaps emanate from Breitkopf. The first movement (i.e., the finale of Hob. XVI: G1) apparently circulated separately, as it appears alone in an old Berlin manuscript. Since Breitkopf listed this sonata separately from a group of six by Haydn in his 1767 catalogue, the cycle may have come into existence in Breitkopf's shop. The minuet of Hob. XVI: 11 comes from the Baryton Trio Hob. XI: 26, composed *ca.* 1766–1767, but the minuet's trio, like the slow movement, is otherwise unknown; that no other trio among the authentic sonatas is in the relative minor, rather than in the parallel minor or in the subdominant, casts further doubt on its authenticity in this context. Thus, Hob. XVI: 11, 15, and 17 must be rejected as authentic sonatas, even though individual movements of Hob. XVI: 11 are possibly Haydn's.

Of the three works for keyboard four hands without authentic data (Hob. XVIIa: 2, C1, and F1), the case for Hob. XVIIa: 2 is the strongest, with a copy in Berlin and an entry in the catalogues of Aloys Fuchs. Musically, too, it is the most impressive and should be regarded as a work by Haydn until another attribution is found. As Hoboken has already indicated, C1 is spurious; the copy in the Öster-reichische Nationalbibliothek seems to have been copied from a print that names Tommaso Giordani (*ca.* 1730–1806) as the composer. F1 (Example III-6) survives in a single source (Kroměříž) of Viennese origin, from the copy shop of Laurent Lausch. Haydn's relationship with Lausch was not a happy one (he was involved in the theft of Haydn's Quartets Op. 50);[34] therefore, the copy is open to question. Internally, the first impression is that the work is an imitation of Haydn's popular "Il maestro e lo scolare" with the alternation of material between the *primo* and *secondo*. However, a number of details speak against it: the lack of rhythmic control in the exposition of the first and second movements; the peculiar shift from the dominant of the sub-mediant to the dominant of the tonic (mm. 39–41) in the first movement; and the chromaticism of the primary material in the finale. F1 is at best doubtful and probably spurious.

Both Es2 and Es3 were discovered in 1962 by Georg Feder in an old copy by the organist Matthäus Benedict Rutka of the Benedictine Abbey at Rajhrad, whose music collection is now a part of the Moravské Múzeum in Brno. Feder argued not unconvincingly for their authenticity on the basis of the Rajhrad source (which also contains Hob. XVI: 14, 13, and 2) and the style.[35] Although doubts had been raised concerning their genuineness, it was not until Es3 was attributed, with a previously unknown finale, to Mariano Romano Kayser in Anthology Roskovsky that the status of both was publicly debated.[36]

The evidence indicates that Es2 and 3 probably contain enough parallels to have stemmed from the same pen. Unfortunately, our present control over Haydn's keyboard music from before 1766 and the available sampling of Kayser's output are not sufficient to form a stylistic judgment. If indeed these two sonatas are from Haydn's hand, they do not convincingly exemplify either his keyboard style or the high level of craftsmanship displayed in other works of the 1760s; they can only be considered plausible products of Haydn's earliest years.

The remaining problems relating to the authenticity of the solo works concern those known in multiple versions. Hob. XVI:4, in the cycle published by Päsler with two minuets (one from Salieri's "Fiera di Venezia"), can be dismissed as having nothing to do with Haydn; the two-movement structure of a fast movement followed by a minuet is perfectly acceptable as genuine Haydn although the existence of a now-missing fast finale in 2/4 or 3/8 time should not be ruled out.[37]

The most difficult cyclic puzzle relates to Hob. XVI:47, which is best known from its 1788 edition by Artaria: a three-movement work in F major consisting of a Moderato in triple meter with an invention-like texture, a Larghetto in compound duple meter, and a duple-meter finale marked Allegro (Example III-10). The first movement also appears as an independent keyboard piece in a copy from Kroměříž and as the closing movement to Hob. XVI:44 in a copy now located at the Öster-reichische Nationalbibliothek (Example III-11). The Gesellschaft der Musik-freunde copy (Anthology Dorsch) consists of the second and third movements of

EXAMPLE III–10. Hob. XVI:47.

EXAMPLE III–11. Hob. XVI:44 and Hob. XVI:47/1.

EXAMPLE III–12. Hob. XVI:47/2, 3, and 4.

EXAMPLE III–13. Hob. XVI:47/2 and 3, and XVII:1.

Hob. XVI:47 with a Tempo di Menuet finale, all in the key of E instead of F (Example III-12).[38] The second and third movements of Hob. XVI:47 also appear in E major in a source from Kroměříž, with Hob XVII:1 as a closing (Example III-13).

The stylistic differences between the first movement and the final two movements of Hob. XVI:47 make the Artaria version very improbable.[39] The cycle formed by Hob. XVI:44 with the first movement of Hob. XVI:47 as a closing can also be dismissed because of the unsatisfactory nature of this movement as a finale; the impossibility of the tonal, temporal, and metric sequence; and the proven independence of the cycle of Hob. XVI:44. The second and third movements of Hob. XVI:47, with Hob. XVII:1 as an ending, can be eliminated because of the existence of the autograph of the Capriccio (the third movement of the cycle) and the improbability of the cyclic tonal sequence E minor–E major–G major. An independent cycle of the movements in E minor and E major is also unlikely, since a sonata of two connected movements is not a part of Haydn's style.

The cyclic arrangement of the Anthology Dorsch copy seems to be the most satisfactory—a slow first movement in 6/8 time, followed by a fast movement in duple meter, with a Tempo di Menuet finale—a cycle found in a number of Haydn's other works.[40] In addition, these three movements have similar thematic material. As common thematic material is not found in any of the other versions considered here, the one in Anthology Dorsch was almost certainly conceived as a single entity.[41]

The remaining problem is whether F or E is the original key. The first portion of Anthology Dorsch appears to have been copied for an instrument having a limited upper range, as no work goes higher than d''', a pitch that would be exceeded by the F-major versions.[42] In addition, only the E-major version requires a keyboard with a short octave. It is difficult to believe that the E-major version would have been both transposed and altered to accommodate the range and the short octave[43] after the F-major version had been completed. Thus E must have been the original key.

Trios

In contrast to the solo sonatas, the trios divide rather clearly bibliographically, stylistically, and chronologically into two groups: an early series, Hob. XV: 1, 2, 33–41, C1, [D1], and f1; and a late series, Hob. XV: 3–32 and C2. The summary data for the works in this genre are therefore presented in two separate parts in Table III-2.

Of the forty-seven contemporary copies and prints surviving in versions as keyboard trios by Haydn, only eight are known in autographs: Hob. XV: 5, 6, 7, 9, 17, 25, 30, and 31.[44] The title pages of the Sieber editions for trios Hob. XV: 11– 13 and 24–26 state that the publications are based "sur l'original de l'auteur," but these claims cannot be corroborated.[45]

In contrast to the solo sonatas, the incipit of only one trio, Hob. XV: 9, is recorded in EK, perhaps as late as ca. 1800.[46] On the other hand, HV lists all but two of the trios found in Oeuvres complettes (Hob. XV: 9 and 30). Additionally, virtually every one of the trios composed after ca. 1784, with the exception of Hob. XV: C2, has strong supporting evidence (see Table III-2), whether it be an authentic copy, an authorized publication, or verification by correspondence or anecdote. Therefore, there can be no reasonable doubt concerning the authenticity of these mature trios.

The early trios (see Table III-2, Part 1) were probably written in some form or another either before or during the 1760s. None survives in autograph; and only Hob. XV: 2 appears in EK, but in its version with baryton. However, Haydn's response to Griesinger about his authorship was totally negative for only one of these surviving trios, Hob. XV: C1. With regard to the copyists, five works are by scribes believed to have been associated with Haydn: Hob. XV: 34 and f1 in copies by one of the so-called Fürnberg copyists;[47] Hob. XV: 2 in a copy from Haydn's estate (HNV 507) by Esterházy Anonymous 23; and Hob. XV: 35 and 41 in copies by Viennese Professional No. 2, the former also a part of Haydn's estate (HNV 513). In addition, Hob. XV: 40 survives in one rather late copy from the Viennese

TABLE III-1

Solo Keyboard Sonatas Attributed to Haydn

Work	Autograph	Entwurf-Katalog	London Catalogue	Haydn Verzeichnis	Oeuvres complettes	Haydn's response (1803)	Authentic copies	Authentic editions	Correspondence and other documents†	Copies by scribes associated with Haydn	Other copies from Vienna and its environs	Breitkopf catalogue	Other early copies	Other early editions (Remarks)	Fuchs catalogues
Hob. XVI:1											A-Wn CS-KRm(2) D-brd-B(Artaria?)				X
Hob. XVI:2											A-Wgm CS-Bm(Rajhrad) D-brd-B(Artaria?)				X
Hob. XVI:2a–e, g, h (music lost)		X		X					2c, p.14						
Hob. XVI:3		X		X							A-Wgm(Dorsch) A-Wgm CS-KRm				X
Hob. XVI:4		X		X							A-Wgm				X
*Hob. XVI:5						+					A-Wn	1763	D-brd-B;D-ddr-A D-ddr-G01 D-ddr-LEm(mvt.2)		X
Hob. XVI:5a(XIV:5)	X	X		X										Note: Auto. is frag.	
Hob. XVI:6	X	X		X		+						1766	D-brd-B;D-ddr-A D-ddr-G01 D-ddr-LEm	Note: Auto. is frag.	X
Hob. XVI:7					X	+					A-Wn CS-KRm	1766	D-ddr-A D-ddr-D1 D-ddr-G01		X
Hob. XVI:8						+					A-Wn	1766 1766	D-ddr-A D-brd-B(2) D-ddr-D1 D-ddr-G01		X
Hob. XVI:9						+						1766	D-ddr-A D-brd-B D-ddr-G01		X
*Hob. XVI:10						+						1767	D-ddr-Bds(mvt.3) D-ddr-G01 GB-Ltyson		X

Hob.					Sources		Editions	Publisher	
Hob. XVI:11			+			1767	D-ddr-Bds(mvt.3) D-ddr-G01 GB-Ltyson		X
*Hob. XVI:12	X	X	+			1767	D-brd-B B-ddr-G01 GB-Ltyson		X
*Hob. XVI:13			+; –		A-Wgm CS-Bm(Rajhrad)	1767	D-ddr-G01 GB-Ltyson		X
*Hob. XVI:14	X	X	+		A-Wn A-Wgm(Dorsch) A-Wgm CS-Bm(Rajhrad)	1767	D-ddr-G01 GB-Ltyson		X
Hob. XVI:15	X								
Hob. XVI:16			+		D-brd-HR		D-brd-DO	Artaria Op. 53 Longman & Broderip Op. 53	
*Hob. XVI:17					CS-KRm		D-brd-DO		
Hob. XVI:18	X pt	X			A-GÖ CS-KRm		D-brd-DO D-brd-Mbs	Artaria Op. 53 Longman & Broderip Op. 53	X
Hob. XVI:19	X	X			A-Wgm(Dorsch) A-Wgm A-Wn A-KRm D-ddr-SW1		D-brd-DO	Artaria Op. 53 Longman & Broderip Op. 53	X
Hob. XVI:20	X pt	X		Artaria Op. 30/6 pp.23–25	A-Wn				
Hob. XVI:21–26	X pt	X		Kurzböck p.21				Hummel Op. 17 (authentic?)	X
Hob. XVI:27	X		+		A-Wgm(Dorsch) A-Wn A-Gk CS-KRm (2) D-ddr-SW1			Hummel Op. 14	X
Hob. XVI:28	X				A-Wn CS-KRm D-ddr-SW1			Hummel Op. 14	X
Hob. XVI:29	X	X			A-Wn CS-KRm(2) D-brd-B			Hummel Op. 14	X
Hob. XVI:30	X				A-Wn(2) CS-KRm D-brd-B D-ddr-SW1			Hummel Op. 14	X
Hob. XVI:31	X				A-Wn CS-KRm(3) D-brd-B(2) D-ddr-SW1			Hummel Op. 14	X

TABLE III-1 (*continued*)

Solo Keyboard Sonatas Attributed to Haydn

Work	Autograph	Entwurf-Katalog	London Catalogue	Haydn Verzeichnis	Oeuvres complettes	Haydn's response (1803)	Authentic copies	Authentic editions	Correspondence and other documents †	Copies by scribes associated with Haydn	Other copies from Vienna and its environs	Breitkopf catalogue	Other early copies	Other early editions (Remarks)	Fuchs catalogues
Hob. XVI:32		X			X						A-Wgm A-Wn(2) CS-KRm D-ddr-SW1			Hummel Op. 14	X
Hob. XVI:33				X							A-GÖ A-Wn CS-KRm D-brd-B			Beardmore & Birchall	X
Hob. XVI:34				X	X						D-brd-B A-Wn; A-GÖ A-Gl A-SF; CS-KRm(3)			André Op. 42 Beardmore & Birchall	X
Hob. XVI:35–39				X	X			Artaria Op. 30	pp.23–25					Hummel Op. 17 (Authentic?)	X
Hob. XVI:40–42				X	X			Bossler Op. 37	p.26					Hummel Op. 33	X
Hob. XVI:43					X						A-GÖ A-Wlandon A-Wn D-brd-B			Beardmore & Birchall	X
Hob. XVI:44				X	X						A-GÖ A-Wn CS-KRm D-brd-Mbs			Artaria Op. 54 Longman & Broderip Op. 54	X
Hob. XVI:45	X	X		X	X						A-GÖ A-SF A-Wn CS-KRm			Artaria Op. 54 Longman & Broderip Op. 54	X
Hob. XVI:46		X		X	X						A-Wn CS-KRm			Artaria Op. 54 Longman & Broderip Op. 54	X

Hob.	Marks	Page†	First edition	Authentic sources	Date / attributions	
Hob. XVI:47	X X		Artaria Op. 55	A-Wgm(Dorsch) A-Wn CS-KRm(2)		X
Hob. XVI:48	X X X	p.36	Breitkopf Bland?	D-brd-B		X
Hob. XVI:49	X X X / X lost?	pp.43–45	Artaria Op. 66			X
Hob. XVI:50	X? X slow mvt.	pp.52–53	Caulfield Op. 79 / Artaria (slow)			X slow mvt.
Hob. XVI:51	X? X	pp.52–53	Breitkopf Op. 93			X
Hob. XVI:52	X? X X		Longman, Clementi Op. 78 / Artaria Op. 82			
Hob. XVI:C1				A-Wn		
Hob. XVI:C2				I-Gi(1)		
*Hob. XVI:D1				F-Pc		
Hob. XVI:Es1	[H-Bn]			D-brd-DO		
Hob. XVI:Es2				CS-Bm(Rajhrad)		
*Hob. XVI:Es3				CS-Bm(Rajhrad) / H-Bn		
Hob. XVI:G1				A-M A-Wgm A-Wn CS-KRm		
Hob. XVI:B1				A-Wn		
Hob. XVII:D1				A-Wn		
*Göttweig Sonatas				A-GÖ		
Frankfurt Sonatas				D-brd-F		
Hob. XVIIa:1	X			A-Wn(mvt. 1) CS-KRm / A-Eh	1778 Skillern; Hummel; Artaria	X
Hob. XVIIa:2				CS-KRm / D-ddr-Dlb	Artaria	
*Hob. XVIIa:C1				D-brd-B / A-Wn		X
Hob. XVIIa:F1				CS-KRm / A-Wn		

+ = positive

− = negative

0 = could not recall

* = conflicting attributions

† Page numbers refer to documents in Essays I and II.

TABLE III-2, PART 1

Early Keyboard Trios Attributed to Haydn

Work	Autograph	Entwurf-Katalog	London Catalogue	Haydn Verzeichnis	Oeuvres complettes	Haydn's response (1803)	Authentic copies	Authentic editions	Correspondence and other documents †	Copies by scribes associated with Haydn	Other copies from Vienna and its environs	Breitkopf catalogue	Other early copies	Other early editions (Remarks)	Fuchs catalogues
Hob. XV:1		X			X	+					CS-KRm, D-brd-B		D-ddr-GO1	Hummel	X
Hob. XV:2		X		X		+	H-Bn, GB-Lbm	Forster, Op. 42	pp.30–32		CS-KRm(3), D-brd-B				
Hob. XV:33 (music lost)											D-brd-B	1771			
Hob. XV:34						+				CS-KRm	CS-Bm (Rajhrad), CS-Bm (Strassnitz)	1771	A-Ssp		
Hob. XV:35						+	H-Bn				CS-KRm	1771	D-brd-B		X
Hob. XV:36						+					A-GÖ, A-Wgm	1774			X
Hob. XV:37						+					A-Wn, CS-KRm, D-brd-B, D-brd-B(mvt.3)	1766	D-brd-B(2), D-ddr-GO1, D-ddr-D1, D-ddr-LEm	Hummel, Op. 4	X
Hob. XV:38						+					CS-KRm, D-brd-B(mvt.2)		D-ddr-D1, D-ddr-LEm(2)		X
Hob. XV:39											D-brd-B		D-brd-B(3)	Hummel, Op. 4	
Hob. XV:40						0					A-Wn		D-brd-MGmi, D-ddr-D1		

Hob. XV:41	CS-KRm	+/–	A-ST A-Wn CS-KRm D-brd-B	1767	D-brd-B D-ddr-D1 D-ddr-LEm		
Hob. XV:deest.			CS-KRm			(Landon No. 42)	
*Hob. XV:C1		–	A-Wgm CS-KRm D-brd-B	1766	D-brd-B D-ddr-D1 D-ddr-G01 D-ddr-SW1	Hummel, Op. 4	X
Hob. XV:D1 (music lost)		–		1771			
Hob. XV:f1	CS-KRm	0			D-ddr-D1		

+ = positive

– = negative

0 = could not recall

* = conflicting attributions

† Page numbers refer to documents in Essays I and II.

TABLE III-2, PART 2

Keyboard Trios after ca. 1784 Attributed to Haydn

	Autograph	Entwurf-Katalog	London Catalogue	Haydn Verzeichnis	Oeuvres complettes	Haydn's response (1803)	Authentic copies	Authentic editions	Correspondence and other documents †	Copies by scribes associated with Haydn	Other copies from Vienna and its environs	Breitkopf catalogue	Other early copies	Other early editions (Remarks)	Fuchs catalogues
*Hob. XV:3					X	–	G-Lbm	Forster Op. 40	pp.27–28						X
*Hob. XV:4				X	X	+	G-Lbm	Forster Op. 40	pp.27–28						X
Hob. XV:5	X pt			X	X	+	CS-KRm GB-Lbm	Forster Op. 40	pp.27–28						X
Hob. XV:6–8	X6 7			X	X			Artaria Op. 40	pp.29–32					Forster Op. 43 (7 is sketch auto.)	X
Hob. XV:9	X	X			X		GB-Lbm	Forster Op. 42	pp.30–32						
Hob. XV:10				X	X		GB-Lbm	Forster Op. 42	pp.30–32					Hoffmeister	X
Hob. XV:11–13	?			X	X			Artaria Op. 57	pp.34–35					Longman & Broderip Op. 58 (auto. owned by Sieber?)	X
Hob. XV:14				X	X			Artaria Op. 61 L&B Op. 68	p.46						X
Hob. XV:15–17	X 17			X	X		16-I-Mc	Bland Artaria Op. 63	pp.38–42					(17 auto. is sketch)	X

						Publisher / Opus	†	Notes		
Hob. XV:18–20		X	X	X		L&B Op. 70	p.47		X	X
Hob. XV:21–23		X	X	X	22-H-Bn slow mvt.	Preston Op. 71	p.47		X	X
Hob. XV:24–26	? X 25		X	X		L&B Op. 73 ?Sieber Op. 83, 84	p.47	(auto. owned by Sieber?; 25 auto. is sketch)		X
Hob. XV:27–29	X	X		X		L&B Op. 75 Artaria Op. 78				X
Hob. XV:30	X pt			X	H-Bn	Artaria Op. 79 Breitkopf Op. 88	p.55			X
Hob. XV:31	X		X	X		Traeg [Nadermann]	pp.51–52, 58–59	(London Catalogue: mvt. 2)		X
Hob. XV:32	X		X			Artaria Op. 70 Bland Preston	pp.45–46			X
Hob. XV:C2								Pollet (Some sections arr. from symphony movements; see Feder/GROVE 6, p.389)		

+ = positive
− = negative
0 = could not recall
* = conflicting attributions
† Page numbers refer to documents in Essays I and II.
L&B = Longman & Broderip

firm of Traeg, with whom Haydn had business dealings;[48] while Hob. XV: 36, 37, and C1 are transmitted in what seem to be Viennese copies. Thus, to varying degrees all the early trios have some claim to legitimacy based on external evidence.

Only one of the early and two of the later trios have conflicting attributions: Hob. XV:C1, 3, and 4. Hob. XV:C1 was discovered under Wagenseil's name (*WWV* 449) by Michelle Fillion in a collection containing other works by the Viennese Hofklaviermeister at the Benediktiner-Frauenstift Nonnberg in Salzburg. However, Fillion was able to establish that the Wagenseil attribution may very well stem from the same source as the Kroměříž copy, which attributes the work to Haydn, or one related to it. The provenance of the Wagenseil copy cannot be determined since its watermark is indecipherable and the scribe cannot be definitely identified. The existence of seven sources—two Viennese and five German, the latter probably all related to Breitkopf copies—speaks strongly for Haydn's authorship. Furthermore, a number of characteristics point to Haydn as the composer: 1. Haydn's early trios always begin with the keyboard taking the leading line and the violin subsequently repeating the material, whereas trios by Haydn's contemporaries almost always begin with the violin followed by the keyboard. 2. The string instruments in Haydn's works play an important concertante role, whereas in Wagenseil they tend to be more contributory. 3. The module of activity in Haydn tends to be somewhat larger and more articulated than in Wagenseil. Therefore, even though Haydn denied authorship of this trio, both the sources and the style sustain the attribution of Hob. XV:C1 as at least plausibly authentic.[49]

On the other hand, both external and internal evidence for Hob. XV:3 and 4 seem to indicate that these trios are not by Haydn, despite the fact that they appeared under his name in some of the very best of sources: an authentic edition— Forster's Op. 40, *Oeuvres complettes*, and a contract made by William Forster with Haydn in 1786, plus the words "di me Giuseppe Haydn" on the title pages of the *Stichvorlagen*. In 1803, while still claiming Hob. XV:3, Haydn attributed Hob. XV:4 to his brother Michael, an indication that prompted Saint-Foix in 1931 to assign both works to Michael on the basis of style.[50] The difficulty with Saint-Foix's hypothesis is that Haydn's brother is not known to have written any chamber music with keyboard, therefore calling into question Joseph's attribution.

It was not until thirty years after the appearance of Saint-Foix's study that the discussion concerning these trios was resumed from both the bibliographic and the stylistic aspects by Tyson, Schwarting, Stockmeier, Benton, and Fruewald.[51] The result is a tight case for Ignaz Pleyel's authorship, the main points of which are supported by written documents, printed editions, and style. Among the written documents are John Calcott's account; Framéry's *Notice*, which presumably derives from Pleyel; and a slip of paper from *ca.* 1822 in Tyson's copy of an edition of the trios attributed to Pleyel, with indications of a court hearing.[52] All the printed sources attributing the works to Haydn either stem from or are related to the Forster edition; a series of prints attributing them to Pleyel date from as early as 1791 (Sieber) and include one published by Pleyel himself. As for style considerations, an exhaustive study by Schwarting concludes that Haydn could not possibly have composed the Trios Hob. XV:3–4; both, according to Benton, have strong similarities to Pleyel's Trios Op. 23 as well as to his Symphony in F major (Benton 136).[53] Finally, it should be pointed out that Haydn frequently used or incorporated parts of works composed by his students: it is known that he requested minuets from Eybler, incorporated some of Pleyel's music for *Feuersbrunst* and *L'Infedelta delusa*, and had Sigismund Neukomm produce some of the arrangements for Thomson's collections of national song. If there had been no open legal conflict between Forster and the rival publisher Longman & Broderip concerning the authorship of these trios, if both composers had not found themselves in London as rivals, and if Pleyel himself had not been so enterprising by using his thematic materials in several versions, today we would still be wondering how two trios with such first-rate sources could be so second-rate musically.

Besides Hob. XV:3 and 4 there is only one spurious composition within this category: the aforementioned Hob. XV:C2, which has no positive bibliographic or stylistic Haydn attributes.

Concerning the authenticity of the cycle, Hob. XV:39 and 40 survive in multiple versions. In addition to an unknown slow movement, Hob. XV:39 is a compilation of three movements from three solo keyboard sonatas: a fast first movement from Hob. XVI:9, the first movement of Hob. XVI:8, and a minuet and trio arranged from Hob. XVI:9 and 5. The fact that this cycle seems to have emanated from Hummel, a publishing house known to have tampered with Haydn's music on other occasions, speaks against its authenticity on the most objective grounds.[54] Furthermore, the accompaniments are so unlike those in Haydn's other early trios and the slow movement is so impoverished (Example III-14) that XV:39 is unquestionably spurious. In 1958 Horst Heussner discovered an additional movement for Hob. XV:40—an Adagio that appears to be a minuet—within a copy from the Hessisches Musikarchiv der Philipps-Universität.[55] But it should be rejected since none of the other sources contain the movement, the source itself is not especially valuable, the movement was inserted into the manuscript, and its overall style is unconvincing.

EXAMPLE III–14. Hob. XV:39/2, mm. 1–8.

TABLE III-3

Accompanied Divertimentos and Concertinos Attributed to Haydn

Work	Autograph	Entwurf-Katalog	London Catalogue	Haydn Verzeichnis	Oeuvres complettes	Haydn's response (1803)	Authentic copies	Authentic editions	Correspondence and other documents†	Copies by scribes associated with Haydn	Other copies from Vienna and its environs	Breitkopf catalogue	Other early copies	Other early editions (Remarks)	Fuchs catalogues
Hob. XIV:1	X	X		X		+				CS-KRm	A-SCH D-brd-B	1766	A-Ssp D-ddr-D1	Hummel Op. 4	X
Hob. XIV:2 (music lost)		X		X											X
*Hob. XIV:3	X	X		X							A-Eh A-L CS-KRm H-Bn CS-Pnm		D-brd-B		X
Hob. XIV:4	X	X		X		+					A-Wgm(2) CS-KRm CS-Bm(Rajhrad) A-Wgm(Dorsch)	1773	D-brd-B		X
Hob. XIV:7							H-Bn		?p.34						
Hob. XIV:8							H-Bn		?p.34						
Hob. XIV:9							H-Bn		?p.34						
Hob. XIV:10							A-Wgm D-brd-B								

Work		Sources	Date	Source	Note	
Hob. XIV:11	X	A-Gö / A-Wn / CS-KRm	1771	D-brd-B	(auto. lost)	X
Hob. XIV:12		CS-KRm / D-brd-B	1772	D-ddr-SW1		
Hob. XIV:13						X
Hob. XIV:C1	−?	A-Wn / CS-KRm	1772	D-brd-D0		X
Hob. XIV:C2		CS-KRm				
*Hob. XIV:C3		CS-KRm				X
*Hob. XIV:Es1					Fentum	
*Hob. XIV:F1					Girard	
*Hob. XIV:F2				B-Bc		
Hob. XIV:G1 (music lost)			1774			X
*Hob. XVII:G1		CS-KRm				
Hob. XVIII:F2		CS-KRm				
[Hob. XIV:] D1		CS-KRm				

+ = positive
− = negative
0 = could not recall
* = conflicting attributions
†Page numbers refer to documents in Essays I and II.

Accompanied Divertimentos and Concertinos

To the works included by Hoboken in *Gruppe* XIV—known by their copies and other citations as accompanied divertimentos, concertinos, or concertos, chiefly with two violins and bass for the accompaniment—should be added Hob. XVIII:F2, XVII:G1, and (not in Hoboken) D1 (see Table III-3). Only two of the works from Hoboken's *Gruppe* XIV are known from autographs: Hob. XIV:4, which is today in the National Széchényi Library in Budapest; and Hob. XIV:11, which was seen by C. F. Pohl but is now lost.[56] Three other works were entered in *EK*: Hob. XIV:1, 2 and 3.[57] Hob. XIV:7, 8, and 9 survive in copies by the Esterházy copyist Anonymous 23, which were a part of Haydn's library at the time of his death (*HNV* 508–10); these may also be the same three works that the composer was trying to sell to the English publisher William Forster in a letter of 8 April 1787.[58] Hob. XIV:10 is transmitted in two copies by Haydn's personal scribe, the senior Elssler, and both indicate that there are accompanying parts, now missing.[59] Thus, nine works have strong Haydn traditions.

For Hob. XIV:12, 13, C1 and C2, [Hob. XIV]:D1, XVII:G1, and XVIII:F2, the sources are more problematical. Of Hob. XIV:12 and 13, 12 seems to have the stronger source tradition, with several German and Austrian copies; while XIV:13 survives only in a less than satisfactory copy at Donaueschingen; stylistically there are no arguments against admitting these works into the Haydn canon. Hob. XIV:C1 comes down to us in versions with and without accompaniment: while its second and third movements are the most acceptable stylistically, the first and last cannot be totally rejected.[60] The source situation for Hob. XIV:C2 is just as weak, with a single copy at Kroměříž by an otherwise unknown scribe. However, from a musical standpoint this tiny divertimento seems at least plausible: for example, the rhythmic acceleration in the first violin part during one of the few moments in the first movement (mm. 20–23) when it is independent of the keyboard; the sustained trill in the keyboard with active accompanying voices in the minuet, paralleling the unquestionably authentic Hob. XIV:3; and the use of Haydn's preferred formula for every large-dimension cadence.[61] This divertimento, however, may be incomplete: both a trio for the minuet and a 3/8 or 2/4 finale seem possible. Like Hob. XIV:C2, XVIII:F2 survives only at Kroměříž, but this time in a Viennese copy. A good source with positive stylistic factors admits it as a plausible Haydn work.

The Concertino [Hob. XIV]:D1 and Hob. XVII:G1, which come down to us in a single Viennese copy at Kroměříž, have been unrecognized in the Haydn literature (Example III-15).[62] The manuscript itself emanates from Vienna and begins with a set of variations (Hob. XVII:G1) in G major followed by an unknown minuet in C major with a *minore* trio. The possibilities of the latter two movements forming a cycle or part of one seems highly unlikely: variations are used as first movements, but minuets are always in the principal key. The melody seems to have some association with Dittersdorf,[63] while the variations are unusually primitive; the theme, the first two variations, and the fourth only increase the speed of the keyboard accompaniment in the left hand, from quarter notes to oscillating

EXAMPLE III–15. Hob. XVII:G1 and [Hob. XIV]:D1.

eighths to rolling triplets and Alberti sixteenths, leaving the melody unaltered. Throughout, the string accompaniment essentially repeats the materials used for the theme. It is particularly difficult to make any judgment concerning the minuet without further source evidence. Thus despite the importance of Kroměříž as a source for Haydn's keyboard music, the weight of the internal evidence indicates that the work is spurious.

The title Concertino for [Hob. XIV]: D1 is a generic indication at variance with Haydn's practice for other works of this sort; i.e., concertinos consist of a Fast–Slow–Fast movement sequence, while a divertimento—the term that seems more appropriate for D1—has a Fast–Minuet–Fast cycle.[64] Even though it appears in the same manuscript with a spurious composition, D1 seems at first almost acceptable as an unknown accompanied work by Haydn: the writing is compact and attractive and the piece has the rhythmic drive that so frequently eluded Haydn's contemporaries. On the other hand, the accompaniment is voiced rather peculiarly for Haydn, the first violin often playing a third above the keyboard line. Furthermore, the work contains not a single "Haydn cadence," and the cello line that serves to activate the end of the phrase has no counterpart in the other works for this setting. Thus, even considering the strength of the source, D1 must be regarded as one of the spurious compositions.

The first movement of "Il maestro e lo scolare" is also transmitted to us in an arrangement for keyboard four hands, two violins, and bass, framed by a previously unknown Moderato in a rudimentary sonata form and a miniature rondo finale (Example III-16).[65] While the outer movements are not unattractive, there is no

EXAMPLE III–16. Hob. XVIIa: 1 and deest.

reason from either external—it is a copy of Italian origin—or internal data to consider this "Divertimento" any further.

The remaining divertimentos listed by Hoboken, with the questionable exception of the lost Hob. XIV:G1, are not by Haydn, as they have other attributions and lack any source basis that might suggest the Viennese master. Hob. XIV:C3 is attributed to Haydn only in the catalogues of Aloys Fuchs. Its attribution to Wagenseil in Breitkopf 1766 and 1778 as well as in a Parisian print from 1778 is confirmed stylistically by the small-dimension motivic and sub-phrase repetitions.[66] Hob. XIV:Es1 is found at Kroměříž in two copies: one as a solo work attributed to Joseph Anton Steffan and another with an accompaniment for two violins and bass attributed to Haydn. A third copy at the Brussels Conservatory also indicates Steffan. Since the integrity of the solo setting and the sources point toward Steffan, the Haydn attribution can be discounted.[67] Hob. XIV:F1 is attributed only to Haydn in two early nineteenth-century editions by Fentum and Girard, publishing houses with which the composer had no known contact. Both the Breitkopf catalogue of 1774 and the Sarasin catalogue attribute the work to Joseph Aloys Schmittbaur.[68] Since Haydn never wrote any other work for this setting (flute, viola, cello, and keyboard), there is no reason to doubt Schmittbaur's authorship. Hob. XIV:F2, like F1, is also scored for a setting without precedent for Haydn (oboe, violin, viola, cello, and keyboard); has unacceptable Haydn sources; and occurs in a posthumous adaptation attributing the work to its probable author, Johann Christian Bach.[69]

Klavierstücke

The sources for the twenty-three *Klavierstücke* catalogued by Hoboken in *Gruppe* XVII[70] divide into three groups (see Table III-4): Hob. XVII: 1–6 and 9, with sources of real strength;[71] Hob. XVII: 7, 8, 10, and 12, whose sources require that the works be seriously considered;[72] and Hob. XVII:C1–A3, whose generally weak sources raise immediate doubts about their authenticity.

The seven *Klavierstücke* of the first series are represented by six entries in *HV*, but only one in *EK*, three autographs, one authentic copy, six publications by

Artaria (most from a period in 1788 and 1789 when the Viennese publisher might very well have issued some unauthorized prints[73]), and six in *Oeuvres complettes*. Of these, only the Variations Hob. XVII:2 raises any textual problems that need to be considered here: is the original tonality G major or A major, and what are the authentic number and sequence of the variations?

The keys and make-up of the two principal sources, Anthology Dorsch and Weimar, together with those of the Artaria print, *Oeuvres complettes*, and other copies from Kroměříž and Prague are shown in Table III-5. The most striking characteristic of the twenty variations in the two principal sources is their architecture, an aspect totally destroyed in the Artaria print. On the largest dimension, this twenty-variation version divides into two large sections: the theme through Variation 8; and Variation 9, which commences with the unornamented theme in the left hand, through Variation 20. The initial presentation of the theme, a minuet, forms a structural pair with the Variation 1 because of the tessitura and, most important, the continuation of the triplet rhythm. The next three variations are also united: 2 and 4 parallel each other rhythmically (eighth notes) and texturally, with Variation 3 forming a link to the theme and Variation 1 by the use of triplets. Variations 5 and 6 form another rhythmic pair (sixteenth notes), while 7, with its more anacrustic sixteenths, intensifies the activities of its two predecessors. Variation 8 closes the first section by transforming the minuet into a *polacca*.

Although Variation 9 shapes the large dimension by returning to the theme, it also stands at the center of a group of three variations (8-10) that show increased rhythmic and textural activity. In contrast, Variation 11 is more severe in style, with its chromatic suspensions. Variations 12 and 13 form a pair not only through rhythmic articulation but also in that 13 increases the length of the upbeat over Variation 12. Variation 15 is in the French overture style, which is prepared by the dotted rhythms of 14, just as 16 prepares for the toccata of Variation 17. Variations 18 and 19 use rhythmic ostinatos, the latter remarkable for changes in sonority and range. The final variation encompasses the widest range and sonority—it is the only one to demand the short octave—which are complemented by the broader feeling of rhythmic movement both in the structure of the bass line and in the octaves of the upper voices.

None of the other versions come close to achieving this coherence. On musical grounds, the Artaria print does not seem to be authentic; it is difficult to believe that Haydn would have blundered with his own masterpiece at a time—the late 1780s—when sophisticated architecture was a hallmark of his style.[74]

The other question concerning Hob. XVII:2 is its tonality. If *EK* did not show the correction from G major to A major (see Plate 2), one would conclude that Hob. XVII:2 was originally in G major. However, Anthology Dorsch is known to have other works transposed downward to accommodate an instrument whose top note was d'''.[75] Furthermore, since the preponderance of contemporary sources does seem to favor A major and the Weimar twenty-variation set occurs in this key, one is led to hypothesize that the original *EK* entry in G major represents a transposed version.

The second group—Hob. XVII:7, 8, 10, and 12—poses problems that can

TABLE III-4

Klavierstücke Attributed to Haydn

	Autograph	Entwurf-Katalog	London Catalogue	Haydn Verzeichnis	Oeuvres complettes	Haydn's response (1803)	Authentic copies	Authentic editions	Correspondence and other documents †	Copies by scribes associated with Haydn	Other copies from Vienna and its environs	Breitkopf catalogue	Other early copies	Other early editions (Remarks)	Fuchs catalogues
Hob. XVII:1	X			X	X						A-Wgm(Dorsch) A-Wn			Artaria	X
Hob. XVII:2		X		X	X						A-Wgm(Dorsch) CS-KRm	1771	CS-Pn (D-ddr-WRtl)	Artaria	X
Hob. XVII:3				X	X						A-Wgm(Dorsch) A-Wgm(2) A-Wn A-Eh D-brd-B	1774	D-brd-B D-brd-D0	Artaria	X
Hob. XVII:4				X	X			Artaria	pp.35–46		A-Wn(2)		CS-Pn (Osek)		X
Hob. XVII:5				X	X			Artaria	p.45		A-Wn		D-brd-B GB-Lryson		X
Hob. XVII:6	X			X	X		A-Wn A-Wgm	Artaria (?)							X
Hob. XVII:7											A-Wn CS-KRm D-brd-B	1766	D-brd-HR		X

Hob.		A-Wn(2) D-brd-B	D-ddr-SW1	Daube	X
Hob. XVII:8					X
Hob. XVII:9	X				
Hob. XVII:10	Artaria (?)			(auto is sketch) Artaria Op. 46	
Hob. XVII:11				Artaria = Hob. XVII:12?	
Hob. XVII:12				Artaria	
Hob. XVII:C1			D-brd-D0	Bossler	
Hob. XVII:C2		A-Wn			
Hob. XVII:F1					
Hob. XVII:F2			A-Wn		
*Hob. XVII:F3		A-Wgm			
Hob. XVII:G1			D-brd-HR		
Hob. XVII:G2				Baillon Poro	
Hob. XVII:A1			D-brd-SI		
(music lost)					
Hob. XVII:A2		A-Wn			
Hob. XVII:A3			I-MoE		

+ = positive
− = negative
0 = could not recall
* = conflicting attributions
† Page numbers refer to documents in Essays I and II.

TABLE III-5

Versions of Variations Hob. XVII:2

G Major Anthology Dorsch	A Major *Oeuvres complettes*	A Major Artaria	G Major CS-KRm	A Major CS-Pn	A Major Weimar*
Theme	Theme	Theme	Theme	Theme	Theme
1	1	1	1	1	1
2	2	5	2	2	2
3	5	6		5	3
4	6	2	4	6	4
5	3	7	5	4	5
6	4	3		8	6
7	7	13		12	7
8	8	14	8	11	8
9	9	16		7	9
10	10	New		14	10
11	11	17	11	16	11
12	12	10	12	10	12
13	13			20	13
14	14			17	14
15				15	15
16			16	19	16
17	17		17	13	17
18	18		18		18
19	15				19
20	16		20		20

* Copy lost, source used by Soldan/KLAVIERSTÜCKE.

only be solved by examining the works themselves in relation to their sources. Hob. XVII:7 (Hob. XV:42) has a source pattern not unlike many other early keyboard works: two groups, German and Viennese. In addition, it occurs in two versions: the variations alone, as indicated in the 1766 Breitkopf catalogue; and the variations preceded by a seventy-seven-measure introduction that has more the character of a finale even though it ends on the dominant leading to the variations proper. This second form, which occurs in the Kroměříž version, has no precedent in Haydn. Indeed, the fact that some other Kroměříž sources contain peculiar groupings further calls it into question. Nevertheless, it is difficult to judge these movements as not by Haydn or as questionable; both individually and together they are, oddly enough, musically plausible. Unfortunately, neither of the published versions, one by H. C. R. Landon and one by the Haydn-Institut, is totally satisfactory. The latter chose to treat the two movements as separate pieces without accompaniment,[76] while the former published both movements together but with the peculiar accompaniment from Kroměříž.[77] The most satisfactory version seems to be the two movements together in a solo keyboard setting.

The complex background of Hob. XVII:8 raises questions as to the authenticity of the setting as well as the number and ordering of the variations. Its roots go back to a baryton trio that survives in several versions;[78] while the variations for keyboard come down to us in two different versions and two different keys (D major and A major), as shown in Table III-6 and Example III-17. The *Pianoforte* indication on the title page of the variations in A major suggests that they were composed later than the D-major version, although "per il Pianoforte" is written in another hand. The D-major version consists of three variations not found in any other source. Its theme is merely a transcription of the baryton trio; the right hand equals the baryton part, while the left plays the viola and bass parts. In many of the variations, the texture is more idiomatic to the keyboard, with Alberti bass accompaniments and the like. Particularly uncharacteristic of Haydn is the use of the same or rapid surface rhythms in both hands (Example III-18), simultaneous duple and triple subdivisions of the beat, and the same texture throughout the set. Furthermore, parallel octaves occur in the theme and in Variation 8; there are appoggiaturas with doubled resolutions; and the cadences are relatively static. In the ordering of the variations, the D-major version departs from while the one in A major conforms to the other sources, although the latter does have a coda that is very unlike anything found in Haydn's keyboard works (Example III-19). Moreover, its wide spacings and unusually thin textures do not point to Haydn.[79] In the end, both versions must be the product of someone other than Haydn.

In view of the date of Artaria's publication and its limited range, Hob. XVII: 10 seems to be a transcription from the musical clock piece Hob. XIX: 27. The text of the print seems to come from the autograph of the clock piece; if it were an aural transcription from the clock itself, the accuracy of the reading would probably have been seriously diminished (Example III-20) and the variants of the clock version from the autograph would be apparent. At the least, Artaria provided an arrangement that was corrected and approved by Haydn. At the most, it is an arrangement, or work later arranged for the clock, stemming from the composer himself.[80]

Hob. XVII: 12, an Andante with four variations, was first published by Artaria in July 1807.[81] That it has no earlier sources weighs against its authenticity, since Haydn had ceased to compose four years previously. Musically, two details further support a negative conclusion: the rhythmic layout of the sequence of variations (Variation 1, sixteenths; Variation 2, triplet sixteenths; Variation 3, sixteenths); and the harmonic language and voice leading of the theme (Example III-21), which pervades all the variations, is very unlike Haydn. Thus, from this second group of works, Hob. XVII: 8 and 12 can be rejected as having nothing to do with Haydn; 7 can be judged as plausible; and 10, with reservations, as a plausible Haydn arrangement.

As mentioned above, the third group, Hob. XVII: C1–A3 is marked by generally weak sources. Hob. XVII: C1, a set of variations on the ubiquitous *Mahlbarough*, is ascribed to Haydn in an old copy from Donaueschingen. It seems to derive its attribution from a Bossler print that contains as its third work the "Roxelane" Variations from Symphony No. 63, but it does not actually identify Haydn as the author of the first two compositions, one of which is Hob. XVII: C1. Even on the Donaueschingen manuscript, the attribution is given on the title and second pages by another hand. Musically, the variations have nothing to recommend

TABLE III-6

Versions of Hob. XI:2/XVII:8

	Baryton Trio Hob. XI:2/I	Daube Der Musikalische Dilettante (pp. 69–72) for 2 violins and bass? Hob. XI:2/I	Trio for viola, cello, and bass Hob. XI:2bis/III Version A	Trio for 2 violins and bass Hob. XI:2bis/III Version B	Trio for cello, violin, and bass Hob. XI:2bis/III Version C	Variazioni per Cembalo Hob. XVII:8	Variations per il Pianoforte Hob. XVII:8
Key	A Major	A Major	G Major	G Major	G Major	D Major	A Major
Tempo marking	Allegretto	Allegretto	Allegro	Allegretto	Allegretto	Andantino	(Thema)
Var. 1	A	A	A	A	A	A	A
Var. 2	B	B	B	B	B	C	B
Var. 3	C	C	C	C	C	E	C
Var. 4	E	D	D	D	D	D	D
Var. 5	F	E	E	E	E	B	E
Var. 6		da capo (F)	F			(G)	Coda
Var. 7						(H)	
Var. 8						(I)	

EXAMPLE III–17. Variations in Hob. XI:2/XVII:8.

EXAMPLE III–18. Hob. XVII:8, mm. 17–20, 97–99.

EXAMPLE III–19. Hob. XVII:8, Coda, mm. 97–104.

EXAMPLE III–20. Hob. XVII:10 and XIX:27.

EXAMPLE III–21. Hob. XVII:12, mm. 1–8.

Haydn's authorship. Hob. XVII:C2 consists of "Drei Praeambeln für Orgel" bound together with a series of miscellaneous-sized copies of keyboard music at the Österreichische Nationalbibliothek.[82] The script of the copy itself suggests Viennese origin. As the title implies, these are written-out improvisations, based on the old *Regola dell'Ottava* described by Emanuel Bach and others. Since these preludes postdate Haydn's extant works for organ and none of them are improvisatory in style, there is really no basis on which to categorize them as other than doubtful. One wonders, however, if a more likely author might be the Viennese composer Joseph Hayda (fl. 1780s), "one of the finest organists of his time, especially praised for his improvisations. . . ."[83] Hob. XVII:F2 carries its attribution to Haydn only in the card catalogue in the Österreichische Nationalbibliothek.[84] Stylistically there is no reason to believe Haydn to be the composer. Hob. XVII:F3 is another battle sonata, this time representing *La Battaile de Rosbach*, which has been attributed not only to Haydn but also to J. C. Bach,[85] Emanuel Bach (Wq. 272), one "E. Bach," and Graun. Whoever the author is, Haydn might have said the same thing that Emanuel Bach wrote to J. C. Westphal on 4 August 1787 concerning what is probably the same work: "The *Bataille* you mention is not by me. Such-like is not my style."[86] Hob. XVII:G2 has as its only source an edition by a Parisian publisher, Baillon, with whom Haydn had no known connection. Musically, there is no reason to honor the attribution: both the large structure and the details speak against Haydn's authorship.

Hob. XVII:A1 is lost, but the two other variation sets in A major (A2 and A3) survive. Hob. XVII:A2 is found only in a single manuscript, where it follows the Pleyel trios Hob. XV:3–4, and contains no indication of its author. The variations themselves are unlike Haydn's other works in this form: as in the spurious Hob. XVII:8, XVII:A2 employs identical rhythmic motion in soprano and bass for long stretches; there are sections of duplets vs. triplets in the two hands; and the same accompaniment figures are seen predominating in more than one variation. Finally, Hob. XVII:A3 survives at the Estense Library in Modena in the hand of an Italian copyist under the title "Variazioni per Piano Forte."[87] As pointed out for Hob. XVII:8, if the work stemmed from Haydn, its style has nothing to do with those works titled for the modern instrument. Stylistically it has many of the characteristics of A2; note especially the peculiar chromatic alteration so unlike Haydn in m. 2 of the theme (Example III-22). The works of this third group are therefore either spurious or at best doubtful.

EXAMPLE III–22. Hob. XVII:A3.

Concertos

Of the seventeen concertos listed by Hoboken in *Gruppe* XVIII (see Table III-7), five possibly carry the authority of an entry in *EK*,[88] four of these are also listed in *HV*, and one is extant in an autograph (Hob. XVIII:1). However, because of the ambiguity of the *EK* entry "e ancora altri Due Concerti p. l'organo in C" without incipits, Hob. XVIII:5, 8, and 10 must be regarded as straddling the authentic and plausible categories. Oddly enough, one work listed by its incipits in *EK*, Hob. XVIII:2, survives in two copies at Berlin—one attributed to Haydn and the other to Baldassare Galuppi (1706–1785)—and one copy at the Österreichische Na-

TABLE III-7

Concertos Attributed to Haydn

	Autograph	Entwurf-Katalog	London Catalogue	Haydn Verzeichnis	Oeuvres complettes	Haydn's response (1803)	Authentic copies	Authentic editions	Correspondence and other documents †	Copies by scribes associated with Haydn	Other copies from Vienna and its environs	Breitkopf catalogue	Other early copies	Other early editions (Remarks)	Fuchs catalogues
Hob. XVIII:1	X	X		X						CS-KRm	A-GÖ; A-M A-Wgm(2) CS-Bm(2)(Rajhrad) A-Lambrecht	1763	D-brd-B D-brd-ZL		X
*Hob. XVIII:2	X	X		X							A-GÖ A-SCH A-SEI; A-Wn CS-KRm D-brd-B	1767	D-brd-B		X
Hob. XVIII:3		X		X								1771	D-brd-B D-ddr-SW1	Le Duc	X
Hob. XVIII:4		X		X							CS-KRm(2)	1782/84	D-brd-DO D-brd-NEhz	Boyer, Schmitt	X
*Hob. XVIII:5											A-Eh-CS-Bm (Rajhrad)	1763	D-brd-MGmi		X
Hob. XVIII:6		X									A-SCH CS-KRm CS-Bm(Rajhrad) D-brd-B	1766	I-Bi(1) D-brd-ZL; D-ddr-Dlb D-ddr-LEm D-ddr-SW1		X

*Hob. XVIII:7			CS-Bm(Rajhrad), CS-KRm(2)	1766	D-brd-B	Gardon	X
*Hob. XVIII:8			A-M, CS-Bm(Rajhrad), CS-KRm	1766	D-brd-B		X
Hob. XVIII:9				1767	D-brd-B, D-brd-ZL		X
Hob. XVIII:10			A-Wgm	1771			X
Hob. XVIII:11	Artaria(?)	CS-KRm			B-Bc, D-brd-B, F-Sim	Boyer, Schmitt	X
Hob. XVIII:C1					CS-BRnm		
Hob. XVIII:Es1	p.34		D-brd-B		D-brd-B		
*Hob. XVIII:F1					D-brd-B		
*Hob. XVIII:F3					CH-E		
*[Hob. XVIII:]F4					CS-Pn		
*Hob. XVIII:G1			CS-KRm				
*Hob. XVIII:G2						Skillern	

+ = positive
− = negative
0 = could not recall
* = conflicting attributions
† Page numbers refer to documents in Essays I and II.

tionalbibliothek accidentally bound with two other movements, which have nothing to do with this concerto. The Galuppi attribution, not discussed by Larsen, was observed in 1938 by Carl Bittner, who noted on the Haydn copy "The D Major Concerto attributed to Joseph Haydn (Mus. ms. 10067) is probably an arrangement of a D Major Concerto by B. Galluppi (Mus. ms. 6975)."[89] The differences between the two Berlin sources, however, do not support Bittner's hypothesis, as their textual vagaries fall within the bounds that could occur in the transmission of copies. In any case, the Galuppi copy seems textually superior in some respects to the Haydn. If the work is not by Haydn, it is the only one to appear in *EK* that is not clearly authentic.[90]

Of the remaining six of eleven concertos listed as genuine by Hoboken, none is explicitly entered in *EK*. Only the famous Concerto in D major Hob. XVIII:11 appears in any possibly authoritative sources; while 5, 7, 8, and 10 continue a pattern of distribution already seen among other early and presumed authentic trios and solo sonatas. Of these, Hob. XVIII:7 is an arrangement of the first and last movements of Hob. XV:40 with a new Adagio. The Kroměříž copy of this arrangement attributes it to Wagenseil, but it is difficult to imagine Wagenseil arranging a Haydn trio. Stylistically there are reasons to doubt Wagenseil's and Haydn's authorship of the Adagio or of the new concerto ritornellos, which contain material not found in the solos. Until more convincing sources are found, Hob. XVIII:7 can only be considered doubtful.[91]

The Hofmann attribution for Hob. XVIII:8 in Berlin, which was corrected to Haydn, must have been an error; the lack of any other Hofmann attribution and the local sources assigning it to Haydn demand no further bibliographic discussion. Stylistically, the simplicity of the melodic line in the slow movement is at odds with the elaborate surface rhythms associated with Hofmann. The Wagenseil attribution of Hob. XVIII:5 in a single source (A-Eh) can also be doubted; it and Hob. XVIII:8 are really stylistic twins.

On the other hand, the authenticity of Hob. XVIII:9 has been questioned by Georg Feder,[92] on the basis of both external and internal evidence. As can be seen from Table III-7, it seems to have been transmitted only in German sources (Berlin and Zeil?) and through Breitkopf (1767). Furthermore, the range exceeds d''', Haydn's normal compass for keyboard works from before *ca.* 1766, and the orchestra has no viola. The redundancy of material, the either contrapuntal or staid textures of the first movement, the unusually severe style of the slow movement, and the 3/8 Tempo di Menuet finale are stylistically at odds with Haydn's other authentic keyboard concertos. Therefore, it should be considered doubtful.

Among the seven concertos designated as doubtful by Hoboken, all should be considered spurious. At first glance, Hob. XVIII:G1 (Example III-23) seems to be the best candidate from the source standpoint: it comes down to us in an old Viennese copy from Kroměříž with "Spect. ad me J. H." in the lower right corner. In contrast to the bold hand of the copy associated with Joseph Georg Haroldt, this notation is in the more characteristic, small, wiry letters often associated with Haydn himself; however, under closer examination this author has concluded that the inscription is in Haroldt's hand. Furthermore, Hob. XVIII:G1 is especially

EXAMPLE III–23. Hob. XVIII:G1.

EXAMPLE III–24. Hob. XVIII:G2.

unconvincing, with its plethora of dynamic and expressive markings: "dolce assai" for the wind instruments, "poco forte" and "un poco crescendo"; a slow movement with the heading "Andante ma con Guste e sempre piano"; the generally fussy melodic style; and the uncharacteristic treatment of the winds. Overall, its style is more reminiscent of the works of Joseph Anton Steffan, although we have no sources to confirm this hypothesis.[93]

Hob. XVIII:G2 (Example III-24), a concerto for two keyboards, could be given serious consideration solely on the basis of style. However, its only Haydn attribution comes from a 1782 edition by the London publisher Skillern, who had no known association with the composer even though he did publish possibly the earliest edition of *Il maestro e lo scolare* (Hob. XVIIa:1). A copy at the Staatsbibliothek Preussischer Kulturbesitz attributes it to Joseph Anton Steffan,[94] who is certainly the rightful author.

The Organ Concerto Hob. XVIII:C1 (Example III-25) survives only in a late copy (1823) of Slovakian provenance; its title and first pages merely indicate "Authore Haÿden." These circumstances alone—location, date, and only the family name—exclude it from serious consideration, a conclusion supported by the style: the keyboard range exceeds that of any of the known organ works by Haydn; the chromatic alteration in the opening ritornello is exceptional; and the treatment of the surface rhythm as well as the overall quality speak against Haydn's authorship.

For the remaining works, the following can be noted: Hob. XVIII:Es1 is attributed to Haydn by another hand in a single surviving copy in Berlin; although Hob. XVIII:F1 carries Haydn's name at Berlin, it is now known in another source attributing it to the Abbé Vogler (1749–1814).[95] Both works are stylistically so alien to Haydn that they cannot be accepted. According to the Breitkopf catalogue of 1766, a copy at Berlin, as well as an early print, Hob. XVIII:F3 is by Johann Georg Lang (1724–ca. 1794); the Haydn copy is from Einsiedeln, a location not known for reliable Haydn sources.[96]

The Organ Concerto [Hob. XVIII]:F4 is not listed in Hoboken but was published in a modern edition under Haydn's name, based on a local copy from the Ursulinenkloster (Alžbétinky) now in the Národné Múzeum in Prague (see Example III-26). As Feder has pointed out, there are two copies at Kroměříž, one at Schlägl, and an entry in Breitkopf 1770, all of which name the Viennese composer Leopold Hofmann.[97] To the sources mentioned by Feder, one should probably

EXAMPLE III–25. Hob. XVIII:C1.

EXAMPLE III–26. [Hob. XVIII]:F4.

add the best Hofmann source, a collection of keyboard concertos at the Öster-reichische Nationalbibliothek associated with the Imperial family (Anthology Imperial, S.m.11085).

Five of the authentic concertos (Hob. XVIII:1, 2, 4, 5, and 8) pose problems with regard to their instrumentation. The surviving autograph for the first movement of Hob. XVIII:1 indicates individual lines for Clarino 1mo, Clarino 2do, Oboe 1mo, Oboe 2do, Violino 1mo, 2do, Viola, Organo, and Basso, which fill all the staves on the page. Unfortunately, the *clarini* parts are left blank. The second movement is scored for strings alone with the instruction "Oboe Adagio Tacent," and the finale re-indicates the presence of the two oboes but continues to leave the upper two lines unfilled, this time without the indication for *clarini*. This situation suggests that Haydn originally intended to compose *clarini* parts and then decided not to; or that the *clarini* lines were written directly on the parts themselves, thereby saving the effort of recopying them. If the latter were the case, it would both account for the lack of indication in the finale and open up the possibility of Haydn's intention to write a timpani part. The autograph itself does reject the possibility of horn parts, which are found in a number of eighteenth-century copies, and the setting for strings alone. Parts for *clarini* and timpani are found in several copies, including an early one from Kroměříž in the hand of the possibly authentic Haydn copyist Viennese Professional No. 2. Despite a seemingly good source situation, musically they arouse reservations: Example III-27 reveals how these parts fail to integrate into the prevailing textures of the string and oboe parts.[98]

Of the two other C-major organ concertos, Hob. XVIII:5 comes down to us in versions for two oboes and two horns from Rajhrad, for *clarini* and timpani in a source of German origin, as well as for strings alone in both the 1763 Breitkopf catalogue and a further German source. All these wind parts must be rejected for their failure to integrate into the texture in a way one expects of Haydn. For Hob. XVIII:8, two groups of brass and percussion parts have been transmitted to us:[99] a set now in Berlin in which they are indicated as "ad lib"; and another set surviving in Moravia from both Rajhrad and Kroměříž, the latter indicating horns in place of trumpets. There can be no definitive answer as to whether these parts are authentic; certainly Heussner's objection that works without violas cannot have trumpets and drums must be rejected, especially in an era when the viola was so frequently "ad libitum" to the bass line.[100] In terms of general practice in eighteenth-century Austrian liturgical music, compositions in C major usually follow the tradition of the mass, which calls for trumpets and drums during the festive periods and holidays. Thus, the added *clarini* and timpani parts to both Hob. XVIII:5 and 8 have a strong historical tradition, if not an authentic one; horns seem less appropriate.

The D-major Concerto Hob. XVIII:2 seems most acceptable with a scoring for strings alone; the extra parts exist only in the Berlin Haydn copy (oboes, *clarini*, and timpani), although Aloys Fuchs inscribed two oboes and two horns in his thematic catalogues.[101] The brilliant *clarini* parts seem very unlike Haydn, both from their function—at times they double the strings in principal lines—and from their rhythmic figures; the syncopations seem very peculiar indeed. In terms of Haydn's practice during this period (1750s–1760s), authentic trumpet parts seem to occur

EXAMPLE III–27. Hob. XVIII:1 (CS-KRm), mm. 1–13.

EXAMPLE III–28. Hob. XVIII:4/2, mm. 1–9.

in symphonies in C major only and not in those in D major, which are instead scored for the standard chamber setting of two oboes and two horns. The added oboe parts also seem unorganic and textually of little value.

The only harpsichord concerto to pose difficulties of authentic instrumentation is Hob. XVIII:4, which appeared in two editions by Boyer and Hummel with oboe and horn parts. Unfortunately, the two sets of wind parts are different.[102] Regarding the other important sources, the manuscript copies from Kroměříž are for strings alone, as is the entry in the Fuchs catalogue. The wind parts in the Boyer print are very skillfully done, and whether "cors et hautbois ad libitum" on the title page indicates that those instruments were added for publication cannot be determined. However, the lush color of the solo oboe above the strings, although rather striking, is not what we might expect of Haydn (Example III-28).

Arrangements

It is immediately obvious from the various *Anhänge* to Hoboken's *Gruppen* that Haydn's works, whatever their original settings, were arranged for numerous combinations meant mainly for *Hausmusik*. These arrangements, perhaps more than anything else, accounted for Haydn's enviable reputation throughout the Continent. However, except for a very few, these arrangements—ranging from the skillful to the deplorable—were done without the composer's approval or knowledge.

Since other gifted composers could execute an arrangement that could pass as coming directly from Haydn's pen, one must depend exclusively on external evidence. For example, the authenticity of the string trio setting (violin, viola, and cello) for Hob. XVI:40–42 cannot be definitively settled, although the authenticity of the keyboard version cannot be questioned; the skill of the string setting and the distribution of sonorities in the keyboard version certainly leave open the possibilities that the trio setting is authentic. On the other hand, Haydn wrote only one other work (Hob. V:8) for this setting (at least two decades earlier), the publisher of the trio setting (Hofmeister) is not known to have published any authorized Haydn prints, and Hofmeister himself was a skilled composer and transcriber of other composers' works (e.g., Mozart).

Autographs for keyboard arrangements do exist for the following: Quartet Op. 33/5/4 (an abbreviated version); Quartet Op. 74/3/2; Derbyshire Marches; and Quartet Op. 76/3/2. In addition, the keyboard arrangements of Symphonies 69/1–3 and 73/1, 2, and 4 may be by Haydn.[103]

Even though Haydn executed the quartet transcription, there seems to be little doubt that he did not transcribe the *Seven Last Words* for keyboard. He wrote to Artaria on 23 June 1787, "I compliment you on the piano score, which is very good and has been prepared with the greatest care." Although it has been pointed out that Haydn could have been praising Artaria for the engraving, the opposite view is further supported by comparing the title pages of the quartet and keyboard arrangements: the former explicitly states that the composition of both the work and the transcription were by Haydn, while the latter credits Haydn with only the work itself. More ambiguous is a 1788 letter sent to Artaria by Haydn's brother Johann: "I take the liberty of asking you to send me the Seven Words for the *Clavier* in his arrangement."[104]

Although most of these adaptations have not gained legitimacy in current editions, several have been published many times: the so-called Violin Sonatas; the "Roxelane" Variations; and the arrangement of Hob. II:11 (discussed above), published in Päsler's edition. The Variations can be dismissed, since there is no evidence for the legitimacy of the arrangement. A number of works published as violin sonatas continue to be played and are believed by some to be authentic although none have any claim to legitimacy. The origins of these sonatas—identified by numbers from the Peters edition—are as follows: the first Sonata (in G major) is the Keyboard Trio Hob. XV:32 without cello; the second through fifth Sonatas (in D, E-flat, A, and G) are the solo keyboard Sonatas Hob. XVI:24–26 and 43 respectively (Hob. XVI:43 has been transposed from A-flat major to G major, and the accompaniments [violin parts] to Hob. XVI:24–26 are probably by Charles Burncy);[105] the sixth Sonata (in C major) is an arrangement from a keyboard sonata version of the Divertimento Hob. II:11; and the seventh and eighth Sonatas (in F major and G major) are arrangements by A. E. Müller of the String Quartets

Op. 77. However, the concept of the violin sonata was not completely alien to Haydn: there is at least one work that the composer himself reportedly presented at various times for violin and keyboard, the "Dream Sonata." [106] Haydn was also to use this piece as the last movement of the Keyboard Trio Hob. XV:31. In 1803, when Prince Esterházy requested a sonata for Madame Moreau, he provided both movements of the trio as a violin sonata (i.e., he omitted the cello part). [107]

Works Transmitted in Dual Settings

A number of keyboard works for which Haydn's authorship has been established or hypothesized are plagued by further questions as to their original and/or authentic setting(s). Although the two terms, *original* and *authentic*, may be seen in some quarters as synonymous, an important distinction exists: an original version must always be authentic, but an authentic version need not be the original one. Therefore, one can envision a situation in which a composition might be used in one instance as a solo keyboard work and later with an accompaniment. [108]

Let us first discuss those works whose dual versions are almost certainly genuine. Hob. XV:22/2 without the accompanying parts exists in an authentic copy on British paper by Johann Elssler with Haydn's signature and autograph corrections; it was also part of Haydn's estate (*HNV* 515). Stylistically it can stand on its own, and the solo setting appears to be the original version of the trio's slow movement. Hob. XIV:2 may have existed in as many as three keyboard versions: for keyboard trio (Hob. XV:2); for keyboard, baryton, and two violins, presumably with bass (Hob. XIV:2), now lost; and possibly for keyboard, two violins, and cello, also lost. Although two of the versions are lost, the existence of the one with baryton can be verified by entries in the authentic catalogues. The final version is hypothesized from the title page of the copy of the keyboard trio setting from Haydn's estate (*HNV* 507) in the hand of Esterházy Anonymous 23: "Divertimento per il Clavicembalo à Due Violini con Violoncello." There are a number of internal characteristics that point to the possibility that the surviving keyboard version is an arrangement: e.g., the violin begins the first movement with the principal material, whereas Haydn more normally commences with the keyboard; and the string parts are unusually simple. Since none of Haydn's surviving divertimentos for keyboard, two violins, and cello offer the second violin an important role, it is possible that the trio version is a slightly revised accompanied divertimento without the second violin.

Among the less-convincing arrangements, are the first and last movements of Hob. XVIII:7. It appears that they were created out of Keyboard Trio Hob. XV:40/1 and 3 by adding initial and terminal ritornellos. Feder has shown Hob. XVIII:7 to be an organ concerto, with only small changes executed to accommodate the keyboard text of the original trio version of the two movements to the range of the organ. [109]

Hob. XIV:C1, XVI:1, XVI:3, XVI:G1, and XVII:7 come down to us in accompanied versions from copies at Kroměříž. None of these accompaniments seem to have originated with Haydn. Hob. XIV:C1 exists in two copies as a solo sonata

in Vienna and as an accompanied divertimento with two violins and bass in the
1772 Breitkopf catalogue. Although it can be played without the accompaniment,
what survives at Kroměříž is not a keyboard trio, as published by Landon, but the
second violin and cello parts of a three-part string accompaniment.[110] In the case of
Hob. XVII:7, the version as a keyboard trio is so unlike Haydn's textural approach
in either the early or the mature trios (i.e., the violin part slavishly accompanies the
keyboard) that it too must be rejected. Hob. XVI: 1, 3, and G1 exist at Kroměříž
with accompaniments for two violins and bass; the solo keyboard parts are good
Viennese copies. In Hob. XVI: 1 and 3, the two violin and cello parts are on a
different paper from the solo part; and for Hob. XVI:3, the suspicious "Spectat ad
me Josephum Haroldt" is once again inscribed on the cover.[111] The accompaniment itself bears no resemblance to Haydn's practice in the accompanied divertimentos: the second violin part contains extended rests and lengthy sustained notes
and chords.

    Hob. XIV:7 and 10 may have originated as solo keyboard divertimentos with
the accompaniments added at a later date. For Hob. XIV: 10, the two authentic
Elssler, Sr., copies may have originally differed in their setting: at the Gesellschaft
der Musikfreunde the copy has only the title "Divertimento," but the later wrap-
pers state "Divertimento f. Pfte, Vl & Vcl"; while at Berlin the copy is entitled
"Divertimento N⁰ 1 con Violini."[112] Musically the piece is perfectly satisfactory
without the accompaniment; it is difficult to imagine how an accompaniment
would enhance it to any appreciable degree. The situation for Hob. XIV:7 is more
complex, as two versions are extant in two important sources: an authentic copy
with the accompaniments (by Esterházy Professional No. 23) owned by Haydn;
and in Anthology Dorsch, where it is a solo keyboard work. The origin of these
accompanying parts must be seriously questioned—even if one wants to consider a
very early date—as they are incongruent and carelessly done. In the opening measures, the first violin part doubles the descending thirty-second notes of the key-

EXAMPLE III–29. Hob. XIV:7/1, mm. 1–3.

EXAMPLE III–30. Hob. XIV:7/1, mm. 5–6, 37–38.

EXAMPLE III–31. Hob. XIV:7/1, m. 7.

EXAMPLE III–32. Hob. XIV:7/1, mm. 50–52.

board; this figure is eliminated in the violin part with every subsequent appearance of the opening two-measure phrase, while the rest of the accompaniment is maintained (Example III-29). This scoring seems peculiar when one considers that Haydn invariably avoids an awkward entry by beginning on the downbeat, by having the strings enter after a pick-up, or, as in the case of the early trios, by having the initial material stated first by the keyboard without accompaniment,

TABLE III-8

Authenticity Status of Keyboard Works Attributed to Haydn

Authentic	Probably Authentic	Plausible	Doubtful	Spurious
Accompanied Divertimentos and Concertinos				
Hob. XIV:1	Hob. XIV:7	Hob. XIV:12	Hob. XIV:C1/1, 4	Hob. XIV:C3
Hob. XIV:2	(keyboard part)	Hob. XIV:13	(Hob. XIV:G1)	[Hob. XIV:]D1
Hob. XIV:3	Hob. XIV:8	Hob. XIV:C1/2, 3		Hob. XIV:Es1
Hob. XIV:4	Hob. XIV:9	Hob. XIV:C2		Hob. XIV:F1
Hob. XIV:10		Hob. XVIII:F2		Hob. XIV:F2
Hob. XIV:11		Hob. XIV:7		Hob. XVII:G1
		(accompaniment)		

Accompanied Divertimentos and Concertinos (spanning header)

Keyboard Trios

Authentic	Probably Authentic	Plausible	Doubtful	Spurious
Hob. XV:2	Hob. XV:1	Hob. XV:36	(Hob. XV:D1)	Hob. XV:3
Hob. XV:5	(Hob. XV:33)	Hob. XV:C1		Hob. XV:4
Hob. XV:6–8	Hob. XV:34			Hob. XV:39/1, 3,
Hob. XV:9	Hob. XV:35			4 (setting)
Hob. XV:10	Hob. XV:37			Hob. XV:39/2
Hob. XV:11–13	Hob. XV:38			Hob. XV:40
Hob. XV:14	Hob. XV:40			(Adagio)
Hob. XV:15–17	Hob. XV:41			Hob. XV:C2
Hob. XV:18–20	Hob. XV:f1			
Hob. XV:21–23				
Hob. XV:24–26				
Hob. XV:27–29				
Hob. XV:30				
Hob. XV:31				
Hob. XV:32				

Solo Sonatas

Authentic	Probably Authentic	Plausible	Doubtful	Spurious
(Hob. XVI:2a–e, g, h)	Hob. XVI:7	Hob. XVI:1	Hob. XVI:47/1	Hob. XVI:11/2,
Hob. XVI:3	Hob. XVI:8	Hob. XVI:2	Hob. XVI:Es3/3	3 (trio and
Hob. XVI:4/1, 2	Hob. XVI:9	Hob. XVI:5		cycle)
Hob. XVI:5 (*recte*	Hob. XVI:10	Hob. XVI:16		Hob. XVI:15
XVI:5a)	Hob. XVI:12	Hob. XVII:D1		(setting)
Hob. XVI:6	Hob. XVI:13	Hob. XVI:Es2		Hob. XVI:17
Hob. XVI:14	Hob. XVI:33	Hob. XVI:Es3/1, 2		Hob. XVI:4/3, 4
Hob. XVI:18	Hob. XVI:34	Hob. XVI:G1		Hob. XVI:C1
Hob. XVI:19	Hob. XVI:43			Hob. XVI:C2
Hob. XVI:20	Hob. XVI:44			Hob. XVI:D1
Hob. XVI:21–26	Hob. XVI:47/2, 3, 4			Hob. XVI:Es1
Hob. XVI:27–32				(setting)
Hob. XVI:35–39				Hob. XVI:B1
Hob. XVI:40–42				Frankfurt Sonatas
Hob. XVI:45				Göttweig Sonatas
Hob. XVI:46				
Hob. XVI:48				
Hob. XVI:49				
Hob. XVI:50				
Hob. XVI:51				
Hob. XVI:52				

Klavierstücke

Authentic	Probably Authentic	Plausible	Doubtful	Spurious
Hob. XVII:1		Hob. XVII:7	Hob. XVII:C2	Hob. XVII:8
Hob. XVII:2		(= Landon Trio	(Hob. XVII:A1)	(setting)
Hob. XVII:3		No. 15)		Hob. XVII:12

TABLE III-8 (*continued*)

Authenticity Status of Keyboard Works Attributed to Haydn

Authentic	Probably Authentic	Plausible	Doubtful	Spurious
		Klavierstücke (*continued*)		
Hob. XVII:4		Hob. XVII:10		Hob. XVII:C1
Hob. XVII:5				Hob. XVII:F2
Hob. XVII:6				Hob. XVII:F3
Hob. XVII:9				Hob. XVII:G2
				Hob. XVII:A2
				Hob. XVII:A3
Hob. XVIIa:1		Hob. XVIIa:2		Hob. XVIIa:C1
				Hob. XVIIa:F1
		Concertos		
Hob. XVIII:1	Hob. XVIII:5		Hob. XVIII:7	Hob. XVIII:C1
Hob. XVIII:2	Hob. XVIII:8		Hob. XVIII:9	Hob. XVIII:Es1
Hob. XVIII:3	Hob. XVIII:10			Hob. XVIII:F1
Hob. XVIII:4				Hob. XVIII:F3
Hob. XVIII:6				[Hob. XVIII:]F4
Hob. XVIII:11				Hob. XVIII:G1
				Hob. XVIII:G2

and then with the violin. Also suspicious are the simultaneous double stops in the violin parts, the awkward voice leading in the first violin of the corresponding portion in the recapitulation (Example III-30), and the unison doubling of the keyboard figuration in mm. 7–9 (Example III-31). However, Hob. XIV:7 cannot be categorized as a solo sonata with total certainty, as the unembellished cadence at the end of the first movement is more reminiscent of an accompanied work (Example III-32). Indeed, the fact that the cadence is neither embellished nor rhythmically activated by the accompaniment gives further support to the belief that the accompaniment might not have originated with Haydn. Nonetheless, since it occurs in an authentic source the accompaniment must be accepted with reservations.

Table III-8 summarizes this essay: Works listed as "authentic" have written documentation by Haydn himself or prints and copies executed under his direction; "probably authentic" works have strong connections with Haydn and/or are totally convincing from a stylistic criterion; "plausible" works have weaker stylistic associations and/or the sources are not particularly strong, yet there is no reason to exclude them from the canon; "doubtful" works have insufficient evidence to proclaim them absolutely spurious, in terms of the source itself or of the style, yet the probability of their being genuine Haydn seems minimal; and "spurious" works have been rejected on both source and stylistic grounds. In general, those listed in the first, second, and fifth columns can be accepted as such with little further discussion, whereas those indicated as plausible or doubtful in the third and fourth columns need continued questioning until new sources or documents are discovered.

Essay IV

DATING AND CHRONOLOGY

In Essay III the authenticity of the more than 150 keyboard compositions that come down to us in copies and prints under Haydn's name were reviewed and placed on a continuum from authentic to spurious. In the present essay only the original versions of the various works will be examined, not any arrangements or alternate settings.

As one might expect, the weak source situation for the generally acknowledged early works has resulted in many efforts during the twentieth century to fashion a chronology, none of which have been completely accepted. For the mature works, an overall chronology has been accepted, even though there are still some *lacunae* in the exact datings. This essay will therefore discuss the validity and results of the various methods applied to the keyboard works and present new hypotheses concerning their date and order to those previously offered by Päsler, Strunk, Larsen, Feder, C. Landon, H. C. R. Landon and others.[1]

Traditionally, the establishment of a chronology has emphasized external evidence: dated autographs, correspondence, contemporary and early catalogues, and information about or derived from copies and prints. But for Haydn's keyboard music much of this information is missing or unreliable. Few autographs of the keyboard works survive, and Haydn dated them only with the year in a shortened form (e.g., 761). While the autographs may therefore provide the most reliable evidence for dating, the correspondence is the most precise: for identifiable works one can date relevant activities down to the month and day. Unfortunately, Haydn's correspondence with publishers and others began only in the 1780s. Publishers' and archival catalogues often provide a terminal date; the enterprising Breitkopf first advertised manuscript copies of Haydn's keyboard works in 1763. However, keyboard music generally does not appear in archival catalogues, the entry for Haydn sonatas in the inventory from the Benedictine Cloister at Rajhrad being an exception. The catalogues of private collectors and scholars such as Aloys Fuchs, C. F. Pohl, and Artaria can yield facts about autographs and copies no longer available, but only rarely are the needed data for Haydn's keyboard works found. Finally, information culled from the copies themselves is less precise and reliable, unless one has an extensive bank of corollary evidence. Unfortunately, this evidence simply does not exist for Haydn's pre-Esterházy works, and few of the later ones are known in copies.

Given the less-than-satisfactory state of the traditional external evidence, Georg Feder has also attempted to provide terminal dates by identifying Haydn's orthographical practices and the highest keyboard pitch required. His study of the former has contributed three guidelines for dating Haydn's early works: before 1762 Haydn used the eighth note as a *Vorschlag*, but after 1762 one-half the length of the principal note is notated; in 1760 Haydn changed his spelling from Minuetti, Minuet, and Minuetto, to Menuet; and Haydn normally dated his autographs beginning in 1760.[2] The problem with this approach is not in the method itself but with the limitations of its application since there are so few extant autographs; the method's reliability diminishes when it is applied to copies, since copyists were careless when dealing with such details. Feder has also observed that into the middle of the 1760s the highest note of Haydn's datable keyboard works (including obligatory keyboard parts in cantatas) was normally d''', occasionally e flat''', and many times e'''; since f''' appears for the first time in a series of works *ca.* 1768–1769, Feder has concluded that Haydn may have acquired a new keyboard instrument after his home burned in August 1768 and that any work with this pitch must have been composed after that date.[3] However, Feder's hypothesis presupposes that Haydn composed for only one instrument. Since by 1760 keyboards whose range exceeded d''' were known to exist in Vienna, and the Esterházy court probably had instruments of different types and compasses, his hypothesis cannot be accepted without a reservation.[4] Nevertheless, since it is the only external evidence available that can be applied uniformly to all the keyboard works, Table IV-1 presents these data.

Internal or stylistic evidence can be even more elusive in determining a chronology. The practice of seeing a composer evolve from one phase to another along a path that culminated with Beethoven led to certain of Haydn's works being placed chronologically in order to elucidate this progression. The series of steps to this Parnassus, however, is not relevant for Haydn's environment: the keyboard works were probably tailored more to practical requirements of the moment—the needs of students, the taste of a patron, and the technical abilities of the women for whom they were composed. A more defensible approach is to pursue stylistic aspects, such as thematic similarities, that are not affected to the same degree by external circumstances. Since Haydn's compositional process involved an initial improvisation, it certainly seems probable that in some instances a recently used idea would serve as a starting point for another work.

With an appreciation of the difficulties in the dating and ordering of the works, let us first examine the *Entwurf-Katalog* (*EK*), which in Essay III was considered the most important extant document with regard to authenticity apart from the autographs themselves. But what is its significance with regard to the dating and chronology of the keyboard works themselves? First it should be noticed that *EK* has two types of entries: the main groups, with the incipits in the right-hand column and their identifications on the left; and entries added at a later time on the left. Then, some of the questions that should be posed are: Why are some keyboard

TABLE IV-1

Haydn's Keyboard Works According to Highest Pitch
(including cantatas with obligatory keyboard parts)

Highest Pitch	Work
c'''	Hob. XIV:10; Hob. XVI:G1; Hob. XVIII:1, 2, 5, 6, 8, 10
c♯'''	Hob. XV:f1; Hob. XVI:13
(d♭''')	
d'''	Hob. XIV:3, 4, 7, 9, 11, 12, 13, C1, C2; Hob. XVIII:F2; Hob. XV:1, 33, 34, 36, 37, 38, 40, 41, C1; Hob. XVI:1–12, 14, 16, 19, Es2, Es3, 45, 47; Hob. XVII:D1; Hob. XVII:1, 7, 10; Hob. XVIII:3
e♭'''	Hob. XIV:1; Hob. XVI:28
e'''	Hob. XV:35, 9, 28; Hob. XVI:22, 27, 30–32, 34, 36; Hob. XVII:2; Cantatas: "Qual dubbio" (1764), "Destatevi" (1763), "Applausus" (1768), "Saper vorrei se m'ami" (1796) "Dr. Harrington's Compliment" (1792–1795)
f'''	Hob. XIV:8; Hob. XV:2, 5–8, 10–27, 29–32 Hob. XVI:18, 20; Hob. XIV:5 (*recte* XVI:5a); Hob. XVI:21, 23–26, 29, 33, 35, 37–44, 46, 48, 49, 51, 52; Hob. XVII:3, 4, 5, 6, 9; Hob. XVIII:4, 11 Cantatas: "Arianna a Naxos" (1789), "Lines from the Battle of the Nile" (1800); "Guarda qui, che lo vedrai" (1796)
a'''	Hob. XVI:50

works not listed in *EK*? Is *EK* a compilation of all Haydn's works then in his memory or ownership? Is *EK* more or less à tally of compositions written or used after Haydn entered the service of the Esterházy court in answer to the Prince's directive in the fall of 1765?[5] *EK* may have served several purposes; i.e., it included works that Haydn had newly composed and/or had used in some capacity at court. Perhaps the early keyboard trios are not listed because there was no occasion to use them in the service of the Prince. Also missing from the keyboard list is the 1765 Capriccio on "Acht Sauschneider müssen seyn" (suggesting that this special piece may have been an outside commission[6]) as well as a number of presumed early solo sonatas, accompanied divertimentos, and concertinos.

There are, however, other plausible explanations for the relatively small number of keyboard works found in *EK*. First, it is known that during the 1750s, after his association with Porpora, Haydn moved to new quarters on the Seilerstätte, where all his possessions were stolen. Some of the music circulating in copies was probably recoverable. Thus, one can explain the relatively large number of early concertos listed—more than half of the authentic survivors—since they would have been copied in parts and perhaps kept in places other than Haydn's own quarters. Second, according to Griesinger, "Only a few originals [of the early sonatas] have remained with him; he gave them away and considered it an honor if people took them."[7] Finally, if Haydn composed "diligently" before working for Porpora, there is no reason to believe he did not compose at the same pace afterwards; that he could not recall all these works five, ten, or fifteen years later is to be expected.

Table IV-2 (see also Plate 2) provides a summary list of the keyboard music

TABLE IV-2

Keyboard Works in the Entwurf-Katalog *(EK)*
(except for Hob. XV:9, which was added ca. *or after 1800)*

Works		Remarks	
Left	Right	Left	Right
EK 19			
	Hob. XVIII:1		Autograph [1756], Breitkopf 1763
	Hob. XVIII:2		Breitkopf 1767
EK 20			
Hob. XVIII:6	2 Concertos for Organ in C (Hob. XVIII:5 and 8?)	Breitkopf 1766	Breitkopf 1763 (Hob. XVIII:5)? Breitkopf 1768 (Hob. XVIII:8)?
	Hob. XIV:1		Breitkopf 1766
6 Sonatas 1774	Hob. XVIII:3	Published by Kurzböck 1774	Breitkopf 1771, Fuchs 1770
6 Sonatas 1776	Hob. XVIIa:1	Professional Viennese copies dated 1776	Theme to Baryton Trio Hob. XI:38/i (1767)
	Hob. XVI:2a		Music lost
	Hob. XVI:2b		Music lost
EK 21			
	Hob. XVI:19		Autograph 1767
	Hob. XVI:2c		Music lost—Griesinger anecdote 1770 (1767?)
	Hob. XVI:2d		Music lost
Hob. XVI:14	Hob. XVI:2e		Music lost
	Hob. XVI:45		Autograph 1766
EK 22			
	Hob. XVI:46		
Hob. XVIII:4	Hob. XVI:2g	Larsen *ca.* 1770, Breitkopf 1782–1784	Music lost
	Hob. XVI:2h		Music lost
	Hob. XVI:3		Theme to Baryton Trio Hob. XI:37 (1767)
	Hob. XVI:4		
EK 23			
Hob. XIV:3	Hob. XIV:2	Breitkopf 1771 (Hofmann)	Theme to Baryton Trio Hob. XI:103 (*ca.* 1772)
	Hob. XIV:4		Autograph 1764
	Hob. XIV:5		
	Hob. XVI:6		Autograph (before 1760?)
	Hob. XVII:2		

listed in *EK*. Most of the works in the right-hand column (except the concertos) seem to date from about 1765 or later—that is, the date Haydn began to have a need for an inventory—with one apparent exception: Hob. XVI:6 survives in an autograph fragment without date, but with the *Vorschläge* written as small eighth notes and with the spelling "Minuet," which point to a period before *ca.* 1760. With three criteria in agreement, it seems difficult to dispute Feder's dating method, although this sonata should probably be placed as late as the *terminus* allows.[8]

Of the other extant works listed in the right-hand column of *EK*, several come down to us in dated autographs: Hob. XVIII:1 (1756), Hob. XVI:19 (1767), Hob. XVI:45 (1766), and Hob. XIV:4 (1764). Two others give some idea of their date of composition from thematic similarities with datable baryton works: Hob. XVIIa:1 "Il maestro e lo scolare" (1767) and Hob. XIV:2 (*ca.* 1772). The earliest known date for Hob. XIV:1 (1766) is an entry in the Breitkopf catalogue.

The added works in the left-hand column and the nonthematic entries at the top of *EK* 20 were presumably added later, after all the staves for thematic entries were filled. Only one concerto listed at the top of *EK* 20 can be definitely identified as the "Concerto per Violino e Cembalo in F" (Hob. XVIII:6) listed in Breitkopf for 1766 and perhaps dated 1756 by Haydn;[9] the two additional Concertos in C for Organ could be any two of three known works: Hob. XVIII:5, 8, or 10, which are also listed in Breitkopf for 1763, 1766, and 1771.[10] The two sets of sonatas are Hob. XVI:21–26 and 27–32, the former the so-called Esterházy Sonatas printed by Kurzböck, and the latter a set distributed through a professional Viennese copy firm. Hob. XVIII:4 was inadvertently entered on *EK* 20, crossed out, and rewritten on *EK* 22. Larsen believed this entry was made *ca.* 1770,[11] a date that, if one considers stylistic factors, may be several years too early. That it is entered above the 1774 and 1776 sets of sonatas is not adequate evidence, for these could have been entered together any time after 1776. However, from the watermarks on the copy at Kroměříž there is reason to hypothesize that this concerto was contemporary with the 1776 set of sonatas and the D-major Concerto Hob. XVIII:11, which are not entered in *EK*. Malcolm Cole, in a study of the instrumental rondo, believes that both concerto finales come from about the same time.[12] Furthermore, if the Fuchs catalogue entry for Hob. XVIII:3 is correct, i.e., composed in 1770,[13] we have a logical, if not a proven, chronological progression: Hob. XVIII:3, 4, and 11. The placement of the entry for Hob. XIV:3 dates it from after the period when most of the other works were entered in the catalogue.

When compared to other genres listed in *EK*, the keyboard works are not as completely accounted for as the symphonies and the compositions for baryton. Furthermore, whereas the entries for the symphonies and baryton divertimentos give a number of important clues for chronology and dating, most of the incipits for the keyboard music seem to have been inscribed at one time (or over a relatively short period) during the late 1760s.[14] Some of the keyboard genres are also almost totally missing from *EK*: only a single keyboard trio is listed (Hob. XV:9), and it seems to have been entered around or after the year 1800; while incipits are given for fewer than half the keyboard concertos and only a few of the other accompanied works and solo keyboard pieces.[15] Finally, except for the concertos, it seems that all but one of the keyboard works listed (Hob. XVI:6) were probably composed after Haydn's employment by the Esterházy family.

Unfortunately, therefore, *EK* provides only a limited amount of useful information for determining the date and order of the keyboard works. Nonetheless, the clues it offers are important and in a few cases the only ones. In the following discussions the data from *EK* will be combined with other external evidence and stylistic observations in order to establish a chronology for each of the five genres.

Solo Sonatas

A chronology for the solo sonatas was first published by Karl Päsler in 1918 for the never-completed Breitkopf & Härtel collected edition of Haydn's works. For nearly half a century, Päsler's chronology was generally accepted except for the elimination of some spurious early sonatas and the placement twenty years too late of Hob. XVI:44, 45, 46, and 47 because of Päsler's heavy reliance on Artaria's printed editions.[16] It was not until 1963, with the appearance of Georg Feder's "Probleme einer Neuordnung der Klaviersonaten Haydns," a scholarly prelude to his subsequent volumes of the *Joseph Haydn Werke*, and Christa Landon's edition for the *Wiener Urtext Ausgabe* of Universal Edition in 1966, that Päsler's order was extensively revised. In 1969 Feder presented a revised chronology in his first volume of the solo sonatas. Today there is still scholarly disagreement as to the dating and chronology of primarily the early sonatas but also of some of the works placed during the 1770s and early 1780s.

The central difficulty of a chronology for the early solo sonatas—as is also true of the keyboard trios, accompanied divertimentos, and concertinos—is the lack of documentation. Feder attacks it in "Probleme" by distinguishing early works composed in either the *Kenner* or *Liebhaber* styles from those that do not belong clearly to either category. The latter he considers to be Haydn's earliest solo keyboard works from *ca.* 1750; the former are placed in two chronologically parallel columns according to the predominant style. Feder subsequently revised this arrangement into two groups of nine works each: *frühe Sonaten* and *kleine Sonaten*.[17] Concerning the chronology in her edition, Christa Landon writes:

> Most of the early keyboard compositions were probably written before 1761. . . .
> To add a presumed date to the not yet distinctive works before the middle of the
> 1760s seemed of little point to the editor; hardly any such clues exist with regard to
> the keyboard works. The chronological order in our edition can be regarded merely
> as an attempt.[18]

Unlike those of Feder and Landon, Newman's ordering, published in *The Sonata in the Classic Era*,[19] is not based on primary sources but on a compilation of information from several important Haydn editions and studies: Päsler's prefaces to the 1918 *Gesamtausgabe*, the information in Hoboken's *Verzeichnis*, and an article on Haydn by Jens Peter Larsen and H. C. Robbins Landon.[20] The comparison of the chronologies of the early solo sonatas presented in Table IV-3 is remarkable for its total lack of agreement as to the ordering of these early works and therefore as to the development of Haydn's style. Given this unsatisfactory situation, one could also look for clues in the ordering of some of the old sources, as listed in Table IV-4. In 1963 Feder suggested that the ordering of the five works in the Rajhrad manuscript, all of which are in a "comparatively dense and concert-worthy

TABLE IV-3

Comparison of Chronologies of Early Solo Keyboard Sonatas

Päsler, B. & H. Gesamtausgabe (1918)	Newman, SCE (1963)	C. Landon, Sonatas (1966)	Feder, "Probleme" (1963)	Feder, Klaviersonaten (1969)
XVI:1	XVI:1	XVI:8	XVI:1	*Neun Frühe*
XVI:2	XVI:2	XVI:7	XVI:5	XVI:16
XVI:3	XVI:7	XVI:9	XVI:16	XVI:5
XVI:4	XVI:8	XVI:G1	XVI:12	XVI:12
XVI:5	XVI:9	XVI:11		XVI:13
XVI:6	XVI:5	XVI:10	*Kenner*	XVI:14
XVI:7	XVI:3	XVII:D1	XVI:13	XVI:6
XVI:8	XVI:4	XVI:5	XVI:2	XVI:2
XVI:9	XVI:10	XVI:4	XVI:6	XVI:Es2
XVI:10	XVI:11	XVI:1	XVI:Es2	XVI:Es3
XVI:11	XVI:12	XVI:2	XVI:14	
XVI:12	XVI:13	XVI:12	XVI:Es3	*Neun Kleine*
XVI:13	XVI:14	XVI:6		XVI:1
XVI:14		XVI:3	*Liebhaber*	XVI:7
XVI:15ᵃ		XVI:13	XVI:9	XVI:8
XVI:16		XVI:14	XVI:11	XVI:9
XVI:17ᵃ		XVI:Es2, Es3,47ᵇ	XVI:G1	XVI:10
			XIV:C1	XVI:G1
			XVII:D1	XVII:D1
			XVI:7&8	XVI:3
			XVI:10	XVI:4
			XVI:3&4	

ᵃNow considered spurious.

ᵇHob. XVI:47/2, 3, 4 (E-minor version).

TABLE IV-4

Order of Keyboard Sonatas in Old Sources

Anthology Dorsch	Rajhrad	Anthology Vienna	Breitkopf Catalogue
XVI:13	XVI:14	XVI:14	1763–XVI:5
XVII:1	XVI:13	XVI:13	1766–XVI:6
XVI:19	XVI:2	XVI:2	XVI:8
XVII:2	XVI:Es2		XVI:7
XVI:47	XVI:Es3		XVI:9
XIV:7			XVII:7
XVII:3			1767–XVI:10
XVI:27			XVI:11
XVI:14			XVI:12
			XVI:13
			XVI:14

style" for the *Kenner*, might provide the best clue.[21] It should also be noted that the first portion of the Rajhrad collection duplicates the order of three sonatas in Anthology Vienna, which appears to have been copied sometime during the late 1760s and early 1770s. However, Anthology Dorsch may be the most important source for keyboard works from the 1760s, as it contains sonatas from *EK* as well as other compositions seemingly from the same period.

All but a few of the early solo sonatas reveal a high degree of skill and polish despite their simplicity of style, small dimension, and ease of execution. For example, one can find few sonatas with as strong a slow movement as Hob. XVI:2 or as finely honed a melodic curve as Hob. XVI:8/3. Because of the paucity of external evidence, however, one must depend on internal evidence. For the following discussion the author has chosen to make chronological conclusions based on an evolutionary approach to style.

Of the sonatas generally considered early—that is, composed before 1766— Hob. XVI:16, 5, Es2, and Es3 in the main do not display the skillful approach to syntax seen in the others and therefore are probably among the very earliest of those extant. Hob. XVI:12, which has been placed rather early in Feder's listing, is clearly well crafted, despite the more seamless structure of the first movement. Hob. XVII:D1 and Hob. XVI:G1 are stylistically close to the earliest sonatas; while Hob. XVI:1, 7, 9, 10, and 12 are possibly somewhat later products of the 1750s. Hob. XVI:2, 6, 8, and 13 are perhaps from about 1760; while Hob. XVI:3, 4, and 14, which appear in *EK*, may have been composed sometime during the 1760s. Of these, Hob. XVI:14 may be the latest, as evidenced by its placement in Anthology Dorsch.

From the second half of the 1760s, two dated autographs in fair copies are extant: Hob. XVI:45 (1766) and Hob. XVI:19 (1767). On the basis of the entries in *EK* and their overall style, Hob. XVI:46 and 18, and Hob. XIV:5 (*recte* XVI:5a) belong with this group. Hob. XVI:47, which is also present in Anthology Dorsch, probably stems from this same time or a little earlier, as do "Il maestro e lo scolare" (Hob. XVIIa:1) and the other four-hand sonata, Hob. XVIIa:2, if it is authentic.

Hob. XVI:44 and 18 cause problems in dating and placement. Hob. XVI:44 has been dated 1766 in *MGG*, *ca.* 1771–1773 by Feder, and *ca.* 1766–67? by C. Landon. Feder has observed that Hob. XVI:44 is a stylistic twin to Hob. XVI:18,[22] while Rosen thinks its "coordination of harmony, accent, and regular cadence would place it later than 1770, and perhaps after 1774."[23] In addition, Hob. XVI:44 is absent from *EK*, suggesting that it postdates the other works inscribed there. Although Hob. XVI:18 does not appear in *EK*, its style suggests that it is contemporary with other keyboard works that were registered there.

Hob. XVI:20, the next sonata to appear in a dated (1771) autograph, is also absent from *EK*. Unfortunately, the autograph date itself cannot be taken at absolute face value, for Haydn's orthography for the final numeral is not clearly written, and the autograph is incomplete. More specifically, the date occurs on what begins as a fair copy of the first movement (see Plate 10), but starting with its development section is only a sketch. The finale that follows breaks off at the end of a page, intimating that it may have been completed. At the bottom of the last sheet is material for the end of the first movement; there is no slow movement. Perhaps most puzzling is that Haydn apparently chose not to publish or distribute this sonata until 1780, and then as the sixth of the Auenbrugger group. Two interpretations are thus possible: either Hob. XVI:20 was completed *ca.* 1771 but thought inappropriate for the intended audience of the 1774 and 1776 sets; or it was set aside with the incomplete state of the first movement and returned to at a later date, perhaps at the end of the decade. Since Haydn frequently accelerated his tempo indications when revising after the passage of time,[24] the latter possibility is supported by the quickening of the tempo found in the first edition: for the first movement the autograph has "Moderato," while the Artaria print reads "Allegro Moderato." Haydn's use of dynamics is also expanded in the 1780 edition. While all of this is conjecture, it should be emphasized that for this particular sonata, the presence of a date on the autograph should not be accepted without question.

During the 1770s, Haydn distributed the bulk of his sonatas in three *opere* of six works: the Esterházy Sonatas, Hob. XVI:21–26; the six Sonatas of the year 1776, Hob. XVI:27–32; and the Auenbrugger Sonatas, Hob. XVI:35–39 plus Hob. XVI:20. The Esterházy Sonatas were published in an authorized edition by Kurzböck and announced in the *Wienerisches Diarium* on 26 February 1774. This advertisement, coupled with the date of 1773 on the autograph of the fragments that survive of 21, 22, 23, and 26, each with a number, suggests that the sonatas were composed as a set and that the order is perhaps the one of composition. From the appearance of the script the final sonata, numbered Sonata 6[ta], seems to have been written in a great hurry. The autograph does not include the middle movement, a "menuet al rovescio," which apparently was transcribed as an afterthought from the Symphony No. 47, composed in 1772.[25] The minuet transcription, the unusual brevity of the finale, and the character of the notation on the autograph itself point to a shortage of time, perhaps a publication deadline.[26] The first sonata of the Esterházy set was probably begun after the completion of *Philemon und Baucis* and other operatic responsibilities in the fall of 1773; and with time allowed for setting and proofreading—although the text of the print leaves the latter open to question—the last one was probably composed near the end of the year.

Hob. XVI:27–32 were distributed through professional Viennese scribes; there can be no doubt of the correlation of these works with the reference to six sonatas from 1776 in *EK* since they survive in dated copies at Schwerin, Kroměříž, Graz, and Vienna. However, the one sonata that survives in partial autograph, Hob. XVI:29, is dated 1774, leaving open the possibility that others in the set also stem from an earlier date. One of the best candidates for such dating is the G-major Sonata Hob. XVI:27, which does not extend beyond d‴ and is also found in the first part of Anthology Dorsch, which may date from the late 1760s.

Like the Esterházy set, the Auenbrugger Sonatas were distributed in an authorized edition, which was announced by Artaria in the *Wiener-Zeitung* on 12 April 1780. Besides the appended XVI:20, others from the set could possibly have been written earlier; for example, the Minuet of Hob. XVI:36 contains a quotation from the "Night Watchman's Song," which Haydn seems otherwise to have used only in instrumental works up to about 1774.[27] Furthermore, Haydn discovered his use of the same thematic material in Hob. XVI:36/2 and Hob. XVI:39/1 only after they had been engraved, leading one to suspect that Hob. XVI:39—"the 5th and last sonata," mentioned in the letter of 8 February 1780—postdated the other by some length of time. Along with Hob. XVI:39, both Hob. XVI:35 and 37 with their "con brio" opening movements are indeed more advanced, whereas the moderato tempos and minuet *cum* trio finales of Hob. XVI:36 and 38 hark back to an earlier style. Therefore, the 1780 set includes possibly two sonatas—or partial sonatas—held in reserve by Haydn for some time.

Among the works of the 1770s to be placed are three sonatas not associated with an authorized print or copy: Hob. XVI:43, 33, and 34. They appeared in an unauthorized edition in three parts by Beardmore & Birchall entitled *A Fifth Sett of Sonatas*, entered at Stationer's Hall on 26 July 1783 (Hob. XVI:43), 27 November 1783 (Hob. XVI:33), and 15 January 1784 (Hob. XVI:34). In addition, they were distributed in possibly authorized copies, with Hob. XVI:43 by one of the scribes who participated in the "1776 set" and Hob. XVI:33 in two copies dated 1778, one of which carries the day: 17 January. If the Moderato or Allegro Moderato first movements (in which the basic pulse is the eighth note) and the 3/8 and Tempo di Menuet finales (a prominent feature of the 1774 set) of Hob. XVI:43 and 33 are contrasted with the Allegro con brio first movements and fast finales in either 6/8 or 2/4 found among the Auenbrugger Sonatas, it then becomes possible to place all three sonatas tentatively within the context of these two styles: Hob. XVI:33 and 43 are from the mid-1770s, while Hob. XVI:34 with its newer tendencies belongs with the most advanced works of the Auenbrugger group.[28]

The final eight solo sonatas span the decade from *ca.* 1784 to *ca.* 1794: three for Marie Esterházy, Hob. XVI:40–42; one for Breitkopf & Härtel's *Musikalischer Pot-pourri*, Hob. XVI:48; the E-flat major sonata for Marianna von Genzinger, Hob. XVI:49; and the three sonatas written for England, Hob. XVI:50–52. The

Marie Esterházy sonatas, advertised in the *Frankfurter Staatsristretto* on 31 August 1784, were printed in an authentic edition by Bossler. We know little else about their exact date. From Haydn's other activities during 1784 we can hypothesize that they were probably composed before the Keyboard Trio Hob. XV:6 and after the first performance of *Armida*, i.e., between March and mid-summer of 1784. The great C-major Sonata Hob. XVI:48 was probably not begun until after Breitkopf's request of 10 January 1789 and finished, according to Haydn's correspondence, by 6 April of that year.

Letters exchanged with Marianna von Genzinger give us a complete history for Hob. XVI:49. As early as June 1789 Haydn wished to write a sonata for her, for he wrote on 20 June 1790 that the "sonata was intended for Your Grace already a year ago." On 6 June, Haydn had said he would be able to deliver the new work in two weeks, but on the twentieth he wrote that "only the Adagio . . . has been finished quite recently" and the "last movement contains the very Minuet and Trio which your Grace asked from me in your last letter." Therefore, the autograph date of 1 June 1790 is probably the day when the first movement was set down from sketches that may have been in existence for as long as a year; then the finale was written, perhaps during the first part of June 1790; and finally the slow movement, sometime before 20 June.

Clarity of this sort does not surround the three solo sonatas written during Haydn's stay in England: only one survives in autograph, Hob. XVI:52, with the date of 1794. This Sonata and Hob. XVI:50 and 51 have been regarded in some quarters as an *opera* written for Therese Jansen Bartolozzi, yet only the final printed edition of Hob. XVI:50 and the autograph of 52 support this association. As is well known, Hob. XVI:50 demands the use of a pedal in the first movement and the pitch a''' in the finale; neither is required in Hob. XVI:52. Since Hob. XVI:52 is dated before the marriage of Therese Jansen to Bartolozzi on 16 May 1795, perhaps Hob. XVI:50 was composed for a new *fortepiano* that she acquired at the time of or soon after her wedding. It may also explain the revisions to the slow movement, which had already appeared separately in an Artaria print in June 1794: they were perhaps a result of the character of our hypothesized new instrument for this virtuoso.[29] While Hob. XVI:50 and 52 are big and difficult sonatas, Hob. XVI:51 is a more lyrically conceived work composed for an "English lady." If it was written for Rebecca Schröter,[30] it could have been composed any time from 1791 until Haydn's final departure from England in 1795.

A proposed chronology with estimated dates of composition for the early and mature solo keyboard sonatas is given in Table IV-5.

Trios

Beginning with the nineteenth-century editions, the keyboard trios known to performers numbered thirty-one, and only two works composed before 1784 were included: Hob. XV:1 and 2. Although Hoboken included the relatively unknown early trios in his *Gruppe* XV, his numberings provide a jumbled picture of their chronology: the traditional thirty-one in Larsen's chronological order appear first,

TABLE IV-5

Proposed Chronology for Solo Sonatas

Date	Work
Pre-Esterházy	
Very earliest (*ca.* 1750–1755)	Hob. XVI:16, 5, Es2, Es3
1750s	Hob. XVII:D1, XVI:G1
	Hob. XVI:1, 7, 9, 10, 12
ca. 1760	Hob. XVI:2, 6, 8, 13
Esterházy	
ca. 1761/2–*ca.* 1767	Hob. XVI:3, 4, 14
ca. 1765	Hob. XVI:47/2, 3, 4
	(E-minor version)
1766	Hob. XVI:45
	Hob. XVIIa:1, 2
1767	Hob. XVI:19
ca. 1767/68	Hob. XVI:46
	Hob. XIV:5
	Hob. XVI:18
ca. 1770	Hob. XVI:44
Autumn/winter 1773	Hob. XVI:21–26

	"1776" Sonatas	Auenbrugger Sonatas	Others
Possibly late 1760s; no later than 1776	Hob. XVI:27		
Begun 1771 (finished by 1780)		Hob. XVI:20	
1774	Hob. XVI:29		
Possibly before 1774; no later than 1776	Hob. XVI:28, 30, 31, 32		
Mid-1770s		Hob. XVI:36, 38	Hob. XVI:33, 43
Late 1770s to 1780		Hob. XVI:35, 37, 39	

Date	Work
ca. 1780–1783	Hob. XVI:34
March to mid-summer 1784	Hob. XVI:40–42
Mid-January to 6 April 1789	Hob. XVI:48
June 1789 to June 1790	Hob. XVI:49
London	
Early(?) 1794 (1793?)	Hob. XVI:50/2
1791–1796	Hob. XVI:51
1794	Hob. XVI:52
16 May to 15 August 1795	Hob. XVI:50/1 & 3

the newly authenticated trio setting of Hob. XV:32 follows, and then the early trios begin with the numbering XV:33. Thus, it was not until the publication of the Doblinger edition by H. C. R. Landon in 1970[31] and two volumes of the *Joseph Haydn Werke* under the direction of Georg Feder in 1970 and 1974[32] that all the keyboard trios were accessible in a plausible chronological sequence.

Concerning the dating of the early trios, Landon's list is prefaced by the following remarks:

As far as the early works are concerned, . . . we have no exact date of composition and in many cases no positive proof of Haydn's authorship. Thus we were forced to proceed from the known to the unknown, i.e. to list first those works for which we have some kind of dates, then to proceed to those for which we have no dates at all.[33]

Landon places the early works *ca.* 1755–1760 and orders them beginning with Hummel's Op. 4, followed by the Breitkopf catalogue entries, and ending with the Kroměříž manuscripts as follows:

Hob. XV:37	Breitkopf 1766, Hummel Op. 4/1 (1767)
Hob. XV:C1	Breitkopf 1766, Hummel Op. 4/2 (1767)
Hob. XIV:6	Hummel Op. 4/3 (1767)
Hob. XV:39	Hummel Op. 4/4 (1767)
Hob. XV:1	Breitkopf 1766, Hummel Op. 4/5 (1767)
Hob. XV:40	Breitkopf 1766
Hob. XV:41	Breitkopf 1767
Hob. XV:33	Breitkopf 1771 (lost)
Hob. XV:D1	Breitkopf 1771
Hob. XV:35	Breitkopf 1771
Hob. XV:34	Breitkopf 1771
Hob. XV:36	Breitkopf 1774
Hob. XV:38	Kroměříž Ms. *ca.* 1760
Hob. XV:f1	Kroměříž Ms. *ca.* 1760
(Hob. deest)	Kroměříž Ms. *ca.* 1760
	(second movement Breitkopf 1766) and
(Hob. XIV:C1)	Kroměříž Ms. *ca.* 1760

Although entitled "Chronological List," it is, as Landon himself implies, only a systematic one.

Feder's chronology for the early trios is fashioned out of a combination of external evidence, including his own methods of dating the sources and, to a lesser extent, internal factors. The result is as viable as the available data permit:

up to 1760	Hob. XV:36, C1, 37, 38, 34, f1, 41, 33 (lost)
ca. 1760	Hob. XV:40
ca. 1760–1762	Hob. XV:1
ca. 1764–1765	Hob. XV:35
ca. 1767–1771	Hob. XV:2 and
(before 1771)	Hob. XV:D1

It seems to this author that there is not enough evidence to separate Hob. XV:40 from the Trios dated "up to 1760": all of them form a stylistic unit in that their first movements depend heavily on the trio sonata concept. Feder's first three are without question the most primitive: Hob. XV:36 begins with an unconvincing, peculiarly shaped theme and is the closest to the older suite with two dance-styled movements;[34] Hob. XV:C1 also displays a primitive style; and the sequence of movements in Hob. XV:37 (Slow–Fast–Minuet) is rather retrospective. Since Hob. XV:34 belongs with the trios that begin to depart from the trio sonata idea, it should be placed somewhat later within its group. Hob. XV:1 and 35 seem to be in reverse order: the two form a stylistic pair in their departure from the trio sonata beginning, yet Hob. XV: 1 seems to be the later work (e.g., the trio of the minuet). Feder's belief that the Capriccio of Hob. XV: 35 may have something to do with the Capriccio of Hob. XVII: 1 from 1765 also must be questioned, since they belong to different traditions: Hob. XV: 35 is of the perpetual-motion type found in the works of Monn, while Hob. XVII: 1 is a synthesis of the Emanuel Bach Fantasia concept with the Capriccio based on pre-existent material.[35]

Feder dates Hob. XV: 2 *ca.* 1767–1771, but Landon hypothesizes that it was composed *ca.* 1772 for baryton and revised *ca.* 1785 into the keyboard trio setting. Landon's dating seems to be circumstantially the stronger: during the 1780s, with the peak demands on his time and energy in his duties as an opera conductor, Haydn was forced to palm off two trios of Pleyel as his own because of the demand to publish works of this type. Since Hob. XV: 2 seems to be a transcription of XIV: 2, it certainly could give the appearance of an earlier work. As there are no other works for keyboard trio from the same period (late 1760s or early 1770s) with which it can be compared, the date of the transcription is left open to speculation. All the sources for the trio setting seem to be considerably later than the period 1767–1771.

Haydn composed no more trios until the mid-1780s, and then did so primarily as a result of contacts with Viennese and English publishers. Unlike the early trios, the works of this period are documented by advertisements, contracts, correspondence, entries at Stationer's Hall, and publishers' notes of receipt on the *Stichvorlagen*. Together with the available dated autographs, these facts can therefore be used to arrive at a reasonable terminal date of composition. For example, Hob. XV: 9, 2, and 10 were sent to Forster's on 28 October 1785 and advertised on 4 February 1786; and the C-major Fantasia Hob. XVII: 4 was completed by 29 March 1789, sent to Artaria on 6 April, and issued by 5 July.[36] Under normal circumstances it apparently took about three months from the day the completed work left Haydn until it was available to the public.

One can also ascertain how long it took Haydn to compose a keyboard trio under normal circumstances. For example, his letter to Artaria dated 11 January 1790, in which he wrote, "the first sonata [trio] is ready now, the 2nd in two weeks, and third by the end of Carnival," indicates that Haydn would compose the second trio before the beginning of the operatic season at Esterháza, but the third would take longer, as the operatic activities would begin in February. This timing is generally in agreement with Webster's hypothesis that the composition of a quartet took one month or less;[37] since the trios were usually shorter, a minimum of two weeks, as Haydn stated, seems very probable.

Before Haydn arrived in London in 1791 he had published fourteen authentic trios in authorized editions. The first one, Hob. XV: 5, was sent to William Forster on 24 or 25 October 1784, arrived in London on 8 November, and was published as Op. 40, together with two spurious works (Hob. XV: 3 and 4) in early 1785. Hob. XV: 5 was probably composed in September–October 1784, although the watermark on some copies could allow a date earlier in the 1780s.

The next set, Hob. XV: 6–8, also to appear as Op. 40 but this time under the

aegis of Artaria, was engraved by 26 November 1785, with the proofs corrected by
Haydn before 10 December 1785. The autographs for Hob. XV:6 and 7 are dated
1784 and 1785 respectively. The Artaria edition is ordered like the Hoboken numbers, while that of Forster is 6, 8, 7. Since the Artaria edition is without question
authentic, its ordering must be preferred: Hob. XV:6, late 1784 to early 1785;
Hob. XV:7 and 8 before autumn 1785. These dates seem most plausible since
Haydn was to compose two more trios, Hob. XV:9 and 10, and transcribe or have
transcribed Hob. XV:2 for Forster's Op. 42, which was sent to London on 28 October 1785 and arrived there on 26 December 1785. Thus, Hob. XV:9 and 10
and the trio version of XV:2 were possibly written in the late summer or early fall
of 1785.

Following a break of several years, Hob. XV:11, 12, and 13 appeared in an
Artaria print that was announced in the *Wiener-Zeitung* on 1 July 1789 and was
available four days later. Although no autographs survive, the correspondence provides the most-precise history for any keyboard *opera* save Hob. XVI:49:

10 August 1788	Haydn offers to compose three quartets or three accompanied sonatas by the end of December.
17 August 1788	Artaria prefers sonatas.
26 October 1788	In process of composition.
16 November 1788	One and one-half sonatas completed.
8 March 1789	Still working on them (presumably the remaining sonatas).
29 March 1789	Rewrote Hob. XV:13 "according to your taste . . . with variations."

Thus by November 1788, Hob. XV:11 and the first part of 12 were probably
completed. Perhaps delayed by the start of the operatic season, Haydn was still
working on the remainder of the set in early March, but they must have been completed a few days thereafter. During the last week of March the first movement of
Hob. XV:13 was rewritten as variations; it was presumably the last trio to be
composed.

Haydn's plans for the next set—Hob. XV:14, 15, and 16—were to compose
them by the end of the Carnival season. From a letter of his it can be surmised that
Hob. XV:14 was finished by 11 January 1790; Haydn completed Hob. XV:16 by
12 April and Hob. XV:15 by 19(?) April.[38] Hob. XV:15 and 16 were published
by John Bland in late June 1790. According to the announcement in the *Wiener-
Zeitung*, all three trios were subsequently published by Artaria before 20 October
1790. Since it is possible that the two trios sent to Bland were written before
Hob. XV:14—which might explain the delay of the appearance of the Artaria edition—the ordering is open to question.

Hob. XV:17 together with 15 and 16 were the three trios that Haydn wrote for
John Bland's series *Le Tout Ensemble*. Hob. XV:17 was presumably finished before 20 June 1790, as Haydn told Marianna von Genzinger on that date about a
"brand new trio" that may have been contained in an envelope that arrived in London with the inscription "Haydn 12 July 1790." Thus it can be hypothetically

dated during the spring of that year. However, the date of Bland's edition is not secure: it could have appeared any time between 28 June 1790—bringing the contents of the envelope into question—and 12 February 1792.[39] Artaria's edition was not announced until late November 1792. Presumably, Hob. XV:17 was composed in 1790 and issued sometime after mid-July.

For the trios composed in London, i.e., after January 1791, we have fewer documents: the arrangements for their publication were presumably made through in-person contacts. It has generally been hypothesized that Haydn composed no trios during the first London sojourn because he was too busy with the six new symphonies, the concertante symphony, the opera *L'anima del filosofo*, and various other smaller vocal works. The one work for which this hypothesis may be incorrect is Hob. XV:32, which was published in two London editions in 1794 by Preston and Bland as a trio and not in its once better-known setting as a violin sonata. Tyson believes that this G-major Trio is referred to in a letter of 2 March 1792 written to Marianna von Genzinger, an idea that can be neither confirmed nor refuted. However, if it is not the sonata referred to, it seems unlikely that it was composed as an isolated work unless it was requested for a series such as Bland's *Le Tout Ensemble*.

All but one of the trios written during or for the second London visit were published in four sets:

Hob. XV:18–20	Longman & Broderip	Registered Stationer's Hall 17 November 1794; advertised 25 November 1794 in *The Sun*.
Hob. XV:21–23	Preston	Registered Stationer's Hall 23 May 1795; advertised *Morning Chronicle* 13 June 1795.
Hob. XV:24–26	Longman & Broderip	Announced 9 October 1795; registered Stationer's Hall 31 October 1795.
Hob. XV:27–29	Longman & Broderip	Announced 20 April 1797 in *The Oracle*; registered Stationer's Hall 27 April 1797.

It is possible, but not too likely, that Trios Hob. XV:18–20 were composed in 1793 along with other works that we know Haydn was preparing for London; the lateness of their appearance in 1794, however, makes one believe that they were not written in Vienna. The slow movement of Hob. XV:22 appears as a separate keyboard piece in a copy on English paper with Haydn's corrections, so it was probably composed earlier than the other movements in the second set of trios, Hob. XV:21–23. The slow movement of Hob. XV:26 (part of the third set, Hob. XV:24–26) is also to be found in Symphony No. 102, which can be dated 1795; a sketch for the slow movement of Hob. XV:25 is also found on the same sheet with an incipit catalogue for all the London Symphonies. Therefore, Trios Hob. XV:24–26 were possibly written between May and August 1795.

In Haydn's London catalogue (*LV*) of works "vom 2ten Jan. 1791 bis 1795 in

England komponirt" are listed "3 Sonates for Broderip," "3 Sonates for Preston," "3 Sonates for Broderip," and "3 Sonates for Miss Janson." These sonatas have traditionally been cited as Hob. XV:18–20, XV:21–23, XV:24–26, and (the three solo keyboard sonatas) Hob. XVI:50–52 respectively. However, there is no other evidence to suggest that the three solo sonatas constituted an *opera*. Since the other three groups are in fact trios, it follows that this entry could refer to Hob. XV:27–29 and not Hob. XVI:50–52. If a date of composition while in London is accepted, their late date of publication could be explained by the probability that they were Therese Jansen Bartolozzi's property and were—like her two solo sonatas—later published from her copies or autographs.[40] Hob. XV:27–29 may therefore predate some of the other late ones, but could have been written no later than 1795. All that one can be certain of is that they were published in April 1797 and dedicated to Mrs. Bartolozzi.

Regarding the last two single trios of the "traditional" thirty-one, Hob. XV:31 was composed in two distinct stages: the autograph of the first movement is dated 1795, presumably while Haydn was still in England; while the finale was originally entitled "Sonata, Jacob's Dream by Dr. Haydn 1794." The entire trio was not published until 1803 by Traeg in Vienna: "edition faite d'après le manuscrit original." Thus, the finale to Hob. XV:31 possibly precedes Hob. XV:21–23 and the

TABLE IV-6

Proposed Chronology for the Mature Keyboard Trios
(Beginning ca. *1784)*

Date	Work
Vienna	
September–October 1784	Hob. XV:5
Late 1784 to early 1785	Hob. XV:6
No later than autumn 1785	Hob. XV:7–8
Late summer or early autumn 1785	Hob. XV:9, 10, 2
August to 16 November 1788	Hob. XV:11 and part of 12
Up to mid-March 1789	Remainder of Hob. XV:12 and 13
Rewritten end of March, completed by 29 March	Hob. XV:13/1
Finished 11 January 1790	Hob. XV:14
Finished by 12 April 1790	Hob. XV:16
Finished by 19(?) April 1790	Hob. XV:15
Finished by 20 June 1790	Hob. XV:17
London	
1791 to early 1792	Hob. XV:32
Before autumn 1794	Hob. XV:18–20
	Hob. XV:22/2 for keyboard solo
1794	Hob. XV:31/2
Late 1794 and/or early 1795	Hob. XV:31/1
Late 1794 to early 1795	Hob. XV:21–23
1794 to 1795	Hob. XV:27–29
Spring and summer 1795 after Symphony No. 104	Hob. XV:24–26
Vienna	
Finished by 9 November 1796	Hob. XV:30

first Longman & Broderip set (Hob. XV : 18–20). Only Hob. XV : 30 is known to have been finished in Vienna after Haydn's final return from England. Intended for Breitkopf & Härtel, it was delivered to the firm by Joseph Weigl, Jr., who left the Imperial city about 9 November 1796.

In summary, a proposed chronology for the mature keyboard trios is given in Table IV-6.

Accompanied Divertimentos and Concertinos

In contrast to the concern about the solo sonatas and the trios, there has been little discussion of the dating and order of the accompanied divertimentos and concertinos. A few comments have been made in prefatory remarks to editions by H. C. R. Landon and Horst Walter, stating that the works are for the most part from around 1760, a period during which Haydn was presumably employed by Count Morzin.[41] It should be emphasized, however, that we have no real documentary evidence for this period. We are not even certain of the exact dates of this Morzin appointment, nor do we know anything about its special requirements, such as whether the Count and Countess favored the keyboard to the extent that Nikolaus Esterházy did the baryton. The 1760 date apparently derives from the lost autograph of Hob. XIV : 11; Landon seems to place less emphasis on the fact that the autograph of Hob. XIV : 4 has a 1764 date. However, the following examination of the sources and other documented circumstances suggests that in general the "around 1760" dating may not be wholly justified.

Hob. XIV : 3 survives in several old copies; the two that this writer examined seem to date from the third quarter of the eighteenth century, i.e., from around 1771, when it was entered in the Breitkopf catalogue under Leopold Hofmann's name.[42] Its placement as one of the left-hand entries in *EK* signifies that it may have originated as late as the end of the 1760s, or at least not earlier than its counterpart on the same page, Hob. XIV : 4, which is dated 1764.

Hob. XIV : 7, 8, and 9 seem to form a group; all survive in copies by Esterházy Anonymous 23 on papers with watermarks that tend to place them during the 1780s. The late date of these authentic copies is possibly confirmed by a letter of 8 April 1787 to William Forster in which Haydn offered "three little *Clavier Divertimentos* for beginners with violin(s?) and bass." It seems unlikely that these pieces were keyboard trios; regardless, Forster must have rejected them, for they never reached print. All three, according to the notation of the appoggiaturas, seem to have originated after 1762. Hob. XIV : 7 also appears in Anthology Dorsch, whose first portion can be dated probably before 1770;[43] therefore it was seemingly composed at the latest during the 1760s. The first movement and trio of the minuet of Hob. XIV : 8 are transcribed in or from the Baryton Trio Hob. XI : 110, which can be dated April 1772. The short length of Hob. XIV : 9 may lead one to believe it to be very early, but Haydn probably created tiny, polished compositions of this type even after his early years, perhaps as teaching pieces for the boys in the Esterházy Kapelle.

Such a hypothesis is supported by the source situation of another miniature from this genre, Hob. XIV:10. It comes down to us in two copies by Joseph Elssler, Sr., who died in 1782, after serving as Haydn's personal copyist for a number of years. One copy contains the autograph of Haydn's song "Der schlaue Pudel," dating from sometime around 1780; the other contains fanfares for Prince Esterházy. The notation indicates that Hob. XIV:10 originated during or after 1762, and the papers seem to place it in the 1770s or 1780s.[44] Since the work was used by Haydn during the Esterházy years but did not appear in *EK*, it may have originated during the 1770s.

Hob. XIV:C2 probably belongs with the small works from the Esterházy years—Hob. XIV:3, 9, and 10. It survives in a single copy at Kroměříž with the indication "Menuet." In contrast, a series of larger works—Hob. XIV:12 and 13 and Hob. XVIII:F2—all seem on the basis of the orthography to come from around 1760. Hob. XIV:1, which appears in the Breitkopf catalogue for 1766, distinguishes itself by its occasionally elaborate parts for horns, which parallel those in a number of other works from this period: the Horn Concerto Hob. VIId:3 (1762), the Divertimento Hob. IV:5 (1767), Symphony No. 31 (1765), Divertimento in D major (Hob. II:D22),[45] and Symphony No. 72. (The Divertimento and Symphony No. 72 seem also to emanate from the 1760s.[46]) If one were to consider only the keyboard range, then all but Hob. XIV:1 and 8 would probably date from the mid-1760s or earlier: the former has e flat''', the latter f''' as its highest note, while none of the remaining works go higher than d'''. Although the highest note might be a general determining factor in chronology, its applicability to works for students may be deceiving; one can hypothesize that the keyboard students at the court used the older instruments, which may have had a smaller range.

A possible chronology of these works is given in Table IV-7. The last five works listed—Hob. XIV:3, the three works known in authentic copies (Hob. XIV:8, 9, and 10), and Hob. XIV:C2—contain notational practices indicating

TABLE IV-7

Proposed Chronology for the Accompanied Divertimentos and Concertinos

Date	Work	Inclusion in *EK*
ca. 1760	Hob. XIV:12	
	Hob. XIV:13	None in *EK*
	Hob. XVIII:F2	
1760	Hob. XIV:11	
ca. 1765 but before 1766	Hob. XIV:1	
1764	Hob. XIV:4	All but XIV:7 in
After 1762 but before *ca.* 1770	Hob. XIV:7	*EK*, right-hand
ca. 1765 but before *ca.* 1770	Hob. XIV:2 (music lost)	column
ca. 1770	Hob. XIV:3	
After 1762	Hob. XIV:C2	Only XIV:3 in
ca. 1772	Hob. XIV:9	*EK*, left-hand
Before 1782	Hob. XIV:10	column
Before 1787	Hob. XIV:8	

dates after 1762. Since all but Hob. XIV:3 are missing from *EK* and all but C2 exist in Esterházy copies, they perhaps postdate the entries in *EK*.

Klavierstücke

The *Klavierstücke*, in terms of both external and internal evidence, offer the most information with regard to dating and chronology. The Introduction and Variations Hob. XVII:7 is the earliest work of this group and probably belongs with the sonatas of the 1750s. The Capriccio in G major Hob. XVII:1 and the masterly F-minor Variations Hob. XVII:6 survive in autographs dated 1765 and 1793 respectively. The remaining pieces that are not arrangements fall into place within these borders as discussed below and summarized in Table IV-8.

TABLE IV-8

Proposed Chronology for the Klavierstücke

Date	Work
1750s but before 1766	Hob. XVII:7/1, 2
ca. 1765	Hob. XVII:2
1765	Hob. XVII:1
ca. 1770 but before 1774	Hob. XVII:3
ca. 1785–1786	Hob. XVII:9
Finished by 29 March 1789	Hob. XVII:4
22–29 November 1790	Hob. XVII:5
1793	Hob. XVII:6
?1793–1794	Hob. XVII:10

Hob. XVII:2, the Variations in A major, is found in Anthology Dorsch, entered in *EK*, and listed in the 1771 Breitkopf catalogue. Along with Hob. XVI:47, XVIIa:1, and the 1765 Capriccio, it requires the short octave, and thus probably originated *ca.* 1765. The Variations in E-flat major Hob. XVII:3 is based on a theme also found in the Minuet of the E-flat major Quartet from Op. 9; and it cannot be disputed that the version for keyboard derives from this source.[47] Since Opus 9 dates from late 1769 to 1770,[48] these variations probably originated very close to that time, after the bulk of the incipits were inscribed in *EK* but before their entry in the Breitkopf catalogue of 1774. Hob. XVII:9 was published by Artaria in September 1786. A *Partiturskizze* for it, which also contains sketches for Symphony No. 84 and the aria Hob. XXIVb:7, dates it from as early as the second half of 1785.[49] Fantasia in C major Hob. XVII:4 and Hob. XVII:5 can be placed almost exactly from contemporary correspondence: the former was finished by 29 March 1789, at about the same time as Hob. XV:13; and the latter was probably composed sometime during the week of 22–29 November 1790. Hob. XVII:10 was published in 1794 and—if authentic in this setting—most likely arranged no earlier than 1793 in view of its textural relationship to the *Flötenuhr* piece Hob. XIX:27.

Concertos

In the earlier discussion of the keyboard entries in *EK*, it was hypothesized that the D-major Concerto Hob. XVIII:11—not in *EK*—together with Hob. XVIII:4—entered first on *EK* 20 and then on *EK* 22—may date from the middle of the 1770s; and that Hob. XVIII:3—entered in the right-hand column of *EK*—seems to have predated these two works. In addition, according to the notation of its appoggiaturas, Hob. XVIII:3 probably could not have been composed before 1762, and its highest pitch places it before 1767. An absolute terminal date for Hob. XVIII:3 based on the Breitkopf catalogue would be 1771; a copy from Kroměříž of Hob. XVIII:4 is dated 1781. Hob. XVIII:11 may well have been performed at a private concert in Vienna on 28 February 1780,[50] but a firm *terminus* remains its Artaria print of 1784.

Hob. XVIII:3 seems to have been preceded by the Double Concerto in F major for violin and keyboard Hob. XVIII:6. Although Haydn at one time recalled a 1756 date,[51] the orthographical evidence seems to favor one after 1762; it is listed in the Breitkopf catalogue of 1766. Thus it probably comes from *ca.* 1762–1765, although an earlier period is stylistically possible.

For the remaining concertos, one returns to the same type of speculation required for the early sonatas and accompanied works. Haydn also identified Hob. XVIII:1 as 1756, a date presumably not inscribed on the autograph until *ca.* 1800.[52] The orthographical evidence and the fact that this concerto has been associated with Therese Keller's taking of vows in 1756 support this delayed inscription. Hob. XVIII:2 seems to form a stylistic pair with Hob. XVIII:1, although from an evolutionary viewpoint it probably preceded it.[53] Another pair, Hob. XVIII:5 and 8, might be somewhat later than Hob. XVIII:1 and 2. Hob. XVIII:10 survives in a 1793 copy; the Breitkopf catalogue registers it in 1771, but the notation of the appoggiaturas indicates 1762 or earlier. Because of its polished style, this little concerto should probably be placed close to this *terminus*.

The proposed chronology for the authentic keyboard concertos given in Table IV-9 tends to reflect what is known about Haydn historically and stylistically from

TABLE IV-9

Proposed Chronology for the Concertos

Date	Work
?1756 or earlier	Hob. XVIII:2
1756 (?)	Hob. XVIII:1
?Mid-1750s	Hob. XVIII:5 and 8
ca. 1760–1762	Hob. XVIII:10
?1756 to before 1766	Hob. XVIII:6
Not before 1762 but before 1767	Hob. XVIII:3
?Mid-1770s but no later than 1781	Hob. XVIII:4
?Mid-1770s but no later than 1784 (1780?)	Hob. XVIII:11

the 1750s to the mid-1770s. The first six or seven works with their highest pitch of c''' are believed to have been organ concertos; during the 1750s and possibly into 1760 Haydn seems to have made a portion of his livelihood from playing this instrument for the Barmherzigen Brüder in Leopoldstadt as well as for the chapel of Count Harrach. After his service with the Esterházy family, the three "cembalo" concertos reflect the tendency toward a more popular style, which is fully realized in the rondo finales of Hob. XVIII:4 and 11.

Haydn's keyboard works were mainly composed in four chronological groups: before 1761; the later 1760s up to *ca.* 1780; 1784 to 1790; and 1794 to 1795. Teaching and performing activities are evident in the first group; the second—at least during the 1770s—provided a means of furthering his reputation with the *Kenner* and *Liebhaber* of Viennese society; the third satisfied the demands of Viennese as well as foreign publishers; and during the fourth Haydn composed not only for the public at large but also for the virtuosos resident in London.[54] These chronological groupings thus reflect the spread and solidification of Haydn's reputation.

Comparing the believed and known dates of composition for the string quartets, symphonies, operas, and other substantial genres after Haydn's appointment with the Esterházy family, one sees that Haydn was able to contend with as many as three major genres at a time. Before 1773 the total output of works is absolutely staggering. Following the commencement of his duties as opera composer and conductor in 1776, the number of symphonies decreases while string quartets, solo keyboard sonatas, and trios are alternately produced. Perhaps affected by the stimulation and social demands of English life[55] as well as by contractual pressures, the pattern then changes: in the first English period Haydn concentrated on opera, other vocal works, and orchestral music, while in the second he focused more on *Hausmusik*—keyboard trios and sonatas, canons, English canzonettas, and the flute trios. He never wrote symphonies or operas after his last return from London, but devoted himself to quartets, masses, and oratorios—the first for the noble Viennese connoisseurs, the second for Marie Esterházy's name day, and the last for the public at large. Even though only one new keyboard work, Hob. XV:30, was completed after his 1795 return, the documents indicate that Haydn intended to compose more sonatas and trios for Viennese, German, and English publishers.[56] That he did not may have been merely a reflection of the other demands made on his time. These non-keyboard compositions certainly provided an adequate income for the aging composer; perhaps the pragmatic old gentleman held the possibility of new keyboard works as future securities upon which he never needed to draw.

Essay V

THE QUESTION OF KEYBOARD IDIOM

It is known from both tradition and the extant documents that Haydn had access to and probably used the full gamut of keyboard instruments: organ, harpsichord, clavichord, and *fortepiano*. Attempts to establish the way these instruments relate to Haydn's stylistic development and which one is most appropriate for a specific work have resulted in widely divergent conclusions. For example, some commentators believe that Haydn began to compose for the *fortepiano* as early as 1760, while others place this change in the 1760s, 1770s, or even as late as the mid-1780s. Thus, it is necessary to reexamine the question of idiom by combining our knowledge of keyboard instruments and music in Vienna and its environs as well as in London, the available Haydn documents, and the relevant aspects of style as seen in more than one hundred keyboard works.[1]

The instruments under consideration all have individual characteristics. The organ, essentially a wind instrument activated by keys, permits the performer the least flexibility with regard to ornamental dynamics. Of the stringed keyboards, the harpsichord is its closest neighbor in this respect: for both, the performer has control of the large dimension by the use of various stops and registrations. On the other hand, the two differ in their ability to sustain a given sound: on the harpsichord a rapid decay occurs, while on the organ the dynamic level can be sustained at the pleasure of the performer. In addition, very limited dynamic nuances are possible on the harpsichord by the manner in which the keys are struck.[2]

Modeled on Italian designs, Austrian organs and harpsichords were quite different from those commonly used in France and North Germany: the stops were relatively few, a single manual was the norm, and pedals were used sparingly. Thus, music by Austrian composers conceived for these instruments has relatively little to do with present-day concepts of the organ and harpsichord based on the multicoloristic effects of the French and the elaborate pedal parts of the North German schools.

However, one should not ignore the fact that the nobles in Vienna and the wealthy Esterházys were very much taken by French taste in general: it is only necessary to cite the Prince's desire to imitate Versailles in the construction of Esterháza. French music also played a more significant role in the musical life of the Esterházys than has been generally acknowledged.[3] It follows that French harpsichords were probably among those available to Haydn.

Another group is formed by the clavichord and *fortepiano* on which the performer can control dynamics by the weight of touch. In the case of the clavichord, where the string is struck and the contact is maintained as long as the key remains depressed, there are two ways for the performer to affect the nature of the vibration after the sound has begun: the *Bebung*, a vibrato effect indicated by a series of dots covered by a slur over a single pitch; and the *Tragen der Töne* (or portamento), notated with dots covered by a slur (♩♩♩♩) enclosing several notes.[4] The clavichord's dynamic capabilities range from very to moderately soft, which restricted its use to solo performance and the accompaniment of lieder. It is likely that the new *fortepiano* eventually superseded all its stringed keyboard predecessors because it had the harpsichord's power as well as the clavichord's graduated dynamics and *Tragen der Töne*.

Each of these instruments had a defined function within the various institutions and social classes of eighteenth-century society. Although they could all be used for accompaniment of some sort, the situation most appropriate to each instrument was quite different. The harpsichord was used mainly in the theater and court chamber, as its restricted expressive capabilities were especially appropriate to the stylized court opera and chamber music. The organ was "indispensable in church music with its fugues, large choruses, and sustained style"; and as does the institution in which it is housed, "it provides splendor and maintains order."[5] The clavichord was used for music in the home; its mechanical simplicity, low cost, restricted dynamic range, and capabilities of expression rendered it best suited for the environment of middle-class life. It was recommended for the most intimate and deepest expression. The *fortepiano*, on the other hand, available in both a square form and a grand design, was appropriate for both *Hausmusik* and public performance.

While these musical, social, and expressive distinctions may seem clear enough to provide a basis for judging which instruments were intended for specific works, composers and publishers were reluctant to draw these lines too heavily and risk limiting a given work's market. Thus, many title pages allowed the options of either harpsichord or *fortepiano*; *Flügel*, *Cembalo*, *Clavicembalo*, and *Clavecin* generally meant harpsichord but were also used in a generic sense, while *Fortepiano*, *Pianoforte*, and *Hammerflügel* indicated the piano.[6] In addition, *Clavier* could be used as either a generic term for all keyboard instruments (e.g., "Clavier Sonate,") or a specific term for the clavichord (e.g., "Sonate fürs Clavier.")[7] Finally, pieces intended for organ were often not distinguished from others by title, but were simply known as for the *Clavier*, *Cembalo*, etc. Distinguishing organ works by South German, Austrian, and Italian composers from those for the harpsichord in genres common to both instruments, like the concerto, is nearly impossible: the composers seemed to make little or no overt stylistic distinction.

However, range can separate concertos performable on the organ, and therefore plausibly intended for it, from those for harpsichord.[8] As discussed in Essay IV, the range of the stringed keyboards was expanding during the mid-eighteenth century. Older instruments commonly did not go beyond c''', newer ones added d''', e''', and f'''. While it was a relatively simple matter to purchase a new harpsichord, clavichord, or *fortepiano*, or even to have an older one modified, it was a major undertaking to expand the range of an organ, possibly entailing architectural alterations and aesthetic considerations. Therefore, organ works composed in Austria up to the end of the eighteenth century rarely exceeded c'''.[9]

The shift from the harpsichord and organ to the touch-sensitive instruments, particularly the *fortepiano*, is intimately tied to the change of style that took place during the mid-century. Since keyboard instruments were so basic to the musical education of composers and performers, their limitations and capabilities must have had a profound effect on the way the various musical parameters interacted within a particular work. With the touch-sensitive instruments it was possible to achieve certain kinds of rhythmic stress and dynamic nuance that altered the requirements for various other musical components and changed the whole character of the thematic line. Indeed, the generation of composers learning their craft during the mid-century were required to adapt to and adopt not just the new instruments but an entirely new language.[10]

Haydn's Keyboard Instruments

It is unfortunate that there are very few specific descriptions of the keyboards to which Haydn had access during his compositional life. The first keyboard instrument that he came into contact with was probably the organ. If the chapel of the Harrach castle or the parish church in Rohrau had no instrument, there is little doubt that when Haydn went to study with a relative in Hainburg in 1737 or 1738, he must have become acquainted with the organ and perhaps the clavichord. While at the Kapellhaus in Vienna, where he had both lessons and duties as a choirboy, he certainly learned about the various species of keyboard instruments in common use. The first instrument that Haydn himself probably owned was an "old worm-eaten clavier" (a clavichord), which he used while he lived in the attic of the Michaelerhaus; he may very well have lost it or another instrument when his living quarters in the Seilerstätte were robbed sometime between the end of Porpora's Viennese residence (1752–1757) and the Morzin appointment (*ca.* 1759–1761).[11] During the 1750s, when Haydn taught a number of students, accompanied for Porpora, was a temporary resident at several noble estates (Mannersdorf, Weinzierl, and the Morzin residences), and held various positions as an organist, he surely acquired a knowledge that went beyond specific types of instruments to their individual "personalities."

There can be no doubt that as Vice- and full Kapellmeister to the Esterházy family, Haydn had access to a number of different instruments, but for a variety of reasons none of the keyboards used for their chamber and theater performances survive. Fires destroyed the contents of Haydn's home in 1768, when a keyboard is believed to have been a casualty,[12] and again in 1776; the Esterháza theater also burned, and according to the *Pressburger Zeitung* "the beautiful *Flieg* [*sic*] of the famous *Kapellmeister* Haydn" was destroyed;[13] eighteenth-century keyboard instruments were not valued during the nineteenth century, when the modern piano was considered the supreme instrument to the exclusion of all others; Haydn's family had little interest in preserving such items (one of his *fortepiani* reportedly became a feeding and storage bin for grain[14]); and what remained of the Esterházy instruments was pillaged during the last years of World War II. One might expect to find purchase orders, repair bills, and inventories to document the instruments used for chamber and theater. However, these documents seem not to have survived. The same lack of specificity that characterizes Haydn's musical autographs and letters is typical of the various repair bills, which frequently refer to the instruments in local dialects.[15]

There is but a single report of a performance on the *fortepiano* during the 1770s at Esterháza. One G. F. von Rotenstein, who was at the princely residence during the visit of Empress Maria Theresa in 1773, wrote of a concert at which a musician was heard playing a *Piano-forte*.[16] Unfortunately, we know nothing of Rotenstein's ability to distinguish among the keyboard instruments, and Haydn's name is not mentioned in this account.

One must wait until the 1780s for documents concerning specific instruments. Repair bills from the organ builder Anton Walter for work at Esterháza and Haydn's negative comments about Walter's *fortepiani*—"Only one out of ten can be called really good, and besides he is extraordinarily expensive"[17]—have led to the belief that Haydn used one of Walter's instruments. This hypothesis is further supported by the survival of a Walter piano with the number 18, with a direct connection to Eisenstadt, now in the collections of the Burgenländisches Landesmuseum. Whether this instrument was known to Haydn we cannot verify, even though the response and sound of this particular keyboard confirms Haydn's opinion. Haydn himself preferred the instruments made by Schanz, one of which he owned during the late 1780s and another of which was purchased for Frau von Genzinger on Haydn's recommendation: "His *fortepiani* have an unusual lightness and a pleasing action. It is most necessary for Your Grace to have a good *fortepiano*. . . ."[18] The Kunsthistorisches Museum in Vienna owns several keyboards catalogued as having been in the possession of Joseph Haydn. Horst Walter has cast doubt on several of these attributions, including the Schanz *Tafelklavier* (i.e., a square *fortepiano*): the price Haydn paid for his Schanz keyboard was so high that it must have been of the grand design.[19]

Fortunately, it is easier to identify the organs for which Haydn might have composed church music, at least in Eisenstadt, as no fewer than seven still survive: the single-manual organ in the chapel of the Barmherzigen Brüder hospital, built *ca.* 1750–1770; the single-manual instrument in the Franziskanerkirche, built around 1750; the two-manual instrument of the Stadtpfarrkirche (St. Martin's); the small instrument in the chapel of the palace at Eisenstadt, built *ca.* 1800; the old and new instruments of the Bergkirche, the former now in the Haydn-Haus in Eisenstadt and the latter a two-manual one constructed in 1797 by Johann Gottfried Malleck and used for the performances of most of Haydn's late masses; and a small instrument at the Kalvarienberg.

When Haydn arrived in London he was immediately exposed to the products of Johannes Broadwood, the instrument maker to the royal family. He took up residence with Salomon and had a room at the Broadwood firm nearby, presumably furnished with one of its famous *fortepiani*. (According to Gyrowetz, Haydn composed the slow movement of Symphony No. 94 on a square piano, possibly a Broadwood.[20]) From his active social life in the British capital and associations with a number of talented pianists, Haydn also became familiar with instruments produced by Clagget and Stodart, two other important makers then active in London.

Nevertheless, when Haydn returned to Vienna he chose to take an instrument built by Longman & Broderip with a compass "From FF in the bass with the added keys up to c alt." After Haydn's death this instrument came into the possession of his long-time friend the Abbé Maximillian Stadler.[21]

Several other keyboards, acquired after his return from London, are known to have been in Haydn's house in the Vienna suburb of Gumpendorf. One is described in the *Nachlass Verzeichnis* (*HNV*) as "a French piano fitted with mahogany and decorated with metal moulding [with a compass] from low F to high C—five and one half octaves with the usual stops (Veränderungen) by Erard et Frères Compagnie."[22] Haydn acknowledged the arrival from Paris of the Erard *fortepiano* in a letter of 20 May 1801; after noting some damage that occurred during transport, he concluded: "I must pay you the compliment that this *fortepiano*, from its outward as well as inner beauties is the greatest masterpiece of its kind I have ever seen or heard."[23] Although this Erard has not survived, it is presumably similar to the one sent to Beethoven, which is now in the Kunsthistorisches Museum in Vienna.[24] Haydn seems to have owned two other instruments: a *fortepiano*, which he sold on 1 April 1809 (see Plate 1),[25] and the clavichord on which he played "Gott erhalte Franz den Kaiser" during the last months of his life.

Apart from the Eisenstadt organs, the only authenticated extant Haydn instrument is a clavichord built by a comparatively little-known maker, Johann Bohak, in Vienna in 1794. The documents indicate that this keyboard was used in Eisenstadt and was later transmitted through a private English owner, a Miss Chapman, to the collection of the Royal College of Music, in London. Thus, Haydn occasionally used this instrument when he was in residence in Eisenstadt after the reactivation of the Esterházy Kapelle in the mid-1790s.[26] Despite the lack of additional documentation, Haydn probably used a clavichord throughout a good part of his creative life.

The two authentic portraits of Haydn sitting at a keyboard are not reliable indicators of his association with a particular instrument. Although there is no known documentation to prove that the actual keyboards pictured are anything more than a convention, the first of these portraits (Plate 9) was done by Frau Haydn's erstwhile lover, Ludwig Guttenbrunn, who was employed by the Esterházy family until 1772 and was also in London when Haydn arrived there in 1791.[27] Guttenbrunn apparently prepared two versions of the portrait, the second of which—according

PLATE 9. Haydn at the keyboard, by Ludwig Guttenbrunn (early 1770s or 1790s?). (A-Eh)

to Somfai—served as the basis for Schiavonetti's London engraving in 1792. Somfai's first version, if it does date from the early 1770s and if the presence of the keyboard is more than a convention, supports the belief that Haydn had available at a relatively early date a square *fortepiano* of the English type. (The depiction in the portrait of a fairly young man cannot be accepted by itself as documentation for dating since idealization of portraiture to the point of misrepresentation was fairly common at this time.) The second portrait, a Johann Neidl engraving after a painting by Johann Zitterer, was issued by Artaria in two versions in 1800. In one of the versions (see Frontispiece) Haydn is seated at a square keyboard instrument with his left hand on the keys and his right near his face, and the slow movement of the "Surprise" Symphony (No. 94) is on the music rack.[28]

Thus, with regard to the specific keyboard instruments that Haydn owned or had access to, the circumstances of their survival do not parallel his output. While we can identify the organs Haydn knew, he composed relatively little music for that instrument. On the other hand, of the stringed keyboards, for which he wrote numerous works throughout most of his creative life, only one survives and it was used after he had ceased composing for the instrument. To continue the pursuit of the question of idiom for these works, let us then enlarge our scope to the city of Vienna and examine the authentic documentation, as well as the works themselves.

The Fortepiano *in Vienna*

To ascertain the availability and acceptance of the new *fortepiano* by the Viennese keyboardists to whom Haydn's music would have been dedicated or sold, as well as by other composers active in Vienna during Haydn's creative life, the first line of evidence must be the publications offered by Viennese firms and advertised in the *Wienerisches Diarium* until the end of the century. A perusal of this material suggests that the *fortepiano* did not gain sufficient acceptance in eighteenth-century Viennese society to become the first or only choice on title pages of prints. Before 1780, which marks the beginning of music publishing by Artaria, only two *opera* available in Vienna included "*fortepiano*" on their title pages, and then only as a second option: Boccherini's "Six Sonatas for the Harpsichord or Pianoforte with an accomp. for 1 Violin or German Flute, Op. 3," advertised in 1776; and Johann Christian Bach's "6 Concertos pour le Clavecin ou le Pianoforte avec accomp. de 2 Violons & Basse, Op. 4," announced in 1777.[29] Perhaps the most convincing evidence stems from the title page of works by Leopold Koželuch, the most popular keyboard composer of the last quarter of the century in the Imperial city: despite the fact that the *Jahrbuch der Tonkunst 1796* states that "few authors have written so much for the *fortepiano* as he," and Koželuch required his students to play the instrument,[30] the Viennese prints of his keyboard music carry the designation *clavecin* or offer the *fortepiano* as a second choice.[31] Mozart used dynamic signs as early as 1774; the first documentation of his "delight" with Stein's *fortepiano* dates from 1777. His preference for the *fortepiano* after 1781 cannot be questioned. Nevertheless, the title pages of contemporary Viennese publications generally present the option of the *fortepiano* only after the harpsichord; exceptions are a few prints from Hofmeister (e.g., K. 331, 481, and 511) and Artaria's editions of the C-minor Fantasy and Sonata, K. 475 and 457, where the *fortepiano* is listed either first or as the only instrument.[32] As late as 1802 even Beethoven's compositions still carried the harpsichord or *fortepiano* option on their Viennese title pages.[33]

A second line of evidence stems from contemporary reports concerning performances in Vienna. Although we now know that the first public *fortepiano* performance took place in 1763 in the old Burgtheater,[34] it is clear that the instrument did not immediately find favor among the most important resident musicians. When Charles Burney—a reliable witness—visited Vienna in 1772, he wrote in detail about the instruments used. Among others, the Emperor, the Countess Thun, Gluck, Marianna Martines, Hasse, Wagenseil, and Gassmann played the harpsichord; only two other persons played the clavichord—Vanhal and "a child of eight or nine years"; and one the *fortepiano*.[35] One year later, in 1773, we know that Friedrich the Great sent a large *Cembalo* by Shudi to the Empress Maria Theresa: the Prussian king owned *fortepiani* from Silbermann's workshop,[36] yet he sent a harpsichord. Presumably the harpsichord was still the norm.

It was not until 1777 that the Countess Thun, mentioned by Burney, and the powerful Count Johann Rudolf Czernin acquired *fortepiani* made by Stein of Augsburg.[37] In this same year Stein himself made a pilgrimage to Vienna, where his talented daughter performed at court on one of his *fortepiani*.[38] Four years later, in the famous Mozart/Clementi contest, Mozart used the Countess Thun's instrument; Clementi, however, played on a *fortepiano* from the Imperial court that was out of tune and had three sticking keys. That the court instrument was in such poor repair suggests that it was not normally used, and—one might add—since Mozart arranged to have the borrowed Stein instrument present, he must have been well aware of its condition.[39]

There are, however, indications that by the middle of the century the more touch-sensitive instruments, the *fortepiano* and the clavichord, were favored by some composers affiliated with the court. Although none of the surviving musical manuscripts used by the Imperial family containing music by Wagenseil, Birck, Steffan, Leopold Hofmann, and others contain dynamic markings or other touch-sensitive indications, works by Birck and Steffan distributed outside the court circle require dynamic shadings. In 1757 Wenzel Raimond Birck (1718–1763) published his *Trattenimenti per Clavicembalo*,[40] which demands not only fortes and pianos but also contains the expressive indications amabile, crescendo, cantabile, and dolce. In some contexts the dynamics are strictly registrational and therefore easily negotiable on the harpsichord, while others suggest the necessity of a touch-sensitive instrument. Although this date seems early for the *fortepiano*, at the very least these pieces were conceived for the clavichord. If so, this publication is the only known verifiable print of music for North Germany's favorite instrument from a composer at the Viennese court (Example V-1).

Birck's younger contemporary Joseph Anton Steffan was, apart from Mozart and Haydn, the earliest and most effective composer for the *fortepiano* in Vienna. While his first two published *opere* follow to some extent the harpsichord style found in the works of his teacher Georg Christoph Wagenseil, his Op. 3, published

EXAMPLE V–1. Birck. *Trattenimenti*, mm. 13–26.

EXAMPLE V–2. Steffan. Capriccio 3 (Šetková 49; A-Wgm), mm. 35–43.

in two parts *ca.* 1763,[41] requires sforzando in addition to forte, piano, and dolce. As in the Birck *Trattenimenti*, many of these dynamic markings are registrational, but others could only indicate the clavichord or the *fortepiano*. In some of Steffan's later works there can be no question of his interest in the *fortepiano*, since some solo keyboard compositions and concertos explicitly indicate on the title page "per il Forte Piano," "Forte e Piano," "Clavi Cembalo d'espressione," or "Cembalo di Forte Piano."[42] Among the most idiomatic of these works (i.e., requiring techniques not possible on the harpsichord) are the *Capricci*, which survive in a copy at the Gesellschaft der Musikfreunde.[43] Unfortunately, none can be dated with any precision, but it seems that many of them originated during the 1780s (see Example V-2).[44]

A final line of evidence has to do with our knowledge of the Viennese artisans who built these instruments. Once again we are plagued by the inability to date their activities precisely. Although by the late 1770s instruments by Stein of Augsburg had been ordered by residents of the Imperial city, Stein's firm did not move there from Bavaria until 1794.[45] Haydn's correspondence indicates his awareness during the 1780s of the workmanship of both Wenzel Schanz and Anton Walter, who together with the Stein/Streicher firm were apparently for the Viennese the most important producers of *fortepiani*. However, the Esterházy documents reveal that Anton Walter also maintained, repaired, and rebuilt all types of keyboards;[46] the demand for the *fortepiano* apparently did not take up the bulk of his time.

Just as it can be said that the Viennese *fortepiani* as a group have a more delicate action and intimate tone quality than their more powerful English counterparts, one commentator—presumably J. A. Schonfeld—published a comparative description of the *fortepiani* by Walter, Schanz, and Stein/Streicher:

> The one artist who has become the most famous so far (and who, in fact, was the first creator of these instruments here) is Herr Walter. . . . His *Fortepiani* speak clearly with a full, bell-like tone and a strong, resonant bass. At first the sound is somewhat dull; but when it is played for a while, it becomes very clear—especially in the treble. However, if it is played a great deal, the sound becomes harsh and steely; nonetheless, this can be remedied by releathering the hammers. The instruments of this master often suffer a flaw, which must be watched for when selecting one: the treble and bass are not always evenly balanced. In some the bass is too thick for the treble; in others, too strong; and in still others, too harsh. . . . The second master of good repute is Herr Schanz. . . . [The] sound [of his instruments] is not as strong as . . . Walter's instruments, but it is just as clear and for the most part, more pleasing. They also have a lighter action because the keys have a shorter fall and are not so wide. Actually, they are almost copies of the *Fortepiano* made by the Augsburg artist, Stein. This master also makes many smaller *Fortepiani* in the English shape [square], which are easily played and have a rather big sound. . . . The third great master, or rather mistress, is Madame Streicher. . . . Her instruments do not have the strength of Walter's, but in evenness of sound, clarity, and a gentle sweetness that seems to float, they are matchless. The sounds blend together; the action needs a light touch, resilient fingers, and a sensitive heart. . . . Generally speaking, it is clear that we have, as it were, two original instrument makers,

namely, Walter and Streicher, and that the rest imitate either the one or the other. Many especially copy Walter because they come from his school.

Inasmuch as there are two original instrument makers, we divide our instruments into two types: the Walter and Streicher varieties. Likewise, we seem to have two types of great pianists. One of these loves to treat the ears to a powerful clamor. So, they play with a full sound and extraordinary speed; they practice the fastest scales and octaves. All this demands strength and composure. In accomplishing this they do not have enough control to maintain a certain moderation, and so they need a *Fortepiano* that will not snap. For this kind of virtuoso we recommend the Walter *Fortepiano*. The other type of great pianist seeks nourishment for the soul and loves not only clear but also soft, sweet playing. These pianists can choose no better instrument than a Streicher, or the so-called Stein variety. Virtuosos who fall between these two types will also have no trouble finding a good instrument whatever their taste.[47]

Haydn's Keyboard Terminology

Central to any discussion of idiom is the examination of the titles of the keyboard works in existing autographs as well as in authentic copies, prints, and catalogues (see Table V-1). In the entries in the *Entwurf-Katalog (EK)*, on p. 20 (see Plate 2) the terms "Cembalo" and "Clavicembalo" both appear, while p. 21 has the term "Cembalo" exclusively, p. 22 "Clavicembalo," and p. 23 "Cembalo." The distinction between "Cembalo" and "Clavicembalo" here is apparently of limited, if any, significance. In the first place, the terms seem to be used interchangeably, and variances occur between authentic sources for the same work; e.g., for Hob. XVI:45 *EK* uses "Cembalo" while the autograph designates "Clavi Cembalo." Second, although many of the sonatas and divertimentos were distributed in sets of three or six, *EK* only allows five works per page. Since the sonata at the top of *EK* 22 was probably composed about the same time and distributed with that at the bottom of *EK* 21, one might expect *EK* to have the same terminology, but that is not the case.

The autographs themselves do not enlighten us appreciably. For the three earliest works (before and *ca.* 1760), Haydn inscribed "per il Organo" on Hob. XVIII: 1, "Cembalo" on Hob. XIV: 11, and "Clavicembalo" on Hob. XVI: 6. During the 1760s he continued to use "Clavicembalo" or its shortened form "Cembalo." For the following decade and through most of the 1780s, these terms were still employed—even for the C-minor Sonata Hob. XVI: 20, which has a number of dynamic and expressive markings. It is not until the E-flat major Sonata Hob. XVI: 49 of 1789–1790 that Haydn writes for the first time "Forte-piano" on the title page of the autograph. However, this occurrence should not be taken as a "watershed," for Haydn later reverted to less-precise designations.

The authorized prints of the solo sonatas and trios indicate *fortepiano* or its equivalent somewhat earlier than the autograph of Hob. XVI: 49. The first presumably authentic print of the so-called Esterházy Sonatas Hob. XVI: 21–26, published by Kurzböck in 1774, allows for only the harpsichord on the title page, but the 1780 print of the Auenbrugger Sonatas Hob. XVI: 35–39, 20 consists of works "per il Clavicembalo o Forte Piano," the preferred designation for

TABLE V-1

Authentic Evidence of Keyboard Terminology
(correspondence excluded)

Work by Hob. *Gruppe*	*Entwurf-Katalog*	Autograph	Authentic copy (Hob. XIV–XVII) or *HV* * (Hob. XVIII)	Authorized print
Hob. XIV:1	Cembalo			
Hob. XIV:2	Cembalo			
Hob. XIV:4	Cembalo	Cembalo		
Hob. XIV:7			Clavicembalo	
Hob. XIV:8			Clavicembalo	
Hob. XIV:9			Clavicembalo	
Hob. XIV:10			Clavicembalo	
Hob. XIV:11		Cembalo		
Hob. XV:2	(Cembalo)		Cembalo	
Hob. XV:5			Clavi Cembalo	Harpsichord or Piano Forte
Hob. XV:6–8				Clauecin [*sic*] ou Piano-Forte
Hob. XV:9	Cembalo (*ca.* 1800)		Clavecin o piano forte	Harpsichord or Piano Forte
Hob. XV:10				Harpsichord or Piano Forte
Hob. XV:11–13				Clavicembalo o Forte-Piano
Hob. XV:14				Clavecin ou Piano-Forte
Hob. XV:15–16				Forte Piano, ou Clavecin
Hob. XV:17				Forte-Piano ou Clavecin
Hob. XV:18–20				Piano-Forte
Hob. XV:21–23				Piano Forte
Hob. XV:24–26				Piano Forte
Hob. XV:27–29				Piano-Forte
Hob. XV:30				Clavecin ou Piano-Forte
Hob. XV:31				Piano Forte
Hob. XV:32				Piano-Forte
Hob. XV:35			Clavicembalo	
Hob. XVI:2a–e, g, h	Cembalo and Clavicembalo			
Hob. XVI:3	Clavicembalo			
Hob. XVI:4	Clavicembalo			
Hob. XVI:6	Cembalo	Clavicembalo		
Hob. XIV:5 (XVI:5a)	Cembalo			
Hob. XVI:14	Cembalo			
Hob. XVI:19	Cembalo			
Hob. XVI:20		Clavi Cembalo		
Hob. XVI:21–26		Cembalo		Clavi-Cembalo
Hob. XVI:27–32		29. Clavicembalo		
Hob. XVI:35–39, 20				Clavicembalo, o Forte Piano
Hob. XVI:40–42				Pianoforte
Hob. XVI:45	Cembalo			
Hob. XVI:46	Cembalo			
Hob. XVI:48				
Hob. XVI:49		Forte-piano		
Hob. XVI:50				Piano Forte
Hob. XVI:51				
Hob. XVI:52				Clavecin ou Piano-Forte

TABLE V-1 *(continued)*

Work by Hob. *Gruppe*	*Entwurf-Katalog*	Autograph	Authentic copy (Hob. XIV–XVII) or *HV** (Hob. XVIII)	Authorized print
Hob. XVII:2	Cembalo			
Hob. XVII:4				Clavicembalo o Forte-Piano
Hob. XVII:5				Clavecin ou Piano Forte
Hob. XVII:6			Piano Forte	Clavecin ou Piano-Forte
Hob. XVIIa:1	Clavicembalo			Clavicembalo o Piano Forte
Hob. XVIII:1	Clavicembalo	Organo	Organo	
Hob. XVIII:2	Clavicembalo		Clavicembalo	
Hob. XVIII:3	Clavicembalo		Clavicembalo	
Hob. XVIII:4			Clavicembalo	
Hob. XVIII:5	(Organo)			
Hob. XVIII:6	Cembalo			
Hob. XVIII:8	(Organo)			
Hob. XVIII:10	(Organo)			
Hob. XVIII:11				Clavicembalo ó Fortepiano

* The *Haydn Verzeichnis* (*HV*), which derives from *Oeuvres complettes* and *EK*, applies only to the concertos.

Artaria's prints. Hob. XVIII:11, the only concerto to receive a possibly authorized print (1784), also follows Artaria's general practice. The three sonatas for Marie Esterházy, Hob. XVI:40–42, as published by Bossler also in 1784, specify the "Fortepiano."

In the case of the authentic prints of the trios, the first edition (1785) by Forster of Hob. XV:5 together with Hob. XV:3 and 4 allows the option of "Harpsichord or Piano Forte." This designation or its equivalent is found consistently in prints until about 1790, when John Bland published Hob. XV:16 and 15 with "Forte Piano" as the first option, before the harpsichord; however, since these two works probably belonged to the series of *Le Tout Ensemble*, the inscription must not be taken at face value. Although the Viennese publications of Haydn's trios continued to offer an option, by 1794 the English prints began to use only *fortepiano* or its equivalent. The first Viennese print to use "Piano-forte" alone for a Haydn trio (Hob. XV:31) was that issued by Traeg in 1803.

In Haydn's correspondence a keyboard instrument is referred to only once with regard to a performance: the famous letter concerning the 1768 "Applausus" cantata mentions the expected practice of using the cembalo ("Cembalisten"). However, there are numerous letters to publishers beginning in 1780[48] in which Haydn refers to specific keyboard works. Although these references do not have the same authority as the catalogue entries, autographs, and authentic copies, certain conclusions can be derived from them, as seen in Table V-2. First, Haydn uses the term *Clavier* in a generic sense. Second, used as an adjective, "Clavier" seems to have been associated with multimovement musical genres. Even in the famous letter to Artaria of 26 October 1788, "Clavier Sonaten" is employed in conjunction with the request to purchase a new Schanz *fortepiano* in order to compose them. Only in

TABLE V-2

Keyboard Terminology Found in Haydn's Correspondence

Date of Letter	Publisher	Work	Haydn's Terminology
31 January 1780	Artaria	Hob. XVI:20?	Clavier Sonate
ca. 25 July 1782	Artaria	Hob. XV:?	Clavier Sonaten
10 December 1785	Artaria	Hob. XV:6–8	Clavier Sonaten
1786	Forster	Hob. XV:3–5, 9, 2, 10	Clavecin
8 April 1787	Forster	Hob. XVIII:11	Clavier Concert
	Forster	Hob. XIV:7–9?	3 kleine Clavier Divertimenten
	Forster	Hob. XVI:34?	Sonate fürs Clavier
21 June 1787	Artaria	Seven Words	Clavier Auszug
23 June 1787	Artaria	Seven Words	Clavierauszug
2 August 1787	Artaria	Seven Words	Clavierauszug
10, 17 August 1788	Artaria	Hob. XV:11–13	Clavier Sonaten
26 October 1788	Artaria	Hob. XV:11–13	3 Clavier Sonaten . . . ein neues Fortepiano
8 March 1789	Breitkopf	Hob. XVI:48?	Clavier Sonaten
29 March 1789	Artaria	Hob. XVII:4	fortepiano
5 April 1789	Breitkopf	Hob. XVI:48?	Clavier Sonaten
5 April 1789	Sieber	?	Clavier Sonaten
5 July 1789	Artaria	Seven Words	Clavier Auszug
11 January 1790	Bland	Hob. XV:14–16?	Clavier Sonaten
22 November 1790	Artaria	Hob. XVII:5	Forte piano
9 November 1796	Breitkopf	Hob. XV:30	Clavier Sonate
1 July 1800	Breitkopf	?	Clavier Sonaten

one case does Haydn use a variant of "Clavier Sonaten": the citation "Sonate fürs Clavier," which may signal Hob. XVI:34 or one other work to be for the clavichord.[49]

The correspondence also contains an important letter written to Marianna von Genzinger concerning the E-flat major Sonata Hob. XVI:49. For this work we need not rely on secondary sources, and the authentic evidence is consistent: both the correspondence and the title page of the autograph explicitly state *fortepiano*. Furthermore, Hob. XVI:49 is more than a work for any *fortepiano*; it was composed for an instrument by a specific maker, Wenzel Schanz.[50]

The previous sections surveying the external evidence for the character of the various keyboard instruments, the instruments Haydn knew, and Haydn's terminology have only outlined the complications that surround the selection of the proper instrument for the performance of Haydn's keyboard music. Since the documents speak against the conclusion that some kind of decisive "turning point" occurred, the best conclusion one can draw is that Haydn was well aware of the attributes of the available keyboard instruments and that at times he composed with one or more in mind. In turning to the works themselves, let us pose two different but related questions: Which works did Haydn compose with touch-sensitive instruments in mind? In which works did he begin to realize most fully the character of the different instruments?

Dynamic Markings and Tragen der Töne

The first question is best dealt with through identifying the presence in Haydn's keyboard works of dynamic markings and the aforementioned *Tragen der Töne*, both of which can only be fully achieved on touch-sensitive instruments. Yet not even the presence of dynamic markings means that a touch-sensitive instrument is an absolute requirement, as dynamic effects can be achieved by judicious changes in texture, sonority, harmony, and ornamentation. Indeed, in a number of Haydn's works from the 1770s where authentic dynamic indications are first present, they are underlined by some of the same techniques that would attain like effects on the instruments without marked touch sensitivity; this differentiation aids in explaining the logic behind title pages that indicate the two types of instruments. Thus, we have two classes of dynamic markings: those whose effect could be achieved by their context on a touch-insensitive instrument, and those achievable only on a touch-sensitive instrument.

The following types of dynamic markings in Haydn's keyboard works fall into the first category: sforzando on a dissonance; sforzando with an ornament; dynamic coordinated with complementary changes in texture or sonority; dynamic doubled by or present only in an accompanying voice; and crescendo in an accompanying part in a passage of active rhythmic acceleration. On the other hand, dynamic markings not realizable from their musical context are of the following types: dynamic intensification with the thinning of sonority and the reverse; dynamic change with no change in texture; sforzando or dynamic without dissonance; ornament followed by sforzando; crescendo with other elements relatively static; and more refined indications such as mezza voce, calando, perdendosi, etc.

With these classifications in mind, let us now examine the keyboard works in which dynamic markings and *Tragen der Töne* indications appear in order to establish which keyboard works were composed by Haydn with touch-sensitive instruments in mind. For this discussion, only authentic and other highly regarded sources will be used.

The earliest appearance of dynamic markings was in the initial movements of solo sonatas from just before or during the first half of the 1770s. In these works Haydn often used dynamic markings only in the sonata-form movements and dispensed with them in such sectionally oriented structures as rondos and variation sets. Perhaps the earliest markings are to be found in Hob. XVI:46/1 and 18/1. In the latter, dynamics occur in the middle section of the exposition and in the retransition. A touch-sensitive instrument seems required for the musical continuity of the first instance and for the counteractivity of texture and dynamics of the second; i.e., as the dynamics increase, the number of voices remains the same or decreases (Example V-3).

Although Hob. XVI:18 cannot be dated precisely, the autograph of the frequently discussed Hob. XVI:20 gives us a potential starting date of 1771. Whether we adhere to the autograph or to the authentic Artaria edition of 1780 (see Plates 10 and 11), there is no question that the dynamic markings require a touch-sensitive instrument. A comparison of the exposition of the first movement

EXAMPLE V–3. Hob. XVI: 18/1, mm. 12–17, 69–75.

in the autograph and in the authentic first edition of Hob. XVI: 20 from nine years later provides a picture of Haydn's changing use of dynamics. The forte added to the first edition in m. 9 only confirms, as does the piano in m. 10, a dynamic already implied by the texture. The famous alternating forte and piano in m. 14 of both the autograph and the print does not lose its total effect on a harpsichord because of the motion of the melodic line—ascending for forte and descending for piano—and the possibility of a slightly more pronounced attack achievable on the harpsichord for the forte pitches. Yet in the second part of the transition in both the exposition (mm. 20–26) and recapitulation the harpsichord is no longer a possible alternative, since the forte and piano, as in Hob. XVI: 18, operate "counter to" the sonorities. Furthermore, in the first edition a pianissimo is added to mm. 76 and 87, and a fortissimo to m. 92, requiring more than two levels of shading. Thus, in terms of the dynamic effects required, the 1771 autograph of the C-minor Sonata does not represent an advance over Hob. XVI: 18, except that the shadings are more numerous and are used at a smaller dimension. However, with the 1780 edition the necessity of a touch-sensitive instrument is intensified.

Dynamic markings also are found in the E-flat major Variations Hob. XVII: 3 from *ca.* 1770–before 1774. However, they seem to have been taken from the original theme as found in the String Quartet Op. 9/2/3, as the variations themselves contain no shadings. Composed about the same time are the six sonatas for Nikolaus Esterházy, Hob. XVI: 21–26, which contain but a single dynamic marking, a forte in the autograph of Hob. XVI: 22/1. Its placement in m. 41, one measure before the recapitulation, is not musically convincing.

PLATE 10. The first two pages of the autograph for Hob.
XVI:20/1. (F-Pn)

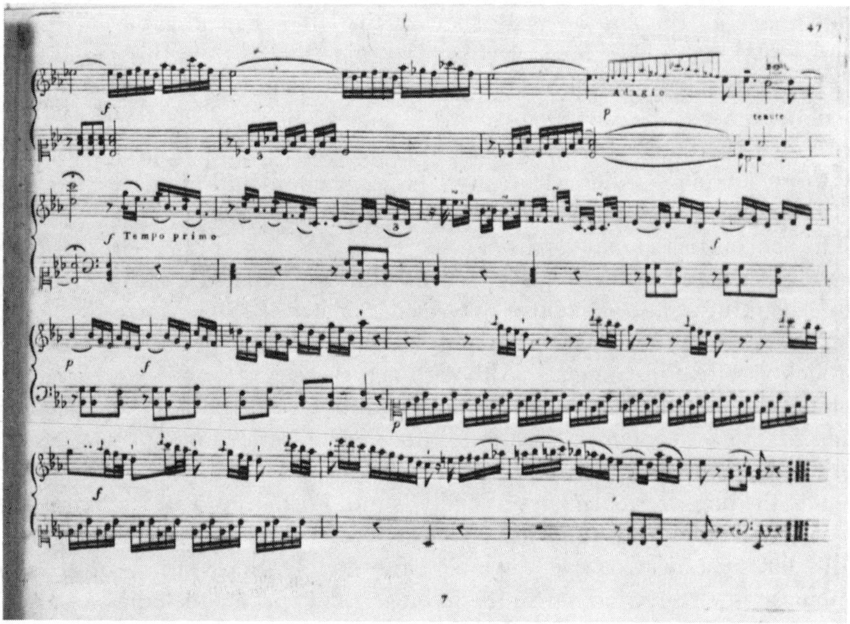

PLATE 11. The first two pages of the authentic edition by Artaria of Hob. XVI:20/1. (Author's collection)

As distributed in presumably authentic Viennese copies, Hob. XVI:27–32 also contain dynamic markings in only one sonata, that in F major Hob. XVI:29 composed in 1774 (see Example V-18). Unfortunately, the autograph lacks dynamics, and the copies themselves are inconsistent in their placement. Nevertheless, an important conclusion can be drawn from this example: it is the first source to make extensive use of dynamics in contexts that do not allow other musical elements to compensate for touch. Measure 10 brings to mind m. 14 of Hob. XVI:20: forte and piano alternate and are coordinated with a rising eighth-note passage. However, in the 1774 example these dynamics are not supported by the texture but operate in contradiction to it: the fortes apply to a single sound while the pianos are written for a triple simultaneity. On the other hand, the dynamic changes in mm. 21–23 are unlike anything seen previously in a Haydn keyboard work; in fact, a "crescendo" appears only twice in other sonatas from this decade—once in the E-flat major Auenbrugger Sonata Hob. XVI:38 and once in the D-major Esterházy Sonata Hob. XVI:42—and is not encountered again until the late 1780s, although both "calando" and "perdendosi" are used in the meantime. In these measures of Hob. XVI:29, the crescendo depends strictly on touch, as every other element remains constant.

Of the Auenbrugger Sonatas Hob. XVI:35–39, 20 published in 1780, all except Hob. XVI:37 contain dynamic markings. Viewed as a set, however, these sonatas "per il Clavicembalo o Forte Piano" must have represented in their use of dynamics a publisher's ideal: some are more suitable for the harpsichord, some more suitable for the *fortepiano*. But few of the latter depend so heavily on their dynamic markings for the total effect as to exclude the set from the sizable market of harpsichord owners as, for example, the late works for London very well might have done. Indeed, one cannot cite many instances where the effect of the dynamics could not be felt either from the musical context or by careful preparation, e.g., shortening a note preceding a sforzando. Here dynamic indications are fairly common in movements not in sonata form.

The sonatas that are not a part of a set (Hob. XVI:33, 43, 34) present no new dynamic effects; they seem less progressive with regard to idiom than some of those in the Auenbrugger set. The three Esterházy Sonatas of 1784, Hob. XVI:40–42, like Hob. XVI:29, mark another important turning point in Haydn's writing for the touch-sensitive instruments. Although the Bossler print of these sonatas—in all probability an authentic one—is unclear in its placement and interpretation of dynamics, the set contains a greater number of indications irrespective of movement form, requires the use of accents (fz) within the context of a soft level, and demands shadings from pianissimo to fortissimo. Furthermore, it can immediately be seen that the sforzandos and ornaments are used outside of the contexts expected for the harpsichord (Example V-4): e.g., the double graces in m. 19 are purely harmonic in their function, while the following fz is purely melodic and does not affect the integrity of the barline. Indeed, one receives the distinct impression that the solo works with the detailed indications, as in Hob. XVI:20, 29, and 40–42, were compositions for specific touch-sensitive instruments and performers.

The two concertos composed perhaps during the 1770s, Hob. XVIII:4 and

EXAMPLE V−4. Hob. XVI:40/1, mm. 12−24.

EXAMPLE V−5. Hob. XVIII:4/2, mm. 21−28.

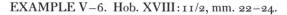

EXAMPLE V−6. Hob. XVIII:11/2, mm. 22−24.

11, do contain dynamic indications in the early sources but just in isolated passages: for example, Hob. XVIII:4 contains sforzandos in the slow movement of the Boyer print and one of the Kroměříž copies (Example V-5). Nevertheless, these dynamics do not require a *fortepiano*: in Hob. XVIII:4 the impact of the intervals themselves provides the sforzando, while in Hob. XVIII:11 (Example V-6) the dissonance has the same effect.

About the same time that the prints of the Esterházy Sonatas and the two concertos appeared, Haydn returned to the composition of keyboard trios. The dynamics in the keyboard parts of these new trios do not continue in the style of Hob. XVI:40–42, but more closely approximate the solo works of the 1770s. However, this difference is partially compensated for by the dynamic capabilities of the violin or flute and cello: at times a dynamic marking occurs in one of the accompanying parts but is absent in the keyboard.

In the first of these trios, Hob. XV:5 (Example V-7), the implied forte and the ensuing piano in the initial measures are underlined also by the texture and the tutti/solo effects. The fz of the third measure, although within the context of piano, is achievable on the harpsichord because of the quick arpeggiated approach to a''. The remainder of the movement has no shadings. The second movement of Hob. XV:5 (Example V-8) continues to use dynamics in a manner still effective on the harpsichord; perhaps the fact that in m. 47 dynamics appear for the violin only speaks for the possibility that the accompanying instruments provide dynamic color for the monochromatic harpsichord, an interpretation supported by the increase of sonority and the more closed position in the keyboard part. Throughout this entire movement, only two measures (mm. 33 and 69) lose their effectiveness on the harpsichord. The same ambivalence of idiom is seen in the series Hob. XV:6–9.

The next set of three trios, Hob. XV:11–13, should represent a significant change in style: Haydn wrote to Artaria that he needed a new Schanz *fortepiano* to compose them. Yet they contain little convincing evidence that the arrival of the new instrument affected Haydn's compositions as profoundly as might be expected. Their innovations with regard to dynamics are as follows: In Hob. XV:11/1 (Example V-9), the strings enter with a piano dynamic in m. 64 not to support a new dynamic level but to color an existing one; and in mm. 67–68 combined changes in dynamics, sonority, and texture occur. In the opening measures of Hob. XV:12/1 (Example V-10) the strings are piano while the keyboard continues forte. And in

EXAMPLE V–7. Hob. XV:5/1, mm. 1–3.

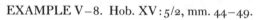

EXAMPLE V–8. Hob. XV: 5/2, mm. 44–49.

EXAMPLE V–9. Hob. XV: 11/1, mm. 60–70.

EXAMPLE V–10. Hob. XV:12/1, mm. 1–7.

EXAMPLE V–11. Hob. XV:13/2, mm. 255–59.

the final measures of Hob. XV:13/2 (Example V-11) piano and forte quickly alternate, but the sonorities remain constant. All these excerpts are best realized with a *fortepiano*. Perhaps the most immediate clue to their conception for a new type of instrument is the use of pizzicato in the accompaniment of Hob. XV:12/2: with the harpsichord this color would be redundant as the plucking of strings in the accompaniment would lend only a new shade to the same effect, whereas with the *fortepiano* it provides a more percussive articulation.[51]

Beginning with Hob. XV:14, published in 1790, the shadings begin to approximate that of the 1784 solo sonatas in detail although not in scope. At the very beginning of the Rondo finale (Example V-12), the combined effect of downbeat with the written-out Haydn ornament (m. 2) followed by an accented syncopation on the second eighth is nearly the antithesis of instruments that are not touch-sensitive in that the downbeat is melodically stressed without support, followed by the fz with bass support. This passage requires four different levels of stress for the first four eighth notes of the movement, effects most easily achievable on a touch-sensitive instrument like Haydn's new Schanz *fortepiano*.

EXAMPLE V–12. Hob. XV:14/3, mm. 1–4.

During the late 1780s Haydn's writing for a touch-sensitive keyboard peaked in three solo works: the C-major and E-flat major Sonatas Hob. XVI:48 and 49 and the Fantasia in C major Hob. XVII:4. The Fantasia, although it does not contain markings as detailed as those in the C-major Sonata, requires touch sensitivity not only to fulfill the dynamic indications but also to underline its middle- and small-dimension structure. Passages such as the one beginning in m.88 (Example V-13) require levels of accentuation to delineate the profile of figuration both within the measure as well as within groups of three, six, and twelve measures. In addition, the subito pianissimo of m. 116, the hand-crossing passage requiring one hand to change dynamics while the other remains constant, and the instruction "tenuto, intanto, finiché non si sente più il suono" (mm. 192 and 302) all point to the *forte-piano* or clavichord (Example V-14).

Of the two sonatas, the one in C major contains the most explicit and the greatest variety of markings in any work dating from before Haydn's journeys to England. Most striking in the first movement is the total independence of dynamics from other previously dynamic-forming elements; i.e., the diminuendo in m. 2 on a rising pitch; the piano in m. 9 followed by a pianissimo in m. 10 with a roll-device, which on the harpsichord would be used for accentuation; and the pianissimo in m. 22, which occurs in the most tensive moment of the entire opening thematic statement (see Example X-43). The markings in the E-flat major Sonata, as in many of the earlier works, are less explicit. This contrast in treatment is perhaps explained by the circumstances of composition: the E-flat major Sonata was written for a keyboardist with whom Haydn had close contact—"There is much in [the Adagio] that I will point out to Your Grace . . ."—while the C-major Sonata was part of a commission from Breitkopf. In the latter case Haydn was writing for the unknown connoisseur, who perhaps needed direction in the new type of expression, for it too is "somewhat difficult but full of feeling."[52]

Although the *Liebhaber* Variations in C major Hob. XVII:5 from 1790 have no dynamics at all, the masterly F-minor Variations Hob. XVII:6 of 1793 takes up the progression toward works requiring extreme touch sensitivity. The indications found in both the autograph and the authentic copies provide a virtual summary of

EXAMPLE V–13. Hob. XVII:4, mm. 88–114.

EXAMPLE V–14. Hob. XVII:4, mm. 115–31, 191–98.

Haydn's repertoire by the year 1793: tenute, mezza voce, cresc., $>$, $\mathcal{>}$, piano, forte, fz, $<$, ff, pp, and forte e tenuto.

The gulf noted above between the number and type of dynamic indications in the trios as opposed to the solo works holds true for those composed in London. The touch-sensitive aspects of Haydn's last three solo sonatas support the hypothesis that they were written for different instruments or performers: the type and number of dynamics in Hob. XVI:51 clearly set it apart from Hob. XVI:52 and 50, which are remarkable for the way in which they consistently combine dynamics and sonority for the grandest effects. The only completely new dynamic effect occurs in Hob. XVI:50, in which a passage for the open pedal commences a long crescendo (Example V-15).

A second characteristic of touch-sensitive keyboard instruments is the notation of the *Bebung* and *Tragen der Töne*. Although there is no example of the *Bebung* in Haydn's keyboard works, the *Tragen der Töne* is used sparingly beginning in the 1770s, becomes more prominent during the 1780s, and is found with relative frequency after 1790, a situation parallel to the usage of dynamic markings. Its presence in both keyboard trios and solo works, including Hob. XVI:49 ("per il Forte piano"), rules out Haydn's use of the articulation exclusively for the clavichord; it is merely indicative of a touch-sensitive instrument.

Tragen der Töne appears first in the Variations in E-flat major Hob. XVII:3, composed *ca.* 1770 but before 1774; however, like the dynamics, its use is confined to the theme and derives from the bowings of the string quartet version. Perhaps of greater import is the use of this device in Hob. XVI:24/2, 38/1, and possibly 32/1, all sonatas from the 1770s. During the 1780s and 1790s the *Tragen der Töne* is

EXAMPLE V−15. Hob. XVI:50/1, mm. 120−24.

EXAMPLE V−16. Hob. XVII:6, mm. 50−51.

used with the same lack of consistency seen in the 1770s. In Hob. XVII:6 from 1793 Haydn even notated it with a rest between each pitch (Example V-16).

Realization of Idiomatic Styles

The second question posed goes beyond the problem of touch sensitivity: in which works did Haydn begin to realize the potentialities and limitations of the various keyboard instruments? The answer, of course, can only be speculative. The hypothesis offered here is that the realization of any one style also affects the opposite polarity. Thus, when Haydn became conscious of the special qualities of one keyboard, the potentialities and limitations of the others probably came into sharper focus.

Haydn's concertos for organ do not seem to develop in the same way as those for the stringed keyboards. A comparison of those works for organ that do not exceed c''' (Hob. XVIII: 1, 2, 5, 6, 8, and 10)[53] with those for harpsichord or *forte-piano* that do (Hob. XVIII:3, 4, and 11) reveals that the latter have a more active surface rhythm. This difference in rhythmic activity—which may well emanate from differences in the instruments' attack and release of sound—is especially evident when comparing the secular works for obbligato cembalo and voices from the 1760s—the two Esterházy (Hob. XXIVa:3–4) and the "Applausus" (Hob. XXIVa:6) cantatas—with the two liturgical works with obbligato organ from the 1770s. Registration markings are known to exist only in the Rajhrad copy of Hob. XVIII:5.

Haydn's earliest solo sonatas (before 1766) seem to be the most neutral in terms of instrument but are probably in the main for the harpsichord. Although Haydn had the readiest access to a clavichord when writing his very earliest solo compositions, it cannot be accepted as the first choice: 1. No pervading stylistic distinction with regard to instrument can be found between the ensemble pieces (i.e., trios, accompanied divertimentos, and concertinos) and the solo pieces; since the former were without question composed for the harpsichord, the latter are probably for the same instrument. 2. Since Haydn's early solo divertimentos seem to be modeled on the type of keyboard sonata composed and distributed in Vienna during the 1750s and early 1760s, works that appear to have been written for the harpsichord, it follows that Haydn's were also for this instrument.[54] 3. In his autobiographical sketch Haydn states that he learned the true fundamentals of *Setzkunst* from Porpora; since most of the keyboard works are highly skillful and stylistically homogeneous, they were most likely for the type of instrument Porpora presumably used, an Italian harpsichord. 4. Not a single Haydn source contains the notation for the *Bebung*, the only explicit and exclusive indication for the clavichord.

During the 1760s Haydn also came into contact with new keyboards that had additional keys and the short octave. The original version of Hob. XVI:47, the Variations in A major Hob. XVII:2, "Il maestro e lo scolare" Hob. XVIIa:1, and the Sauschneider Capriccio Hob. XVII:1 (1765) all have stretches for the left hand that can be negotiated only with the short octave;[55] there is no internal evidence from these works of the 1760s to lead one to believe that the instrument was a *fortepiano*. The fact that f''' appeared in several works from the late 1760s suggests that Haydn may have secured a new instrument after his house burned in August 1768.

The highly expressive solo keyboard compositions with dynamic markings from the late 1760s and early 1770s seem most appropriate for the clavichord, especially since the *fortepiano* was not greatly cultivated in Vienna until around 1780.

The intense character of these works—especially the great C-minor Sonata Hob. XVI: 20—also points to the clavichord tradition; since the *fortepiano* did not achieve a reputation as a "lonely, melancholy, inexpressibly sweet instrument,"[56] it is almost certain that these sonatas were composed for the clavichord. Larsen's statement that the C-minor Sonata was much too modern to have been written for the clavichord cannot be accepted:[57] this idea seems to result from viewing history by moving backward in time from the period of full development of the *fortepiano* style. Since dynamics have always been relative rather than absolute indications, the dynamic range in the C-minor Sonata must not be taken to mean anything approaching modern levels of volume; one of the most famous and idiomatic works for the clavichord, C. P. E. Bach's "Abschied vom Silbermannschen Clavier," also has a notated dynamic range from pianissimo to fortissimo.

Although in terms of their overall style, most of the remaining solo sonatas up

EXAMPLE V–17. Hob. XVI:26/1, mm. 1–29.

EXAMPLE V–17 (*continued*)

EXAMPLE V–18. Hob. XVI:29/1, mm. 1–31.

EXAMPLE V–18 (*continued*)

to the mid-1770s are probably for the harpsichord, there is a significant movement toward idiomatic realization in these works. By way of example, the exposition of Hob. XVI:26/1 from 1773 (Example V-17) typifies the crystallization of a style appropriate for a harpsichord with limited coloristic possibilities, while that of its chronological neighbor, Hob. XVI:29/1 from 1774 (Example V-18), exhibits a *fortepiano* style. In the later work, dynamics are present in a reliable source, suggesting that it was conceived for a touch-sensitive instrument if not for the *fortepiano* specifically, while in the earlier movement no overt characteristics of idiomatic style are evident.

It is also useful to consider these two movements from the viewpoint of compensatory activity. In Hob. XVI:26/1 the limited dynamic and coloristic capabilities of the harpsichord are compensated for by shifts of texture, figuration, and tessitura at the phrase and subphrase level. For example, the transfer of material from one octave to another in the opening bars, the subsequent contrapuntal texture (mm. 11–13), and the active three-voice fabric beginning in m. 14 result in a series of well-defined but short ideas. These ideas are further underlined by the prevalence of beat marking and the relatively fast harmonic rhythm; in addition, rhythmic stress is often created by ornaments or chromaticism.

Some of the same elements that provide activity at the level of the phrase and the subphrase in Hob. XVI:26/1 are used in Hob. XVI:29/1 to define the structure of the exposition (mm. 1–14, 15–26, 27–31). Although a contrast of register occurs in the opening statement, the effect is streamlined and the surface and harmonic rhythms are less erratic. In mm. 7–10 the alternating forte/piano sequences with the one-against-three-voice sonority are in total opposition to a harpsichord style, and the structural use of the crescendo beginning in m. 22 contributes to the resolution of the tonal conflict in mm. 26–27. The repetitions with no change of register found in mm. 15–20 imply dynamic nuances possible only on the newer instrument. In sum, the capabilities of the *fortepiano* are successfully realized in the first movement of Hob. XVI:29 to the degree that the functional divisions of the exposition emerge with unusual clarity.

Like Hob. XVI:26 and 29, the remaining sonatas of the "1776 set" as well as the Auenbrugger Sonatas published in 1780 reveal a mixture of styles, some for harpsichord and others for a touch-sensitive instrument, a characteristic that also seems evident in the miscellaneous sonatas of this period, Hob. XVI:33, 43, and 34.

During the 1780s up to Haydn's departure for England, his keyboard works are for the most part *fortepiano* compositions.[58] Among these, the solo works can be divided into those from the time before Haydn acquired his Schanz *fortepiano* in 1788 (which include the three Sonatas for Princess Esterházy Hob. XVI:40–42) and after (the great C-major and E-flat major Sonatas Hob. XVI:48 and 49, and the Fantasia Hob. XVII:4). Circumstantial evidence seems to favor the *fortepiano* built by Anton Walter for the three Esterházy Sonatas: the Esterházy bills of payment to him for working on the keyboard instruments at Esterháza during the 1780s; Haydn's references to Walter in a 1781 letter; and Haydn's evaluative comments, indicating a thorough familiarity with a number of his instruments in his 1790 letter recommending the Schanz instrument to Frau von Genzinger. The keyboard trios of this period remain in the mixed style of the keyboard sonatas of the previous decade; while the *fortepiano* is to be preferred, the harpsichord is a very serviceable alternative. The last work Haydn composed before departing for London, the little Variations in C major Hob. XVII:5, was written for the *fortepiano*, according to the contract with Artaria, but could be effectively performed on the harpsichord or clavichord. Its use of the *Tragen der Töne*, however, favors a touch-sensitive instrument.

Even though Haydn had an opportunity to become acquainted with the London *fortepiani* after 1790, the F-minor Variations Hob. XVII:6 must have been written with a Viennese instrument in mind; it was composed in Vienna during 1793 for a Viennese virtuoso, Barbara von Ployer. The ideal performance of these variations would be on either a Schanz *fortepiano* or a clavichord, as its demands seem to parallel the C-major Sonata Hob. XVI:48.

In England there was a profound difference between the grand—used and owned mainly by the rich, the virtuosos, and serious students—and the square *fortepiano*, which presumably found a place in the living quarters of most amateurs. The former had a wider dynamic range, especially on the louder end of the spectrum, and a fuller sound; while the latter had a somewhat restricted strength and a more delicate touch. Haydn composed two of the last three solo sonatas and one set of trios for the professional Miss Jansen (Mrs. Bartolozzi). Among the three solo sonatas Hob. XVI:50–52, those in C major and E-flat major seem more appropriate on one of the large instruments of grand design;[59] while the D-major Sonata—with its lighter sonorities and fewer dynamics—seems better suited to the popular square instrument. It is perhaps for this type of keyboard that most of the late piano

TABLE V-3

Preferred Instruments for Haydn's Keyboard Works

Work by Genre	Preferred Instrument	Other possible instrument	Remarks
Hob. XIV:1–4, 7–13, C1, C2, Hob. XVIII:F1	Harpsichord		
Hob. XV:1, 2, 34, 35, 36, 37, 38, 40, 41, C1, F1		Harpsichord	
Hob. XV:5	*Fortepiano*	Harpsichord	Most dynamics realizable from musical context without a touch-sensitive instrument.
Hob. XV:6	*Fortepiano*	Harpsichord	Performance on harpsichord decidedly less satisfactory than on *fortepiano* but still a possibility.
Hob. XV:7	*Fortepiano*	Harpsichord	Many dynamics realizable on harpsichord or by accompaniment. Pizzicato in slow movement coloristically favors *fortepiano*.
Hob. XV:8	*Fortepiano*	Harpsichord	Finale requires *fortepiano* more than first movement, where only a few dynamics require touch sensitivity.
Hob. XV:9	*Fortepiano*	Harpsichord	Few dynamic marks and most realizable from context or accompaniment, except finale, mm. 129–31.
Hob. XV:10	*Fortepiano*	Harpsichord	Although few dynamic indications, structure of the finale would be lost without their realization in mm. 198–205.
Hob. XV:11	*Fortepiano*	Harpsichord	In mm. 180–81 the opposition of texture and dynamics underlines the required *fortepiano*.
Hob. XV:12	*Fortepiano*	Harpsichord	In mm. 150–51 the sforzandos are only possible on *fortepiano*. Pizzicato in slow movement. In general few dynamic markings; finale contains only one for the last two measures.
Hob. XV:13	*Fortepiano*	Harpsichord	Sforzando in m. 1 and following preceded by staccato; i.e., by shortening the previous note; its effect is musically partially possible on the harpsichord. Dynamics of the finale are mostly registrational with the exception of the close.
Hob. XV:14	*Fortepiano*		In first and second movements most dynamics are registrational. However, the *Tragen der Töne* and sforzandos in first movement require *fortepiano*.
Hob. XV:15	*Fortepiano*	Harpsichord	Most dynamics registrational, hence realizable on harpsichord.
Hob. XV:16	*Fortepiano*	Harpsichord	Except for sforzandos and crescendos, a work performable on the harpsichord.
Hob. XV:17	*Fortepiano*	Harpsichord	*Tragen der Töne* points toward the touch-sensitive instrument even though the dynamics are mostly registrational.

Hob. XV:18	*Fortepiano*		The first use of mezza voce in the keyboard part of these trios.
Hob. XV:19	*Fortepiano*	Harpsichord	Dynamics remain mainly registrational except for accents.
Hob. XV:20	*Fortepiano*		The effect of mm. 60 ff. in the first movement is only achievable on *fortepiano*.
Hob. XV:21	*Fortepiano*		First movement, m. 91, has crescendo while the second calls for *Tragen der Töne*. Otherwise notable for lack of dynamic indications. Second movement, mezza voce.
Hob. XV:22	*Fortepiano*		Opposition of texture and sonority in opening measures make *fortepiano* a necessity. Crescendo and *Tragen der Töne* in slow movement. Finale least pianistically oriented.
Hob. XV:23	*Fortepiano*		Differentiation of sforzando from accent (beginning in m. 21) rules out harpsichord as an option, as do the final measures of slow movement and mm. 75–77 of the finale.
Hob. XV:24	*Fortepiano*	(Harpsichord)	With the exception of accentual ones, dynamics mainly registrational.
Hob. XV:25	*Fortepiano*	(Harpsichord)	First movement contains no dynamics; second requires only *Tragen der Töne* for one measure. Except for the sforzandos, all keyboard dynamics are realizable from context or in the accompaniment.
Hob. XV:26	*Fortepiano*		The only work of this set where the harpsichord is not a possibility.
Hob. XV:27	*Fortepiano*		The number and different types of dynamics in the first and second movements place this in the same category as Hob. XVI:50 and 52. The finale strongly contrasts with them by its few touch-sensitive indications.
Hob. XV:28	*Fortepiano*		Compared with the first work in this set, the use of dynamics is very limited. Special note should be made of the ensemble color of the opening, which points toward the *fortepiano*.
Hob. XV:29	*Fortepiano*		Dynamic requirements only begin to approach those of Hob. XV:27/1 and 2. The mezza voce of second movement and the hemiola of mm. 31–34 are especially notable.
Hob. XV:30	*Fortepiano*		See especially the phrase repetitions in the first movement and the sforzandos and beginning of the slow movement.
Hob. XV:31	*Fortepiano*	Harpsichord	Even though this work was composed for a known *fortepiano* performer, all the dynamics are registrational; i.e., harpsichord is a perfectly viable alternative.
Hob. XV:32	*Fortepiano*	Harpsichord	In the same style of idiomatic writing as the works from the late 1780s.
Hob. XVI:16	Harpsichord	Clavichord	
Hob. XVI:5	Harpsichord	Clavichord	
Hob. XVI:Es2	Harpsichord	Clavichord	
Hob. XVI:Es3	Harpsichord	Clavichord	
Hob. XVII:D1	Harpsichord	Clavichord	
Hob. XVI:G1	Harpsichord	Clavichord	
Hob. XVI:1	Harpsichord	Clavichord	The use of ornaments in the first movement seems particularly characteristic of the harpsichord.

TABLE V-3 (*continued*)

Work by Genre	Preferred Instrument	Other possible instrument	Remarks
Hob. XVI:7	Harpsichord	Clavichord	
Hob. XVI:9	Harpsichord	Clavichord	
Hob. XVI:10	Harpsichord	Clavichord	
Hob. XVI:12	Harpsichord	Clavichord	
Hob. XVI:2	Clavichord	Harpsichord ⎫	The expressive character of the slow movements separates these two sonatas from the others and possibly indicates the clavichord as the preferred instrument.
Hob. XVI:6	Clavichord	Harpsichord ⎭	
Hob. XVI:8	Harpsichord	Clavichord	
Hob. XVI:13	Harpsichord	Clavichord	
Hob. XVI:3	Harpsichord	Clavichord	The use of ornaments points toward a harpsichord style.
Hob. XVI:4	Harpsichord	Clavichord	
Hob. XVI:14	Harpsichord	Clavichord	
Hob. XVI:47	Harpsichord (short octave)	Clavichord	
Hob. XVI:45	Harpsichord	Clavichord	
Hob. XVIIa:1	Harpsichord	Clavichord	
Hob. XVIIa:2	Harpsichord	Clavichord	
Hob. XVI:19	Harpsichord	Clavichord	
Hob. XVI:46	Clavichord	Harpsichord	A single forte occurs in m. 75 of the first movement. Note the expressive slow movement.
Hob. XIV:5 (XVI:5a)	Harpsichord	Clavichord	
Hob. XVI:18	Clavichord	*Fortepiano,* Harpsichord	Piano and forte dynamics mixed with ornaments functioning as they might in a work for harpsichord.
Hob. XVI:44	Clavichord	Harpsichord ⎫	The minor key and expressive nature seem to favor the clavichord for the two sonatas. Extensive dynamic indications in first and last movements of Hob. XVI:20 require the touch-sensitive instrument.
Hob. XVI:20	Clavichord	*Fortepiano,* Harpsichord ⎭	
Hob. XVI:21	Harpsichord	Clavichord	Contains a single forte dynamic in first movement.
Hob. XVI:22	Harpsichord	Clavichord	The slow movement seems more effective on a touch-sensitive instrument,
Hob. XVI:23	Clavichord	Harpsichord	even though the ornamentation is for the harpsichord.
Hob. XVI:24	Clavichord	*Fortepiano,* Harpsichord	*Tragen der Töne* in the slow movement seems to favor a touch-sensitive instrument, although little would be lost if it were performed on a harpsichord.
Hob. XVI:25	Harpsichord		Stylistically from all parameters one of Haydn's most convincing harpsichord
Hob. XVI:26	Harpsichord	Harpsichord	works from this period. See the comparison of it with Hob. XVI:29.

Hob. XVI:27	Harpsichord		
Hob. XVI:28	Harpsichord		
Hob. XVI:29	*Pianoforte*	Clavichord	The dynamics in the first movement, even though from an important secondary source (absent from autograph), are probably authentic. They cannot be realized in any way on a harpsichord.
Hob. XVI:30	Harpsichord		
Hob. XVI:31	Harpsichord		
Hob. XVI:32	Clavichord	Clavichord	*Tragen der Töne* in secondary source, if authentic, requires a touch-sensitive instrument.
Hob. XVI:35	*Fortepiano*	*Fortepiano,* Harpsichord	Since many of the dynamics can be achieved from their musical context, the harpsichord remains a viable choice.
Hob. XVI:36	*Fortepiano*	Clavichord, Harpsichord	Dynamic usage strongly favors a touch-sensitive instrument, but the ornamentation and texture do not rule out the harpsichord.
Hob. XVI:37	Harpsichord	Clavichord, Harpsichord	Dynamics in finale are terraced; perhaps they are registrational clues for the harpsichord.
Hob. XVI:38	*Pianoforte*	*Fortepiano,* Clavichord	Indications for crescendo and accents on weak part of beat require touch-sensitive instrument. However, as in other works from this series, enough textual and ornamental support exists for a not ineffective harpsichord performance.
Hob. XVI:39	*Fortepiano*	Clavichord, Harpsichord	Compare the dynamics with like movement in Hob. XVI:36; Hob. XVI:39 contains more dynamics that cannot be realized on the harpsichord.
Hob. XVI:33	Harpsichord	Clavichord, Harpsichord	Closely approximates style of Esterházy Sonatas (1773) and "Anno 1776" Sonatas.
Hob. XVI:43	*Fortepiano*	Clavichord, *Pianoforte*	Dynamics at three levels—*pp*, *p*, and *f*—strongly favor a touch-sensitive instrument.
Hob. XVI:34	Walter *Fortepiano*	Clavichord, Harpsichord	Most dynamics realizable on harpsichord; the perdendosi of slow movement requires a touch-sensitive instrument.
Hob. XVI:40–42	Walter *Fortepiano*	Clavichord, Harpsichord	The fullest realization of a touch-sensitive instrument style to date. Harpsichord is now no longer a viable alternative.
Hob. XVI:48	Schanz *Fortepiano,* Clavichord	Clavichord	Together with the F-minor Variations Hob. XVII:6, Haydn's most detailed use of dynamics. Haydn may have intended this work for the clavichord, as he referred to it as "Sonate fürs Clavier."
Hob. XVI:49	Schanz *Fortepiano*		Haydn himself said this work could only be realized on the *fortepiano.*
Hob. XVI:51	Square *Fortepiano*	Clavichord	A more intimate and technically easier work that does not demand the big sonorities of Hob. XVI:52 and 50; hence the preference for a small instrument.
Hob. XVI:52	Grand *Fortepiano*		*Tragen der Töne* and numerous dynamic markings.
Hob. XVI:50	Grand *Fortepiano*		Compass to a''' with *una corda, Tragen der Töne,* and numerous dynamic markings.

TABLE V-3 (*continued*)

Work by Genre	Preferred Instrument	Other possible instrument	Remarks
Hob. XVII:1	Harpsichord (short octave)	Clavichord	
Hob. XVII:2	Harpsichord (short octave)	Clavichord	
Hob. XVII:3	Harpsichord	Clavichord	Dynamics and *Tragen der Töne* present but only in the theme as found in its original version as string quartet.
Hob. XVII:4	*Schanz Fortepiano*	Clavichord	Numerous dynamic markings.
Hob. XVII:5	*Schanz Fortepiano*	Clavichord	*Tragen der Töne.*
Hob. XVII:6	*Schanz Fortepiano*	Clavichord	*Tragen der Töne.*
Hob. XVII:7	Harpsichord	Clavichord	
Hob. XVII:9	*Fortepiano*	Clavichord	*Tragen der Töne.*
Hob. XVII:10	Harpsichord	*Fortepiano,* Clavichord	
Hob. XVIII:1	Organ	Harpsichord	
Hob. XVIII:2	Organ	Harpsichord	
Hob. XVIII:3	Harpsichord		
Hob. XVIII:4	*Fortepiano*	Harpsichord	Sforzandos occur in slow movement of Boyer print and in Kroměříž copy; effect realizable on harpsichord.
Hob. XVIII:5	Organ	Harpsichord	
Hob. XVIII:6	Organ	Harpsichord	
Hob. XVIII:8	Organ	Harpsichord	
Hob. XVIII:10	Organ	Harpsichord	
Hob. XVIII:11	*Fortepiano*	Harpsichord	Sforzandos occur in slow movement; effect realizable on harpsichord.

trios, as well as the English Canzonettas and many of the other London vocal works, were conceived, although a song such as "Fidelity" and the Trios Hob. XV:27–29 might benefit from the use of the larger instrument.

Table V-3 summarizes the external and internal evidence for each authentic or plausibly authentic keyboard work and the resulting selection of the preferred instrument(s) for its performance. Although the remarks offered may be neither definitive nor complete, they point out the significant touch-sensitive requirements for specific works. While the preferences of this list are personal and could probably never be realized by any one performer, it may provide some insight into the ways Haydn's keyboard music might be most effectively realized.

It should be remembered, however, that emphasizing the differences among these eighteenth-century instruments may obscure a more important consideration for the twentieth-century performer: that is, the differences between the harpsichord and *fortepiano* of the eighteenth century are not nearly as pronounced as the disparity between the modern Steinway or Bösendorfer piano and the old Stein or Walter *fortepiano*. The instrument made in Germany and Austria during the eighteenth century had a brightness and crispness of articulation that seems to have had little aesthetic connection to the more massive and darker-sounding large English pianos that are the true ancestors of the modern instrument.

Performances of Haydn's sonatas, trios, divertimentos, concertos, and pieces—especially the pre-London ones—therefore lose much of their character when performed on today's instruments. Yet if only the twentieth-century piano is available for concert performance, the performer who has an understanding of the characteristics of the keyboard(s) for which a given work may have been intended can potentially achieve a more satisfying performance than one who has not.

Essay VI

THE VIENNESE
KEYBOARD TRADITION

The background for Haydn's stylistic development has to a large extent been neglected. Since a scientific approach to the source problems of Haydn's output was only established in the 1930s by Jens Peter Larsen[1] and further substantial work was impossible, because of the world situation, until about 1950, scholars are still mainly occupied with bibliographic and stylistic problems pertaining to Haydn himself. Although much of the repertoire of Haydn's environment is now physically accessible, most of the music for ensemble—i.e., accompanied divertimentos, keyboard trios, and concertos—still requires that scores be constructed from parts; thus, the availability of ensemble music in a format usable for study remains for the future. As a result, the solo repertoire can be dealt with here in some detail, whereas the ensemble works can only be surveyed.

The first references to a Viennese repertoire were made by Hermann Abert, who essentially saw Haydn's keyboard style as emanating from two sources: the Wagenseil divertimento, and the more elevated style of Carl Phillip Emanuel Bach.[2] This viewpoint dominated the literature until 1975, when Bettina Wackernagel carefully reviewed the known and accessible keyboard music by Wagenseil, the brothers Monn, Steffan, and Mozart, as well as some foreign products by Galuppi, Rutini, and Emanuel Bach; her aim was not to establish a possible Viennese repertoire for Haydn's early sonatas but to examine formal, melodic, and procedural similarities.[3]

The first line of attack in establishing a Viennese repertoire relevant to Haydn would be documentation close to the composer himself. Unfortunately, for the early years we have no idea of his knowledge of other composers' music except as he expressed it during the 1790s while in England and to Dies and Griesinger during the first years of the nineteenth century. Haydn seems to have had little interest in personally collecting keyboard music by his contemporaries; most of what he owned was apparently given to him. However, even though Haydn implied that he was a self-made professional in his early years, he must have been acquainted with a wide repertoire by his elders and peers.

A second goal of this essay is to provide a survey of Viennese keyboard music up to and somewhat beyond the period when Haydn's personality as a keyboard composer was established, thereby elucidating his special contributions to the Viennese keyboard tradition. Thus for the solo sonata we will focus not only on matters of syntax but also on the evolution from the suite to the sonata cycle; for the accompanied keyboard music, texture and setting; and for the concertos, the transition from a first-movement form oriented toward the ritornello to one more like a sonata structure.

The Imperial Repertoire

By the second half of the seventeenth century, Vienna had become a center of keyboard composition and performance. The Baroque tradition of a suite of dances, unified by tonality and diversified by style, prevailed at court from *ca.* 1658 until *ca.* 1750, i.e., from the beginning of the reign of Leopold I until that of Maria Theresa. The repertoire composed and performed for the court was intended for amusement within the private chamber of the Imperial family. The Habsburgs were personally involved with music making: Leopold I (reigned 1658–1705) was himself a composer and kept more than a hundred musicians on the Imperial payrolls. His successor, Joseph I, reigned only six years. He was followed by Karl VI (reigned 1711–1740), a keyboard player, who further increased the size of the Hofkapelle to 140 members and employed one of the most important Baroque composers, Johann Joseph Fux.

During the reign of Maria Theresa (reigned 1740–1780), keyboard composition and performance activities within the Imperial chambers reached their highest point during the period 1749–*ca.* 1765, when the prolific Georg Christoph Wagenseil was court keyboard composer and music teacher not only to the Empress—who was a skilled player[4]—but also to her children. Her eldest son, Emperor Joseph II, was a violist, cellist, singer, and keyboardist and held regular musicales in his chambers. Two contemporary paintings now in the Kunsthistorisches Museum in Vienna attest to the musical interests of the Empress's progeny: in one, Joseph II is seated at the keyboard flanked by two of his sisters holding music (Plate 12); the other shows Maria Antonia performing at the keyboard (Plate 13).

Yet the musical tastes of the Imperial family apparently only slowly departed from suite-oriented works. The deaths of Emperor Karl VI in 1740 and his Kapellmeister Fux in 1741 did not so much mark a revolution in style as a quickened evolution: solo and accompanied divertimentos/sonatas with little or no relationship to the suite did not begin to be composed by the court musicians until the 1750s.

Some of the repertoire performed at the Imperial court during the reign of Maria Theresa is contained in three manuscripts at the Osterreichische Nationalbibliothek (Anthology Imperial): S.m. 11084 and 11085, music books apparently written for the Archduchess Maria Elisabeth (1743–1808); and S.m. 3348, pos-

PLATE 12. Joseph II seated at the keyboard flanked by his sisters, Marianne and Elisabeth (b. 1780). Oil painting by Joseph Hauzinger. (Kunsthistorisches Museum, Vienna)

PLATE 13. Maria Antonia (*ca.* 1770) seated at the keyboard.
Oil painting by Franz Xaver Wagenschön. (Kunsthistorisches
Museum, Vienna)

sibly a collection used by Archduchess Maria Anna (1738–1789). Even though
S.m. 11084 and 11085 are now bound with the Archduchesses' book plates, they
are not true collections: the watermarks change, several copyists are found (but not
in consecutive order), and the *Primo* and *Secondo* parts to the same compositions
are bound in the same volume.[5] In contrast, S.m. 3348 is more unified: the works
are all by Wagenseil; a single copyist was used for the entire first part and a second
completed the collection. Together, the three manuscripts contain twenty-seven
concertos, two concertinos, a trio, three suites, and five divertimentos by Wagenseil;
six concertos, a trio, and three partitas by Hofmann; a concerto and a concerto
movement by Steffan; a concerto by Matielli; a divertimento by Loserth; two concertos by Agnesi; and a trio (Hob. XV:41) and a concertino (Hob. XIV:11) by
Haydn.

While the dominance of Wagenseil is not surprising, it is difficult to believe that
works by his pupil Joseph Anton Steffan would play such a small role, since Steffan
was Klaviermeister to Maria Carolina (1752–1814) and a future Queen of France,
Maria Antonia (1755–1793). During the early years of the nineteenth century a
large collection of Steffan's keyboard music became part of the archive at the castle
in Kroměříž, a residence of the archbishop of Olomütz. It seems likely that this
collection was at one time part of the Imperial holdings since on external grounds it
segregates itself from other keyboard copies in the archbishop's archive. Also con-
spicuous by their absence are compositions by Wenzel Raimond Birck, the music
teacher to the three archdukes Joseph (1741–1790), Karl (1745–1761), and
Leopold (1747–1792). Although the documentation is still incomplete, it is clear
that the Imperial keyboard repertoire was dominated by Wagenseil and his students during Haydn's early years.

Solo Keyboard Works

SOURCES

Prints. Outside the Imperial court, some music was available to the Viennese
public in prints. During the first half of the eighteenth century, only one print of
keyboard music was published in Vienna: *72 Versetl Sammt 12 Toccaten* by the
Imperial court organist Gottlieb Muffat (1690–1770) in 1726.[6] More than a
quarter of a century was to pass before Wagenseil's Op. 1 (a set of six divertimentos) appeared in 1753. It was soon followed by the publication of three more sets
of six divertimentos by Wagenseil—Op. 2 (*ca.* 1755), Op. 3 (*ca.* 1761), and
Op. 4 (1763)—and his three divertimentos (1761); the *Trattenimenti* (1757) by
Wenzel Raimond Birck; and the six-sonata sets Op. 1 (*ca.* 1759) and Op. 2 (1760),
the three-sonata sets Op. 3 (1763–before 1771) and another without opus number
(1771–*ca.* 1776), plus *40 Preludi* (1760) by Joseph Anton Steffan.[7]

This meager list does not represent the only keyboard prints on the market
during the mid-century; advertisements in the *Wienerisches Diarium* and other
catalogues show that a number of works written and published by foreigners were
readily available to the Viennese public. From 1737 to 1780—when Artaria issued
its first set of sonatas by Haydn—in addition to works by C.P.E. Bach (which are

identified in Essay VII), no fewer than sixty-five *opere* were advertised in the Imperial city.[8]

Before 1760 the "foreign" solo keyboard music available in printed form was not dominated by any single composer as much as by one publisher: Johann Ulrich Haffner of Nürnberg. His beautifully engraved works were sold by Peter Conrad Monath, who carried more of Haffner's products than did any other Viennese bookseller, perhaps because of his Nürnberg family ties—Augustin Bernardi, Georg Bauer, and Johann Jakob Lidl. As a result, from *ca.* 1742 through the mid-1760s Vienna was inundated by keyboard music from Germany and Italy. Unfortunately, none of these works exhibited a strong stylistic profile except for those of Domenico Scarlatti. One wonders why not a single notice has been located for the keyboard anthologies for which the Nürnberg house was so famous: *Oeuvres mêlées* (1755–1765 or 1766), twelve volumes containing seventy-two sonatas by German composers;[9] *Raccolta musicale* (1756–1765), five volumes containing thirty sonatas by Italian composers;[10] and *Collection recreative* (1758–1761 or 1762), two volumes containing twelve sonatas by German composers.[11] The only evidence we have for the importation of any of these anthologies is a late one: the 1799 catalogue of Johann Traeg, who advertised all twelve volumes of *Oeuvres mêlées*. However, we do not know whether he was selling Haffner's prints or, as is more likely, manuscript copies.

After 1760 a greater number of German prints of solo keyboard music became available, with publications from Hummel, Hartknoch, Lotter, Gerle, Hande, and Breitkopf. It seems odd that so few from Breitkopf made their way to Vienna, even though a large number of Viennese products are found in the Leipzig dealer's thematic catalogue. Preston of London and the Bureau d'Abonnement Musical of Paris are the only non-German firms represented. In the years after 1780 there was a trend toward greater diversity; and by 1799, according to Traeg, a staggering number and variety of keyboard works from d'Anglebert to Beethoven were available in the Imperial city.[12]

Manuscript Copies. In contrast to the situation in London and Paris, printed music was not the only way to measure what the Viennese keyboardists were playing, for the professional copy shops were at the center of music distribution. As Charles Burney reported in 1772:

> here, among other things, I was plagued with copyists the whole evening; they began to regard me as a greedy and indiscriminate purchaser of whatever trash they should offer; but I was forced to hold my hand, not only from buying bad music, but good. For everything is very dear at Vienna, and nothing more so than music, of which none is printed.[13]

Unfortunately, very few manuscript collections from the mid-century period survive. Symphonies and string quartets are preserved in great numbers, but keyboard music was used again and again and when worn, was discarded. Many of these works were used for pedagogical purposes and were thought not worthy of preservation. Among the surviving collections, excluding those of the Imperial family described above, two anthologies remain unrivalled: a two-volume set of unknown provenance now in the Gesellschaft der Musikfreunde in Vienna (Anthology Vienna) and two volumes, Ms. mus. 749 and 753, in the National Széchényi Library in Budapest (Anthology Roskovsky).

Anthology Vienna, the more careful compilation, was probably assembled sometime during the 1760s or early 1770s, but no later than *ca.* 1780. It consists of seventy-one attributed works that reflect the availability of a solo keyboard repertoire from various geographic areas: Italy (Agnesi, Alberti, Fiorroni, Martino, Sampani, Toselli [?]);[14] Germany (Platti), perhaps from Breitkopf and Haffner sources; Bohemia (Brixi); and Vienna, from both prints and manuscripts (Buchhammer, Haydn, Hofmann, Matielli, Monn, Schlöger, Steffan, Umstatt, Wagenseil, and Vanhal).

The two Budapest volumes—Anthology Roskovsky—are part of a larger series of seven tomes copied and collected by Pater Panteleon Roskovsky (1734–1789), a Franciscan monk resident in Bratislava, Pest, and other locations.[15] Their contents are broader both geographically and chronologically. Besides the better-known Viennese (Birck, Fux, Kohaut, Monn, Muffat, Reutter, Steffan, Tuma, Umstatt, and Wagenseil) and some lesser lights from the Imperial city (Peyer, Römer, and Schmidt), Italians (Agnesi [?Alberti], Palladini, Platti, Rutini, and Vento) and Germans (J. L. Krebs and Handel) are well represented. In addition, the anthology preserves compositions by Hungarian (Csermak, Ninger, and Roskovsky) and Austrian (Ehrenhardt and Zechner) monks as well as by a series of otherwise unknown composers (Fillenbaum, Kayser, Obermäyer, Ruge, and Wachowski). Some 145 works are identified, and about 120 more are not explicitly attributed.[16] In short, the Roskovsky volumes offer the most extensive anthology of the eighteenth-century repertoire available in the Imperial lands.

In addition to their presence in these *Sammelbände*, a series of Viennese composers are represented in separate copies. At the Nationalbibliothek in Vienna, S.m. 1079 is devoted chiefly to music by Wenzel Raimond Birck (1718–1763). The manuscript begins with an explanation of the musical elements, followed by dances and suite/divertimentos by Birck, and concludes with an aria by Galuppi and a group of figured bass exercises. As some are Birck autographs, one might hypothesize that this book was a *Klavierschule* for Joseph II.

An unusually rich series of solo keyboard copies, housed in the Staatsbibliothek Preussischer Kulturbesitz in West Berlin, includes works by Matthias Georg Monn, Johann Christoph Monn, Joseph Anton Steffan, Leopold Hofmann, Georg Christoph Wagenseil, and Georg Reutter d.J. (?), among others. It remains a mystery how many of these Viennese copies came into the possession of the Staatsbibliothek. Since some works by Fux are in the hand of a copyist referred to by Riedel as having been associated with the Baron Gottfried van Swieten,[17] some of this material may have emanated from the mostly lost *Nachlass* of this musical collector and connoisseur.

Probably the most comprehensive collection is to be found at the archbishop's castle/residence at Kroměříž, in Moravia. In addition to nearly all the keyboard works by Joseph Anton Steffan, this relatively well known but little explored archive contains five capriccios, a character piece, twenty sonatas, and two variation sets by Vanhal; three divertimentos/sonatas by M. G. Monn; nine pieces and seven divertimentos and sonatas by J. C. Monn; three sets of variations by Giuseppa Auerhammer; twenty-six two- and four-hand sonatas by Leopold Koželuch; twelve sonatas by Wagenseil; and twenty-six sonatas attributed to Joseph Haydn. In general, the bulk of this music seems to originate after 1750; in the final decades of the century the archbishops' interest in keyboard music seems to have waned.[18]

STYLE

There can be no question that the solo keyboard repertoire to which Haydn could have been exposed went far beyond that proposed by Abert and surveyed by Wackernagel. Although it is impossible here to offer a comprehensive treatment,[19] we shall discuss the works of some of the most important native and resident composers as they relate to Haydn's early sonatas. No effort will be made to establish thematic connections as a direct influence from one composer to another: the triadic melodies, stock accompaniments, *galant* cadences, etc., frequently chosen as significant observations are merely formulas of the age. Rather, the focus will be on movement and cyclic typologies, with some further remarks on syntax and other special aspects.

From Suite to Sonata. The most important developments in seventeenth-century Viennese solo keyboard compositions are to be found in the works of Johann Jakob Froberger (1616–1667). Froberger was familiar with a broad spectrum of Continental keyboard music: he studied with Frescobaldi in Rome, and he was intimately acquainted with the French school through his associations with Gaultier, Chambonnières, and Louis Couperin. His most important contribution was the establishment of the keyboard suite not as an *ordre* but as an established cycle consisting of an allemande, a courante, and a sarabande, to which a gigue was added or interpolated in later sources. In the larger view this development was one of the early steps toward the eighteenth-century keyboard partita/divertimento/sonata.[20]

The keyboard music of Johann Joseph Fux (1660–1741),[21] which was still being distributed in copies during the last decades of the eighteenth century, serves as the most important link in the transmission of the synthesized Franco/German/Italianate keyboard styles of Froberger. Although Fux's works are characterized by the dense textures, fabrics, and ornaments also seen in Froberger, they display a more flexible approach to the suite, while retaining the essential outline of Froberger's cycle (as shown by brackets):

E.115 Allemande–Courante–Sarabande–Aria–Menuet–Gigue–Menuet
E.116 Aria–Rigaudon–Passepied–Echeggiata–Gigue–Menuet

K.405 Allemande–Courante–Gavotte–Menuet in Rondeaux–Sarabande–
Gigue

E.117 Allemande–Courante–Bourée–Menuet + Double–Aria–Gigue

E.70 (Version 1)   French Overture–Courante–Sarabande–Rigaudon–Menuet

1 + 2–Gigue–Menuet 3

E.70 (Version 2)   French Overture–Allemande + Double–Rigaudon–

Sarabande–Courante–Menuet 1,2,3–Gigue

K.404   Capriccio (Praelude)–Fuga 4/4–Adagio 3/4–Fuga da capo–Allegretto 3/4 "La Superbia"–Gustuoso 3/4 "Arietta"–Tempo giusto 2/4 "L'Humilta"–Affettuso 3/4 "La vera pace"–Allegro 2/4 Finale

E.114   Harpeggio 4/4–Fuga 4/4–Aria Passagiata 4/4

Here three types can be distinguished: those that consist of a series of dances without a prelude, those preceded by a French Overture, and those that commence with an improvisatory prelude. Various aspects of these cycles were continued by later generations. Two characteristics should be especially noted: the presence in all but two of a minuet (which plays such a central role in the mid-century divertimento/sonata that it is often—particularly in the *minore* trios—the center of aesthetic gravity), and the improvisatory prelude. Riedel correctly described K.404 as approaching the Viennese keyboard divertimento/sonata of the mid-century.[22]

The First Generation of Composers after Fux. The Viennese composers of keyboard music that constituted the first generation after Fux set the vogue to which the young Haydn was subjected (see Table VI-1). Even though documentation of a direct association with Haydn exists only for Georg Reutter d.J., the Kapellmeister at St. Stephen's when Haydn was a member of the choir school, to deny the importance of Wagenseil and his contemporaries for Haydn's formative years would be to ignore the musical environment offered by the Imperial capital.

Georg Christoph Wagenseil (1715–1777) was among the most respected of the Viennese keyboard composers and one of Fux's own students. After changing from the study of law to music, Wagenseil was appointed Hofscholar (1735) at the Imperial court. In 1741 he became organist to the widow of Karl VI, Elisabeth Christine, and eventually took up the position of Hofklaviermeister (1749), i.e., keyboard teacher and composer for the Imperial family. In a two-year concert tour (1756–1758), Wagenseil established himself as one of Europe's premier keyboardists,[23] a reputation that was still obvious to Charles Burney in 1772 even though Wagenseil's health had deteriorated.[24] C. F. D. Schubart described him as "one of the first *Clavier* virtuosos of his time. . . . He himself plays with unusual expression and improvises fugues with considerable skill."[25]

Among Wagenseil's solo keyboard cycles are works titled Divertimento, Sonata, Suite, and Partita. His use of these terms, however, does not follow textbook prescriptions, for each type may contain all dances (pure suites), a mixture of dances and free movements (mixed suites), or only one dance—the minuet and trio—(new divertimento/sonata). The contents and titles of these cycles are summarized in Table VI-2. These sets are so varied that it is difficult to draw conclusions with regard to number of movements, movement types, and generic terms, except to

TABLE VI-1

The Viennese Keyboard Tradition Beginning with Fux

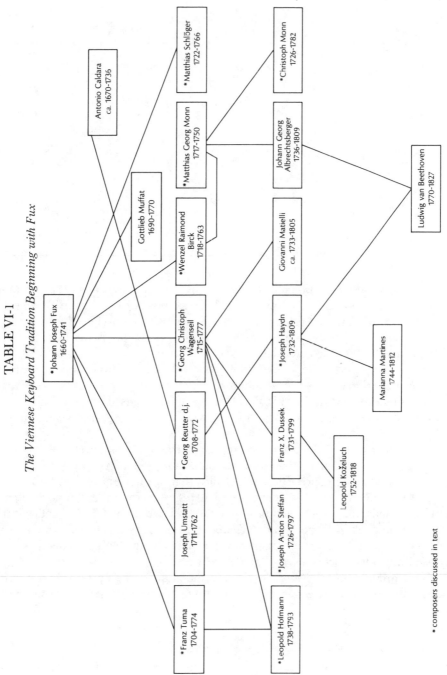

Antonio Caldara
ca. 1670-1735

*Johann Joseph Fux
1660-1741

Gottlieb Muffat
1690-1770

*Matthias Schlöger
1722-1766

*Matthias Georg Monn
1717-1750

*Christoph Monn
1726-1782

*Wenzel Raimond
Birck
1718-1763

Johann Georg
Albrechtsberger
1736-1809

*Georg Christoph
Wagenseil
1715-1777

Giovanni Matielli
ca. 1733-1805

Ludwig van Beethoven
1770-1827

*Georg Reutter d.j.
1708-1772

*Joseph Haydn
1732-1809

Marianna Martines
1744-1812

Joseph Umstatt
1711-1762

Franz X. Dussek
1731-1799

*Joseph Anton Steffan
1726-1797

Leopold Koželuch
1752-1818

*Franz Tuma
1704-1774

*Leopold Hofmann
1738-1793

* composers discussed in text

TABLE VI-2

Summary of Wagenseil's Solo Keyboard Cycles[26]

No. of Movements	Pure Suites	Mixed Suites	New Divertimentos/ Sonatas
2	2	1	2
3	3	12	34
4	1	11	4
5	1	3	
6	2	2	
7	1	1	
8		1	
Title			
Partita	4	1	2
Suite	4	9	7
Sonata	2	5	3
Divertimento		16	27
(?) Lesson			1

note that the new divertimento/sonata employs fewer movements (two to four), whereas the pure and mixed suites may have as few as two or as many as eight. "Divertimento" is not used for pure suites; it seems to be preferred for the mixed and new divertimento/sonata types. Surprisingly, "Sonata" is the least preferred title among those of the new style.

Each of the pure suites,[27] like the keyboard works of Fux, contains a minuet movement, and examples can be found of the arpeggiated prelude (in WWV 59) and the French Overture (in WWV 17). However, Wagenseil never uses more than two of the dances from the Froberger cycle, while Fux on several occasions employs all four.

A number of new characteristics appear in the thirty-one cycles of the mixed style: fast first movements that are not dances; movements that begin as stylized dances but carry no dance titles; and finales that are not gigues but rather more neutral movements: very fast or fast pieces in 3/8 or 2/4, and the Tempo di Menuet or minuet and trio. It is still not uncommon to find two minuet movements within a cycle: the minuet with trio; and the Tempo di Menuet, which takes on a more specialized role as a finale. In addition, several sicilianos (a standard slow movement type), duple-meter scherzos, and polonaises occur.

This group features a more stylized formulation of the cycle. Whereas in the pure suites no two cycles were alike; now there are several that appear more than once:

WWV

7,9,13,16,29,36	Fast–Minuet and Trio–Gigue
33,34,68	Fast–Minuet and Trio–Slow (Siciliano)–Tempo di Menuet
39,40	Fast–Slow–Minuet + Trio or Tempo di Menuet–Gigue
43,50	Prelude–Fast–Minuet + Trio–Fast 3/8

Nine of the thirty-one cycles contain movements with titles such as Preludio, usually a series of arpeggios with toccata-like sections (WWV 60); Capriccio, here in toccata style (WWV 73); Ricercarta (WWV 50), an extended movement not unlike the first Prelude to Bach's *Well-Tempered Clavier*;[28] Intrada (WWV 75), a march with dotted rhythms; and a French Overture (WWV 75).

In the new divertimento/sonata, a uniformity in the number of movements is immediately evident: three-movement sequences account for all but six of forty works, the others having two or four movements. The three-movement sonatas divide into one of three cyclic patterns: Fast–Minuet + Trio–Fast (thirteen examples); Fast–Slow–Fast (five examples); and Fast–Slow or Moderate–Minuet + Trio or Tempo di Menuet (sixteen examples).

But do the pure suites, mixed suites, and new divertimentos/sonatas represent a chronological evolution? Although a chronology for Wagenseil is not yet possible, one can turn to the six collections published from 1753 to 1765, including the one published by Haffner: of the thirty-three cycles, all—except for six in the mixed style—belong to the new divertimento/sonata type. Since nearly all these prints can be proven to be authentic and are probably fairly representative of Wagenseil for these dozen or so years, it can be said that by the 1750s and early 1760s, the new divertimento/sonata was the predominant cyclic type.

Although Wagenseil is a pivotal figure in the evolution from the suite to the sonata, the works themselves are at best disappointing: the composer seems to connect one empty idea to another with little, if any, compensatory activity.[29] For example, in Op. 1/5, the exposition (Example VI-1) is based entirely on scale passages, trills, and stock accompaniments. Even though this criticism could be leveled at other composers from the period, few were so relentless in the sameness of the texture and the predictability of the two-measure phrase rhythms.

Ironically, it was these weaknesses that established Wagenseil's historical importance. In comparison with the suites of Fux and Gottlieb Muffat (the latter published in his *Componimenti Musicali* [Augsburg, 1736]), Wagenseil's solo output significantly departed from the stylized dances, thick textures, and continuous syntax of his predecessors, replacing them with less-characterized movements, thin two- and three-voiced fabrics, and a more modular phrase structure. In the end, however, it must be concluded that Wagenseil's reputation rested more on his abilities as a teacher and performer and on the prestige generated by many published *opere* than on the quality of his music.

A second student of Fux, the little-known Wenzel Raimond Birck (Pürck, Pürk, Pirck, etc.; 1718–1763),[30] was, like Wagenseil, Hofscholar (1726–38) and later (1734) court organist and music teacher to the Imperial family. The 1757 print *Trattenimenti per Clavicembalo* (whose title page states that Birck was "Maestro di Tre Serenissimi Archduchi"), S.m. 1079 at the Österreichische National-bibliothek, and a few examples from one of the Roskovsky manuscripts (Ms. mus. 749) constitute his known keyboard output. The *Trattenimenti* ("entertainments") is divided into two large tonally unified suites or *balli*, each preceded by a series of movements that approximates a sonata cycle: the first in four (Fast–Slow–

EXAMPLE VI–1. Wagenseil, Divertimento Op. 1/5/1
(WWV 64), mm. 1–29.

EXAMPLE VI–1 (*continued*)

Variations–Fugue) and the second in three (Fast–Slow–Fast). Its entire plan seems to be modeled after François Couperin's *Les Nations*:

Trattenimento I^{mo}
Allegro 4/4
Adagio 4/4
Aria con sei variazioni: Tempo Giusto 3/4
Fuga: Non troppo presto 4/4
Ballo piccolo
   Aria Amoroso 3/4
   Minuettino galante 3/8
   Contredanse: Allegretto 3/8, 2/4, 3/4
   Sarabanda: Dolce 3/4
   Bourée: Tempo graziosa 2/4
   La petite Allemande: Poco allegro 3/8
   Scaramuccia: Lento 12/8
   Furlàna: Presto 2/4
   Menuetto ouvero La Quaglia 3/4

Trattenimento II^{do} *per Pantomimi*
Spiritoso e presto 4/4
Andante sempre dolce 3/4
Presto 2/4
Pierot: Tempo moderato 3/8
La Gelosa: Presto 3/8
Pierot: Allg. molto 3/8
Polacca 3/4
Gavotta: Allegro 2/4
Aria Seria: Larghetto 3/4
Ninfe e Pastori: Allegro 2/4
Lour Serieux 3/4
Pastore Armante: Tempo moderato 2/4
La Promessa: Maestoso 4/4
Tempo di Menuetto 3/4
La Zinghera: Larghetto 2/4
Contredanse: Allegro 3/8   Presto 2/4
L'Allemandes Agréables
Finale: Più Presto 3/8

The plan presents a synthesis of the light and elevated styles in the mid-century Viennese tradition: the fugue with the chromatic subject, which closes the sonata-like composition[31] of the first part; and the extended suites, which mix main and supplementary dance movements with character pieces. The latter recall not only Fux's K.404 but more markedly works by French composers of the so-called first *galant* school.

The manuscript S.m. 1079 contains seven or eight cyclic compositions in addition to some individual minuets, a ballet, and an aria. Within this apparent autograph, Birck uses the three different titles Parthia, Divertimento, and Ballo, none of which assumes a generic identity.

According to the classifications applied to Wagenseil's suites, of Birck's thirteen or fourteen extant cycles (excluding the two *balli*), four are of the more progressive divertimento/sonata type and the remaining are mixed suites. Yet, like Wagenseil's works, aspects of the tradition established by Fux are still evident: the ever-present minuet, the use of titles such as scherzo and capriccio as well as those with more specific programmatic or characteristic implications, and the improvisatory prelude movement.

Birck's works arouse more interest than do Wagenseil's; rarely does Birck revert in such length to the melodic and rhythmic clichés and formulas so evident in the works of his better-known contemporary. Although Birck also uses the exact repetition of two-measure units, one can find more advanced antecedent/consequent formulations. Furthermore, he seems to have a special talent for employing advanced textures: massive chords of seven and eight notes and rapid alternations of register (Example VI-2). Most astonishing is the extensive use of dynamic markings in the 1757 print (see Example V-1). Birck is certainly one of the more attractive of the unknown mid-century Viennese composers.

Two other composers active at the court were probably students of Fux: Franz Tuma (1704–1774), a member of the Kapelle of Karl VI's widow; and Matthias Schlöger (1722–1766), Hof-Klaviermeister and teacher to Maria Carolina and Maria Antonia. Anthology Roskovsky contains the only known keyboard works attributable to Tuma: two four-movement Partitas,[32] both belonging to the new divertimento/sonata type. Syntactically they do not change the established view of Tuma as an essentially conservative composer. He was less oriented than Wagenseil toward modular phrases and composed in a more Baroque idiom, while the quality of his works is at least a notch or two higher. Matthias Schlöger's works have been said to include "new stylistic elements of great promise."[33] Although Schlöger was a keyboard teacher at the court, only a single solo keyboard work survives in Anthology Vienna, a three-movement Divertimento, Fast–Slow–Fast without a minuet, which confirms the above comment. In the exposition of the first movement (Example VI-3), the phrase continuations and expansions go beyond the one- and two-measure repetitions and sequences so prevalent in Wagenseil.[34]

Outside the court circle, the best-known composer of the post-Fux generation is Matthias Georg Monn (1717–1750).[35] At one time he was the organist at the Karlskirche, and he may have studied with Birck. Considering that all of Monn's cyclic keyboard works were written before 1750, the number, type, and order of

*F♯, E, F♯, better

EXAMPLE VI–2. Birck, *Trattenimento* 1/3, mm. 1–4, 81–83, 101–103.

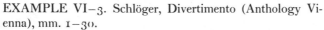

EXAMPLE VI–3. Schlöger, Divertimento (Anthology Vienna), mm. 1–30.

EXAMPLE VI–4. Monn, Sonata 1/1 (Fischer 45), mm. 1–9.

EXAMPLE VI–5. Monn, Sonata 9/1 (Fischer 58), mm. 1–17.

movements are rather advanced; of fifteen listed by Fischer, only one (No. 50) is a pure suite, five are mixed, one (Slow–Fast) is probably for the liturgy, and the remaining eight belong to the new divertimento/sonata type, as does one work in Anthology Vienna that is not listed by Fischer. Once again the minuet is an ever-present component. Also encountered are those arpeggiated preluding pieces that precede the first substantial fast movement of the cycle. Monn's sonatas are the most conservative in style. Their expository materials are almost entirely generated through *Fortspinnung* (Example VI-4). At other times the syntax seems more progressive (Example VI-5), but even here Monn eventually reverts to the older growth process.

In sum, it was Wagenseil—if only by virtue of the wide distribution his works received—who led the way for the change from a cycle oriented toward the suite to the new divertimento/sonata type in which dance movements and styles become relatively insignificant. However, Wagenseil and his generation failed to find a satisfactory solution to the syntactical problems of the mid-century style that confronted them: either they continued to write in an essentially Baroque style, or they depended on the repetition of one- and two-measure units.

The Second Generation after Fux: Students of Wagenseil and Others. Wagenseil replaced Fux as the leading musical personality in Theresian Vienna; according to Hiller, Wagenseil was "in omni genere notissimus."[36] One need only remember the names and reputations of some of his many students—Joseph Anton Steffan (1726–1797), Franz X. Dussek (1731–1799), Giovanni Anton Matielli (*ca.* 1733–1805), and Leopold Hofmann (1738–1793), who, if not of the first rank, were among the most-admired Viennese musicians of their era.

Without doubt the most talented was Steffan, who was the most-advanced composer of keyboard music among the Viennese *Kleinmeister* of his generation; a favored student of Wagenseil, he established his name through the publication of a number of keyboard Divertimentos and Sonatas beginning in the 1750s. In 1766 he succeeded Schlöger as Klaviermeister to the Archduchesses Maria Carolina and Maria Antonia.[37] In the same year the *Wienerisches Diarium* stated:

> There is no denying his novelty, the beautiful and unaffected turns of phrase in which art and nature seem bound together. His concertos, divertimentos, galanteries, variations, and preludes for *Clavier* will always be acclaimed by connoisseurs. . . . His works reveal a spirit which can create real delight whenever he wants. His Allegros are for the most part amusing and charming, full of fun and solid ideas, however mournfully the previous Adagio may have sighed.[38]

After retiring from his court appointment, Steffan established himself as one of the most important teachers and composers in the salons of the gentry and the chambers of the aristocracy.

A prolific composer, Steffan produced for keyboard forty-one sonatas and divertimentos, six sets of variations, more than forty concertos, characteristic/programmatic pieces, and almost a dozen accompanied works.[39] In addition, the five capriccios, forty preludes (1762), and ninety cadenzas (1783) point to his strong improvisatory bent. Looking at his solo works in their entirety, one is struck by the absence of titles such as Partita and Suite and the limited use of the term Divertimento (ten examples) in contrast to Sonata (thirty-one examples). As far as can be ascertained, Steffan never used "Divertimento" after 1768 and began to employ the term "Sonata" first in his Op. 2, of 1760, even though his mentor Wagenseil continued to use "Divertimento." The number of movements in the cycles still ranges from one to thirteen, but there is a strong preference for those in two, three, and four movements: three examples have only one movement; eight have two movements; seventeen have three; ten have four; and there are one each of cycles with five, six, and thirteen movements.

Steffan used a number of dance and characteristic pieces from the earlier generation, but they are less common than with Wagenseil; the Polonaise and Capriccio are the most frequently encountered, with the Courante ("Currant") the only vestige from the standard Froberger suite. Other suite-related movements are the Villanesca Gallante (Šetková No. 4 and No. 15), Contredanse Angloise (Šetková No. 5), and Inglese (Šetková No. 18). Even though some cycles have two minuet movements, the minuet is no longer present in nine sonatas. Many of Steffan's introductions take on a character totally different from the arpeggiated preludes of his predecessors; while they may retain the spirit of improvisation, they have a formal and expressive substance that provides contrast as well as balance to the ensuing Allegro.[40]

The cycles lean strongly toward the new sonata/divertimento type. Excluding the one-movement and programmatic sonatas, only one keyboard work is a pure suite, Op. 1/4 (Šetková No. 4.); eight are mixed; and twenty-eight are of the new divertimento/sonata type. The tonal practices also depart from the suite: related keys other than the tonic are used for internal movements and trios of the minuets. These progressive tendencies are evident even in the fifteen sonatas published before 1764.

A comparison of the first-movement expositions of Steffan's Op. 1/2 from *ca.* 1763(?) (Example VI-6) and Wagenseil's Op. 3/1 from *ca.* 1761 (Example VI-7) shows Steffan's musical syntax to be decidedly more up-to-date than his teacher's. Wagenseil's exposition contains only the primary, transition, and closing functions, whereas Steffan's also includes seven measures that have a secondary function. For Steffan each function is clearly defined by surface and phrase rhythms, melodic materials, and rests. As in Example VI-1, Wagenseil's themes are lacking in distinction, a trait not compensated for by their context. Furthermore, the range of Steffan's sonorities and his harmonic language enhance the melodic ideas, as do the dynamics—which even at this early date require a touch-sensitive instrument.

Leopold Hofmann, a somewhat younger Wagenseil student, is best known for the disparaging remarks Haydn made about some of his songs.[41] Nevertheless, Hofmann achieved a reputation almost comparable to Wagenseil's; he eventually attained the position of Kapellmeister at St. Stephen's with Mozart as his deputy. We have only ten extant solo keyboard cycles by Hofmann; they may date from the period when he was Hofklaviermeister to the Archduchess Maria Josepha, who died in the fall of 1767.[42] All are in the newer style and are titled Partita and Divertimento. Only one is in four movements (Fast–Slow–Minuet–Fast); the rest are in two (Allegro or Vivace and Tempo di Menuet or Minuet with Trio).

Hofmann's sonatas are miniatures that remind one of some early Haydn sonatas. Hofmann's expositions, like Wagenseil's, usually have only the primary, transition, and closing functions; but they tend to be less homogeneous than Wagenseil's, and the movements never disintegrate so completely into a series of clichés. Perhaps the most-advanced first-movement exposition is found in the third sonata of a series of six from Kroměříž (Example VI-8).

The keyboard cycles of Johann Christoph Monn [Mann] (1726–1782), the brother of M. G. Monn, cause difficulties of fraternal attribution. Those listed in

EXAMPLE VI–6. Steffan, Divertimento Op. 1/2/1 (Šetková 2), mm. 1–51.

EXAMPLE VI–7. Wagenseil, Divertimento Op. 3/1/1
(WWV 41), mm. 1–42.

EXAMPLE VI–8. Hofmann, Divertimento 3/1 (CS-KRm), mm. 1–30.

Fischer's catalogue are equally divided between cycles of mixed character and the newer divertimento/sonata. Other works from Kroměříž attributed to Christoph but not listed by Fischer might tip the scales to the more conservative side, for they tend more toward the dance suite.[43] Some works definitely bring to mind the earlier traditions: the arpeggiated prelude, the incorporation of more than one minuet or minuet-styled movement per cycle, and the Allegro "Paese" and the Allegro assai "Villanesca" all recall divertimentos from the Wagenseil circle.

However, Monn's musical language is the most advanced and controlled of any Viennese *Kleinmeister* of his generation save for Steffan. In Example VI-9 the initial measures of the E-flat major Sonata (Fischer No. 98) reveal his ability to provide contrast and continuity without the disjointed effect of Wagenseil's modular structures. Monn begins with three hammerstrokes (x) that provide a contrast to the linear (y) motion that follows. The repetition complements the opening but substitutes a full close in m. 6 for the half-cadence of m. 3. The continuation leading to the transition is derived from the rhythm of y and the chord outline of x. The

EXAMPLE VI–9. J. C. Monn, Sonata in E-flat Major/1
(Fischer 98), mm. 1–20.

secondary and closing sections rhythmically parallel the primary and transition
sections, lending a balanced continuity to the entire exposition.

The Second Generation after Fux: Joseph Haydn. Within the context of the Viennese tradition, Haydn's early solo sonatas occupy a pivotal position in the evolution
of the sonata cycle. All are of the new divertimento/sonata type and in two to four
movements. Specific dances, except for the minuet, are totally absent, and the only
titled characteristic type is the duple-metered "scherzo" employed as a finale;
Haydn does not even use the compound duple-meter movements of the gigue/hunt
typology so popular in the solo sonatas of his contemporaries. He does, however,
exploit the favorite type of slow movement: a cantilena with accompanying pulsating eighth notes reminiscent of a written-out *continuo* part. None of Haydn's solo
sonatas contain the arpeggiated preludes found in a significant number of cycles

from Fux to Steffan. Furthermore, Haydn does not precede any of the extant sonatas with an introductory movement, although in some of the later sonatas a central
movement may function as a prelude to the finale.

As in nearly all the Viennese divertimentos/sonatas, a minuet or minuet-styled
movement is part of the cycle. In the unquestionably authentic sonatas Haydn
never uses more than one minuet movement, but he does continue the tradition of
the minuet in the major mode and the trio in the parallel minor. In a few instances
syncopated rhythms pervade the trio, a characteristic seen in the cycles by his
Viennese contemporaries and predecessors. When employed by Haydn as a finale,
the minuet is occasionally extended by a series of variations, a characteristic of
Leopold Hofmann's sonatas. In Haydn's sonatas of the mid- to late 1760s, the minuet is omitted from the cycle, as is also true of works by Steffan.

Haydn's solo sonatas of the mid- to late 1760s and Steffan's are completely segregated from those of their Viennese contemporaries: they are cyclic works of un-
paralleled seriousness that ultimately lead to the sonata as a genre of real stature.
During the 1780s, Haydn was in attendance at the salon of the von Greiners,
where Steffan was a favored guest. There, he must have become familiar with both
Steffan and his keyboard music. However, Steffan is not mentioned in any extant
Haydn documents, and there is no evidence from the 1760s of any direct connection between them.[44] It is therefore possible that these earlier parallel developments
were merely coincidental.

Accompanied Keyboard Works

The origins of accompanied keyboard music in the Viennese milieu remain a mystery. It is possible to trace the tradition from suite to sonata in solo keyboard works
from Froberger to *ca.* 1770, but no parallel repertoire exists to explain the presence
of accompanied settings in Vienna. According to the *Wienerisches Diarium*, only
three such publications were advertised before 1750 and a total of forty-one up
to 1780.[45] The first print by a Viennese, Wagenseil's Op. 5, appeared in 1770.
However, it was not until the mid-1770s that a number of accompanied settings
received notice. By 1799 accompanied keyboard music occupied as much space
in Traeg's catalogue as did works for one and two keyboards without accompaniment.

In contrast to solo settings, manuscripts of accompanied works are less prevalent, and there seem to be no *Sammelbände*[46] for this repertoire. The only trios to
be found in collections are those in the volumes of Anthology Imperial. Manuscript
sources of individual compositions are at the same locations that took on such importance for the solo keyboard sonata. The collection at Kroměříž is again one of
the principal sources for this repertory, and it provides a general beginning date for
the composition of works in this genre: the latter half of the mid-century period
(*ca.* 1755–1770). The creative lives of the composers of these works[47]—Wagenseil,
Dussek, Leopold Hofmann, J. C. Monn, Steffan, Johann Vanhal, and Anton
Zimmermann—support such a hypothesis: the fact that Fux did not contribute to

this genre, nor did any of his students from the first generation save Wagenseil, also points to the rise of accompanied keyboard music as a relatively late phenomenon, and then it only achieved secondary status to a composer's solo output.

In addition to the standard settings for keyboard and violin and for keyboard, violin, and bass, the repertoire contains a broader spectrum of instrumentation than heretofore assumed. It includes the flute as an option to the violin or as the preferred accompanying treble instrument (Hofmann and Vanhal); accompaniments for two violins and bass and, in the case of one work by Wagenseil, with the instruments indicated "con sordino" (WWV 268); and settings for a variety of combinations: flute, violin, and bass or cello (Dussek, Hofmann, and Steffan); violin, cello, and bass (Hofmann); two flutes and bass (Hofmann); flute, violin, bass, and two horns (Steffan); violin and viola (Wagenseil and Zimmermann); viola and cello (Vanhal); cello obbligato and violin *ad lib* (Wagenseil); and the modern piano quartet—violin, viola, and cello (Zimmermann).

The titles continue to be the expected Sonata, Divertimento, and Trio or Terzetto. Suite and Partita, however, are used only once, while Concerto is used to indicate the relationship among the various parts (i.e., at least one of the voices in addition to the keyboard is obligatory and operates as a full partner). Although Concertino is reserved primarily for settings with three or more accompanying parts, the term may indicate a chamber rather than orchestral setting (i.e., concertino vs. ripieno, solo vs. orchestra) and/or a miniature concerto if the movement sequence is Fast–Slow–Fast.

In contrast to the solo repertoire, the accompanied works contain few vestiges of the suite; only one by Johann Christoph Monn conforms to the older type with more than four movements (Fast–Slow–Ballet with Variations–Minuet and Trio–Fast). Besides nine cycles of Fast–Slow–Fast; three of Fast (Moderate)–Slow–Minuet and Trio, eight of Fast–Slow–Tempo di Menuet, six of Fast–Slow–Minuet and Trio–Fast, and two of Fast–Minuet and Trio–Fast, others less prevalent in early solo keyboard music come to the fore. There are ten instances of two movements consisting of Moderate, Slow, or Fast followed by a minuet and trio or a Tempo di Menuet; and a number of three- and four-movement orderings: one consists of Moderate–Slower–Fast, one of Slow–Fast–Moderate/Fast, three of Fast–Slow–Moderate to Slow in Variation form, two of Slow–Fast–Variations, and one of Moderate/Fast–Fast–Minuet and Trio–Fast. The two- and three-movement cycles provide a model for keyboard trios during the last two decades of the century.[48]

Before 1780 Haydn composed thirteen or more keyboard trios and possibly more than a dozen accompanied keyboard divertimentos/concertinos with two violins and bass, making him the most productive composer of accompanied keyboard music in Vienna during the mid-century period. However, his output is more restricted in terms of setting, as he composed only two works with an accompaniment other than violin and cello or two violins and bass: a keyboard trio with a pair of horns (Hob. XIV : 1) and a lost work adding a baryton to his normal accompanied divertimento setting (Hob. XIV : 2).

The exceptional structures and movement typologies in Haydn's trios can also be found in the compositions of his contemporaries. Hob. XV:33, today known only by its incipits, is the only accompanied setting to hark back to the older suite; of similar ancestry is a work by his contemporary Christoph Monn (Fischer No. 103). Hob. XV:36 and Hob. XV:C1 are Haydn's only trios with two dance movements—containing a polonaise and a fast minuet and two minuets respectively; these trios bring to mind Wagenseil's solo divertimentos. In contrast, Hob. XV:37, with its Slow–Fast–Minuet sequence, belongs to the tradition of the Viennese *da chiesa* trio sonata. Single movements also relate to established types and styles: the Capriccio of Hob. XV:35/1, the French Overture rhythms of Hob. XV:1/1, the elaborately ornamented slow movements of Hob. XV:33 and 41, and the slow finales in variation form of Hob. XV:2 and C1. The first three seem to find their origins in the Viennese solo rather than in the accompanied repertoire; Fillion has shown that Hob. XV:1 may be modeled on Wagenseil's G-minor solo Divertimento WWV 58.[49] The slow finales in variation form are also present in accompanied works by both Vanhal and Zimmermann.

In terms of texture, Haydn's early accompanied works—like those of his contemporaries—share small motives among the various instruments. In Haydn's trios, however, the primary material is always presented first by the right hand of the keyboard and then by the violin; his contemporaries are more likely to begin with the violin and follow with the keyboard.[50] The upper two voices (i.e., the right hand of the keyboard and the violin) of the trio setting also act as they might in a trio sonata, with the left hand and the bass part maintaining a Baroque role.

Thus, Haydn's early accompanied keyboard sonatas derived a great deal from his contemporaries. With the exception of his limited settings (i.e., keyboard and strings *a due* and *a tre*), his works are a reflection of Viennese trends in general during the 1750s and 1760s. Even though the entire issue of *Priorität* in terms of the invention of a genre is a risky one, Haydn probably played as vital a role in the development of accompanied keyboard music as he did in the primal stages of the modern string quartet and symphony. His contributions to the accompanied keyboard genres differ only in the consistency with which they were cultivated: no original keyboard trios were composed from *ca.* 1765 to *ca.* 1783, and he may have ceased writing accompanied divertimentos and concertinos during the 1770s or early 1780s, if not earlier.

Concertos

Although there has been a tendency to trace the origins of the keyboard concerto to J. S. Bach, whose two sons disseminated the tradition in North Germany and England, that assumption is falsely grounded. The elder Bach's model was the Italian violin concerto.[51] To view the Viennese product as an outgrowth of events in Weimar, Cöthen, and Leipzig is clearly unacceptable, for a similar cultural environment existed at the Imperial court. During the first half of the eighteenth century and even earlier, Vienna was saturated with Italian composers, performers, and, presumably, concertos; certainly, the keyboard concertos of the elder Monn or Wagenseil could have been composed independently of any North German influence.[52] M. G. Monn died in 1750, so his concertos pre-date the mid-century mark, as do—most probably—the first concertos of Wagenseil, who had been employed since March 1741 as organist in the chapel of Elisabeth Christine, the widow of Karl VI. Yet before 1750 only foreign concertos by Leffloth and Platti were advertised in the *Wienerisches Diarium*,[53] and even after that date relatively few by the Bach sons and other North Germans appear.

The assumption that the keyboard concerto in Vienna was a small work, scored for two violins and bass, infused with the "divertimento spirit," and of little consequence[54] does not stand the test of a survey of the works themselves. The scoring of the Viennese concerto probably has a greater variety of and interest in color than its North German counterpart, even if all of Mozart's contributions are eliminated. Not uncommon are scorings for three- and four-part strings and for strings with winds and timpani—including flutes, oboes, horns, and clarini. There are even works in which the keyboard is pitted against soloists within the orchestra, such as the concertos by Leopold Hofmann with a solo oboe and obligatory horn parts and those by Steffan and by Wagenseil that feature a solo violin in the slow movement. Furthermore, the dimensions of the Viennese concerto seem to be appreciably larger than the qualifier "divertimento spirit" might allow. Before the 1780s there were clearly two places where concertos were used: in church, where the individual movements became interludes and substitutions for various portions of the Mass proper;[55] and at court, where the Imperial family played them for amusement in their chambers. It is no wonder that the keyboard concertos that come down to us resulted mainly from an ecclesiastical and/or court appointment.

For sources and repertoire, the most important collection is Anthology Imperial. In addition, the *Wienerisches Diarium* advertised sixteen works by 1780,[56] and by the late 1790s, Traeg was offering about 150 keyboard concertos. As final evidence of the independent Viennese development of this genre, the concertos offered by Traeg are more confined to works by Viennese residents than are those for solo keyboard.

NATIVE VIENNESE COMPOSERS

M. G. Monn to L. Hofmann. Possibly the earliest Viennese keyboard concertos are by M. G. Monn to whom seven works (Fischer Nos. 35, 36, 40–44) have been attributed without question.[57] All are strongly oriented toward a Baroque style in their beat marking, surface rhythmic homogeneity, fast harmonic rhythm, spun-out melodies, and motivic play. In addition, the first movements are in ritornello form with four or five tuttis and three or four solos; the structural downbeat and thematic correspondence among the sections required for a recapitulation are generally absent; and the tonic often does not return until the final statement of the ritornello. Their overall structure thus essentially conforms to the Baroque stereotype. On the other hand, the opening ritornello/tutti is frequently a strongly articulated three-section affair, underlined by contrasts in dynamics and texture.[58]

Most of the slow movements have a cantilena texture, the Adagio of the C-major Concerto (Fischer No. 35) being one of the more elaborate melodically. Three are ritornello forms but with only three tuttis, and their total effect is very close to a binary structure. Fischer No. 35 begins with the solo; and the slow movement of the E-flat major Concerto (Fischer No. 44) is basically a solo sonata movement in binary form. The finales are of four types: two are 3/4 Allegros characterized by rhythmic drive;[59] two are 3/8 Presto or Allegro; one is a 3/8 Tempo di Menuetto; and two are fast movements in 2/4 in the style of sonata finales sometimes titled "scherzo." The ritornello structure again predominates.[60]

Unfortunately, the concertos of Wenzel Raimond Birck, a possibly significant link from the old to the new, are no longer extant. They must have been distributed rather widely, for the Breitkopf catalogue lists three with an accompaniment for strings *a quattro* in 1763, 1767, and 1775.[61]

While it is highly probable that Haydn was acquainted with Matthias Georg Monn's works, Haydn's associations with Georg Reutter d.J. carry authentic documentation. His keyboard concertos in F major and C major, which survive undated in copies at the Gesellschaft der Musikfreunde, are scored for two violins and bass and seem to be intended for the harpsichord, as their highest tone is d'''. Reutter's concertos have a more progressive musical syntax than Monn's, but their harmonic language is less colorful. One of Reutter's slow movements is remarkable

EXAMPLE VI–10. Reutter, Concerto in C Major/2 (A-Wgm 16286), mm. 1–8.

for its similarity to the slow movements in Haydn's early solo Sonatas Hob. XVI: 1 and 6 (Example VI-10). Both finales are ritornello forms enclosed by repeats.

The most prolific producer of keyboard concertos during the mid-century period was, once again, Georg Christoph Wagenseil. His output numbers more than eighty works for one and two keyboards with orchestra. Of those for which data are available, sixty-three are scored for strings *a tre* and eight for strings *a quattro*;[62] the remaining dozen or so require from one to three pairs of wind instruments in addition. The emphasis on strings may reflect the fact that these works were for the most part composed for the entertainment of the Imperial family. In this capacity, many are in the modern sense on the border of chamber music; it is not known if the strings were played by more than one performer to a part. Those with larger and more diverse scorings were perhaps for special occasions, the chapel, or even a private concertlike environment.[63]

It was shown above that Wagenseil held a crucial position in the transition from suitelike cycles to the more modern sonata in the solo keyboard works. Here he can be given a place of importance in the development of a new type of concerto. However, for the concertos it is not a change that affects the formation of the cycle— they are all in a Fast–Slow–Fast sequence—but rather the structure of the individual movements: the first movements can be seen to evolve from a form strictly governed by the ritornello principle to one that more consistently reflects its synthesis with sonata form. Since in the older structure the initial material did not return in the tonic key until the final tutti, the presence of a recapitulation before the final tutti-ritornello, i.e., during the penultimate tutti and/or final solo, is crucial to this synthesis. Only one of the first movements of the authentic concertos by M. G. Monn has a recapitulation, while of the available sample of twenty-five first movements in ritornello form by Wagenseil,[64] twenty-two have a recapitulation before the final tutti.

Most of the middle movements employ highly embellished melodies in a cantilena texture. One might expect a binary or small ritornello form with one or two solo sections, but that is not the case: Wagenseil again uses the large ritornello structure of the first movement with a recapitulatory downbeat combining theme and key in the area of the penultimate ritornello and final solo. Most of the binary movements are from smaller works whose first movements were derived from or possibly based on a solo divertimento.

All but two of Wagenseil's finales from the sample of twenty-five are in triple meter (3/4 or 3/8), and more than a third are in Tempo di Menuet. In contrast to the previous movements, binary form with indicated repetitions is the only structure encountered. As happens in the first movements using this framework, a ritornello or tutti/solo plan is interpolated. A shape in which the binary frame is preceded by a tutti section, e.g., in WWV 283

$$R \, \|{:}\, S \, R \,{:}\| \, |{:}\, S \, R \, S \, R \,{:}\|$$

held special interest for the next generation of Viennese composers.[65]

Wagenseil's student Leopold Hofmann composed many more concertos than solo divertimentos/sonatas; according to Jan LaRue, he produced more than thirty keyboard concertos.[66] Although in the concertos his musical ideas do not differ appreciably in quality or interest from those of his mentor Wagenseil, Hofmann used the structures in different ways. Within a sample of seventeen available works,[67] nine first movements use a binary frame for the ritornello, with two of them—as in WWV 283—preceded by a ritornello. Perhaps all nine are based on solo divertimentos/sonatas now lost, even though only one of the known solo divertimentos can be matched to them. Hofmann almost always made use of a recapitulatory form, but—unlike Wagenseil—usually commenced the reprise with the penultimate tutti not the final solo, thereby strengthening its effect. In some of these recapitulations the tutti is followed immediately by the solo restatement of the initial material, while in a few others the solo continues the phrase of the tutti—a device reminiscent of some Mozart concertos in which the keyboard emerges out of the orchestral beginning in the recapitulation.

Although Hofmann's slow movements are also mostly cantilenas, their tonalities depart from a mid-century orientation in that the major mode is preferred.[68] Ritornellos now account for nearly two-thirds of the structures and tend to be less strongly articulated.

The majority of the finales are of a very fast tempo in 2/4, 3/8, or 3/4, but more than a third are still in the aristocratic Tempo di Menuets. One of the most interesting aspects of the fourteen movements in binary form is the syntactical relationship of the opening tutti to the subsequent solo: here the tutti ends in a half cadence followed by the solo commencing with the same material, thereby effecting an antecedent-consequent statement.[69] For the first time there is a finale in the form of theme with variations, a structure enhanced by its scoring with concertante oboe.

An even more prolific composer of keyboard concertos after Wagenseil's generation was Joseph Anton Steffan, to whom forty-two are attributed.[70] A few of his late concertos (after ca. 1789?) have received some attention because of their explicit indications for the *fortepiano*, lengthy slow introductions, and flexible rhythmic/improvisatory style, but the early works have had little study. Even from the seven available early Steffan concertos[71] it is clear that during the 1760s recapitulatory ritornello forms, as well as binary frames preceded by a ritornello, were already an established Viennese tradition.

Haydn and the Viennese Tradition. The position of Haydn's concertos within the Viennese environment is considerably different from that of his solo and accompanied works. While Haydn seems to have been a major contributor to these other mediums and their development, the keyboard concerto was of real interest to him only before his employment by the Esterházys in 1761. Because of his lack of interest, it is one of the few genres in which Haydn failed to develop a personal style.

Rather than being innovative, Haydn's early concertos fit well within the tradition of his Viennese colleagues. If the setting is genuine, Hob. XVIII:7—an arrangement of Hob. XV:40—recalls procedures of transcription and arrangement found in Wagenseil and Hofmann. Although the process in the examples not by Haydn is closer to a transcription than a total reworking, Hob. XVIII:7 and 10 probably belong to a wider tradition that will be further elucidated once a tighter bibliographic control of both the solo sonata and the concerto is achieved. Perhaps also deriving from this heritage of transcriptions and arrangements is the structure that imbeds the tutti/solo of the ritornello principle into a binary frame. Within the first movements in ritornello form, Haydn often used the Viennese recapitulatory practices, discussed above, with regard to the placement of the structural downbeat and the synthesis of recapitulatory function with ritornello in the penultimate tutti and final solo. In addition, one can cite the similar cantilena slow movements and the use of binary/ritornello forms for finales. Haydn's concertos differ from those of his Viennese contemporaries in that they tend to be less virtuosic and to contain fewer measures of empty figuration.

In the Viennese keyboard tradition and repertoire Haydn's output was decisive in the areas of the keyboard trio and the solo sonata. Haydn was the central figure in the early propagation of the keyboard trios; later he established the piano trio as a primary genre of the Classic style. In his solo sonatas, Haydn transformed the Wagenseil divertimento from a suitelike genre of little consequence to the elevated sonatas of late Classicism. In the course of this process during the 1760s, Haydn expanded not only their depth of expression but also their length, formal complexity, harmonic language, and keyboard idiom to the extent that the divertimentos of Wagenseil and his students seem unlikely ancestors.

Essay VII

JOSEPH HAYDN AND
C. P. E. BACH:
THE QUESTION OF INFLUENCE

The problems of influence, causation, and origins have traditionally been of concern to historians. One of the central explanations for the development of Haydn's style during the mysterious period between his dismissal from the choir school at St. Stephen's about 1749 and his recorded employment with the Esterházy family in May 1761 has been his relationship with the leading musician of North Germany, Carl Philipp Emanuel Bach. Today it is still common to find a biography that presents the scenario of Haydn playing C. P. E. Bach's sonatas at a well-worn clavichord on the sixth floor of the Michaelerhaus in the cold of winter.

The association of Haydn and Emanuel Bach appeals to many traditional viewpoints: for the evolutionist, it provides a line from Johann Sebastian Bach to the so-called Viennese Classical School; for those who view history in the Carlylian manner, as the product of interactions of great men, it provides a link between two of the most imaginative minds of the eighteenth century; and for the nationalists, it emphasizes the joining of Protestant and Catholic, North and South—albeit both German. The result, however, has been a rather indistinct view: instead of attempting to clarify, define, and corroborate—or even doubt—certain aspects of this ubiquitous association, there has been a tendency to synthesize and obscure. That is unfortunate, since a return to the origins of the idea with consideration of corroborative evidence tends to cast doubt on some of those very aspects of the C. P. E. Bach/Haydn relationship that have been most fully exploited.

Early Documents and Their Dissemination

The earliest substantive statement[1] concerning Haydn and Bach appeared in the October 1784 issue of the *European Magazine and London Review*, an influential publication among intellectual circles in England and on the Continent. This issue contained a biographical "Account" as well as a review of the Keyboard Sonatas Hob. XVI: 21–32. The statements concerning Haydn and Bach included a reference to a feud between the two, which was subsequently denied by Bach in a letter published by a Hamburg newspaper. Although the reliability of the author (or authors) can therefore be questioned, the sketch and the review provide the earliest and most specific reference to a stylistic relationship:

> With these advantages, it is no wonder if we now behold Haydn outstrip all his competitors. And as envy never fails to pursue merit, the masters in Germany were so jealous of his rising fame, that they entered into a combination against him in order to decry his works and ridicule his compositions; nay, they even carried it so far as to write against him; and many pamphlets in the German language appeared in print to depreciate him in the public esteem, alledging his works were too flighty, trifling, and wild, accusing him at the same time as the inventor of a new musical doctrine, and introducing a species of sounds totally unknown in that country. . . .
>
> Amongst the number of professors who wrote against our rising author was Philip-Emanuel Bach of Hamburgh (formerly of Berlin); and the only notice Haydn took of their scurrility and abuse was, to publish lessons written in imitation of the several stiles of his enemies, in which their peculiarities were so closely cópied, and their extraneous passages (particularly those of Bach of Hamburgh) so inimitably burlesqued, that they all felt the poignancy of his musical wit, confessed its truth, and were silent.
>
> This anecdote will account for a number of strange passages that are here and there dispersed throughout several of the sonatas that have been reprinted in England from the German copies, of which we shall point out the few following passages by way of illustration. Among others, Six Sonatas for the Piano-Forte or Harpsichord, Opera 13 and 14, are expressly composed in order to ridicule Bach of Hamburgh. No one can peruse the second part of the second sonata in the thirteenth opera, and the whole of the third sonata in the same work, and believe Haydn in earnest, writing from his own natural genius, and committing his chaste and original thoughts upon paper. On the contrary, the stile of Bach is closely copied, without the passages being stolen, in which his capricious manner, odd breaks, whimsical modulations, and very often childish manner, mixed with an affectation of profound science, are finely hit off and burlesqued.[2]

The review, which is given in Essay II, specifically refers to the canonic minuet in Haydn's Sonata Hob. XVI: 25 as an imitation of Bach. While minuets in canon represent an important Viennese tradition, in Bach's sonatas they are rarities, and canonic minuets are nonexistent.[3]

Although the origins of this account are unknown, its importance is not so much in its content as in the tradition it fostered. In the following year this essay was translated into German by Carl Friedrich Cramer and published in his *Magazin der Musik* for April 7. Cramer, a connoisseur of Haydn's music, characterized the passages on C. P. E. Bach as "vile attacks . . . against one of the foremost German artists" and continued:

> How ashamed Haydn must feel at heart to be extolled by a panegyrist at the expense of a man whose studies he, I know for certain, himself willingly thanks for a great

TABLE VII-1

Distribution and Influence of 1784 Account

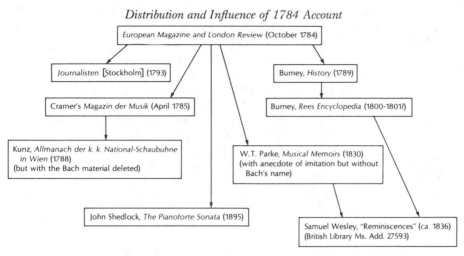

part of his excellence, and who values him in return without envy or spite. . . . It need not be pointed out to us Germans that the historical reports of Bach's hostility toward Haydn etc. are merely trumped-up tales, and that, with the exception of the passages which are meant to praise Haydn (yet how vague, how wishy-washy!), the entire essay is fiction.[4]

This essay of false information, as Cramer termed it, probably only gained further attention through his publication. As can be seen in Table VII-1, the "Account" can be traced as a source for at least four English, another German, and one Swedish publication over the period of a century.

Although the influence of the *European Magazine and London Review* was widespread, Georg August Griesinger's *Biographische Notizen* affected our image of the Haydn/Bach relationship more directly:

> *Haydn erhielt seine Entlassung aus dem Kapellhause im sechszehnten Jahr, weil seine Stimme gebrochen war;* er konnte nicht die mindeste Unterstützung von seinen armen Eltern erwarten, und musste daher suchen, sich blos durch sein Talent fortzubringen. *Er bezog in Wien ein armseliges Dachstübchen (im Hause Nr. 1220. am Michaelerplatze) ohne Ofen, worin er kaum gegen den Regen geschützt war. Unbekannt mit den Annehmlichkeiten des Lebens war seine ganze Zeit zwischen Lektiongeben, dem Studium seiner Kunst, und praktischer Musik getheilt. Er spielte bey Nachtmusiken und in den Orchestern ums Geld mit, und er übte sich fleissig in der Komposition, denn* "wenn ich an meinem alten, von Würmern zerfressenen Klavier sass, beneidete ich keinen König um sein Glück." Um diese Zeit fielen Haydn die sechs ersten Sonaten von Emanuel Bach in die Hände; "da kam ich nicht mehr von meinem Klavier hinweg, bis sie durchgespielt waren, und wer mich gründlich kennt, der muss finden, dass ich dem Emanuel Bach sehr vieles verdanke, dass ich ihn verstanden und fleissig studirt habe; Emanuel Bach liess mir auch selbst einmal ein Kompliment darüber machen."

In demselben Hause, worin Joseph Haydn einquartiert war, wohnte auch der berühmte Dichter Metastasio. Dieser liess ein Fräulein Martinez erziehen, Haydn musste ihr Unterricht im Singen und Klavierspielen geben, und erhielt dafür drey Jahre lang die Kost umsonst.

Haydn received his dismissal from the choir school when he was sixteen because his voice had broken; he could not expect the least support from his poor parents and thus had to try to support himself by his talent alone. *He moved into a miserable attic room in Vienna (in the house at No. 1220 in the Michaelerplatz) without a stove, where he was scarcely protected from the rain. Unacquainted with the comforts of life, his entire time was divided between giving lessons, studying his art, and performing. He played in serenades and in orchestras for money, and he practiced composing diligently, for "whenever I sat at my old worm-eaten Klavier, I didn't envy any king his good fortune."* About this time Haydn got hold of the first six sonatas by Emanuel Bach: "I didn't leave my *Klavier* at all until they were played through, and whoever knows me very well, must realize that I owe Emanuel Bach a great deal, and that I have understood and studied him diligently. Emanuel Bach even paid me a compliment about that once."

In the same house where Joseph Haydn lived, also lived the famous poet Metastasio. He was educating a Fräulein Martines. Haydn had to give her instruction in singing and Klavier playing and for three years received his board for doing it.[5]

Based on a series of visits to Haydn, Griesinger's material was apparently rearranged into a chronological continuity. The question then is not *whether* Haydn had an encounter with C. P. E. Bach's sonatas but *when*. If one compares Bertuch's account of Haydn's early years, originally published in 1805 in *Journal des Luxus und der Moden*—which Bertuch himself later confirmed as based on Griesinger's not yet published material (indicated by the italicized passages in the Griesinger excerpts)—with the final presentation in 1809, one can hypothesize that the entire C. P. E. Bach episode was inserted by Griesinger at a later date:

Mit dem sechzehnten Jahre erhielt Haydn seine Entlassung von der Stephanskirche, weil seine Stimme gebrochen war. Höchst kümmerlich musste er sich nun eine lange Reihe von Jahren hindurch in Wien fortbringen. Er wohnte in einem sechsten Stockwerke; seine Dachwohnung hatte weder Ofen noch Fenster, der Hauch fror des Winters auf seiner Bettdecke, und das Wasser, welches er sich des Morgens am Brunnen zum Waschen holte, war bei seiner Ankunft in den höheren Regionen oft schon zum Eisklumpen verwandelt. Haydn gab Lectionen, er spielte in den Orchestern mit, wo es etwas zu verdienen gab, seine Armuth entfernte ihn von den Menschen, und er fand sein einziges Glück an einem alten, von würmern zerfressenen Klavier. Er komponirte wacker darauf los, sein Genius liess ihn nicht ruhen. Eine Fräulein Martini [sic], die mit Metastasio in Verbindung stand, unterrichtete er im Singen und Klavierspielen, und erhielt dagegen drei Jahre lang dort die Kost umsonst.

With his sixteenth year Haydn received his dismissal from St. Stephen's Church because his voice had broken. In greatest need, he had to endure a succession of years in Vienna. He lived on the sixth floor; his attic room had neither stove nor window. In the winter his breath froze on his bedcovers, and the water that he fetched from the fountain for washing in the morning was often already changed into ice by the time he returned to those higher reaches. He gave lessons; he played in orchestras when there was something to be earned. His poverty separated him from people, and he found his only happiness at an old worm-eaten *Klavier*. He continued composing eagerly at it; his genius would not let him rest. To a Fräulein Martini [*sic*], who was connected with Metastasio, he gave lessons in singing and *Klavier* playing and for this received his board for three years.[6]

My hypothesis is that the portion of the paragraph ending with "whenever I sat at my old worm-eaten *Klavier*, I didn't envy any king for his good fortune" and the following reference to C. P. E. Bach were not spoken by Haydn during a single conversation with Griesinger.[7] Griesinger himself provides a caveat with the lead-in "About this time." It must then be asked, how confining is "About this time," when stated almost half a century after the fact?

Griesinger's paragraph also raises some other questions of origin: the scenario of a protagonist in a *Dachwohnung* or other isolated room playing his heart out at an old *Klavier* turns up in the well-known novel *Anton Reiser* by Karl Phillip Moritz, from the second half of the 1780s:

> He shut himself up in his room where he had repaired an old, dilapidated *Klavier* as well as he knew how and had tuned it with great trouble. He sat at this *Klavier* the whole day and, as he knew how to read music, he learned to sing and play almost all the arias from *Die Jagd, Der Tod Abels*, etc. by himself.[8]

Whether Griesinger knew this work cannot be ascertained, but certainly the similarity is a strong one. The same paragraph is also echoed in the *Gazetteer* [London] for February 1787 in a report from Gaetano Bartolozzi:

> The Prince of Esterhagy [*sic*], to whom this great composer is *Maitre de Chapelle*, though he affects the highest admiration of the works of Haydn, who is constantly employed in his service, yet his only reward is a pittance which the most obscure fiddler in London would disdain to accept, together with a miserable apartment in the barracks, in which are his bed and an old spinnet, or clavichord.[9]

In addition we might question what is meant by "the first six sonatas of Emanuel Bach." Pohl and nearly everyone after him have assumed that Haydn studied the first print of Bach's keyboard works, the so-called Prussian Sonatas (Wq. 48).[10] Since this set is not designated as Op. 1 on the title page, this hypothesis is slippery. Indeed, the only source that could have identified Bach's first publication of sonatas would have been J. J. C. Bode's German translation of Burney's *The Present State of Music in Germany, the Netherlands, and the United Provinces*. The translation, published in 1772–1773, replaced Burney's first-hand reports with Bach's autobiography: in the list of works, the "Prussian" sonata set (1742) is given as Bach's first major publication.[11] If Haydn actually made reference to Bach's "Opus 1," three other prints that had "Opus 1" in their titles would be more plausible: an unauthorized 1761 print containing Wq. 62/8 and 13, 65/9–10, 8, and 22, titled *Six Sonates . . . Oeuvre 1ᵉʳ* from Huberty in Paris; *Six Sonates . . .*

l'usage des Dames (Wq. 54); and the first set of *Kenner und Liebhaber* Sonatas (Wq. 55). The first and third publications have special credibility. The Huberty print was available in Vienna through the Parisian publisher's agent, Van Ghelen; his shop was in the Michaelerhaus, where Haydn lived, worked, and studied some time during the 1750s. Van Ghelen also sold a number of other publications that Haydn owned, works by Marpurg, Mattheson, Fux, and Kirnberger. The *Kenner und Liebhaber* sonatas published in 1779 were subscribed to in multiple copies by both Haydn's friend Baron Gottfried van Swieten and his publisher, Artaria (see Table VII-2).

A final argument to discredit Griesinger's reference to Bach is his possible regional chauvinism. Griesinger came to Vienna as Royal Councillor to the Saxon Legation, and some of his earliest meetings with Haydn in 1799 were at the instigation of Gottfried Härtel. His biographical notes were originally intended for the *Allgemeine Musikalische Zeitung*, which was published by Breitkopf & Härtel of Leipzig. Thus, the Saxon/Leipzig background of Griesinger and his employer may have made Haydn's connection with the most famous musical family of this geographical region a necessity for the potential audience.

Whereas many people read the London "Account" and even quoted it, Griesinger's biography gained a distribution and public credibility through its 1809 publication in the *Allgemeine Musikalische Zeitung*,[12] the most widely read and respected music journal of its day, and through a reprinting in book form under the *aegis* of Breitkopf & Härtel in 1810 and 1819 that should not be underestimated. It was read, translated, copied, and paraphrased; it served as the basis for nearly every biographical sketch and tribute after Haydn's death: Le Breton (1810), Choron and Fayolle (1810), Gerber (1812),[13] Baur (1816), *English Musical Gazette* (1819), *Neujahrstück der Allgemeinen Musik Gesellschaft in Zürich* (1830), Fétis (1839), and Wurzbach (1862), among many others.

In contrast, the impact of Albert Christoph Dies's *Biographische Nachrichten* has been somewhat limited, even though it too is based on a series of visits to the aged composer. It received only one printing in 1810 and was not republished until 1959.[14] The book may have been ignored because Dies, a landscape painter, did not have Griesinger's important connections, and because the loquacity of the biography cast suspicion on his reliability.[15] However, Dies's book is the only authentic biographical source that refers to Haydn's possession of Emanuel Bach's *Versuch über die wahre Art das Clavier zu spielen*.

> However, what interested him most was to make use of the important discovery that I mentioned above, and by a serious study of theory to be able to learn to bring order to his artistic creations (which, as we all know, he loves above all). He decided to buy a good book; but which one? He couldn't answer, and he had his reasons for not asking someone's advice. Since he didn't know how to choose, he left it almost to chance, intending first to leaf around in a book a little to judge it before he spent, perhaps for nothing, a whole month's income.
>
> Haydn ventured to enter a bookstore and ask for a good theoretical text. The bookdealer named Carl Philipp Emanuel Bach's writings the newest and best.

Haydn wanted to see, to be convinced; he began to read, understood, found what he was looking for, paid for the book and carried it off, quite satisfied.

That Haydn tried to make Bach's principles his own, that he studied them untiringly, is already to be noted in his youthful works from that time. At nineteen years of age, he wrote quartets which made him known as a well-versed genius to the lovers of music. So quickly had Haydn understood. In time he bought the later writings of Bach. In his judgment, Bach's writings are the best, most fundamental, and most useful works that have ever appeared as textbooks.[16]

Even this reference to Haydn and C. P. E. Bach is not without confusion: the factuality of the statement on the early string quartets from Haydn's nineteenth year has been questioned by both Finscher and Webster.[17] However, the remainder of the statement seems clear: Haydn bought a book by C. P. E. Bach. A number of commentators have tried to place this incident during the 1750s, as the first part of the *Versuch* appeared in 1753. But Dies was referring to a theoretical work; while the first part of Bach's treatise deals with problems of performance, both technical and interpretive, the second covers intervals, thorough bass accompaniment, and improvisation. It thus seems more likely that Haydn acquired Parts I and II, both of which were published by 1762.

The most troublesome aspect of this story is that neither part or their musical supplements were found in Haydn's library, as known from the *Haydn Bibliothek Verzeichnis* (*HBV*), ca. 1804, and the *Haydn Nachlass Verzeichnis* (*HNV*), 1809. Although this discrepancy might be explained by the various fires that occurred in Haydn's household during the 1760s and 1770s, this argument can be countered by the presence in the library of many of the other authors mentioned by the early biographers—Mattheson, Heinichen, and Fux.[18]

The most completely satisfying firsthand statements derive from Haydn's friend Abbé Maximilian Stadler. His version of the Bach–Haydn relationship has been made known primarily through Friedrich Rochlitz's introduction to an essay on Emanuel Bach.[19] Stadler himself stated:

> As a boy gifted with genius, [Haydn] had the opportunity to study singing and instruments. The learned masters, among them Reutter, Porpora, and the books of Fux, Mattheson, etc., willingly imparted instructions to this diligent pupil. He heard with interest the masterpieces of Holzbauer, Wagenseil, [and] Hasse, which then were improving the musical tastes of the time, and many other composers of Vienna who were, so to speak, his predecessors; he himself began to compose early, and whoever possesses and examines his first *Klavier* sonatas and violin divertimentos will easily see that he had modeled himself after Wagenseil and his kind. Later he took in hand the foreign "products" such as those of C. P. E. Bach, etc., studied them, and while remaining faithful to his own special tastes, through this study he still molded more and more the realization of his own ideas, among which his quartets with fugues can serve as examples.[20]

Stadler gives the distinct impression that Haydn's early stylistic development can be viewed in two phases: a period during which Haydn absorbed the style of his

TABLE VII-2

Publications of Bach's Solo Keyboard Works: Availability in Vienna

Wq.	Title	Publication date	Dealer and date in *Wienerisches Diarium/Wiener Zeitung* notices up to 1779	Prints now extant in Vienna	Traeg Catalogue, 1799 + = included − = absent	Viennese subscribers, Remarks
48	Sei Sonate per Cembalo, che all' Augusta Maestà di Frederico, Re di Prussia	1742	1756 Bauer		+	Also possibly sold by Monath, 1746
49	Sei Sonate per Cembalo, dedicate all' Altezza Serenissima di Carlo Eugenio, Duca di Wirtemberg . . . Op. 2	1744		A-Wgm A-Wn	+	Also possibly sold by Monath, 1746
63	Achtzehn Probe-Stücken in sechs Sonaten	1753	1773 Ghelen 1763 Schmid of Regensburg		−	
62/9	Oeuvres mêlées, I	1755			+	
62/13	Raccolta delle più nuove Composizioni di Clavicembalo . . . Fatta Stampare dal Sign. Feder. Guiglielmo Marpurg	1756			−	
62/15	Raccolta delle più nuove Composizioni di Clavicembalo . . . Fatta stampare dal Sign. Feder. Guiglielmo Marpurg.	1757			−	
62/4	Oeuvres mêlées, III	1757			+	
62/5	Oeuvres mêlées, IV	1757–58			+	
62/22	Collection récréative Op. 1	1758–61			+	
62/16	Oeuvres mêlées, V	1758–61			+	
50	Sechs Sonaten für Clavier mit veränderten Reprisen	1760	1767 ⎱ Trattner 1769 ⎰ 1773 Krütchen	A-Wgm A-Wn	+	
51	Fortsetzung von Sechs Sonaten	1761		A-M A-Wgm	+	
62/1, 6, 8, 11, 12	Musikalisches Allerley	1761	1768 ⎱ 1770 Trattner 1777 ⎰		−	
62/7	Collection récréative Op. 2	1761			−	
62/2	Nebenstunden der berlinischen Musen	1762			−	
62/3	Marpurg's Clavierstücke mit einem practischen Unterricht für Anfänger und Geübtern	1763			−	

62/10, 14, 18, 19, 20	Musikalisches Mancherley	1762–63			+	
52	Zweite Forstezung von Sechs Sonaten	1763	1769 Trattner	A-Wgm	+	
62/21	Oeuvres mêlées XI	1765			+	
112	Clavierstücke Verschniedener Art	1766?	1769	A-Wn	–	
62/17	Oeuvres mêlées XII	1766 Bernardi	1769	A-Wn	+	
113–114	Kurze und leichte Clavierstücke mit veränderten Reprisen . . .	1766			+	
53	Sechs leichte Claviersonaten		1771 Ghelen	A-Wgm / A-Wn	–	
54	Six sonates pour le clavecin, à l'usage des Dames . . . Op. 1	1769?	1775 Ghelen / 1777 / Trattner; Artaria?	A-M / A-Wgm	+	
62/23	Musikalisches Vielerley	1773	1776		–	
24	Six sonates pour le clavecin . . . Oeu. 1er		1777 Ghelen / Trattner / 1772? Ghelen		+	
62/8, 65/10, 22, 62/13, 65/9, 18						
55	Sechs Clavier-sonaten für Kenner und Liebhaber . . . Erste Sammlung (K + L)	1779		A-M / A-Wgm	+	Artaria, 12 copies / van Swieten, 12 copies
56	Clavier-sonaten nebst einigen Rondos fürs Fortepiano, K + L 2	1780		A-Wgm (2 examples) / A-Wn	+	Baron von Braun, 1 copy / van Swieten, 12 copies
57	Clavier-sonaten nebst einigen Rondos fürs Fortepiano, K + L 3	1781		A-Wgm (2 examples) / A-Wn	+	Artaria, 12 copies / van Swieten, 12 copies / HBV 69; HNV 263
58	Clavier-sonaten und freye Fantasien nebst einigen Rondos, K + L 4	1783		A-Wgm (2 examples) / A-Wn	+	Artaria, 6 copies / van Braun, 2 copies
59	Clavier-sonaten und freye Fantasien nebst einigen Rondos, K + L 5	1785		A-Wgm (2 examples) / A-Wn	+	Artaria, 12 copies / Baron von Braun, 1 copy / van Swieten, 12 copies / HBV 117; HNV 264
60	Una Sonata per il Cembalo	1785		A-Wgm	–	
61	Clavier-sonaten und freye Fantasien nebst einigen Rondos, K + L 6	1787		A-Wgm / A-Wgm (2 examples) / A-Wn	+	Artaria, 6 copies / van Swieten, 12 copies
53b	Sechs neue Sonatinen welche bey der 3ten [4ten?] Auflage	1786?				
	Tonstücke für das Clavier	1762 Kraus	1762 Trattner		+	

Viennese predecessors, including works by Holzbauer, Wagenseil, and others, which were models for his early keyboard sonatas and violin divertimentos; and a somewhat later period during which he studied the "products" of foreign composers, among them C. P. E. Bach. Stadler seems to be a reliable source, for he had known Haydn for many years and, unlike Dies and Griesinger, had gathered his information long before the composer's mental faculties had begun to deteriorate. Stadler seems not to have had a special viewpoint to espouse; his comments reflect what we know of Haydn's stylistic development from his works; and an evolution from local Viennese influences toward more Continental ones is logical for a developing talent.

The remaining important sources date from the London period. In the preface to *A Selection of Sacred Music* Christian Ignaz Latrobe wrote:

> Bach, Charles Philip Emanuel . . . Haydn considers him as the author of all modern elegance and gracefulness in execution; and in conversation with me want [*sic*] so far as to say, with his usual modesty, that but for studying Bachs' [*sic*] Works, he had himself been a clumsy Composer.[21]

Perhaps the most interesting statement concerning Haydn and Bach is found in a little-known encyclopedia article by Charles Burney, *ca.* 1800:

> For the practice [of Music], [Haydn] studied with particular attention, the pieces of Emanuel Bach, whom he made his model in writing for keyed instruments, as he candidly confessed to us when in England, in the same manner as Pope had formed himself upon Dryden.[22]

Since Burney was a member of the circle of the lexicographer and critic Samuel Johnson, the analogy of Dryden—Pope with Bach—Haydn as examples of stylistic parallels can be pursued from Johnson's well-known essay on Pope. Burney seems to have had in mind the opening paragraph:

> He [Pope] professed to have learned his poetry from Dryden, whom, whenever an opportunity was presented, he praised through his whole life with unvaried liberality.

Other statements by Johnson also seem uncanny:

> Dryden's page is a natural field, rising into inequalities, and diversified by the varied exuberance of abundant vegetation; Pope's is a velvet lawn, shaven by the scythe, and leveled by the roller.

> If the flights of Dryden therefore are higher, Pope continues longer on the wing. If of Dryden's fire the blaze is brighter, of Pope's the heat is more regular and constant. Dryden often surpasses expectation, and Pope never falls below it. Dryden is read with frequent astonishment, and Pope with perpetual delight.[23]

Several questions arise as one consults other early sources in which one might expect mention of Haydn and C. P. E. Bach and yet finds none. For example, both composers are discussed but no relationship is drawn by Carl Ludwig Junker in his *Zwanzig Componisten* (Bern, 1776). Indeed, there are no sources before the 1780s that refer to a Bach–Haydn relationship. More significantly, Bach does not appear in Haydn's autobiographical sketch of 1776, which otherwise seems to be one of the most explicit documents concerning his early years and in which Haydn mentions that Porpora taught him the fundamentals of composition. Instead, the seemingly firsthand reports of Haydn's acknowledgment of his indebtedness to Bach first date from his London visits.[24] Were they a result of inquiries from Haydn's English friends who knew of the 1784 "Account"? Did his friends jog his memory and cause Haydn to recall experiences from the 1750s and 1760s that he had forgotten when he wrote his autobiographical sketch in the 1770s, but later remembered somewhat confusedly in his conversations with Dies and Griesinger? Given the present state of documentation, it is impossible to resolve all these discrepancies.

The validity of the Bach–Haydn relationship can be pursued through more recent musicological literature, where it has grown far beyond the restraints of the early documents (and the constraints of historical method). The conclusions drawn from it can be tested against the known distribution of Emanuel Bach's works in eighteenth-century Vienna. How well will the resulting distinct linkages between Haydn and Bach stand up to this additional scrutiny? Did Haydn play, study, and admire the keyboard sonatas of C. P. E. Bach? Did Haydn study the *Versuch*? Did Bach influence Haydn's stylistic development as seen in the latter's keyboard sonatas?

The Musicological
Literature of the Twentieth Century

The musicological literature of the present century is mostly concerned with the widely disseminated view that Emanuel Bach's music had a significant and observable impact on Haydn. It has been marked by an unusual enthusiasm to find interactions among great men and plagued by errors of both judgment and fact. Unconvincing stylistic parallels have been used to conclude that Bach's style was an ever-present factor in Haydn's works, and there are errors of dating, chronology, and identification, as well as a regional chauvinism among non-Austrian German scholars. If these shortcomings were only isolated phenomena they could be overlooked; but they have originated from authoritative scholars and publishers and thus have created their own "traditions."

The infrequent use of actual musical examples to demonstrate parallels between Bach and Haydn immediately raises doubts about the viability of the espoused relationship; when examples have been cited, they appear to this author to be unconvincing or otherwise untenable. These problems begin as early as the "Account" and reviews that appeared in the 1784 *European Magazine and London Review*. Subsequent examples have been presented, albeit somewhat apologetically, by such scholars as E. F. Schmid, an authority on the music of both Haydn and Bach.[25] In 1932 he cited one pair of excerpts from Hob. XVI:22/2 and Wq. 78/1,

measures whose parallels are not apparent to either eye or ear: the similarities of
mode and, to a lesser extent, texture are of a most common type and certainly form
no criterion on which to base an influence. Schmid explains that the sensitive/ex-
pressive aspect and Bach's language in general are the important factors in the six
measures shown.

More recently, H. C. R. Landon explained the similarities found in the third
sonata from Bach's Württemberg set and Haydn's D-major Sonata, Hob. XVI: 19:

> In 1765, Haydn's whole sonata technique has begun to change. There is now a real
> development section, a new sense of tension generated by the organised use of
> motifs. The development sections of the two works . . . show how much of the spirit
> if not the letter of the new *anti-galant* writing comes from C. P. E. Bach.[26]

Hob. XVI: 19 was first referred to in a 1915 article by Rudolf Steglich as one of the
sonatas from Op. 13–14 reviewed in the October 1784 issue of the *European
Magazine and London Review;*[27] it is now known that this sonata had no part in
these *opere*. Landon was not the only one to perpetuate this error, for his distinguished company includes Schmid, Abert, Geiringer, and Finscher.[28]

Geiringer tends to cite Bach's influence whenever Haydn chose to compose
anything out of the ordinary.

> The second sonata shows some marks of the influence of Philipp Emanuel Bach,
> which was to assume much larger proportions in the years to come. The syncopa-
> tions and unison passages, the passionate and quite personal character of the largo,
> with its sudden contrasts of mood, are unmistakably of north-German origin.
>   The closer we come to Haydn's third period, the clearer become the indications
> of the influence of Philipp Emanuel Bach. Number 46, written between 1765 and
> 1768, contains a wide-contoured adagio in D-flat Major, testifying, with its pathos
> and sudden changes of mood, to the impact of the north-German master's music on
> Prince Esterházy's conductor. . . .
>   In the first movement [of Hob. XVI: 20] the beginning of the development ex-
> hibits Haydn's art as constituting a link between the music of P. E. Bach and that of
> Beethoven. . . . Haydn now wrote rondos in which, as in the works of Philipp
> Emanuel Bach, each entrance of the main theme displays new figuration. . . . The
> quartets of Op. 17 show how closely Haydn approached the art of P. E. Bach during
> this period.[29]

Geiringer also cites the "sudden half-tone progressions" in the first movement of
the Quartet Op. 55/2.[30] Perhaps most surprising is his assertion that the first movement of the Sonata Hob. XVI: 52 "uses all of the devices of Bach's style";[31] it has
been more commonly thought that its boldness derived from the composer's exposure to the music of the "London Pianoforte School."[32] Geiringer is not alone in
the indiscriminate invoking of the North German composer's name with regard to
Haydn's style; this practice is also found in widely read discussions by Philip
Radcliffe[33] and Rosemary Hughes.[34] Many of the characteristics cited by Geiringer,
Hughes, and Radcliffe can also be found in other compositions of the period from
Viennese sources and other geographic areas on the Continent; half-step slips, sud-

den changes in mood, first movements of moderate pace, repeated notes, rolling sextuplets, and the like were hardly the exclusive properties of Bach's or Haydn's music.

One also suspects that regional chauvinism has colored scholarly views of the Haydn–Bach relationship. When Hermann Abert wrote his still valuable and important stylistic survey of Haydn's solo sonatas, perhaps the professor from Kiel was being too much of a North German in suggesting that Haydn's keyboard music of the 1760s represents a synthesis of North German and Viennese styles.[35] In a recent monograph, Ludwig Finscher cites Emanuel Bach frequently in his discussion of the history of the string quartet in relation to Haydn.[36] Most surprisingly, he suggests that the chamber music quality of *opere* 1 and 2 might have come from Bach's trio sonata "Gespräch zwischen einem Sanguineo und Melancholico," composed in 1749 and published two years later.[37] The idea that chamber music in Haydn derives from Bach not only is weak history but also minimizes the options available to one of the most resourceful of musical minds.

In establishing an interaction between one composer and another, complete control of the chronology is essential; Bach could not have influenced Haydn unless the works in question were available to Haydn before the modeled work was composed. Still one reads in the preface to Franz Eibner's 1975 edition of Haydn's *Klavierstücke* that the Capriccio in G major Hob. XVII:1 "adopts the characteristic Ph. E. Bach rondo, evolved from a single theme."[38] While there is no question that Haydn had an opportunity to familiarize himself with the rondos from the third and fifth *Kenner und Liebhaber* collections, he could not have studied them before 1780, the year they appeared in printed form. Since Haydn's G-major Capriccio dates from 1765 and Bach did not begin to compose rondos of this type until the late 1770s, even the possibility of Haydn's seeing prepublication manuscript copies is excluded.[39]

After this examination of the early documents and their striking embellishment in some of the more visible literature on Haydn's music, one might be tempted to dismiss the entire concept of a Bach–Haydn connection. But in light of the variety of early independent sources that contain this idea—the anonymous writer in the *European Magazine*, Burney, Latrobe, Stadler, Dies, and Griesinger—there must be some basis for it. Therefore, let us look at the evidence for the availability of Bach's works in Haydn's surroundings.

Distribution of Emanuel Bach's Works in Vienna

The distribution of Emanuel Bach's works in eighteenth-century Vienna[40] and the likelihood of their reaching Haydn or the circle of his acquaintances can be determined by advertisements in the *Wienerisches Diarium/Wiener-Zeitung*;[41] extant copies of prints in Austrian archives, monasteries, and libraries; the catalogues of the Viennese music dealer Johann Traeg, first issued in 1799;[42] the subscription lists for Bach's works; and the catalogues of Haydn's library, *HBV* and *HNV* (see Table VII-2). Because of the difficulties of identifying concertos and chamber works, only solo keyboard works have been included. Although such information has its limitations, it is certainly superior to approaches that do not even attempt to define the repertoire.

The largest single source in Vienna was the music dealer and publisher Johann Traeg (*ca.* 1747–1805), who offered the most comprehensive catalogue of music that could be purchased in the Imperial city. Traeg's listing for Emanuel Bach includes ninety-six keyboard sonatas; six collections for *Kenner und Liebhaber* of sonatas, rondos, and fantasias; sixteen keyboard concertos, and various other chamber works. Since Traeg's activities can be traced back only to 1782,[43] his list can give us but a glimmer of the works available in Vienna before his ascendancy. Haydn's association with Traeg was an important one; it goes back to 1789, when Traeg served as Immanuel Breitkopf's representative in Vienna, a role he was to retain until the end of Haydn's creative life. Unfortunately, there is no documentary evidence of Haydn's having acquired any music from him other than his own.

The dealers who advertised Bach's works in the *Wienerisches Diarium/Wiener-Zeitung* give us some idea of which of the Hamburg Bach's compositions Haydn had the possibility of seeing or acquiring before Traeg became active in 1782. Since the central portion of the city of Vienna was small, all these dealers would have been convenient to the two known residences of Haydn during the 1750s, in the Michaelerplatz and Seilerstadt, as well as to the Esterházy Palace on the Wallnerstrasse for the later decades.[44]

It is obvious from Table VII-2 that nearly every major publication of solo keyboard music by Emanuel Bach was available in the Imperial capital. But only for Bach's latest publications, the *Kenner und Liebhaber* volumes, do we have direct or highly plausible evidence that Haydn had opportunities to see the prints: all five sets were subscribed to by Haydn's publisher Artaria and/or Baron Gottfried van Swieten. Baron von Braun, an excellent keyboardist himself, subscribed for three sets; his wife was Josephine von Braun, to whom Haydn dedicated the first Viennese edition of the F-minor Variations Hob. XVII:6.[45] Indeed, Haydn probably received his copies of the third and fifth installments of the *Kenner und Liebhaber* set from Artaria directly, as his letter of 16 February 1788 requests: "In addition, I ask that the 2 latest *Clavier* works by C. P. Emanuel Bach be sent to me."[46]

The inventories of his library show that Haydn acquired manuscript copies of the following solo and ensemble keyboard works by Emanuel Bach:

Freye Fantasie Wq. 67 (*HBV* 181, *HNV* 541)
Trio a Cembalo e Violino Wq. 80 (*HBV* 180, *HNV* 542)
Quartetto für Clavier, Flöte, und Bratsche Wq. 93 (*HBV* 178, *HNV* 543)
Quartetto für Clavier, Flöte, und Bratsche Wq. 94 (*HBV* 179, *HNV* 543)
Concerto [Two keyboards] Wq. 47 (*HBV* 177, *HNV* 544)

The copyists and papers of all are of German and not Austrian origin; Wq. 93 and 94 are by one scribe and Wq. 47, 67, and 80 by another. Since Wq. 47 was composed in 1788, Wq. 67 and 80 were probably acquired after this date. Wq. 93

and 94 contain the inscriptions "Mense. Jan: 88" and "g[estochen] 27 Jan. 88" respectively.[47]

Exactly when these copies came into Haydn's possession cannot be determined. E. F. Schmid believed that Haydn acquired some during his stopover in Hamburg on his return from London in 1795 and others, listed in *HNV* but not *HBV*, from the estate of Baron Gottfried van Swieten, who died in 1803.[48] Copies acquired on the latter occasion could not have had any influence on Haydn, since by 1803 he had already proclaimed the end of his creative career with the two movements for the Quartet Op. 103. It is difficult to believe, however, that if Haydn was at the sale of the Baron's *Nachlass*, that he would not have recovered the autographs and other documents relating to *The Creation* and *The Seasons*, which were reportedly in the Baron's possession.

Finally, the Abbé Maximilian Stadler leads us to conclude that the study of Emanuel Bach was not unfashionable in Vienna among Haydn's circle. Stadler's is especially revealing, as it mentions Johann Georg Albrechtsberger (1736–1809) and Robert Kimmerling (1737–1799), both of whom had important connections with the Benedictine Abbey at Melk, as did Stadler himself. According to Stadler, Albrechtsberger—one of Haydn's friends for nearly half a century—"studied diligently the works of Sebastian and Philipp Bach"; while the Regens Chori at Melk, Kimmerling, who studied with Haydn around 1760 and later became one of his "trusted friends," was "an excellent tenor and keyboard player [who] made himself familiar with Graun's and Philipp Emanuel Bach's works and studied them assiduously." Today Kimmerling's library survives at Melk with one work by Galuppi, in which Kimmerling inscribed that it was recommended to him by Haydn, and prints of C. P. E. Bach's Sonatas Wq. 51, 54, and 55—none of which were available before 1760.[49]

From Table VII-2 and the subsequent discussion we can draw the following conclusions concerning Haydn and a Viennese tradition for Bach's music with obbligato keyboard:

1. Haydn owned Wq. 47, 57, 59, 67, 80, 93, and 94.

2. A strong tradition in Vienna—and within Haydn's circle (e.g., copies at Melk and/or publications sold by Ghelen)—makes it plausible that Haydn could have additionally known Wq. 51, 53, 54, 55, 56, 57, 58, 61, 62 (8, 13, 23, 24), and 65 (9, 10, 18, 22).

3. The following were also available in Vienna during Haydn's creative life: Wq. 48, 49, 50, 52, 53b, 60, 62 (1, 3?, 4–6, 8–12, 16–21), 112, 113, and 114.

4. There is no evidence of the following being available in Vienna during Haydn's creative life: Wq. 62 (2, 3, 7, 13, 15, 22).

Since some of the earliest documents and much of the literature on this topic have emphasized that Haydn learned of Bach's music during the 1750s, the next task is to establish a chronological sequence of the availability in Vienna of this repertoire. Table VII-3 shows that little would have been available in Vienna during the 1750s, but that contact in the 1760s is quite plausible. Furthermore, the so-called Prussian and Württemberg Sonatas (Wq. 48 and 49), which are fre-

TABLE VII-3

Chronology for Available Published Solo Keyboard Works of C. P. E. Bach in Vienna

Earliest Date of Viennese Availability*	Acquired by Haydn	Strong Tradition for Vienna and Haydn	Procurable in Vienna
before 1749			Wq. 49
1750			
1751			
1752			
1753			
1754			
1755			Wq. 62/9
1756			Wq. 48
1757			Wq. 62/4, 62/5
1758			Wq. 62/16
1759			
1760			
1761		Wq. 51	
1762			Wq. 62/10,14,18,19,20
1763			Wq. 62/3?
1764			
1765			Wq. 112
1766			Wq. 62/17
1767			Wq. 50
1768			Wq. 62/1,6,8,11,12
1769			Wq. 52,113,114
1770			
1771		Wq. 53	
1772		Wq. 62/8,13; 65/9,10,18,22	
1773			
1774			
1775		Wq. 54	
1776		Wq. 62/23,24	
1777			
1778			
1779		Wq. 55	
1780		Wq. 56	
1781		Wq. 57	
1782			
1783		Wq. 58	
1784			
1785			Wq. 60
1786			Wq. 53b
1787		Wq. 61	
1788	Wq. 57,59		
1789			
after 1790	Wq. 47,67,80,93,94		

*For later dates see Table VII-2.
N. B. Wq. 62/21 not datable.

quently mentioned in relation to Haydn, have a relatively weak tradition in the Imperial capital.[50] Irrefutable documentation of Haydn's acquisition of Bach's works exists only for the 1780s. Thus, one needs to be more cautious than has heretofore been the case with regard to the possibility that Bach's musical creations influenced Haydn.

As for Haydn's acquaintance with Bach's *Versuch*, Dies mentions the book directly, but his anecdote can be questioned on the basis of its context. The treatise is not listed in the two catalogues of Haydn's library (*HBV* and *HNV*). The first part was published in 1753, the second in 1762, but neither was advertised in the *Wienerisches Diarium* until 1763. It thus seems that neither part of Bach's *Versuch* was generally available in the Imperial capital until after the appearance of Part II in 1762.

Haydn's own autographs suggest a contact with Part I just at this time, for there is evidence that Bach's advice for notating appoggiaturas was read by Haydn. In Part I of the *Versuch* Bach writes:

> Because of the former circumstance [i.e., the variable value of some *Vorschläge*], these *Vorschläge* have quite recently begun to be indicated according to their true value, instead of all of them being marked with 8th-notes. Previously, *Vorschläge* of such variable length were not yet introduced. However, in today's style, unable to rely on rules about their length, we cannot do without exact indication, since all kinds [of lengths] occur with all kinds of notes.[51]

Significantly, Haydn discontinued his practice of notating the *Vorschläge* with a small eighth note for the first time in 1762; beginning with *Acide* he followed Bach's advice, i.e., notating the *Vorschläge* as half the value of the following note.[52] Thus it seems that Dies's reference to studying the *Versuch* has credence, although the incident did not occur in the 1750s, as his biography suggests, but in the next decade.

Haydn's Music and Emanuel Bach

In surveying the sonatas of Emanuel Bach and of Haydn, one must ask in what kind of work by Bach can one identify style traits that might be found in Haydn. In his autobiography, Bach distinguishes two types of his own compositions: those written for others; and those composed for himself, which were "written with complete freedom."[53] If any of his works had an ascertainable stylistic impact on another composer, they would have to belong to the second type. However, few of Emanuel Bach's more original works were published, and those that reached distribution in Vienna—the *Württemberg* and *Kenner und Liebhaber* sets—either had a weak Viennese tradition or appeared long after Haydn's keyboard style had reached relative maturity.

Instead of following the well-worn path in search of formal or thematic similarities among the works of Bach and Haydn,[54] let us turn to Bach's *Versuch*, which is in many respects the strongest candidate for a Haydn connection. Two important concepts in the *Versuch* merit discussion in relation to Haydn's output and style: the varied reprise; and the fantasia—which Bach believed to be the highest form of improvisation.

The idea of the varied reprise was promulgated by Bach not only in the *Versuch* but also in the *Sechs Sonaten für Clavier mit veränderten Reprisen* (Wq. 50), published in 1760 and distributed in Vienna by 1767 if not earlier. The latter contained an extensive introduction justifying the publication of works with written-out embellishments in the repetitions of the two parts of the sonata-form structure. While Haydn may have been influenced by this introduction and by Bach's example in F major from his *Probestücke* (eighteen pieces in six sonatas, written to illustrate discussions in the *Versuch*), he seems to have avoided some of the hallmarks of Bach's use of the principle: Bach varied movements in bipartite as well as tripartite binary structures; he used the variation idea as a large dimension device, i.e., he systematically varied the entire repeated section of a sonata form movement; he permitted changes in the bass line (Wq. 50/3); and he applied the practice to all movements of the cycle. In contrast, Haydn employed the varied reprise mainly in tripartite movements; left the bass line intact; for the most part used varied repetitions at the level of the phrase rather than of the section; and when employing Bach's principle at the large dimension, restricted it mainly to slow movements, i.e., those that in eighteenth-century practice would probably have been varied in much the same fashion as an aria.

It is interesting to note that Haydn's adaptation of the varied reprise to the large dimension of slow movements occurs in string quartets and duos composed after the time that Wq. 50 and the *Versuch* became available in Vienna: Quartets Op. 9/2 and 4 (1769–1770 [1766–1770]), Quartet Op. 17/4 (1771), Quartet Op. 20/6 (1772), Quartet Op. 33/3 (1781), String Duos Hob. VI:3 and 6 (*ca.* 1765–1775?).[55] There is only one instance in which Haydn obscures the structural downbeat of a first movement in the manner of Bach: the beginning of the recapitulation of the String Quartet Op. 9/1. However, this example has a totally different effect from that found in Bach; the musical idea does not lose its identity because the primary theme has a strong profile and because Haydn has applied the embellishment with care. The first occurrence in Haydn's keyboard music of the varied reprise in Bach's fashion is in the slow movement of Hob. XVI:38, composed during the mid-1770s. In movements other than slow ones, it is used more at the phrase level beginning in the late 1760s to early 1770s. It has been argued that the final sonata in one movement of Wq. 50, which has two varied restatements of a C-minor theme separated by two related couplets in C major, served as a model for Haydn's "hybrid" or synthesized variations. However, works by Giovanni Martini and by Wagenseil use similar if not identical procedures, indicating that the practice was a Continental one that perhaps stemmed from an expected performance practice written out in only a few examples.[56] Haydn's rondo finale of Hob. XVI:19, from 1767, varies the reprises of the rondo theme, a not unexpected occurrence; but in contrast to Bach, Haydn uses unrelated and contrasting episodes, thus excluding Wq. 50/6 as a meaningful model during the 1760s.

Since Haydn was always aware of the structural results when adding melodic variations to his sonata and part forms, once again a statement from the *Versuch* constitutes a more persuasive description of Haydn's approach than anything found in Bach's own compositions:

> Not everything should be changed, or else it would become a new piece. . . . This [varying] must be done with no small consideration; there must be constant reference to preceding and following ideas. There must be a concept of the whole piece so that an even mixture of the brilliant and the simple, the fiery and the calm, the sad and the cheerful, the vocal and the instrumental, will be preserved. In *Clavier* pieces the bass may also be altered from what it was, as long as the harmony remains the same. Generally, despite the many [elaborate?] variations, which are now in fashion, the basic outlines of the piece, which allow the recognition of the affect, must, nonetheless, shine through.[57]

Haydn's concept of the Fantasia/Capriccio also seems to have been affected by Bach's statements in the *Versuch*, which were adapted by Haydn to fit his own personal style. Bach describes the "Free Fantasia" in the tradition of the unmeasured prelude. Although Haydn never wrote a work in the tradition of the German toccata or the French prelude, elements and techniques discussed by Bach are found in a number of instrumental works composed by Haydn after 1762. Most of them have the generic titles Capriccio and Fantasia, which Haydn apparently used interchangeably, as evidenced by his correspondence with Artaria concerning the 1789 Fantasia Hob. XVII: 4.[58] To the above group one should properly add "Chaos," from *The Creation*, perhaps the capstone to Haydn's career as an experimenter. Thus, the following works[59] or movements should be considered for discussion:

[Hob. XV: 35/1	Keyboard Trio in A major, "Capriccio"	*ca.* 1764–1765]
Hob. XVII: 1	Capriccio in G major, "Acht Sauschneider müssen seyn"	1765
Hob. III: 32/2	String Quartet Op. 20/2, "Capriccio"	1772
[Hob. I: 53/4	Symphony in D major (Version A)	1777?]
Hob. I: 86/2	Symphony in D major, "Capriccio"	1786
Hob. XVII: 4	Fantasia in C major	1789
Hob. III: 80/2	String Quartet Op. 76/6	1797
Hob. XXI: 2	"Chaos," from *The Creation*	1798

Hob. XV: 35 can be eliminated from further comment, as its use of the Capriccio style relates to toccata-like movements found in cyclic works of Matthias Georg Monn (1717–1750).[60] Since the authenticity of the finale to Version A of Symphony No. 53 is highly questionable,[61] it too should be excluded, even though it has some characteristics in common with Hob. XVII: 1: e.g., they both exploit a single thematic idea within a larger-dimension repetition structure. In addition, neither Hob. XV: 35 nor Hob. I: 53 is particularly remarkable for harmonic boldness, the hallmark of Bach's concept of the Fantasia.

The chronology of the remaining works remarkably corresponds to that of the documents. Haydn's first encounter with Bach's *Versuch* probably occurred during the 1760s, along with some other keyboard works then available in Vienna: these encounters are paralleled in Haydn's Capriccio Hob. XVII:1 and in the second movement of Op. 20/2. A second phase came during the 1780s, after a thirteen-year break, with the composition of the orchestral Capriccio in Symphony No. 86 and the keyboard Fantasia Hob. XVII:4, i.e., about the time of the appearance of the "Account" in the *European Magazine* and several years before reports of Haydn's statements in England about his indebtedness to Emanuel Bach. After his return from England, Haydn produced the Op. 76 Quartet Fantasia and *The Creation* "Chaos" in close proximity. Did he restudy the *Versuch* periodically and use it as a textbook, as he had done with Fux's *Gradus*?

Let us now look at each work in more detail, with emphasis on the keyboard works. The G-major Capriccio Hob. XVII:1 synthesizes the capriccio based on preexistent musical material with Bach's description of the Fantasia. Here, the combination of the Austrian folk song "Acht Sauschneider müssen seyn"[62] and its attendant simple harmonies provides a foil for elaborate tonal events. Certainly the folk song fulfills one of Bach's basic ideas: the tonality must be firmly established before it can be departed from, and the more elaborate the excursion, the stronger must be the tonal confirmation.[63]

Bach also emphasizes fashioning a bass out of descending and ascending scales, which can be rearranged and embellished with chromatic pitches, a prescription that derives from the *Regola dell'Ottava*.[64] Bach offers a large number of examples with figures and publishes two entire examples: the "Hamlet" Fantasia in C minor, as a part of the *Probestücke*, and a smaller work in D major at the end of the *Versuch* itself. A comparison of the bass line on which the D-major Fantasia is fashioned with its treatment in the Fantasia itself shows that Bach does not advocate treating all the pitches of the matrix with equal weight.[65]

Haydn's G-major Capriccio is formulated on similar principles (Example VII-1). At the large dimension, it begins by moving from G major through the circle of fifths to E minor, and then by means of the relative major (G) to C. After a rather weak tonic recapitulation, the key of B minor appears—i.e., the relative minor of the dominant—and with a lengthy chromatic descent, the piece lands on C major. The remainder of this section (to m. 352) also stresses fifth relationships as well as the related major to the tonic's minor.

In concluding this Capriccio Haydn also followed Bach's advice: "The organ points on the tonic suffice to establish the key at the beginning and the end. Before the closing, organ points on the dominant can also be used to good effect."[66] Haydn dispensed with the initial organ point perhaps because of the strong tonal orientation of the folk material, but the close does use both dominant and tonic pedal points, which are enhanced by the surface rhythmic activity (mm. 352–53) and by references to the lowered leading tone. The interruption of the dominant pedal by the diminished seventh of B flat in m. 348 also seems to follow Bach's *Versuch* (Example VII-2):

EXAMPLE VII–1. Hob. XVII: 1.

It is felicitous in improvisation to appear to modulate to another key using a formal cadence, but then to take another turn. This and other deceptions make a fantasy good; only they must not happen all the time so that normal progressions are completely hidden by them.[67]

Bach defined another aspect of the Fantasia/Capriccio: "A free fantasia consists of varied harmonic settings which can be expressed in all kinds of figures and mo-

EXAMPLE VII–2. Hob. XVII:1, mm. 347–55.

tives."[68] This sentence provides one of the stronger arguments for Haydn's studying the *Versuch* rather than Bach's music, since the two composers have such different approaches to keyboard figuration and sonority. Whereas Bach's examples
illustrate the French prelude and German toccata styles—the latter with its strong
rhythmic contrasts—Haydn opts for a strong metric organization with graduated
levels of rhythmic activity at both the large and small dimensions by employing
various rhythmic resources: surface, harmonic, tonal, and textural rhythms.

Hob. XVII:1, written in 1765, demonstrates this difference with its large-
dimension rhythmic organization consisting of two parts of almost equal length.
Part one, consisting of 189 bars of a total of 368, can be divided into three parallel
subsections at mm. 1, 34, and 62. Each section is characterized by a rhythmic acceleration and the return of the Sauschneider tune, until the rhythmic relaxation of
mm. 165–89. In the third section, after its initial statement, the tune is repeated
four more times (mm. 85, 114, 133, 157), but with cadential articulations of diminished strength. This decrease in cadential strength, together with the slowing
of the surface and harmonic rhythms beginning in m. 156, prepares for the otherwise incongruous nature of mm. 165–89.

In contrast, part two emphasizes in broad statements the stability of rhythm
and texture that divide it into two large subsections and a coda. Each subsection is
marked by three commencements of the Sauschneider tune, the third of which returns in the tonic, and to the rhythmic activity of the opening of the Capriccio. The
tonic at the end of the first subsection, which changes mode in order to veer toward
B flat, returns to the home key with a dominant pedal and is enhanced by a bifocal
deception (V_7 of B flat to V_7 of G) before the final statement of the tune over an
embellished dominant pedal.

The most distinctive section from the harmonic standpoint is the close of part
one: it consists of the longest chromatic descent of the movement, which, when
resolved to C major (m. 190), results in an unusual tonal color that affects one's
perception of the returns to the tonic that precede (m. 133) and follow (m. 265)

(Example VII-3). Once again Haydn seems to have heeded Bach's guidelines for the Fantasia: "those places which begin sections in a key somewhat remote from the established one, must be held onto longer than the others,"[69] for these measures contain the slowest and most regular harmonic rhythm of the entire Capriccio. Finally, the similarities between Bach's prescriptions and Haydn's music for mm. 165–89 seem inescapable in light of the following quotation:

> Broken chords that repeat both the chord tones and neighboring ones are especially agreeable, since they provide more variations than a simple arpeggio, where the tones are repeated again and again just as they lie under the hand. In all broken triads or figures based on triads, it is possible to ornament each interval by adding the lower major or minor second, though without letting it sound through.[70]

The second chronological example—the "Capriccio," from the String Quartet Op. 20/2—also seems to follow the conceptual lines laid down by Emanuel Bach. One wonders, however, if by 1772 Haydn had not had an opportunity to study the "Hamlet" Fantasia, which served as the last piece in the *Probestücke*: both works are in C minor, and Haydn translates some of the rhythmic freedoms, expressive articulations, dynamics, and recitative/arioso sections of Bach's keyboard examples to the idiom of the string quartet.

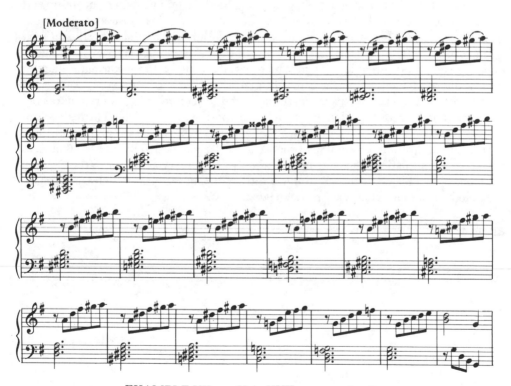

EXAMPLE VII–3. Hob. XVII:1, mm. 165–89.

After a break of some fourteen years, the next "Capriccio"—the slow movement of the "Paris" Symphony No. 86—is far removed in setting from the keyboard and string quartet idioms, even though the orchestra is treated with a chamberlike delicacy. Here the resemblance to Bach's *Versuch* and the two Fantasias possibly known to Haydn (i.e., the "Hamlet" Fantasia and the D-major work printed in the *Versuch*) seems at best remote. Yet this movement contains the rhythmic surprises, striking harmonies, chromaticisms, and recitative/arioso styles associated with the Bachian concept. Structurally it consists of a series of events whose sequence is never predictable, a characteristic that was a hallmark of both men. Haydn's opening statement, so regular at the beginning, with its three four-measure groups, only serves to emphasize the ensuing irregularities.

When Haydn returned to the keyboard fantasia in 1789, Hob. XVII:4, like its 1765 counterpart, was based on a folk song. The tune "Dŏ Bäuren håt d'Kåtz valor'n" provides the primary melodic material, and the text itself serves as the basis for a character piece in which the farmer's wife tries to capture her elusive cat. The hunting motifs, sudden changes in register, and rising chromatic scales are musical ideas that can easily be associated with the text.

In this Fantasia, however, the Bachian freedoms are no longer basic to Haydn's concept of the genre as Haydn now moves from the less-stereotyped structures of the earlier works to a shape grounded in the fundamental principles of rondo and sonata form (Example VII-4). The first section is one of his most-specialized and best-articulated three-part expositions, i.e., P (primary material)–T (transitional material)–K (closing material). The remainder is essentially a series of harmonically stable and unstable areas in which developmental and recapitulatory activities interrupt one another at carefully graduated levels of emphasis. As for the middle dimension of the structure, the second return of primary material marks the beginning of a recapitulation in which both expository material and entire development sections return. The use of primary material to kick off a developmental area is an intensification of a common practice of the Classic period in general; that is, in many recapitulations the statement of the primary material is followed by a brief expansion. This habit brings to mind the 1765 Capriccio, in which the primary melodic material initiates a series of new sections.

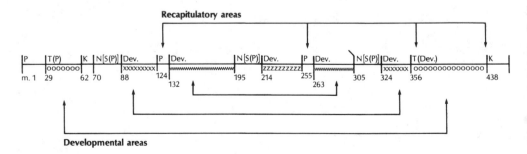

EXAMPLE VII–4. Hob. XVII:4.

EXAMPLE VII–5. Hob. XVII:4, mm. 191–98, 440–58.

By this time Haydn employed only isolated techniques suggested by Bach (Example VII-5): the slide of the dominant up a semitone at the return of the secondary material (mm. 192–95 and 302–305), the lengthy chromatic ascents in the approach to the primary material (mm. 114–24 and 445–53), the terminal pedal point (mm. 422–34), the strong deceptive resolution (mm. 444–45), and the chromatic and scalar bass line, which brings to mind the *Regola dell'Ottava*.[71]

The first measure of the great Fantasia from the Quartet in E-flat major Op. 76/6 immediately calls our attention to the special emphasis that is to be placed on tonal excursion. It is in B major, even though there is no key signature at the beginning. As in Bach's ideal model, there is no question that a key has been established:[72] the basic outline is to be found in the simple and symmetrical structure of the bass line, which includes a half-step "slip" (Bach's *semitonium modi*) (Example VII-6). The similarities of this movement to the 1765 and 1789 keyboard pieces

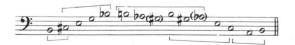

EXAMPLE VII–6. String Quartet Op. 76/6/2.

should not be overlooked. The 1765 Capriccio moves systematically downward through the circle of fifths, but both have a central section that restates the tonic and boldly departs from it before resuming the systematic plan. Op. 76/6 also recalls the 1789 Fantasia, as scale passages serve to connect the principal thematic material. Finally, all three examples use a pedal point to reaffirm the tonic tonality and the closing function.[73]

The introduction to Haydn's *The Creation*, "Chaos," has been discussed from standpoints varying from the philosophy of the Enlightenment to Heinrich Schenker's well-known analysis.[74] It can also be viewed from the standpoint of Haydn's own theoretical studies, whether it be Fux's *Gradus* or Bach's *Versuch*. In this orchestral work a number of passages recall, more or less, Bach's keyboard style in the Fantasia: the ascending triplets in mm. 10−13, the bassoon figures in mm. 21−24, the clarinet arpeggios in mm. 27−30 and the following glissando, the flute passages in mm. 36−39 and 45−47, the bassoon afterthought to m. 49, and

EXAMPLE VII−7. "Chaos" from *The Creation*, mm. 1−58.

the mysterious rhythm and articulation of the *tutti* chords in mm. 48–49. Most important, "Chaos" represents the most pervasive use of the *Regola dell'Ottava*: the three divisions of the movement—the exposition, development, and recapitulation—correspond to the descending, ascending, and descending scales (as shown by the asterisks in Example VII-7). As expected in an eighteenth-century structure, the first section is open, the middle is more active tonally, and it leads directly to the final section, which is closed.

The above works were chosen for discussion as they belong to a category of composition for which Bach was especially revered and which the North German master dealt with at some length in the *Versuch*. However, many of the same techniques discussed by Bach can be found in other Haydn compositions whose dates seem to cluster around those of his Capriccios and Fantasias. For example, the deceptive cadence and the descending bass line of Haydn's sonata form retransitions seem to become a significant characteristic during the mid-1760s.[75] An enharmonic modulation[76] is first found in the slow movement of the Symphony No. 45 ("The Farewell"), i.e., just after the composition of the Quartets Op. 20. Certain other techniques seem to be held in reserve until the 1780s, when they are exploited to their fullest: the *semitonium modi*[77] is seen in Op. 54/2/1, Op. 55/2/2, Hob. XVI:48/1, Hob. XV:27/1, and Op. 76/3/1 as well as in the Fantasia discussed above, while the enharmonic modulation seems to be used in epidemic proportions during the last two decades of the composer's creative activities: Symphonies No. 93/2 and 102/2; Quartets Op. 50/2/1, Op. 71/3/1, Op. 76/1/4, Op. 76/6/2, Op. 77/2/1; Keyboard Trios Hob. XV:14/2, XV:7/3, XV:26/1, XV:27/2–3, XV:28/1, XV:30/2, XV:31/2; and the "Scena da Bernice."

While the question of influence is always difficult to ascertain, when dealing with "secondary" masters echoes of other composers are often not so well hidden. However, in the case of personalities like Haydn and Bach, two of the most original composers of their century, the supposition that one could find passages in Bach's works that served as obvious models for Haydn is absurd: in Haydn's hands Bach's sonatas would have undergone a complete metamorphosis.[78]

The influence of a treatise, however, seems—at least in the case of Haydn—to be a defensible historical approach: few would question the importance of Fux's *Gradus* for Haydn's music.[79] Indeed, Haydn's contrapuntal style evolves from Fux's *Gradus* not unlike the way his Capriccios and Fantasias reflect Bach's *Versuch*—from saturation during the 1760s and early 1770s to selectivity in later years. While the impact of Bach's *Versuch* may not be as pervasive as that of Fux's *Gradus*, the chain of evidence is strong: the anecdote offered by Dies, the known dates of availability of the *Versuch* in Vienna, the change in Haydn's *Vorschlag* notation beginning in 1762, the use of the varied reprise (albeit in a different form) beginning in the late 1760s, and the composition of the 1765 Capriccio and later works of the Fantasia type. Finally, if we return to the quotations from Griesinger and Dies, both stress the idea of repeated study and understanding, concepts that in themselves seem most appropriate to a treatise such as Bach's *Versuch*.

PART TWO

Style

Essay VIII

TOWARD DEFINING GENRE AND GENRE TYPES

When Hoboken enumerated Haydn's instrumental output for his thematic catalogue in 1957, he organized it according to the traditional settings established during the late eighteenth and early nineteenth centuries, when the various keyboard genres were highly unified and discrete entities. Indeed, in the works of Mozart and Beethoven the solo sonata, piano trio, and piano quartet are in practice clearly defined genres. But the usefulness of such categories is diminished in Haydn's keyboard music: the genres are less clearly defined, some are interrelated, and within a given setting subgroups exist.

Since the 1960s several Haydn scholars have attempted to develop meaningful categories for the solo keyboard cycles; here, therefore, that genre will receive relatively little discussion. However, the remaining accompanied and concerted works have not been subjected to such careful scrutiny with regard to their generic titles, setting, cycles, and movement forms and types. These works have thus been allotted the bulk of the discussion in the ensuing survey of Haydn's concepts of genre as found in the keyboard music, a summary of which is provided by Table VIII-1.

Solo Keyboard Works

SONATAS

In the old copies and prints as well as in *EK*, the solo cycles up to 1771 are headed by the titles "Divertimento" or "Partita."[1] But to assign special characteristics to the Divertimentos and to the Partitas is well nigh impossible, for in their makeup there is no distinction. Although Haydn holds the term "Sonata" in reserve until 1771 for the impressive Sonata in C minor Hob. XVI:20, one should not attach too much significance to this event, for the solo cycles from the late 1760s are also works of substance although they have the older title "Divertimento."

The early solo sonatas (up to *ca.* 1765) were classified in 1963 by Georg Feder (see Table IV–3) into *Kenner* and *Liebhaber* (connoisseur and amateur) styles,[2]

TABLE VIII-1
Haydn's Keyboard Genre Types

SOLO KEYBOARD

Sonatas

Two-hand

- **Early**
  - *Frühe Sonaten* | *Kleine Frühe Sonaten*

Frühe Sonaten	*Kleine Frühe Sonaten*
XVI:16	XVI:1
XVI:5	XVI:7
XVI:12	XVI:8
XVI:13	XVI:9
XVI:14	XVI:10
XVI:6	XVI:G1
XVI:2	XVII:D1
XVI:Es2	XVI:3
XVI:Es3	XVI:4

- **Mature**

XVI:47
XVI:45
XVI:19
XVI:5
(recte XVI:5a)
XVI:46
XVI:20
XVI:18
XVI:44
XVI:21-26
XVI:27-32
XVI:35-39
XVI:43
XVI:33
XVI:34
XVI:40-42
XVI:48
XVI:49
XVI:50
XVI:51
XVI:52

Four-hand

Kenner	*Liebhaber*
XVIIa:2	XVIIa:1

Klavierstücke

Kenner

Capriccio/Fantasia	*Variation*
XVII:1	XVII:2
XVII:4	XVII:3
	XVII:6

Liebhaber

Variation	*Piece*
XVII:5	XVII:9
XVII:7	

ACCOMPANIED KEYBOARD

Keyboard Trios (Accompanied Sonatas)

Early (Trio-Sonata Texture)	Transitional	Mature
XV:36	XV:1	XV:5
XV:C1	XV:35	XV:6-8
XV:37	XV:2	XV:9
XV:38		XV:10
XV:34		XV:11-13
XV:f1		XV:14
XV:41		XV:15-16
XV:33		XV:17
(music lost)		XV:32
XV:40		XV:18-20
		XV:21-23
		XV:24-26
		XV:27-29
		XV:30
		XV:31

Accompanied Divertimentos and Concertinos

Divertimentos (Fast-Minuet-Fast)

Optional Accompaniment		Obligatory Accompaniment	
Kenner	*Liebhaber*	*Kenner*	*Liebhaber*
XIV:7	XIV:10	XIV:1	XIV:3
	XIV:C1	XIV:2	XIV:9
		XIV:4	XIV:C2
		XIV:8	

Concertinos (Fast-Slow-Fast)

XIV:11
XIV:12
XIV:13
XVIII:F2

CONCERTOS
(Fast-Slow-Fast)

Small

Ritornello/Binary (Transitional)	Ritornello
XVIII:10	XVIII:5
	XVIII:8

Large

Concertante	Virtuoso
XVIII:6	XVIII:1
	XVIII:2
	XVIII:3
	XVIII:4
	XVIII:11

with a third category for those less advanced: Hob. XVI:1, 5, 16, and 12 were considered the most primitive; Hob. XVI:13, 2, 6, Es2, 14, and Es3 for the *Kenner*; and Hob. XVI:9, [11], G1, XIV:C1, XVII:D1, and XVI:7, 8, 10, 3, 4 for the *Liebhaber*. When the solo sonatas were published in *Joseph Haydn Werke* in 1966, Feder redefined these categories and proposed two groups: "Neun frühe Sonaten" (Hob. XVI:16, 5, 12, 13, 14, 6, 2, Es2, and Es3), and "Neun kleine frühen Sonaten" (Hob. XVI:1, 7, 8, 9, 10, G1, XVII:D1, XVI:3, and 4).[3]

The sonatas that follow from after *ca.* 1765 are for *Kenner* and professionals. In this case, László Somfai designed a needed outline of "genre typology" along sociological and stylistic grounds—based mainly on cyclic structure, technical demands, and movement styles—and used it to divide the five works composed from *ca.* 1765 to the early 1770s into two types: the three-movement early "concert sonata" (Hob. XVI:19, 20, and 46); and the two-movement early "chamber sonata" (Hob. XVI:18 and 44). The former then provided the basis on which Somfai categorized the three-movement Esterházy "court sonatas" (Hob. XVI:21, 23, and 24), the "dilettante sonatas" of the year 1776 (Hob. XVI:27, 28, 29, 31, and 32), the "dilettante concert" style of the Auenbrugger set (Hob. XVI:35, 36, 37, 38, and 39), and the late "grand sonatas" (Hob. XVI:50 and 52). From the early "chamber sonata"—which also includes Hob. XIV:5 (*recte* XVI:5a), XVI:45, 25, 26, and 30—emerges the two-movement "Damensonate" of the 1780s (Hob. XVI:41, 42, 43, 48) and 1790s (Hob. XVI:51). For the remaining works, Somfai views Hob. XVI:22 and 34 as syntheses of the "concert and court types" and the "dilettante concert and grand sonatas" respectively, while the Genzinger Sonata Hob. XVI:49 derives from both the "Damen" and "grand" sonatas.[4]

Although undeniably stimulating and useful, the titles that Somfai applies are misleading from a historical viewpoint: such terms as "chamber" and "concert" are questionable, because none of the works in the two groups can be confirmed as having a background in either the court chamber or the public concert. Instead, these keyboard sonatas appear in the main to be *Hausmusik*, even if they were used in the residences of the aristocracy and perhaps even occasionally in a concertlike environment.[5] Indeed, all the sonatas—with the possible exception of Somfai's "grand" sonatas—were in the best sense "dilettante" and "Damen" sonatas, as evidenced by the nearly unanimous dedications to women, in contrast to the solely male dedications for the string quartets.[6]

KLAVIERSTÜCKE

Five of the eight *Klavierstücke* parallel the advanced language and idiom of the mature solo sonatas and keyboard trios. The two big variation sets, Hob. XVII:2 and 3, are truly independent works, while the famous F-minor Variations Hob. XVII:6—also known from authentic sources as "Sonata" and, somewhat surprisingly, "un piccolo divertimento"—is less extended and may well have been intended originally as the first movement of a sonata not unlike Hob. XVI:48.

Both of the Capriccios/Fantasias, Hob. XVII:1 and 4—Haydn used these terms interchangeably—are based on Austrian/South German folk tunes and signal important advances in Haydn's keyboard writing at two different points in his stylistic development, *ca.* 1765 and 1788–89. Were these two works intended to serve as preludes to solo sonatas, as was common in eighteenth-century practice? The G-major Capriccio Hob. XVII:1 from 1765 has been transmitted in an old copy from Kroměříž that contains the solo Sonata Hob. XVI:47 (see Example III-13). Although the tonality of the E-minor/E-major version of Hob. XVI:47 is possible, the Capriccio occurs in the manuscript after rather than before the sonata. Furthermore, it would be tempting to associate this work with one of the other sonatas of the 1760s, but the size of the Capriccio itself seems to exclude it from such consideration. On the other hand, the C-major Fantasia Hob. XVII:4 was composed at about the same time (1788–89) that Haydn was working on the two-movement C-major Sonata Hob. XVI:48 and—unlike its G-major counterpart—the Fantasia, in terms of both tonality and size, might be successfully combined with this sonata.

Accompanied Keyboard Works

TRIOS

If one looks beyond their setting, the works of Hoboken's Group XV clearly divide into two categories: the early trios (Hob. XV:34, 36–38, 40, 41, C1, and f1) and three transitional ones (Hob. XV:1, 2, and 35); and the twenty-eight mature trios dating roughly from 1784 to 1796.

The trios of the first category are known from contemporary copies under the common titles "Divertimento," "Partita," "Concerto," "Trio," and "Capriccio"

PLATE 14. An eighteenth-century keyboard trio performance. Detail from the title page of Artaria's edition (Op. 80) of Hob. XV:10. (A-Wn)

(Hob. XV : 35); the term "Sonata" is also found, but chiefly in prints. As with the solo sonatas, these titles have little meaning in terms of either style or cyclic structure: indeed, the only term found here that seems to have had a precise meaning is "Concerto," which may simply refer to the concertante and obligatory nature of the violin part.

The fabric of Haydn's early trios (Hob. XV : 34, 36–38, 40, 41, CI, and fI) is a hybrid of the Baroque violin sonata and the newer accompanied style. Most of the first movements begin with the keyboard alone presenting the initial material, immediately followed by a solo violin repetition with the keyboard assuming a *basso continuo* role—sometimes indicated with figures; the cello simply doubles the bass line throughout. These characteristics bring to mind the trio texture found in a number of Baroque violin sonatas: the violin and the right hand of the keyboard are the two upper voices, while the left hand and cello realize and play the bass. Other portions of the first movements as well as most of the ensuing movements use the so-called accompanied texture: the violin either plays in unison or forms thirds and sixths with the right hand of the keyboard, participates in motivic play, and—less frequently—has independent material.[7] Thus, in Haydn's early trios the violin is an indispensable part of the texture; it does not function in the optional manner found in many examples of eighteenth-century accompanied keyboard music by other composers frequently used to illustrate this genre.[8]

The opening statement of Hob. XV : 40 begins to reveal a synthesis of trio sonata and accompanied textures that marks a transitional style; the new approach is more pronounced in Hob. XV : 1, 35 and —perhaps with less validity—in the possibly transcribed Hob. XV : 2. In XV : 35 the violin and keyboard share material democratically (Example VIII-1), without strong indications of the old trio sonata. In addition, there are passages in which the violin and cello are perceived as playing together (Example VIII-2); the keyboard and violin perform in a three-part sonority without the cello (Example VIII-3); and, in the first and last movements, the technical demands on all players exceed previous expectations. In Hob. XV : 1 these developments are taken further: the opening phrase places the violin and keyboard on equal footing; the cello and violin are at times of equal importance (Example VIII-4); the violin independently carries the melodic material in the trio of the minuet; and double stops—supported by the cello—are used in the finale when the keyboard part becomes more linear (Example VIII-5). Without question, both of these works adumbrate the mature trios of the 1780s.[9]

In contrast to the early solo sonatas, these early trios are unusually uniform in size and difficulty. Excluding the transitional works, there are no movements as large and demanding as the most difficult of the early solo sonatas or as small and simple as the easiest of them. It seems likely that the trios were conceived with a single keyboardist or ensemble in mind.

The late trios all carry the title "Sonata for keyboard with accompaniments for a violin and cello" or its equivalent. This designation accurately describes their texture: the violin performs as an accompanying instrument as well as more soloistically; and, in general, the cello part supports the keyboard bass. This latter function, however, is more flexible in these works than has been recognized by such

EXAMPLE VIII–1. Hob. XV:35/1, mm. 1–8.

EXAMPLE VIII–2. Hob. XV:35/1, mm. 67–69.

commentators as Donald Francis Tovey, who recommended that the late trios be played as violin sonatas and even rewrote some of the cello parts in conformity with nineteenth-century practice.[10] Such an expectation has resulted in widespread criticism of the mature trios, even by the Haydn enthusiast Marion M. Scott in 1932:

> The problems of trio-writing for pianoforte and strings are extremely delicate. To do him justice Haydn did not know they existed. Indeed, they did *not* exist dur-

EXAMPLE VIII–3. Hob. XV:35/1, mm. 138–41.

EXAMPLE VIII–4. Hob. XV:1/1, mm. 1–2, 8–9.

ing the major portion of his working life. If he had met them earlier he might have solved them as thoroughly as those of the string quartet. They only emerged towards the end of his career, because they were bound up with slow changing of clavier and harpsichord for the modern pianoforte. . . .

If we recollect the tone of the claviers—or pianofortes—of his day, we have the explanation of his peculiar scoring. In thirty-one Trios in print, as Prof. Tovey says, "hardly for a dozen notes in the whole collection is it (the 'cello) allowed to diverge

EXAMPLE VIII–5. Hob. XV:1/3, mm. 74–78.

from the bass of the pianoforte. The only movement in real trio writing . . . is the Adagio at the beginning of the two-movement work in A major."

What sounded well in Haydn's time is wrong for today. The thick doubling of the bass dulls the lower edge of the score; . . . it bores 'cello players to the point at which they retaliate by leaving the Trios alone.

. . . It is only fair, however, to admit that he was perfectly content to carry on his "continuo" technique in the trios long after Mozart and Beethoven [*sic*] had shown him a better way.[11]

Within four months after publication, Scott's and Tovey's viewpoint was roundly rejoined by Arthur T. Froggatt:

In the thirty-one published trios there are seven hundred and forty-four bars in which the 'cello part differs from the pianoforte bass—an average of twenty-four bars to a trio. In this calculation I take no account of difference of octave, or of repeated notes, but only of a difference in the twelve notes of the scale. I have not counted the number of notes: possibly three hundred.

. . . Mozart wrote seven trios with a 'cello part, all composed between 1786 and 1788 . . . there are nine hundred and ten bars in which the 'cello doubles the pianoforte bass. (In the adagio of the first Trio, K. 254, it does nothing else.) As for Beethoven, there is not one of his trios in which the 'cello does not occasionally double the pianoforte bass; in the last and finest, Op. 97, there are a hundred and seventy-seven bars in which the 'cello (according to Miss Scott's gospel) goes astray.[12]

Tovey was correct to some extent: Haydn's late trios do tend more toward the violin sonata. This inclination is one that the composer himself acknowledged by taking one of his own works for violin and piano ("The Dream"), adding a cello part and a new first movement, and publishing it as a trio; later, when Haydn needed a gift of a "violin sonata" for Madame Moreau, the work was copied again with a second new first movement, but without the cello part. The exception to this generic concept is Hob. XV:9/1, in which the cello uses the higher positions and participates in true duet style with the violin (Example VIII-6).

EXAMPLE VIII–6. Hob. XV:9/1, mm. 1–8.

Apart from their settings, however, the mature trios and late solo sonatas follow the same evolutionary path: two- and three-movement cycles predominate, variation and part forms gain an importance comparable to the sonata form, and the same movement styles (e.g., siciliano, contradance, etc.) are favored. Thus, the title "Sonata"—which Haydn used interchangeably for solo sonatas and keyboard trios in letters to publishers, in the London Verzeichnis (*LV*), and in the Haydn Verzeichnis (*HV*)—is a valid one.

DIVERTIMENTOS AND CONCERTINOS

The works enumerated by Hoboken in *Gruppe* XIV, to which should be added Hob. XVIII:F2, come down to us in contemporary copies with such titles as "Concerto," "Concertino," or "Divertimento," and all but two are scored for keyboard, two violins, and bass. Haydn himself used the terms "Concertino" on the autograph for Hob. XIV:11 and "Divertimento" on the autograph for Hob. XIV:4 and in *EK* for Hob. XIV:3. "Divertimento" is also the title on the presumed authentic copies of Hob. XIV:7–9, which were a part of Haydn's *Nachlass*. A consistent distinction in terminology is made among these authentic examples: those called "Divertimento" consist of a Fast–Minuet–Fast sequence, whereas in the "Concertino" the minuet is replaced by an expressive cantilena slow movement. If we go beyond the authentic sources, the same generic distinction still holds true: those labeled "Concertino" are related to the cyclic form of the concertos, while those labeled "Divertimento" relate to the early solo and other accompanied sonata cycles.

On the other hand, in both the Concertinos and Divertimentos of Hob. XIV, the movements are mainly in binary-based forms and do not, except for short cadential tuttis, even hint at a ritornello/concerto structure. In both, the two accompanying violins and the bass perform the same basic functions: they normally double the keyboard; they sometimes simplify the keyboard line; they occasionally contribute independent material; and the first violin only rarely participates in motivic play with the keyboard. Especially in the Divertimentos, the strings seem merely to be supporting an insecure performer (Example VIII-7); in three Divertimentos Hob. XIV:7, 10, and C1 the accompaniment could even be considered optional.

The distinction between works for *Kenner* and those for *Liebhaber* that Feder applied to the early solo sonatas is also relevant for these Divertimentos. For example, Hob. XIV:9, 10, and C2 are comparable to the smallest of the *Liebhaber* solo sonatas (Hob. XVI:7 and 8) in dimension and difficulty. But this *Kenner/ Liebhaber* polarity is not as evident for the four Concertinos even though their size and difficulty remain within the boundaries of the early solo sonatas.

Concertos

The three Concertinos of Hob. XIV and the little Concerto XVIII:F2 differ from most of the larger concertos of Hoboken's Group XVIII in that they never approach the ritornello/concerto form. But this distinction, while certainly useful, is not as well defined as one might presume; for Hob. XVIII:5, 8, and 10 are intermediary works that form a bridge from the "Concertinos" placed by Hoboken in *Gruppe* XIV to the full-fledged concertante and solo Concertos of *Gruppe* XVIII. Hob. XVIII:10 represents a true formal and textural synthesis of the concertino and concerto genres: repeats divide the first movement into a binary form, but it still preserves elements of the ritornello both in the thematic structure and in the tutti/solo contrasts. Hob. XVIII:10 is also unlike the full-fledged concertos in its decidedly different approach to the keyboard/string relationship: one finds sections

EXAMPLE VIII–7. Hob. XIV:9/1, mm. 1–9.

for the tutti with the keyboard playing *continuo*, the keyboard and strings doubling, and the keyboard accompanying the strings (mvt. 1, m. 35), as well as concertante sections. Hob. XVIII: 5 and 8 stand closer to 10 because of their less-demanding nature and probable liturgical function as organ concertos.[13] Hob. XVIII: 6 is a concerto for solo violin, the right hand of the keyboard, the left-hand keyboard *basso continuo*, and strings; it thus harks back to the concerto grosso for two solo treble instruments. The remaining early works (XVIII: 1 and 2) are full-fledged mid-century concertos, while the later ones (XVIII: 3, 4, and 11) are fine examples of the Classic concerto in a totally mature realization.

This overview of Haydn's approach to genre in the keyboard music reveals a series of work groups interrelated by more than the inclusion of a keyboard instrument. Of the early output, the solo sonatas and accompanied divertimentos for keyboard, two violins, and bass are related by their cyclic structures and technical demands. Closely allied are the concertinos: both maintain the same relationship of the solo to the accompanying group. Yet the concertinos are also miniature concertos, as evidenced by their cyclic plan and similarity in movement structures and textures with the smaller concertos in Hob. XVIII. Of the early works, it is only the keyboard trios that stand apart, with their mixture of trio-sonata and accompanied textures.

Concerning the mature works, those entitled "Sonata"—whether they be keyboard trios or solo sonatas—are uniform in cyclic makeup, movement forms, and overall style. The mature concertos (Hob. XVIII: 3, 4, and 11) also begin to consolidate form and style in a manner not seen in their predecessors.

The picture that emerges of Haydn's keyboard settings and genres is therefore one quite different from the standard Classic repertoire as established by works of Mozart and Beethoven with similar settings. Nothing in the output of either composer approaches the practices found in early Haydn. Mozart's piano trios, quartets, and the quintet with wind instruments are completely alien to Haydn's early trios, divertimentos, concertinos, and concertos: Mozart exploited the dramatic possibilities by pitting the keyboard against a competitive block of sound and savored the give-and-take among the parts, a concept only rarely found in Haydn's ensemble works. On the other hand, Beethoven was more interested in the full spectrum of the piano's sonority in the solo sonatas and its ability to compete with and dominate its partners in both chamber and concerted orchestral music. Here, one could argue for a few of Haydn's late solo sonatas and trios as one foundation for the Beethovenian approach.

Haydn's concept of genre and setting is clearly couched in a totally different tradition, one that flourished in Vienna during the mid-eighteenth century, and one to which Mozart and Beethoven had little exposure. Here, there existed two basic types: solo keyboard settings, including *Klavierstücke*, along with accompanied sonatas, divertimentos, and concertinos, which used forms that depended little on contrasts and confrontations of the keyboard with other instruments; and the concerto, in which these contrasts and confrontations were the essence of the solo/tutti polarity and ritornello form.

Essay IX

THE CONCERTOS:
STRUCTURE AND STYLE

Of all the genres to which Haydn contributed, only two have been deprecated in the past: the operas and the concertos.[1] Although the judgments expressed have been based on incomplete knowledge of the works themselves and the inevitable comparisons with Mozart's contributions, it must be admitted that most of Haydn's keyboard concertos pre-date his stellar works for solo and accompanied keyboard, string quartet, and orchestra. For the following discussion, the nine authentic concertos are divided into two groups: those created before *ca.* 1765 (Hob. XVIII: 1, 2, 5, 6, 8, and 10), and those from the mature Esterházy years (Hob. XVIII: 3, 4, and 11).

Cycle and Movement Types

The cyclic structure of all the keyboard concertos is totally predictable: it always follows the Fast–Slow–Fast plan. As will also be seen in the solo sonatas, the first movements of the early works emphasize marchlike themes and Moderato or Allegro moderato tempos in duple or quadruple meters with either quarter or eighth notes serving as the beat. Of the later works, Hob. XVIII: 3/1 and 11/1 are in the "con brio" style, which begins to appear in the solo sonatas during the 1770s. Concerto form or some modification of it is common to all first movements.

The central movements favor Adagio and Largo tempos and for the most part are in a contrasting triple meter. Formally more diverse than the first movements, their keys strikingly favor the major mode with an equal preference for the dominant and the subdominant. Although all the slow movements are cantilenas, they are of different types: Hob. XVIII: 1 and 6 are in 4/4 with elaborate melodic lines; Hob. XVIII: 2, 5, 8, and 10 are stylistically related movements in triple meter; Hob. XVIII: 3 and 4 are in a more streamlined lyric style than their predecessors; and Hob. XVIII: 11 is an appropriate, synthesized culmination of the above types.

The finales are all in a fast tempo (Presto, Allegro, and Allegro molto) and generally in 3/8 for the early works or 2/4 for the later ones. The 3/8 finale has gener-

PLATE 15. A performance of a keyboard concerto. Engraving by J. E. Mansfeld, 1785. (Author's collection)

ally been considered a lightweight movement with little thematic identity, but that is not true of many of these concertos: certainly such a characterization is not appropriate for Hob. XVIII: 1 and 6, whose finales almost balance their opening movements. All but the two late ones in rondo form (Hob. XVIII: 4 and 11) use some sort of ritornello scheme, at times framed with two sets of repetitions.

First Movements

It is useful to compare Haydn's first-movement structures with eighteenth-century concerto forms: the so-called Baroque ritornello, Koch's now well-known descriptions, and the textbook Classic concerto form (see Table IX-1).[2] In the Baroque ritornello form, the contrasts of ritornello (tutti) vs. episode (solo) establish the basic principle. The movement commences with the ritornello stated in its entirety, cadencing in the tonic; each subsequent statement is normally in a different related key and often presents only portions of the ritornello, except for the last, in which the entire section is restated in the tonic. In contrast, the solo episodes are modulatory and feature idiomatic figuration, but may also incorporate ideas from the ritornello. Koch's 1793 description emphasizes the synthesis of ritornello and what

TABLE IX-1

Eighteenth-Century Concerto Forms

	Opening Tutti	First Solo	Second Tutti
Baroque	Ritornello	Episode	Ritornello
theme:	P ⟶ K	(P)	P*
key:	I I	I	Related
Koch/1793	Ritornello (*Nebenperiode* 1)	Exposition (*Hauptperiode* 1)	Ritornello (*Nebenperiode* 2)
Koch/1802	Ritornello	Solo Exposition	Ritornello
Classic	Exposition 1	Exposition 2	
theme:	P-T-(S)-K	P-T-S-K ⟶	
key:	I⟶(V)⟶I / i⟶(III)⟶i	I∿V / i∿III	

	Second Solo	Third Tutti/Solo	Final Tutti
Baroque	Episode	Ritornello Episode	Ritornello
theme:	(P)	P* (P)	P ⟶ K
key:	Related	New Related	I ⟶ I
Koch/1793	Development (*Hauptperiode* 2) Ritornello (*Nebenperiode* 3)	Recapitulation (*Hauptperiode* 3)	Ritornello (*Nebenperiode* 4)
Koch/1802	Solo ⟶		Ritornello
Classic	Development	Recapitulation	Closing Tutti
theme:	Reworking or New	P-T-S-K ⟶	
key:	∿(vi or III)∿	I / i ⟶	

∿ = modulatory areas   * only partial restatements

we today would call sonata form.[3] His treatise essentially views the concerto as a sonata form with the three solo sections as the exposition, development, and recapitulation and the four tuttis (ritornellos) surrounding them forming an introduction, interludes, or closings. In Koch's *Lexikon* of 1802, the tutti between the development and the recapitulation is eliminated,[4] and the scheme approximates the so-called Classic concerto form.

All but one of the first movements of the pre-Esterházy concertos conform to one of Koch's models; Hob. XVIII: 10, uses a binary form molded around a ritornello/tutti-solo structure:

‖:.R S R.‖:.R S R S R.‖

The late concertos Hob. XVIII: 4 and 11 have first movements closer to the late eighteenth-century stereotype; Hob. XVIII: 3/1 bridges the two groups.

<h3 align="center">OPENING TUTTI/RITORNELLO</h3>

In the early concertos the initial ritornello ranges from ten to twenty measures of four quarters and is usually laid out in three to four thematic sections corresponding roughly to the functions of a sonata-form exposition, even though all end on a tonic cadence. Somewhat surprisingly, the ritornellos often begin with ideas in parallel and/or complementary, if not symmetrical, structures. Four of the opening phrases (Example IX-1) use repetitive thematic construction (Hob. XVIII: 1, 5, 8, and 10), even though only one (Hob. XVIII: 10) is also symmetrical. In three of these examples, the stronger punctuation is used, as in some of the sonatas, at the mid-point of the statement rather than its end, which remains harmonically

EXAMPLE IX–1. Hob. XVIII: 1/1, mm. 1–8; 5/1, mm. 1–5; 8/1, mm. 1–5; and 10/1, mm. 1–8.

EXAMPLE IX–2. Hob. XVIII:2/1, mm. 1–2, and 6/1, mm. 1–5.

open. Hob. XVIII:2 and 6 achieve much the same impression through forte and piano dynamic markings, even though they are confined to the half-measure (Example IX-2).

In the continuations, which suggest a T function, greater reliance is placed on *Fortspinnung* than on repetition. Except for Hob. XVIII:10, all close in a related key with strong articulations, often ending on full or half cadences and at times followed by a pause.[5] Nonetheless, the cadential arrival in the new tonality does not represent a plateau of stability, as Haydn returns decisively to the tonic within a few measures.

The material following the cadence in the related key takes on the S function in Hob. XVIII:1, 2, and 5, which is enhanced by a lower dynamic level and/or a reduction of the instrumentation. At this point Hob. XVIII:6 and 8 act more like a retransition, with their allusions to the supertonic just before S or K.

The closing (K), as will be seen in the early solo and accompanied sonatas, is often the most organized shape because of its repetition of harmonically stable thematic ideas. Closure is enhanced by dynamic contrast (Hob. XVIII:1), by returning to materials from the opening (Hob. XVIII:6), and by an allusion to the subdominant (Hob. XVIII:5 and 6).

While the details of the structure of the opening tuttis in these early concertos reveal a composer of promise, overall they are disappointing. The main weakness of the larger concertos, Hob. XVIII:1, 2, and 6, is a structural one due to the stringing together of a series of short ideas. In both the large and the small works the common problem is the combination of moderate tempos and a lack of distinctive thematic material, in contrast to the memorable themes and driving rhythms of their Italian Baroque counterparts.

Hob. XVIII:3/1, from the 1760s, reveals a greater breadth, coherence, and drive in its opening ritornello; it is Haydn's first entirely successful synthesis of content, form, and style in these concertos. A comparison of the ritornellos of Hob. XVIII:1 from 1756(?) and Hob. XVIII:3 from about a decade later dramatically shows this change. From all external aspects, the earlier concerto should give a feeling of breadth—with its *maestoso* indication and surface rhythms—in contrast to the faster tempo and high activity of Hob. XVIII:3. Yet, the dynamic changes in Hob. XVIII:1 are chiefly ornamental, and those that might be construed as structural are obscured by the decorative functions; while in Hob. XVIII:3 the dynamics clearly define three of the four structural areas of the ritornello. Regarding the thematic material itself, Hob. XVIII:3 is strongly directionalized in its melodic contour: P is dominated by ascents and descents within the measure, T by descent over several measures followed by single- and half-measure ascents, and S by descents; while K, although beginning with the initial thematic material, synthesizes the melodic contour of the previous functions. The thematic material in Hob. XVIII:1 lacks such patterning and direction. Finally, the harmonic rhythm in Hob. XVIII:3 is more differentiated than in Hob. XVIII:1; in the later concerto each pattern aids in defining a function, while the earlier work's patterns are less profiled. Thus, in Hob. XVIII:3 Haydn skillfully controls nonmelodic components to provide coherence and contrast. This ritornello reveals a striking stylistic advance, which is also seen in Haydn's other forms from the 1760s.

The opening ritornello to the next later concerto, Hob. XVIII:4, is less interesting historically. Its overall shape retains the practice of the previous work, with

EXAMPLE IX–3. Hob. XVIII:11/1.

four well-defined functions, some of which approach a form of classic specialization: P is presented in a nine-measure compound phrase structure; T uses one-measure sequences; and K repeatedly outlines the tonic and dominant seventh chords.

Another stylistic leap occurs with the famous D-major Concerto Hob. XVIII: 11. Its forty-eight-measure opening ritornello is more intricate than and nearly twice as long as its predecessors and thoroughly exemplifies the first tutti/exposition of the late eighteenth-century model. Now the sonata form functions are clearly delineated in the materials presented. The structural articulations are no longer just cadences but closings to each of the functions.[6] Since the melodies are so thoroughly conceived in phrase groups, Haydn can extract motives for specialized treatment; i.e., the rhythmic motive in m. 1 is confined to expository functions, but m. 2 is exploited in the development (Example IX-3).

FIRST SOLO/EXPOSITION

The first solo in each of Haydn's early keyboard concertos begins with the same material that commenced the ritornello. In several instances P is embellished. The new material presented in T often consists of figuration that either continues or builds upon P's level of rhythmic activity. However, one must admit that in the early concertos, Haydn's changes are not especially idiomatic, for the figuration is not always of a type tailored for the keyboard, and the alterations are confined to the right hand.

In three examples—one of the least idiomatic (Hob. XVIII:8), the most idiomatic (Hob. XVIII:1), and the Double Concerto for keyboard and violin (Hob. XVIII:6), which has the problem of synthesizing violin and keyboard idioms—one can observe more closely Haydn's alterations of the opening material for the first solo. In Hob. XVIII:8 the rocket contour of m. 4 from P of the ritornello is altered in m. 20 of the first solo to a broken chord (Example IX-4), a difference more indicative of tutti and solo styles than of string and keyboard;[7] throughout the first solo, the left hand contains no idiomatic figuration whatsoever. The alterations in Hob. XVIII:1 (Example IX-5) more effectively distinguish the solo from the tutti: the soloist immediately embellishes P, and stronger idiomatic writing also occurs in T—the right hand arpeggios (mm. 56–59), the broken thirds in the left hand (mm. 61–64), and the arpeggios covering more than three octaves (mm. 71–72). Immediate embellishment of P is also found in the Double Concerto Hob.

EXAMPLE IX–4. Hob. XVIII:8/1, mm. 4–5, 20–21.

EXAMPLE IX–5. Hob. XVIII: 1/1, mm. 40–48 (cf. Example IX–1).

EXAMPLE IX–6. Hob. XVIII: 6/1, mm. 33–37 (cf. Example IX–2).

XVIII: 6 (Example IX-6), but here we can see that Haydn does not distinguish idiomatically between the keyboard and violin soloists; even the figurations are abstract rather than being tailored to the idioms of the individual solo instruments. In all three examples, the alterations to the material of the first solo provide a higher level of rhythmic activity than that of the opening tutti and are therefore structural in conception.

Throughout the concertos of the first group the functions in the first solo are generally more strongly defined than in the first ritornello: P materials are extended; T becomes specialized; and S and/or K at times display structures highly organized through repetition, which enhance the feeling of closure. Despite this overall profile, one can distinguish without regard for chronology two different approaches: Hob. XVIII: 2, 5, and 10 have a sonata-like continuity, i.e., the first solo is equivalent to a solo sonata exposition; while the discreet orchestral interjections in Hob. XVIII: 1, 6, and 8 bring to mind the solo sections of older Baroque concertos. Yet these categories are not exclusive, for within some works of the first group dialoguing may take place toward the end of the solo, and orchestral interjections do occur.

In the first solo of the earliest mature concerto, Hob. XVIII: 3, one again finds a dramatic change—now with regard to the idiomatic treatment of the keyboard instrument (Example IX-7). Although P is altered immediately and in a manner not unlike that of the early works, in T a variety of ideas peculiar to the keyboard— broken chords, rapid parallel thirds, and sextuplet finger swirls—are presented, but still only for the right hand. Perhaps as a result of this partial immersion in idiomatic writing, the solo is conceived in a new manner, becoming less and less like the ritornello. The orchestra plays a secondary role throughout, lacking even the interjections of the earlier works; indeed, it could be silent during the entire first solo, for the players only double the left hand, support the cadences, sustain

EXAMPLE IX–7. Hob. XVIII:3/1, mm. 27–56.

EXAMPLE IX–7. (*continued*)

TABLE IX-2

Delineation of Structure in Hob: XVIII:11

Measure	Function	Texture
49	P	Solo alone.
60	P^k	Solo accompanied by orchestral strings.
69	1T	Dialoguing tutti orchestra vs. solo alone, then solo with orchestral punctuation.
77	2T	Orchestra presents simplified version of solo figurations.
84	3T	Solo alone with orchestral punctuation.
91	S	Orchestra doubles keyboard then to simplification of keyboard part.
103	K	Solo alone with orchestral punctuation.

the broken chords, and harmonically enrich the keyboard part. This strong separation of tutti and solo activity is reminiscent of Baroque practice.

The first solo of the following G-major Concerto Hob. XVIII:4 takes the same general approach as its predecessor; but in the late D-major Concerto Hob. XVIII:11 these structural tendencies are cast aside. Now the keyboard seems less couched in flashy and figural writing, and the melodic material is immensely well suited to the harpsichord; the overall structure closely follows the opening ritornello, giving the general impression of a second exposition; and the relationship between the keyboard and the orchestra is developed with dramatic results. By using half a dozen different textures and colors, Haydn underlines the structural functions (see Table IX-2). The overall impression given by this solo is, therefore, very close to the late eighteenth-century model. It has been suggested that this work was modeled on Mozart's concertos, which were being performed in Vienna at the time of its publication by Artaria (1784), but there is evidence that Hob. XVIII:11 may date from the 1770s.[8]

SECOND TUTTI/RITORNELLO

The tutti that follows the first solo is one of the few remnants of the Baroque concerto that cannot be associated in any way with sonata form. The first solo is always longer than the opening tutti, in part because of its tonal function; and the second tutti is considerably shorter than the first. To some degree these changes in length reflect the function of the second tutti within a given movement as a whole.

In the six early concertos, the second tutti is always between one-third and one-half the length of the opening tutti. The second tuttis of Hob. XVIII: 1, 2, 6, and 8 have a strong K function that reinforces the related key, begins with material other than P, and ends with the first tutti's closing. They are thus orchestral continuations of the previous solo. The two remaining early concertos offer quite different approaches. In Hob. XVIII: 10, a movement enclosed by repeats, the second tutti acts like a development (after the double bar), as it begins with the repetition of the opening measures of the first tutti in the dominant. The second tutti of Hob. XVIII: 5 is a compressed version of the opening ritornello, presenting material from only P and K.

While in Hob. XVIII: 5 it is difficult to make a strong case for Haydn's balancing the second tutti with the first, for two of the Esterházy Concertos, Hob. XVIII: 3 and 4, such a hypothesis cannot be dismissed. They too begin with the initial material, but this time their expanded lengths of 80 and 75 percent respectively of the opening tutti could be perceived as an effective counterpart.

Although the second tutti of Hob. XVIII: 11 is slightly more than one-third the size of the opening, this work reveals the most sophistication. Harmonically, this fourteen-measure interlude moves from the dominant to the submediant, the key in which the next section begins, using the motive from P that is to be exploited so fully in the ensuing section. Thus, it serves as an organic extension of K as well as a transition to the second solo.

SECOND SOLO/DEVELOPMENT

During the mid-century period the second solo begins to take on a double role: from the Baroque perspective it is the fourth major unit of ritornello form, while according to Koch and the textbook models it takes on characteristics of a development section, with its tonal activity and motivic play. Even among Haydn's earliest concertos one can find important distinctions with regard to the differing functions of the first and second solo sections, and in the mature works the second solo is more specialized and segregated.

The second solos of the six early concertos tend to be about one-third longer than the first solos, and all commence with the same material as the opening tutti and first solo but in a related key: five in the dominant and one, in Hob. XVIII: 6, in the submediant. After the statement of the initial material—with little if any alteration of the original—a tonal shift takes place for the five in the dominant key: to the tonic in Hob. XVIII: 1, 8, and 10; and to the submediant—the ultimate tonal destination of all of these development sections—in Hob. XVIII: 2 and 5. The assertion of the tonic immediately after the beginning of the development may seem a self-defeating move, but it was apparently not uncommon during the mid-century; it appears in development sections of a number of Haydn's early works in different genres as well as in works by other Continental composers.[9] After these initial tonal shifts, Haydn continues with a large modulatory section, which appropriately occupies the middle of this central solo.

Haydn's handling of this modulatory section is always skillful and adumbrates the kind of intellectual approach to structure for which his works are so admired. In contrast to the early solo and ensemble keyboard works, often with miniature proportions, these extended excursions offer a special opportunity for examining another aspect of Haydn's early style: the descending and ascending patterns of the bass line, which lend direction to the harmonic organization.[10] In all but one of the early concertos, the small-dimension harmonic movement revolves around the submediant; Hob. XVIII: 2, probably the earliest concerto, wanders somewhat aimlessly but becomes more focused after the establishment of the submediant.

In terms of thematic development, these modulatory sections for the most part contain new material, while previously presented ideas are often used to frame the entire second solo and in some instances enhance tonal stability by occurring at the same time as the main tonal area is established; e.g., in Hob. XVIII: 1 and 6, the arrival in the submediant is coordinated with the return of S. In the developments of the smaller concertos Hob. XVIII: 5 and 8, a previous idea (a motive from P) is treated sequentially. In the case of Hob. XVIII: 5 (Example IX-8), P is divided between the keyboard and the first violin; in the course of its five measures, it is reduced from a half- to a quarter-measure unit. Such dialoguing occurs elsewhere only in Hob. XVIII: 10, but without any unit reduction or reference to previous material. Surprisingly, not even in the Double Concerto Hob. XVIII: 6 do the two soloists exchange motives from previous material.

The second solo of the first mature concerto, Hob. XVIII: 3, has some similarities to the previous six works: it begins with material from the opening of the solo and moves by its seventh measure to the submediant, although here it is not the principal tonality of the section. While one might have expected Haydn to increase the level of solo/orchestral interplay, the solo remains the dominating force, with the orchestra providing only supporting accompaniment. Yet this development section is far in advance of the early works, for here Haydn concentrates on phrase rhythms in different dimensions. As can be seen in Example IX-9, the development is in six sections, with the rhythmic acceleration reaching a plateau in the fourth and longest section, a stable fifth section, and a final section in which the surface rhythmic acceleration is coordinated with a return to the highest pitch (d‴) then available to Haydn on the keyboard.

Hob. XVIII: 4 consolidates the accomplishments of the previous concerto: the development carries over characteristics of the earlier work—the rhythmic accelerations, the total dominance by the keyboard, the idiomatic figurations, and the return of material from the solo in the development—but does not work them out as fully or as skillfully as does its predecessor. For example, the return to material from the first solo (m. 119) does not prepare for the final burst of energy that closes the second, but merely defines the two major sections of the development. The rhyth-

EXAMPLE IX–8. Hob. XVIII:5/1, mm. 45–53.

mic drive in general is only provided by surface and harmonic rhythms, and is not combined with sophisticated phrase rhythms ordered strategically, as in Hob. XVIII:3.

The final work in D major, Hob. XVIII:11, is the only one saturated with thematic development. In the discussion (pp. 254–55) of the first solo and the second

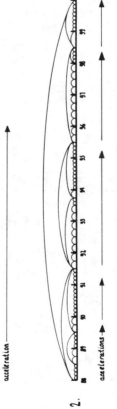

1.   acceleration

2.   accelerations

3.   accelerations

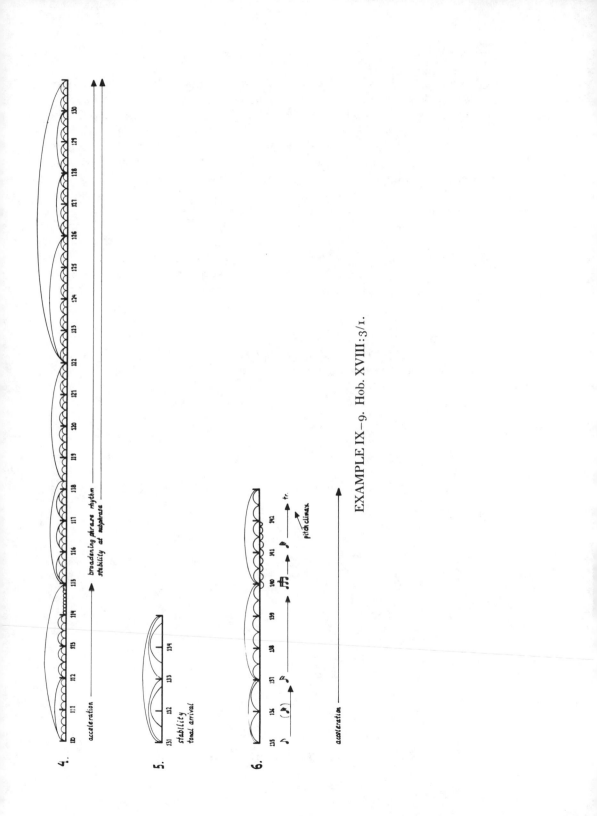

EXAMPLE IX–9. Hob. XVIII:3/1.

tutti, it was pointed out that Haydn had already introduced the motivic activities of the development section by highlighting the second measure of the opening material. The development itself begins not in the dominant but in the relative minor, previously seen only in the Double Concerto Hob. XVIII:6. As expected, P commences the section, but here the entire opening phrase is stated before the second measure is developed in twelve measures of two- and one-measure groups moving up and down through the string section. The return to the tonic in the seventh measure (m. 133) to commence the actual motivic working-out is an antiquated gesture prominent in the works of the 1750s and early 1760s.

The second section presents one of the K themes, while the third combines these elements with another cadential idea used in both the previous tutti and the solo sections. The three sections are also strongly distinguished by their harmonic-rhythmic patterns (Example IX-10) [11] and articulations. Overall, this development brings to mind the thematic reduction and variation for which Beethoven has been so highly touted.

THIRD TUTTI/RITORNELLO AND SOLO/RECAPITULATION
The third internal tutti is found in only five of the six early first movements; when it occurs, it is often the briefest, but usually only slightly shorter than the preceding

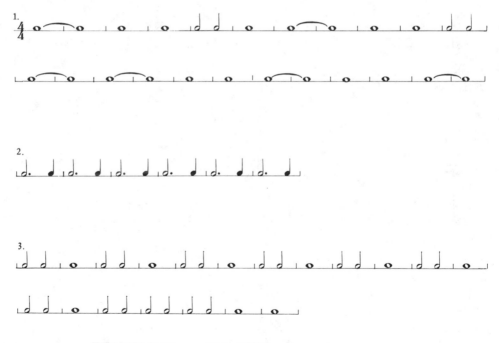

EXAMPLE IX–10. Hob. XVIII:11/1, mm. 127–49, 150–55, 156–74.

tutti. In all but Hob. XVIII:8, where it is recapitulatory, it functions as a further closing to the previous solo or as a retransition from the main tonality of the development to the preparatory dominant for the recapitulation.

Of the later group, Hob. XVIII:3 continues the practice found in the earlier works with its closing/retransition function. In contrast, both Hob. XVIII:4 and 11 take as their model Hob. XVIII:8: the orchestra provides the structural downbeat for the recapitulation with P in the tonic, after which the solo reenters as an echo of its material. With this emphasis on the recapitulation of P together with the tonic key, Haydn underlines the relationship of first-movement concerto form to that of the sonata.[12]

The third solo can be considered from the perspective of three functions: recapitulation, development, and closure. The first implies parallels with the opening ritornello and solo, the second with the activities of the second solo; and the third is characteristic of the end of the opening tutti, first solo, and second tutti.

The third solo functions as a tonal and thematic recapitulation in all the early concertos. While these third solos may have other parallels with the opening ritornello and solo, they are not strong enough to have the effect of a recapitulation in the same sense as in Haydn's solo and accompanied sonatas: the remainder of the material is either presented in a different order or excluded to a degree not found in the other keyboard genres before the late 1780s.

Of the early concertos, development is emphasized in the third solo of Hob. XVIII:1, 6, and 10. In Hob. XVIII:10 the developmental aspects of the second solo are immediately continued with the reestablishment of the tonic key; the dialoguing of the keyboard and the first violin develops the principal material in sequence for six measures. On the other hand, in Hob. XVIII:1 and 6 traits of the exposition as well as the development are stressed within the recapitulation. In Hob. XVIII:1, T begins with a striking new tutti chord that follows P,[13] the closing to T is replaced by further development, and S—similar to the second solo—is stated in the minor mode. Next follows the first recapitulation of the contrasting material from the first tutti (mm. 24–31). Something quite similar also takes place in Hob. XVIII:6, where S is a restatement of the *minore* presentation in the development. Also of special interest here is the alteration that takes place in T: the violin and keyboard exchange figurations from the exposition.

If the beginning of the third solo emphasizes recapitulation, the central section development, the last—as expected—is concerned with closure. Since a sense of conclusion is present in the opening ritornello—which ends in the tonic—and often some of this material is repeated in the subsequent solos and tuttis, it becomes almost imperative for Haydn to enhance closure in the final solo and tutti. Only Hob. XVIII:6/1 uses a cadenza to underline this function. Other means are more prominent in these early works: the introduction of the subdominant; greater emphasis on cadential formulas; and an increase of textural activity between the solo and tutti. The emphasis on cadential formulas and activities is the most pervasive—nowhere is this function isolated in the final orchestral tutti; rather closure begins some time before the end of the third, recapitulatory solo. It may be effected by repetition of cadential material, such as the threefold one in Hob. XVIII:1 and 6; by preparation for the cadence beginning nine measures before the conclusion of the solo in Hob. XVIII:10; or by expansion of the solo section after the statement of previous materials associated with closure earlier in the movement, as in Hob. XVIII:5 and 8.

The third solo of the first mature concerto, Hob. XVIII:3, continues to use the same structural principles as in the previous ones, with a continued emphasis on idiomatic figuration. Otherwise, it does not demonstrate any significant departures from the earlier group. That, however, does not hold true for Hob. XVIII:4 and 11. In both instances, the recapitulation begins with the previous orchestral tutti, as in Hob. XVIII:8, and is merely emphasized by the keyboard's repetition of P. In Hob. XVIII:4, after this double statement of P, development is literally resumed, resulting in the recapitulatory statement's being almost parenthetical (Example IX-11); indeed, the third solo is almost entirely given over to idiomatic figuration, buttressed by P, T—presently played by the keyboard—and K from the opening ritornello, which now leads to a cadenza before the final orchestral close. The brief development in the recapitulation of Hob. XVIII:11 occurs just before the cadenza and again focuses on the continued working-out of the second measure of P, which is again presented in stretto with the keyboard and orchestra overlapping (cf. mm. 104–106) by a single beat (Example IX-12). Nevertheless, the overall effect is one of a recapitulation, as close as Haydn comes to the late eighteenth-century model.

FINAL TUTTI/RITORNELLO

The sole function of the final tutti is to bring the entire movement to a satisfying conclusion. In addition to repeated cadences, there is a return of material that operated as K either within or at the conclusion of the ritornello. It is only in the later works (Hob. XVIII:3, 4, and 11) that Haydn consistently interpolates a solo cadenza as part of the final tutti.

Regardless of the period of their origin, the first movements of these concertos mix ritornello with sonata principles in a manner best described by Koch. The earlier works contain a number of different solutions toward this fusion. One is enclosed by repeats, thereby retaining the basic binary shape of sonata form; the other five works hint at a sonata structure through the embellishment—if only temporarily—of a new key area in the opening ritornello, the expository nature of the first solo, thematic development in the second solo, and a tonic recapitulation in the penultimate tutti or solo. In the later Esterházy Concertos the first movement has a different process of growth. Hob. XVIII:3 is thematically the most homogeneous and idiomatic of them all; its spirit also recalls the old Baroque model. Hob. XVIII:11, made up of the most diverse material, is the most sophisticated and advanced. Hob. XVIII:4, whose chronological placement is between these two works, is a compromise between these two extremes. The first movement of each of these mature concertos informs us of something different regarding Haydn's artistic development, and all three are thoroughly satisfying.

EXAMPLE IX–11. Hob. XVIII:4/1, mm. 137–50.

EXAMPLE IX–11 (*continued*)

EXAMPLE IX–12. Hob. XVIII:11/1, mm. 235–40.

Second Movements

Among the early concertos, the slow movements of Hob. XVIII: 1, 2, and 6 employ the ritornello principle. As in many slow movements in other types of compositions, Hob. XVIII: 1 and 2 lack a structural downbeat to articulate the recapitulation; although in both concertos the initial material is restated in subsequent solos and tuttis, it never returns in the tonic after the opening ritornello and first solo. The effect is a structure more binary in orientation. Like their first movements, both have a certain diffuseness attributable to the multiplicity of ideas; again, Hob. XVIII: 1 seems slightly more cogently organized than Hob. XVIII: 2.

The Double Concerto Hob. XVIII: 6 is quite another matter, as the tutti and the solo themes are different. The statements in the expected tonic, dominant, and again tonic of the initial material of the first tutti ritornello provide structural pillars for the solos. The solo, however, repeats its initial material only in the development, leaving the third tutti to provide the recapitulatory downbeat. Tutti/solo distinctions are further underlined in the orchestra by the use of arco in the tuttis and pizzicato in the solos. On the other hand, Haydn minimizes the importance of the tutti by choosing melodic material that lacks any of the memorability associated with ritornello themes. Perhaps the unusual approach to this slow movement is a result of an attempt to accommodate the material to two soloists in the context of a slower tempo.[14]

Hob. XVIII: 5/2 and 10/2 have two traits that distinguish them from the above group: they each begin with a solo section; and the primary role of the tutti is to close each part. In fact, the orchestra's participation is minimal. Hob. XVIII: 8/2 is marked by a great deal more tutti/solo dialogue. The orchestra not only articulates the beginning and end of the two sections but also converses with the solo, closes and connects phrases, and begins the recapitulation with the opening material, which is then taken up by the keyboard.

The slow movements of Hob. XVIII: 3, 4, and 11 are remarkably different from those of the earlier concertos in that they emphasize simple and memorable lyricism. Indeed, one might be tempted to say that of Haydn's keyboard works written from *ca.* 1760 to 1785, these compositions are among the most inspired (Example IX-13). Apart from their lyricism, two other important factors contribute to their success. First, Haydn holds in reserve their highest pitches until late in the move-

EXAMPLE IX–13. Hob. XVIII: 3/2, mm. 1–6, and 11/2, mm. 1–4 (see also Example III-28).

EXAMPLE IX−14. Hob. XVIII:11/2, mm. 53−58.

ment: d‴ in Hob. XVIII:3, c‴ in 4, and f‴ in 11. In Hob. XVIII:4 the general tessitura is fairly low until the end; and in Hob. XVIII:11 Haydn uses an octave leap to reach f‴ (m. 53), the highest pitch on the normal keyboard during the 1780s and one not expected within the context of a movement whose principal key is A major (Example IX-14).[15] Second, the phrases and subphrases are expanded upon repetition. In Hob. XVIII:3 the opening six-measure material is restated in lengths of eight (twice) and ten measures; in Hob. XVIII:4 the second and third subphrases add a single measure to each repetition; and in Hob. XVIII:11 the second subphrase is expanded from four- to five- to eight-measure statements. The result is a new structural breadth.

All three later slow movements have totally different approaches to the growth process. In Hob. XVIII:3 the orchestra begins and closes the movement, framing the binary structure for the solo material, of which only the first half is repeated. Hob. XVIII:4, which begins with a lengthy tutti, is a ritornello/sonata form without development; tuttis occur at the ends of the exposition and the recapitulation, but at no point during the movement is P presented in a key other than the tonic. Hob. XVIII:11 is much like Hob. XVIII:4, except that developmental solo material is introduced before the tutti-initiated recapitulation. The rearrangement of phrases and subphrases and the delay of the restatement of "b," however, lends to Hob. XVIII:11 a high degree of structural expectation:

Tutti a + b
     4   4

Solo a a c d d Tutti b Solo b
     4 4 5 5 5   5   8

Tutti a Solo c d cadenza Tutti b
     4   6 7   5

As Hob. XVIII:11 demonstrates, the hallmark of these later slow movements is a well-articulated form permitting even its complexities to emerge with simplicity and directness. It was precisely this combination that made Haydn's style so palatable to both connoisseurs and amateurs, a characteristic that comes to the fore in the finales of these concertos as well as in the solo sonatas beginning *ca.* 1780.

Finales

The finales of the early concertos are of two types: those that approximate the first-movement ritornello form (Hob. XVIII:1, 2, and 6); and those with a binary structure (Hob. XVIII:5, 8, and 10).[16]

In Hob. XVIII:1, 2, and 6, parallels with the first movements go beyond the similarity of a structural stereotype: all have opening tuttis that recall first-movement dimensions, and each tutti touches on a related key—the dominant in Hob. XVIII:2 and 6 and the subdominant in Hob. XVIII:1.[17] The first solos, as expected, all begin with the same material as the tutti, but in Hob. XVIII:1 and 6 they are embellished. In Hob. XVIII:2 the effect of the structural downbeat at the beginning of the solo is lessened in another way: the closing of the opening tutti uses P. Within all three concertos, the first solo has substantial T sections and references to the dominant minor; the second tutti has a closing function; and the second solo/development commences with P. In the last section, Hob. XVIII:1/3, as does its first movement, almost immediately returns to the tonic, with the tutti stating the opening theme in its original form; all three finales continue with extensive modulatory areas using bass patterns not unlike those in their first movements. In Hob. XVIII:1 and 2, the third tutti functions as a transition/closing; in Hob. XVIII:6 it serves as the beginning of a recapitulation, and the solo follows in the minor with the idiomatic variant found at the beginning of the second solo/development, a procedure that recalls the first movement. The third solo of Hob. XVIII:1 also begins in the minor with an idiomatic version—perhaps in this case to offset the unaltered tonic tutti restatement in the ninth measure of the development. Otherwise, the remainder of the third solo may reflect the first solo (Hob. XVIII:1), be a synthesis of the first ritornello and solo (Hob. XVIII:2), or select and scramble thematic materials to enhance closure (Hob. XVIII:6). Only Hob. XVIII:2 alludes to the subdominant to underline its conclusion.

Hob. XVIII:5 and 8 begin with open-ended tuttis that are relatively short and perceived as the antecedent phrase of the solo's consequent, with the solo subsequently continuing to perform the usual sonata form functions (Example IX-15). Both finales stand apart from their ritornello counterparts and from mid-century sonata-form practice by beginning the development section with something other than P and not moving to the related minor; Hob. XVIII:8 commences with K, while Hob. XVIII:5 recalls T but in the tonic. As expected, all the developments depend rather heavily on sequences and dialoguing.

Despite the relative simplicity of these early finales, Hob. XVIII:10 shows a rather sophisticated use of K with three levels of closure: one for the tutti, one for the exposition (first solo) and development, and one for the recapitulation, which contains references to the subdominant and gathers the previous K material together.

Tutti <u>P   1K</u>
       I   I

Exposition <u>P   2K</u>
(*Solo* 1)   I   V

Development <u>P   2K</u>
           V   VI

Recapitulation <u>P   2K + 1K</u>
             I   I

The result is an increase in anticipation of the conclusion to the finale.

Of the three later concertos, the finale of the earliest, Hob. XVIII: 3, continues to use the big ritornello form found in three of the earlier works, but again—like its first two movements—it has little in common with its predecessors. Rather, the closest parallel is found in its own first movement: the material of the tuttis and solos, except for the initial idea, is totally different; the solos emphasize idiomatic figuration; and some of the same sophisticated approaches to rhythm are present.

EXAMPLE IX–15. Hob. XVIII:8/3, mm. 1–12.

To some extent, the separation of solo and tutti is further enhanced in the finale, for the solo/development ignores P material.

The ritornello theme of Hob. XVIII:3 is appropriate for a rondo, but it is not until the finales of the last two concertos, Hob. XVIII:4 and 11, that the synthesis of rondo style and form is completely realized. Since the rondo and ritornello forms are to some degree confused and especially problematical in some of Haydn's works, it may be helpful to define them: The rondo theme is always closed, and in its function as a reprise, it recurs in the tonic, while the episodes are in a contrasting key and/or mode. By contrast, the ritornello, except for its first and final statements, is open and usually in a key other than the tonic, while the episodes often provide modulatory links between the ritornellos/tuttis.

It should be emphasized that in his rondo form, Haydn continues to practice the development of a single idea. Therefore, the "textbook" definition that the episodes of a rondo must contrast melodically with the reprise does not hold true; the rondo is a key-area form, and every reprise and episode may be based on the same material. In the 1780s, the German music historian Johann Forkel confirmed the key-area principle of Classic forms and, in fact, stated that the best rondos are those based on a single theme.[18]

The finale of Haydn's G-major Concerto Hob. XVIII:4 entitled "Rondo: Presto," is such a Classic rondo form, as illustrated in Example IX-16. The rationale for B beginning at m. 84 is that the new key of D major is established after a lengthy T, which closes with material that includes ideas from all the major sections of the form. The first statements of both A and B conclude with a pause in all voices and are closed sections followed by transitions that end with open punctuations. The second transition (m. 106) begins with the A material in E minor and leads with a Haydnesque up-beat to four measures of A (mm. 125–28) in G major (Example IX-17). The central episode, C, is well articulated by a sudden shift to the tonic minor; one may be led to believe, because of the parallel shift to the minor and the succeeding concentration on the second measure of the primary theme (Paxn), that this episode is another transition, but the more extensive thematic development confirms its true function.

Some may be reluctant to identify a second A section of only four measures (mm. 125–28). Malcolm Cole viewed this movement mainly in terms of thematic activity and described a central couplet as "a genuine development" touching on E minor (m. 106), G major ("a false recapitulation," m. 125) and G minor (m. 129), eventually coming to the "real reprise" (m. 162).[19] However, a false recapitulation is usually not in the tonic key, and there are many rondos from the period with equally abbreviated refrains. Furthermore, Haydn's long preparation for this return in the second transition (m. 106) is perhaps of more articulatory importance than the length of A's return. If this lengthy preparation is compared with the nonexistent preparation for B, the difference becomes even stronger; Haydn thrusts into the first episode immediately and without pause after the closing to the first T. The third refrain (m. 162) has an even stronger preparation, which underlines its recapitulatory function.

The emphasis on a single theme and its motivic and tonal development casts

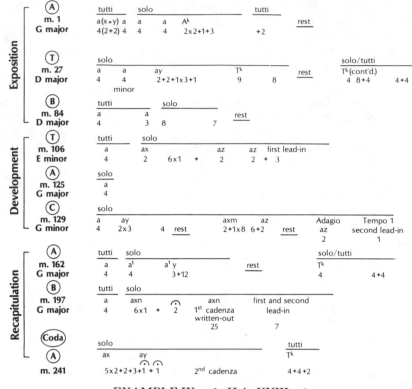

EXAMPLE IX–16. Hob. XVIII:4/3.

this movement into the realm of the sonata-rondo. Here, the central development section is not limited to the central episode (m. 129), but actually commences with the second transition (m. 106) and concludes with the recapitulation (m. 162). If the movement is seen as a sonata form, the reprise at m. 125 is another instance of returning to the tonic during the course of a development section. If this movement does date from the mid-1770s, it ranks as one of the earliest and most complex examples of its type in Haydn's output.

The rondo themes of both Hob. XVIII:4/3 and 11/3 have a rhythmic and intervallic simplicity associated with the contradance and allied folk idioms, but their shapes are relatively complex. The first four measures of Hob. XVIII:4/3 are notable for their motivic construction: the rhythm of the accompaniment of m. 1 becomes the principal material of m. 2 (Example IX-18). That permits a reinterpretation of the theme by changing the placement of the *Hauptrhythmus* in the musical fabric, beginning in m. 110. On a slightly larger level, Haydn divides the two two-measure groups to be worked out in the various sections: some concentrate on the first two measures (ax) and others on the last two (ay).

EXAMPLE IX–17. Hob. XVIII:4/3, mm. 106–34.

EXAMPLE IX–18. Hob. XVIII:4/3.

Greater complexity marks the rondo theme of Hob. XVIII:11 (Example IX-19): it contains three elements (xyz) treated in such a way as to produce an acceleration that continues through the conclusion of the transition to the episode. The first statement consists of a six-measure group of three two-measure cells, the third being a repetition of the second. The two-measure cells of the next six measures are perceived as still faster because of the more active intervallic shape of z and the surprise ending with x^2. Beginning with T at m. 25, x and z are further worked out in two four-measure groups and then compressed into three two-measure and finally into half-measure units (m. 40); this acceleration is underlined

EXAMPLE IX–19. Hob. XVIII:11/3, mm. 1–12, 25–41.

EXAMPLE IX–20. Hob. XVIII:11/3, mm. 60–77.

by surface rhythmic intensification and the elimination of z^2, which provided moments of repose.

The same technique is used even more effectively in mm. 51–77, comprising B and a closing section. Beginning with six measures in the dominant that duplicate the material of the reprise, a downward scale of rushing sixteenths leads to a large closing section, which commences with two four-measure groups and concludes with four two-measure segments. In the four measures beginning with m. 60 (Example IX-20), m. 62 is an intensification of m. 60, and mm. 61 and 63 have more movement than do mm. 60 and 62; beginning with m. 69 the previous motivic sequence is reordered, the subphrase is compressed, and the surface rhythm is intensified. This activity is further enhanced by the syncopations in the second violin, the repeated eighth notes in the bass, and the pedal point broken by the harmonic motion in the horns.

The second episode, C (m. 78), consists of two parts: the first, like its counterpart in Hob. XVIII:4/3, is an unusually strong development notable for its increased rhythmic activity on several levels; while the second is an effective *minore* that derives from the harmony of the reprise. The second reprise (m. 201) is delayed until after the second episode and is limited to a single thirteen-measure statement; as in the rondo of Hob. XVIII:4, its brevity is compensated for by a lengthy preparation. The third episode, like the development of the first movement of XVIII:11, begins in B minor. The rondo closes after a restatement of the reprise and a transition to a lengthy coda. Thus, Hob. XVIII:11/3 is an irregular rondo in six sections: A–B(A)–C–A–D–A–Coda.

This finale is best known for its folklike material of eastern European deriva-tion, as indicated by its title: "Rondo all'Ungarese."[20] The folk elements are strong-est in the first transition, with its *acciaccaturas* (see Example IX-19), the demonic whirling character of the closing to the episode (see Example IX-20), and the *minore* (m. 150). Such a use of folklike materials is not peculiar to Haydn and was not an uncommon practice for Classic concerto finales. Indeed, Hob. XVIII:11/3 gained its popularity not so much from Haydn's skillfulness as from its modishness, for it fulfilled the expectations of a wide public.

Thus, Haydn only distinguishes the finales of the early concertos from their first movements with regard to their meter; in terms of dimension, structure, and style, their overall profiles are remarkably similar. In the last three concertos, how-ever, the finale gains a stronger identity; beginning with Hob. XVIII:3, it has the character of a duple-metered contradance. It is not only this new style but also the rondo structure and sense of movement that bring to Hob. XVIII:4/3 and 11/3 a real finale character. Their exuberance is totally appropriate to the public concert rather than to the church or the aristocratic salon, for which the earlier works may have been intended.

The early concertos are valuable in that they reveal something about Haydn's style during a time when it is extremely difficult to construct a distinctive profile for his artistic development. In some respects they might be the best genre to illuminate an otherwise dark area, for here we have the only very early instrumental works to be dated: Haydn assigned the date 1756 to Hob. XVIII:1 and possibly to the Double Concerto Hob. XVIII:6.[21] One can also argue for the musical worth of these early works: along with those of the Monns, Steffan, and Emanuel Bach, they are among the most skillful mid-century keyboard concertos. Although the larger concertos can be criticised for a certain garrulousness, in some movements the or-ganization of the rhythm in the first solo, the shape of the developments, and the sense of closure found in the third solo/recapitulation foreshadow Haydn's later, more successful, efforts.

The three Esterházy works have special qualities that for the most part have yet to be acknowledged. If Hob. XVIII:3—the first mature keyboard concerto—was written during the early to mid-1760s, it is one of Haydn's most exciting and skill-ful works from this period. It also resolved the problem of synthesizing the older concerto form with a more advanced musical and formal syntax. As will be seen in Essay X, Hob. XVIII:3/1 reveals the same evolutionary path found perhaps a dec-ade earlier in the solo sonatas, in that Haydn turns from a big work with a plethora of ideas to one that uses more homogeneous materials. The slow movement of Hob. XVIII:3, a pure cantilena, eschews the elaborately embellished melody for one that is simple and direct, but subtly shaped, thus providing an effective foil for the energetic finale.

Besides its own inherent value, Hob. XVIII:4/1 is an important precursor to Hob. XVIII:11, for it constitutes a return to the integration of solo and orchestra. Hob. XVIII:4/2 and 4/3 build on the model provided in Hob. XVIII:3: the rhythmic flexibility of the slow movement, a Haydn trait beginning in the late 1760s, is more evident, and the rondo-finale idea is now securely in place.

With Hob. XVIII:11 Haydn achieves a mastery of theme, form, and idiom; this work in its own way rivals Mozart's Viennese concertos. It closes Haydn's keyboard concerto output; thereafter Haydn composed comparable works only for the cello and trumpet, instruments for which Mozart produced no mature efforts. Perhaps Haydn felt, even though such a self-appraisal seems unjustified for the Esterházy works, that the tendency to compare him with his younger colleague in the realm of the concerto was too strong for his own psychological comfort.[22]

Essay X

THE SOLO AND ENSEMBLE KEYBOARD MUSIC: STRUCTURE AND STYLE

Unlike the concertos, which were composed sporadically over a period of some two or three decades, the solo and accompanied keyboard music listed in Hoboken's *Gruppen* XIV, XV, XVI, XVII, and XVIIa spans nearly half a century in Haydn's creative life with some consistency of production. Rather than looking at early and mature phases, into which the concerto output was divided, here we will consider the earliest works, which date from before *ca.* 1765; the sonatas and other works from *ca.* 1765 to *ca.* 1771, which reveal an unexpected maturity; a series of publicly distributed *opere* from *ca.* 1774 to 1784; the sonatas, trios, and pieces of the late 1780s; and finally the works for London and Vienna from the 1790s. Thus, this survey will begin with Haydn's earliest and not completely successful efforts from *ca.* 1750 and conclude with the acknowledged masterpieces of the 1790s, thereby presenting a total overview of his stylistic development as a keyboard composer.

The Earliest Works, before ca. *1765*

CYCLE AND MOVEMENT TYPES

The cycles of the keyboard works from before *ca.* 1765 present a different configuration of tempos, keys, meters, and forms than is found in the early symphonies and string quartets. While the quartets are consistently five-movement affairs and the symphonies stabilize by the early 1760s into four, the keyboard sonatas of this time range from as many as six to as few as two movements, with the prevailing number three. Haydn's first movements are predominantly sonata forms in fast duple or quadruple meter, although a few begin with a movement that is marked by a slow tempo or conveys this impression by subdivision of the beat. In the final two movements of the solo sonatas an interdependence of tempo and meter exists: if the second is moderato or slower the finale will almost always be a minuet, but if the central movement is a minuet, the finale will be an energetic 2/4 or 3/8. Yet in the accompanied divertimentos and concertinos of Hob. XIV, the central movements are either slow (concertinos) or minuets (divertimentos), and none of the finales are minuets. Nearly all the cycles are in keys that do not exceed three sharps or flats. About three-quarters of the cycles remain in the same major tonality or the parallel minor for all movements, or they change to the related minor or the subdominant for the slow movement. Central minuets are always in the tonic.

However, tonality may not be the only unifying force in these early cycles; some gain coherence through their incipits. Despite the existing controversy that surrounds the topic of thematic unity in multimovement works from the second half of the eighteenth century, in these early sonatas one can find more examples than in any of Haydn's later works.[1]

Before *ca.* 1765 the "dynamic or climactic" curve is totally different from what might be surmised from familiarity with the better-known works of the Viennese masters:[2] here, the initial movement is not clearly the strongest, as Haydn presents a number of other options. The minuet's trio or the slow movement often becomes without hesitation the strongest member, whereas the finale is rarely afforded this position unless it balances the opening movement. In some cases the first two or even three movements could be viewed as equally significant.

FIRST MOVEMENTS

The most prominent type of early first movement draws upon the march intrada with dotted rhythms and embellished flourishes. A number of them also employ the hammerstroke: one or several massive chords open the piece. Others begin with four thirty-second-note pick-ups, a derivation from the five-finger motives so prominent in Wagenseil. With their prevailing Alberti and rolling triplet accompaniments, Hob. XVI: 1/1 and 3/1 seem particularly Italianate. In still a third type, the first movements are cantilenas and create the impression of a slow tempo: Hob. XVI: 12, XV: 36, and 37 confine their main musical interest to the violin or the right hand of the keyboard, while the left hand and the cello provide unobtrusive support.

The first movements of Hob. XVI: 16, 5, and Es2 clearly depart from the usually polished products: they do not present a unified style either together or individually. Instead, one might regard them as probes in different compositional directions. Certainly the most primitive is Hob. XVI: 16/1. It is not constructed along the lines of sonata form, but is a binary structure with two parallel sections in each part: an opening andante in cantilena style connected by a cadenza to a fast section. Here one may wish to attribute the disorganized impression to the cliché-ridden melodic materials of dotted rhythms, triplets, trills, and various broken-chord figurations, but they are not the problem, for they were to be Haydn's vocabulary for even the most successful sonatas. Rather, Hob. XVI: 16/1 fails to cohere because there is no organic connection among the materials nor are they underlined by any sort of rhythmic strategy. Hob. XVI: 5/1 has surface unity in both tempo and motive, but the motive (♪♫)—which is found in nearly every measure—seldom fulfills its anacrusic expectations, as the downbeat is frequently left empty. In addition, the harmonic rhythm consists of spurts and stops, which merely add to the ploddings of the movement as a whole. The dimensions of Hob. XVI: 5/1 are twice those of XVI: 16/1, but its effect is much the same: two sections without any underlying coherence.

These problems are confronted in Hob. XVI: Es2 with more sophistication. The harmonic language is more effectively employed, and, instead of a binary structure, a big tripartite sonata form is used.[3] Its breadth is conveyed in the opening P section (Example X-1), which is laid out in a big three-part form (a, a¹, a) and followed by well-articulated T and SK functions. But its exposition still lacks direction: the patterning of the harmonic rhythm is reminiscent of Hob. XVI: 5/1; the melodic curve has no goal in either the small or large dimension; and the surface rhythms are oriented toward small anacrusic gestures, again reminiscent of Hob. XVI: 5/1. Yet the movement perhaps could have achieved far more than the other two if it were not so packed with cadences employed so indiscriminately. In the P section alone they occur in mm. 2, 3 (twice), 4, 5, 6, 6-7, and 11 (three times). P's final punctuations in m. 11 seem more appropriate for the end of an exposition, while the covered cadences that follow articulate too frequently and too decisively. Perhaps Haydn's awareness of the problems of this exposition resulted in Pa being stated in the second half only once at the beginning of the development

EXAMPLE X–1. Hob. XVI:Es2/1, mm. 1–12.

EXAMPLE X–2. Hob. XVI: 12/1, mm. 1–20.

and of the abbreviated recapitulation, which is further shortened by replacing T with a cadenza-like flourish—a device also used in Hob. XVI: 16/1.

The first turning point in these early works is to be found in Hob. XVI: 12/1 (Example X-2). In XVI: 16, 5, and Es2, either motivic diversity or unity was stressed, but here Haydn opts for a melodic line that "spins out" in a Baroque manner. In spite of its slower tempo, a sense of movement and coherence are achieved, first by carefully graded levels of harmonic rhythmic activity: P accelerates from half to quarter notes, T duplicates this pattern, and SK accelerates from quarters to eighths before returning to quarter-note units for the exposition's conclusion. Second, the carefully controlled melodic curve hovers around a''' and b''', reaches to c-sharp''' in m. 13, and then descends for the final cadence. Finally, the cadences are carefully weighted: m. 4—authentic imperfect weak; mm. 6 and 7—authentic imperfect strong; m. 11—half; and finally in m. 18—authentic perfect strong. This strategic arrangement lends the exposition a coherence that goes far beyond the previous efforts.

While Hob. XVI: 12/1 moves in a new direction, it hardly represents Haydn's final solution to the problems of first-movement form: the materials are differentiated but are unified often by a motive and always by carefully controlled cadential activity. These common denominators are present in the smallest as well as the largest movements.

Hob. XVI:8 (Example X-3), the sonata Christa Landon placed earliest in her 1966 edition, is among the smallest, but its first movement displays a craftsmanship that defies its size. Each of the exposition's three functions (P, T, K) is clearly defined by its harmonic rhythm, melodic range, and cadential strength, but not by any distinctive melodic gestures. The cadences emphasize the arrival in the related key, again resulting in a sense of movement. The development uses the motives of the exposition rearranged: the upbeat dotted rhythm of P, followed by the off-beats of T and then the triplets of P, in the space of three measures. The following bars reduce the opening three measures to two-measure modules based on P, and then return to a single three-measure statement, resulting in a small but impressive thematic development.

EXAMPLE X-3. Hob. XVI:8/1, mm. 1–27.

The absence of tonal activity is not uncharacteristic of these early works; in fact a development section in the tonic—or one that returns to the tonic after the statement of P in the dominant—is not unusual nor was it regarded as a defective solution during the eighteenth century. But to presume that for Haydn motivic development and tonal inactivity are the rule in these early works would be a misconception: often the relative minor will be strongly articulated or emphasized.[4] Thus, these movements are frequently organized around three tonal areas: tonic, dominant, and submediant.

The importance of the submediant in Hob. XVI: 1/1 is exceptional: in the recapitulation P returns not in C major but in A minor (Example X-4). This tonality is actually reached during the development; it begins with P on the G minor, but immediately moves toward the submediant, which is confirmed by a half-cadence and a pause. Six measures of A minor follow and lead into the beginning of P at the point of recapitulation; it is not until m. 35 that the tonic convincingly returns. Although for Haydn, beginning the recapitulation in a key other than the tonic was rare, this practice was common in eighteenth- and early nineteenth-century Viennese first movements.[5] Except for the primitive Hob. XVI: 16 and 5, only two other opening movements lack a strong structural downbeat at the beginning of the

EXAMPLE X–4. Hob. XVI: 1/1, mm. 18–35.

EXAMPLE X–4 (*continued*)

recapitulation: Hob. XVI:6/1, an expanded binary form; and Hob. XVI:3/1. In the latter, the recapitulation commences in the tonic minor; to assure the listener that it is indeed the return, the initial four measures are stated twice rather than once.

The most noteworthy achievement of these early solo sonatas is Hob. XVI:2/1 (Example X-5). Here Haydn successfully handles a number of different themes bound together by a motive (*) that recurs in all the functional sections (1P, 1T, 1Sb, 3Sa¹, and K[1P]). Tonally, the first part of the exposition heads for the dominant, and that key occupies half the exposition. Harmonically, Haydn provides both tonal areas with some coloration so that the opening (1P) and closing (3S and K)—firmly entrenched in their respective keys—are followed and preceded by

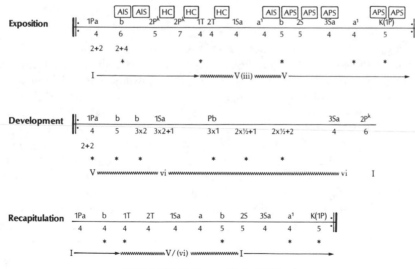

EXAMPLE X–5. Hob. XVI:2/1.

less-stable areas (2P^k and 1S, 2S). Such a procedure of weakening the tonic and gradually strengthening the dominant—which is common in the exposition of the later sonata forms—could be represented as follows:

$$\|{:}\quad P\quad \text{pre-T}\quad T\quad \text{post-T}\quad S\quad K\quad {:}\|$$

Although in many of Haydn's other sonatas from this period the area in the related key is either represented only by K or by an ambiguous SK, in Hob. XVI:2, S and K are solidly formed; 1S and 3S together with K are similar in structure and of equal length, with 2S forming the core of the related key area.

The development of Hob. XVI:2/1 is also impressive. Beginning in the usual fashion with 1P, the module of activity diminishes from a nine-measure phrase to two-measure groups (1Pb, 1Sa), then to single measures, and finally to half measures, with the shrinking module coordinated with harmonic instability. The entire passage is buttressed on either side by the relative minor. The greater tonal stability and broadening at the conclusion of the development prepare for the recapitulation. The development closes with 2P^k; its absence from the recapitulation is the only significant alteration in that section of the form.

Finally, the first movements of the early keyboard trios constitute a real departure from the above description of the early solo sonatas, accompanied divertimentos, and concertinos, primarily as a result of the violin/keyboard partnership: P is always stated in two parallel phrases, the first by the keyboard and the second by the violin. However, the shape is not that of a closed form, for the first cadence is usually a full one and the second a half close. Additionally, in both T and the development, motivic play appears to be more active as a result of the violin/keyboard exchange. However, in just one instance (Hob. XV:41/1) does Haydn take advantage of the added sonority to heighten the structural downbeat at the recapitulation (Example X-6).

CENTRAL MOVEMENTS

In the central slow or moderato movements the cantilena predominates, with three subtypes distinguishable: the simple cantilena, in which a single rhythmic value dominates; the elaborate cantilena, in which the rhythmic subdivisions are unusually fussy and complex, i.e., the melodies are fully ornamented; and the mixed cantilena, in which internal melodic contrasts exist at the phrase and section level but the rhythm of the line remains uncomplicated.

Among the early solo sonatas there are three exceptional slow movements, all linear in concept: Hob. XVI:3/2, Es2/2, and XVI:8/3. Among the sonatas whose first movements were cited as the earliest (Hob. XVI:16, 5, Es2), Hob. XVI:Es2 alone contains a slow movement. Like its first movement, it reveals characteristics that point to a very early genesis: in the first part strong cadences articulate three rather than two tonalities (C minor, G minor, and B-flat major), and it is marked by exact or nearly exact repetitions of two- and one-measure groups that impede its movement.

EXAMPLE X–6. Hob. XV:41/1, mm. 1–4, 83–86.

Hob. XVI:8/3 (Example X-7), Haydn's tiniest slow movement, is a finely honed miniature compared with the sprawling Es2/2. M. 3 reaches beyond the line in m. 1 by a major third, which is underlined by a momentary halt in the bass. The apex is reached by another upward skip of a third (m. 5), with which the melodic line immediately begins its descent. The penultimate measure stalls the motion, underlining the closure of m. 9. Each event within this nine-measure piece is carefully calculated.

In contrast, Hob. XVI:3/2 is the only slow movement in a full sonata form. The exposition is "complete" with four clearly differentiated functions: P is a two-part parallel statement; T begins with the head motive of P; S is clearly laid out by another double statement; and K attains closure with repeated cadences. Its development is comparable to that of Hob. XVI:2/1, with the initial restatement of P, the working-out of material from T and S, and a full-fledged retransition. This highly differentiated and exceptional slow movement provides a decided contrast to the homogeneity of the sonata's opening piece.

The majority of the remaining second movements, the cantilenas, belong to the mainstream of mid-century Viennese keyboard music. In fact, Hob. XVI:1/2 and 6/3 derive from the slow movement of a Reutter keyboard concerto,[6] a modeling that affects the texture as well as the rhythmic and melodic configurations. The two

EXAMPLE X–7. Hob. XVI:8/3, mm. 1–9.

Haydn works are quite different, and it is difficult to hypothesize which was written first, for both reveal primitive as well as more advanced traits. On the one hand,
Hob. XVI:1/2 has archaic cadences without the third, but in its second part the
melody tellingly reaches for c''' nearly a dozen times before d''', the highest pitch on
the keyboard, is struck; while on the other, Hob. XVI:6/3 lacks any climactic contour and articulates its continuous flow by cadenzas, which mark its binary structure, a procedure employed in some of the earliest opening movements. Nevertheless, both cantilena movements are superior to the proposed model by Haydn's
erstwhile teacher.

Unlike these simple cantilenas, XVI:2/2, with its elaborate style, well matches
the accomplishments of its first movement. The contrasting materials are unified
not only by the pulsating accompaniment but also by a control of the melodic curve
that spans each part of the binary structure. Even the smallest figurative motive is
no longer allowed to bear exact repetition (cf. mm. 1–3, 9–11, 12–14). Without
question, this movement could be called Haydn's most "sensitive" among the early
works; its rhythmic variety, ornamentation, and chromatic melodies seem almost
North German in their aesthetic stance. Although one might wish to believe that
behind such a movement lurks the shadow of C. P. E. Bach, no work of Bach's
available in Vienna before 1760 could have served as its model.[7]

The cantilenas of the accompanied works match neither the expressive intensity nor the sense of structure found in the solo sonatas. Hob. XV:41/3 is the only
trio to contain a slow movement of this type: its melody and ornamentation are
reminiscent of those by Wagenseil and by Hofmann. But one's suspicions are
aroused as to its authenticity for this cycle, because the violin merely plays with the
pulsating eighths of the left hand; perhaps it once belonged to a solo sonata. Within

the concertinos, the cantilenas are miniature concerto movements, with the violins and bass providing support, introductions, occasional independent interjections, and closings.

DANCE MOVEMENTS

With the single exception of a rather jocular polonaise, Hob. XV:36/2, all the dance movements that occupy either the central or the final position of the cycle are minuets in some form, and all but one are in an aristocratic style, in contrast to the more rustic style seen in a few of Haydn's later keyboard movements and in the later string quartets and symphonies in particular. Characteristic of the keyboard movements are dotted rhythms, rolling triplets, trills and other ornaments, half-cadences ending on the third beat for internal punctuation, and weak final cadences (Example X-8). Ideas of motivic size molded by other elements into two-, four-, and eight-bar sentences are stressed. Their textures rarely exceed two or three voices. The only early rustic minuet occurs in the inauthentic cycle Hob. XVI:11 (Example X-9). Its unison opening and disjunct melodic line are completely foreign to the aristocratic type; deep melodic and textural contrasts and strong cadences, enhanced by pauses and longer note values, decisively articulate phrase and strain. Hob. XV:36/3 and XVI:16/3, two minuets in a quicker tempo, preserve a somewhat lightened aristocratic style. Finally, the minuet style of Hob. XV:C1/3 differs not only by having an Adagio tempo but also by the variations that follow.

In the more than thirty early minuets that have trios, most retain the tonality but change the mode. This preference, common during the mid-century, can best be understood by considering the relationship of the central cadence of the trio to

EXAMPLE X–8. Hob. XVI:2/3, mm. 1–10.

EXAMPLE X–9. Hob. XVI:11/3, mm. 1–8.

the tonality of the minuet: for example, a trio in the tonic minor presents a stronger contrast than one in the subdominant. In this instance, the internal cadence of a trio in the subdominant major would be on the tonic major, whereas in the tonic minor it would be on its relative major.

Yet the deep contrasts usually provided by the trio in these early minuets are only partially a result of a preference for the minor mode. In some cases, the minuet's aristocratic stance is replaced by a less-stylized and more-introspective section, which is further underlined by syncopation (Hob. XVI:2/3), a more continuous syntax (Hob. XVI:6/3), chromatic progressions (Hob. XVI:12/2), or irregular phrase lengths (Hob. XVI:1/3). In addition, contrasts in sonority occur in a few of the solo as well as in most of the accompanied sonatas: sections of the trio in a lower or higher range; and in the keyboard trios, a more soloistic role for the violin that may occur throughout (Hob. XV:41/2) or in brief imitative passages (Hob. XV:40/3). In Hob. XIV:1/2, scored for keyboard trio plus two horns, only the strings and keyboard participate.

Four-fifths of the minuets are rounded binary forms, many of which are surprisingly individual. For example, in the first section of Hob. XVI:9/2, Haydn constructs two asymmetrical phrases of similar material, with the section after the double bar consisting of related and new material in four-measure segments. It is exceptional for all three parts of the rounded binary to be the same length, as in Hob. XVI:11/3.

The harmonic structure of the first strain is open in most of the minuets—all but one have a cadence in a related key, while the initial cadence of the second strain is usually in the tonic. The remaining minuets are closed for the conclusion of both strains. As a result of the occasional use of the initial material in the first part of the second section, the minuet proper at times is like a sonata form with an embryonic development (e.g., Hob. XVI:9/2 and 4/2).

In some of the minuets the reprise of the initial section is expanded in the second half, strengthening the sense of closure (e.g., Hob. XV:38/2, Hob. XV:41/2, and Hob. XVI:10/2 and 4/2). And for the *da capo* of others, a repetition of the final phrase is indicated in at least two extant sources: the autograph for Hob. XIV:5/2 (*recte* XVI:5a/2) and a copy of Hob. XVI:2/3. Certainly a *reprisa* should be considered for further examples; it may be especially appropriate for concluding minuets.

NON-MINUET FINALES

Besides the minuet, two additional finale types derive from sonatas by Haydn's contemporaries: the scherzo in duple meter, and the 3/8 Presto/Allegro. Whether they begin with a pick-up or on the downbeat, unrelenting energy characterizes their surface rhythms. Even though only one is entitled "Scherzo," Hob. XVI:9/3, the common tradition of all the duple-metered Prestos or Allegros is unmistakable; their progeny are the contradance-rondo finales. Nevertheless, the two can be readily distinguished: none of the early scherzos begin with the two sixteenth-note pick-ups that mark the contradance-rondo finales. The 3/8 Presto/Allegro finales are less inspired and have few descendants.

The early non-minuet finales use *da capo*, binary, or sonata form. Whether they are in 2/4 or 3/8, they are much less distinctive than their first movements. In the sonatas with the most-primitive first movements, the finales—as well as the middle movements—seem to have caused Haydn fewer problems of coherence; even in the more-mature early sonatas with sophisticated initial pieces, the finale is often diminutive in character if not size. Surprisingly, the most interesting of these non-minuet finales are in binary form.

Among the most-accomplished binary finales are Hob. XVI: 14/3, XV: 38/3, and XIV: 12/3. For Hob. XVI: 14/3 Haydn experiments with the phrase lengths and shape of P:

$$
\begin{array}{ll}
\text{m. 1} & \dfrac{\text{Pa} \quad \text{b} \quad \text{a}^1 \quad \text{c}}{2+3 \quad\; 2+3} \\[2ex]
\text{m. 11} & \dfrac{1\text{T}(\text{Pa}^2)}{2 \times 2} \\[2ex]
\left\{ \begin{array}{l} \text{m. 32} \\[2ex] \text{m. 36} \end{array} \right. & \begin{array}{l} \dfrac{\text{Sa}(\text{Pa}^3)}{2+2} \\[2ex] \dfrac{\text{Sa}^1(\text{Pa}^4)}{4} \end{array}
\end{array}
$$

As a result of the manipulations in the first part, Haydn does not open the second part with P but with new material, which dominates its first portion. In the two other finales, Haydn uses contrasting material in S of the first part and alters the thematic presentation in the second part. These examples are clearly exceptional, since thematic reordering is seldom found in either binary or sonata structures before *ca.* 1765.

Haydn uses the variation form for the finale of Hob. XV: C1, the initial movement of Hob. XVII: D1, and the *Klavierstück* Hob. XVII: 7.[8] All three emphasize figurations generated from the harmonies of the bass rather than embellishment of the melody and so tend to be more Baroque than Classic in their orientation. For example, in Hob. XVII: D1/1 the bass is identical in all the variations,[9] and the figurations are controlled by the harmonies generated from the bass rather than by the original theme (Example X-10). The symmetrical phrases of the theme are strictly maintained in all but the first variation. Such regularity is more characteristic of these variations than of any other formal stereotype. All three pieces using the variation form have the same rhythmic structure: the first variation has small note values, the penultimate variation has larger ones, and the last has the smallest.

The early keyboard works reveal a considerable achievement in Haydn's ability to sustain interest in the larger first-movement structure. Searching in several directions, Haydn at times emphasizes homogeneity and other times contrast. Even though one of his first successful efforts uses undifferentiated material, the most impressive first movement has contrasting ideas connected by a recurring motive. Progress toward the development of a coherently structured exposition is also evi-

EXAMPLE X–10. Hob. XVII:D1/1.

EXAMPLE X–10 (*continued*)

dent in the strategic placement of cadences of varying weight, a concern for a large-dimension pitch curve, and controlled harmonic-rhythmic flow. Development sections have also become highly sophisticated not only in synthesizing separately stated thematic ideas but by combining a module of decreasing size with increasing tonal instability. Recapitulations are rarely only a *da capo* of the exposition's themes.

Overall, these sonatas, divertimentos, concertinos, and trios are in the mainstream of the Viennese tradition. But the examination of Haydn's use of many of the same movement types, figurations, and other rhythmic and melodic materials commonly used by his predecessors and contemporaries only heightens our appreciation of his accomplishments before his first mature works, from the mid-1760s.

Maturity, ca. 1765–ca. 1771

During the second half of the 1760s and into the early 1770s, Haydn's style underwent a substantive change. It was first identified in the symphonies by Théodore de Wyzewa, who attempted to explain their deeper expression as a *crise romantique*; in Germany the same concept became a part, or, more accurately, a precursor of the literary *Sturm und Drang*.[10] Although neither label is truly applicable to Haydn, it cannot be denied that an important style change occurred in some of his works during the second half of the 1760s and into the early 1770s. It is within his keyboard music that this change is the most striking: whereas before *ca.* 1765 the sonatas, divertimentos, concertinos, and trios were for the most part small in size and superficial in expression, they became larger and correspondingly deeper in character. And with the new keyboard style the instrument became a medium for elevated thoughts rather than for diversionary musings.

EARLIEST MANIFESTATIONS OF THE NEW STYLE

The first hints of this change occur in three compositions composed around 1765: the G-major Capriccio Hob. XVII: 1 on "Acht Sauschneider müssen seyn";[11] the

EXAMPLE X–11. Hob. XVII:2, mm. 1–32.

twenty Variations in A major Hob. XVII:2; and the Sonata in E Hob. XVI:47. All three are large compositions; in fact, the Capriccio and the Variations are among Haydn's longest keyboard movements.

In Hob. XVII:2 Haydn goes beyond a concern for relating one variation to another,[12] as he turns to the problem of recurring structural patterns in the strophe. The theme (Example X-11) is divided by the overall binary form, i.e., ‖: 8 :‖: 8 :‖, with rolling triplets in the left hand to provide continuity. However, the first variation's syntax could be parsed as follows:

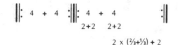

Structural changes such as these can be found in each adjacent variation, even though nearly all of them continue a single figuration throughout a strophe. This trait, combined with both a departure from the harmonic framework of the theme and the employment of characteristic styles, results in one of the most important variation sets of the Classic period. In toto, Hob. XVII: 2 provides a model for solving the structural problems inherent in the variation form, with its large-dimension architecture and changing shapes within the strophe.

The Sonata Hob. XVI:47 is substantially different from any other keyboard composition that Haydn had composed up to this time. Its three movements are arranged as in a trio sonata; the first is a slow 6/8 minor-mode siciliano, which directly links with a driving major-mode Allegro 2/4; and the last is a Tempo di Menuet. Not only are the first two movements joined, but all three are unified by their incipits.[13] In the central movement (Example X-12), this cyclic motive is used as the basis for the most intensive development of a single idea in all of Haydn's keyboard music. The initial idea is employed in both P and S. At the opening of the development, after its literal restatement in the dominant minor, it is first combined with an idea from m. 15 of the exposition; then, in m. 62, it is stated in a form similar to that previously presented in S. In m. 69 it is reworked into a brief symmetrical phrase. Another permutation, in m. 73, is closely related to the second half of S (m. 18). A final climactic passage, beginning in m. 90, takes place in the recapitulation, where the motive assumes a level of recurrence reminiscent of the energy of Baroque rhythm.

The Tempo di Menuet finale is also tightly organized around this motive; up to the first repeat it initiates nearly every phrase. However, unlike the plan of the preceding movement, the recapitulation's structural downbeat is not set forth clearly: the motive is varied in m. 40, concluded by a strong tonic cadence in m. 43, and then followed with a dominant pedal, so that it is not until m. 54 that a completely convincing return occurs. Perhaps Haydn created this solution to scuttle the expectation of return so completely accomplished in the previous movements.

However, to label these movements "monothematic"—a term frequently applied to Haydn's works—would be clearly incorrect. In fact, the application of this term to Haydn's sonata forms should be avoided: more often than not, only a very small portion—at the most the first two or three measures—or the initial phrase will return in a varied form.[14] This procedure highlights the tonal—rather than the thematic—structure by having the P theme herald the new key. While thematic repetition is central to Haydn's style, even more significant are the endless mutations a theme may undergo and still maintain its identity.

Hob. XVI:47 is clearly a significant work. It points toward the better-known sonatas of this period and beyond in the linkage of movements, the use of the minor mode to open the cycle, the replacement of the minuet and trio by a Tempo di

EXAMPLE X–12. Hob. XVI:47/2, mm. 1–8, 19–25, 50–95.

EXAMPLE X–12 (*continued*)

EXAMPLE X–13. Hob. XVI:45/1, mm. 1–12.

Menuet, and the complete working-out of a given compositional problem. Nevertheless, to presume that Hob. XVI:47 was the only transitional work of this period is probably a mistake: Hob. XIV:5 (*recte* XVI:5a), which survives only in a fragment, and perhaps the lost works in minor keys known from the *Entwurf-Katalog* (see Plate 2) might have provided the "missing links."

SIX PROGRESSIVE SOLO SONATAS

First Movements. The first movements of the six remaining solo sonatas (Hob. XVI:18, 45, 19, 46, 44, and 20) all belong to the newer style in their breadth of conception, which is immediately apparent from their P sections.[15] In each case we are dealing with broadly conceived structures that are often symmetrical. Even the earliest of those that can be definitely dated—Hob. XVI:45 of 1766—provides an unusually sophisticated precedent (Example X-13). The surface rhythmic acceleration, the upward melodic direction, and the sustained chord rhythm of the first two measures is offset by the more-relaxed rhythmic flow, the downward melodic direction, and the faster chord rhythm of the following two measures. With the repetition of these two units, some of these characteristics are intensified, and the

EXAMPLE X–14. Hob. XVI:46/1, mm. 1–11.

final phrase is extended to emphasize closure. The same principles can be also seen in the other five sonatas. The one important characteristic lacking in Hob. XVI:45 is the almost improvisatory feeling created within these highly formalized statements. For instance, Hob. XVI:18 begins as an elegant march with stiff dotted rhythms that are destroyed by the septuplets of m. 7; in Hob. XVI:46 (Example X-14), the improvisatory aspect is so fully imbedded within a sophisticated shape that the opening itself is a syntactical paradox.

This new approach to P in the solo sonatas of this period thus spawns a totally different exposition structure. Rather than being characterized by a tonal drive to the related key area (S and K), the material of the tonic asserts itself more powerfully, so that the two principal tonal areas are more balanced in strength. In between P and SK there is now an expansive transition that often dominates the entire exposition.[16] In this central section Haydn sometimes provides a modulating transition, but more often the secondary key is reached relatively early though not established until considerably later. One way that Haydn underlines the tension of this central section—a practice that became almost commonplace during the 1770s—is by introducing deceptive resolutions or a suspension of activity, creating again a sensation of improvisation.

Nowhere are these characteristics more completely illustrated than in the justly celebrated C-minor Sonata Hob. XVI:20/1 (see Plate 11). It begins with an eight-measure P that contains two four-measure phrases: the first has two two-measure segments, the second of which spins out from m. 2; the second four-measure phrase parallels the first, with carefully controlled changes in harmony and rhythm. The first phrase moves to a weak half-cadence on the tonic; the second suggests the mediant in m. 6, reaches a climax, and then concludes—by way of the Neapolitan sixth—with an authentic cadence deepened by the succeeding quarter rest in m. 8. In T, the architectonic structure of the opening period slowly disintegrates (3 × 2, 3 × 1, 4 × ¼) before turning into a free fantasia culminating on a dominant-ninth chord coloristically voiced. One would now expect a resolution confirming the related key. Instead, the new tonic occurs in first inversion and builds to a second climax, which is followed by a rest in m. 31 that parallels m. 8. The complete resolution is delayed until m. 32. The related key area is thus comparable in length and articulation to the opening statement. Although it appears to be new, T derives from previous material: m. 10 is elaborated in mm. 20–24, and mm. 27–29 are associated with the opening, since the same rhythmic motive (♩ ♪♩ ♪) now becomes the chord rhythm.

In all six solo sonatas the development section of the first movement begins with P, but in all except Hob. XVI:19/1 it is so altered from its opening that it provides a disruption from the initial statement: in Hob. XVI:20 and 44 the symmetry is destroyed; in XVI:46 it becomes more regular; and in XVI:45 the opening motive is presented in the dominant minor. The middle portion is often expanded by a single figuration and usually ends with a well-defined retransition. A climax occurs at the end of the middle portion or during the retransition. Even in Hob. XVI:45, the least-impressive development, one can discern the combining of a rhythmic and a pitch climax just before the recapitulation. Hob. XVI:19 and 46

EXAMPLE X–15. Hob. XVI:44/1, mm. 46–53.

do not bring every resource together to achieve an all-powerful moment, but XVI: 20 and 44 are especially notable in this respect. In the latter (Example X-15), it occurs at the end of the development, where P is restated in its simplest texture and then is suddenly treated to stretto, rises to e-flat''', and achieves its thickest sonority with six simultaneities.[17] In Hob. XVI: 20 Haydn leaves no doubt as to its climax: the highest dynamic marking accompanies a figuration that is nothing less than a wash of color.

But these climactic moments are hardly isolated events within their development sections, for they relate to what has previously happened. In the case of Hob. XVI: 44/1, the climax is set up by the development's opening, where the contrapuntal potentialities of P are suggested. What follows is a thematic recapitulation of the exposition that suddenly terminates with an improvisatory flourish and a pause; but all of this is structurally parenthetical, for the retransition completes the activity begun by P. In the C-minor Sonata Hob. XVI: 20/1 the use of material in the development can be viewed in two ways. First, in its relationship to the exposition:

$$\|\colon\ \text{P}\quad \text{T}\quad \text{K}\ \colon\|\colon\quad (\text{P})\qquad \text{K}\longrightarrow\text{climax}\quad \text{T}$$

Here, the repetition of P after the double bar is merely an interruption of the lengthy K that follows. Secondly, K in the development can be viewed as an interruption of the PT sequence established in the exposition:

$\|: \quad$ P $\quad$ (K $\longrightarrow$ climax) $\quad$ T

Nonetheless, when compared to the stark contrasts of rhythmic relaxation and activity within the exposition, the development presents an impression of overall stability.

The recapitulations in these six sonatas are even less a repetition of the exposition's thematic material. The most significant alterations are the elimination of part of P and all or part of T, and the reorganization and sometimes developmental expansion of the PT juncture. Since P now establishes the tonic, as opposed to providing a beginning whose purpose is to drive toward the related key, in the recapitulation it is no longer necessary to reassert the tonic so strongly, since S and K will return in the home key. Thus, the strong final cadence at the end of P in the exposition is superfluous and is replaced by an open punctuation.

Although the resulting lengthy section in the tonic contributes decisively to the long-range feeling of closure, only Hob. XVI:44/1 (Example X-16) is reformulated to underline this function. Haydn first states S in its original form and then embellishes it; this material leads to a cadenza-like passage above a diminished-seventh chord; and K follows. This sequence is reminiscent of Hob. XVI:20/1, but in that instance no functional differentiation was made, as the closure-enhancing passage occurred in both the exposition and the recapitulation (mm. 22–26 and 55–90).

EXAMPLE X–16. Hob. XVI:44/1, mm. 64–72.

P plays a significant role in the coherence of the first movements and in defining the functions of exposition, development, and recapitulation. As in some of the earlier works, it is stated at the beginning of each of the three sections. However, since P is now formulated in two clear-cut phrases, the first is restricted to a reprise function, and the second—when retained—is treated to variation, which leads directly to further newly formulated events.[18]

Exposition	Development	Recapitulation
Pa Pa^1	Pa Pa$^{1^1}$	Pa Pa$^{1^2}$
or	or	or
Pa Pb	Pa Pb^1	Pa Pb^2

Middle Movements. The four middle movements are completely different from those of the earlier sonatas: none are minuets with trios, none retain the same tonic as the first movement, and none are cantilenas. All but one (Hob. XVI:45) are true slow movements, and they consistently achieve an importance that approaches that of the first movement. Both Hob. XVI:19/2 and XVI:46/2 require, as do some from before *ca.* 1765, improvised cadenzas.[19]

Allusion to a concerto style, as suggested by the presence of cadenzas, is fully realized only in Hob. XVI:19/2, a binary form with distinct tuttis and solos; the

EXAMPLE X–17. Hob. XVI:19/2, mm. 1–20.

tuttis (mm. 1–15, 50–66, 74–78, and 113–15) lie in a high tessitura, the solos in a bass-baritone range (Example X-17). Perhaps Haydn transcribed this movement from one of the lost concertos for bassoon or "Contra Violone."[20] If this hypothesis is correct, the orchestral effect of contrasting ranges and colors suggested by the keyboard version would be rather special, from what is known of Haydn's extant concertos. Whatever the origin of Hob. XVI:19/2, it employs a concept that was antiquated by the mid-1760s.

Haydn also draws on the past in Hob. XVI:46/2 and 20/2, both of which use Baroque "walking" basses and initially hint at a type of continuous bass variation. Hob XVI:46/2 carries the suggestion farther, with two complete four-measure statements, which disintegrates with the following phrase. The second part deals with this idea mostly in four-measure, modulating segments from its opening in m. 29 to m. 52, when the flow is disrupted by a fermata. An unusually lengthy coda begins in m. 60; the descending motive returns in a modified form in mm. 66–70. The bass of the final group of measures oscillates between half-steps, the interval that initiated the "passacaglia" idea. Although this movement is in sonata form, the continuity of the materials, the placement of the fermatas, the lack of a strong recapitulation, and the two framing repetitions create a principally bipartite rather than tripartite shape.

Hob. XVI:20/2 is much more continuous than XVI:46/2, as moving eighth-notes persist in nearly every measure. In this instance the tension is not created by breaking the flow with fermatas; rather, it results from the first part of the second half of the binary being extended five measures and reaching a climax that outclasses that of Hob. XVI:20/1. Once again the strongest moment is strategically prepared, not only by the length of part one but also by the placement of the sonorities in a low tessitura and their restricted range. In the first part of the second half, these restrictions and the shape of part one are maintained. By m. 43 the persistent eighths turn to quarters; in two measures the syncopated melody leaps and skips, the tessitura rises; and, finally, with the top and the bottom parts moving in contrary motion, the highest pitch (f‴) is reached in the right hand and the greatest space in sonority occurs with the left. It is not only the sense of tension that unites this movement with the first but also its tonally ambiguous beginning, which could just as easily have been C minor, the tonic of the first movement, as A-flat major.

Finales. The finales contain a variety of styles and forms, but none revert to the minuet and trio. Hob. XVI:45/3 and 20/3 might be seen as outgrowths of the fast minuet finale found in a few works before *ca.* 1765, but the almost demonic drive of Hob. XVI:20/3 would certainly exclude it from this tradition. Now, it is the Tempo di Menuet of Hob. XVI:44 and the fast duple-meter finale in the style of the contradance of Hob. XVI:19 and 46—in either a sonata, variation, or part-form—that establish a firm tradition until the 1790s.

An example of the second type, Hob. XVI:19/3, marks Haydn's first use of a synthesized form: a rondo with the refrain treated to variation.[21] The uniform rhythmic velocity of each variation, the alterations in the original bass line and harmony (mm. 54–56), and the use of techniques independent of embellishment in the final variations are significant departures from the earlier variation sets. The absence of embellishment in the first strain of the last variation lends to this section (mm. 101–108) the additional function of recapitulation; even the cadence (mm. 104–107) is simplified. For the final strain Haydn further enhances the recapitulatory feeling of closure by writing out the repeat and then indicating that the entire second strain is to be played again. The strophic variation aspects dominate the structure of the rondo's refrains, since none are abbreviated. As a result, the reprises are afforded a larger proportion than in any other rondo. Although Hob. XVI: 19/3 is one of Haydn's least-complex examples because of the absence of transitions, this movement is the beginning of an important tradition of synthesized structures that was fully exploited during the next decades.

The Tempo di Menuet of the two-movement Hob. XVI: 44 also adumbrates a characteristic that gained in importance: the thematic connection of contrasting sections in part forms. In this ABAB structure, A and B share a head-motive as well as a similar cadential formula. In addition, in contrast to Hob. XVI: 19/3, each of the repeats after the first is written out, so that recapitulation is combined with variation. This procedure recalls the treatment of P in sonata form.

Of the four finales in sonata form (Hob. XVI: 18, 45, 46, and 20), only Hob. XVI: 20/3 presents a completely new concept. Like its first movement, P is a balanced two-part (a–a¹) period in which the second part is stated an octave lower; this relationship is retained for the beginning of the development, and it generates a double reprise (Example X-18), which occupies nearly half of the movement. In the first reprise 1T is excluded; 2T and 3T are recapitulated and are followed by an extensive area derived from 4T. In the second reprise Pa′ and then 4T, 5T, 6T, and 7T return, with the exposition's K concluding the movement.[22]

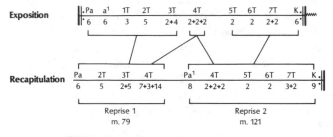

EXAMPLE X–18. Hob. XVI: 20/3.

CONSERVATIVE SONATAS AND VARIATIONS

While the aforementioned six sonatas each represent to some degree the great strides that Haydn made during the mid-to-late 1760s and into the first year or so of the 1770s, this new style for *Kenner* was not one that Haydn used exclusively. He continued to compose large-scale works for the *Liebhaber* that had neither technical and musical difficulties nor pre–Romantic murmurings. Among the more conservative sonatas are two works for keyboard four hands, Hob. XVIIa: 1 and 2, and the Quintet for keyboard, baryton, and strings, which survives only as the Keyboard Trio Hob. XV: 2.

Hob. XVIIa:1 and 2 each consist of two movements in the Fast–Minuet pattern of Hob. XVI:18 and 44, but instead of a sonata form, XVIIa:1/1 is a set of variations known as "Il maestro e lo scolare." It lacks all the most progressive aspects of variation form and technique already described; its diminutions, regular phrase lengths, and *maestro/scolare* imitation within each strophe provide nothing unexpected. In short, it is a piece that would please many, cause only rank beginners any difficulties, and thoroughly annoy only a few of the sophisticated.

Hob. XV:2 hardly seems to belong to this period in terms of cyclic structure or of style: its finale, an Adagio with variations, superficially recalls the very early Hob. XV:C1/3. But despite its commonplace materials, the movement deals with a compositional problem provided by an unusual theme: the phrases are asymmetrical,[23] and three of the four are based on the same material—a syntax whose redundancy does not seem very conducive to successful variations (Example X-19). Haydn's solution is to group the four variations into pairs; the first two contain embellishments that are closely related to the theme and are concertante in style, while the remaining two maintain only the original bass and employ an accompanied texture. The rhythmic plan of the set underlines these pairs with an acceler-

EXAMPLE X–19. Hob. XV:2/3, mm. 1–18.

ation and then—more peculiarly—a rhythmic relaxation for Variations 3 and 4. Even more ingenious are the distribution of the individual pitches of the theme between the violin and the keyboard in Variation 1 and the democratic division of the principal line at the level of the phrase: the violin has the primary role in the initial and final phrases, the keyboard in the two internal ones.

The twelve Variations in E-flat major Hob. XVII: 3, based on a theme from the String Quartet Op. 9/2, is less conservative; it does not probe large-scale architecture and characteristic styles but change of activity within the strophe. Rather than having each variation continue with the same figure, in Hob. XVII: 3 Haydn may change at virtually any dimension: the section, phrase, subphrase, or even measure. These alterations within a strophe are a direct outgrowth of varying the form-shaping articulations seen in Hob. XVII: 2, from some five years earlier. Haydn's fascination during the 1760s with variation practice transformed one of the most rigid and pedestrian of eighteenth-century stereotypes into a most interesting aspect of his stylistic development in the coming decades.

The Publicly Distributed Opere, ca. 1774–1785

With the decade *ca.* 1774–1785, Haydn's activity as a keyboard composer again changed radically. Whereas previously he concentrated on works for private use that only coincidentally found their way into copies and prints, he now composed *opere* meant for public distribution and presumably financial rewards. Although the greater part of this period was occupied with solo sonatas, at the end of the decade solo settings became secondary to keyboard trios, which dominated Haydn's keyboard output until the mid-1790s.

During the 1770s almost all of Haydn's solo keyboard output is found in three sets: Six Sonatas for Nikolaus Esterházy Hob. XVI: 21–26, published in 1774; Six Sonatas Hob. XVI: 27–32 distributed by professional Viennese copyists in 1776; and Six Sonatas Hob. XVI: 35–39 and 20, dedicated to the Auenbrugger sisters and published by Artaria in 1780. But these *opere* were not planned compositional units, even though one can surmise that Haydn carefully selected the sonatas that would constitute a marketable group to the music-purchasing public: the 1780 set contains a sonata begun in 1771 (Hob. XVI: 20), and some other works could very well have been composed considerably earlier than their date of distribution. Also, Sonatas Hob. XVI: 33, 34, and 43, dating from this time, may well have been intended for one of these sets but were subsequently rejected.

Nevertheless, each set of six sonatas begins with an easily accessible sonata in C major or G major, opening with marchlike rhythms, and concludes with a most esoteric work. Some first movements in these sets are marked Moderato or Allegro Moderato and have dotted rhythms, two are in triple meter, and three marked Moderato require subdivision of the beat. The Auenbrugger set contains an additional esoteric sonata in C-sharp minor (Hob. XVI: 36), a reflection of the esteem that Haydn held for the sisters to whom they were dedicated. Each set also has its share of progressive and conservative second and third movements.

THE ESTERHÁZY SONATAS

As a whole, the six Esterházy Sonatas Hob. XVI:21–26 are the most conservative; not one is in a minor key. The first of the series begins with a homogeneous movement that stresses dotted rhythms and concludes with a finale in 3/8 time; both recall Haydn's pre–1765 style if not syntax. Also in an older style are the Andante in a diminutive 3/8 time of the second sonata, the siciliano of the third, and the miniature Presto 2/4 finale of the sixth. In addition, the canonic and "rovescio" minuets of the fifth and sixth sonatas have a strong Viennese tradition. This posture, rather than that of the late 1760s, must have been chosen to please their dedicatee, Prince Nikolaus Esterházy.

First Movements. All the first movements are in sonata form, and all but one commence with a P theme of two or more phrases of the same material; i.e., the initial function is a direct descendant of the P themes from the most advanced works of the previous group. Now, however, the medial cadence returns to being stronger than the terminal one. Perhaps the most significant aspect concerns the makeup of the T sections, which are appreciably more advanced in their increased length and emphasis on the development of P.[24] In Hob. XVI:21/i the dotted rhythm and chordal outline of the melody are elaborated. In Hob. XVI:22/i (Example X-20) the sequential sixteenth-note group in mm. 9–11 is derived from m. 5, which in turn is an inversion of the figure from the initial measure. In Hob. XVI:23/i and 24/i the opening ideas are worked out in a modulating sequence. In Hob. XVI:25/i a statement of the opening motive in the relative minor leads to a cadenza-like flourish for one and a half measures, punctuated by a half-cadence on the dominant. And in Hob. XVI:26/i, the most elaborate of the set, a transposed statement of the initial motive (m. 9) is followed by a series of sequences (mm. 11–21), concluding with a deceptive cadence.

The sections in the related key are especially notable for allusions to or entire phrases in the minor mode. Although change of mode is a common device during the eighteenth century, Haydn's use of the minor in S and/or K takes on a specialized role: since it is not possible to have a functioning "minor dominant," by turning to the minor after the establishment of the new key, the effect is to destroy any lingering concept of P's tonic. Afterward, the exposition is always closed by a return to the major. Unlike P, S may use a deceptive cadence in the midst of or just before the SK area. Both practices are found in Hob. XVI:21/i, in which a passage firmly in the dominant (mm. 19–22) is followed by a more tonally elaborate

EXAMPLE X–20. Hob. XVI:22/i, mm. 1, 5, 9–11.

section (mm. 23–35). After an authentic-perfect-strong dominant cadence, the parallel minor is introduced (mm. 36–40). A final period with a deceptive cadence at the midpoint (m. 51) closes the exposition. In the initial section (mm. 21–32) of Hob. XVI:23/1, the parallel minor (mm. 29–32) is introduced by a deceptive cadence; another brief allusion to the minor is found in m. 38. The minor section (mm. 40–45) of Hob. XVI:24/1 provides a moment of comparative instability framed by two stable sections in the major (mm. 35–39 and after m. 46).

In contrast to the most advanced first movements from the previous period, just one of the Esterházy expositions (Hob. XVI:26/1) interrupts the continuous flow of the beat, and then only momentarily. Gone is any sense of improvisation. Instead, five of the six expositions are constructed with related materials and with a quickening of the overall surface rhythm as the section progresses. The exposition of Hob. XVI:24, with its two thematically parallel parts, is the exception.

All six developments begin with material from P; three begin on the dominant, two on the tonic, and one on the dominant of the submediant. After the opening, Haydn employs two different approaches: following the order of the exposition rather closely, with each idea improvised on in turn; and superimposing a completely new structure on the expository materials. In both cases there is a heavy dependence on idiomatic figurations when modulatory activity is stressed.

The first type of development is found in Hob. XVI:21/1, 23/1, and 24/1. In XVI:21/1, P is presented in a single statement, T and S are elaborated upon in turn, new figuration follows, and K now in single-measure sequences serves as a retransition. Only one detail disturbs the rather placid presentation: in mm. 85–86, the upper part triadically ascends to f‴, the highest pitch of the entire movement, and is then disrupted by a sonority of seven simultaneities whose dotted rhythms recall an earlier passage in the development. One has the feeling that the improvisatory wandering of mm. 80–86 was "snapped back" to discipline by this disruption.

A rather special example of the first type is Hob. XVI:24/1, whose exposition in two thematically parallel parts generates a like development: the first consists of 1P followed by T, the second of 2P followed by its concluding figuration (m. 38). The retransition deals with the movement's main motive (𝄾♪♫ | ♩), which becomes expanded to a longer anacrusis (𝄾♪♫♫ | ♩).[25]

On the other hand, each of the reformulated developments of the second type has a logic of its own. Despite its brevity, the development of Hob. XVI:22/1 (Example X-21) is a model of structural acumen: here Haydn depends on one device, the articulatory power of the movement's opening sonority. Beginning on the dominant of the submediant, the first six measures elide the first two beats of m. 1 with the third and fourth beats of m. 12. The second part, mm. 31–36, corresponds to mm. 1 and 2, but then expands upon m. 7 for three additional measures, reaching a climactic fermata. The remaining five measures bring back mm. 16–19, followed by a retransition. In Hob. XVI:25/1 the development also uses P in a similar fashion, but here the recurrence of P is one part of a larger plan for the entire movement: P recurs at T of the exposition; at the beginning, middle, and end of the development; and is restated in an unadulterated form at the beginning

EXAMPLE X–21. Hob. XVI:22/1, mm. 25–42.

of the recapitulation. Hob. XVI:26/1 recalls the parenthetical approach of Hob. XVI:44/1 by beginning the development with Pa and ending with Pb (m. 55), both on the tonic; between these two points come K, new material, and T—a partial retrograde of the exposition's order.

The recapitulations follow many of the procedures seen in the previous period. In this respect, the first sonata (Hob. XVI:21/1) again is the most conservative, for it presents the most regular recapitulation of the set. Hob. XVI:22/1 and 23/1 are notable for their addition of a prolonged dominant to underline closure. Previously, this device was used in Hob. XVI:20 in both exposition and recapitulation and only in the recapitulation of Hob. XVI:44/1. Haydn must have thought that XVI:44/1 was the more successful of the two, for XVI:20/1—which today is the more admired movement—was not duplicated. In Hob. XVI:22/1 this dominant prolongation (mm. 48–54) is sustained longer and not resolved until some seventeen measures later. In the following sonata, Hob. XVI:23, Haydn again has a long-range strategy, but the order of events is juggled and the resolution is gradually established: weak resolutions occur three times (mm. 111, 114, and 121), but a decisive articulation is delayed until m. 123.

If Hob. XVI:24/1 had been composed a decade later, Haydn might have treated its recapitulation differently: with its exposition of two parallel parts, one part could easily have been excluded or considerably tightened. Instead, the second part is only briefly expanded by a deceptive resolution and followed by a brief working-out of its main motive. In the recapitulation of Hob. XVI:25/1, Pb, which was ignored in the development, is briefly developed; and in XVI:26/1, the recapitulation, although rather regular, begins on the half-bar and excludes the part of P previously used as a retransition, a device reminiscent of the early sonatas (e.g., Hob. XVI:2/1).

Second Movements. Only the first four sonatas contain slow movements and all but the first (Hob. XVI:21) are in the tonic minor. This choice of key and mode again recalls the sonatas before *ca.* 1765. More telling, however, is their character: only one (Hob. XVI:23) approaches the depth of expression found in those from *ca.* 1765–*ca.* 1771, and it contains no remarkable events. All three slow movements are cantilenas of homogeneous materials, reminiscent of the earliest examples.

Perhaps the most successful is the only one in a major key, Hob. XVI:21/2. Within the context of its otherwise rhythmically rigid cycle and of the other slow movements of this set, it is an experiment in contrasting rhythmic flow. The opening dozen measures are almost like a composed improvisation; the right hand contains a variety of durations while the left fails to establish any strong sense of meter. The continuity of motion that begins in m. 13 is continued after the double bar up to the recapitulation. If the repeats of both parts are observed, the shape of the movement can be perceived through this rhythmic polarity.

The overall conservative neutrality of these sonatas can be further seen in Haydn's failure to exploit fully the possibilities of the *attacca* to the finale in Hob. XVI:24. Since it is a sonata form without development, the length of one of the final functions of the two parallel parts could have been appreciably lengthened or shortened to underline the beginning of the finale. In the recapitulation, although K has been eliminated, S remains approximately the same length and thus produces little of the anticipatory tension found in some of the previous slow movements.

Only Hob. XVI:26 has a minuet at its center: a Menuet and Trio al rovescio, i.e., the second half of each is a retrograde of the first. Its presence in this position again recalls the earliest cycles. A transcription from Symphony No. 47 of the previous year, it must have provided some extra amusement for at least the performer: in the original edition the keyboardist was presented with the problem of realizing the retrograde, as only the forward portion was engraved.

Finales. The finales include two sonata forms (in Hob. XVI:21 and 23), two variation sets (in Hob. XVI:22 and 24), one minuet with trio (in Hob. XVI:25), and one miniature rounded binary (in Hob. XVI:26). Hob XVI:21 and 23 present no new sonata-form procedures and tend to continue a finale tradition of less-formal adventure, more homogeneity, and much energy. Hob. XVI:26/3 also belongs to this tradition, but in this instance Haydn was in such a hurry to complete the set that he produced little more than a trifle, one that seems a more appropriate conclusion to one of the small sonatas from before 1765 rather than to the impressive first movement of this cycle.[26] The Presto that closes Hob. XVI:24 is the earliest example of the fast triple-meter scherzo that gained some favor in later works. The minuets of Hob. XVI:22 and 25 belong to another tradition, the relaxed and elegant conclusion; and the latter, a canonic minuet, has an extensive Viennese ancestry.[27]

In terms of Haydn's stylistic development, the two sets of variations are of the greatest significance. The aristocratic Tempo di Menuet of Hob. XVI:22, like XVI:44/2, is one of Haydn's earliest variations that alternates two themes in differing modes. Additionally, it is another early example of formal synthesis: since the *minore* theme is open, the structural effect is that of a part form with variation. The written-out repeats with pure and embellished restatements of the major-mode theme provide within each couplet both recapitulation and variation. Even though Hob. XVI:24/3 has only a single variation of A, it is an important predecessor of Haydn's ternary and other part forms in which the episodes are free adaptations of the refrain's materials.

THE SONATAS "ANNO 1776" AND HOB. XVI:43 AND 33
Although one can rightly attribute the conservatism of the Esterházy Sonatas to the fact that they were written for his patron, Haydn must have had additional motivations: these six works were in a real sense his debut as a composer of fullfledged keyboard sonatas and he certainly would not have wished to offend or "tax" the tastes of the Viennese public. Thus, one is not surprised to find that the sonatas "anno 1776" (Hob. XVI:27–32) plus XVI:43 and 33, which were also publicly distributed, do not re-embrace the style of the late 1760s.

Unencumbered by the deadline imposed on the Esterházy Sonatas, all eight of these works are in three movements with none of the short cuts evident in the earlier set. Except for one, the cycles are of two types, both of which were prominent before *ca.* 1765:

Fast–Minuet–Fast   Hob. XVI:27, 28, 32, 43

Fast–Slow–Minuet   Hob. XVI:29, 30, 33

(The exception, Hob. XVI:31, merely substitutes a triple-meter slow movement for the minuet in the first type; it is the only cycle to imitate the later 1765–1771 group.) Except for the minuets with trios, sonata form dominates the first and second movements. In the finales, variation sets or part forms in which embellished returns play an important function account for all but Hob. XVI:32, a sonata structure; the finales, therefore, now also attain formalization. Three sonatas link movements together: the second movement and finale are joined in Hob. XVI:31 and 33, and all three movements are joined in XVI:30.

First Movements. Although part of the 1776 set, Hob. XVI:27 may well have originated earlier.[28] The first movement's homogeneous and continuous rhythmic flow through most of the exposition, recapitulation, and the entire development certainly seems conservative. In contrast to the exposition, which is entirely in major, the development emphasizes the minor mode and works on a single idea; the latter brings to mind Hob. XVI:45/1. The somewhat unremarkable material of XVI:27/1, however, is counterbalanced by a highly polished presentation.

Hob. XVI:27/1 is not the only movement to recall a sonata from the late 1760s: the figuration of Hob. XVI:31/1 is reminiscent of Hob. XVI:46/1. But more significant than the thematic similarities are the differences: whereas XVI:46/1 emphasizes irregularities of syntax, the exposition to XVI:31/1 is one of the most regular—three two-measure pairs, two four-measure pairs, and a four-measure conclusion. Its development follows the gestalt of the exposition, with the exception of five measures of "singing allegro" material. The model for the exposition and recapitulation of Hob. XVI:28/1 seems to have been Hob. XVI:20/1 (1771): both have big initial statements, cadenzas that confirm the new key in both exposition and recapitulation, and an epilogue to K. In both Hob. XVI:28/1 and 31/1, the surface similarities to earlier sonatas are striking. However, the originality with which these same devices were first used during the 1760s, in contrast to their regular and perfunctory employment in these works from the 1770s, is particularly noteworthy.

At first perusal one might think that Hob. XVI:30/1 belongs with the first movements of XVI:28 and 31, for everything about it seems commonplace: the turns and dotted rhythms of P, the horn motives of P^k and K signaling "farewell" to P as well as to the entire exposition, and the inversion of material from left to right hands. One would not even raise an eyebrow at the development and the generally regular recapitulation. However, at the conclusion of the movement the exposition's penultimate material is extended, the horn motive is excluded, a broken dominant-seventh flourish on the tonic intrudes and is deceptively resolved to C-sharp major with doubled, fully voiced chords, and the second movement begins; the first movement therefore becomes one enormous gesture preparing for the dramatic link to the Adagio. It is tempting to seek a connection between this dramatic intrusion and a similar one in Emanuel Bach's Sonata in A major Wq. 55/4, but although Bach's sonata was composed in 1764, it was not available in Vienna until 1779, when it was published as a part of the *Kenner und Liebhaber* sets.[29]

The first movements of Hob. XVI:29 and 32 are the most original of the set. Since we have already called attention to the exposition of Hob. XVI:29 as Haydn's first realization of a *fortepiano* idiom,[30] only the development (Example X-22) requires comment here. Although it follows the plan of the exposition, the opening foreshadows the kind of concentrated motivic treatment highly admired and frequently imitated in the early decades of the nineteenth century: Pax (m. 1) is thrice stated with mounting harmonic intensity, Pay (m. 2) is then taken up, Pax interrupts, and Pay is developed in a pair of three-measure statements before breaking into free figuration. A similar procedure occurs in the second part, where arpeggiated material disintegrates into a pointillistic texture (mm. 54–55) just before the retransition.

EXAMPLE X–22. Hob. XVI:29/1, mm. 32–44, 51–60.

For the Sonata in B minor Hob. XVI:32, as in XVI:29, Haydn provides a strong profile to P at both the motivic and the phrase levels. At the beginning of T the potentialities of Pa are exposed, but Haydn holds them in reserve and instead sets up a sophisticated tonal struggle between the leading tones of the tonic minor (B) and its related major (D). The first part (mm. 9–12) acts like a normal T in the minor mode, with the flattening of the leading tone (m. 11) followed by a half-close in the new key of D major. However, in the second part (mm. 13–24), which

EXAMPLE X–23. Hob. XVI:32/1, mm. 20–23.

one would expect to be solidly entrenched in the related tonality, Haydn establishes a bifocal situation by flattening the leading tone of the new key (C sharp to
C natural) and reinstating the A sharp of the old tonality over a tonic pedal of the
new. The crucial moment is m. 21 (Example X-23): in the first half C sharp and
A sharp coexist, while in the second the leading tone of the minor key is flattened, this time making way for authentic cadences in the relative major (mm.
23–24) and their extension in K, during which A sharp makes a fleeting final
appearance.[31] The development (Example X-24) begins with two measures that
totally disrupt Pax's intervallic content. Pa is then stabilized on the subdominant
and a sequence ensues on Pb. T (Pax) returns with its importance underlined by
the added octave in the bass and proceeds to develop Pay in continuous, single-
beat units. In a mere nineteen measures Haydn has created one of his greatest developments to date.

    Of the remaining two works in the 1776 group, Hob. XVI:33 has the stronger
initial movement and would have little difficulty in being exchanged with one of
the other first movements of the 1776 set. However, XVI:43/1 is closer in style to
Hob. XVI:27–29 and is probably the weakest of this series of sonatas: it is built on
commonplace thematic materials that fail to be revived by the predominant rolling-
triplet accompaniment. Only the cadenza-like passage breaks this pattern, for it
serves as the retransition to the recapitulation and not to confirm S.

    Second Movements. Of the four central slow movements, those of Hob. XVI:30,
31, and 33 lead directly to their finales. Indeed, Hob. XVI:30/2 functions entirely
as an interlude between two substantial formal structures. Parallels between the
initial movements of Hob. XVI:31 and Hob. XVI:46 have already been noted;
they are similar also in the passacaglia-like style of their second movements. However, whereas the first movement of Hob. XVI:31 is a relative disappointment, its
central movement is comparable to its stylistic parallel. The moving bass is more
persistent than that of Hob. XVI:46/2, the texture less disrupted, and the control
of range and sonority impressive (see mm. 16–18). The reprise sends the listener
mixed signals: on the one hand, the lengthy dominant preparation heightens an

EXAMPLE X–24. Hob. XVI:32/1, mm. 29–48.

expectation for resolution, while on the other, its shortness makes the beginning of the finale appear premature. Hob. XVI:33/2, a sonata-form movement, uses the same general structural principle of shortening the reprise, but again one is confused: since both the development and the recapitulation begin as a varied reprise, the overall shape of the movement is not verifiable until the final measures.

Only the sonata-form Adagio of Hob. XVI:29 stands independently. As in its first movement, broad structural gestures are emphasized in the exposition: eight measures of rather stark sonorities, a middle dominated by Alberti figurations, and a closing returning to the fabric of the first. Since the development returns to the figurations of the exposition's central section, once again we find a slow movement whose primary shape is determined by alternating sonorities and rhythms. Although the Alberti figurations might seem commonplace, Haydn does not use them in a "singing" context. Instead, he presents a detached and almost breathless melody.

The four central minuets are in the aristocratic style, with trios, even though such a designation is lacking in Hob. XVI:32. The real oddity among these otherwise stylistically homogeneous minuets is Hob. XVI:43/2, whose opening intervals refer to the beginning of the first movement; more important, however, as a whole it is a caricature of an aristocratic style. The "Trio" is extremely peculiar; it remains in the same mode and key as the "Menuetto" and uses a "singing allegro" texture throughout.

Finales. The use of variation form or procedures in all but one finale indicates an effort to appeal to the public with a favored structural stereotype. But Haydn was not satisfied with composing one predictable strophe after another. In earlier sets, he searched for solutions to the problems of the standard variation form, but always within the confines of the strophic structure. In these sonatas, however, the strophe is violated, and in the part forms embellishment of repeated material becomes a principle.

In the finales to Hob. XVI:27 and 28, nonstrophic forms are employed for the third variation. The theme of Hob. XVI:27/3 is a rounded binary:

$$\|{:}\ \underset{4}{a}\quad \underset{4}{b}\ {:}\|{:}\ \underset{4}{c}\quad \underset{4}{d}\quad \underset{4}{a}\quad \underset{4}{b^1}\ {:}\|$$

The episodic third variation (Example X-25), however, first presents phrases a and b in a recapitulatory manner. In the written-out repetition, the mode is changed to the parallel minor, and the melody is altered. The ensuing developmental passage consists of a repeated symmetrical eight-measure period based on the initial subphrase (a) of the theme, a cadential motive ($\quad$) treated sequentially (mm. 90–92), and an inversion (mm. 93–96) of the preceding four measures. The resulting compression by one-third undermines the "strophic rhythm" so characteristic of variations.

The finale of Hob. XVI:30 is more conservative. As he did in Hob. XV:2/3, Haydn unifies the first two variations by his treatment of the theme: in Variation 1 the initial four measures of each strain are embellished more than the last portion, whereas in Variation 2 the reverse occurs. A new feature is the hint of motivic development within a strophic framework in Variation 2. The third—with its invention-like texture—and fourth variations form another pair similar to the first two: in Variation 3 the second half of each strain is closer to the theme, whereas in Variation 4 that occurs only in the first strain. The recapitulatory final variation with written-out repeats also departs from the previous sets: only the initial subphrases of both strains are restated as given in the theme.

Yet a further expansion of the developmental concept of variation within a strophic framework can be seen in Hob. XVI:31/3 (Example X-26): the second and third variations emphasize single aspects of the theme and first variation. In the first strain of the second variation the theme is treated to changes in color, harmony, and texture, and the second strain concentrates on the development of the initial motive of the theme: a fragment treated sequentially in mm. 41–44 is inverted in mm. 45–48. Variation 3, a *minore*, is built on the embellishment of the original bass line of m. 20 of Variation 1, which is initially presented in the bass and then inverted in the soprano.

The double strophic variation of Hob. XVI:33/3 is another instance of motivically related themes (Example X–27). Here, this device is true not only of the melody but also of the bass. The first variation distinguishes itself by replacing the original pick-up notes to each four-measure phrase with the headmotive of the second theme, a process that further obscures the shape of the set. Although previous events diminish the initial effect of the close, Haydn again synthesizes recapitulation and variation in the final section (beginning in m. 65) and brings the movement to a brilliant conclusion.

Experimentation with the concept of recapitulation is also a significant aspect of the finale to Hob. XVI:29, an A B A¹ A form in which the structural downbeat is obscured. The listener is thus confronted with the reprise of A as a variation; only the return to the major mode and the initial two intervals of the theme are left un-

EXAMPLE X–25. Hob. XVI:27/3, Var. 3, mm. 73–104.

EXAMPLE X–26. Hob. XVI:31/3, mm. 1–16, 33–56.

altered. As in Hob. XVI:33/3, the effect of the real return to A is understandably diminished. Yet this movement is another step toward those later ternary forms with episodes derived from the refrain.

Compared to an earlier rondo, Hob. XVI:19/3, Hob. XVI:43/3 is more complex. Most obvious is the addition of a third episode, but more significant are the occurrence of variation procedures at new points in the structure, the employment of homogeneous material, and the use of transitions organically related to the refrain. For each refrain Haydn selects different phrases for variation; the first return duplicates the refrain only in the initial eight (mm. 57–64) and final three (mm. 88–90) measures, but the most distant variant is reserved for the central

EXAMPLE X–27. Hob. XVI:33/3.

phrase (mm. 78–82). Although all of the phrases are varied in the second return, the same recapitulatory concept is applied; the initial and final phrases are closest to the opening refrain. The final refrain is characterized throughout not by embellishment but by octave displacement and expansion—the latter via repetition, the addition of a fermata, and a cadenza-like flourish, all of which eliminate any potential monotony. The episodes are less coherent and structurally more dependent than those of Hob. XVI:19/3. The transition to the first episode (mm. 27–32) derives from the refrain, as do the central section of the episode proper (mm. 37–42, cf. m. 1) and the retransition (mm. 46–56, cf. m. 15). On the other hand, for the second and third episodes Haydn provides new material and relates the beginning of the coda (m. 219) to the brief transition to the third episode.

The only sonata-form finale appropriately belongs to the final and most serious sonata of the set, Hob. XVI:32. Yet it has a totally different plan than its opening movement: rather than a three-part exposition in which the establishment of the related key is delayed, this exposition is in two parts; a very brief transition that emerges from P is followed by a lengthy area (SK), in which the related key is repeatedly reaffirmed. Each half is further defined by its surface rhythm—the first all eighth notes, the second sixteenths. The development plays on the contrapuntal possibilities of P, and SK is so modified that it does not insistently confirm any key. The recapitulation contains a shortened version of P, and the version of SK is not that of the exposition but of the development (Example X-28). The contrapuntal orientation of P and the need for further stabilization of the movement result in a final statement of the subject in octaves, an ending derived from the Viennese fugue.[32] Despite these differences, both the first movement and the finale are notable for their simultaneous, bifocal activities; at the beginning of T in the first movement the right hand stresses B, the left D; in the recapitulation of SK in the finale, the right hand centers on B and the left initially on D.

Situated between the 1774 Esterházy Sonatas and the 1780 Auenbrugger set, those of "anno 1776" plus Hob. XVI:43 and 33 represent a compromise between the progressive works of the 1760s and the more conservative sonatas published in 1774. Yet the overall, moderating effect of this group of works results not so much from the bringing together of entirely progressive and conservative sonatas into an *opera*, as in the combination of polarities within a sonata cycle or even a single movement. An example of the former are the unusually strong contrasts of style and expression between the accessible outer movements and austere central ones of Hob. XVI:30 and 31. Polarities within single movements are found in the variations of Hob. XVI:27/3 and 28/3, where regular strophes are disrupted by irregular and developmental ones, and the double variations of Hob. XVI:33/3 with their ambiguous beginnings.

Among the sonata forms, the imposed regularity in Hob. XVI:31/1 is only a preparation for a violent disruption. More impressive is the working-out process in the developments of Hob. XVI:29/1 and 32/1, which contain some of the earliest and most-controlled instances of thematic reduction.

THE AUENBRUGGER SONATAS AND HOB. XVI:34

The Auenbrugger Sonatas Hob. XVI:35–39 were published in 1780 together with Hob. XVI:20 (discussed above), which was begun in 1771. Thus, as with the 1776 set, these sonatas were not all new, and that may account for two movements based on the same material, Hob. XVI:36/2 and 39/1. Perhaps the E-minor Sonata Hob. XVI:34, which is in general stylistically congruent with several of the other sonatas of this group, was originally to have been the last of the series, but the esoteric C-minor Sonata Hob. XVI:20 was substituted, possibly because of the reputation of the dedicatees (the sisters Auenbrugger) and/or the similarities of Hob. XVI:34/1 and Hob. XVI:39/3.

The cycles of the six works from this period, Hob. XVI:35–39 and 34, present a relatively uniform layout compared to the 1776 sonatas. All are in three move-

EXAMPLE X–28. Hob. XVI:32/3, mm. 38–53, 105–22, 154–71.

EXAMPLE X–28 (*continued*)

ments, and all but one use the Fast–Slow–Fast pattern.[33] The first movements include two instances of the older Moderato or Allegro Moderato type, but modern "con brio" and Presto movements predominate; Hob. XVI:39/1 looks forward to the initial movements of later cycles, with variations replacing the usual sonata form. The central movements are no longer Andantes but slower, with the more introspective Adagio and Largo markings; two revert to the older Baroque dance styles of the siciliano (Hob. XVI:38) and sarabande (Hob. XVI:37) and are linked directly to their finales, one of which (Hob. XVI:37/3) is characterized as "innocentemente." The juxtaposition of these two elevated dance styles with the lighter-weight rustic minuet (XVI:38) and contradance (XVI:37) conclusions must have perturbed the North German critics. In contrast to the 1776 set, none of the finales use the variation as the main structure.

First Movements. The functional parts of the five sonata-form first movements contain the same types of expositions as in the previous set: two built from homogeneous material (Hob. XVI:35 and 34), one in three parts (P–T–K) with a very lengthy T (Hob. XVI:37), one divided into two sections by the repetition of the opening of P as S (Hob. XVI:38), and one in which P's motivic character is so concentrated that it distinctively shapes the entire movement (Hob. XVI:36). The developments of Hob. XVI:35/1 and 34/1 continue in the manner of their expositions, without any really striking gestures. Hob. XVI:37/1, like its earlier structural counterpart, Hob. XVI:32/1, has a small development but does not have such a masterly motivic treatment. Instead, it reverts to an old and empty device, the sequence coupled with suspensions, which here is preceded by P and followed by a retransition astutely based on material that established the related key. Hob. XVI:38/1 (Example X-29) delays the return of P until the fourth measure of the development and eases into it by a half-step. From this point on the development seems like two short improvisational meanderings on P (mm. 32 and 40), interrupted by its concluding bars (cf. mm. 46–47 and 7–8). The logic of such a procedure is only revealed in m. 48, a false reprise on the submediant, which is followed in the next measure by the totally unexpected recapitulation. Except for the first movements of Hob. XVI:35 and 36, the recapitulations for the most part

EXAMPLE X–29. Hob. XVI:38/1, mm. 29–48.

continue the procedures seen earlier. Hob. XVI: 35/1 is one of the rare instances in which Haydn provides a coda: in this case the material developed in the expansion after the downbeat of the recapitulation (mm. 111–18) is restated in a stabilized form.

Hob. XVI: 36/1 (Example X-30) is the most impressive first movement of the set, in some ways surpassing the earlier Hob. XVI: 20/1. Its strength is to be found in the manipulation of the various members of the initial phrase: Pax, Pay, Paz, and Pam. Pax is immediately worked out sequentially (mm. 7–16), after which Pay is given similar treatment (mm. 17–21). In the development, the material appears in reverse order: mm. 34–43 equal mm. 12–21, mm. 44–47 equal mm. 1–4, then Paz is treated sequentially. In the recapitulation, further aspects of the opening phrase are exploited: after Pay is extended (mm. 65–72), the hitherto-ignored Pam is treated to rhythmic extension (m. 73), followed by the return to Pay. For the conclusion, Pax is brought to a climax with a rhythmic stretto (m. 93). Although the presentation of these motives is altered considerably for the recapitulation, the length is left unchanged—only one measure is subtracted from P and one is added to 2T. The exposition and recapitulation are therefore equal in overall length, although the movement is pervaded by internal irregularities as a result of the full but completely controlled exploitation of the motivic structure of P.[34]

Hob. XVI: 39/1 and 36/2. As Haydn himself informed Artaria just before their publication, the double-strophic variations of Hob. XVI: 36/2 and the mostly strophic variations of Hob. XVI: 39/1 are based on the same material. In Hob. XVI: 39/1 (Example X-31) the opening phrase is restated before the beginning of each variation (mm. 33–36 and 76–79), while in Hob. XVI: 36/2 (Example X-32) the opening is restated before the variations of the major-mode theme (mm. 31–34 and 65–68) and before the coda (mm. 85–88). Hob. XVI: 39/1 tends toward greater homogeneity since the two episodes (mm. 17–32 and 53–75) are closely related to the theme. In fact, the first episode could be mistaken for the second theme of a double variation set except there are no further sections in this key. The second episode develops the dotted rhythm of the theme, bringing to mind a previous Haydn device: the developmental variation. Hob. XVI: 36/2 provides another example of Haydn's originality: in the single variation of the minor mode theme, only the initial two measures of each strain retain an identity with its first statement. The coda in Hob. XVI: 39/1 derives from the first variation and the theme, while that of Hob. XVI: 36/2 contributes a final thematic variant.

The procedures in Hob. XVI: 36/2 and 39/1 demonstrate the growing fluidity of Haydn's conception of part and variation forms. With the introduction of developmental strophes and the use of recapitulatory events, the variations become more and more like part forms. Indeed, if it were not for the structural use of tonality, one would be pressed to draw viable distinctions between these two structures.[35]

Middle Movements. The middle movements of Hob. XVI: 37, 38, and 34 are linked to their finales using the same principles previously examined. Hob. XVI: 37/2 is noteworthy not only for its structural alteration but also for its richness of harmonic color, which foreshadows later intermovement transitions. Its first part modulates to the relative major (F); the second part, which has no repeats,

EXAMPLE X-30. Hob. XVI:36/1, mm. 1–21, 34–50, 65–82, 93–97.

EXAMPLE X–30 (*continued*)

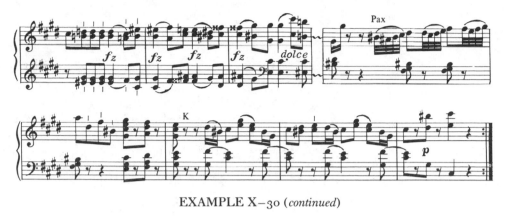

EXAMPLE X–30 (*continued*)

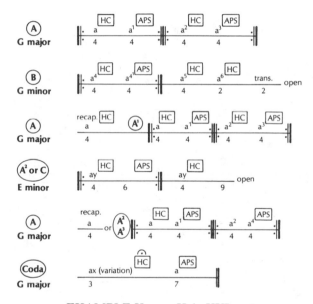

EXAMPLE X–31. Hob. XVI:39/1.

immediately disrupts and foretells the advent of the finale with its opening D-major chord and the Neapolitan harmony in m. 16, which passes to the concluding dominant pedal. Hob. XVI:38/2 is notable not for means of linkage but because it is one of the few examples that essentially duplicates Emanuel Bach's varied reprise;[36] i.e., it consists of an exposition (mm. 1–13) and a strophic variation (mm. 14–26) in place of the usual repetition. A second variation (beginning in m. 33) of only the first phrase of the theme constitutes the recapitulation.[37]

A lengthy cadenza, occupying nearly one-fifth of the piece, occurs before the final closing of Hob. XVI:39/2; this central movement is completely independent

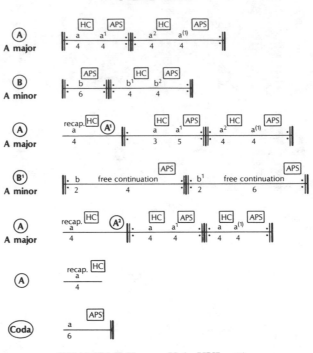

EXAMPLE X–32. Hob. XVI:36/2.

EXAMPLE X–33. Hob. XVI:36/3, mm. 1–8.

of its finale. The Adagio of Hob. XVI:35 is the most commonplace; it fits well into this popular sonata.

Finales. The two minuets in this group are complete departures from the expected aristocratic posture. Hob. XVI:38/3 is thoroughly rustic, while Hob. XVI:36/3 (Example X-33) is one of Haydn's excursions into folk materials: embedded into the upper line is the "Nightwatchman's Song," which Haydn quoted numerous times during the 1760s and 1770s.[38] This tune must have generated the exotic harmonies of mm. 4–5 and the parallel octaves of mm. 7–8. Contending with the seven sharps of C-sharp major and the double sharp needed for realizing an ornament in the trio must have tested the abilities even of the Auenbrugger sisters.

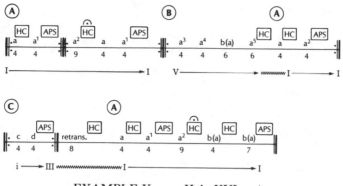

EXAMPLE X–34. Hob. XVI:35/3.

Of the three rondos, Hob. XVI:35/3 has the most unusual overall plan, as the refrains and episodes are enclosed by repeats (Example X-34). The use of opening material throughout A and B points to a practice that predominates during the 1780s. In Hob. XVI:37/3 all the refrains and episodes are of equal length and in closed forms. The regular internal structure of the refrain:

$$\|\!: \ 4+4 \ :\|\!\|\!: \ 4+4+4 \ :\|$$

sets into relief the first episode,

$$\|\!: \ 4+4 \ :\|\!\|\!: \ 6+6 \ :\|$$

as well as the 4 + 3 + 6 division of the retransition (Example X-35), whose final six measures use one of Haydn's favorite devices, an extended anticipation. Only the final refrain is varied by an Alberti bass, which effects a rhythmic acceleration that contributes to closure. The "Vivace molto innocentemente" of Hob. XVI:34 is on the surface A B A¹ B¹ A², with B derived from A but in the opposite mode. The similarity of their head-motives and the use of written-out repeats lead to an ambiguity very much like that of Hob. XVI:33/3 of the 1776 set. In this instance, though, the sense of identity is further confused, as B¹ employs the Alberti accompaniment associated with A. In these rondos Haydn is experimenting with unity and ambiguity by enclosing refrains and episodes with repeats, using similar and derived thematic ideas, and constructing both refrains and episodes as strophes with internal differences.

The sonata structure that concludes Hob. XVI:39 begins with a motive whose simplicity permits melodic and rhythmic permutation while retaining its identity. Although cleverly constructed and packed with techniques that few composers could employ with such facility, it is one of the least distinctive pieces of the Auenbrugger set. As was the case with the last sonata to be composed for the Esterházy set, Haydn may have been pressed to meet a deadline.

EXAMPLE X–35. Hob. XVI:37/3, mm. 81–109.

In Essay V, on keyboard idiom, we concluded that from their musical requirements these sonatas were a publisher's ideal, for there were few measures that would lose their effect on either the harpsichord or the *fortepiano*. With regard to their overall style and form, one could say much the same: the published set contained two difficult sonatas (Hob. XVI:36 and 20) of an intellectual bent, two up-to-date ones of universal popular appeal (Hob. XVI:35 and 37), one slightly old-fashioned sonata (Hob. XVI:38), and a work of mixed character (Hob. XVI:39). Although some may complain that the set does not "wear well," it was probably this group of works that completely established Haydn as a recognized keyboard composer.

THE SONATAS FOR PRINCESS ESTERHÁZY

Haydn's interest in appealing to the public at large is further pursued in the next set, Hob. XVI:40–42, published in 1784. Instead of six works there are just three, and each is in two movements. Even though this brevity was necessitated by Haydn's overwhelming duties as Esterházy opera conductor, not one movement has been slighted: each pursues its objectives to perfection. His growing interest in variation and part forms, first seen during the 1770s, is patently evident here, as the set has not even a hint of a minuet and only one piece in sonata form.

First Movements. The single sonata form, Hob. XVI:41/1, stylistically resembles the march of Hob. XVI:18/1. It has less rhythmic flexibility than its counterpart from the late 1760s, and in this aspect it is more reminiscent of movements dominated by a single rhythmic figure and tempo from the 1770s. As in Hob. XVI:30/1, the thematic material of 41/1 hints at a "characteristic" sonata, with its opening march and closing fanfares. The exposition is in three parts with an extended central section. The development commences neither with P nor on the dominant, but with K on the lowered mediant; this departure from established practice was of great importance for the late 1780s and 1790s. As in Hob. XVI:43/1, a cadenza-like passage before the retransition breaks the movement's pace; in the recapitulation, closure is enhanced by veering toward the subdominant (m. 135) as part of an extended cadence before K.

The two first movements in variation form are totally different from each other in content and form: Hob. XVI:40/1 is an Allegretto innocente in 6/8—a coquettish pastoral; while Hob. XVI:42/1 is an elaborate Andante con espressione in simple triple meter. The former is an A B A^1 B^1 A^2, like the "innocentemente" finale of Hob. XVI:34; while the latter is a variation on a single theme with a central section in the minor.

The most significant aspect of Hob. XVI:42/1 (Example X-36) is its theme, which appears to be an embellishment of an ungiven melody. Additionally, the opening phrases are rather elaborately ornamented in the internal return. As a consequence, the two other variations also yield more variants than strophes. This treatment results in a new large-dimension rhythmic plan: the increase of surface rhythmic activity within each strophe is more prominent than that of the entire movement. Nevertheless, the final variation retains its recapitulatory character. The central B section (mm. 41–58) is difficult to classify, for it is really a developmental variation that approaches in form the structure of the theme but could also be seen as an episode of the ternary structure. By removing the cadence at the midpoint of the first strain and shortening the second part, Haydn obscures the structure of the theme. Even with the addition of a retransition (mm. 59–61), the total length is one measure shorter than the second strain of a normal strophe. Thus, Haydn retains the size of the main units, while scrambling the internal phrases. This is but one more instance of structural synthesis in which part- and variation-form principles are difficult to distinguish.

Compared with Hob. XVI:42/1 above and 34/3 of the Auenbrugger set, Hob. XVI:40/1 seems almost reactionary: the two themes in opposite modes have no significant similarities, their structure is maintained, the procedures of embellishment are normal, and each strain has indicated repeats. The purpose of all this predictability is not revealed until the last variation of A, where Haydn creates an admirably controlled disruption that is the climax of the entire set. In the first strain of this final variation, the flourishes (mm. 76–77) and the "calando" merely hint at the events of the second strain. A dense figuration (mm. 81–83) leads to a burst of

EXAMPLE X–36. Hob. XVI:42/1, mm. 1–20, 41–62.

EXAMPLE X–36 (*continued*)

fortissimo, expands the structure of the second strain, and sustains its tension with another "calando," during which a dominant-seventh chord is built for the return of the initial phrase. This return is upset by the biggest sonorities of the entire movement and concluded by a flourish before the final phrase.

Finales. The Presto finale of Hob. XVI:40 (Example X-37) is also formally straightforward, as the episode of this ternary form contrasts with the refrain in every imaginable way. Notable here is the use of embellishment within the refrains. In the initial statement of the refrain Haydn modifies the second part at its return (m. 15) by varying the first subphrase (a^2) and replacing the second with new material (d). The refrain's second statement has a somewhat different embellishment scheme: the first four measures are identical to those of the initial statement, and

Refrain (A) ‖: a a¹ b :‖: c a² d b :‖
        4   3   3   4   4   3   3

Episode (B) e   e   e¹   f(e)   g   h
         4   4   4   4   3   5

Refrain (A) a   a¹'   b¹   a^(1)   a¹'   b¹ ‖:c¹ a²' d¹ b²:‖
        4   3   3   4   3   3   4   4   3   3

EXAMPLE X–37. Hob. XVI:40/2.

                       1   2   3

‖:ax+y b :‖: ax¹ ay¹ c   ax² ay² d   ax³ e
  4   4   5   6   6   2   12   6   6   4
2+2

              4   5

ax⁴ ay³ f ay⁴ c¹   ax⁵ ay⁴ ay⁵ ay⁶ ay⁷ :‖
 5   5   6   6   5   5   4   6   2   2

EXAMPLE X–38. Hob. XVI:42/2.

the next six (a¹' and b¹) are varied; while in the written-out repetition, the initial four measures are varied but the final six are repeats of previous variants.

The other two finales are also "con brio" pieces, but their speed is enhanced by linear textures that convey the impression of an invention with occasional added voices and inverted counterpoint. Eighteenth-century performers were certainly tested by the rapid tempos, numerous accidentals, and the five flats of the episode of Hob. XVI:41/2. This work uses many of Haydn's standard devices for a ternary structure—thematically related episode and written-out repeats with variation. By contrast, Hob. XVI:42/2 (Example X-38) is a singular binary form. The first part presents two compact four-measure phrases that prepare one for a miniature along the lines of Hob. XVI:26/3. Surprisingly, the second part has an expansive section in five divisions that stretches the material to more than ninety measures; each section commences and/or concludes with the initial idea, and all except the last interpolate new material. The open cadences of the first three sections, the rhythmic drive, and the pervading polyphony create its pressing character.

In style and in musical and technical difficulty, the ordering of the Sonatas for Princess Esterházy follows the same rationale as that of the Auenbrugger group, i.e., they progress from the easily understood to the most esoteric. The G-major Sonata Hob. XVI:40 is the most accessible and up-to-date, with two straightforward, immediately appealing movements. The second sonata, Hob. XVI:41, is somewhat old-fashioned and neutral. It begins with a march-styled sonata form and concludes with an invention. The third, Hob. XVI:42, is the most difficult. The first movement is clearly experimental and demands the utmost sensitivity from the performer; the conclusion is a singular example of structural distortion with a tiny first strain and an expansive second one.

THREE SETS OF KEYBOARD TRIOS

The 1784 Esterházy Sonatas closed an era of nearly two decades during which the solo setting was the predominant one for Haydn. Only five additional sonatas—two from the late 1780s and three from the London years—and four *Klavierstücke* date from after 1784. At the behest of publishers in both Vienna and England, Haydn turned instead to the keyboard trio. From *ca.* 1784 to 1796 he completed no fewer than twenty-eight trios, which literally replaced the solo sonatas with those for keyboard "with an accompaniment for violin and cello." Yet despite the change in setting, the stylistic evolution evidenced in the solo sonatas during the previous thirty-five years is continued in the trios.

Right on the heels of Hob. XVI:40–42, Haydn published three sets of keyboard trios: Hob. XV:3, 4, and 5; Hob. XV:6, 7, and 8; and Hob. XV:9, 10, and 2. As discussed in Essays II and III, Hob. XV:3 and 4 were composed by Ignaz Pleyel; and Hob. XV:2, which we have already considered, originated from a quintet for keyboard, baryton, and strings from some years earlier.[39] Thus, during 1784 and 1785 Haydn actually produced only six authentic and completely new trios.

Hob. XV:5. The only authentic trio from its set, Hob. XV:5 heralds Haydn's new style of writing trios and turns away from the delicate style of the previous Esterházy solo sonatas. Almost as if to attract attention, Hob. XV:5 no longer employs the trio sonata idiom in either its orchestration or its syntax, even though its structure is the old Slow–Fast–Minuet. The opening of the first movement, Adagio non tanto, reminds one of a symphonic introduction with the tutti playing in octaves, a sonority found only rarely in the previous keyboard trios (see Example V-7). Its introductory function is confirmed by the fact that P never returns in this annunciatory garb; in S(P), at the beginning of the development, and for the recapitulation it is totally transformed. Long symphonic lines are also stressed in the development: six measures for the keyboard, five for the violin, and a nine-measure retransition in dialogue. Since S duplicates P, it is not recapitulated, so the second half of the reprise consists of a cadenza.

The orchestral character of the opening movement is continued in the Allegro. P begins with hammerstrokes and fanfares, T consists of a keyboard/violin dialogue with a flood of sixteenth notes, S—preceded by fermatas—provides a strong thematic contrast to P in a double statement, and K returns to the fanfare. The development begins neither with P nor in the dominant, but with S on the submediant, now a favorite tonal beginning. Within several measures the subdominant is set up and confirmed by a false reprise, after which the submediant returns for the real developmental activity. None of Haydn's previous development sections for keyboard achieved the clarity found in this example, a result of not only the differentiated thematic material but also the strong contrasts of harmonic stability and movement. After the recapitulation, in which a large portion of T is excluded, the coda uses the same material (S) with which the development began; its effect can only be realized if both repeats are taken.

In contrast to the assertiveness of the first two movements, the finale returns to a structure from the 1770s: a theme with a single variation and a recapitulatory coda, a plan that nearly duplicates Hob. XVI:24/3. In the variation, the principal material is distributed at the level of the strain between the violin and the keyboard, not unlike the plan of Hob. XV:2/3. In the coda, the recapitulatory aspect is reduced to a minimum.

Hob. XV:5, like Hob. XVI:47 from *ca.* 1765, offers a sequence whose tempo and style present mixed signals. In both works, the central movement could function as either the initial movement or a finale; each is followed by a concluding piece in triple meter.

Hob. XV:6–8. Two sonatas from the next set, Hob. XV:6 and 8, are in two movements, a fast one followed by a ternary Tempo di Menuetto. The third trio, Hob. XV:7, is Haydn's first three-movement cycle without a single sonata form. Hob. XV:6/1 and 8/1 retain the symphonic idiom of Hob. XV:5/2, while Hob. XV:7 is in a chamber style that depends more on detailed realizations than on grand gestures.

Although in Hob. XV:6/1 and 8/1 Haydn does not approach the level of contrasting themes seen in XV:5/2, he uses some of the heavy articulations found in Hob. XV:5 to underline the structure: hammerstroke beginnings, closing subfunctions, fermatas, and grand pauses. Both expositions use the dialoguing and flood of sixteenths in the T-S area, but they are decidedly different: Hob. XV:6/1 provides another example of an exposition in which S begins with P transposed, whereas XV:8/1 is through-composed. As a result, the recapitulation of XV:8/1 is approximately the same length as the exposition, while that of XV:6/1 deletes S and is about twenty measures shorter—a tightening that became a common practice. However, the most notable aspect of Hob. XV:6/1 is the clever treatment of S (Example X-39): in the exposition it gradually disintegrates from a two-measure module down to a half measure (mm. 34–52), while in the development it is put back together (mm. 68–90) only to be dismantled again for the retransition (mm. 97–109). Both developments commence with P on the "dominant minor"; but in XV:6/1 this opening is merely a false start, and P is repeated on the tonic minor. In XV:6/1 both statements of P at the beginning of the development depart from the expected straightforward gesture by a suspension of activity that is reminiscent of Hob. XVI:20/1.

The minuets in the Auenbrugger Sonatas made important departures from the predominantly aristocratic style: one was rustic and another acquired exotic overtones by imbedding the "Nightwatchman's Song" in its main part. In the present set of trios Hob. XV:6/2 is an aristocratic minuet, while Hob. XV:8/2 broadens the repertoire by its flowing lyricism. However, the finales of Hob. XV:6 and 8 are structural twins: both are ternary, both are in the minor, the episodes of both fea-

EXAMPLE X–39. Hob. XV:6/1, mm. 34–52, 68–88, 97–112.

EXAMPLE X–39 (*continued*)

EXAMPLE X–39 (*continued*)

EXAMPLE X–39 (*continued*)

ture the violin and begin with a head-motive derived from the refrain, both change the repetition scheme with the return of A, and both have codas.

While in Hob. XV:6 and 8 the weight of the cycle is centered in the first movement, Hob. XV:7 begins with its lightest movement, a set of variations. In view of the many experiments with this stereotype Haydn had previously undertaken, this set is decidedly old-fashioned: each strain is strictly strophic; each maintains the repetitions, and none are written out; the violin and keyboard take the lead in alternate variations; and the usual diminutions are present. To find a variation series as conservative, one must return to some of Haydn's earliest works. Its only progressive aspect is the nature of the theme, whose elaborateness approaches a variation; thus, the less-elaborate first variation is more like "the theme." The first part of the siciliano Hob. XV:7/2 appears to be a continuation of the conservative opening, but in the second part the tension is skillfully increased for the *attacca* to the finale: the diminished-seventh chord is highlighted by the only dynamic marking of the movement (m. 18), followed by a descending line (mm. 19–25) resolved deceptively (m. 26), which eventually comes to rest on a dominant pedal.

Hob. XV:7/3 is the first of an impressive series of rondos, a form to which, from this point until the London period, Haydn afforded special treatment. Since in this case both the refrain and the first episode (B) are built from the same material, and the differentiated second episode (C) is very short, it is to date among Haydn's most

thematically concentrated rondos, one that could even be called "monothematic"—
a term certainly more appropriate here than applied to Haydn's sonata form. Unexpectedly, the greatest weight of the structure does not reside in either the refrain or
the second episode (C), but in B, which consists of A in the *minore* and a lengthy
development. Its high point is an enharmonic movement from E flat to D sharp and
two subsequent false reprises in B major and B minor just before the refrain finally
returns to the D-major tonic. This double false reprise leaves one wondering
whether the *minore* of the episode or the *maggiore* of the refrain will return.[40]

Hob. XV:9 and 10. The first trio of the third set begins, as did XV:5, with a
slow movement, but Hob. XV:9/1 is a totally different type of piece. It signals a
turn toward a chamber orientation, which characterizes both trios of this set.
Rather than beginning with a tutti passage in octaves, the keyboard and the strings
are now thoroughly concertante. Indeed, in this movement, the cello takes its most
prominent role in all the Haydn trios (see Example VIII-6); at one point the violin
and cello even play a duo while the keyboard accompanies. Finally, at the end of the
recapitulation the written-out cadenza in tempo confirms the fully concertante texture. Hob. XV:9/1 is more like a misplaced central movement than an introduction.

In another reversal, the finale is reminiscent of an opening piece, a sonata form
in quadruple meter. The big initial sonority, the double statement of P, and the
strong reiterated cadences at first give the impression of a movement in a symphonic style, but the exposition is now more continuous, for none of its cadential
articulations are reinforced by rests in all parts. As a result, the P, T, S, and K
functions are defined by changes in orchestration and harmonic rhythm, the repetition of P as S, the deceptive cadence between S and K, and the harmonically
colorful passage that heightens the arrival of K. The development begins somewhat tentatively, but by its twelfth measure P arrives in the subdominant and commences a most assured plan. P subsequently disintegrates with greater textural activity and a reduction in the size of the phrase module. For the recapitulation S(P)
is not eliminated but is enhanced by a momentary turn toward the subdominant in
P^k and by deceptive cadential progressions. The weight given to S(P) here hints at
a later recapitulatory solution for the S(P) exposition.

The comparable movement to Hob. XV:9/2 is Hob. XV:10/1. After the symphonic opening in octaves, its chamber-music character is conveyed not only by
unbroken cadential articulations but also by the subsequent linear garb of P and
the delicate triplets of T. Only K returns to the character of the beginning. The
opening of the development is one of Haydn's most-effective juxtapositions: the end
of K is repeated in the minor. Otherwise, standard procedures are used: the restatement of P is followed by a free fantasia, expansion, or working-out section, which
concludes in the submediant and is followed by a big retransition. In the recapitulation the feeling of closure is strengthened over the exposition in subtle ways: the
6/4 chords are reinforced (cf. mm. 41–42 and 137–38), and one authentic cadence
is added to K (cf. mm. 45 and 142).

The finale Hob. XV:10/2 is another instance of experimentation with the synthesis of structural procedures: Haydn embeds sonata-form development within
the episode of a ternary form. However, since the first part of A ends with a full

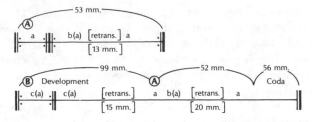

EXAMPLE X–40. Hob. XV:10/2.

tonic cadence, the refrain itself is a small ternary shape. The episode is not just a section related to the refrain; it contains a level of modulatory activity present in Haydn's sonata forms. Within the larger ternary scheme, the structural upbeat leading to the return of the opening material grows in significance. Each time it reappears it is lengthened (Example X-40). These retransitions, together with the internal structure of A, hint at a full-fledged rondo, which is obviated by the binary repeats. The unusually large coda reintroduces harmonic deception to underline closure. With its homogeneous themes, this movement is related to Hob. XV:7/3 and at the same time foreshadows the multiple formal interpretations of XVI:48/2.

As we have already pointed out, these works are a total break from the trios written during the 1750s and 1760s. Yet Haydn seems not to have been at all certain what direction the new trios should take. In the first three trios, Hob. XV:5–7, the bigger movements are conceived as symphonies in their approach to both heavy formal articulations and textures in which the tutti plays in unison. The later trios, Hob. XV:8–10, are less-assertive and less-extroverted chamber works, with the cello and violin operating more independently of the keyboard. But these chamber trios are also characterized by some uncertainty regarding their cyclic structure: styles that earlier found specialized places in the solo sonatas are now in the "wrong" position. Was a mixture of symphonic and chamber styles with various cyclic types another commercial ploy? It may well be that Haydn viewed the trio—in contrast to the solo sonata—as music not for the ladies alone, and that he expected the variations and the minuets to appeal to the women, the bolder sonata forms and rondos to the men.

Years of Extraordinary Achievements, 1788–1790

HOB. XV: 11–13

It was three years later, in 1788 and 1789, that Haydn returned to the composition of keyboard trios, yet Hob. XV:11–13 adopted the same formulae used previously: two trios in two movements, one in three; one first movement in variation form in duple meter, two in sonata form; the single slow movement a siciliano; and the finales triple-meter dances or duple-meter rondos.[41]

Even though the cyclic features of the set are not pathbreaking, the two sonata forms Hob. XV:11/1 and 12/1—together with the initial movements of Sym-

phonies Nos. 88 and 92—are among Haydn's most notable architectural achievements from one of the most extraordinary periods of his creative life.

   In the exposition of Hob. XV : 11/1 (Example X-41) nothing happens that has
not already been observed: S begins with P transposed, the development is introduced without pause by a powerful deception—the dominant moves to the diminished seventh of the submediant—and its presentation of the materials bears no
resemblance to their occurrence in the exposition. 1K replaces the usual repetition
of P after the disruption (1N) and, as expected, is the most stable event until the
false reprise. Instead of only eight measures of stability, the false reprise holds its
plateau for nearly sixteen measures. Subsequently, 1N + 3T receives much less
harmonic stability and much more textural activity, concluding with a pedal in
which the module of activity is the quarter note. Thus, the development consists of
two stable sections followed by unstable sections that are inversely proportional in
duration. The recapitulation consists of only P and K separated by new material, so
that its total length is about one-half that of the exposition; the level of exclusion is a
direct result of the exposition's S(P) structure and the development's false reprise.
The interdependence of the events in the development and recapitulation is carried
much further than observed earlier: the development from the false reprise to its
end plus the entire recapitulation nearly equals the length of the exposition. In addition, the stronger articulation is not held in reserve for the recapitulation but occurs in the preparation for the false reprise.

   For Hob. XV : 12/1 the interest is also centered in the development and the recapitulation. From the plethora of ideas found in the exposition, one would expect
the development to be lengthy and loose in its construction, but it is short and concentrated. In fact, it is a fugato that begins by combining P and 2S (m. 71), continues with a stretto on P (m. 79), and concludes with a retransition. In the recapitulation Haydn concentrates not on the exclusion of functions, but on smaller
alterations that occur within nearly every phrase. Only the first twelve measures

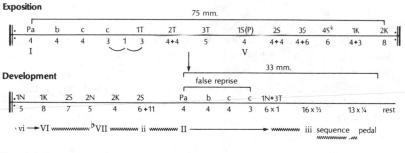

EXAMPLE X-41. Hob. XV:11/1.

remain untouched. The high point is reached with P stated in octaves by the entire ensemble. With P's contrapuntal elaboration in the development, one is again reminded of the Viennese tradition of concluding a fugue with the subject in unison.

Hob. XV: 12/2 is also rather special. The dance rhythms of a siciliano are hinted at in the pizzicato accompaniment, and the melody is extensively altered by metric, rhythmic, ornamental, and chromatic complications. One of its most extraordinary moments occurs in the "search" for the final cadence (Example X-42): the writing shared here by the violin and the right hand of the keyboard brings to mind some of the outstanding slow movements from the string quartets of this time (e.g., Op. 50/6 and Op. 54/2).

The finale of Hob. XV: 12 continues the developmental/part-form tradition seen in Hob. XV: 7/3 and XV: 10/2. As in Hob. XV: 7/3, the first episode is in the parallel minor rather than in the dominant, and it is not preceded by a transition. Instead, the first episode is unrelated to the reprise, and a big development occupies its expected location, the second episode. For the refrains Haydn embellishes only the final eight measures, a procedure that recalls the treatment of P in sonata form. Thus, this finale makes a significant contribution toward the synthesis of sonata and rondo procedures.[42]

Hob. XV: 13/2 is also an important sonata-form movement. The transformation of P in both function and character is stressed during the course of the exposition; i.e., at the opening, P is a symphonic fanfare, while in S it becomes lyrical and is placed in the rich baritone register. The ending of P is also elaborated by repetition and expansion. The development further exploits the possibilities of P by isolating its initial dotted rhythm; on this motive a climax is reached with a surprising slip from E minor to a boldly stated F-major triad. A similar event occurs in the recapitulation, now intensified by an augmented sixth chord. The coda also deals with the dotted motive as it wanders in and out of the flattened-sixth degree. One wonders if this highly concentrated piece was originally the first movement of the trio but was moved to second position when the publisher Artaria requested a replacement.

HOB. XVI: 48 AND 49

At the end of the 1780s, Haydn returned to solo keyboard composition with the two sonatas Hob. XVI: 48 and 49 and the Fantasia in C major Hob. XVII: 4.[43] The cyclic plans of the sonatas are similar to those of the trios—Hob. XVI: 48 in two movements and Hob. XVI: 49 in three—but the content of Hob. XVI: 48 is more evenly balanced than has been the case heretofore.

In Hob. XVI: 48/1 Haydn turned from the tiresome strophic variations of the trios to a practice that builds on the accomplishments of the previous solo sonatas; in fact, this unusual movement could be dubbed a "fantasy variation." It is essentially a double variation on one theme presented in both major and minor. The superior shape and expressive content of the initial statement distinguish this movement from Haydn's other variations. The theme itself is an elaboration of an ungiven melody and emphasizes interval over line. Rests articulate the initial strain into irregular modules (2 + 2 + 1 + 3 + 2), while the harmonic structure adds

EXAMPLE X–42. Hob. XV:12/2, mm. 69–85.

EXAMPLE X-43. Hob. XVI:48/1, mm. 1-26.

EXAMPLE X–43 (*continued*)

motion to the phrase. This small-dimension structure generates a middle-dimension form perhaps unique among variation sets from the late eighteenth century (Example X-43). The passacaglia-like repetitions of two- and three-bar harmonic modules of the theme are undermined by the direction of the bass line. Surface rhythmic patterns do not coordinate with any other element. The employment of dynamics is especially effective: the lowest level occurs at the points of densest sonority and greatest harmonic tension. The rising tessitura and the ascending motives of the bass in the first strain are followed by a downward motion in the first bars of the second. The ascending and descending motion of the two parts of the major-mode theme is retained for the minor mode along with the expected melodic relationship.

Haydn's usual series of strophic modules—perhaps broken by one irregular unit—is here replaced by a more complex solution at the large dimension (Ex-

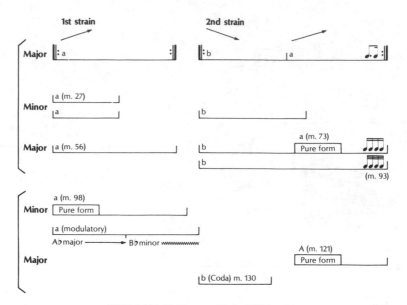

EXAMPLE X–44. Hob. XVI:48/1.

ample X-44): after the binary statement in major (mm. 1–26), the following section in minor (mm. 27–55) emphasizes by repetition the first strain of the major
theme, the next section in major (mm. 56–97) the second strain, the subsequent
minor and modulatory areas the first strain (mm. 98–120), and the final section in
major (beginning with m. 121) the second strain.

Unlike the order of the other sets, here the initial material does not appear in its
purest melodic form until mm. 73–76, while the surface rhythm is systematically
accelerated only in cadential measures (mm. 23–26 and 78–81) and reaches its
peak of activity earlier than expected (mm. 94–97), about two-thirds of the way
through the movement. Only after this point does a statement of the pure form of
the initial module coincide with the beginning of a section (m. 98). A combination
of tonal action and rhythmic activity provides a dramatic climax before the more-
subdued conclusion in major (m. 121).

The finale of Hob. XVI:48 is the first complete realization of the sonata rondo
in the keyboard works and the most concentrated use of a single theme within this
part form. The exposition (Example X-45) consists of a chromatically tinged refrain (P), a thematically related transition (T), and a first couplet (S); P and S now
have the required tonic-dominant relationship. The first return of the refrain is unusual in that no variation by embellishment occurs; indeed, the maintenance of the
refrain in its pure form is a decided break from previous practice. The second episode develops material from the refrain and the first episode, as in Hob. XV:12/3.
However, the alterations in the recapitulation are most striking in that they are
typical of sonata form movements from this time: the recapitulation of the refrain
and the first episode is nearly equal in length to the initial statement of the refrain.

EXAMPLE X–45. Hob. XVI:48/2, mm. 1–6, 31–33, 54–59.

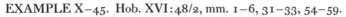

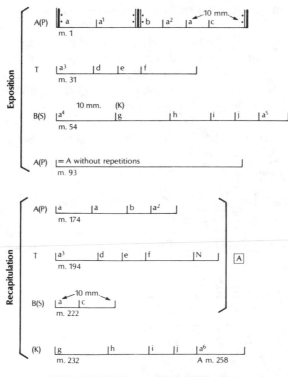

EXAMPLE X–46. Hob. XVI:48/2.

That is accomplished by eliminating repetitions within the refrain, replacing the initial ten measures of the episode with the final ten measures of the refrain, and adding four final measures that intensify the cadence. On another level, as in the earlier Hob. XV: 10/2, this economic use of material in the exposition and the re-sulting redefinition of function permit differing formal interpretations; its reprise (Example X-46) can be seen as a sonata form recapitulation with the primary area telescoped, as a five-part rondo with module "ac" functioning as an interrupted closing of the refrain, and as a seven-part rondo with the final eight measures acting as the final statement of the refrain.

Thus, in the two-movement cycle of Hob. XVI:48 Haydn reveals his special interests outside the realm of sonata form: the variations are totally liberated from a rigid strophic/figurative structure, and the rondo is infused with thematic unity and development. On another level, this solo keyboard sonata is a synthesis of a *Liebhaber* cyclic plan—two movements, one a variation and the other a rondo—with a content clearly meant for *Kenner*, as is the case with the most sophisticated of Haydn's works. It is all the more surprising that until now Hob. XVI:48 has elicited little discussion in the literature.

No lack of discussion exists for Hob. XVI:49, however, as its first movement has fascinated such commentators as Mersmann, Schenker, and Cone; Abert even con-sidered it Haydn's complete achievement of a Classic idiom.[44] Its three-movement cycle is unified not only by key but also by meter and theme. Metric variety is to be expected in Haydn's cycles, and seldom are two adjacent movements in the same meter; yet, in this work, not only are all three in triple meter but also they take the quarter note as the beat. Because of such a cyclic plan, Haydn's intent regarding tempo should be carefully considered: were the first and last movements meant to be in the same tempo, with the central Adagio e cantabile taking the speed of the previous quarter for its eighth, so that the duration of the sextuplets in the middle movement would equal the triplets of the finale with the dotted motive underlining the contrast in speed? As for the thematic unification, the beginning of the develop-ment section (m. 65) of the first movement is related to the second section of the

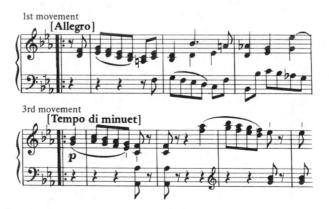

EXAMPLE X–47. Hob. XVI:49/1, mm. 65–67, and 49/3, mm. 25–28.

EXAMPLE X–48. Hob. XVI:49/1, mm. 1–4, 3–15, 21–22,
25–29, 43–46, 53–55, 59–61.

first part (m. 25) of the finale, an observation that becomes more convincing when
one notes that Hob. XVI: 49/3 is Haydn's only ternary form in which the refrain
has two independent parts (Example X-47).

Hob. XVI: 49/1 commences with a large initial statement consisting of three
four-measure phrases, a structure that is more characteristic of the initial statements from *ca.* 1788–1790 than of any other time. The essence of the entire movement resides in the anacrustic motive, which is stretched from two and three eighth
notes to entire functional sections (Example X-48). T is notable for its control of
contour. Again introduced by P—which is subtly varied by its chord rhythm—the
main part of S (beginning in m. 28) contains two enormous periods of fourteen and
eighteen measures each. S ends with a parenthesis (mm. 53–60) to its cadence,
which features the anacrustic rhythm. The exposition concludes over a pedal point
with passing chromatic movement that serves to enhance the related key.

For the development of Hob. XVI:49/1 (Example X-49) Haydn uses what,
during the 1780s, was a common formula: an initial section, a point of arrival with
the return of P and its continuation (S), and a retransition. However, in this instance the initial section—a continuation of K—is unusually long, delaying the
structural downbeat for seventeen measures. After the return of P, the central section modulates in uniform modules joined by the submediant, with which it begins
and ends. All of this is presented with the least amount of disturbance, for each
section presents a single texture, a single surface rhythm, and regular tonal move-

EXAMPLE X–49. Hob. XVI:49/1, mm. 65–131.

EXAMPLE X–49 (*continued*)

ment. Within such a context, the retransition—a mutation of the parenthesis to the S cadence—is indeed a strange effect. Whereas in the exposition, it was an incomplete triad on the lowered seventh with its root added later, now it mainly consists of incomplete seventh chords with the missing pitch subsequently stated alone. Upon repetition, the combination of this rhythmic motive and the initial idea results in duple meter superimposed on the existing triple meter, culminating in a cadenza leading to the recapitulation. Like the development's initial section, this retransition is an exceptionally big gesture whose gravitational strength and originality immediately bring to mind Beethoven. After the rather regular recapitulation, in which S(P) is eliminated, the coda expands K and brings back T, which did not appear in the development. Although Hob. XVI:49/1 is not an unusually large movement, it gains breadth through the employment of anacrustic ideas within a function or section that unify the entire movement.

For the slow movement of Hob. XVI:49 Haydn again applies—now more extensively than heretofore—variation at the phrase rather than at the section level, resulting in eleven variants of the initial statement (Example X-50); the opening A section with its written-out repetitions therefore recalls many of Haydn's earlier recapitulatory variations. The *minore* episode, a developmental variation, is one of the most romantically conceived utterances in all the sonatas. Since for the reprise Haydn unrelentingly adheres to the structure of the initial statement, one is jolted by the deceptive cadence that initiates the coda (mm. 108–109).

The Tempo di Menuet finale is another example of a part form in which the points of thematic and modal contrast and arrival are not coordinated. It can thus be viewed as three possible shapes: A B A¹ A², A A¹ A, or A B A (Example X-51).

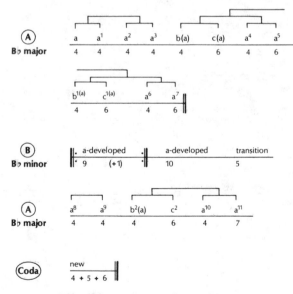

EXAMPLE X–50. Hob. XVI:49/2.

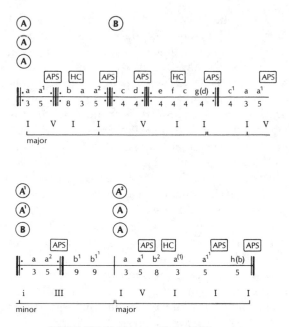

EXAMPLE X–51. Hob. XVI:49/3.

For a minuet-styled movement, the initial eight-measure group is noteworthy: its phrase structure, like its larger form, is couched in ambiguity, for it can be parsed as either 3 + 5 or 4 + 4.

HOB. XV:14–17

During the time that Haydn was composing Hob. XVI:49, he was concurrently working on four additional keyboard trios: Hob. XV:14, 16, 15, and 17. The most significant of the series, the A-flat major Trio Hob. XV:14, has an E-major Adagio—the slowest middle movement of this group—which leads directly to the finale. In view of this and other tonal juxtapositions and the brilliant writing of the second and third movements, it is not surprising that Haydn programmed this work for one of the Salomon concerts during his first London visit. The keyboard part was performed by the young Hummel. In the context of the style of the "London" Symphonies, Hob. XV:14 was no oddity, for its combining of the popular with the esoteric was characteristic only of Haydn.

The first movement of Hob. XV:14 is a *galant* march reminiscent of earlier solo sonatas, with its moderated tempo, dotted rhythms, and ornamental turns. However, this seemingly aristocratic posture is a charade, since Haydn treats the material, as in Hob. XVI:49/1, in a fully Classic idiom. P is conceived on an even larger scale than in the previous solo sonata: it totals twenty-four measures and is organized architectonically. This big compound statement elides with T, a rather common practice in the trios of this time. The sequences, violin/keyboard dialogue, and regularly changing chord rhythm of the transition segregate it from P, whose stability, texture, and accelerating harmonic rhythm within each phrase strongly differentiate P and T. The secondary key is again introduced by P; new material, symmetrically organized, follows; and a big closing brings back the turning figure of P. Thus, S is also a well-defined section: S(P), new S, and S^k.

As in Hob. XVI:49/1, the development begins with K, but now with pedals on the mediant and submediant followed by a grand pause. At this point one would expect P to return in a new key; instead, T is presented on the lowered seventh degree, which becomes the dominant of C flat, and then P finally arrives in B major (C flat) in an almost pure version for eighteen measures.[45] This presentation of a stabilized thematic idea in a very distant key is indicative of Haydn's Classic moderation: i.e., if one element is radicalized, another must be conserved. The recapitulation also begins with an enharmonic relationship: K ends on the dominant of G sharp, and P begins in A flat. Because of the nature of the exposition and the development, the recapitulation—as was seen earlier in Hob. XV:11/1—is shortened to P, S^k, and K, thus containing only the barest essentials: return and closure.[46]

The first section of the ternary slow movement of Hob. XV:14 adumbrates a type of theme seen in the opening measures of the "London" Symphonies Nos. 98/2 and 99/3, a triple-meter hymn of utmost simplicity. The refrain contains only one unusual harmony, and it is characteristically underlined by *fz*. The episode is one of Haydn's most striking creations: pizzicato strings accompany the keyboard in a rhythmically controlled virtuoso fantasy, just the sort of writing that would have spotlighted the young Hummel. The reprise is surprisingly unvaried. Perhaps it was an attempt to set off the transition to the finale, which establishes another enharmonic dominant.

Designated "Rondo," the finale (Example X-52) is really closer to a sonata form with two sets of repeats: the refrain acts more like a P section, as it is not strongly articulated; and the episode in the dominant begins with a transposed P introducing S. What does recall Haydn's other rondos is the use of the head-motive as a reiterated lead-in, which here cleverly occurs for every episode and return of the refrain save for the "recapitulation." Each lead-in is tonally different and unexpected. Only the one for the repetition of the exposition is a conventional dominant-seventh preparation. Haydn mixes signals most completely during the development, for during its course B(A) [or S(P)] is introduced in the subdominant. An

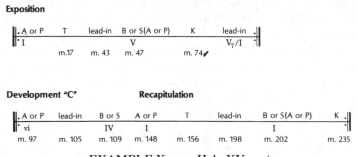

EXAMPLE X–52. Hob. XV:14/3.

eighteenth-century Viennese connoisseur could interpret this device as a bifocal recapitulation in the subdominant, known from chamber and symphonic works by such composers as Christoph Sonnleithner and Gassmann.[47] The delayed return of P after the development's beginning might be seen as a reversed return of the main rondo components, which is often found where B is based on A, or as a simple false reprise. Regardless of the interpretation, one would have expected B(A) [or S(P)] to have been excluded in the recapitulation or at most to return once more as the final reprise, but unexpectedly every function is recapitulated.

This striking trio, the solo Sonatas Hob. XVI:48 and 49, and the Fantasia Hob. XVII:4 exemplify the unusual directions of Haydn's experiments during the late 1780s. Hob. XV:14, above all, reveals Haydn's capabilities in manipulating tonal activity. No longer restricted to development sections, enharmonic movement and unusual tonal juxtapositions lend the cycle a coherence as effective as the unifying thematic and metric elements in Hob. XVI:49.

If Haydn had continued to pursue the most-advanced aspects of Hob. XV:14, he would probably have lost a good portion of his admiring public. Thus, it is not surprising that the other three trios—Hob. XV:16, 15, and 17—retreat to a much more conservative stance; in fact, they are the only accompanied works since the 1750s and early 1760s to begin with the keyboard alone. Perhaps that was a concession to the *Liebhaber* who did not need to be concerned about an initial unprepared entrance.

Unlike the instrumentation of Haydn's other trios, these three are scored for the flute rather than the violin as the preferred instrument. Of course, the entire fabric of the sound is changed, especially when the trio is played on instruments of the time. Otherwise, except for restrictions of range and the absence of double stops, there is little distinction between these flute parts and those designated for the violin; the tessitura is low even for an eighteenth-century flute, and in one instance, it is required to play a line clearly conceived for crossing strings. So, as seen in Essay V with regard to the keyboard instruments themselves, the scoring does not exclude any of the likely options.

Hob. XV:15 and 16 each contain three movements; Hob. XV:17 has only two. All three trios begin with a sonata-form Allegro in quadruple meter. The two central movements (Hob. XV:15/2 and 16/2) are Andantes in 6/8, a possible concession to the flute's pastoral associations. The finales of the three-movement works are rondos, and Hob. XV:17/2 concludes with a Tempo di Menuet.

The similarity of Hob. XV:16 and 15 extends beyond their cyclic structure, for their first movements are nearly twins: both begin with introductory material; they have a similar thematic idea in their T/S areas; their development sections do not use P but concentrate on their T/S themes; and their developments emphasize the supertonic, flattened seventh, and submediant. Nevertheless, each has its points of individuality. Hob. XV:16/1 temporarily establishes the lowered mediant before S in the exposition and at the beginning of the coda; the latter has an astonishing cadential disruption by an augmented-sixth chord that resolves to the Neapolitan. K charmingly uses a "Lebewohl" horn motive, with its open fifths and thirds. The first measure of Hob. XV:15/1 recalls the String Quartet Op. 33/5/1, in which the consequent comes before the antecedent phrase, a ruse that finally finds its proper place at the very end of the movement.

The two central movements again explore synthesized forms. In Hob. XV : 16/2, a binary structure, variation pervades nearly every repeated phrase. The movement is linked uneventfully to the finale. On the other hand, Hob. XV : 15/2 limits variation to the episode of its ternary form, although even here the treatment is distinctive:

$$
\begin{array}{ccccccccc}
\text{d} & \text{e} & \text{d}^1 & \text{e}^1 & \text{f} & \text{g} & \text{h} & \text{d}^1 & \text{e}^2 \\
2 & 4 & 2 & 4 & 3 & 4 & 5 & 2 & 5 \\
\end{array}
$$

m. 17   Var. 1   Var. 2

Var. 2 incorporates a procedure more often found in the sonata forms; that is, the treatment of the initial phrase is more closely related to a preceding variant than to its original form.

Hob. XV : 15/3 is another monothematic sonata-rondo, though both episodes as well as the coda contain some new material. Once again Haydn uses a lead-in to the refrain, but here each return becomes extended. As in the other rondos from this period, there is almost no embellishment, a practice also found in the extended rondo Hob. XV : 16/3 (A B A C A D A), which is notable for its sparing use of thematic development.

Hob. XV : 17/1 returns to an older style. In this 4/4 Allegro the eighth note is the primary unit and the functions are less differentiated than in Hob. XV : 16/1 and 15/1. The first part of the development, as is now expected, avoids the opening material, instead concerning itself with a reduction of K; the second part centers on D flat, a Neapolitan to the tonic's dominant.[48] For the recapitulation Haydn predictably tightens his material: S follows directly after P, resulting in one more substantially shortened reprise. Except for a climax of range and sonority toward the end of the development (mm. 62–63), which is followed by a deceptive resolution, the finale is remarkably conventional.

Just before departing for London, Haydn wrote his final work distinctly geared to the *Liebhaber*, the C-major Variations on a single theme Hob. XVII : 5. If its date of composition were not known with certainty, one might assume that this work originated during the 1770s, as little of the advanced style of Hob. XVI : 48/1 is revealed; the Variations are actually closer to Hob. XVII : 3. Two details, however, separate Hob. XVII : 5 from the norm of the 1770s: the inclusion of five eighth notes within a single measure (m. 62); and a link between the *minore* Var. 5 and *maggiore* Var. 6.

As a group, the nine solo and accompanied sonatas and the two *Klavierstücke* from the late 1780s are Haydn's most progressive to that time. Especially notable are the advances in the treatment of harmony and tonality. Haydn broadens his vocabulary not only to more distant relationships but also to enharmonic ones. The rondos contain very little in the way of variation procedures, as Haydn concentrates on monothematicism, thematic development, and increasingly extended and unusual approaches to the refrain. In structures other than rondos, however, variation procedures are used in new and individual ways. As for the sonata forms, the developments are less likely to be concerned with P and the recapitulations tend to be substantially shortened.

The remarkable nature of these works recalls the sonatas of the late 1760s: here in the late 1780s to 1790 we find a series of highly original, experimental, and accomplished pieces (Hob. XVI:48, 49, XV:14 and XVII:4) set side-by-side with works whose character is less demanding. However, the differences between the sophisticated and easy pieces of the 1760s (e.g., Hob. XVI:46 vs. Hob. XV:2 or XVIIa:1) were deeper than those between the two groups of trios from the late 1780s to 1790. In a sense this lack of differentiation is what Haydn had been working toward since the 1760s, for in the *opere* of the 1770s one could still classify individual sonatas as belonging to one style or another. It was precisely this coalescence that contributed to the enormous popularity of Haydn's music during the 1790s.

The London and Viennese Works of the 1790s

HOB. XV:32

During his first stay in London (1791–1792), Haydn was occupied with the composition of symphonies and other contracted obligations; apparently the only keyboard work he completed was the Keyboard Trio Hob. XV:32. It is certainly not one of his more important efforts, being a hybrid of some earlier pieces. Overall, it reminds one of the 1784 Esterházy Sonata in the same key, Hob. XVI:40: both begin with variations in 6/8 and conclude with a fast movement in 4/4; and the first movements are pastorales, with Haydn's characteristic accents on the third eighth note.[49] The structure of Hob. XV:32/1, a ternary variation, is closer to the plan of Hob. XVI:49/2: although the episode is thematically independent of the refrain, its phrase structure duplicates the opening while the refrain's return again combines recapitulation with variation. The sonata-form finale contains nothing surprising. As in the works of the late 1780s, the beginning of P is ignored in the development; instead, it commences with a rather obscure motive from m. 9 and expands on material from S and K. The retransition, a section Haydn often exploits to the fullest, is left in an undeveloped state (Example X-53). Haydn shows very little interest in the thematic material of either movement; the themes are neither distinctive in and of themselves nor enhanced during their re-presentations.

HOB. XVII:6

While Hob. XV:32 was meant for immediate publication and was presumably produced with speed, skill, and a notable lack of depth, the same cannot be said of the F-minor Variations Hob. XVII:6, composed in 1793, after Haydn's return to Vienna. It is an experimental variation set, yet it is completely different from Hob. XVI:48/1. In a very real sense Hob. XVII:6 consolidates two different tendencies from the previous decade: the strictly strophic approach coexists with the dramatic

EXAMPLE X–53. Hob. XV:32/2, mm. 85–92.

aspects of some of the less rigidly conceived sets. It uses two alternating themes, and the overall impression is one of a *marcia funebre* in the minor with a trio in the major. However, within the restraints imposed by this characteristic style, the material is set forth in the most flexible manner possible, with changes of range affecting the motive as well as the phrase. The first variation abandons every aspect of the *minore* theme except its harmony, while the second (mm. 99–127) is composed along more figural lines. In both, Haydn retains the bold Neapolitan intrusion (m. 25) of the second strain.

The variations of the "trio" take on a new twist. Each begins with the melody in an almost pure form, which highlights the second theme rather than the opening *minore*. With the structural regularity imposed on the variations of both themes, their similar rhythmic motion, and the recapitulatory aspects reserved for the second theme, the reprise of the opening theme in its original state becomes an event that causes one to expect a continuation of the strophic form. But Haydn breaks the pattern by eliminating the cadence originally in m. 22, returning to the initial phrase in m. 23, and following with the now referential Neapolitan chord of m. 25. The coda, which follows immediately, creates a dramatic tension without precedent; it is partially resolved in m. 180 but not completed until the very end of the piece.[50]

HOB. XV: 18 – 20

In 1793 or 1794 Haydn composed another set, the trios Hob. XV: 18–20. At various times Haydn incorporated a previously independent movement into a cycle, but in this group it is possible that he exchanged movements within the set. Hob. XV: 18 consists of three movements, all utilizing the same tonic; Hob. XV: 19 and 20, however, contain unusual key schemes (G minor: i-VI-i; B-flat major: I-vi-I) that could easily be ironed out by exchanging the two slow movements, although the two resulting adjacent variation forms in Hob. XV: 19 would be a collocation previously reserved only for sonata movements. In addition, this set is the first in which all three trios have three movements.

Hob. XV: 18/1 begins with a series of hammerstrokes, what Somfai would call "noise-killers."[51] Although we have previously seen strong beginnings whose effect was much the same, in this instance it is a gesture that takes place outside of the structure's activity; that is, it is functionally identical to the beginnings of some quartets from Op. 71 and Op. 74. Perhaps Haydn expected to program this work during the 1794–95 concert season, just as he had done with Hob. XV: 14.

The exposition of Hob. XV: 18/1 begins with a broadly conceived opening theme characteristic of works from the late 1780s onward. The double statements are like variations whose second strophe is irregular:

But this irregularity was no accident, for the material contained within Pbx + y is to gain significance in articulating the main sections. Characteristically, P overlaps T, during the course of which dialoguing is emphasized. S once again commences with P transposed, but here it merely provides a tonal oasis after which the instability of T returns. K too is internally unstable both rhythmically—with syncopations, tempo change, and a fermata—as well as harmonically—with an augmented triad—but is stabilized by the repetition of Pby. The development begins with Pbx—a gesture of almost Beethovenian irony—before P is restated in the subdominant and ends on the dominant of the submediant. This chord resolves to the dominant of the flattened dominant, which initiates a working-out section that concludes with K. This plan harks back to an older one in that P precedes a central developmental section. For the recapitulation Haydn tightens P, alters S, and extends K to include all of Pb, an ending that requires that the repeat be taken. Thus, Hob. XV: 18/1 contains a number of distinctive events: opening hammerstrokes, P treated as a theme with variations, P generating two motives (Pbx and y) that articulate the structure, an exposition shaped in five sections (P-T-S(P)-T-K), and a development that continues to expand tonal vocabulary and juxtaposition even though its thematic plan is retrospective.

Haydn returns in Hob. XV: 18/2 to one of his favorite types, a 6/8 Andante in ternary variation form. In this movement, which leads without pause to the finale,

EXAMPLE X-54. Hob. XV:18/3, mm. 1-8.

he provides a restrained and almost introverted statement with *mezza voce* and piano dynamics; its entire purpose is to provide a stark foil for the exuberant finale.

Hob. XV:18/3 is the first of a series of finales in triple meter that have absolutely nothing to do with the Tempo di Menuet. One of Haydn's digressions into Eastern European folk music, characterized by Szabolcsi as a "Hungarian Polonaise,"[52] its tremendous energy and charm are achieved by unrelenting surface rhythms (only once is the flow broken), syncopations, and the *accacciaturas*, which form extended upbeats (Example X-54). That this movement has not achieved the popularity of a later counterpart (Hob. XV:25/3) can be attributed only to a general lack of appreciation for Haydn's trios.

Hob. XV:19 begins with the ubiquitous set of variations on two themes. Instead of having similar head-motives, the end of the first and the beginning of the second theme are melodically related. Charles Rosen has shown how the coda is shaped by expanding the structure of the second theme; i.e., each structural articulation is maintained while the mid-sections are further developed.[53] Because of the nature of the thematic relationship, this expanded variation of the second theme sends confused signals as to its function, since it is situated immediately after the previous variation. In its larger form, Hob. XV:19/1 seems to owe something to the F-minor Variations Hob. XVII:6: both have two themes the first of which is in the minor; both are in a march style; and both end with a substantial coda. But here the coda is not a dramatic event; rather, it transforms the major mode section from a trio of a march to a gigue in a miniature sonata form.

Whatever Haydn's original intent with regard to Hob. XV:19/2, this slow movement is the perfect antidote to the sectional nature of the variations: an extremely smooth and continuous piece that never once pauses until the final cadence. Rhythmically, the exposition quickens its principal durations from sixteenth notes to sextuplets, which continue for the entire development and recapitulation. One wonders if the rhythmic organization of this movement was at the back of Beethoven's mind during his writing of the second movements of Op. 18/1 and Op. 13.

The Presto finale of Hob. XV:19 is a concise sonata structure. In fact, its exposition is so tight that the functions of P and T are combined in the opening compound statement: the first phrase ends with a tonic half-cadence, while the second terminates with a full "dominant minor" cadence, which is then juxtaposed with the relative major. The development is packed with tonal activity: during twenty-one measures the minor subdominant, the flattened seventh, and the "dominant minor" are established. Haydn's expanded recapitulation recalls the coda of the first movement, especially in the similarities of their final measures (Example X-55).

The variation principle as applied to P in Hob. XV:18/1 is so expanded in Hob. XV:20/1 that it brings to mind Haydn's finest example of this procedure, Hob. XVI:50/1. In Hob. XV:20/1 (Example X-56) the initial two measures receive four permutations in the exposition. Three come at the introduction of T and serve to destabilize until S arrives with the fourth variation—a new approach to Haydn's now common S(P). At the same time the accelerating surface rhythms tend to underline all four functions (P, T, S, K). One peculiarity of the exposition is that at the very beginning and several times thereafter the highest available pitch on the keyboard, f''', is used. Since the general thrust of the pitch curve is downward, it is therefore more notable that the development contains its own climax (m. 54), which is realized by coordinating curve, pitch, dynamics, and harmony. The retransition, which derives from P, winds down from this climax but creates its own tension with colorful chords, modulations, and chromaticism. In the recapitulation Haydn eliminates one section, but compared to the pruning that an exposition of this type might generate, the treatment seems conservative.

This extraordinary opening movement is hardly matched by the variations—solo con mano sinistra—and the finale. The central movement adopts an almost antiquated format for the theme and the first two variations; it is oriented toward the older bass variation of the earliest works. Only in the third variation does Haydn break the leisurely pace with a flood of figurational thirty-second notes so common to "hack works" in this form. The ternary-minuet finale has a delightful touch of gypsy flavor in the minore episode, but in the reprise's return the variation sounds facile. This may have been another instance of Haydn's working against a deadline and slighting the conclusion of a set.

EXAMPLE X–55. Hob. XV:19/1, mm. 156–63, and 19/3, mm. 118–25.

Exposition

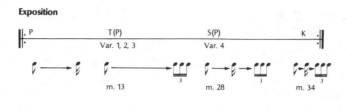

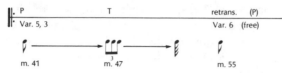

Development

EXAMPLE X–56. Hob. XV:20/1.

HOB. XVI:52

The virtuoso nature of Hob. XV:20/1 is expanded upon in the solo Sonata Hob. XVI:52, composed in 1794, the same year in which Hob. XV:18–20 appeared. A big sonata in every sense, it requires power, dexterity, and expression. Each movement has its own personality: the first is extroverted, the second supersensitive, and the third witty. It is this combination of requisites and character that has retained for Hob. XVI:52 a secure place in the repertoire.[54]

Its opening sonorities and dotted rhythms were to be Haydn's most impressive opening keyboard gesture. This ceremonial march, derived from the French overture, has nothing to do with the *galant* ones from the previous sonatas. Preceded by strong pedals and cadences, the characteristic head-motive solidifies the exposition as it powerfully introduces each function. The material placed between these pillars is totally different: rather than mass, line and figure are stressed. Even the contrasting part of S (beginning in m. 27), a perfect *Flötenuhr* theme, is effective within this context. Except for the opening two measures of the development, where it appears in skeletal form, the principal motive does not return until the reprise; S essentially takes over P's expository function by dividing the development in two parts, appearing first in the submediant and then in the Neapolitan (E = F flat). The recapitulation is conservatively tightened in a manner similar to that of Hob. XV:20/1. As in a number of sonata forms that follow—including the finale of this sonata—there is no indication that the development and recapitulation are to be repeated.

When Haydn presented S in the Neapolitan in the first movement, one could not have predicted that this key was to serve as the tonality of the slow movement, a monothematic Adagio in ternary variation form. Here there is nothing mechanical or superficial, for the impression is one of a spontaneous but extremely skilled and expressive improvisation. The notation in the autograph only serves to underline its spontaneity, with many flourishes written in small notes and two measures containing an extra beat (mm. 40 and 48).[55]

A tonal deception at the beginning of the finale relates it to the central slow movement; the isolated G natural with which it begins creates the impression that the key is E minor. Such a conclusion is thwarted with the entry of E flat, but this tonic is not confirmed until some two dozen bars later. Although the finale is bound to the previous movement by tonal uncertainty, it distinguishes itself from the first two movements in its surface rhythmic treatment: previously the continuum provided by the beat was violated only once, whereas in the finale the linear and anacrustic orientation of the themes imparts a great deal of forward motion, which highlights its dozen stops and spurts. Other witticisms result from use of the *fz*: the first intrusion of the dominant (m. 17), and the stress on the fourth eighth note (mm. 44–48) shifting to a quarter-note downbeat (m. 50). Overall, this finale makes few concessions to its position in the cycle, for in every way it is almost the equal of the first movement.

HOB. XVI: 51

Totally different in character but possibly coming from the same year, is XVI: 51; it has none of the "grand" style of Hob. XVI: 52. The first movement is a mainly lyrical Andante, while the finale is a jesting Presto in triple meter. Not even a hint of the big sonorities and the formidable technical demands of Hob. XVI: 52/1 are present in this D-major Sonata.[56]

The opening movement dispenses with both repeats. As is often the case in such sonata forms from Mozart to Brahms, the development begins with P in the tonic, giving the impression that the exposition is being repeated. Even though Haydn varies P at this point, the embellishments evolve from the exposition:

Exposition   Pa + a¹
Development   Pa¹ + a²

The opening of the recapitulation does not repeat the exposition but the development. Thus, Haydn's treatment of the initial motive departs from his usual plan.

Instead of continuing with the opening march-like material to make a compound statement, the initial key area is extended by presenting a new and contrasting idea (2P) marked cantabile. Haydn deepens its lyricism by a totally new sonority, melodic octaves. 2P becomes T by a simple chromatic alteration, which is characteristically emphasized with a sforzando. S is again conceived in two large periods. The development, after the ambiguous repetition of P in the tonic, works on S and then builds to a harmonic and pitch climax on 2P/T, which is subsequently eliminated from the recapitulation.

In recent times, the first movement has been described as Schubertian,[57] but it is the second movement that is laid out in what was to be one of Schubert's favorite structures: A B A B A. The use of accents, however, is particularly Haydnesque. Here one can find a series of different applications that result in a highly flexible approach to meter (Example X-57): stressed pick-ups, hemiola anticipating the

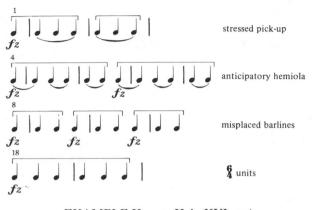

EXAMPLE X–57. Hob. XVI:51/2.

bar lines by a quarter beat, misplaced bar lines, and 3/4 measures combined to form 6/4 units. Although the sforzando has been used previously, in no single movement has it been exploited so completely. In size and musical demands, this work reminds one of the 1783–84 Sonatas Hob. XVI:40–42, but its style is completely within the mainstream of the 1790s.

HOB. XV: 21 – 23

In 1795 the three trios dedicated to Marie Esterházy, Hob. XV:21–23, appeared. The external similarities of this group to Hob. XV:18–20 are striking: each trio has three movements, two of the opening movements (Hob. XV:21 and 22) are in sonata form, and one (Hob. XV:23) is a variation set; the slow movement of Hob. XV:23 is a triple-meter Adagio ma non troppo; and two of the finales (Hob. XV:22 and 23) are triple-meter Allegros. In addition, two of the trios (Hob. XV:21 and 22) are in the major mode; Hob. XV:23, the one that begins with variations, is in the minor. Thus Haydn seems to have modeled this second set of London trios on the first. Indeed, certain cycles could easily be transferred from one set to the other without appreciably changing the effect of the group.

On the other hand, Hob. XV:21 is the only keyboard trio to begin with a slow introduction, a practice Haydn usually reserved for the symphonies. As in the London Symphonies, this introduction is thematically and metrically related to the main body of the movement; in this case, the Adagio pastorale is transformed into a bucolic gigue with drones and pedals, which serve as the affective basis for another impressive sonata form.

Thematic transformation was previously seen in Hob. XV:19/1, where it occurred as an expanded variation. This concept also finds a place in the exposition of Hob. XV:21/1: both P and S begin with identical material, and S concludes with an idea derived from P^k (Example X-58). Haydn has thus modified a now common practice—the theme of P introducing S—to accommodate a current preference for incorporating variation into sonata form. The interrelationship of the development

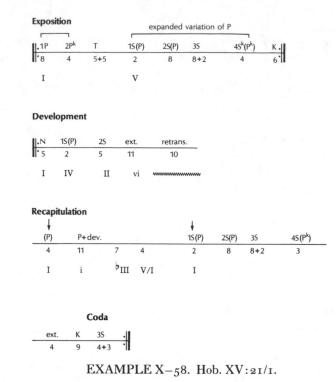

EXAMPLE X–58. Hob. XV:21/1.

and recapitulation is, as in Hob. XV: 18/1, generated from the exposition's structure. For the development Haydn uses his normal plan and saturates it with tonal activity. In the recapitulation, the developmentlike section that usually follows an abbreviated statement of P in the tonic is expanded and moves toward a tonality more distant from the tonic than any found in the actual development section. The result is twofold: the brief statement of P in the tonic becomes parenthetical; and 1S(P) becomes the stronger structural downbeat. Therefore, in this example Haydn provides another solution to the recapitulatory problem posed by the S(P) exposition.

The Andante molto of Hob. XV: 21/2 is an appropriate, affective sequel to these pastoral and rustic qualities, for it is in the style of a Romanza with ingratiating melodies, simple harmonies, straightforward textures, and a part-form structure. The embellishments in the repetitions are so beautifully integrated into the simplicity of the initial presentation that they could easily serve as examples of the tasteful embellishments to which eighteenth-century treatises refer. Continuity of texture and theme hold this cantilena movement together, allowing very closely related changes in key and mode (tonic minor, submediant, subdominant) to provide contrast.

For the finale Haydn continues the pastorale atmosphere by combining a contradance with allusions to a hunting scene: horn harmonies are buttressed by a pedal trill. One would expect such a picture to be framed by a rondo; indeed, the repeat of and heavily articulated end to the opening idea would confirm such an expectation. Instead, there ensues an unusually large sonata form that separates the exposition's functions with repeats:

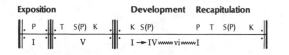

Otherwise, a tonal formula somewhat reminiscent of the first movement is used: the development begins in the tonic and presents S(P) in the subdominant; while for the recapitulation, P turns to the tonic minor after four measures and resumes the development.

The unity of characteristic styles that holds Hob. XV:21 together is not found in the E-flat major Trio Hob. XV:22, which is in part a *pasticcio* cycle: its middle movement was originally a solo keyboard piece, or possibly a rejected slow movement for a solo sonata, to which accompanying parts were added. This may also explain its tertian relationship to the key of the cycle (E-flat, G, E-flat). Indeed, the Poco Adagio seems to be rather bland when compared to the striking moments that mark the opening and closing movements, which have a noticeably similar motive that appears in their respective S sections (cf. mm. 66–68 of the first movement, mm. 16–24 of the last).

The first movement's main points of interest generate from P^k (Example X-59), whose strength derives from the neutrality of P and its own harmonic progressions, which assert the tonic in a singularly impressive manner. When P returns as the beginning of S, one anticipates a repetition of P^k as well. Instead, it is replaced in both the exposition and the recapitulation by its very antithesis: a deceptive cadence that moves to the chord of G-flat major in the exposition and C-flat major in the recapitulation for eight and nine measures respectively before returning to the related key. When this material is restated in the development, it asserts with a full cadence the most distant key possible—the flattened leading tone (D flat). But this development does more than legitimize the deception of the exposition; it is the most impressive yet penned by Haydn. There is nothing unusual about beginning this section with K on the dominant, but the density of the line, the polyphonic texture, and the length of the elaboration set it apart; throughout, such procedures as imitation, inversion, permutation, and reduction are fluently applied.

The finales of Hob. XV:22 and 23 resemble Hob. XV:18/3: they are triple-meter pieces that have little if anything to do with the Tempo di Menuet. However, the extravagances of rhythmic drive and syncopation found in Hob. XV:18/3 are considerably moderated in Hob. XV:22/3, for only the beginning of the latter reveals the slightest hint of the former's exuberance. As in the first movement, it is the tonal activity—which is now centered in the development—that gains one's attention. With wild arpeggios, the development moves rapidly through the submediant, the supertonic, and the lowered-seventh degree (D flat, which becomes enharmonically respelled as C sharp); it then settles on the raised-fourth degree

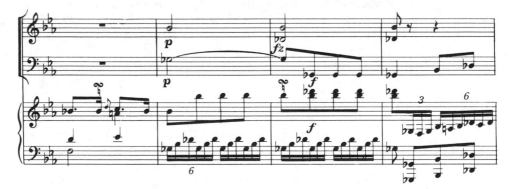

EXAMPLE X–59. Hob. XV: 22/1, mm. 9–20, 46–59.

EXAMPLE X–59 (*continued*)

EXAMPLE X–60. Hob. XV:22/3.

with S, establishes C sharp, deceptively presents P in the Neapolitan, asserts G, and finally slips back to E-flat major. As can be seen from Example X-60, most of these keys are related by thirds, one of the prominent secondary relationships Haydn used during the 1790s.

Even though the cycle of Hob. XV:23 is nearly a twin to Hob. XV:19, their opening movements are strikingly different: Hob. XV:19/1 is dominated by figurative changes, whereas the variations in XV:23/1 are primarily based on texture and fabric. The latter approach is immediately apparent, as the *minore* theme's treatment of sound changes with nearly every phrase. The *maggiore* theme also changes its fabric, but its contrapuntal aspects are more complex: contrary motion among the voices is underlined by characteristic accents that disrupt the barline's effect. During the course of the variations the *minore* is treated austerely, while the *maggiore* is full of extroverted brilliance. Thus, the cadenza at the beginning of the coda, following a *maggiore* variation, seems entirely appropriate.

Hob. XV:23/2 looks forward to Hob. XV:26/2 in its elaborate—almost fussy—treatment of melody. At the same time it harks back to Hob. XVI:38/2, as it is one more instance of Haydn's employing a sonata form with a varied reprise in the manner of C. P. E. Bach. Overall, the second movement demands considerably more of the performer than does the first: not only virtuosity, but also sensitivity and intelligence are required to conquer its difficulties.

For the finale of this D-major Trio, a small-dimension sonata form is once again employed. As in Hob. XV:22/3, emphasis is placed on hemiola shifts. Just as the 3/4 measure seems established, a sforzando intrudes on a weak beat. In a very real sense this movement anticipates Haydn's most rhythmically disruptive piece, the finale to the Quartet Op. 76/6.

HOB. XV: 31

Hob. XV:31 is another pasticcio cycle, as the finale of this two-movement affair was originally a 1794 character piece entitled "The Dream," to which a new first movement was added by early 1795. The first movement owes something to Hob. XV:23/1 in its thematic material—triadic outlines that extend over the barlines—and, to a lesser degree, in its use of counterpoint. The structure of Hob. XV:31/1, however, is another example of the synthesis of variation and rondo, but here they are combined in a different manner. The movement opens with a statement in the unusual key of E-flat minor and follows with a complementary theme in the major, related to the first by the inversion of its head-motive. Since both are closed forms, use the minor-major modes, and are thematically related, one is prepared for a series of double variations. But with the return of the *minore* theme in a pure form, such an expectation is scuttled. A second episode in B major—an enharmonic third below E flat—is then presented; it is followed by the *minore* in a full-fledged variation, which concludes the movement without a hint of a reprise function. It is thus a rondo:

A	B(A)	A	C	A variation
E-flat minor	E-flat major	E-flat minor	B major	E-flat minor

Haydn's previous models for such a movement would also lead one to anticipate that the first reprise would use variation, and that the third would either combine variation and recapitulation or be entirely recapitulatory. These departures—the initial orientation toward double variations, the key of the second episode, and the use of six flats—mark this movement as one of the composer's most individual efforts.

Despite the fact that the second movement, which is in E-flat major, originated apart from the first, the two present a coherent cycle. The episode of the ternary-form finale recalls both E-flat minor and B major, and the movement ends with a partial variation using the sextuplets found at the conclusion of the initial movement. Such similarities certainly suggest that the first movement was conceived as an organic partner to this once-independent finale, which was written for the virtuoso Therese Jansen Bartolozzi and an amateur violinist.

HOB. XV: 27–29

Haydn also composed a series of trios, Hob. XV:27–29, for Therese Bartolozzi. As a group they are similar to the previous London sets except for the absence of a cycle in the minor mode. Notable again are the tonalities chosen for the two central movements: the major submediant in Hob. XV:27 and the lower enharmonic third (E-flat to B major) in Hob. XV:29.

Consisting of two big sonata-form movements that frame a central Andante, Hob. XV:27 is the most virtuosic of all the Haydn trios. It recalls the big E-flat major solo Sonata Hob. XVI:52 of 1794, which is also dedicated to Mrs. Bartolozzi. The power of the solo sonata is immediately conveyed in the trio's thematically integrated hammerstrokes, and its brilliance is duplicated throughout. P is highly unified; 2P, beginning in m. 5, grows directly out of m. 4. It is almost as if the composer were searching for a more decisive cadence with which to conclude 1P: the first attempt is deceptive (m. 8) and the last complete (m. 12). Haydn's use of harmonic deception within P is repeated at other important junctures: just before T (V_7 of IV to V_7 of V), just before the entry of P in the development (V of I to the Neapolitan of V), and before the retransition.

In the exposition as a whole, Haydn continues to reemploy thematic ideas for different functions, but now he goes beyond the simple transposition of P; as seen in Example X-61, the ideas are related, so that S and S^k become an expanded variation of P and P^k. The development is in three parts, each of which works on elements of 2P: for the first part, 2P is reduced to its smallest half-step component; for the second, which begins with 1P, 2P spawns an old-fashioned fugato; and for the third, 2P serves as the basis for a wash of color that culminates in a potent half-step dissonance. Thus, the deceptive cadence of the exposition calls our attention not only to the overall harmonic activity but also to 2P itself, which was to become the basis of virtually the entire development. Haydn purges the recapitulation of many of the harmonic deceptions found in the exposition, lending it a new stability. Additionally, the themes are tightened and reordered so that the recapitulation places greater weight on closure (e.g., P^k is repeated before K). As a whole, the movement is marked by an unusual number of sforzandos, many of which characteristically set into relief the more colorful harmonies. Indeed, Hob. XV:27/1 often reminds one of Beethoven in the use of dynamics, developmental procedures, and grand gestures.[58]

For the Andante Haydn turns again to a congenial siciliano in ternary form. Beneath this facade, however, is an unusually sophisticated opening section in which the phrase rhythms are cleverly manipulated and elongated by embellished fermatas:

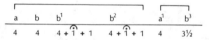

The reprise further alters the syntax:

Since nearly all the fermatas are underlined by deceptive resolutions, the cadential activity recalls the first movement. In addition, the stormy middle section, with its exploitation of color—which arrives prematurely because of the shortened b^3—has a strong association with the opening movement's retransition; the fact that this episode is a potent development section further strengthens the association. As was often the case during the 1790s, Haydn chooses to work on one of the more obscure motives, here a six- to seven-note idea descending from the embellished fermatas.

Formal synthesis of another sort is found in the finale of Hob. XV:27, a sonata

EXAMPLE X–61. Hob. XV:27/1, mm. 1–7, 12–14, 19–20, 38–40.

EXAMPLE X–61 (*continued*)

form with hints of rondo influence. At the very beginning, the anacrusic theme (Example X-62)—which is laid out in an incomplete rounded binary—recalls the expanded structure of a large-scale refrain rather than a sonata-form P section. P's central portion is a short development in the parallel minor with a retransition that effectively juxtaposes an A natural in m. 34 with the E flat and A flat of the previous measure. T and S are combined by a flood of sixteenths, which is partially relieved by a less-active K. Only two motives are dealt with in the actual development: the head-motive of K and the material previously worked out in the central portion of P. Since this part of P carried a retransition function and was given the most extended treatment, the overall effect of the development is that of one big preparation for the recapitulation. Both motivically and harmonically, this development section is one of the most powerful. By concentrating on the minor mode, the tonalities employed have a stronger effect; and the tonal rhythms again recall Beethoven, with their alternation of activity and stasis. By way of the dominant of A major, Haydn lands directly on C major for the recapitulation, in another prominent example of third relations in these late works. In the recapitulation only that portion of P that occurred after its "retransition" is heard again; the remainder is altered to emphasize the initial expectation of a rondo:

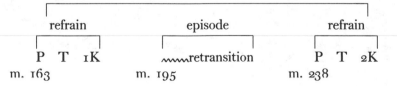

Just before the episode's retransition, another purely coloristic passage binds the finale to the previous movements. Indeed, the entire finale exceeds the accomplishments of Hob. XVI:52/3 and matches the flair of the conclusions to the London Symphonies.

The second trio, in E major, Hob. XV:28, is a less-driven and more-intimate sonata, with all the movements in the same key and only the first employing sonata

EXAMPLE X–62. Hob. XV:27/3, mm. 1–36.

EXAMPLE X–62 (*continued*)

form. In contrast to Hob. XV:27/1, the exposition of Hob. XV:28/1 returns to
the S(P) shape in the clearest possible manner. The singularity of P—scored for
pizzicato strings doubling a graced melody—not only sets it apart from every other
Haydn beginning but also contributes to the strength of the articulation for the
S(P) area and shapes the entire movement to a degree unmatched by any theme; its
individuality overshadows everything else. P also occurs in two "strophic variations": the first immediately after the first presentation of P, the second in the development. While the first variation is a standard embellished one, the second is presented in a simplified form as a chorale with as many as eight simultaneities. If
viewed in the context of variation forms, this event recalls Hob. XVI:48/1 and to a
lesser extent a few of the trios and other sonatas in which the "theme" is more
elaborate than the variation. On the other hand, within a sonata-form context the
purest version of P is thus stated in a tonality far removed from the tonic, the enharmonic respelling of G sharp as A flat.[59]

This initial movement conveys an up-to-date style and almost ethereal warmth
that does not prepare one for the antiquated and stark atmosphere of the following
Allegretto. For the first time in almost two decades, Haydn reverts to a triple-meter
movement that at the outset creates the impression of continuous variations on a
Baroque bass. Each of its larger sections is defined by tonality and orchestration:

Introduction	E minor	Strings and keyboard in octaves
Part 1	E minor	Keyboard Solo
Part 2	G major	Ostinato in left hand of keyboard and strings, melody in right hand.
Part 3	E minor	Ostinato in right hand of keyboard and violin, melody in left hand of keyboard and cello.
Coda	E minor	Keyboard flourishes accompanied by strings

The concluding flourishes introduced by deceptive cadences underline the anti-quated effect, as they recall the toccata/fantasia.

For the finale, the atmosphere of the first movement returns. In this leisurely triple-meter piece, there is none of the character of a minuet. But it is not without surprises: there is a passionate *minore* with an enharmonic excursion and a fantasia-like flourish near the end. The former recalls the opening movement, the latter the end of the second. Thus, Hob. XV:28 is a cycle unified beyond tonality.

Hob. XV:29 begins with a rondo/variation movement in the same style as Hob. XV:19/1, 23/1, and 31/1, i.e., a duple-meter march that usually employs dotted rhythms. Compared with that of the chronologically closest Hob. XV:31/1, its overall plan is more orthodox:

```
 ┌─────────┬────────────────────────────────────────────────┐
 A        B(A)    A reprise + variation    C(A)    A abbreviated Coda
major     minor          major                  ᴡᴡᴡᴡmajor
```

For Hob. XV:29/2 Haydn selected a siciliano "innocentemente" and, within an E-flat major cycle, chose B major as its key. In every earlier instance of this tonal juxtaposition, E-flat minor played a special role—B major being the enharmonic respelling of its sixth degree. In this slow movement, an E-flat major chord follows the dominant of B major at the beginning of the long preparation for the finale. The overall structure of this piece (Example X-63) consists of three open parts, each of which is progressively less shackled by, but grows out of, the shape of the first. In this context the move to E-flat major, although surprising, does not seem totally out of place.

The "Finale in the German Style" Hob. XV:29/3, or, as it was called in the

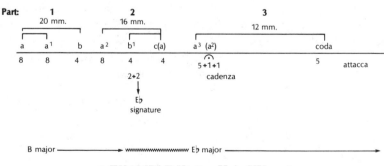

EXAMPLE X–63. Hob. XV:29/2.

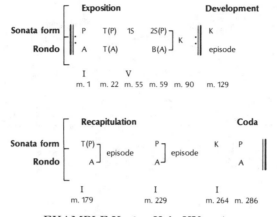

EXAMPLE X–64. Hob. XV:29/3.

Continental editions, "Allemande," is another conclusion that exploits a national idiom. Haydn's earlier dances called Allemande or "Deutscher Tanz" were no longer than several eight-bar strains; this one, however, takes up more than 300 measures. Its "German Style" comes from the character of the wide-ranging broken arpeggios of the melody and the stomping Ländler background. The disturbance of the strong triple pulse in mm. 32–34 (mm. 201–203) and mm. 162–65 calls attention not only to the rhythm but also to the harmonic peculiarities. In total shape Haydn returns to the principles of Hob. XV:27/3: a sonata form with rondo elements (Example X-64). The exposition again uses P within S, but now S(P) occurs in second rather than in first place. Since T and S are based on P, K is the only other function to gain a completely separate profile.[60]

During the course of the second part, which has no repeats, the refrain returns three times. Haydn mixes signals as to the function of each return: the first is approached like a recapitulation, but it then uses the violin/keyboard dialoguing from T; the second is preceded by material reminiscent of S, but it then duplicates P; and the last combines P with the scales of K for an impressive conclusion. In sum, this movement brings together two unlikely partners, a popular dance style and a sophisticated structure.

HOB. XV:24–26

The final set of London trios, Hob. XV:24–26, dedicated to Rebecca Schröter, Haydn's closest female friend, are a masterly contribution to the medium. As a group these trios present a total contrast to those composed for Mrs. Bartolozzi (Hob. XV:27–29), even though the structure of the set is the same: they are less driven, less predicated on coloristic writing, and less technically demanding. Even the F-sharp minor Trio Hob. XV:26 fails to conjure up anything of the character of Haydn's only symphony in this key, No. 45, "The Farewell." Most indicative of the difference in technical demands are their finales: two of the trios end with Moderato triple-metered movements, while the third—the famous Hungarian rondo of

EXAMPLE X–65. Hob. XV:24/1, mm. 1–13.

Hob. XV:25—sounds more difficult than it really is. None make use of the sonata principle, in contrast to Hob. XV:27–29, in which two use developmental forms. Finally, whereas in the Bartolozzi set two of the slow movements are in remote keys, in the Schröter trios two merely change mode and the third uses the major submediant.

Hob. XV:24 commences with a "noise-killer" chord that implies a symphonic character, but its first movement is in a chamber rather than in a concert style. As in Hob. XV:20/1, variation procedures are extensively incorporated into a sonata structure. Of seminal importance is the second presentation of Pa (Example X-65), with its deceptive beginning on the first inversion of the supertonic, which is heavily articulated by the preceding fermatas. This presentation generates T and much of the development section, all of which provides contrast to the root position presentation of the beginning of P and S(P).

Its slow movement in D minor is a 6/8 Andante that surprisingly contains nothing reminiscent of a siciliano. Variation is applied, as expected, for the repetitions; but the sudden establishment of the supertonic in mm. 15–16 (the same deception that occurred in the midst of the first movement's P) is entirely unexpected. Thus, as in the earlier Hob. XVI:52/1 and 2, Haydn binds two movements together by recalling the most striking tonal event of the first. The Allegro ma dolce finale stresses linear writing. In the central *minore* the polyphony and rhythm are intensified as the upbeat of A is extended from ♫♩ | ♩ to ᵞ♫♫♩ | ♩ .

Hob. XV:25 is the most popular of all the Haydn trios. It is also one of the more unusual among these London efforts: it does not contain a single sonata form, and the treatment of the part forms in the opening and final movements is atypical. Hob. XV:25/1 is distinctive among the variation rondos in that variation aspects spill over into the episodes. The first episode (mm. 22–42) is related to the reprise in a manner more characteristic of the first and second themes of many variation sets; both B and C begin with the same head-motive, and C continues the style of the first variation of A with its sextuplet rhythm. In toto, the diminutions present an accelerating surface rhythm that recalls some earlier single-theme strophic variations:

Haydn contributes his richest melodic utterance to the Poco Adagio slow movement. Here each repetition of the main theme is rescored so that the melody receives its most intense setting and soars to its highest point with the reprise.

The finale of Hob. XV:25 is the famous rondo "in the Gypsies' Style."[61] It seems that a composer's most popular works, if not spurious, are at least unusual manifestations of his style, and this rondo fits this characterization. At the outset, the two-section refrain is noteworthy. In its first section the opening strain has a written-out repetition with a change in scoring. In contrast, the second section of the refrain has two strains with written-out exact repetitions. Only the first section of the refrain is recapitulated, and each return begins with the second orchestration of the opening phrase. Also exceptional are Haydn's use of the same tonic-minor tonality for the two episodes and the total melodic independence of the episodes from the refrain. Even though this finale was best known during the eighteenth century as a separate piece in many different settings,[62] its impact is best appreciated within the context of this keyboard trio cycle, for the Andante and Poco Adagio hardly prepare one for its burst of energy.

The opening sonata-form movement of Hob. XV:26 (Example X-66) initially seems spiritually closer to the E-major Trio Hob. XV:28 of the Bartolozzi set, but during its course expressive aspects gradually surface. An increase in tension is created by the recapitulation, which relates more to the development than to the exposition. The exposition leaves the tonic minor after nine measures; the development works in reverse, beginning in the tonic major and continuing with a string of minor tonalities. The most poignant moment of Hob. XV:26/1 occurs when 1K, the most distinctive material of the exposition, is sequentially treated in the minor, ending with the tonic's diminished-seventh chord. The recapitulation— which is identified only by its opening phrase—not only remains in the minor but is completely reformulated so that it becomes a continuation of the development. 1K reappears earlier than expected in order to build to a second climax, rendering

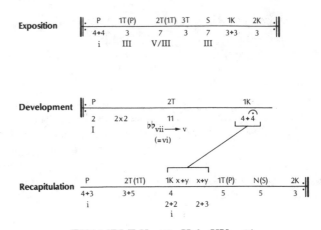

EXAMPLE X–66. Hob. XV:26/1.

the opening of the recapitulation as merely a parenthetical event. This movement is thus similar to the trios of the late 1780s, with their radically altered recapitulations, as well as to Hob. XV:21/1, which thoroughly exploits the parenthetical concept.

The Adagio cantabile of Hob. XV:26, which Haydn later adapted for Symphony No. 102/2, is the culmination of his slow movements with an unusually elaborate melody. Once again, perhaps because of the ensemble problem posed by the ornaments, the violin and cello for the most part provide support. In fact, the cello part in the trio resembles an orchestral bass line, while in the symphony it is more chamberlike. Much of the established mood is continued in the Tempo di Menuet finale; it too has an underlying intensity that betrays itself with occasional sforzandos and unexpected harmonic shifts.

HOB. XVI:50

Hob. XVI:50 was probably the last work Haydn completed before returning to Vienna, and it was the last of some half dozen trios and sonatas he wrote for Mrs. Bartolozzi. Although each individual movement is masterly, the cycle itself reveals signs of haste. It is a compilation, as the slow movement was completed before Haydn returned to London in 1794. Unlike the other works proven to have been composed for Mrs. Bartolozzi, this one lacks a balance between the opening movement and the finale. The conclusion is a diminutive piece, whose dimensions would be more appropriate for Hob. XVI:51; it was made to appear longer in the first edition by writing out the repeats. Still, the two outer movements are bound by a jesting character. Hob. XVI:50 is another tribute to the technical and musical prowess of Mrs. Bartolozzi; the first movement implies that she had dexterity and power and must also have been a remarkable colorist.

Hob. XVI:50/1 (Example X-67) is the fullest flowering of variation procedures in Haydn's sonata form. Although some of the other Bartolozzi sonatas gained distinction from their "grand" primary themes, here Haydn initiates the exposition

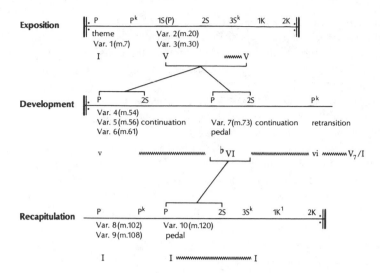

EXAMPLE X–67. Hob. XVI:50/1.

with a more common idea that gains in interest from a series of permutations and continuations that include a full gamut of textures—from unadorned monophony to invertible counterpoint. P achieves its climactic presentations not in the grand sonorities of m. 7 but in its most mysterious garb: a pedal passage that first leads to the recapitulation and later to the concluding measures.

The exposition of this remarkable movement employs an S(P) structure with a series of heavy cadences similar to those of Hob. XVI:52/1. One wonders, however, if the S section was not at one point thirteen measures shorter, for the cadence at m. 33 is more completely resolved in mm. 46–47. These thirteen parenthetical measures of 2S and 3S^k, however, lend breadth, harmonic color, and additional tension to what would otherwise have been for its time an unusually neutral exposition.[63] The development is enlarged from the formula of P / continuation / retransition, to P / continuation / P / continuation / retransition, with both continuation sections deriving from and having the same effect as 2S. The first P (Var. 4–6) and its continuation are what one would expect in the development, except for the conclusion on the dominant of the dominant's Neapolitan. Haydn then again presents P (Var. 7) in the dominant's Neapolitan with an indication for the use of the pedal; the most distant tonality is thus underlined by the softest dynamic level and a dark, low register. During the second continuation, as the dynamic level increases, the tonality moves to the submediant, which commences the return to the recapitulation. This retransition expands the final motive of P^k (mm. 16–19)—also fleetingly used at the end of the first continuation—from three to some thirteen measures, which conclude with a massive dominant seventh. Such a sequence of events beginning with Var. 7 results in a structural tension matched only by the retransition in Hob. XVI:49/1. The first part of the recapitulation follows the exposition with the usual modifications, while the second commences not with 1S(P) but a bright presentation of P with a pedal passage in a high register (Var. 10), after which the sequence of the exposition is resumed. Thus, as in Hob. XV:26/1, Haydn predicates the recapitulation on the development as well as on the exposition.

Even though the slow movement of Hob. XVI:50 was composed earlier, it seems totally appropriate to the improvisatory and expressive playing of Mrs. Bartolozzi, not unlike that required for Hob. XVI:52/2. Before incorporating this piece in the sonata, however, Haydn made small modifications to deepen some sonorities and loosen a few ornamental flourishes. Hob. XVI:50/2 also bears some similarity to the first movement, not only in the varied repetitions of the opening materials but also in its larger structure: the recapitulation is expanded by replacing T (mm. 9–12) with a half dozen measures from the beginning of the development (cf. mm. 24–30 and 42–47). Additionally, the tension that this interpolation lends to the recapitulation is continued in the coda with halting allusions to P.[64]

Beethoven is again anticipated in the triple-meter Allegro molto finale, for it is in every way a scherzo. One wonders why Haydn did not use the term here—as well as in the earlier Hob. XV:24/3 and XVI:51/2—for he employed it frequently in the string quartets. Part of the answer may be found in the Viennese keyboard tradition of the duple-meter "scherzo" finale, the fact that these three movements do not use the *da capo* form of the quartets, and that they all are finales not central movements. Nonetheless, Hob. XVI:50/3 is one of Haydn's most complete realizations of a jesting character, with its opening seven-measure phrase, unresolved harmonies combined with a pause (mm. 9–11), reorganization of phrase rhythm (m. 69), kinetic repetitions (mm. 53–56), and quiet premature conclusion. Despite its small size, the movement provides the climax of the cycle: the range is extended by a major third and for the first time reaches a‴.

HOB. XV:30

Haydn's final keyboard work, the E-flat major Trio Hob. XV:30, was completed if not entirely composed after his return to Vienna in 1795. Its cycle uses the formula found in many of the London trios: a big sonata-form first movement followed by a slow movement in a rather distant tonality—here, the major of E-flat's relative minor—that connects to a triple-meter ternary finale.

If Beethoven's style was approached in Hob. XVI:50/3, the exposition of Hob. XV:30/1 seems to recall Mozart. One is immediately reminded of the younger composer by the wealth and number of ideas presented: There are two distinct themes within P, S, and K. Both 2P and S employ a singing allegro texture, which occurs frequently in Mozart but is not especially characteristic of Haydn.[65] Finally, the surface rhythms tend to accelerate only within a thematic idea, the harmonic rhythms have a more distinct patterning, and there is a shift to a melancholy minor for 2S.

Not satisfied merely to present a series of striking and discrete themes, Haydn subtly unifies his ideas not only by the S(P) relationship—obscured here by variation—but also by both a chordal motive buried in the initial measure and a series of slurred eighth-note pairs in 2P and 2S. The chordal motive receives ingenious treatment: it serves as accompaniment, counterpoint, and melody. Such strong motivic ties allow the harmonic structure to be subjected to stronger deceptions; in the exposition 2P ends on the dominant while 1T begins on the dominant seventh of the submediant, and 1K is delayed by a shift to the diminished seventh of the supertonic.

The wealth of expository themes is matched by the richness of tonal activity in the development. This section begins on the dominant seventh of G flat, which immediately follows the exposition's concluding B-flat major. After four introductory measures, P appears in C-flat major, the dominant's Neapolitan, and 2P is developed in E-flat minor. The continuation—or expansion—area uses material from K and is articulated by a shift to D-flat major. E-flat minor returns and is followed by F minor and C minor. The development concludes as it began, with another deception: the dominant of the submediant resolves to the dominant seventh of the subdominant before reaching the tonic.

Compared with the first-movement recapitulations of Hob. XV:26 and Hob. XVI:50, that of Hob. XV:30 is also Mozartean in its unusual regularity. Haydn not only provides greater harmonic continuity in the recapitulation but also expands the surface rhythmic accelerations from the level of the theme to that of the entire recapitulation. This change in the rhythmic plan results in a breadth that goes far beyond the exposition, with its series of discretely presented ideas.

The designation Andante con moto in 3/8—the smallest measure in the late slow movements—suggests that Haydn was attempting to assure a tempo of some pace for this ternary form. A slow tempo would give the chromatic inflections added for the reprise variations more than the apparently intended ornamental significance. The episode as well as the two refrains are conceived with a strong linear orientation, as are many of Haydn's late textures; even the inner voices of the essentially homophonic refrains reveal the easy craftsmanship of a master. The rhythmic motion increases in the episode and remains at this intensity for most of the refrain's return and the coda. Rather than modulating to the dominant of E-flat major at its conclusion, Haydn simply ends on the dominant of C minor which is immediately followed by E-flat major for the beginning of the finale. This tonal relationship finds its roots in the Baroque practice of the dominant of the relative minor functioning as the dominant of its related major.[66]

Haydn's contrapuntal facility is also evident in the ternary finale, a triple-meter Presto that brings to mind the Allemande of Hob. XV:29. Its episode in E-flat minor takes a now almost predictable enharmonic excursion to C-flat major respelled as B major. The coda again reveals the rhythmic control that has pervaded this entire trio, with its sudden rush from eighths to triplets for a breathtaking conclusion.

Although apparently not perceived by Haydn as his farewell to keyboard composition, this final trio does bring together many of the elements of the composer's late style in a highly personal utterance.[67] The distant tonalities, harmonic deceptions, counterpoint, and rhythmic strategies are handled with such skill that they almost pass without notice. Indeed, these artifices are combined with such attractive materials that the trio must have appealed to a broad spectrum of the eighteenth-century public, from the complete artist and scholar, who demanded the most sophisticated of musical experiences, to the amateur, who only desired delight.

One can view these final London and Viennese keyboard compositions in two distinct groups: the Sonatas and Trios written for Therese Jansen Bartolozzi, which display a virtuosity certainly beyond the reach of most of the nonprofessional London pianists; and those composed for the amateur musician of taste and technical skill, such as the Widow Schröter. We have already considered in some detail their manifold structural aspects, including the treatment of tonality and theme, as well as their strong tendencies toward structural synthesis. Yet, perhaps the one trait that decisively separates these sonatas and trios from the earlier ones is the rich variety of types used for the finales. That is especially true of those in triple meter: scherzo—Hob. XVI:50, 51; Hungarian polonaise—Hob. XV:18; allemande—Hob. XV:31, 29; Tempo di Menuet—Hob. XV:26; fast minuet—Hob. XV:20, 22, 23; Allegro—Hob. XV:28; and Allegro ma dolce—Hob. XV:24. Those not in triple meters include an Allegro 4/4 (Hob. XV:32), a gigue-Presto 6/8 (Hob. XV:19), and four 2/4 Prestos, the most remarkable of which is the "Rondo in the Gypsies' Style" (Hob. XV:25/3). In these finales Haydn moved from the duple-meter contradance toward triple-meter types that encompass the lively and brilliant style of the scherzo and the allemande, as well as the more moderate and elegant minuet and Allegro ma dolce.

Conclusion

Haydn was interested in the architecture of every aspect of his keyboard output. He treated with the utmost care the grouping of cycles into sets to make them commercially viable, the organization of movements into unified cycles, the treatment of individual formal stereotypes, the building of sections and functions within forms, and the growth of individual phrases. To be sure, some movements coming at the end of a set were without doubt perfunctory efforts because he ran short of time, but they are hardly representative. What is really astonishing is that with the exception of set structure, Haydn never completely duplicates procedures and materials.

The grouping of works into sets first began in the 1770s with three *opere* of six solo sonatas. At this time Haydn carefully mixed progressive, conservative, popular, and learned compositions within a single set to make them commercially viable. Often the most impressive sonata would be placed last and the most conservative or popular first. Sonatas in the major mode predominate, and no more than two of the six are in minor. During the 1780s—beginning with the solo sonatas for Marie Esterházy of 1783–84—the grouping is reduced to three works, and this number became the standard for the trios of the 1780s and 1790s. Although the solo sonata set for Marie Esterházy contains only two-movement cycles, in the trio sets that follow, two- and three-movement cycles exist in the same *opera*. Normally two trios are in the major mode, and the one in minor frequently commences with a part and/or variation form.

The character of the sonatas and trios themselves was determined not only by commercial viability but just as much if not more by the tastes and/or abilities of those to whom they were dedicated. Compared with the striking works of the late 1760s and early 1770s, the six sonatas for Nikolaus Esterházy from 1773 are decidedly tailored to conservative tastes. On the other hand, the two sonatas for the Auenbrugger sisters that are in the minor mode are among Haydn's most sophisticated keyboard writing. The sonatas for Marie Esterházy from 1783–1784 lead one to believe that she was a performer with a light, rapid touch and a fine sense of timing, while from the single one for Maria Anna von Genzinger (Hob. XVI:49), one can surmise that her playing combined sophistication, expression, and elegance. Therese Jansen Bartolozzi was certainly the most brilliant pianist for whom Haydn expressly wrote; her works are characterized by virtuosity, sensitivity, power, and color.

Although Haydn's keyboard cycles contain as many as six or as few as two movements, it is the two- and three-movement types that appear fairly consistently over nearly five decades. The two-movement sonatas contain either a fast first movement (which includes pieces as slow as Moderato) almost always in sonata form, followed by a minuet type; or a slow first movement (as fast as Allegretto), often using variation- or part-form concepts, followed by a quick finale. Among the three-movement sonatas, Haydn employs five different plans: Fast–Slow–Fast; Fast–Slow–Minuet or Minuet–Styled; Fast–Minuet–Fast; Slow–Slow–Fast; and Slow–Fast–Minuet. Sonata form is preferred for the initial movement except in the Slow–Slow–Fast plan, where the formal preference is more closely related to the two-movement Slow–Fast cycles.

As for tonality, the primary keys of the extant keyboard works never exceed four sharps or flats, and the major mode predominates. Virtually all the two-movement sonatas retain the same key and mode; and in those with more than two movements, the minuet types never depart from the tonic. The monotonal, suite-like orientation of the early cycles was totally rejected by *ca.* 1788. In works such as Hob. XV:14, 19, 29, and XVI:52, from after 1788, tonality is used not only as a means of unity and low-level contrast but also for the special coloration that can be achieved by unusual juxtapositions of key. Thus, the early monotonal sonatas reflect the Viennese mid-century style, while the late ones foreshadow an emerging nineteenth-century tradition.[68]

As expected, Haydn relied on more than key to achieve cyclic unification. Within some of his earliest works, one can tentatively postulate that several similar incipits are efforts at unification. Besides the actual linkage of movements, the sonatas after 1765 gain coherence from procedures that are subtler, more convincing, and more individual. For instance, there may be internal motivic similarities, the recurrence of a striking harmony or tonality, an emphasis on color, an appropriate series of characteristic styles, or a proportional metric/tempo sequence. The resulting cycle coheres more through organic means and less through melodic contrivance.

One can also see some evolution in the dynamic curve of a cycle. In the earliest cycles there are several possibilities for the aesthetic center of gravity, including the trio of the minuet. After *ca.* 1765 the strongest movement is usually the first or second, with the finale being more diversionary. It is only after 1790 that in a few sonatas the climax is reserved for the concluding piece. This new dynamic curve of the cycle is not similar to the one in some of Beethoven's works: in Haydn's case, it usually results from a weakening of the opening movement's importance rather than from a pronounced strengthening of the last.

As for movement typologies, before *ca.* 1765 Haydn's opening movements were mainly marches with a few triple-meter dances; cantilenas of varying types, as well as *galant* minuets, dominated in the central movements; and duple-meter scherzos, Allegros or Prestos in 3/8, or *galant* minuets acted as the finales. From the mid-1760s to *ca.* 1771, the central pieces of the solo sonatas were no longer cantilenas but were more linear—with two employing an almost passacaglia-like texture and one modeled on the concerto. The concluding movement tended not to be a minuet with trio but a Tempo di Menuet, a quick movement in triple meter, or a duple-meter contradance-like piece; only the three most conservative works include a *da capo* minuet. During the 1770s and early 1780s Haydn backtracked in some respects to the style of the first period: cantilena slow movements, minuets with trios, and even a single 3/8 Presto finale. However, some minuets incorporated artifices (canon, al rovescio) and quotation ("Nightwatchman's Song"). In addition, previously unused dance and characteristic styles appeared: "innocente" ("innocentemente") sometimes with pastorale overtones, sarabandes, sicilianos, gigues, and a triple-meter scherzo. The most significant new type was a first movement with Allegro con brio and Vivace markings that had lost all its moderato *galant* march associations. Finales now favored duple-meter contradances over the Tempo di Menuet. In the works after 1788, first and internal movements did not change significantly, but the finales of the London sonatas and trios are notable for their variety of predominantly triple-meter styles.

Among the structural stereotypes, it is the sonata form that provides the most complete picture of Haydn's stylistic evolution. In his earliest period one finds a few first movements in which basic operating procedures seem not yet established: some are homogeneous, others diverse. But these works do reveal a mastery in their placement and strength of tonal articulations, motivic unity, and rhythmic flow. Despite the fact that the sonata forms from before *ca.* 1765 are small and technically undemanding, most are highly polished and musically convincing compositions. Their expositions are planned so that the arrival in the related key is their most significant event; i.e., although well established, the tonic is never articulated with the same strength as the secondary key. The developments emphasize thematic rather than tonal activity, for they may remain in a single key or even return to the tonic almost immediately, even though they work over a motive from the exposition. If several ideas are treated, they tend to follow the exposition's order. In a few instances the recapitulation begins without the primary material (P) or in a key other than the tonic; however, the convergence of the tonic and P is the rule. Overall, the recapitulation follows the exposition quite closely. But one already encounters recapitulations in which a portion of the exposition is excluded.

From the mid-1760s into 1771, Haydn's approach changed decisively. The sonata forms became larger in scope and deeper in expression. The exposition now articulated the tonic and related keys with almost equal weight. A transition (T) section, placed between the primary- and secondary-closing (S-K) functions, sometimes occupies more measures than the two key areas combined. During its course, the new key may be approached and withdrawn from before it is established with finality; T may also contain materials that are more improvisatory and in which the rhythmic continuity is broken. The development begins with P—or material from it—in the related key, and it is often followed by a working-out section and concluded with a retransition. As for tonal activity, most development sections from this period tend to center on the submediant to the extent that it assumes the role of a third key area. Just before or in the retransition, several or nearly all the parameters may converge for a climax. These "crescendos" are not isolated events but relate to the following recapitulation, which is now less like its respective exposition: the strong cadence that previously separated P from T has been deleted, replaced by a developmental continuation, and delayed until the conclusion. This delay in cadential articulations underlines the main function of the recapitulation—closure.

Although there are exceptions, from the middle of the 1770s to the middle of the 1780s the sonata forms do not have the depth of expression seen during the mid-1760s to ca. 1771; they can be said to build on the achievements of the previous sonatas but without such strong individual profiles. In many instances P reverts to the type of structure seen in the earliest works, T is more developmental, and S asserts the related key by restating P material transposed and/or by using the minor mode. At times the repetition of the P material at the beginning of S divides the exposition into two sections: P and its continuation; and S(P) with its continuation culminating in K, which becomes more identifiable by both cadential formulas and pedal points. The development and recapitulation most often follow the earlier practices, with some striking exceptions in the minor-mode movements.

From the late 1780s and into the 1790s, Haydn confronted the problems of homogeneity posed by the P–T–S(P)–K exposition structure, including its ramifications for both the development and the recapitulation sections. Some solutions were the exclusion of large portions of thematic material in the reprise, extensive variation of P, the interlocking of a false reprise with the events of the recapitulation, and delayed recognition of the recapitulation until the return of S(P). Tonally, the development contains a broad spectrum of keys, including tertian, Neapolitan, and enharmonic modulations, while thematically they are increasingly concerned with material other than P and an order of presentation less affected by the exposition.

The variation form seems to have fascinated Haydn most during the 1770s and 1780s. In the earliest efforts his Viennese Baroque heritage is evident; the embellishments are generated not so much from the melody as from the bass. The twenty-variation set Hob. XVII:2, composed in the mid-1770s, reveals Haydn's imaginative treatment of the articulations of the phrase within the strophe as well as the overall architecture of the set; and some five years later the concept of a single figuration or characteristic style for each strophe was replaced by changes at the phrase and subphrase level. Still greater freedom is evidenced in works from the 1770s: small changes in the bass line were allowed to occur, the strophic shape could be broken within a variation, two related themes might alternate, and some variations might initially function as a recapitulation. In variation sets from the 1780s the "theme" is sometimes so ornate that the process of variation seems to have changed from one based on increasing complexity to one in which the purest version occurs during the course of the movement rather than at the start. A recapitulatory variation at the end of a set occurred with decreasing frequency during the 1780s and almost disappeared by the time of the London works. In fact, one can say that the variation sets in cyclic works written during the 1790s are generally more conservative than those of the late 1780s.

Although the earliest rondo occurs in the keyboard works during the late 1760s, it is not until two decades later that rondos appear in relatively large numbers. They are normally in five parts, and the two episodes are frequently thematically related to the refrain. Indeed, it is for the rondo rather than the sonata form that the term monothematicism is most appropriate.[69] In the mature specimens the preparation for the refrain's return assumes an unexpected importance; it is characterized by repeated teasing upbeats that anticipate in an unprecedented yet notably Haydnesque manner. The episodes of the late 1780s and 1790s are remarkable for modulatory as well as thematic activity reminiscent of development sections in the sonata forms of this time.

Haydn's very first use of a keyboard rondo in the 1760s (Hob. XVI: 19/3) reveals one of the most distinctive aspects of his style: the amalgamation of characteristics of one formal stereotype with another. Here, the embellishment for the repetition of the refrain results in a variation rondo. Often this takes place when the repeats of a strain are written out, so that the first rendition functions as a recapitulation, the second as a variation. After the mid-1780s, as Haydn seemed to lose interest in the variation as well as its synthesis with the rondo, the sonata-rondo came to the fore. During the 1790s the rondos were therefore less affected by variation, while the "short-rondo" or ternary forms continued to be systematically embellished. There are also a couple of instances of "varied reprises" in the slow-movement rondo forms. Among those in a quick tempo, variation is restricted to the initial phrase or a small portion of P. Certainly if it were not for Haydn's liberating treatment of variation form during the 1770s and 1780s, one could not apply the concept of varied recurrence to the sonata structures of the late 1780s and 1790s.

Haydn's stylistic development in his keyboard compositions is marked by systematic concentration on a distinct set of compositional problems and their solution, followed by the confrontation of a new set. For the sonata form this process took nearly two decades; at first we find a few inept solutions, then a large number of skilled and polished but facile pieces, and finally during the mid- to late 1760s a series of supreme examples.

While many of the sonata-form movements of the next decade do not reach the depth of expression of some earlier pieces, they consistently reveal a high level of craftsmanship and originality, and by the late 1780s the sonata forms combined expression, sophistication, and outright popular appeal. For the variation sets there is also a watershed example from the mid-1760s (Hob. XVII:2), but Haydn experimented with more fundamental procedures from the 1770s to the end of the 1780s. It was not until the 1780s that the rondo emerged as one of his central concerns and achieved equal status with sonata form. Thus, by the 1790s Haydn had carried out a number of imaginative formal experiments in which thematic, harmonic, and rhythmic elements were combined in a masterly way; these achievements were then consolidated in the F-minor Variations, the solo sonatas, and the trios of the London period.

Early in his creative life Haydn asserted himself as a distinctive keyboard composer. In probing into his stylistic development in the solo and ensemble sonatas, we observe his confrontation with problems of form and style and his polished, complex solutions. To be sure, these solutions are often different from those found in his quartets and symphonies, but they are certainly no less worthy. From the Lilliputian solo and accompanied divertimentos to the more expansive sonatas, trios, and *Stücke*, one can conclude, as did the lexicographer Ernst Ludwig Gerber in 1790, that Haydn was "one of our greatest men; great in small things, yet greater in great ones."[70]

BIBLIOGRAPHY

Abert/KLAVIERSONATEN   Abert, Hermann. "Joseph Haydns Klaviersonaten." *ZfMw* III/9–10 (June–July 1921): 535–52.

Abert/KLAVIERWERKE   ———. "Joseph Haydns Klavierwerke." *ZfMw* II/10 (July 1920): 553–73.

ADB   *Allgemeine deutsche Bibliothek*

AfMw   *Archiv für Musikwissenschaft*

AM   *Almanach Musical*

AMu   *Acta Musicologica*

AMZ (Lpzg)   *Allgemeine Musikalische Zeitung* (Leipzig)

Anderson/MOZART LETTERS   Anderson, Emily. *The Letters of Mozart and his Family*, 2 vols. 2d ed. London: Macmillan; New York: St. Martin's Press, 1966.

Andrews/SUBMEDIANT   Andrews, Harold L. "The Submediant in Haydn's Development Sections." *Kongress Washington/ 1975*. Pp. 465–71.

Anthology Dorsch   Anthology owned by Dorsch entitled, "Divertimenta, ac Galantheriae varie a Diversis Autoribus Conscriptae Hauptsächl Del Signore Josef Haydn." A-Wgm: VII 40623.

Anthology Imperial   Anthology used by members of the Imperial Family. Presently bound in 3 vols. A-Wn: S.m. 3348, 11084, and 11085.

Anthology Roskovsky   Anthology in 2 vols. Copied by the Franciscan monk Pater Pantaleonem Roskovsky. H-Bn: Ms. Mus. 753 "Cymbalum Jubilationis." Ms. Mus. 749 "Musaum Pantaleonianum."

Anthology Vienna   Anthology in A-Wgm: SBQ 11537. 2 vols.

Apel/KEYBOARD   Apel, Willi. *The History of Keyboard Music to 1700*. Translated and revised by Hans Tischler. Bloomington: Indiana University Press, 1972.

Bach/AUTOBIOGRAPHY   [Bach, Carl Philip Emanuel.] *Carl Philip Emanuel Bach's Autobiography*. Facsimile of original edition of 1773 with critical annotations by William S. Newman. Hilversum: Frits A. M. Knuf, 1967.

Bach/VERSUCH   ———. *Versuch über die wahre Art das Clavier zu spielen*. 2 vols. Berlin: In Verlegung des Auctoris, 1753–62.

Badura-Skoda/PERFORMANCE   Badura-Skoda, Eva. "Performance Conventions in Beethoven's Early Works." Winter/Carr/BEETHOVEN, pp. 52–76.

Badura-Skoda/PROLEGOMENA   ———. "Prolegomena to a History of the Viennese Fortepiano." *Israel Studies in Musicology* II (1980): 77–99.

Badura-Skoda/REUTTER ————. "Georg Reutter." *MGG* XI:cols. 336–42.

Badura-Skoda/TEUTSCHE ————. "'Teutsche Comoedie-Arien' und Joseph Haydn." *Kongress Graz/1970.* Pp. 59–73.

Bartha/BRIEFE Bartha, Dénes, ed. *Joseph Haydn: Gesammelte Briefe und Aufzeichnungen. Unter Benützung der Quellensammlung von H. C. Robbins Landon.* Kassel: Bärenreiter, 1965.

Bartha/REPERTORY ————. "Haydn's Italian Opera Repertory at Eszterháza Palace." Festschrift Grout. Pp. 172–219.

Bartha/Somfai/HOK ————, and Somfai, László. *Haydn als Opernkapellmeister. Die Haydn-Dokumente der Esterházy-Opernsammlung.* Budapest: Verlag der Ungarischen Akademie der Wissenschaften, 1960.

Becker-Glauch/RISM Becker-Glauch, Irmgard. "Franz Joseph Haydn." *RISM* series A, I/4:140–279.

Benton/PLEYEL Benton, Rita. *Ignace Pleyel: A Thematic Catalogue of His Compositions.* New York: Pendragon Press, 1977.

Benton/RESUMÉ Benton, Rita. "A Resumé of the Haydn-Pleyel 'Trio Controversy' with Some Added Contributions." *H-St* IV/2 (May 1978):114–16.

Bernouilli/SAMMLUNG Bernouilli, Johann. *Sammlung kurzer Reisebeschreibungen.* Description by G. F. von R. [Rotenstein.] IX (1783):294–98.

Bertuch/BEMERKUNGEN Bertuch, Carl. *Bemerkungen auf einer Reise aus Thüringen nach Wien im Winter 1805 bis 1806.* Weimar: Landes-Industrie-Comptoir, 1808–10.

Biba/PÜRK [Birck] Biba, Otto. "Wenzel Raimund Pürk." *MGG* XVI: cols. 1522–23.

Bilson/SCHUBERT Bilson, Malcolm. "Schubert's Piano Music and the Pianos of His Time." *PQ* XXVII (Winter 1978–79):56–61.

BJb *Beethoven-Jahrbuch*

Blümml/MOZART Blümml, Emil Karl. *Aus Mozarts Freundes-und Familienkreis.* Vienna: Strache, 1923.

Bonta/SONATA DA CHIESA Bonta, Stephen. "The Uses of the Sonata da Chiesa." *JAMS* XXII/1 (Spring 1969):54–84.

Botstiber/ARTARIA Artaria, Franz, and Botstiber, Hugo. *Joseph Haydn und das Verlagshaus Artaria. Nach den Briefen des Meisters an das Haus Artaria & Compagnie dargestellt.* Vienna: Artaria & Co., 1909.

Braun/Gerlach/BARYTONTRIOS Braun, Jürgen, and Gerlach, Sonja, eds. *Joseph Haydn: Barytontrios. Nr. 1–24.* XIV/1 of *JHW-HI.* Munich: G. Henle, 1980.

Brook/BREITKOPF Brook, Barry S., ed. *The Breitkopf Thematic Catalogue. The Six Parts and Sixteen Supplements, 1762–1787.* New York: Dover, 1966.

Brown/BACH Brown, A. Peter. "Joseph Haydn and C. P. E. Bach: The Question of Influence." *Kongress Washington/1975.* Pp. 158–64.

Brown/CELERIO ———. "'Celerio, Le Dieu de Clavecin'; An Appraisal of Clementi?" *MT* CXX/1638 (August 1979):645–47.

Brown/CRITICAL ———. "Critical Years for Haydn's Instrumental Music: 1787–1790." *MQ* LXII/3 (July 1976): 374–94.

Brown/EARLIEST ENGLISH ———. "The Earliest English Biography of Haydn." *MQ* LIX/3 (July 1973):339–54.

Brown/EXPOSITION ———. "The Structure of the Exposition in Haydn's Keyboard Sonatas." *MR* XXXVI/2 (May 1975):102–29.

Brown/GENESIS ———. "Tommaso Traëtta and the Genesis of a Haydn Aria." *Chigiana* XXXVI/16 (1979):101–42

Brown/HAYDN-HOFMANN ———. "Joseph Haydn and Leopold Hofmann's 'Street Songs.'" *JAMS* XXXIII/2 (Summer 1980): 356–83.

Brown/MARTINES ———. "Marianna Martines' Autobiography as a New Source for Haydn's Biography during the 1750's." *Haydn-Studien* VI/1.

Brown/NOTES ———. "Notes on Some Eighteenth-Century Viennese Copyists." *JAMS* XXXIV/2 (Summer 1981):325–38.

Brown/PROBLEMS ———. "Problems of Authenticity in Two Haydn Keyboard Works (Hoboken XVI:47 and XIV:7)." *JAMS* XXV/1 (Spring 1972):85–97.

Brown/RAIGERN ———. "Haydn's Keyboard Idiom and the Raigern Sonatas." *Kongress Washington/1975.* Pp. 111–15.

Brown/REALIZATION ———. "Realization of an Idiomatic Keyboard Style in Sonatas of the 1770s." *Kongress Washington/1975.* Pp. 394–400.

Brown/RE-INTRODUCTION ———. "A Re-introduction to Joseph Haydn's Keyboard Works." *PQ* XXI/79 (Fall 1972):42–47.

Brown/SOLO AND ENSEMBLE ———. "The Solo and Ensemble Keyboard Sonatas of Joseph Haydn. A Study of Structure and Style." Ph.D. diss., Northwestern University, 1970.

Brown/UNDERSTANDING ———. "Approaching Musical Classicism— Understanding Styles and Style Change in Eighteenth-Century Instrumental Music." *College Music Symposium* XX/1 (Spring 1980):7–48.

Brown/WACKERNAGEL ———. Review of *Joseph Haydns frühe Klaviersonaten*, by Bettina Wackernagel. *NOTES* XXXIII/1 (September 1976):69–71.

Brown/Berkenstock/HAYDN ———, and Berkenstock, J. T. *Joseph Haydn in Literature: A Bibliography.* Munich: G. Henle, 1974 (*H-St* III/3–4).

Brusatti/HOB. XVI:49 Brusatti, Otto, ed. *Joseph Haydn. Klaviersonate in Es-Dur, Hob. XVI:49, Vollständige Faksimile-Ausgabe.* Graz: Akademische Druck- und Verlagsanstalt, 1982.

BullSIM *Bulletin de la société française des amis de la musique. Revue musicale S.I.M.*

Burney/HISTORY — Burney, Charles. *A General History of Music from the Earliest Ages to the Present Period, to Which is Prefixed a Dissertation on the Music of the Ancients*, 4 vols. London: 1776–89.

Burney/PRESENT STATE — _____. *The Present State of Music in Germany, the Netherlands and United Provinces*, 2 vols. London: Becket, Robson & Robinson, 1773.

Burney/REES (HAYDN) — ———. "Franz Joseph Haydn." *The Cyclopaedia: or Universal Dictionary of Arts, Sciences and Literature*, 39 vols. Edited by Abraham Rees. London: Longman, Hurst, Rees, Orme & Brown, 1819.

BzMw — *Beiträge zur Musikwissenschaft*

Carpani/HAYDINE — Carpani, Giuseppe. *Le Haydine, ovvero lettere su la vita e le opere del celebre maestro Giuseppe Haydn.* Milan: C. Buccinelli, 1812.

Chapman/MODULATION — Chapman, Roger E. "Modulation in Haydn's Piano Trios in the Light of Schoenberg's Theories." *Kongress Washington/1975.* Pp. 471–75.

Chew/NIGHT-WATCHMAN'S — Chew, Geoffrey. "The Night-Watchman's Song Quoted by Haydn and Its Implications." *H-St* III/2 (April 1974): 106–24.

Churgin/GALEAZZI — Churgin, Bathia. "Francesco Galeazzi's Description (1796) of Sonata Form." *JAMS* XXI/2 (Summer 1968): 181–99.

COBBETT'S — *Cobbett's Cyclopedic Survey of Chamber Music.* Edited by Walter Willson Cobbett. 2d ed. London: Oxford University Press, 1963.

Cole/DEVELOPMENT — Cole, Malcolm S[tanley]. "The Development of the Instrumental Rondo Finale from 1750–1800." Ph.D. diss., Princeton University, 1964.

Cole/RONDO — ———. "Rondos, Proper and Improper." *ML* LI/4 (October 1970): 388–99.

Cole/VOGUE — ———. "The Vogue of the Instrumental Rondo in the Late Eighteenth Century." *JAMS* XXII/3 (Fall 1969): 425–55.

Cone/FORM — Cone, Edward T. *Musical Form and Musical Performance.* New York: W. W. Norton, 1968.

Cooper/CLAVICHORD — Cooper, Kenneth. "The Clavichord in the Eighteenth Century." Ph.D. diss., Columbia University, 1971.

CRAMER'S — Cramer's *Magazin der Musik*

Crotch/LECTURES — Crotch, William. Substance of several courses of lectures on music, read in the University of Oxford, and in the Metropolis, 1831.

Cudworth/Brennecke/SCHRÖTER — Cudworth, Charles, and Brennecke, Wilfried. "Johann Samuel Schröter." *MGG* XII: cols. 89–90.

Daffner/ENTWICKLUNG — Daffner, Hugo. *Die Entwicklung des Klavierkonzerts bis Mozart.* (Publikationen der Internationalen Musikgesellschaft. Beihefte. Zweite Folge, 4). Leipzig: Breitkopf und Härtel, 1906.

Dart/INTERPRETATION — Dart, Thurston. *The Interpretation of Music.* London: Hutchinson & Co., 1954.

Davis/HOB. XVIII:F3 — Davis, Shelley G. "Regarding the Authenticity of the 'Haydn' Keyboard Concerto Hoboken XVIII: F3." *Kongress Washington/1975.* Pp. 121–26.

Davis/KOCH — ———. "H.C. Koch, the Classic Concerto, and the Sonata-Form Retransition." *JM* II/1 (Winter 1983):45–61.

Davis/LANG — ———. "The Keyboard Concertos of Johann Georg Lang (1722–1798)." Ph.D. diss., New York University, 1972.

Davis/MOZART — ———. "Harmonic Rhythm in Mozart's Sonata Form." *MR* XXVII/1 (February 1966):25–43.

Deutsch/HOBOKEN — Deutsch, Otto Erich. Review of *Joseph Haydn: Thematisch-bibliographisches Werkverzeichnis*, by Anthony van Hoboken. *MR* XVIII/4 (November 1957):330–36.

Dickinson/HANDBOOK — Dickinson, George Sherman. *A Handbook of Style in Music.* New York: Vassar College, 1965.

Dies/NACHRICHTEN — Dies, Albert Christoph. *Biographische Nachrichten von Joseph Haydn. Nach mündlichen Erzählungen desselben entworfen und herausgegeben von Albert Christoph Dies, Landschaftmahler.* Vienna: Camesinaische Buchhandlung, 1810. All citations from edition by Horst Seeger. Kassel: Bärenreiter, 1964.

Drummond/CONCERTO — Drummond, Pippa. *The German Concerto.* Oxford: Clarendon Press, 1980.

Drury/SEVEN — Drury, Jonathan Daniels. "Haydn's *Seven Last Words*: An Historical and Critical Study." Ph.D. diss., University of Illinois, 1975.

DTOe — *Denkmäler der Tonkunst in Österreich*

Eibner/KLAVIERFASSUNG — Eibner, Franz. "Die authentische Klavierfassung von Haydns Variationen über 'Gott erhalte'." *HYb* VII (1970):281–306.

Eibner/KLAVIERSTÜCKE — ———, and Jarecki, Gerschon, eds. *Joseph Haydn: Klavierstücke.* Mainz: B. Schott's Söhne [1975].

Einstein/MOZART — Einstein, Alfred. *Mozart: His Character and His Work.* New York: Oxford University Press, 1962.

Eitner/QL — Eitner, Robert. "Haydn, Joseph." *Biographisch-bibliographisches Quellen-Lexikon der Musiker und Musikgelehrten der christlichen Zeitrechnung bis zur Mitte des XIX. Jahrhunderts*, vol. V. Leipzig: Breitkopf & Härtel, 1901. Pp. 59–72.

EK — Entwurf-Katalog (Ms.) Copied by Haydn, Joseph Elssler, Sr., and Johann Schellinger. D-ddr-Bds.

EMLR — *European Magazine and London Review*

Engel/QUELLEN — Engel, Hans. "Die Quellen des klassischen Stiles." *Kongress New York/1961.* Vol. I, pp. 285–304; vol. II, pp. 135–39.

Feder/DATIERUNG — Feder, Georg. "Zur Datierung Haydnscher Werke." *Festschrift Hoboken/75th.* Pp. 50–54.

Feder/GROVE 6 ——. "Haydn, (Franz) Joseph—Work-list." *GROVE 6*, vol. 8, pp. 360–401.

Feder/HAYDN R ——. "Franz Joseph Haydn." Riemann/LEXIKON. Vol. I, pp. 499–504.

Feder/HUMMEL ——. "Die Eingriffe des Musikverlegers Hummel in Haydns Werken." Festschrift Fellerer/70. Pp. 88–101.

Feder/KB JHW XII/1 ——. *Kritische Bericht. JHW-H1* XII/1.

Feder/KLAVIERSONATEN ——, ed. *Joseph Haydn: Klaviersonaten. JHW-HI* XVIII/1–3 (1966–70).

Feder/KLAVIERTRIOS ——. "Haydns frühe Klaviertrios. Eine Untersuchung zur Echtheit und Chronologie." *H-St* II/4 (December 1970):289–316.

Feder/KLEINES KONZERT ——. Review of *Joseph Haydn: Kleines Konzert für Klavier/Cembalo. Mf* XVII/4 (October/December 1964):461–62.

Feder/KORREKTUREN ——. "Haydns Korrekturen zum Klavierauszug der 'Jahreszeiten'." Festschrift Dadelsen/60th. Pp. 101–12.

Feder/MANUSCRIPT ——. "Manuscript Sources of Haydn's Works and Their Distribution." Translated by Eugene Hartzell. *HYb* IV (1968):102–39. A translation of Feder/QUELLEN.

Feder/MENSCH ——. "Joseph Haydn als Mensch und Musiker." *JböK* II (1972):43–56.

Feder/NICHT IDENTIFIZIERTEN ——. "Über Haydns Skizzen zu nicht identifizierten Werken." Festschrift Hüschen/65. Pp. 100–11.

Feder/ORGELKONZERTE ——. "Wieviel Orgelkonzerte hat Haydn geschrieben?" *Mf* XXIII/4 (October–December 1970):440–44.

Feder/OSTIGLIA ——. "Eine Haydn-Skizze in Ostiglia." *Studien zur italienisch-deutschen Musikgeschichte*, VIII. Edited by Friedrich Lippmann. Cologne: Arno Volk, 1973. Pp. 224–26.

Feder/PROBLEME ——. "Probleme einer Neuordnung der Klaviersonaten Haydns." Festschrift Blume/70th. Pp. 92–103.

Feder/QUELLEN ——. "Die Überlieferung und Verbreitung der handschriftlichen Quellen zu Haydns Werken (Erste Folge)." *H-St* I/1 (June 1965):3–42.

Feder/SK III ——ed., *Joseph Haydn: Sämtliche Klaviersonaten.* Band III. Munich: Henle, 1972.

Feder/SKIZZEN ——. Bemerkungen zu Haydns Skizzen." *BJb* 1973–77. Pp. 69–86.

Feder/SOURCES ——. "The Sources of the Two Disputed Raigern Sonatas." *Kongress Washington/1975.* Pp. 107–11.

Feder/TYPISCHES ——. "Typisches bei Haydn. Eine Methode der Stiluntersuchung." *ÖMz* XXIV/1 (January 1969): 11–17.

Feder/ZWEI HAYDN ———. "Zwei Haydn zugeschriebene Klaviersonaten." *Kongress Kassel/1962*. Pp. 181–84.

Federhofer/Riedel/FUX Federhofer, Hellmut, and Riedel, Friedrich Wilhelm. "Quellenkundliche Beiträge zur Johann Joseph Fux-Forschung." *AfMw* XXI/2 (August 1964):111–40.

Fellerer/KLAVIERBEARBEITUNG Fellerer, Karl Gustav. "Klavierbearbeitungen Haydnscher Werke im frühen 19. Jahrhundert." Festschrift Larsen/70th. Pp. 301–16.

Festschrift Blume/70th *Festschrift Friedrich Blume zum 70. Geburtstag.* Edited by Anna Amalie Abert and Wilhelm Pfannkuch. Kassel: Bärenreiter, 1963.

Festschrift Dadelsen/60th *Festschrift Georg von Dadelsen zum 60. Geburtstag.* Edited by Thomas Kohlhase und Volker Scherliess. Neuhausen: Hanssler, 1978.

Festschrift Davison *Essays on Music in Honor of Archibald Thompson Davison by His Associates.* Cambridge: Harvard University Department of Music, 1957.

Festschrift Fellerer/70th *Musicae Scientiae Collectanea. Festschrift Karl Gustav Fellerer zum siebzigsten am 7 Juli 1972.* Edited by Heinrich Hüschen. Cologne: Volk, 1973.

Festschrift Geiringer/70th *Studies in Eighteenth-Century Music. A Tribute to Karl Geiringer on His Seventieth Birthday.* Edited by H. C. Robbins Landon and Roger E. Chapman. New York: Oxford University Press, 1970.

Festschrift Grout *New Looks at Italian Opera. Essays in Honor of Donald J. Grout.* Edited by William W. Austin. Ithaca: Cornell University Press, 1968.

Festschrift Hoboken/75th *Anthony van Hoboken. Festschrift zum 75. Geburtstag.* Edited by Joseph Schmidt-Görg. Mainz: B. Schott's Söhne, 1962.

Festschrift Hüschen/70th *Ars Musica. Musica Scientia. Festschrift Heinrich Hüschen zum 65. Geburtstag.* Edited by Detlef Altenburg. Cologne: Gitarre & Laute Verlagsgesellschaft, 1980.

Festschrift King *Music and Bibliography. Essays in Honour of Alec Hyatt King.* Edited by Oliver Neighbour. New York: Clive Bingley, 1980.

Festschrift Kodály/75th *Zenetudományi tanulmányok Kodály Zoltán 75. születésnapjára* (Zenetudományi Tanulmányok, VI). Edited by Bence Szabolcsi and Dénes Bartha. Budapest: Akadémiai Kiadó, 1957.

Festschrift Larsen/70th *Festkrift Jens Peter Larsen 14. VI. 1902–1972.* Edited by Nils Schiørring, Henrik Glahn, and Carsten E. Hatting. Copenhagen: Wilhelm Hansen Musik-Forlag, 1972.

Festschrift Schmidt-Görg/60th *Festschrift Joseph Schmidt-Görg zum 60. Geburtstag.* Edited by Dagmar Weise. Bonn: Beethovenhaus, 1957.

Festschrift Schmidt-Görg/70th   *Colloquium Amicorum. Joseph Schmidt-Görg zum 70. Geburtstag.* Edited by Siegfried Kross and Hans Schmidt. Bonn: Beethovenhaus, 1967.

Festschrift Vötterle/65th   *Musik und Verlag. Karl Vötterle zum 65. Geburtstag am 12 April 1968.* Edited by Richard Baum and Wolfgang Rehm. Kassel: Bärenreiter, 1968.

Fillion/ACCOMPANIED   Fillion, Michelle. "Joseph Haydn's Early Accompanied Keyboard Music and Its Position in Austrian Chamber Music, 1750–1770." Ph.D. diss. Cornell University, 1982.

Fillion/HOB. XV:C1   ———. "Eine bisher unbekannte Quelle für Haydns frühes Klaviertrio Hob. XV:C1." *H-St* V/1 (31 March 1982): 59–63.

Fillion/SONATA-EXPOSITION   ———. "Sonata-Exposition Procedures in Haydn's Keyboard Sonatas." *Kongress Washington/1975.* Pp. 475–81.

Finscher/STREICHQUARTETTS   Finscher, Ludwig. *Studien zur Geschichte des Streichquartetts.* Vol. 1: *Die Entstehung des klassischen Streichquartetts.* Kassel: Bärenreiter, 1974.

Fischer/ENTWICKLUNG   Fischer, Wilhelm. "Zur Entwicklungsgeschichte des Wiener klassischen Stils." *StMw* III (1915): 24–84.

Fischer/VARIATION   Fischer, Kurt von. "Variation." *MGG* XIII: cols. 1274–1309.

Fischer/WIENER   Fischer, Wilhelm. *Wiener Instrumentalmusik vor und um 1750. 2 Auswahl: Matthias Georg Monn, Johann Christoph Mann.* Jahrg. XIX/2, Band 39 of *DTOe.*

Forer/ORGELN   Forer, Alois. *Orgeln in Österreich.* Vienna and Munich: Schroll, 1973.

Framery/NOTICE   Framery, Nicolas Étienne. *Notice sur Joseph Haydn. . . . Contenant quelques particularités de sa vie privée, relatives à sa personne ou à ses ouvrages.* Paris: Barba, 1810.

Franz/MOZARTS KLAVIERBAUER   Franz, Gottfried von. *Mozarts Klavierbauer Anton Walter. MJb* I (1941): 211–17.

Freeman/MELK   Freeman, Robert Norman. "The Practice of Music at Melk Monastery in the Eighteenth Century." Ph.D. diss., University of California, 1971.

Froggatt/TRIOS   Froggatt, Arthur T. "Haydn's Trios." *MT* LXXIII/1074 (August 1932): 741–42.

Fruewald/HAYDN   Fruewald, Scott. "Authenticity Problems in Franz Joseph Haydn's Early Instrumental Works: A Stylistic Investigation." Ph.D. diss., CUNY, 1984.

Fuchs/VERZEICHNISS 1839   Fuchs, Aloys [Alois]. "Thematisches Verzeichniss der sämmtlichen Compositionen von Joseph Haydn . . . 1839." (Ms.) D-brd-Mbs.

Fuchs/VERZEICHNISS 1840   ———. "Thematisches Verzeichniss der sämmtlichen Compositionen von Joseph Haydn . . . Wien 1840." (Ms.) D-ddr-Bds.

Fuller/ACCOMPANIED

Geiringer/HAYDN

Gerber/ATL

Gerber/NTL

Gericke/MUSIKALIENHANDEL

Gerlach/Hob. XVIIa: 1

Gerlach/KLAVIERSTÜCKE

Gerlach/ORDNUNG

Gerlach/RAIGERN

Gerlach/RECONSTRUCTED

Gerlach/Hill/LAUFWERK

Göthel/STEIN

Gotwals/TCP

Graue/HAYDN

Grave/DITTERSDORF

Griesinger/NOTIZEN

Fuller, David. "Accompanied Keyboard Music."
MQ LX/2 (April 1974): 222–45.

Geiringer, Karl. *Haydn. A Creative Life in Music.*
Berkeley: University of California Press, 1982.

Gerber, Ernst Ludwig. "Joseph Haydn." *Histo-
risch-biographisches Lexikon der Tonkünstler. . . ,*
vol. I. Leipzig: J. G. I. Breitkopf, 1790–92. Cols.
609–12.

———. "Joseph Haydn." *Neues historisch-bio-
graphisches Lexikon der Tonkünstler, welches Nachrichten von dem Leben und den Werken musikalischer
Schriftsteller, berühmter Komponisten, Sänger (etc.)
. . . enthält,* vol. II. Leipzig: A. Kühnel, 1812.
Pp. 535–605.

Gericke, Hannelore. *Der Wiener Musikalienhandel
von 1700 bis 1778* (Wiener musikwissenschaftliche
Beiträge, 5). Graz and Cologne: Hermann Böhlaus, 1960.

Gerlach, Sonja, ed. *Joseph Haydn: Divertimento Il
maestro e lo scolare.* Munich: G. Henle, 1982.

———, ed. *Joseph Haydn: Klavierstücke.* Munich:
G. Henle, 1969.

———. "Die chronologische Ordnung von Haydns
Sinfonien zwischen 1774 und 1782." *H-St* II/1
(March 1969): 34–66.

———. "Remarks on the Structure and Harmony
of the Raigern Sonatas." *Kongress Washington/
1975.* Pp. 115–17.

———. "The Reconstructed Original Version of
Haydn's Baryton Trio Hob. XI: 2." *Kongress Wash-
ington/1975.* Pp. 84–87.

Gerlach, Sonja, and Hill, George R., eds. *Joseph
Haydn: Stücke für das Laufwerk [Flötenuhrstücke].*
JHW-HI XXI (1984).

Göthel, Folker. "Familie Stein." *MGG* XII: cols.
1230–34.

Gotwals, Vernon. *Haydn: Two Contemporary Portraits.* Madison: University of Wisconsin Press,
1968.

Graue, Gerald. "Haydn and the London Pianoforte
School." *Kongress Washington/1975.* Pp. 422–31.

Grave, Margaret Grupp. "First-movement Form as
a Measure of Dittersdorf's Symphonic Development." Ph.D. diss., New York University, 1977.

Griesinger, Georg August. "Biographische Notizen über Joseph Haydn." *AMZ* (Lpzg) XI/41–47,
49 (July 12–August 23, 1809; September 6,
1809): 641–49, 657–68, 673–81, 689–99, 705–
13, 721–33, 737–47, 776–81. All citations from
the Franz Grasberger edition. Vienna: Kaltschmid,
1954.

GROVE 2   *Grove's Dictionary of Music and Musicians.* 2d ed.
                              Edited by J. A. Fuller-Maitland. 1900.

GROVE 6   *The New Grove Dictionary of Music and Musicians.*
                              6th ed. Edited by Stanley Sadie. 1980.

Grundmann/CLAVICEMBALO   Grundmann, Herbert. "Per il Clavicembalo o
                              Piano-Forte." Festschrift Schmidt-Görg/70th.
                              Pp. 100–17.

Gyrowetz/AUTOBIOGRAPHY   Gyrowetz, Adalbert. *Biographie des Adalbert Gyro-
                              wetz.* Vienna: Mechitharisten-Buchdruckerei,
                              1848.

Harding/PIANO-FORTE   Harding, Rosamond Evelyn Mary. *The Pianoforte:
                              Its History Traced to the Great Exhibition of 1851.*
                              New York: Da Capo Press, 1973.

Harich/DOCUMENTA   Harich, János [Johann]. "Haydn Documenta."
                              HYb II 1963/64 (1964):2–44; III 1965 (1966):
                              122–52; IV (1968):39–101; VII (1970):47–
                              168; VIII (1971):70–163.

Harich/REPERTOIRE   ———. "Das Repertoire des Opernkapellmeisters
                              Joseph Haydn in Eszterháza (1780–1790)." *HYb* I
                              (1962):9–110.

Hase/BREITKOPF   Hase, Hermann von. *Joseph Haydn und Breitkopf
                              & Härtel. Ein Rückblick bei der Veranstaltung der
                              ersten vollständigen Gesamtausgabe seiner Werke.*
                              Leipzig: Breitkopf & Härtel, 1909.

Haselböck/HAYDN   Haselböck, Franz, ed. *Joseph Haydn.* Drei Praeam-
                              beln h.v. XVII:C2, Andante f-dur h.v. XVII:F2.
                              Hilversum: Harmonia, 1979.

Hatting/HAYDN ODER KAYSER?   Hatting, Carsten E. "Haydn oder Kayser?—Eine
                              Echtheitsfrage." *Mf* XXV/2 (April–June 1972):
                              82–87.

Hatting/KLAVIERMUSIK   ———. "Klaviermusik." *Colloquium Musica Bo-
                              hemica et Europaea. Brno 1970.* N.p.: 1972. Pp.
                              325–48.

HAYDN EMLÉKÉRE   *Haydn Emlékére.* (Zenetudományi Tanulmányok,
                              VIII). Edited by Bence Szabolcsi and Dénes Bar-
                              tha. Budapest: Akadémiai Kiadó, 1960.

HBV   *Haydn Bibliothek Verzeichnis.* British Museum Add.
                              Ms. 32070.

Helm/BACH   Helm, Ernest Eugene. *A New Thematic Catalogue
                              of the Works of Carl Philipp Emanuel Bach.* New
                              Haven: Yale University Press, forthcoming.

Heussner/HAYDN-FUNDE   Heussner, Horst. "Zwei neue Haydn-Funde." *Mf*
                              XIII/4 (October–December 1960):451–55.

Heussner/HOB XV:40   ———, ed. "Joseph Haydn: Trio in F major." Hob.
                              XV:40, *Diletto Musicale* No. 4. Vienna: Doblinger,
                              1959.

Heussner/KONZERT   ———. "Joseph Haydns Konzert (Hoboken XVIII:
                              5). Marginalien zur Quellenüberlieferung." *Mf*
                              XXII/4 (October–December 1969):478–80.

Hill/GASSMANN

Hiller/ENTWURF

Hiller/NACHRICHTEN

HNV

Hoboken/DISCREPANCIES

Hoboken/WERKVERZEICHNIS

Hofer/REUTTER

Hoffmann-Erbrecht/DEUTSCHE UND ITALIENISCHE

Hoffmann-Erbrecht/HAFFNER

Hogwood/HAYDN

Hollis/INSTRUMENTS

H-St
Hughes/HAYDN

HV

HYb
Iffland/FISCHER PROFESSOR

J/NEUE FUNDE

James/CLAVICHORD

Hill, George R. "The Concert Symphonies of Florian Leopold Gassmann." Ph.D. diss., New York University, 1975.

Hiller, J. A. "Entwurf einer musikalischen Bibliothek." *Unterhaltung* (Hamburg), VII (1769):270.

———. "Wien." *Wöchentliche Nachrichten und Anmerkungen die Musik betreffend*, no. 13 (September 23, 1766):97–100.

Haydn Nachlass Verzeichnis. Archiv der Stadt Wien, Persönlichkeiten, 4/1–4.

Hoboken, Anthony van. *Discrepancies in Haydn Biographies*. Translated by Donald Mintz. Washington, D.C.: The Library of Congress, 1962.

———. *Joseph Haydn: Thematisch-bibliographisches Werkverzeichnis*. Vol. I: *Instrumentalwerke*. Vol. II: *Vokalwerke*. Vol. III: *Register, Addenda und Corrigenda*. Mainz: B. Schott's Söhne, 1957–78.

Hofer, N. *Thematisches Verzeichnis der Werke Georg Reutters d.J.* (Ms.) A-Wn.

Hoffmann-Erbrecht, Lothar. *Deutsche und italienische Klaviermusik zur Bachzeit*. Leipzig: Breitkopf & Härtel, 1954.

———. "Der Nürnberger Musikverleger: Johann Ulrich Haffner" and "Nachträge." *AMu*, XXVI (1954):114–26; XXVII (1955):141–42.

Hogwood, Christopher. *Haydn's Visits to England*. London: The Folio Society, 1980.

Hollis, Helen R. *The Musical Instruments of Joseph Haydn: An Introduction*. Washington, D.C.: Smithsonian Institution Press, 1977.

Haydn-Studien

Hughes, Rosemary. *Haydn*. Rev. ed. London: J. M. Dent; New York: Farrar, Straus, and Cudahy, 1962.

"Verzeichniss aller derjenigen Compositionen welche ich mich beyläufig erinnere von meinem 18ten bis in das 73ste Jahr verfertiget zu haben." (Ms.) Copied by Johann Elssler [1805].

The Haydn Yearbook

Iffland, August Wilhelm. "Fischer Professor, Bildhauer, und Maler Maurer in Wien. (Besuch bei Joseph Haydn den 8. September 1808.)" *Almanach fürs Theater* (Berlin, 1811):181–207.

J., V. "Neue Funde an Haydn'schen Kompositionen." *ZfM* C/4 (April 1933):376.

James, Philip. "Haydn's Clavichord and a Sonata Manuscript." *MT* LXXI/1046 (April 1930): 314–16.

JAMS	*Journal of the American Musicological Society*
JböK	*Jahrbuch für österreichische Kulturgeschichte.* I/2 (1971):*Beiträge zur Musikgeschichte des 18. Jahrhunderts.* II (1972):*Joseph Haydn und seine Zeit.*
JbTWP	Schönfeld, Johann Ferdinand, Ritter von. *Jahrbuch der Tonkunst von Wien und Prag.* Vienna: Im von Schönfeldischen Verlag, 1796; facsimile edition, Munich: E. Katzbichler, 1976.
JHW-BH	*Joseph Haydns Werke. Erste kritisch durchgesehene Gesamtausgabe.* Leipzig: Breitkopf & Härtel [1907–33].
JHW-HI	*Joseph Haydn Werke.* Edited by the Joseph Haydn-Institut, Cologne, under the direction of Jens Peter Larsen (1958–61) and Georg Feder (1962–). Munich and Duisburg: G. Henle Verlag, 1958–.
JM	*Journal of Musicology*
JMT	*Journal of Music Theory*
Johannson/FRENCH	Johansson, Cari. *French Music Publishers' Catalogues of the Second Half of the Eighteenth Century.* 2 vols. Stockholm: Almquist & Wiksell, 1955.
Johnson/LIVES	Johnson, Samuel. *Lives of the English Poets*, vol. 2. London: Oxford University Press [1906].
Kamien/HOB. XVI:36	Kamien, Roger. "Aspects of Motivic Elaboration in the Opening Movement of Haydn's Piano Sonata in C-Sharp Minor." *Aspects of Schenkerian Theory.* Edited by David Beach. New Haven: Yale University Press, 1983. Pp. 77–93.
Kamien/SONATA ALLEGRO	———. "The Opening Sonata-Allegro Movements in a Randomly Selected Sample of Solo Keyboard Sonatas Published in the Years 1742–1744 (inclusive)." Ph.D. diss., Princeton University, 1964.
Karajan/HAYDN	Karajan, Th. G. von. *J. Haydn in London: 1791 und 1792.* Vienna: Karl Gerolds Sohn, 1861.
Keller/K. 503	Keller, Hans. "K.503: The Unity of Contrasting Themes and Movements." *MR* XVII (1956):48–58, 120–29.
Kelly/REMINISCENCES	[Kelly, Michael.] *Reminiscences of Michael Kelly, of the King's Theatre and Theatre Royal, Drury Lane, Including a Period of Nearly Half a Century; with Original Anecdotes of Many Distinguished Persons, Political, Literary, and Musical.* 2d ed. London: H. Colburn, 1826. New edition by Roger Fisk. London: Oxford University Press, 1975.
Kinsky/HAMMERKLAVIER	Kinsky, Georg. "Haydn und das Hammerklavier." *ZfMw* XIII/9–10 (June–July 1931):500–501.
Kirkendale/FUGUE	Kirkendale, Warren. *Fugue and Fugato in Rococo and Classical Chamber Music.* 2d ed. Durham: Duke University Press, 1979.
Klier/VOLKSLIEDTHEMA	Klier, Karl M. "Das Volksliedthema eines Haydn-Capriccios." *Das deutsche Volkslied*, XXXIV/7–8 (September–October 1932):88–95, 100–104.

Knight/AUTOBIOGRAPHY [Knight, Ellis Cornelia.] *The Autobiography of Miss Knight*. Edited by Roger Fulford. London: William Kimber, 1960.

Koch/VERSUCH Koch, Heinrich Christoph. *Versuch einer Anleitung zur Composition*. 3 vols. Leipzig: A. F. Böhme, 1782–1793.

Köchel/MOZART/6 Köchel, Ludwig Ritter von. *Chronologisch-thematisches Verzeichnis sämtlicher Tonwerke Wolfgang Amadé Mozarts*. 6th ed. Edited by Franz Giegling, Alexander Weinmann, and Gerd Sievers.

Koller/WERKSTATT Koller, Walter. *Aus der Werkstatt der Wiener Klassiker: Bearbeitung Haydns, Mozarts und Beethovens*. Edited with an introduction by Helmut Hell. Münchner Veröffentlichungen zur Musikgeschichte, No. 23. Tutzing: Hans Schneider, 1975.

Kollman/ESSAY Kollman, Augustus Frederic Christopher. *An Essay on Practical Musical Composition*. London: N.p., 1799; reprint edition, New York: Da Capo Press, 1973.

Kollpacher/MATIELLI Kollpacher, Ingrid. "Giovanni Antonio Matielli." *MGG* VIII: cols. 1789–90.

Kollpacher/MONN ———. "Mathias Georg Monn." *MGG* IX: cols. 470–72.

Kongress Graz/1970 *Der junge Haydn. Wandel von Musikauffassung und Musikaufführung in der österreichischen Musik zwischen Barock und Klassik. Bericht der internationalen Arbeitstagung des Instituts für Aufführungspraxis der Hochschule für Musik und darstellende Kunst in Graz, 29. 6.-2. 7. 1970*. (Beiträge zur Aufführungspraxis, 1). Edited by Vera Schwarz. Graz: Akademische Druck- und Verlagsanstalt, 1972.

Kongress Kassel/1962 *Gesellschaft für Musikforschung. Bericht über den Internationalen Musikwissenschaftlichen Kongress Kassel, 1962*. Edited by Georg Reichert and Martin Just. Kassel: Bärenreiter, 1963.

Kongress New York/1961 *International Musicological Society. Report of Eighth Congress*. Edited by Jan LaRue. New York: American Musicological Society; Kassel: Bärenreiter, 1961.

Kongress Washington/1975 *Haydn Studies. Proceedings of the International Haydn Conference, Washington, D.C., 1975*. Edited by Jens Peter Larsen, Howard Serwer, and James Webster. New York: W. W. Norton, 1981.

Kramer/TWO ASPECTS Kramer, Richard. "On the Dating of Two Aspects in Beethoven's Notation for Piano." *Österreichische Gesellschaft für Musik. Beiträge 76–78: Beethoven-Kolloquium 1977*. Kassel: Bärenreiter, 1978. Pp. 160–73.

Kunsthistorisches Museum/ SAITENKLAVIERE *Katalog der Sammlung alter Musikinstrumente*. Vol. 1: *Saitenklaviere*. Vienna: Kunsthistorisches Museum, 1966.

Landon/C&W   Landon, H. C. Robbins. *Haydn: Chronicle and Works*. 5 vols. Bloomington: Indiana University Press, 1976–80.

Landon/CCLN   ———, ed. *The Collected Correspondence and London Notebooks of Joseph Haydn*. London: Barrie and Rockliff; Fair Lawn, N.J.: Essential Books, 1959.

Landon/DIVERTIMENTO   ———, ed. "Joseph Haydn: Divertimento in D major." [Hob. deest.] *Diletto Musicale* Nr. 86. Vienna: Doblinger, 1960.

Landon/ESSAYS   ———. *Essays on the Viennese Classical Style*. New York: Macmillan, 1970.

Landon/FOREWORD   ———. *The Piano Trios of Joseph Haydn. Foreword to the First Critical Complete Edition*. Vienna: Doblinger, 1970.

Landon/KLAVIERSONATEN   Landon, Christa. *Joseph Haydn: Sämtliche Klaviersonaten*, vols. I–III. (Wiener Urtext Ausgabe). Vienna: Universal, 1963.

Landon/KLAVIERSONATEN KA   ———. *Haydn sämtliche Klaviersonaten. Kritische Anmerkungen*. Vienna: Universal Edition, 1982.

Landon/LETTERS   Landon, H. C. Robbins. "Four New Haydn Letters" *HYb* XIII (1982):213–19.

Landon/ORGAN   Landon, H. C. Robbins, ed. "Joseph Haydn: Concerto per l'organo, Nr. 2." [Hob. XVIII:8 in C major.] *Diletto Musicale* Nr. 80. Vienna: Doblinger, 1962.

Landon/PIANO SONATAS   ———. "Haydn's Piano Sonatas." *Landon/ESSAYS*. Pp. 44–67.

Landon/RT VIb   Landon, Christa. *Kongress Washington/1975*. Pp. 118–20.

Landon/SKETCH   Landon, H. C. Robbins. "Joseph Haydn: A Sketch to Piano Trio No. 30 (Hob. XV:17)." *HYb* XIII (1982):220–27.

Landon/SYMPHONIES   ———. *The Symphonies of Joseph Haydn*. London: Universal Edition, Rockliff, 1955; New York: Macmillan, 1956.

Landon/SYMPHONIES-   ———. *The Symphonies of Joseph Haydn: Supple-
 SUPPLEMENT   ment*. London: Barrie & Rockliff, 1961.

Landon/TRIO   ———, ed. "Joseph Haydn: Trio in D major." [Hob. XV: deest.] *Diletto Musicale* Nr. 533. Vienna: Doblinger, 1976.

Lang/HAYDN-KLAVIER   Lang, Gerhard M. "Das Haydn-Klavier im nö. Landesmuseum." *Kulturberichte aus Niederösterreich* (Vienna) 5 (May 15, 1956):37.

Lang/OPERA   Lang, Paul Henry. "Haydn and the Opera." *MQ* XVIII/2 (April 1932):274–81.

Langley/ENGLISH   Langley, Leanne. "The English Musical Journal in the Early Nineteenth Century." Ph.D. diss., University of North Carolina, 1983.

Larsen/CONTRACT   Larsen, Jens Peter. "A Haydn Contract." *MT* CXVII/1603 (September 1976):737–38.

Larsen/DHK [1 and 2] ——, ed. *Drei Haydn Kataloge in Faksimile mit Einleitung und ergänzenden Themenverzeichnissen.* 2d ed. Copenhagen: Einar Munksgaard, 1941. *Three Haydn Catalogues.* New York: Pendragon, 1979.

Larsen/DISKUSSION ——. "Diskussion." *Kongress Graz/1970.* P. 248.

Larsen/ECHTHEITSPROBLEM I ——. "Das Echtheitsproblem in der Musik des 18. Jahrhunderts." *JböK* II (1972):25–39.

Larsen/ECHTHEITSPROBLEM II ——. "Über Echtheitsprobleme in der Musik der Klassik." *Mf* XXV/1 (January–March 1972): 4–16.

Larsen/HÜB ——. *Die Haydn-Überlieferung.* Copenhagen: Einar Munksgaard, 1939.

Larsen/KLAVIERSONATE ——. *Joseph Haydn. Klaviersonate A-dur.* Munich and Duisburg: G. Henle Verlag, 1958.

Larsen/QUELLE ——. "Eine bisher unbeachtete Quelle zu Haydns frühen Klavierwerken." *Festschrift Schmidt-Görg/60th.* Pp. 188–95.

Larsen/SONATENFORM-PROBLEME ——. "Sonatenform-Probleme." *Festschrift Blume/70th.* Pp. 221–30.

Larsen/Landon/HAYDN ——, and Landon, H. C. Robbins. "Franz Joseph Haydn." *MGG* V: cols. 1857–1933.

LaRue/AUTHENTICATION LaRue, Jan. "Mozart Authentication by Activity Analysis: A Progress Report." *MJb* (1978–79): 209–14.

LaRue/BEETHOVEN ——. "Harmonic Rhythm in the Beethoven Symphonies." *MR* XVIII/1 (February 1957):8–20.

LaRue/BIFOCAL ——. "Bifocal Tonality: an Explanation for Ambiguous Baroque Cadences." *Festschrift Davison.* Pp. 173–84.

LaRue/GUIDELINES ——. *Guidelines for Style Analysis.* New York: W. W. Norton, 1970.

LaRue/MAJOR AND MINOR ——. "Major and Minor Mysteries of Identification in the 18th-Century Symphony." *JAMS* XIII (1960), 181–96.

LaRue/MOZART ——. "Mozart or Dittersdorf." *MJb* (1971–72), 40–49.

LaRue/MULTISTAGE ——. "Multistage Variance: Haydn's Legacy to Beethoven." *JM* I/3 (July 1982):265–74.

LaRue/ON STYLE ——. "On Style Analysis." *JMT* VI/1 (Spring 1962):91–107.

LaRue/SIGNIFICANT ——. "Significant and Coincidental Resemblance Between Classical Themes." *JAMS* XIV/2 (Summer 1961):224–34.

Latrobe/SELECTION Latrobe, Christian Ignatz. *A Selection of Sacred Music from the Work of Some of the Eminent Composers of Germany and Italy.* London, 1806–26.

Loesser/PIANOS Loesser, Arthur. *Men, Women and Pianos: A Social History.* New York: Simon and Schuster, 1954.

Longyear/BINARY-VARIANTS   Longyear, R. M. "Binary Variants of Early Clas-
                                sic Sonata Form." *JMT* XIII/2 (Winter 1969):
                                162–85.

Lowinsky/MOZART   Lowinsky, Edward E. "On Mozart's Rhythm." *MQ*
                                XLII/2 (April 1956):162–86.

Luithlen/EISENSTÄDTER   Luithlen, Victor. "Der Eisenstädter Walterflügel,"
  WALTERFLÜGEL   *MJb* V (1954):206–208.
Luithlen/HAYDN-   ———. "Haydn-Erinnerungen in der Sammlung
  ERINNERUNGEN   alter Musikinstrumente des Kunsthistorischen
                                Museums zu Wien." Festschrift Hoboken/75th.
                                Pp. 110–14.

Luithlen/HAYDN-INSTRUMENTE   ———. "Haydn-Instrumente der Gesellschaft der
                                Musikfreunde in Wien." *ÖK* III/3–4 (March–
                                April 1932):40, 43.

Mann/ELEMENTARBUCH   Mann, Alfred. "Haydn's Elementarbuch: A Docu-
                                ment of Classic Counterpoint Instruction." *Music
                                Forum* III (1973):197–237.

Mann/STUDENT   ———. "Haydn as Student and Critic of Fux."
                                Festschrift Geiringer/70th. Pp. 323–32.

Mann/TEXTREVISION   ———. "Eine Textrevision von der Hand Joseph
                                Haydns." Festschrift Vötterle/65th. Pp. 433–37.

Martines/AUTOBIOGRAPHY   Martines, Marianna. [Autobiography] Letter of 16
                                December 1773 in the Martini Collection (Schnoe-
                                belen No. 3801). I-Bc.

MB   *Musikalische Bibliothek*
MC   *Musikalische Correspondence der teutschen Filar-
                                monischen Gesellschaft*

Mersmann/VERSUCH   Mersmann, Hans. "Versuch einer Phänomenologie
                                der Musik." *ZfMw* V/4–5 (January–February
                                1923):226–69.

Mf   *Die Musikforschung*
MGG   *Die Musik in Geschichte und Gegenwart*
Mitchell/ESSAY   Mitchell, William J., trans. and ed. *Carl Philipp
                                Emanuel Bach: Essay on the True Art of Playing
                                Keyboard Instruments*. New York: W. W. Norton,
                                1949.

Mitchell/SONATAS   ———. "The Haydn Sonatas." *PQ* XV/58 (Winter
                                1966–67):9, 20–23.

MJb   *Mozart-Jahrbuch*
ML   *Music and Letters*
Moritz/REISER   Moritz, Karl Philipp. *Anton Reiser*. Berlin: Fried-
                                rich Maurer, 1785; new ed., Stuttgart: Philipp
                                Reclam jun., 1972.

Mörner/SCHWEDEN   Mörner, C. G. Stellan. "Haydniana aus Schweden
                                um 1800." *H-St* II/1 (March 1969):1–33.

Mörner/WIKMANSON   ———. *Johan Wikmanson und die Brüder Silver-
                                stolpe. Einige Stockholmer Persönlichkeiten im Mu-
                                sikleben des Gustavianischen Zeitalters*. Uppsala:
                                Almquist & Wiksell, 1952.

Morrow/VIENNA

Moss/HOB. XVI:52

Mozart/DOCUMENTA
  ADDENDA

MQ
MR
MRz
MT
Munro/ARRANGEMENT

NB-Jb
Neubacher/KOMPOSITIONS-
  PROZESS

Neumann/ORNAMENTATION

Newman/ACCOMPANIED

Newman/BACH

Newman/COMMUNICATIONS

Newman/PIANISM

Newman/RECOGNITION

Newman/REVIEW C&W

Newman/SCE

Newman/SSB

Niemetschek/MOZART

Morrow, Mary Sue. "Concert Life in Vienna 1780–1810." Ph.D. diss., Indiana University, 1984.

Moss, Lawrence K. "Haydn's Sonata Hob. XVI: 52 (ChL. 62) in E-flat Major: An Analysis of the First Movement." *Kongress Washington/1975*. Pp. 496–501.

Mozart, Wolfgang Amadeus. *Mozart: Die Dokumente seines Lebens: Addenda und Corrigenda*. Edited by Joseph Heinz Eibl. *Neue Ausgabe sämtlicher Werke*. Kassel: Bärenreiter, 1956–. Serie X: 31/1.

The Musical Quarterly
The Music Review
Musikalische Realzeitung
The Musical Times
Munro, Kathleen. "Haydn's Keyboard Arrangement of Symphony No. 96 in D." *Bericht über den Siebenten Internationalen Musikwissenschaftlichen Kongress, Köln 1958*. Edited by Gerald Abraham et al. Kassel: Bärenreiter, 1959. Pp. 197–98.

Neues Beethoven-Jahrbuch
Neubacher, Jürgen. "'Idee' und 'Ausführung.' Zum Kompositionsprozess bei Joseph Haydn." *AfMw* XLI/3 (1984):187–207.

Neumann, Frederick. *Ornamentation in Baroque and Post-Baroque Music: With Special Emphasis on J. S. Bach*. Princeton: Princeton University Press, 1978.

Newman, William S. "Concerning the Accompanied Clavier Sonata." *MQ* XXXIII/3 (July 1947): 327–49.

———. "Emanuel Bach's Autobiography." *MQ* LI/2 (April 1965):363–72.

———. "Communications." *JAMS* XX/3 (Fall 1967):513–15.

———. "The Pianism of Haydn, Mozart, Beethoven, and Schubert . . . Compared." *PQ* XXVII (Spring 1979):14–30.

———. "The Recognition of Sonata Form by Theorists of the 18th and 19th Centuries." *PAMS* (1941):21–29.

———. Review of *Haydn: Chronicle and Works*, by H. C. Robbins Landon. *PQ* XXVI (Winter 1977–78):43–46.

———. *The Sonata in the Classic Era*. Chapel Hill: University of North Carolina Press, 1963.

———. *The Sonata since Beethoven*. Chapel Hill: University of North Carolina Press, 1969.

Niemetschek, Franz. *W. A. Mozarts Leben nach*

Originalquellen. Facsimile edition of first edition with additions from the second of 1808 and an introduction by Dr. Ernst Rychnovsky. Prague: T. Taussig, n.d.

Niemöller/SCHMITTBAUR Niemöller, Klaus Wolfgang. "Joseph Aloys Schmittbaur." *MGG* XI: cols. 1878–81.

NOHM/7 *New Oxford History Of Music*. Vol. 7: *The Age of Enlightenment: 1745–1790*. Edited by Egon Wellesz and Frederick Sternfeld. London: Oxford University Press, 1973.

NOTES *Music Library Association Notes*

Novello/MOZART PILGRIMAGE [Novello, Vincent and Mary.] *A Mozart Pilgrimage. Being the Travel Diaries of Vincent and Mary Novello in the Year 1829*. Transcribed and compiled by Nerina Medici Di Marignano. Edited by Rosemary Hughes. London: Novello, 1955.

ÖK *Österreichische Kunst*

ÖMz *Österreichische Musikzeitschrift*

Olleson/GRIESINGER Olleson, D. Edward. "Georg August Griesinger's Correspondence with Breitkopf & Härtel." *HYb* III, 1965 (1966):5–53.

Olleson/ZINZENDORF ———. "Haydn in the Diaries of Count Karl von Zinzendorf." *HYb* II, 1963/4 (1964):45–63.

Palm/UNBEKANNTE Palm, Albert. "Unbekannte Haydn–Analysen." *HYb* IV(1968):169–94.

PAMS *Papers of the American Musicological Society*

Parke/MEMOIRS Parke, William Thomas. *Musical Memoirs; Comprising an Account of the General State of Music in England, from . . . 1784, to the Year 1830*. 2 vols. London: H. Colburn and R. Bentley, 1830.

Parrish/EARLY PIANO Parrish, Carl. "The Early Piano and Its Influence on Keyboard Technique and Composition in the Eighteenth Century." Ph.D. diss., Harvard University, 1939.

Parrish/HAYDN ———. "Haydn and the Piano." *JAMS* I/3 (Fall 1948):27–34.

Päsler/KLAVIERWERKE Päsler, Karl, ed. *Joseph Haydn: Klavierwerke*. *JHW-BH* XIV/1–3 [1918].

Päsler/NOTIZ ———. "Zur Notiz. Th. de Wyzewa's Publikation 'Une sonate oubliée de Joseph Haydn.'" *ZIMG* XI/6 (March 1910):203–204.

Picton/STEFFAN Picton, Howard. "Joseph Anton Steffan: Concerto in D Major." London: Oxford University Press, 1976.

Pohl/HAYDN Pohl, Carl Ferdinand. *Joseph Haydn*. Vol. I, Berlin: A. Sacco, 1875; Leipzig: Breitkopf & Härtel, 1878. Vol. II, Leipzig: Breitkopf & Härtel, 1882. Vol. III (*Unter Benutzung der von C. F. Pohl hinterlassenen Materialien weitergeführt von Hugo Botstiber*), Leipzig: Breitkopf & Härtel, 1927.

Pohl/SCHRÖTER   ———. "Johann Samuel Schröter." GROVE 2, IV:278–79.

Polák/ZIMMERMAN   Polák, Pavol. "Zur Erforschung der Lebensdaten von Anton Zimmerman." *Musicologica Slovaca* VII (1978):171–211.

Pollack/VIENNESE   Pollack, Carla. "Viennese Solo Keyboard Music, 1740–1770: A Study in the Evolution of the Classical Style." Ph.D. diss., Brandeis University, 1984.

Poole/ENGRAVING   Poole, H. Edmund. "Music Engraving Practice in Eighteenth-Century London." Festschrift King. Pp. 98–131.

Poštolka/KOŽELUCH   Poštolka, Milan. *Leopold Koželuch. Život a dílo.* [Life and Works.] Prague: Státní Hudební Vydavatelstvi, 1964.

PQ   *Piano Quarterly*

PRMA   *Proceedings of the Royal Musical Association*

Prohászka/HOFMANN   Prohászka, Hermine. "Leopold Hofmann." *MGG* VI:cols. 561–65.

PZ   *Pressburger Zeitung*

Radcliffe/KEYBOARD   Radcliffe, Philip. "Keyboard Music," in *The Age of Enlightenment: 1745–90.* NOHM/7. Pp. 574–610.

Radice/PUBLISHERS   Radice, Mark A. "Haydn and his Publishers: A Brief Survey of the Composer's Publishing Activities." *MR* XXXXIV/2 (May 1983):87–94.

Ratner/ARS COMBINATORIA   Ratner, Leonard. "Ars Combinatoria: Chance and Choice in Eighteenth-Century Music." Festschrift Geiringer/70th. Pp. 343–63.

Ratner/CLASSIC   ———. *Classic Music. Expression, Form, and Style.* New York: Schirmer Books, 1980.

Ratner/HARMONIC   ———. "Harmonic Aspects of Classic Form." *JAMS* II/3 (Fall 1949):159–68.

Reichardt/BRIEFE-WIEN   Reichardt, Johann Friedrich. *Vertraute Briefe geschrieben auf einer Reise nach Wien und den Österreichischen Staaten zu Ende des Jahres 1808 und zu Anfang 1809.* 2 vols. Amsterdam: Im Kunst und Industrie-Comtoir, 1810.

Reti/THEMATIC PROCESS   Reti, Rudolph Richard. *The Thematic Process in Music.* New York: Macmillan, 1951.

Riedel/FUX   Riedel, Friedrich Wilhelm, ed. *Johann Joseph Fux: Werke für Tasteninstrumente.* Kassel: Bärenreiter and Graz: Akademische Druck- und Verlagsanstalt, 1964.

Riedel/GÖTTWEIG   ———, ed. *Der Göttweiger Thematische Katalog von 1830.* 2 vols. Munich: Emil Katzbichler, 1979. *Studien zur Landes- und Sozialgeschichte der Musik.* Nr. 2.

Riemann/LEXIKON   *Riemann Musik Lexikon.* Ergänzungsband. Edited by Carl Dahlhaus. 2 vols. Mainz: B. Schott's Söhne, 1972–75.

Riemann/UMSTATT   "Joseph Umstatt." Riemann/LEXIKON, II:815.

Rifkin/BOSSLER — Rifkin, Joshua. "Ein Haydn-Zitat bei Bossler." *H-St* IV/1 (May 1976):55–56.

RILM — *Répertoire international de littérature musicale*

Ripin/KEYBOARD — Ripin, Edwin M. "Haydn and the Keyboard Instruments of His Time." *Kongress Washington/1975.* Pp. 302–308.

RISM — *Répertoire international des sources musicales*

Ritzel/ENTWICKLUNG — Ritzel, Fred. *Die Entwicklung der "Sonatenform" im musiktheoretischen Schrifttum des 18. und 19. Jahrhunderts.* 2d ed. Wiesbaden: Breitkopf & Härtel, 1969.

RMl — *Revue de musicologie*

Rochlitz/FREUNDE — Rochlitz, Friedrich. *Für Freunde der Tonkunst.* 4 vols. Leipzig: Carl Cnobloch, 1824–32.

Roscoe/HAYDN AND LONDON — Roscoe, Christopher. "Haydn and London in the 1780s." *ML* XLIX/3 (July 1968):203–12.

Rosen/CLASSICAL — Rosen, Charles. *The Classical Style: Haydn, Mozart, Beethoven.* New York: Viking Press, 1971.

Rosen/SONATA FORMS — ———. *Sonata Forms.* New York: W. W. Norton, 1980.

Rück/MOZARTS HAMMERFLÜGEL — Rück, Ulrich. "Mozarts Hammerflügel erbaute Anton Walter, Wien." *MJb* VI (1955):246–62.

Rudolf/STORM — Rudolf, Max. "Storm and Stress in Music." *Bach* III (1972) 2:3–13; 3:3–11; 4:8–16.

Saint-Foix/HISTOIRE — Saint-Foix, Georges de. "Histoire de deux trios ignorés de Michel Haydn. Leur influence sur Mozart." *RMl* XII/38 (May 1931):81–88.

Salzer/HAYDN FANTASIA — Salzer, Felix. "Haydn's Fantasia from the String Quartet, Opus 76, No. 6." *Music Forum* IV (1976):161–94.

Sandberger/EINBÜRGERUNG — Sandberger, Adolf. "Zur Einbürgerung der Kunst Josef Haydns in Deutschland." *NB-Jb* VI (1935):5–25.

Sandys/Forster/VIOLIN — Sandys, William, and Forster, Simon Andrew. *The History of the Violin, and Other Instruments Played on with the Bow from the Remotest Times to the Present. Also, an Account of the Principal Makers, English and Foreign, with Numerous Illustrations.* London: J. R. Smith, 1864.

Saslav/TEMPOS — Saslav, Isidor. "Tempos in the String Quartets of Joseph Haydn." D.M. document, Indiana University, 1969.

Schenk/AUTOBIOGRAPHY — Schenk, Johann Baptist. "Autobiographische Skizze." *StMw* XI (1924):75–85.

Schenker/BEITRAG — Schenker, Heinrich. *Ein Beitrag zur Ornamentik. Als Einführung zu Ph. Em. Bachs Klavierwerken. Mitumfassend auch die Ornamentik Haydns, Mozarts und Beethovens etc.* Vienna: Universal-Edition, 1903.

Schenker/C DUR — ———. "Haydn: Sonate C Dur." *Der Tonwille* II/4 (1923):15–18.

Schenker/ES DUR ———. "Haydn: Sonate Es Dur." *Der Tonwille* I/3 (1922):3–21.

Schenker/FIVE ———. *Five Graphic Music Analyses*. Introduction and glossary by Felix Salzer. New York: Dover, 1969.

Schenker/ORGANIC ———. "Organic Structure in Sonata Form." Translated by Orin Grossman. *JMT* XII/2 (1968): 164–83.

Schenker/SCHÖPFUNG ———. "Haydn: Die Schöpfung. Die Vorstellung des Chaos." *Das Meisterwerk in der Musik* II (1926): 159–70.

Schmid/GÖTTWEIGER Schmid, Ernst Fritz. "Die Göttweiger Sonaten von Joseph Haydn." *ZfM* CIV/4 (April 1937):429.

Schmid/HAYDN UND BACH ———. "Joseph Haydn und Carl Philipp Emanuel Bach." *ZfMw* XIV/6 (March 1932):299–312.

Schmid/HOFFMEISTER ———. "Franz Anton Hoffmeister und die 'Göttweiger Sonaten.'" *ZfM* CIV/7–10 (July–October 1937):760–70, 889–95, 992–1000, 1109–17.

Schmidt/DENKSTEINE Schmidt, August. *Denksteine*. Vienna: n.p., 1848.

Schnapper/BUC Schnapper, Edith B. *The British Union-Catalogue of Early Music*. 2 vols. London: Butterworths Scientific Publications, 1957.

Schnerich/ORGELWERK Schnerich, Alfred. "Haydns Orgelwerk." *Alt-Wiener Kalender* (1926):139–43.

Scholz-Michelitsch/WAGENSEIL Scholz-Michelitsch, Helga. "Georg Christoph Wagenseil." *MGG* XIV:cols. 68–74.

Scholz-Michelitsch/WWV ———. *Das Klavierwerk von Georg Christoph Wagenseil*. [and] *Das Orchester- und Kammermusikwerk von Georg Christoph Wagenseil: Thematischer Katalog*. Vienna: Hermann Böhlaus, 1966 and 1972.

Schubart/IDEEN Schubart, Christian Friedrich Daniel. *Ideen zu einer Ästhetik der Tonkunst*. Vienna: J. V. Degen, 1806; new edition, Leipzig: Philipp Reclam jun., 1977.

Schubert/HAYDN G-DUR Schubert, Kurt, ed. *Joseph Haydn: Konzert in G-Dur*. Kassel: Nagels Verlag, 1954.

Schultz/HAYDN F-DUR Schultz, Helmut, ed. *Joseph Haydn: Konzert in F-Dur*. Kassel: Bärenreiter, 1927.

Schwarting/ECHTHEIT Schwarting, Heino. "Über die Echtheit dreier Haydn-Trios." *AfMw* XXII/3 (September 1965): 169–82.

Schwarz/CEMBALOS Schwarz, Vera. "Die Rolle des Cembalos in Österreich nach 1760." *Kongress Graz/1970*. Pp. 249–58.

Scott/CHAMBER Scott, Marion M. "Haydn's Chamber Music." *MT* LXXIII/1069 (March 1932):213–17.

Scott/FANCIES ———. "Haydn: Fresh Facts and Old Fancies." *PRMA* LXVII (1941–42):87–105.

Šetková/ŠTĚPÁN Šetková, Dana. "Josef Antonín Štěpán." *MGG* XII: cols. 1257–61.

Šetková/ŠTĚPÁNA — ———. *Klavírní Dílo Josefa Antonína Štěpána.* Prague: Státní Hudební Vydavatelství, 1965.

Šetková/Straková/ŠTĚPÁN — Šetková, Dana, and Straková, Theodora, eds. *Josef Antonín Štěpán: Composizioni per piano. Musica Antiqua Bohemica*, vol. 64. Prague: Státní Hudební Vydavatelství, 1964.

Shamgar/RHYTHMIC — Shamgar, Beth. "Rhythmic Interplay in the Retransitions of Haydn's Piano Sonatas." *JM* III/1 (Winter 1984):55–68.

Sisman/HYBRID — Sisman, Elaine R. "Haydn's Hybrid Variations." *Kongress Washington/1975.* Pp. 509–15.

Sisman/SMALL — ———. "Small and Expanded Forms: Koch's Model and Haydn's Music." *MQ* LXVIII/4 (October 1982):444–75.

Sisman/VARIATIONS — ———. "Haydn's Variations." Ph.D. diss., Princeton University, 1978.

Śliwiński/WARIACJE — Śliwiński, Zbigniew, ed. *Joseph Haydn: Wariacje na fortepian.* N.p.: Polskie Wydawnictwo Muzyczne, n.d.

Soldan/KLAVIERSTÜCKE — Soldan, Kurt, ed. *Joseph Haydn: Klavierstücke.* Leipzig: Peters, 1939.

Somfai/BAROCK — Somfai, László. "Vom Barock zur Klassik. Umgestaltung der Proportionen und des Gleichgewichts in zyklischen Werken Joseph Haydns." *JböK* II (1972):64–72.

Somfai/ENHARMONIC — ———. "A Bold Enharmonic Modulatory Model in Joseph Haydn's String Quartets." *Festschrift Geiringer/70th.* Pp. 370–81.

Somfai/ISMERETLEN — ——— "Ismeretlen Haydn-kéziratok az eszterházai színház operarepertoárjából." HAYDN EMLÉKÉRE. Pp. 507–26.

Somfai/KEYBOARD — ———. *Haydn: The Complete Keyboard Music.* Notes to the Hungaroton recording of *The Complete Keyboard Solo Music.* SLPX-11614-22, 11625-27, 11800-802. 1975–76.

Somfai/LONDON — ———. "The London Revision of Haydn's Instrumental Style." *PRMA* C (1973–74):159–74.

Somfai/OPUS 3 — ———. "Zur Echtheitsfrage des Haydn'schen 'Opus 3.'" *HYb* III 1965 (1966):153–65.

Somfai/PICTURES — ———. *Joseph Haydn: His Life in Contemporary Pictures.* Translated by Mari Kuttna and Károly Ravasz. London: Faber, 1969.

Somfai/STILFRAGEN — ———. "Stilfragen der Klaviersonaten von Haydn." *ÖMz* XXXVII/3–4 (1982):147–53.

Somfai/ZONGORASZONÁTÁI — ———. *Joseph Haydn Zongoraszonátái.* Budapest: Zenemükiadó, 1979.

Spitzer/AUTHORSHIP — Spitzer, John. "Authorship and Attribution in Western Art Music." Ph.D. diss., Cornell University, 1983.

Stadler/GESCHICHTE — [Stadler, Maximilian.] *Abbé Maximilian Stadler: seine "Materialien zur Geschichte der Musik unter den österreichischen Regenten."* Edited with commentary by Karl Wagner. Kassel: Bärenreiter, 1974.

Steglich/DRESDNER — Steglich, Rudolph. "Karl Philipp Emanuel Bach und der Dresdner Kreuzkantor Gottfried August Homilius im Musikleben ihrer Zeit." *Bach Jahrbuch* XII (1915):39–145.

Steglich/KADENZEN — ———. "Kadenzen in Haydns Klaviersonaten." *ZfM* XCIX/4 (April 1932):295–97.

Steglich/SCHWANBERGS — ———. "Eine Klaviersonate Johann Gottfried Schwanbergs (Schwanenberg[er]s) in der Joseph Haydn Gesamtausgabe." *ZfMw* XV/2 (November 1932):77–79.

Steinberg/TRIOS — Steinberg, Lester. "Sonata Form in the Keyboard Trios of Joseph Haydn." Ph.D. diss., New York University, 1976.

Stern/SCHÖPFUNG — Stern, Martin. "Haydns 'Schöpfung.' Geist und Herkunft des van Swietenschen Librettos. Ein Beitrag zum Thema 'Säkularisation' im Zeitalter der Aufklärung." *H-St* I/3 (October 1966):121–98.

Stevens/CONCERTO — Stevens, Jane R. "An 18th-Century Description of Concerto First-Movement Form." *JAMS* XXIV/1 (Spring 1971):85–95.

Stevens/THEME — ———. "Theme, Harmony, and Texture in Classic-Romantic Descriptions of Concerto First-Movement Form." *JAMS* XXVII/1 (Spring 1974):25–60.

Stieglitz/KLAVIERMUSIK — Stieglitz, Olga. "Josef Haydns Klaviermusik im Lichte der Gegenwart." *Der Klavierlehrer* XXXII/10–11 (May 15–June 1, 1909):145–47, 161–64.

StMw — *Studien zur Musikwissenschaft*

Stockmeier/KB *JHW* XVII/1 — Stockmeier, Wolfgang. *Kritischer Bericht. JHW-HI* XVII/1 (1971).

Stockmeier/KB *JHW* XVII/2 — ———. *Kritischer Bericht. JHW-HI* XVII/2 (1974).

Stockmeier/KLAVIERTRIOS — ———, ed. *Joseph Haydn: Klaviertrios. JHW-HI* XVII/1–2 (1970–74).

Straková/ŠTĚPÁN — Straková, Theodora. "Josef Antonín Štěpán a Haydnovo Divertimento Es Dur." *Časopis Moravského Musea v Brně* XLVI (1961):127–36.

Struck/HAYDN-KONZERT — Struck, Gustav. "Ein neues Haydn-Konzert." *Musica* XI/3 (March 1957):159–60.

Strunk/NOTES — Strunk, William Oliver. "Notes on a Haydn Autograph." *MQ* XX/2 (April 1934):192–205.

Sýkora/DUŠEK — Sýkora, Václav Jan. *František Xaver Dušek: Život a Dílo.* Prague: Státní Nakladetelství Krásné Literatury, Hudby a Umění, 1958.

Szabolcsi/UNGARISCHE — Szabolcsi, Bence. "Joseph Haydn und die ungarische Musik." *BzMw* I/2 (1959):62–73.

Tangeman/TRANSITION

Tangeman, Robert S. "The Transition Passage in Sonata-Form Movements of the Viennese Classical Period (With Special Reference to the Works of Haydn, Mozart, and Beethoven)." Ph.D. diss., Harvard University, 1947.

Tank/DOKUMENTE

Tank, Ulrich. "Die Dokumente der Esterházy-Archive zur fürstlichen Hofkapelle in der Zeit von 1761 bis 1770." *H-St* IV/3–4 (May 1980):129–333.

Taves/EDITIONS

Taves, Jeanette. "A Study of Editions of Haydn's Piano Sonata Hob. XVI:52 (ChL. 62) in E-flat Major." *Kongress Washington/1975.* Pp. 142–44.

Taylor/ANDANTE

Taylor, Robert S., ed. *Andante in B♭ with Variations for piano. Attributed to Joseph Haydn.* Bryn Mawr: Theodore Presser, 1974.

Taylor/VARIATIONS

————. "An Unknown Theme and Variations by Haydn." *The American Music Teacher* XXIV/6 (June–July 1975):33–35.

Temperley/TESTING

Temperley, N. "Testing the Significance of Thematic Relationships." *MR* XXII/3 (August 1961):177–80.

Tenschert/FRAUEN

Tenschert, Roland. *Frauen um Haydn.* Vienna: Donau-Verlag, 1946.

Terry/BACH

Terry, Charles Sanford. *John Christian Bach.* 2d ed. London: Oxford University Press, 1967.

Thomas/GRIESINGER

Thomas, Günter. "Griesingers Briefe über Haydn. Aus seiner Korrespondenz mit Breitkopf & Härtel." *H-St* I/2 (February 1966):49–114.

Todd/HAYDN

Todd, R. Larry. "Joseph Haydn and the *Sturm und Drang*: A Revaluation." *MR* ILI/3 (August 1980):172–96.

Tovey/HOB. XVI:52

Tovey, Donald Francis. "Haydn Pianoforte Sonata in E Flat, No. 1 (1900)." *Essays in Musical Analysis: Chamber Music.* London: Oxford University Press, 1944. Pp. 93–105.

Tovey/MAINSTREAM

————. *The Main Stream of Music and Other Essays.* Collected by Hubert Foss. London: Oxford University Press, 1949.

Tovey/TRIO A

————, ed. "Joseph Haydn: Pianoforte Trio in A major." [Hob. XV:18.] London: Oxford University Press, 1939.

Tovey/TRIO F SHARP

————, ed. "Joseph Haydn: Pianoforte Trio in F-sharp minor." [Hob. XV:26.] London: Oxford University Press, 1951.

Tyson/CLEMENTI

Tyson, Alan. *Thematic Catalogue of the Works of Muzio Clementi.* Tutzing: Hans Schneider, 1967.

Tyson/NEW LIGHT

————. "New Light on a Haydn Trio (Hob. XV:32)." *HYb* I (1962):203–205.

Tyson/REVIEW C&W

————. "On Behalf of Haydn." *Times Literary Supplement,* May 26, 1978, p. 589.

Tyson/STOLEN

———. "Haydn and Two Stolen Trios." *MR* XXII/1 (February 1961):21–27.

Uldall/KLAVIERKONZERT

Uldall, Hans. *Das Klavierkonzert der Berliner Schule*. Sammlung musikwissenschaftlicher Einzeldarstellungen No. 10. Leipzig: Breitkopf & Härtel, 1928; reprint edition, Nendeln/Liechtenstein: Kraus Reprint, 1976.

Ullrich/PARADIES

Ullrich, Hermann. "Maria Theresia von Paradies." *MGG* X: cols. 743–44.

Unverricht/BOSSLER

Unverricht, Hubert. "Haydn und Bossler." Festschrift Larsen/70th. Pp. 285–300.

Unverricht/STREICHTRIOS

———. *Geschichte des Streichtrios*. Tutzing: Hans Schneider, 1969.

Valkó/HAYDN I

Valkó, Arisztid. "Haydn magyarországi műkődése a levéltári akták tükrében." Festschrift Kodály/75th. Pp. 627–67.

Valkó/HAYDN II

———. "Haydn magyarországi műkődése a levéltári akták tükrében II." HAYDN EMLÉKÉRE. Pp. 527–668.

Wackernagel/HAYDN

Wackernagel, Bettina. *Joseph Haydns frühe Klaviersonaten: Ihre Beziehungen zur Klaviermusik um die Mitte des 18. Jahrhunderts*. Tutzing: Hans Schneider, 1975.

Wade/BACH

Wade, Rachel W. "The Keyboard Concertos of Carl Philipp Emanuel Bach: Sources and Style." Ph.D. diss., New York University, 1979.

Wainwright/BROADWOOD

Wainwright, David. *Broadwood By Appointment: A History*. London: Quiller Press, 1982.

Walker/PORPORA

Walker, Frank. "A Chronology of the Life and Works of Nicola Porpora." *Italian Studies* VI. Cambridge, 1951.

Walter/CONCERTINI

Walter, Horst, ed. *Joseph Haydn: Concertini*. Munich: G. Henle, 1969.

Walter/KEYBOARD

———. "Haydn's Keyboard Instruments." *Kongress Washington/1975*. Pp. 213–16.

Walter/KLAVIERE

———. "Haydns Klaviere." *H-St* II/4 (December 1970):256–88.

Walter/KLAVIERKONZERTE

———, ed. *Joseph Haydn: Konzerte für Klavier (Cembalo) und Orchester*. JHW-HI XV/2 (1983).

Walter/TASTENINSTRUMENT

———. "Das Tasteninstrument beim jungen Haydn." *Kongress Graz/1970*. Pp. 237–48.

WD

Wienerisches Diarium

Webster/BASS PART

Webster, James. "The Bass Part in Joseph Haydn's Early String Quartets and in Austrian Chamber Music, 1750–1780." Ph.D. diss., Princeton University, 1973.

Webster/CHAMBER

———. "Towards a History of Viennese Chamber Music in the Early Classical Period." *JAMS* XXVII/2 (Summer 1974):212–47.

Webster/CHRONOLOGY ———. "The Chronology of Haydn's String Quartets." *MQ* LXI/1 (January 1975):17–46.

Webster/EXTERNAL ———. "External Criteria for Determining the Authenticity of Haydn's Music." *Kongress Washington/ 1975.* Pp. 75–78.

Webster/FINSCHER ———. Review of Finscher/*STREICHQUARTETTS. JAMS* XXVIII/3 (Fall 1975):543–49.

Webster/VIOLONCELLO ———. "Violoncello and Double Bass in the Chamber Music of Haydn and his Viennese Contemporaries, 1750–1780." *JAMS* XXIX/3 (Fall 1976): 413–38.

Weinmann/CAPRICCI Weinmann, Alexander, ed. *Joseph Anton Steffan: Capricci.* Munich: G. Henle, 1971.

Weinmann/TRAEG ———. "Johann Traeg." *MGG* XIII: cols. 612–13.

Weinmann/TRAEG FAC ———. *Beiträge zur Geschichte des Alt-Wiener Musikverlages.* Vol. 2, no. 17: *Johann Traeg: Die Musikalienverzeichnisse von 1799 und 1804.* Vienna: Universal, 1973.

Weinmann/WIENER-ZEITUNG ———. "Die Wiener Zeitung als Quelle für die Musikbibliographie." *Festschrift Hoboken/75th.* Pp. 153–60.

Weismann/HAYDN B-DUR Weismann, Wilhelm, ed. *Joseph Haydn: Divertimento B-Dur.* Munich: F. E. C. Leuckart, 1954.

Weiss/COMMUNICATIONS Weiss, Piero. "Communications." *JAMS* XXI/2 (Summer 1968):233–34.

Wellesz/Sternfeld/CONCERTO Wellesz, Egon, and Sternfeld, Frederick. "The Concerto," in *The Age of Enlightenment: 1745–90.* NOHM/7. Pp. 434–502.

Wellesz/Sternfeld/SYMPHONY ———. "The Early Symphony," in *The Age of Enlightenment: 1745–90.* NOHM/7. Pp. 366–433.

Wesley/REMINISCENCES Wesley, Samuel. "Reminiscences." *Ca.* 1836. British Museum Ms. Add. 27593, f. 70.

Wessely/MARTINEZ Wessely, Helene. "Marianne von Martinez." *MGG* VIII: cols. 1716–18.

Wiesel/PRESENCE Wiesel, Meir. "The Presence and Evaluation of Thematic Relationships and Thematic Unity." *Israel Studies in Musicology* I (1978):77–91.

Winter/Carr/BEETHOVEN Winter, Robert, and Carr, Bruce, eds. *Beethoven, Performers, and Critics. The International Beethoven Congress, Detroit 1977.* Detroit: Wayne State University Press, 1980.

Wolf/AUTHENTICITY Wolf, Eugene K. "Authenticity and Stylistic Evidence in the Early Symphony: A Conflicting Attribution between Richter and Stamitz," in *A Musical Offering.* Edited by Edward H. Clinkscale and Claire Brook. New York: Pendragon Press, 1977. Pp. 273–94.

Wolf/RECAPITULATIONS ———. "The Recapitulations in Haydn's London Symphonies." *MQ* LII/1 (January 1966):71–89.

Wolf/STAMITZ   ———. "The Symphonies of Johann Stamitz: Authenticity, Chronology, and Style." 3 vols. Ph.D. diss., New York University, 1972.

Wotquenne/C. P. E. BACH   Wotquenne, Alfred, ed. *Thematisches Verzeichnis der Werke von Carl Philipp Emanuel Bach (1714–1788)*. Wiesbaden: Breitkopf & Härtel, 1964.

Wurzbach/LEXIKON   Wurzbach, Constant von. "Haydn, Franz Joseph." *Biographisches Lexikon des Kaiserthums Österreich*, vol. VIII. Vienna: k. k. Hof- und Staatsdruckerei, 1862. Pp. 108–41.

WWV   *Wagenseil Werkverzeichnis*. See Scholz-Michelitsch/WWV.

Wyzewa/CENTENAIRE   Wyzewa, M. Théodore de. "A propos du centenaire de la mort de Joseph Haydn." *Revue des deux Mondes* LXXIX/51 (June 15, 1909):935–46.

Wyzewa/Saint-Foix SONATE   Wyzewa, [M.] Théodore de, and Saint-Foix, Georges de. "Une sonate oubliée." *BullSIM*, VI/1 (January 15, 1910):34–37.

Zeller/ABWEICHUNGEN   Zeller, Hans Rudolf. "Abweichungen vom Thema." *Musik-Konzepte* 41 (1985), *Joseph Haydn*: 47–67.

ZfM   *Zeitschrift für Musik*

ZfMw   *Zeitschrift für Musikwissenschaft*

ZIMG   *Zeitschrift der Internationalen Musikgesellschaft*

Zinzendorf/DIARIES   Zinzendorf, Count Karl von. "Tagebuch." (Ms.) Vienna, Haus-, Hof- und Staatsarchiv.

NOTES

I. INTRODUCTION: HAYDN AND THE KEYBOARD, A REVISIONIST VIEW

1. See Crotch/LECTURES, pp.140–44, as quoted in Landon/C&W V, pp.412–13, and Newman/REVIEW C&W, p.46; and Newman/PIANISM, pp.15, 17–19, 26–27.
2. See Einstein/MOZART, p.168.
3. Griesinger/NOTIZEN, p.63.
4. The above narrative is summarized from Griesinger/NOTIZEN. Porpora was in Vienna from 1752 to 1757, according to Walker/PORPORA, pp.57–58.
5. Dies/NACHRICHTEN, p.34.
6. Bartha/BRIEFE, pp.42–43.
7. Ibid., pp.58–61.
8. According to G. F. von Rothenstein in Bernouilli/SAMMLUNG IX, p.282, as quoted in Landon/C&W II, p.343.
9. See Harich/DOCUMENTA VII, pp.58, 65, 73, 82.
10. *AMZ* III/11, col.176.
11. Dies/NACHRICHTEN, pp.209–10 (Elssler's account); Stadler/GESCHICHTE, p.133; and Griesinger/NOTIZEN, *passim*.
12. The most complete account of this phase of Haydn's activities is found in Bartha/Somfai/HOK, although it should be supplemented by Harich/REPERTOIRE and Bartha/REPERTORY.
13. As listed in *HNV* and *HBV*. However, the Bach/VERSUCH is not listed.
14. See the Haydn/Genzinger correspondence in Bartha/BRIEFE and Landon/CCLN, as well as in Karajan/HAYDN. Excerpts are given in Essay II, beginning with p.43.
15. Bartha/BRIEFE, p.101.
16. See Essay II, pp.29–30 for the complete quotation.
17. Bartha/BRIEFE, p.127. Concerning this attitude, see Feder/KORREKTUREN.
18. Wesley/REMINISCENCES.
19. Bartha/BRIEFE, p.491.
20. Ibid., pp.250–53, 267–70.
21. See Becker-Glauch/RISM.
22. Parke/MEMOIRS, p.198.
23. Bartha/BRIEFE, p.283; Landon/CCLN, p.135.
24. Harding/PIANO-FORTE, pp.60–64.
25. See Bartha/BRIEFE, pp.499–500, for the list of names.
26. *PZ*, No. 91 (14 November 1800).
27. Mörner/WIKMANSON, p.400.
28. Ibid., p.398; Iffland/FISCHER PROFESSOR. Elssler's report of Haydn's last rendering of the Austrian hymn is given in Pohl/HAYDN III, p.386.

II. THE KEYBOARD WORKS IN BIOGRAPHICAL, CRITICAL, AND MUSICAL DOCUMENTS

1. Griesinger/NOTIZEN, p.14.
2. The earliest Haydn publication for any genre was Chevardière's print of the early string quartets known as Op. 1, in early 1764. See Feder/KB JHW XII/1, p.25.

3. See Bartha/BRIEFE, pp.179–80. Several of Haydn's early string quartets, symphonies, and keyboard trios emanate from a group of scribes called the "Fürnberg copyists" (their work was first noticed in the Fürnberg collection now housed in H-KE).

4. Hob. XVI:6 carries no date. The date of 1756 on Hob. XVIII:1 was added later by Haydn. The date of 1760 on Hob. XIV:11 comes from Pohl; its autograph is presently lost.

5. Concerning Haydn and the Countess Morzin, see Griesinger/NOTIZEN, pp. 14.–15.

6. See Martines/AUTOBIOGRAPHY, where it is stated that her studies with Haydn began when she was seven. The autobiography is published in Brown/MARTINES.

7. See Wessely/MARTINEZ. My spelling of the name conforms to the early Martines documents.

8. Burney/PRESENT STATE I, pp.311–13.

9. Kelly/REMINISCENCES, p.128.

10. *JbTWP*, p.71.

11. Framery/NOTICE, pp.8–12.

12. On this question, see Pohl/HAYDN I, p.188; Hoboken/DISCREPANCIES, pp.7–8; Geiringer/HAYDN, pp.36–37; Olleson/ZINZENDORF, p.47; and Landon/C&W I, p.75.

13. Brook/BREITKOPF, 1763, col.120.

14. On the distribution of these copies, see Essay III.

15. Thomas/GRIESINGER, p.62; see also Essay III, *passim*.

16. Such alterations of the large as well as small dimensions of a composition by Haydn were not unusual for the Amsterdam publisher; see Feder/HUMMEL and Essay III, p.83.

17. Anderson/MOZART LETTERS, pp.191–92; Hoboken/WERKVERZEICHNIS I, p.721; and Fillion/HOB. XV:C1.

18. Hiller/NACHRICHTEN (1768), pp.83–84.

19. Hiller/ENTWURF, as quoted in Unverricht/STREICHTRIOS, p.86.

20. Burney/HISTORY, p.959.

21. Part of a letter dated 6 July 1776. Bartha/BRIEFE, pp.77–78; *facs.* in Somfai/PICTURES, pp.68–71.

22. Some have explained this phenomenon through the historical theory of *Zeitgeist*; i.e., Haydn was one of the first to be caught up in the *Sturm und Drang* movement. See also Essay X, p.289.

23. Klier/VOLKSLIEDTHEMA presents a number of musical versions. Mozart also used the tune in K.32.

24. See Essay VII, pp.222–25, for a full discussion of the Capriccio.

25. For the entire catalogue see Larsen/DHK.

26. Griesinger/NOTIZEN, p.18.

27. Feder/DATIERUNG.

28. Saslav/TEMPOS, p.66.

29. CRAMER'S 1783, p.72; signed "W."

30. *MB* II (1785), p.195, as quoted in Sandberger/EINBÜRGERUNG, p.22. For a new critical edition see Gerlach/HOB XVIIa:1.

31. According to Gericke/MUSIKALIENHANDEL, p.121, and Hoboken/WERKVERZEICHNIS I, p.753.

32. The instrument has been characterized by the twentieth-century baryton virtuoso Riki Gerardy as the "instrument of kings." See notes to the recording Haydn Baryton Trios, His Master's Voice, SLS 5095.

33. As translated from Päsler/KLAVIERWERKE, p.xvii.

34. See Hoboken/WERKVERZEICHNIS I, pp.752–53.

35. Reichardt in *ADB* 33/1 (1778), p.175.

36. *EMLR*, October 1784, p.303. According to Langley/ENGLISH, pp.43–44, the author was probably Samuel Arnold.

37. Based on the appearance of the G-major Sonata in Anthology Dorsch 1 and Larsen's provisional dating of the collection in Larsen/QUELLE; see also Essay IV, p.121.

38. A-Wn, A-Gk, and D-ddr-SW1. These copies may possibly emanate from the shop of Simon Haschke in Vienna. See Brown/NOTES.

39. See Hoboken/WERKVERZEICHNIS I, pp.756–57.

40. *EMLR*, October 1784, p.303. For the author, see note 36 above.

41. In 1771 Haydn seems to have completed at least the exposition of the first movement and the entire finale.

42. Bartha/BRIEFE, p.89.

43. Ibid.

44. Letter of 25 February 1780. Bartha/BRIEFE, pp.90–91.

45. Bartha/BRIEFE, p.92.

46. Feder/KLAVIERSONATEN/2, pp.viii–ix. Dr. Auenbrugger is best known for his development of percussing, a technique for listening to sounds in the chest and abdomen to determine the condition of internal organs.

47. Anderson/MOZART LETTERS, p.236.

48. Feder/KLAVIERSONATEN/2, pp.viii–ix.

49. Hiller/NACHRICHTEN, No. 30, 23 September 1766, p.100.

50. Feder/KLAVIERSONATEN/2, pp.viii–ix.

51. *JbTWP*, p.68.

52. Bartha/BRIEFE, p.92.

53. See Hoboken/WERKVERZEICHNIS I, pp.761–63.

54. *AM* 1781, p.202.

55. A-Wn, S.m. 9820.

56. CRAMER'S, 1787, pp.1287–88.

57. Bartha/BRIEFE, p.115.

58. CRAMER'S, 1783, pp.582–83.

59. Ibid., pp.1075–115; see Bartha/BRIEFE, p.136, and Landon/CCLN, p.45.

60. Bartha/BRIEFE, p.129.

61. Hoboken/WERKVERZEICHNIS I, pp.766–67, is in error on this matter; see Deutsch/HOBOKEN, p.336.

62. Dies/NACHRICHTEN, p.144; Gotwals/TCP, p.164.

63. The assertion in Gerber/NTL II, col.581, that these works were also engraved in Vienna seems to have been an error, as there is no evidence to support another early publication. See Hoboken/WERKVERZEICHNIS I, p.767.

64. Landon/KLAVIERSONATEN/3, pp.ix, xviii.

65. CRAMER's, 1785, p.535; signed "L." These sonatas also appeared in a convincing version for string trio; see Essay III, p.106.

66. See Tyson/STOLEN.

67. Framery/NOTICE, pp.31–34. See also Tyson/STOLEN, p.25 for a later document.

68. Bartha/BRIEFE, p.139.

69. The Adagio in F major (Hob. XVII:9), which was first issued by Artaria in a collection known as Op. 46, can now be dated by its autograph; it therefore has nothing to do with this letter to Nadermann. See Essays III, pp.88–89 and IV, p.131. Nadermann did publish a recently recovered print of Hob. XVII:1 in the early 1790s.

70. Bartha/BRIEFE, p.147.

71. Landon/C&W II, pp.63, 583, 641, 673, 675.

72. Bartha/BRIEFE, p.148.

73. Hoboken/WERKVERZEICHNIS I, p.688. That Artaria was having some of its music engraved outside of Vienna is somewhat surprising considering the number of engraved portraits, scenes, etc., which the firm published by local artists about this same time.

74. See Feder/SKIZZEN.

75. First published in *JHW-HI* XVII/2, p.260.

76. Sandys/Forster/VIOLIN, pp.302–306; also Bartha/BRIEFE, pp.151–55.

77. See Unverricht/BOSSLER, p.294.
78. CRAMER's, 1786, p.1310.
79. Walter/KLAVIERKONZERTE, p.vii. Walter believes the concerto was Hob. XVIII:11.
80. Hoboken/WERKVERZEICHNIS I, pp.816–18, 822–23.
81. CS-KRm II F 40 and A 4903.
82. Hoboken/WERKVERZEICHNIS I, pp.817–18; Walter/KLAVIERKON-ZERTE, p.vi.
83. CS-KRm II G 20.
84. See Szabolcsi/UNGARISCHE.
85. EMLR, October 1784, pp.303–304.
86. CRAMER's, 1785, pp.882–83.
87. Bartha/BRIEFE, p.162.
88. See Essay III, pp.82–83.
89. See Hoboken/WERKVERZEICHNIS I, pp.767, 882.
90. Griesinger/NOTIZEN, pp.7–8.
91. Bartha/BRIEFE, p.191.
92. Ibid., pp.192–93.
93. Ibid., p.195.
94. Ibid., p.196.
95. Ibid., p.198.
96. Ibid., p.202.
97. Blümml/MOZART, p.168. See also the discussion in Koller/WERKSTATT, pp.81–89.
98. This letter harks back to the same idea of 27 November 1787; see Bartha/BRIEFE, pp.182–83.
99. Ibid., p.206.
100. Ibid., p.209.
101. *MRz* No. 36 (1789), p.280, as quoted in Pohl/HAYDN II, p.320.
102. *ADB* 117/1 (1789) as quoted in Pohl/HAYDN II, p.320.
103. Hase/BREITKOPF, pp.4–5.
104. Bartha/BRIEFE, p.200.
105. Ibid., p.203.
106. Gerber/NTL, col. 583.
107. Bartha/BRIEFE, p.204.
108. On Tost, see Landon/C&W II, pp.81–82.
109. See Hoboken/WERKVERZEICHNIS I, pp.746, 770, 786, 807.
110. See Eibner/KLAVIERSTÜCKE, p.xix.
111. See Essay III, pp.71–73.
112. See Bartha/BRIEFE, pp.279–81; Landon/CCLN, pp.131–32. For further discussion, see Radice/PUBLISHERS.
113. See Tyson/NEW LIGHT, pp.203–204.
114. See Landon/LETTERS, pp.214–16.
115. Hoboken/WERKVERZEICHNIS I, p.699.
116. Ibid., pp.698–99.
117. Bartha/BRIEFE, p.223.
118. First published by Feder/SKIZZEN, pp.81–84; facsimile in Landon/SKETCH.
119. Gerber/NTL II, col. 585; see also Hoboken/WERKVERZEICHNIS I, p.700.
120. See Brusatti/HOB. XVI:49 for a facsimile edition of the sonata.
121. Most of the above is summarized from Karajan/HAYDN, p.5; Landon/C&W II, pp.720–23 and CCLN, pp.xxi–xxii.
122. Bartha/BRIEFE, p.237.
123. Ibid., pp.240–41.
124. Ibid., p.242.

125. Ibid., p.244.
126. Ibid., p.245.
127. Ibid., p.280.
128. MC no. 25 (1792), p.195, as quoted in Pohl/HAYDN II, p.316.
129. Bartha/BRIEFE, p.248.
130. *JbTWP*, pp.21–22.
131. The hypothesis here comes from Graue/HAYDN, p.425.
132. Tyson/NEW LIGHT, p.205.
133. Bartha/BRIEFE, pp.267–68, 277.
134. Hoboken/WERKVERZEICHNIS I, p.788.
135. Landon/C&W III, p.157.
136. Hoboken/WERKVERZEICHNIS I, p.697.
137. See Mozart/DOCUMENTA ADDENDA, p.46; and Anderson/MOZART LETTERS II, pp.876–77.
138. See Tenschert/FRAUEN, plates 16, 17.
139. Zinzendorf/DIARIES, as quoted in Mozart/DOCUMENTA ADDENDA, p.45. Barbara was actually the daughter of Franz Kajetan Ployer.
140. She is not mentioned in *JbTWP*, and the other usual biographical sources fail to add any new details after the date of these variations; see also Stadler/GESCHICHTE, p.126.
141. See Hoboken/WERKVERZEICHNIS I, p.792; and *HYb* XIV (1983), p.221. The copy is now in A-Wgm; see Otto Biba's note in *HYb* XV (1984), pp.220–22.
142. But did not remain with him, as it is not listed in *HBV* or *HNV*.
143. See Wurzbach/LEXIKON II, pp.123–24.
144. *AMZ* I (8 May 1799), col. 512.
145. Strunk/NOTES, see plate between pages 196 and 197.
146. Ibid., p.194.
147. *EMLR*, August–December 1796; see also Brown/CELERIO, p.646.
148. According to the watermarks on the autograph in the collecton of the heirs of Steffan Zweig (Albermann) now in the British Library. See Tyson/REVIEW C&W.
149. Dies/NACHRICHTEN, pp.154–55.
150. Reichardt/BRIEFE-WIEN I, p.145.
151. *JbTWP*, pp.38–39.
152. *AMZ* I/33 (15 May 1799), col. 520.
153. Kollman/ESSAY, pp.10–11.
154. Mrs. Schröter had been a keyboard student of Schröter and was described as "a young lady of birth and fortune." After their elopement, which brought the couple into disagreement with her family, Schröter surrendered "all his rights to an annuity of £500." Afterwards, he played only at the concerts of the nobility and in particular those of the Prince of Wales. See Pohl/SCHRÖTER.
155. See Larsen/CONTRACT.
156. Dies/NACHRICHTEN, pp.133–34. Mrs. Schröter's age as described by Haydn needs correction: according to Cudworth/Brennecke/SCHRÖTER, in 1790–91, she must have been in her mid-thirties.
157. H. Landon/C&W III, pp.435–36.
158. See facs., ibid., p.587.
159. Hase/BREITKOPF, p.51.
160. Bartha/BRIEFE, p.302; Landon/CCLN, p.144.
161. *AMZ* (31 July 1805), cols. 711–12.
162. Bartha/BRIEFE, pp.308–309.
163. Ibid., p.309.
164. *AMZ* I, no. 38 (19 June 1799), cols. 599–602. The entire review is given in Landon/C&W, pp.208–10.

165. From the facsimile in Hogwood/HAYDN, p.112. See also Larsen/CONTRACT. Larsen believes the three accompanied sonatas to be the trios for Mrs. Bartolozzi, Hob. XV:27–29, which were published as Op. 75 by Hyde or Longman & Broderip, a firm in which Mr. Hyde was a partner.

166. First published in Feder/OSTIGLIA.

167. Bartha/BRIEFE, p.316.

168. Olleson/GRIESINGER, p.10; and Thomas/GRIESINGER, pp.57–58.

169. Bartha/BRIEFE, pp.345–46.

170. Ibid., p.362. See also Larsen/CONTRACT.

171. *AMZ Intelligenz-Blatt* XIV (June 1799).

172. Olleson/GRIESINGER, p.42; and Thomas/GRIESINGER, pp.96–97.

173. Landon/CCLN, p.221.

174. Bartha/BRIEFE, p.430.

175. See Olleson/GRIESINGER, pp.41–42; and Thomas/GRIESINGER, pp.92–93.

III. AUTHENTICITY

1. See LaRue/MAJOR AND MINOR, pp.181–82.

2. See Larsen/HÜB, p.15; and Webster/EXTERNAL.

3. For recent discussions and important advances, see LaRue/MOZART, LaRue/AUTHENTICATION, Wolf/AUTHENTICITY, Spitzer/AUTHORSHIP, and Fruewald/HAYDN.

4. See Larsen/HÜB, pp.209–50; facsimile edition in Larsen/DHK[1 and 2].

5. The entire letter is published in Bartha/BRIEFE, pp.51–54; and Valkó/HAYDN II, pp.538–39.

6. Bartha/BRIEFE, pp.49–50.

7. See Griesinger/NOTIZEN, p.14, and a discussion of this situation in Essay IV, pp.113–17.

8. See Dies/NACHRICHTEN, pp.217–18; Griesinger/NOTIZEN, pp.31–32; Carpani/HAYDINE, pp.306–307; Bartha/BRIEFE, pp.555–58; Landon/CCLN, pp.309–12; and Landon/C&W III, pp.316–18. For a listing and discussion of the keyboard works, see Essay II, pp.46–47.

9. See Larsen/HUB, pp.251–322; Facs. ed. in Larsen/DHK[1 and 2].

10. British Library Add Ms. 32070.

11. Archiv der Stadt Wien Persönlichkeiten 4/1–4 and A-Wn S.m. 4843A.

12. See the reprint, Brook/BREITKOPF, to which all citations refer.

13. See Fuchs/VERZEICHNISS, 1839 and 1840.

14. All the relevant documents are in Essay II.

15. See Olleson/GRIESINGER and Thomas/GRIESINGER.

16. The document is given in Essay II, p.27. See also Unverricht/BOSSLER and Rifkin/BOSSLER.

17. See Landon/SYMPHONIES, p.611; Feder/QUELLEN; and Brown/NOTES.

18. For further information on Kroměříž, see Essay VI, pp.178–79.

19. The more comprehensive lists and studies are: Eibner/KLAVIERSTÜCKE, Feder/GROVE 6, Feder/KLAVIERSONATEN, Feder/KLAVIERTRIOS, Feder/ORGELKONZERTE, Feder/PROBLEME, Fillion/ACCOMPANIED, Fruewald/HAYDN, Gerlach/KLAVIERSTÜCKE, Hoboken/WERKVERZEICHNIS, Landon/C&W, Landon/FOREWORD, Landon/KLAVIERSONATEN, Landon/ORGAN, Larsen/DHK[1 and 2], Larsen/HÜB, Larsen/Landon/HAYDN, Newman/SCE, Päsler/KLAVIERWERKE, Pohl/HAYDN, Soldan/KLAVIERSTÜCKE, Somfai/KEYBOARD, Somfai/ZONGORSONÁTÁI, and Walter/CONCERTINI. Concerning individual works see the subsequent discussion in the text and their accompanying footnotes.

20. Concerning Haschke, see Gericke/MUSIKALIENHANDEL, pp.104–105; and

Brown/NOTES. In addition, there are seven incipits in *EK* for sonatas whose music is lost (Hob. XVI:2a–e, g, and h).

21. See the discussion of interpreting the London Catalogue in Essay II, pp.46–47.

22. Hob. XVI:5, 10, 12, 13, and 14 were also published *ca.* 1790 by Cooper of London as works by Ignaz Pleyel (1757–1831). Since these works can be documented from the Breitkopf catalogues as Haydn's in 1763 and 1767, and Pleyel did not have a reputation as a *Wunderkind*, this attribution can be dismissed.

23. See Schmid/GÖTTWEIGER and Schmid/HOFFMEISTER.

24. See Feder/PROBLEME, p.96. Feder also lists "Prague Sonatas"; I have rejected them here, as an examination of this manuscript from the monastery at Osek reveals that each work—with the exception of a minuet—already carries an attribution: Haydn—Hob. XVI:29, 31, 32; and Koželuch—Poštolka XII:4, 8–10.

25. Feder/PROBLEME, pp.96–97; and Feder/ZWEI HAYDN.

26. See Feder/PROBLEME, p.96; and Weinmann/WIENER-ZEITUNG, p.157.

27. My thanks to Peter Alexander for examining the Frankfurt copy.

28. See Thomas/GRIESINGER, pp.92–93; and Stockmeier/KB *JHW*-XVII/1, pp.8–9.

29. Steglich/SCHWANBERGS.

30. Feder/KLAVIERSONATEN/1, p.viii; and Landon/KLAVIERSONATEN/1, p.xxi. But see also Badura-Skoda/TEUTSCHE, which cites examples that tend to support the authenticity of the first movement of Hob. XVI:12. Fruewald/HAYDN, pp.110–11, 114, finds XVI:5 spurious and 12 authentic.

31. For example, the Berlin copies of Hob. XVI:1 and 2 are from the Artaria collection. See Larsen/DHK², p.xviii.

32. This work is omitted from C. Landon's edition but included by Feder with reservations about the first movement (Feder/KLAVIERSONATEN/1, p.viii). Fruewald/HAYDN, pp.115–16 finds it spurious. See also Larsen/HÜB, p.302; and Steglich/SCHWANBERGS.

33. In his liner notes for KEYBOARD II, Somfai considers Hob. XVI:43 to be doubtful on both external as well as internal grounds: "If it [Hob. XVI:43] is the work of Haydn at all, it has been preserved by rather secondary sources, and—although so far the Haydn literature has not contested its authenticity—there are grounds for suspicion (the alla breve Moderato combination of the opening movement, the clip-winged thematic material itself; the tiny Menuetto and 'alla *bravura*' rondo—all taken together seems to give an 'à la Haydn' style").

34. Bartha/BRIEFE, pp.179–80; and Landon/CCLN, pp.70–71.

35. Feder/ZWEI HAYDN; and Feder/PROBLEME, p.100.

36. The discovery was made by Carsten Hatting; see his HAYDN ODER KAYSER? The discussions took place at the Haydn Conference in Washington, D.C., in 1975. In that forum I argued that these sonatas were not by Haydn; today I consider his authorship plausible. See the full account in Feder/SOURCES, Brown/RAIGERN, and Gerlach/RAIGERN, including the accompanying discussion. Fruewald/HAYDN, pp.117–20, accepts these sonatas but not the Es3 finale.

37. Indeed, Hob. XVI:9 with the 2/4 scherzo—which Haydn also used with a new middle section in Hob XIV:10—may have had a similar history, i.e., an original two-movement work with an added finale.

38. Larsen/QUELLE.

39. According to H. C. R. Landon, Larsen has suggested that the first movement of this version might be the work of a pupil. See Landon/ESSAYS, p.63.

40. See Hoboken/WERKVERZEICHNIS, *Gruppen* V, X, and XI.

41. Feder at one time thought the Tempo di Menuet to be from a somewhat earlier date than the other two movements in the Gesellschaft der Musikfreunde source. See Feder/PROBLEME, p.102.

42. In Anthology Dorsch, Hob. XVII:2 and 3 were also transposed to accommodate this range. See below, pp.88–89.

43. I am grateful to Georg Feder for calling to my attention the omission of the short octave from my discussion after I had published a more-extended description of this work in Brown/PROBLEMS.

44. The present location of the sketch autograph for Hob. XV:17 is unknown. See Hoboken/WERKVERZEICHNIS, I, p.701; and Stockmeier/KB JHW-XVII/2, pp.33–34.

45. In the case of Hob. XV:11–13, the autograph was presumably owned by Artaria.

46. It is listed not with the other keyboard works, but on *EK* 29.

47. See Stockmeier/KB *JHW*-XVII/1, pp.17–18; and Feder/KLAVIERTRIOS, pp.294–96 and 305. Larsen's questioning of Hob. XV:34 in ECHTHEITSPROBLEM I and II seems totally unjustified; Feder's conclusions thus remain intact.

48. See Stockmeier/KB *JHW*-XVII/1, pp.19–20.

49. Fillion/HOB. XV:C1.

50. Saint-Foix/HISTOIRE.

51. Tyson/STOLEN; Schwarting/ECHTHEIT; Stockmeier/KB *JHW* XVII/1, pp. 36–38; Benton/RESUMÉ; and Fruewald/HAYDN, p.75.

52. Tyson/STOLEN, pp.24–25.

53. Number from Benton/PLEYEL. Benton makes the point in RESUMÉ that self-parody was a not uncommon practice with Pleyel.

54. See Feder/HUMMEL.

55. See Heussner/HAYDN-FUNDE. The movement was published in Heussner/HOB. XV:40.

56. Hoboken/WERKVERZEICHNIS, I, p.677.

57. Hob. XIV:3 is listed in the Breitkopf Catalogue for 1771, col. 431, as by Leopold Hofmann. There seems to be no reason to uphold the Breitkopf attribution; it may have been a mistake—works attributed to Haydn are on the same page—and stylistically there seems little reason to consider Hofmann. The similar incipit in Breitkopf 1767, col. 293 (see Hoboken/WERKVERZEICHNIS, I, p.672), is without question by Hofmann; it is contained in a collection of music belonging to the Archduchess Elizabeth (A-Wn S.m. 11085).

58. See Essay II, pp.33–34.

59. The Gesellschaft der Musikfreunde copy (Q21123) was not known to Hoboken. Its final page contains what are apparently fanfares for Prince Esterházy. The Berlin copy contains the autograph to the song "Der Schlaue Pudel."

60. The second and third movements contain cadences typical of Haydn's early works. See Feder/TYPISCHES, pp.14–15. This work may, however, be more properly a work with an accompaniment; see below, pp.107–108. Fruewald/HAYDN, pp.135–39, considers it authentic with the accompaniment.

61. See Feder/TYPISCHES, pp.14–15.

62. Feder does not mention them in QUELLEN or in PROBLEME. Recently Fruewald/HAYDN, pp.140–41, has rejected D1.

63. Dittersdorf's Symphony C9 (Krebs 1), according to Grave/DITTERSDORF, p.393.

64. See Essay VIII, p.242.

65. Copy in the Burgenländisches Museum, Eisenstadt. My thanks to H. C. R. Landon for bringing this work to my attention and providing me with a copy.

66. Scholz-Michelitsch/WWV, no. 257.

67. Šetková/ŠTĚPÁNA, no. 62. See also Straková/ŠTĚPÁN, where it is hypothesized that the version with the accompaniment is an authentic one, but that the accompaniment was written after the solo version.

68. See Niemöller/SCHMITTBAUR, col. 1880.

69. See Hoboken/WERKVERZEICHNIS, I, p.769; and Terry/BACH, p.310.

70. Hoboken catalogues twenty-four *Klavierstücke* under *Gruppe* XVII. From his list

should be subtracted Hob. XVII:D1, as it is a three-movement work beginning with a set of variations and therefore is legitimately a sonata.

71. For the autograph of Hob. XVII:9 see Feder/NICHT IDENTIFIZIERTEN, p.101.

72. Hoboken XVII:11 may be the same work as Hob. XVII:12.

73. See Essay II, pp.37–38.

74. On this aspect of Haydn's style, see Brown/CRITICAL.

75. See the above discussion of Hob. XVI:47, p.169.

76. See Feder/KLAVIERSONATEN/1, pp.184–85; and Gerlach/KLAVIERSTÜCKE, pp.65–67.

77. Landon/TRIO; Fruewald/HAYDN, pp.156–58, accepts the solo version.

78. See also Braun/Gerlach/BARYTONTRIOS/1, pp.152–53; and Gerlach/RECONSTRUCTED.

79. For the discussion of Hob. XVII:8, I am partially indebted to an unpublished study by René Ramos. Hoboken/WERKVERZEICHNIS, I, p.794, also lists a version in C major at D-ddr-SWl, which was not available for this discussion.

80. See Gerlach/Hill/LAUFWERK, pp.25–27, 83–84.

81. Not listed in Botsiber/ARTARIA. See also Taylor/VARIATIONS; and the modern editions Taylor/ANDANTE and Śliwiński/WARIACJE.

82. Modern edition, Haselböck/HAYDN.

83. Schmidt/DENKSTEINE, p.2n, as quoted in Landon/C&W II, p.665.

84. Modern edition, Haselböck/HAYDN.

85. Terry/BACH, pp.343–44.

86. All attributions are discussed in Helm/BACH.

87. Modern edition, Śliwiński/WARIACJE, pp.55–60.

88. Since they are not all listed by their incipits and Haydn's own written comment in EK (see Plate 12) is ambiguous, the word "possibly" has been used.

89. See Hoboken/WERKVERZEICHNIS, I, pp.815–16.

90. The authenticity of the Missa Rorate Desuper, also listed in EK (p.15), has been questioned.

91. Fruewald/HAYDN, pp.237–38, rejects this version of Hob. XV:40.

92. See Feder/HAYDN R, p.500; and Feder/ORGELKONZERTE, p.442. Fruewald/HAYDN, p.239, also rejects it.

93. Also deemed spurious by Fruewald/HAYDN, p.241.

94. See Šetková/ŠTEPÁNA, No. 135.

95. Hoboken/WERKVERZEICHNIS, III, p.358.

96. See "Concerto No. 4" in Davis/LANG, p.401; and Davis/HOB. XVIII:F3.

97. See Feder/KLEINES KONZERT. Another concerto from Alžbétinky, in B-flat major, is attributed to Haydn by a penciled addition. See Walter/KLAVIERKONZERTE, p.ix.

98. The complete parts as copied by this writer are published in Landon/C&W I, pp.210–13.

99. All are published in a modern edition, by H. C. R. Landon for Doblinger (Diletto Musicale Nr. 80).

100. See Heussner/KONZERT, p.480.

101. See Fuchs/VERZEICHNISS 1839 and 1840.

102. Some of Hummel's other alterations are documented in Feder/HUMMEL. For the wind parts, see Walter/KLAVIERKONZERTE, pp.153–58.

103. For Symphony No. 69 see Bartha/BRIEFE, p.128; for No. 73 see the *Stichvorlage* in A-Wgm; and for the "Gott erhalte" variations see Eibner/KLAVIERFASSUNG. The arrangement of Symphony No. 96, contrary to Munro/ARRANGEMENT, is not authentic.

104. See the discussion in Drury/SEVEN, pp.305–12; and Bartha/BRIEFE, p.188.

105. See Hoboken/WERKVERZEICHNIS, I, p.753.

106. As reported by Dies; for the actual quotation see Essay II, pp.50–51.

107. See Essay II, pp.51–52.

108. Two works can be omitted from consideration because they involve misreadings by Hoboken: XIV:5, which has now been recovered as the solo Sonata XVI:5a; and XIV:6, which is the solo keyboard Sonata XVI:6. In addition, the accompaniments to XV:39 are as suspicious as their cyclic make-up (see above, p.83).

109. See above, p.98.

110. See Feder/KLAVIERTRIOS, p.306.

111. On Haroldt see above, p.68.

112. The Berlin copy is reproduced in Landon/C&W I, pp.546–47.

IV. DATING AND CHRONOLOGY

1. Päsler/KLAVIERWERKE; Strunk/NOTES, pp.204–205; Larsen/HÜB and DHK[1 and 2]; Feder/KLAVIERSONATEN and GROVE 6; Landon/KLAVIERSONATEN; H. C. R. Landon/FOREWORD and various single editions for Doblinger; and also editions of individual and small groups of works by Eibner, Gerlach, Schubert, Schultz, Walter, and Weismann.

2. Feder/DATIERUNG.

3. Feder/PROBLEME, pp.101–102; and Feder/ORGELKONZERTE, pp.440–42. The range of the lieder from the 1780s is quite different, perhaps because of the keyboard part doubling the voice and the traditional use of the clavichord for this repertoire. In any case, they are not congruent with the main body of Haydn's keyboard output.

4. See for example the keyboards described in Kunsthistorisches Museum/SAITEN-KLAVIERE.

5. See Essay III, p.61.

6. But Haydn would have needed the approval of his Prince. Otherwise he would be violating his contract: "The said *Vice-Kapellmeister* shall be under obligation to compose . . . and neither to communicate such compositions to any other person, nor allow them to be copied, but shall retain them for the absolute use of His Highness, and not compose for any other person without the knowledge and permission of His Highness." See Geiringer/HAYDN, p.46. It wasn't until 1779 that the contract was renegotiated without this provision.

7. See Essay II, pp.15–19, for a full quotation of the keyboard works in this document.

8. Feder/PROBLEME, p.101; and Feder/KLAVIERSONATEN/1, p.viii. On the other hand, the dating of Hob. XVI:4 between 1750 and 1760 must be questioned as it comes down to us in a single source, probably from the 1770s. The notation of the appoggiaturas in the *EK* entry seems to point to the post-1762 practice, although it may merely reflect Haydn's new habit. Hob. XVI:14, in view of its placement in *EK*'s left-hand column, was probably composed as late as the corollary evidence indicates: 1766–1767.

9. Landon/C&W I, p.81.

10. The most likely pair stylistically would be Hob. XVIII:5 and 8.

11. Larsen/HÜB, p.233.

12. Cole/DEVELOPMENT, pp.125–26.

13. D-ddr-Bds, HB Kat. Mus. 606, fol. 50a. However, the incipit is listed twice in succession, with the date indicated next to the less-complete second citation.

14. Larsen/HÜB, pp.217–18; and Larsen/DHK[2], p.x.

15. See Larsen/HÜB, p.234; and Larsen/DHK[2], p.xviii.

16. The latter was first determined by Larsen/HÜB, pp.217–18.

17. Feder/PROBLEME, pp.100–101; and Feder/KLAVIERSONATEN/1, pp.v–vi.

18. Landon/KLAVIERSONATEN/1, pp.xx–xxi.

19. Newman/SCE, pp.462–64.

20. Larsen/Landon/HAYDN.

21. Feder/PROBLEME, p.100. This ordering is supportable only to the degree one accepts the authenticity of Es2 and Es3.

22. Feder/PROBLEME, p.102.

23. Rosen/CLASSICAL, p.146n.

24. Saslav/TEMPOS, p.66.

25. See Larsen/KLAVIERSONATE.

26. Perhaps Haydn was attempting to complete the set to assure its printing during 1774, the year of Prince Nikolaus's sixtieth birthday. The dedication is given in Essay II, p.21.

27. See Chew/NIGHT-WATCHMAN'S, pp.106–107. See also Example X–33.

28. See the discussion in Feder/KLAVIERSONATEN/2, pp.vii–viii.

29. The suggestion made in Kramer/TWO ASPECTS that this sonata may date from after Haydn's return to Vienna seems quite unlikely in light of our hypothesis.

30. Concerning Rebecca Schröter, see Essay II, p.54.

31. Landon/FOREWORD.

32. Feder/KLAVIERTRIOS.

33. Landon/FOREWORD, pp.15–16.

34. See Essay VII for the Viennese tradition of two dance movements.

35. See Essay VII, pp.221–25.

36. Within this essay, frequent references to correspondence and other documents are cited and sometimes briefly quoted. All the relevant documents are given in their entirety in Essay II.

37. Webster/CHRONOLOGY, pp.26–29.

38. Landon/LETTERS, pp.214–16.

39. Landon/CCLN, p.95.

40. The title page of the print states that it was "Composed expressly for and Dedicated to Mrs. Bartolozzi." (See Plate 7.)

41. H. C. R. Landon's editions for Doblinger and Walter/CONCERTINI. This hypothesis, however, seems to be losing ground. See Landon/C&W I, pp.267–68, 544–45; and Feder/GROVE 6, pp.387–88.

42. Brook/BREITKOPF, 1771, col. 431.

43. Larsen/QUELLE, p.192.

44. According to the similar watermarks from the Gesellschaft copy in Bartha/Somfai/HOK, p.441.

45. For a modern edition of the D-major Divertimento, see Landon/DIVERTIMENTO.

46. The *con sordino* horns in Hob. XIV : 1 are exceptional in this group, as indicated in Stockmeier/KLAVIERTRIOS/1. From the purely practical standpoint the use of mutes for these parts would cause problems of intonation not normally encountered in Haydn's horn parts.

47. The theme duplicates the dynamics found in the quartet version, but no markings are to be found in the variations that follow.

48. According to Webster/CHRONOLOGY, p.44.

49. Feder/NICHT IDENTIFIZIERTEN, p.101.

50. Walter/KLAVIERKONZERTE, p.vii.

51. See Landon/C&W I, p.217.

52. Presumably during an interview with Griesinger.

53. Both, like the two Rajhrad sonatas (Es2, Es3) seem overextended for their materials.

54. See the evidence in Essay I, pp.7–8, and Essay II, pp.46–55.

55. Haydn wrote to Marianna von Genzinger that he was afflicted by having to attend all sorts of concerts. See Bartha/BRIEFE, p.274.

56. See Essay II, pp.56–57; and Larsen/CONTRACT.

V. THE QUESTION OF KEYBOARD IDIOM

1. The main literature on this topic with regard to Haydn, apart from the prefaces to editions and general studies, is: Brown/REALIZATION, Dart/INTERPRETATION, Feder/PROBLEME, Feder/ORGELKONZERTE, Hollis/INSTRUMENTS, James/CLAVICHORD, Kinsky/HAMMERKLAVIER, Luithlen/EISENSTÄDTER WALTER FLUGEL, Luithlen/HAYDN-ERINNERUNGEN, Luithlen/HAYDN-INSTRUMENTE, Newman/SCE, Parrish/HAYDN, Ripin/KEYBOARD, Somfai/KEYBOARD, Walter/KEYBOARD, Walter/KLAVIERE, and Walter/TASTENINSTRUMENT. Among the more general literature, the most influential have been Päsler/KLAVIERWERKE, Geiringer/HAYDN, Hughes/HAYDN, and Landon/C&W. The most important of these are the articles by Horst Walter, to which this study is indebted for documentary information.

2. This ability, however, is so limited that the harpsichord should not be considered a touch-sensitive instrument.

3. The strongest indication for the importance of French music is the inventory of Esterházy *musicalia* drawn up in 1759, in which the rubrics are: Italian, French, and Miscellaneous. See *HYb* IX, pp.67–88.

4. "Ein gutes Clavichord . . . die Bebung unt [sic] das Tragen der Töne voraus hat, weil ich nach den Anschlage noch jeder Note einen Druck geben kann . . . ," Bach/VERSUCH, I, pp.8–9; Mitchell/ESSAY, pp.36, 156. See also Cooper/CLAVICHORD.

5. Bach/VERSUCH, I, pp.8–9; II, p.1; Mitchell/ESSAY, pp.36, 172.

6. See the discussion of terminology in Schwarz/CEMBALOS, pp.249–50.

7. Cooper/CLAVICHORD, p.7.

8. See Feder/ORGELKONZERTE; and Table IV-1.

9. See the descriptions of instruments in Forer/ORGELN.

10. See the discussion of examples by J. S. Bach, C. P. E. Bach, and Mozart in Brown/UNDERSTANDING. One could argue that the clavichord had been in existence long before the eighteenth century and that an idiomatic style should already have been developed. However, in contrast to the harpsichord, the clavichord never achieved the status of a pre-eminent instrument until the middle of the eighteenth century and then only in North Germany.

11. Griesinger/NOTIZEN, p.13.

12. See Feder/PROBLEME, pp.101–102.

13. *PZ*, 24 November 1779.

14. See Landon/C&W III, p.415, and V, p.383.

15. See Walter/KLAVIERE, pp.257–59, where most of these documents are listed. This listing, however, must now be supplemented by Tank/DOKUMENTE.

16. Landon/C&W II, p.343.

17. Barthe/BRIEFE, p.244.

18. Ibid.

19. Walter/KLAVIERE, p.266.

20. Wainwright/BROADWOOD, pp.75, 185; Gyrowetz/AUTOBIOGRAPHY, p.75.

21. Novello/MOZART PILGRIMAGE, p.157. See also Kramer/TWO ASPECTS.

22. *HNV* No. 79.

23. Landon/C&W V, p.55.

24. Kunsthistorische Museum/SAITENKLAVIERE, pp.35–36, item 27.

25. A-Wn Autographsammlung.

26. James/CLAVICHORD.

27. Concerning this picture see Landon/C&W II, p.343.

28. See the reduced version in Somfai/PICTURES, p.225, h. See also the Hardy portrait, ibid., pp.136–37 (Nos. 247–48).

29. As derived from Gericke/MUSIKALIENHANDEL.

30. See Poštolka/KOŽELUCH, pp.213–80; and *JbTWP*, pp.33–35.

31. These prints carry a great deal of authority, for they were published and sold by the composer's brother, presumably under close supervision.

32. See the numerous references to Stein in Anderson/MOZART LETTERS; and, for the prints, Köchel/MOZART/6. This whole topic of terminology must eventually be studied from the practices of individual publishers; e.g., Hofmeister seemed more inclined to use the *fortepiano* or its equivalent as the first option, while Artaria continued to use the equivalent of harpsichord as the first option until the end of the century.

33. See Grundmann/CLAVICEMBALO, pp.109–13.

34. See Badura-Skoda/PROLEGOMENA, pp.78–80.

35. Burney/PRESENT STATE, pp.221, 257–58, 261–62, 282–83, 292, 311, 313, 318, 329, 341–42, 345, 357, 362, 367.

36. Schwarz/CEMBALOS, p.251.

37. Loesser/PIANOS, p.124.

38. Göthel/STEIN, col. 1231.

39. Anderson/MOZART LETTERS, p.793.

40. Only two copies survive: B-Bc and A-Wgm.

41. Interestingly, the 1771 and 1776 prints require only forte and sforzando.

42. Šetková/ŠTĚPÁNA, pp.162–88.

43. Weinmann/CAPRICCI.

44. See Picton/STEFFAN.

45. Göthel/STEIN, col. 1233.

46. Walter/KLAVIERE, pp.258–59. For more on Walter's *fortepiani*, see Franz/ MOZARTS KLAVIERBAUER; Lang/HAYDN-KLAVIER; Luithlen/EISENSTÄDTER WALTERFLÜGEL; and Rück/MOZARTS HAMMERFLÜGEL.

47. *JbTWP*, pp.87–91. The article clearly does not refer to Wenzel Schanz, who apparently died in 1791, but to a brother who succeeded him. It is assumed that the character of the instrument remained the same.

48. All the letters are derived from the text of Bartha/BRIEFE; many of them are quoted in English in Essay II.

49. See above, p.34. Although both Bartha/BRIEFE, p.163, and H. Landon/CCLN, p.60, believe the work to be Hob. XVI:48, this assertion should be doubted. Larsen/HÜB, p.118, speculates that it is Hob. XVI:34.

50. See Bartha/BRIEFE, p.244.

51. The use of pizzicato occurs in only one work that is here considered for harpsichord, Hob. XV:2. However, this work is a special case since its original form, now lost, was with baryton, an instrument on which the strings can also be plucked.

52. Haydn made this comment to Marianna von Genzinger concerning Hob. XVI:49 (see Essay II, p.44); see also the dynamic markings in the cantata "Arianna a Naxos." Much the same argument might also be applied to the sonatas of the 1760s and 1770s by those who advocate the *fortepiano* for these works.

53. Feder/ORGELKONZERTE.

54. See the discussion of Viennese works for keyboard from this period in Essay VI.

55. See Walter/TASTENINSTRUMENT, p.239.

56. Schubart/IDEEN, pp.222–23.

57. This argument is presented by Larsen in DISKUSSION as well as by Eva Badura-Skoda and others in *Kongress Washington/1975*, pp.216–17.

58. During the early 1780s, Haydn turned to the composition of lieder, a genre that by tradition was accompanied at the clavichord. However, with regard to Haydn we must question this tradition because of the circumstances of the early performances of these works. Haydn had a close association with Franz von Greiner, the father of the famous *Biedermeier* novelist Karoline Pichler, whose salon was an important meeting place for political, literary, and musical personalities of Josephinian Vienna. Presumably Haydn attended these salons. Karoline Greiner Pichler was herself an accomplished keyboardist and a student of Joseph

Anton Steffan, who was one of the very first composers in Vienna to write for the *fortepiano*. Consideration must therefore be given to the *fortepiano* as the preferred accompanying instrument for these works.

59. See also Kramer/TWO ASPECTS regarding the special pedal requirements of Hob. XVI:50.

VI. THE VIENNESE KEYBOARD TRADITION

1. Larsen/HÜB.
2. Abert/KLAVIERSONATEN and Abert/KLAVIERWERKE.
3. Wackernagel/HAYDN; see also the review Brown/WACKERNAGEL.
4. According to Schubart/IDEEN, pp.87–88.
5. From the purely practical standpoint, the volume would be too unwieldy to be held by a rococo music stand. Plates 12 and 13 show performance from a single copy not from a heavy, bound manuscript.
6. Facsimile edition, New York: Broude, 1967.
7. The list is derived from Gericke/MUSIKALIENHANDEL.
8. Ibid.
9. Composers represented are Anton Cajetan Adlgasser, Johann Agrell, Giorg Alb. Appel, Carl Philipp Emanuel Bach, Johann Ernst Bach, Georg Benda, Christlieb Siegmund Binder, Giov. Giac. (Johann Jakob?) Brand, Franz Vollrath Buttstett, Johann Friedrich Daube, Johann Ernst Eberlin, Paul Fischer, Johann Daniel Hardt, Franz Ferdinand Hengsberger, Johann Wilhelm Hertel, Bernhard Hupfeld, Heinrich Philip Johnsen, Johann Balthasar Kehl, Jakob Friedrich Kleinknecht, Johann Gottfried Krebs, Adolph Carl Kunzen, Johann Georg Lang, Philippe Le Roi, Johann Christoph Mann, Leopold Mozart, Johann Gottfried Palschau, Christoph Schaffrath, Johann Adolph Scheibe, Johann Schobert, Johann Gottfried Seifert, Erich Felix Spitz, Franz Anton Stadler, Joseph Ferdinand Timer, Johann Nikalaus Tischer, Joseph Umstatt, Georg Christoph Wagenseil, Johann Christoph Walther, Constantin Joseph Weber, Johann Friedrich Wilhelm Wenckel, Johann Zach, and Justus Friedrich Wilhelm Zachariae.
10. Composers represented are Francesco Araya, Pietro Baldissari, Ferdinando Bertoni, Pietro Chiarini, Baldassare Galuppi, François Krafft, Marianna Martines, Giuseppe Antonio Paganelli, Palladini, Antonio Gaetano Pampini, Fulg. Peroti, Giovan Battista Pescetti, Giovanni Maria or Giovanni Placido Rutini, Pietro Pompeo Sales, Giuseppe (?) Sammartini, Domenico Scarlatti, and Giovanni Battista Serini.
11. Composers represented are Carl Philipp Emanuel Bach, Joachim Busse, Christian Friedrich Carl (?) Fasch, Johann Gottlieb Janitsch, Johann Philipp Kirnberger, Christian Gottfried Krause, Jacques Le Fèvre, Friedrich Wilhelm Marpurg, Friedrich Christian Rackemann, and Wilhelm August Traugott Roth.
12. The information on printed keyboard music in mid-century Vienna was culled from Gericke/MUSIKALIENHANDEL; Hoffmann-Erbrecht/HAFFNER; and Newman/SCE, pp.71–72. For Traeg, see Weinmann/TRAEG and Weinmann/TRAEG FAC.
13. Burney/PRESENT STATE I, pp.367–68.
14. Fiorroni has not been identified any further than this Haffner anthology.
15. On Roskovsky, see Hatting/HAYDN ODER KAYSER?; Riedel/FUX, pp.67–68; and Pollack/VIENNESE, pp.381–96.
16. See Riedel/FUX, pp.67–68; and Pollack/VIENNESE, pp.381–96; for some of the anonymous attributions.
17. Riedel/FUX, facsimile following p.xii.
18. On CS-KRm, see Feder/QUELLEN, pp.26–29.
19. Although "comprehensive" treatment is outside of the scope of this book, since at the time of writing no detailed summaries of the cyclic output of Fux, Wagenseil, Birck, Tuma, Schögler, M. G. Monn, Steffan, Hofmann, and J. C. Monn have been published, they are offered here in order to establish Haydn's place in the Viennese tradition.

20. See Apel/KEYBOARD, pp.566–72.

21. On the problem of attribution—especially those works published in *DTOe*—see Riedel/FUX, pp.vii–viii.

22. Riedel/FUX, p.xii.

23. Scholz-Michelitsch/WAGENSEIL. An important survey of Wagenseil's solo sonatas is found in Pollack/VIENNESE, pp.177–261.

24. Burney/PRESENT STATE I, p.329.

25. Schubart/IDEEN, p.88.

26. Based on Scholz-Michelitsch/WWV.

27. Ibid., WWV 17, 18, 24, 27, 47, 52, 59, 69, 71, and 76.

28. According to Schenk/AUTOBIOGRAPHY, p.77, Wagenseil used the *Well-Tempered Clavier* for teaching.

29. See also Newman/SCE, p.354.

30. Biba/PÜRK. A thematic catalogue appears in Pollack/VIENNESE, pp.406–409, but it does not include A-Wn S.m. 1079.

31. See Kirkendale/FUGUE, pp.109–14.

32. A third composition, consisting of a Prelude and Presto in G major, follows, but comparison with the previous two works makes an attribution to Tuma doubtful.

33. Wellesz/Sternfeld/SYMPHONY, p.395.

34. The keyboard music attributed to Karl Georg Reutter (1708–1772) at D-brd-B Mus. ms. 18395 (see the catalogue by N. Hofer [copies at A-Wn and A-He]) is probably by Reutter's father by virtue of its very conservative syntax. Overall, the works are unremarkable, both musically and historically, and do not contribute to our understanding of Haydn's early sonatas.

35. See thematic catalogues in Fischer/WIENER, and Pollack/VIENNESE, pp.453–86; also Kollpacher/MONN.

36. See Hiller/NACHRICHTEN XIII (1766), p.98.

37. Šetková/ŠTĚPÁN.

38. *WD* XVIII/84 (1766).

39. According to the catalogue in Šetková/ŠTĚPÁNA. For a thorough discussion of Steffan's solo sonatas see Pollack/VIENNESE, pp.262–340.

40. The above summary is based on the catalogue in Šetková/ŠTĚPÁNA, on Šetková/Straková/ŠTĚPÁN, as well as on the author's examination of prints and manuscript copies available at A-Wgm and CS-KRm.

41. See Brown/HAYDN-HOFMANN, and Prohászka/HOFMANN.

42. Thematic catalogues of Hofmann's solo keyboard sonatas are found in Hatting/KLAVIERMUSIK, pp.336–37; and Pollack/VIENNESE, pp.412–25.

43. See Newman/SCE, p.356.

44. See Brown/HAYDN-HOFMANN.

45. Derived from Gericke/MUSIKALIENHANDEL. One hypothesis reportedly advocated by Fischer is that the accompanied tradition in Vienna finds its origin in the "Lauthenconcert" (see Fuller/ACCOMPANIED, pp.222, 234–35). However, only two works that one could possibly construe as belonging to this tradition were advertised in *WD* in 1735 and *ca.* 1743; Philipp Martino, *Galanteriestück: VI Trios, III con Liuto, Flauto Trav. & Fondamento, III con Liuto, Violino & Fondamento*, and Adam Flackenhagen, *Sei concerto a Liuto, Traverso, Oboe or Violino e Violoncello.*

46. The works were assembled into collections only after the individual sonatas were copied. See above, pp.173–76.

47. I am indebted to Michelle Fillion for her unpublished catalogue of this repertoire, upon which the following discussion is based. For a more thorough treatment of accompanied keyboard music in Vienna, see Fillion/ACCOMPANIED.

48. Many of those in two movements are by Anton Zimmermann, some of whose products may be later than 1780.

49. Fillion/ACCOMPANIED, pp.306–307.

50. See Fillion/HOB. XV:C1.

51. See, for example, Daffner/ENTWICKLUNG; Uldall/KLAVIERKONZERT, p.3; Drummond/CONCERTO, pp.4–9, 29, 32–42.

52. The fact that the famous Monn Cello Concerto (Fischer No. 39) comes down to us in a version for keyboard also tends to support an independent development.

53. See Gericke/MUSIKALIENHANDEL.

54. Uldall/KLAVIERKONZERT, pp.86–87. Uldall seems to have made his judgment only on the basis of the D-major Keyboard Concerto by Monn published in Fischer/WIENER.

55. Bonta/SONATA DA CHIESA.

56. According to Gericke/MUSIKALIENHANDEL.

57. Fischer/WIENER, pp.xxviii–xxix. Despite assertions elsewhere (Wellesz/Sternfeld/CONCERTO, p.466), all of Monn's concertos are in three movements. The four-movement work listed by Fischer, No. 38, whose keyboard part is no longer extant, is probably a church sonata with solo organ.

58. For a brief orientation to the problems of concerto form, see below pp.000–00; Stevens/CONCERTO; and Stevens/THEME.

59. See also the finale to Monn's Cello Concerto (Fischer No. 39).

60. Fischer Nos. 123–25 are of questionable paternity and therefore were excluded from the above discussion.

61. Brook/BREITKOPF, cols. 133, 292, and 580.

62. As derived from WWV.

63. On this question see Plate 15, where it appears the strings are not doubled. Probably the most difficult problem with regard to setting is the keyboard instrument for which these works were intended: harpsichord or organ. Organ playing was part of Wagenseil's official duties for nearly a decade, and ten works come down in sources that mention the organ as one of the available options, but only the organ indication for three concertos from Anthology Imperial can be deemed authentic. In these three probably authentic copies, each title page indicates "Clavicembalo" while in the upper right-hand corner "orgl:" is written in an eighteenth-century hand. WWV 261 and 243 remain within the assumed organ compass by not exceeding c''''; WWV 269 exceeds this pitch, raising the further question as to whether it or eighteenth-century Austrian works in general that exceed c'''' are indeed for the organ.

64. The Wagenseil sample includes all those in Anthology Imperial (excluding those for more than one keyboard) as well as the few available works in modern editions; i.e., WWV 5, 41, 253, 256, 258, 261, 265, 266 (231), 267 (232), 269, 278, 279 (234), 282, 283, 289, 291, 297, 299, 300 (238), 301 (239), 309, 312, 313, 316, 322, 329, 331 (243), and 336 (245); and one work in G major not found in WWV. The two concertos published in *Musik Alter Meister* XLII, WWV 295 and 335, are of doubtful authenticity and are therefore not included.

65. In the available concertos by Mattielli, Schlöger, Albrechtsberger, and Michael Haydn, the plan of the Wagenseil concerto is closely followed except for the finale to Michael Haydn's double concerto for viola and organ (Perger No. 55), which is not framed by the binary form. In contrast to other known works by Schlöger, his single known concerto does not display any of the subtleties of syntactic structure seen in the solo divertimento.

66. Wellesz/Sternfeld/CONCERTO, p.468.

67. Including one concerto from A-Wn S.m. 11084, six from S.m. 11085, D-brd-B ms. mus. 10733/1, 4, 7, 11, 12, and 14; and D-ddr-Dlb 3301-0-1, 2, 3, and 7.

68. In one instance, the slow movement of a C-major concerto is placed in the flattened mediant major.

69. This structure is similar to the synthesis of tutti/solo and antecedent/consequent phrases in the first-movement recapitulations.

70. See catalogue in Šetková/ŠTĚPÁNA.

71. Including Šetková 99, 101, 106, 110, 119, 126, and 127. According to external evidence some are from before 1763 and probably none are later than 1776.

VII. JOSEPH HAYDN AND C.P.E. BACH

1. Strictly speaking, the earliest statement concerns C. P. E. Bach's opinion of Haydn's Quartets Op. 33 given in a review in CRAMER'S I (1783), p.153: "I know that Bach in Hamburg . . . has expressed his complete satisfaction with these works of Haydn, especially since they so excellently display skill and artifice." See Schmid/HAYDN UND BACH, p.307.

2. For further commentary and an annotated presentation of this "Account," see Brown/EARLIEST ENGLISH. The reader should note that some of the conclusions there are at odds with some of those expressed here and in Brown/BACH.

3. *EMLR*, October 1784, p.253.

4. CRAMER'S II (1784), pp.585–94.

5. Griesinger/NOTIZEN, p.11.

6. Bertuch/BERMERKUNGEN I, pp.185–86; for the Griesinger acknowledgment see ibid., II, p.54.

7. A comparison of the Dies version of the parallel paragraph also supports this hypothesis; see ESSAY I, p.4.

8. Moritz/REISER, p.300.

9. Roscoe/HAYDN AND LONDON, p.208.

10. Pohl/HAYDN I, pp.133–34.

11. Bach/AUTOBIOGRAPHY, p.203; Newman/BACH, p.368.

12. *AMZ* XI/41–47 and 49 (12 July–23 August 1809 and 6 September 1809).

13. Gerber/NTL, col. 583, also mentions Bach with regard to Hob. XVI:48 but sees the two composers as different. See Essay II, p.43.

14. Horst Seeger, editor (Berlin: Henschelverlag, 1959).

15. See Gotwals/TCP, p.95.

16. Dies/NACHRICHTEN, p.40.

17. See Finscher/STREICHQUARTETTS, pp.138–44; and Webster/CHRONOLOGY, p.38.

18. *HBV*: Mattheson, 5, 9, 27; Heinichen, 8; Fux, 3. *HNV*: Mattheson, 583, 584, 585; Heinichen, 608; Fux, 606.

19. "I [Haydn] should, however, mention which of the excellent masters in particular interested me in my younger years and thus perhaps had the greatest influence on me. So I must name—in vocal music, Gassmann and in instrumental music Emanuel Bach with his *Clavier* matters of every kind. The latter I used to enjoy playing countless times, especially when I felt despondent or burdened by worries. And I was always cheered by them and left the instrument in a good mood." Rochlitz/FREUNDE, p.275, where Abbé Stadler is cited as a source for this information.

20. Stadler/GESCHICHTE, pp.132–33.

21. Latrobe/SELECTION I, p.2, as quoted in Schmid/HAYDN UND BACH, p.301.

22. Burney/REES (HAYDN), n.p.

23. Johnson/LIVES, II, pp.306–309.

24. See Brown/EARLIEST ENGLISH, p.353.

25. Schmid/HAYDN UND BACH, p.303.

26. Landon/PIANO SONATAS, pp.53–55. A more recent attempt to draw musical parallels found in Todd/HAYDN is no more convincing than those given by Schmid and Landon.

27. Steglich/DRESDNER, p.125.

28. Schmid/HAYDN UND BACH, pp.301–302; Abert/KLAVIERWERKE, p.567; Geiringer/HAYDN, p.226; and Finscher/STREICHQUARTETTS, p.150.

29. Geiringer/HAYDN, pp.209, 226, 253–54, and 257. See also p.232.

30. Ibid., p.290.

31. Ibid., p.315.

32. See Graue/HAYDN.

33. Radcliffe/KEYBOARD, p.585. See also pp.587, 593, 596–98, and 602.

34. Hughes/HAYDN, pp.154–55.

35. Abert/KLAVIERWERKE, p.557.

36. See Webster/FINSCHER.

37. Finscher/STREICHQUARTETTS, p.145.

38. Eibner/KLAVIERSTÜCKE, p.xix.

39. Of the remaining important literature, mention should be made of the more measured comments by Heinrich Schenker and by Donald Francis Tovey. In 1908 Schenker completed *Ein Beitrag zur Ornamentik*, the preface of which contains an extensive discussion of Bach with references to the three Viennese masters. One of his examples for comparing Bach and Haydn is from a corrupted text of the Sonata in C-sharp minor Hob. XVI:36 (see translation of Schenker/BEITRAG, p.40). Tovey's article on Haydn's chamber music, originally written for COBBETT'S, makes frequent mention of Haydn and Bach, discussing such topics as the recitative, varied reprise, cadenza, development, modulation, bifocal beginnings (i.e., ambiguity of major/relative minor); see reprint in Tovey/MAINSTREAM, pp.27–29, 34, 35–37, 48, 49, 51, and 57.

Bettina Wackernagel questions these long-held assumptions of Bach–Haydn similarities in her study of Haydn's early keyboard music, i.e., to 1771. She implies that Bach's influence cannot be adequately stylistically documented, and then examines Abert's "thematische Einheit" and "melodisch-stilistische Ähnlichkeiten" as well as Lowinsky/MOZART. Her conclusions cast doubt on the thesis that Haydn used Bach's sonatas as models, but the possibility of a more generalized influence is left open. See Wackernagel/HAYDN, pp.63–102; and Brown/WACKERNAGEL.

40. I am indebted to Eugene Helm for supplying a prepublication copy of his catalogue of C.P.E. Bach's works, which was of great assistance for preparing the following section.

41. Culled from information in Gericke/MUSIKALIENHANDEL.

42. Facsimile edition, Weinmann/TRAEG FAC.

43. Ibid.

44. As mentioned above (p.208), the two dealers with whom Haydn was most likely to do business would have been Ghelen and Artaria, who were located in the Michaelerplatz, adjacent to the Wallnerstrasse.

45. See the subscription lists at the front of the *Kenner und Liebhaber* volumes.

46. Bartha/BRIEFE, p.188.

47. Haydn also owned two of Bach's vocal works: *Heilig*, Wq. 217 (*HBV* 102, *HNV* 265) and *Sturms geistliche Gesänge* II, Wq. 198 (*HNV* 266). According to Wade/BACH, the Concerto Wq. 47 is in the hand of C. P. E. Bach's scribe Michel; thus, so would Wq. 67 and 80.

48. Schmid/HAYDN UND BACH, pp.308–309.

49. Stadler/GESCHICHTE, pp.102 and 150; and Freeman/MELK, p.248.

50. Note that many of the other sonatas listed in the third column of Table VII-2 were available only in anthologies not solely devoted to the sonatas of the Berlin/Hamburg Bach.

51. Bach/VERSUCH I, pp.63–64; see Neumann/ORNAMENTATION, p.184.

52. Feder/DATIERUNG.

53. Bach/AUTOBIOGRAPHY, pp.208–209; Newman/BACH, pp.371–72.

54. There are, however, strong thematic similarities between Wq. 63/2 and Hob. XVI:46/1, and Wq. 50/3 and Hob. XV:35/1.

55. Sisman/VARIATIONS, p.154. The string quartet movements are discussed in Tovey/MAINSTREAM, pp.26–37.

56. Sisman/VARIATIONS, pp.140–45. The idea was first proposed by Radcliffe/KEYBOARD, p.587.

57. Bach/VERSUCH I, pp.132–33.

58. See Essay II, p.35.

59. Although it uses the *Regola dell'Ottava* and has a fantasy character, the first movement of Hob. XVI:48 is not included because it is more a variation form than a fantasia; see note 13 above and Essay X, pp.340–44.

60. See, however, the examples cited *supra*, note 54.

61. Landon/SYMPHONIES, pp.694–99; and Gerlach/ORDNUNG.

62. See Essay II, pp.13–14.

63. Bach/VERSUCH II, pp.327, 328, 340.

64. The *Regola dell'Ottava* was a formula found in many treatises dealing with the basso continuo: a series of diatonic and/or chromatic pitches mostly moving stepwise within the range of an octave.

65. Bach/VERSUCH II, p.326.

66. Ibid., p.330.

67. Ibid.

68. Ibid., pp.326. Bach repeats this idea on p.336.

69. Ibid., p.333.

70. Ibid., p.337.

71. Ibid., pp.326–41.

72. Ibid., p.442.

73. See the important discussions of this work in Somfai/ENHARMONIC and Salzer/HAYDN FANTASIA.

74. See Schenker/SCHÖPFUNG; and Stern/SCHÖPFUNG.

75. Perhaps Haydn's most extensive use of the deceptive cadence is found in the Domine Deus of the "St. Cecilia" Mass, which also comes from the 1760s.

76. Bach/VERSUCH II, p.332.

77. Ibid., p.330.

78. The one instance where Haydn's use of another composer's materials can be directly documented is in Haydn's insertion arias written during the years of the Esterházy operatic establishment. While Haydn may take melodic fragments from these models, the transformation is so complete that if the text were removed, the similarities of the two settings would be deemed coincidental. See Somfai/ISMERETLEN; and Brown/GENESIS.

79. Mann/STUDENT; Mann/TEXTREVISION; and Mann/ELEMENTARBUCH emphasize the importance of Fux's treatise.

VIII. TOWARD DEFINING GENRE AND GENRE TYPES

1. See Webster/CHAMBER for a discussion of various genre designations.

2. Feder/PROBLEME, p.100.

3. Feder/KLAVIERSONATEN/1.

4. Somfai/ZONGORASZONÁTÁI, p.143. Somfai first presented these types at Kongress/Washington 1975, but they were not included in the proceedings; they were later published with some revisions in Somfai/STILFRAGEN.

5. See Badura-Skoda/PERFORMANCE, p.55, on this environment in Vienna through the time of Beethoven. Morrow/VIENNA is a thorough discussion of Viennese concert life; not a single solo keyboard sonata was performed in a public concert from 1781 to 1810.

6. Not mentioned by Somfai and left unclassified by Feder are the two four-hand sonatas, Hob. XVIIa:1 and 2. In accordance with their approaches, Hob. XVIIa:2 would be for the *Kenner*, XVIIa:1 for the *Liebhaber*, and both would be "Damensonaten."

7. See Newman/ACCOMPANIED and Fuller/ACCOMPANIED for the background for this type of setting.

8. Hob. XV:41/2 is the only exception: the violin part is completely dispensable.

9. Hob. XIV:1 also belongs with these trios in a transitional style. It is scored with an additional pair of horns.

10. Tovey rewrote the accompanying parts to Hob. XV:18 and 26 "redistributed for the benefit of Violin and Cello." See Tovey/TRIO F SHARP and Tovey/TRIO A.

11. Scott/CHAMBER, p.215.

12. Froggatt/TRIOS.

13. It has generally been accepted that the C-major Organ Concerto Hob. XVIII:1 was written for the profession of Thérèse Keller as Sister Josepha into the Convent of St. Nicholas of the Order of the Clares in 1756. Haydn had an attachment to Thérèse but in the end married her older sister. See Pohl/HAYDN I, pp.196–97; and Griesinger/NOTIZEN, p.15 (Gotwals/TCP, p.15), and Dies/NACHRICHTEN, pp.45–46 (Gotwals/TCP, p.99).

IX. THE CONCERTOS

1. For example, see Lang/OPERA; and Wellesz/Sternfeld/CONCERTO, p.472.

2. For further recent discussions on the problem of form, see Stevens/CONCERTO; Stevens/THEME; Davis/LANG, pp.148–70; and Davis/KOCH.

3. See Stevens/CONCERTO.

4. On this issue see Davis/KOCH.

5. In one instance (Hob. XVIII:6, mm. 16–20), a closing is provided to the continuation itself.

6. P mm. 12–20, T mm. 25–30, S mm. 35–38, and K mm. 44–48.

7. Much the same can be said for mm. 34–36, which are a variation of mm. 31–34.

8. See Essay II, pp.33–40; and Essay IV, pp.132–33.

9. See Koch/VERSUCH, III, pp.307–308; Wolf/STAMITZ, pp.650–51.

10. See also Essay VII, where this general type of bass line in Haydn's Capriccio/Fantasia works is attributed to the influence of C.P.E. Bach. In the concertos the lines are not so well organized.

11. See LaRue/BEETHOVEN and Davis/MOZART, for a discussion of harmonic-rhythmic patterning in these two composers.

12. See Davis/KOCH on this particular area of the structure.

13. See Symphony No. 37/1, m. 117 for a strikingly similar gesture.

14. It is unfortunate that it is not possible to compare Hob. XVIII:6 with Haydn's only other double concerto, for two horns, which is not extant.

15. Compare this passage to the functionally parallel earlier one in which the melody twists upward and downward, never exceeding e'''.

16. However, Hob. XVIII:1 does repeat the first part, not unlike a binary form.

17. In Hob. XVIII:1 the allusion to the subdominant at the beginning of the finale may indicate some sort of specialized finale function within the tonality of the entire cycle; i.e., the subdominant has been otherwise held in reserve for the latter portions of a movement.

18. Cole/VOGUE, pp.428–31.

19. Cole/DEVELOPMENT, pp.124–25.

20. See Szabolcsi/UNGARISCHE.

21. This date was assigned ca. 1800. See Essay IV, p.132 and Essay VIII, n.13.

22. See the letter in Niemetschek/MOZART, reprinted in Bartha/BRIEFE, p.185, in which Haydn declined an operatic commission for Prague in 1787: "But even then I would be risking much, since the great Mozart can scarcely be compared with anyone."

X. THE SOLO AND ENSEMBLE KEYBOARD MUSIC

1. For example, see Hob. XVI:3, 6, 7, 8, 10, 13, 14, G1, and XVII:D1. The tendency seems less strong in the accompanied works. In the later keyboard cycles even such suspect similarities are no longer present. The entire issue can be pursued in Engel/QUELLEN, Keller/K.503, and Reti/THEMATIC PROCESS, all of which advocate a thematic or motivic connection among movements, while LaRue/SIGNIFICANT, Temperley/TESTING, and Wiesel/PRESENCE are more skeptical.

2. See Newman/SCE, pp.143–47.

3. A substantial survey of sonata form in eighteenth- and nineteenth-century theory and practice can be obtained from Churgin/GALEAZZI; Kamien/SONATA ALLEGRO; Larsen/SONATENFORM-PROBLEME; Newman/COMMUNICATIONS; Newman/ RECOGNITION; Newman/SCE, pp.143–58; Newman/SSB, pp.27–36; Ratner/HAR- MONIC; Ritzel/ENTWICKLUNG; and Weiss/COMMUNICATIONS. For a more syn- tactical approach to Haydn's keyboard music, see Brown/EXPOSITION; Brown/SOLO AND ENSEMBLE; Fillion/SONATA-EXPOSITION; Steinberg/TRIOS; and Tange- man/TRANSITION.

4. See Andrews/SUBMEDIANT.

5. See Hill/GASSMANN, pp.161–96, and particularly pp.178–79.

6. See Essay VI, p.199.

7. See Essay VII, pp.215–19.

8. See Fischer's article on variations in *MGG* and Sisman/VARIATIONS, which ex- pands Fischer's theoretical study and provides a survey of Haydn's variations according to theoretical models.

9. Sisman/VARIATIONS, p.168, considers this to be a "melodic outline" variation.

10. See Wyzewa/CENTENAIRE. For a bibliography of the *Sturm und Drang* litera- ture, see Todd/HAYDN. A complete summary of the idea in music is found in Rudolf/ STORM; and Landon/C&W II, pp.266–393.

11. See Essay VII, pp.222–25 for a detailed discussion of Hob. XVII:1.

12. See Essay III, p.89 for a discussion of the large-dimension plan of Hob. XVII:2.

13. See Essay III, pp.71–73, where the unity of this cycle is pursued.

14. See Brown/EXPOSITION and Fillion/SONATA-EXPOSITION. The "mono- thematic" concept is certainly not peculiar to Haydn; it is a general trait of eighteenth- century Viennese instrumental music.

15. See Schenker/ORGANIC for a discussion of Hob. XVI:44/1.

16. See Larsen/SONATENFORM-PROBLEME, pp.226–27.

17. For a special comment on this retransition as well as on Hob. XVI:23, 27, 28, 30, 34, 41, and 43, see Shamgar/RHYTHMIC.

18. While this model has been alluded to in our discussion of the climax in Hob. XVI:44/1, Charles Rosen in SONATA FORMS, pp.54–55, has pointed to a similar pas- sage in Hob. XVI:20/1. However, Rosen's explanation that it derives from a dramatic proce- dure found in the aria cannot be accepted. For this passage is a direct outgrowth and an intensification of the parallel phrase at the beginning of the development, and the use of the initial part of T as a retransition.

19. See Steglich/KADENZEN.

20. Its autograph was reportedly in the possession of an organist named Czerwenka, who may very well be a descendant of the Esterházy bassoonist Franz Czerwenka (see Bar- tha/Somfai/HOK, pp.172–73). Therefore it is possible that this piece is the slow movement from Haydn's lost bassoon concerto, which is not included in Hoboken but is listed in a short catalogue in Haydn's own hand (reproduced in Hoboken/WERKVERZEICHNIS I). A second possibility, since Hob. XVI:19/2 is in its dominant, is that it is the slow movement of the lost concerto for "Contra Violone," which, from the incipit in *EK*, is in D major.

21. For a survey of the rondo in theory and practice, with extensive sections on Haydn, see Cole/DEVELOPMENT.

22. Similar recapitulatory plans are found in the later string quartets Op. 64/5 and Op. 77/1.

23. See Essay II, p.32 for a contemporary review that mentions the irregularity of this theme.

24. See Larsen/SONATENFORM-PROBLEME, pp.226–27, where this practice is referred to as "Entwicklungspartie."

25. One might have hoped that the manifold possibilities of this motive had been more thoroughly exploited.

26. One senses the same rush to finish a set of works in the finale to the last quartet of the String Quartets Op. 9. See also pp.325, 359, and 378.

27. See Kirkendale/FUGUE, pp.148–49.

28. See Essay IV, p.121.

29. See Essay VII, p.218.

30. See Essay V, pp.163–65.

31. A textual discrepancy exists between Christa Landon's edition of Hob. XVI:32/1 and those by Päsler and Feder. The above discussion is based on the Landon text.

32. See Kirkendale/FUGUE, p.70.

33. Hob. XVI:36 consists of a Fast–Faster–Minuet.

34. See LaRue/MULTISTAGE for a thorough motivic study of this movement.

35. See also Sisman/HYBRID; and Neubacher/KOMPOSITIONSPROZESS.

36. See Essay VII, p.220.

37. Another example of the varied reprise is Symphony No. 102/2. In the keyboard version (Hob. XV:26/2), the variation element is absent because the exposition is not repeated. See also below, p.378.

38. See Chew/NIGHT-WATCHMAN'S.

39. See Essay II, pp.30–32; Essay III, pp.82–83; and below, p.331.

40. That Haydn took particular care in the working-out of this movement can be confirmed by the surviving sketch. See Essay II, pp.30–31.

41. The variations of Hob. XV:13/1 replaced another first movement presumably in sonata form. See Essay II, p.35 and below, p.332.

42. Neither the lyric Tempo di Menuet of Hob. XV:11/2 nor the strophic double variations of XV:13/1 present anything new.

43. The Fantasia is discussed in Essay VII, pp.226–27.

44. Mersmann/VERSUCH, pp.255–62; Schenker/FIVE; Cone/FORM, pp.73–74; and Abert/KLAVIERSONATEN, p.545.

45. See also Somfai/ENHARMONIC and Chapman/MODULATION.

46. See also Palm/UNBEKANNTE, pp.184–86.

47. See Hill/GASSMANN, pp.161–96.

48. As is known from the sketches, part two was originally to have been twice as long. See Essay II, pp.38–42.

49. See also Gabriel's aria "Nun beut die Flur das frische Grün" in *The Creation*.

50. Certainly, Haydn's other solutions for concluding this movement seem hardly adequate beside this final version. See Essay II, pp.48–49.

51. See Somfai/LONDON, pp.166–69.

52. Szabolcsi/UNGARISCHE, p.166.

53. Rosen/CLASSICAL pp.83–88; and Sisman/SMALL, pp.463–72.

54. See also Ratner/CLASSIC, pp.412–21; Schenker/ES DUR; Scott/FANCIES; Moss/HOB. XVI:52; and Tovey/HOB. XVI:52.

55. See Taves/EDITIONS.

56. On the style sources for this work, see Graue/HAYDN.

57. Landon/KLAVIERSONATEN III, p.xv.

58. See Palm/UNBEKANNTE, pp.187–88.

59. See above, p.352, for a similar event in Hob. XV:14/1.

60. A similar type of relationship is found in Symphony No. 92/1. See Brown/CRITICAL, pp.387–90.

61. See Landon/SYMPHONIES-SUPPLEMENT, pp.44–47; and Szabolcsi/UNGARISCHE.

62. According to Hoboken/WERKVERZEICHNIS I, pp.709–10, this movement appeared in arrangements for string quartet, violin duet, keyboard solo, and "in unzähligen anderen Bearbeitungen."

63. For a possible derivation for this passage, see Graue/HAYDN.

64. See also Schenker/C DUR; and Zeller/ABWEICHUNGEN.

65. One notable exception is Hob. XVI:49/1.

66. See LaRue/BIFOCAL.

67. See also Rosen/CLASSICAL, pp.363–64; and Landon/C&W IV, pp.205–208. See Essay II, pp.55–56, for a review of this work, giving an eighteenth-century view of its style.

68. One symphony and three string quartets from the 1790s also use distant tonal relationships for their slow movements: Symphony No. 99 and String Quartet Op. 76/5—mediant major; Op. 76/6—flattened submediant; and Op. 74/3—submediant major. Haydn also began to use remote keys for trios of minuets; see Op. 74/1 and Symphonies Nos. 99 and 104.

69. Forkel believed thematically unified rondos to be the best. See Cole/VOGUE, p.428.

70. Gerber/ATL, col. 610.

General Index

Abert, Hermann, 172, 179, 214–15, 346
Accademia Philharmonica di Bologna, 11
"Acht Sauschneider müssen seyn." *See* Hob. XVII:1
Agnesi, Maria Theresia, 176, 178
Alberti, Domenico, 178
Albrechtsberger, Johann Georg, 43, 217, 431
allemande, 375, 381–82
Allgemeine deutsche Bibliothek, 36
Allgemeine Musikalische Zeitung (Leipzig), 50, 55–56, 208
Almanach Musical, 25
Alžbétinky, convent (Bohemia), 102, 424
D'Anglebert, Jean-Henri, 177
"Anno 1776" Sonatas. *See* Hob. XVI:27–32
Anthology Dorsch (A-Wgm), 71–73, 89, 108, 119–21, 129, 131, 418
Anthology Imperial (A-Wn), 103, 173, 195, 198
Anthology Roskovsky (H-Bn), 70, 178, 186
Anthology Vienna (A-Wgm), 119, 178, 186
appoggiaturas (notation of), 20, 113, 129, 425
Archiv der Stadt Wien, 421
Arnold, Samuel, 417
Artaria (Viennese publisher), 6, 23–27 (plate), 29–30 (plate), 33–35, 37–38, 45, 53 (plate), 62, 71, 88–89, 93, 106, 112, 120–21, 125–26, 132, 140–41, 146, 148, 151 (plate), 208, 216, 254, 340, 422, 428, 433
attacca, 306, 336
Auenbrugger, Katharina, 24–25, 316, 383
Auenbrugger, Leopold von, 25, 418
Auenbrugger, Marianna, 24–25, 316, 383
Auenbrugger Sonatas. *See* Hob. XVI:35–39 [20]
Auerhammer, Giuseppa, 179
authenticity, 27–28, 60–111
autographs, 44, 48–49, 58, 73, 103, 119–20, 122, 131

Bach, Carl Philipp Emanuel, 203–29, 284, 367, 429, 432, 433; works, 97, 125, 161, 172, 176, 207–208, 213–29, 308, 433; *Versuch,* 5, 96, 208–209, 213, 219–29
Bach, Johann Christian, 54, 88, 97, 140
Bach, Johann Sebastian, 183, 197–98, 217, 430

Badura-Skoda, Eva, 422
Baillon (French publisher), 97
Banger (English publisher), 56
Barmherzigen Brüder in Leopoldstadt, 4, 133, 137
Barthelemon, Cecilia, 8
Bartolozzi, Gaetano, 50, 122, 207
Bartolozzi, Therese Jansen, 8, 46, 50–54 (plate), 64, 122, 128, 165, 368, 375–76, 378, 421
baryton, 70, 94
La Battaile de Rosbach. See Hob. XVII:F3
Batton, Kanon, 30
Bauer, Georg, 177
Baur, Samuel, 208
Bay, Mr. (English publisher), 56
Beardmore & Birchall (English publisher), 25, 121
Bebung, 159–60
Beethoven, Ludwig van, 3, 50, 113, 138, 141, 177, 233, 240, 244, 260, 350, 357, 359, 369, 380, 384
Benton, Rita, 82–83
Bergkirche (Eisenstadt), 137–38
Berlin, 100, 102–103, 108
Bernardi, Augustin, 177
Bertini, (Benoît-) Auguste, 50
Bertuch, Carl, 206
Bibliothèque Nationale (Paris), 68
Birck (Pürck, Pürk, Pirck), Wenzel Raimond, 141–43*, 176, *178,* 183–87*, 199
Bittner, Carl, 100
Bland, John (English publisher), 34, 38, 46, 62, 126–27, 146
Boccherini, Luigi, 140
Bode, J. J. C., 207
Bohak, Johann, 138
Bösendorfer (piano manufacturer), 171
Bossler, Heinrich Philipp (German publisher), 27, 30, 32 (plate), 62, 93, 122, 146
Botstiber, Hugo, 37–38
Boyer (French publisher), 33, 105
Brahms, Johannes, 362
Brand, Carl Maria, 62
Bratislava, 178
Braun, Baroness Josephine von, 49–50, 216
Braun, Peter Freiherr von, 49–50, 216

Page numbers in italics refer to main discussions. Asterisks indicate musical examples.

Vanhal (Vanhall), Johann, 38, 61, 141, 178–79, 195–97
variation, 287, 290–91, 301–302, 318, 327–30, 332, 338, 346, 385–86; at the phrase, 350; bass, 359; continuous, 373; developmental, 312–13, 327; embellished themes, 336, 340; expanded, 358, 363, 369; fantasy, 340; nonstrophic, 312, 344; strophic, 313, 320, 373; on two themes, 307, 327, 340, 355–56, 367; procedures, 312–15, 330, 354–55, 359, 376; reprise, 381; rondo, 220, 269–73, 299–300, 314–15, 368, 374, 377, 386; sets, 307, 336, 355, 363, 386; ternary, 330, 354–55, 357, 361
varied reprise, 220, 311, 323, 367, 386
Vento, Mattia, 178
Vestris, Madame, 50
Vienna, 6, 60, 121, 275, 284
Viennese tradition, 289, 340
Vogler, Georg Joseph, 102
Vorschlag, 113, 115, 219, 229

Wachowski, Joseph, 178
Wackernagel, Bettina, 172, 179, 433
Wagenseil, Georg Christoph, 14, 100, 141, 172–76, 178, 180, 189, 195, 200–202, 209, 212, 220, 276, 284, 429; works, 14, 82, 88, 176–78, 180–86*, 192*, 195–98, 200–201, 431
Waldburg-Zeil, 100

walking bass, 299, 310
Walter, Anton (piano maker), 6, 137, 143–44, 165, 171
Walter, Horst, 129, 137
Webster, James, 125, 209
Weigl, Joseph, 55, 129
Weimar, 89
Weinzierl Castle, 136
Werner, Gregor Joseph, 4, 61
Wesley, Samuel, 6
Westphal, Johann Christoph, 97
Wiener Urtext Ausgabe, 117
Wiener-Zeitung, 25, 35, 38, 58, 121, 126, 215–16
Wienerisches Diarium, 20, 120, 140, 176, 189, 195, 215–16, 219, 430
Witzey (Viczay), Countess Marianne née Countess Grassalkovics, 29–30
Wolfegg paper mill, 69
Wurzbach, Constant von, 208
Wyzewa, Théodore de, 289

Zechner, Johann Georg, 178
Zeitgeist, 417
Zimmermann, Anton, 195–97, 430
Zinzendorf, Count Karl von, 48
Zitterer, Johann (painter), 140
Zweig, Steffan, 420
Zwettl, Cistercian abbey (Niederösterreich), 4

INDEX OF WORKS
(according to Hoboken/WERKVERZEICHNIS)

Page numbers in italics refer to main discussions. Asterisks indicate musical examples.

Editor: Natalie Wrubel
Book designer: Matthew Williamson
Jacket designer: Matthew Williamson
Production coordinator: Harriet Curry
Typeface: Linotron Monticello with Caslon display
Typesetter: G & S Typesetters, Inc.
Music typesetter: Melvin Wildberger
Printer and binder: Maple Vail Book Manufacturing Group
Paper: 50 lb. Decision Opaque

A. PETER BROWN is Professor of Musicology at
Indiana University. He is author of *Performing
Haydn's* The Creation: *Reconstructing the Earliest
Renditions*, other books and articles on eighteenth-
and nineteenth-century music, and critical editions
of scores from this period.